METALLURGY IN NUMISMATICS 6

Metallurgy in Numismatics 6

Mines, Metals, and Money
Ancient World Studies in Science, Archaeology and History

EDITED BY

KENNETH A. SHEEDY
and GILLAN DAVIS

AUSTRALIAN CENTRE FOR ANCIENT
NUMISMATIC STUDIES

MACQUARIE UNIVERSITY

THE ROYAL NUMISMATIC SOCIETY

SPECIAL PUBLICATION NO. 56

LONDON

2020

ROYAL NUMISMATIC SOCIETY SPECIAL PUBLICATIONS
GENERAL EDITOR: ROGER BLAND

To our daughters:
Lucy Clare Sheedy, Rebecca Allen and Tamara Davis

© The authors 2020
The Royal Numismatic Society Special Publication No. 56

All rights reserved. No part of this publication may be reproduced, stored in any retrieval system, or transmitted in any form or by any means, electronic, mechanical, photocopying, recording, or otherwise without prior permission of the publisher in writing.

ISBN 0–901405–37–X

British Library Cataloguing in Publication data
A CIP catalogue record is available from the British Library

Set by New Leaf Design, Malton, North Yorkshire
Printed by Gutenberg Press Ltd, Tarxien, Malta

CONTENTS

Contributors	vii
Preface PROFESSOR J.H. KROLL	xi
Foreword DR GEORGE KAKAVAS	xii

1. Introduction   KENNETH A. SHEEDY AND GILLAN DAVIS   1

PART 1. GEOLOGY AND MINING   7

2. Mines, Metals and Money in Attica and the Ancient World: The Geological Context   JAMES ROSS, PANAGIOTIS VOUDOURIS, VASILIOS MELFOS AND MARKOS VAXEVANOPOULOS   9

3. Aegean Mining Technologies in Antiquity: A Traceological Approach: The Laurion Mines (Greece)   DENIS MORIN, PATRICK ROSENTHAL, ADONIS PHOTIADES, IRENE ZANANIRI, SERGE DELPECH, RICHARD HERBACH AND DENIS JACQUEMOT   23

4. Ari - A Classical Mining District at Anavyssos (Attica)   HANS LOHMANN   43

5. The Exploitation of the Argentiferous Ores in the Lavreotike Peninsula, Attica, in Antiquity: Some Remarks on Recent Evidence   ELENI ANDRIKOU   59

6. The Role of Changing Settlement Structures in Reconstructing the Mining History of Archaic Laurion   SOPHIA NOMICOS   67

7. Metal Production Chain at Pangaeon Mountain, Eastern Macedonia, Greece   MARKOS VAXEVANOPOULOS, MICHALIS VAVELIDIS, DIMITRA MALAMIDOU AND VASILIS MELFOS   75

PART 2. ANALYSIS   85

8. The Minting/Mining Nexus: New Understandings of Archaic Greek Silver Coinage from Lead Isotope Analysis   ZOFIA ANNA STOS-GALE AND GILLAN DAVIS   87

9. Silver for the Greek Colonies: Issues, Analysis and Preliminary Results from a Large-scale Coin Sampling Project   THOMAS BIRCH, FLEUR KEMMERS, SABINE KLEIN, H.-MICHAEL SEITZ AND HEIDI E. HÖFER   101

10. Elemental Composition of Gold and Silver Coins of Siphnos   KENNETH A. SHEEDY, DAMIAN B. GORE, MARYSE BLET-LEMARQUAND, BERNHARD WEISSER AND GILLAN DAVIS   149

11. The Gold of the Lydians   PAUL CRADDOCK AND NICHOLAS CAHILL   165

12. The Gold of Lysimachus. Elemental Analysis of the Collection of the Bibliothèque Nationale de France using LA-ICP-MS   FRÉDÉRIQUE DUYRAT AND MARYSE BLET-LEMARQUAND   175

13.	Depth Profile LA-ICP-MS Analysis of Ancient Gold Coins MARYSE BLET-LEMARQUAND, SYLVIA NIETO-PELLETIER AND BERNARD GRATUZE	195
14.	Studies in Athenian Silver Coinage: Analysis of Archaic 'Owl' Tetradrachms GILLAN DAVIS, KENNETH A. SHEEDY AND DAMIAN B. GORE	207
15.	The Silver of the Owls: Assessment of Available Analyses Performed on Athenian Silver Coinage (Fifth - Third Centuries BC) CHRISTOPHE FLAMENT	215
16.	Metallic Composition of Ancient Imitative Owls – Preliminary Analyses THOMAS FAUCHER	223
17.	Neutron Diffraction Texture Analysis for Numismatics VLADIMIR LUZIN, KENNETH A. SHEEDY, SCOTT R. OLSEN, FILOMENA SALVEMINI AND MAX AVDEEV	239
18.	Neutron Imaging for Numismatics FILOMENA SALVEMINI, KENNETH A. SHEEDY, SCOTT R. OLSEN, VLADIMIR LUZIN AND ULF GARBE	247

PART 3. ARCHAEOLOGY AND MUSEUMS 261

19.	The Acropolis, 1886 Hoard (IGCH 12) Revisited PANAGIOTIS TSELEKAS	263
20.	A Small Numismatic Group from the Ancient Road of Koile OLGA DAKOURA-VOGIATZOGLOU AND EVA APOSTOLOU	275
21.	The Enigmatic Tool from the Sanctuary of Poseidon at Sounion: New Evidence ZETTA THEODOROPOULOU POLYCHRONIADIS AND ALEXANDROS ANDREOU	291
22.	Methods of Conservation of Ancient Silver Coins used at the Numismatic Museum, Athens GEORGE KAKAVAS, ELENI KONTOU AND NIKOLETA KATSIKOSTA	303
23.	The Role of the Numismatic Museum of Athens in Determining the Authenticity of Coins: The Contribution of Scientific Analysis GEORGE KAKAVAS AND ELENI KONTOU	317

CONTRIBUTORS

Alexandros Andreou
Athens Numismatic Museum, Greece

Eleni Andrikou
Hellenic Ministry of Culture
Ephorate of Antiquities of East Attica, Greece

Eva Apostolou
Athens Numismatic Museum, Greece

Max Avdeev
Australian Centre for Neutron Scattering, Australian Nuclear Science and Technology Organisation, New Illawarra Rd, Lucas Heights NSW 2234, Australia

Thomas Birch
Centre for Urban Network Evolutions (UrbNet), Aarhus University, School of Culture and Society, Moesgård Allé 20, 4230-221, 8270 Højbjerg, Denmark

Maryse Blet-Lemarquand
IRAMAT-CEB, CNRS / Université d'Orléans, 3D rue de la Férollerie; CS 60061; F-45071 Orléans cedex 2, France

Nicholas Cahill
Department of Art History, University of Wisconsin-Madison, United States

Paul Craddock
Emeritus Scientist, Department of Conservation and Scientific Research, British Museum, Great Russell Street, London WC1B 3DG, United Kingdom

Olga Dakoura-Vogiatzoglou
Retired. Formerly Athens Ephorate, Greece

Gillan Davis
Department of Ancient History, Macquarie University, NSW, 2109, Australia

Serge Delpech
Equipe Interdisciplinaire d'Etudes et de Recherches Archéologiques sur les Mines Anciennes et le Patrimoine Industriel (ERMINA), France

Frédérique Duyrat
Bibliothèque nationale de France, 58, rue de Richelieu, F-75084 Paris Cedex 02, France

Thomas Faucher
IRAMAT-CEB, CNRS / Université d'Orléans, 3D rue de la Férollerie; CS 60061; F-45071 Orléans cedex 2, France

Christophe Flament
Département de Langues et littératures classiques, Université de Namur, Belgium

Ulf Garbe
Australian Centre for Neutron Scattering, Australian Nuclear Science and Technology Organisation, New Illawarra Rd, Lucas Heights NSW 2234, Australia

Damian B. Gore
Department of Environmental Sciences, Macquarie University, NSW, 2109, Australia

Bernard Gratuze
IRAMAT-CEB, CNRS / Université d'Orléans, 3D rue de la Férollerie; CS 60061; F-45071 Orléans cedex 2, France

Richard Herbach
Laboratoire TRACES, (Travaux et Recherches Archéologiques sur les Cultures, les Espaces et les Sociétés) UMR CNRS 5608, Université Jean-Jaurès, Toulouse, France

Heidi E. Höfer
Institut für Geowissenschaften, Goethe-Universität, Altenhöferallee 1, D-60438 Frankfurt am Main, Germany

Denis Jacquemot
Equipe Interdisciplinaire d'Etudes et de Recherches Archéologiques sur les Mines Anciennes et le Patrimoine Industriel (ERMINA), France

George Kakavas
Athens Numismatic Museum, Greece

Nikoleta Katsikosta
Athens Numismatic Museum, Greece

Fleur Kemmers
Institut für Archäologische Wissenschaften, Abt. II, Goethe-Universität, Norbert-Wollheim-Platz 1, Hauspostfach 27, D-60629 Frankfurt am Main, Germany

Sabine Klein
Archäometallurgie, Deutsches Bergbau-Museum, Herner Straße 45, D-44791 Bochum, Deutschland and FIERCE, Frankfurt Isotope & Element Research Centre, Goethe Universität, Altenhöferallee 1, 60438 Frankfurt am Main, Germany

Eleni Kontou
Athens Numismatic Museum, Greece

Hans Lohmann
Institute of Archaeological Studies, Ruhr-Universität Bochum, Am Bergbaumuseum 31, D-44791 Bochum, Germany

Vladimir Luzin
Australian Centre for Neutron Scattering, Australian Nuclear Science and Technology Organisation, New Illawarra Rd, Lucas Heights NSW 2234, Australia

Dimitra Malamidou
Ephorate of Antiquities of Kavala-Thasos, Ministry of Culture, Kavala, Greece

Vasilios Melfos
Department of Mineralogy, Petrology and Economic Geology, Faculty of Geology, Aristotle University of Thessaloniki, Thessaloniki 54124, Greece

Denis Morin
Laboratoire TRACES, (Travaux et Recherches Archéologiques sur les Cultures, les Espaces et les Sociétés) UMR CNRS 5608, Université Jean-Jaurès, Toulouse, France

Sophia Nomicos
Institut für Klassische Archäologie und Christliche Archäologie/Archäologisches Museum Westfälische-Wilhelms Universität Münster, Domplatz 20-22, 48143 Münster, Germany

Sylvia Nieto-Pelletier
IRAMAT-CEB, CNRS / Université d'Orléans, 3D rue de la Férollerie; CS 60061; F-45071 Orléans cedex 2, France

Scott R. Olsen
Australian Centre for Neutron Scattering, Australian Nuclear Science and Technology Organisation, New Illawarra Rd, Lucas Heights NSW 2234, Australia

Adonis Photiades
Department of General Geology & Geological Mapping, Institute of Geology and Mineral Exploration, Athens, Greece

Zetta Theodoropoulou Polychroniadis
Chair, Greek Archaeological Committee UK

Patrick Rosenthal
Laboratoire Chrono-environnement, UMR CNRS 6249, Université Bourgogne-Franche-Comté, Besançon, France

James Ross
School of Earth Sciences, University of Western Australia, Crawley, WA 6009, Australia

Filomena Salvemini
Australian Centre for Neutron Scattering, Australian Nuclear Science and Technology Organisation, New Illawarra Rd, Lucas Heights NSW 2234, Australia

H.-Michael Seitz
Institut für Geowissenschaften, Goethe-Universität, Altenhöferallee 1, D-60438 Frankfurt am Main, Deutschland and FIERCE, Frankfurt Isotope & Element Research Centre, Goethe Universität, Altenhöferallee 1, 60438 Frankfurt am Main, Germany

Kenneth A. Sheedy
The Australian Centre for Ancient Numismatic Studies, and Department of Ancient History, Macquarie University, NSW, 2109, Australia

Zofia Anna Stos-Gale
Retired. Formerly Isotrace Laboratory, University of Oxford, United Kingdom

Panagiotis Tselekas
School of History and Archaeology, Faculty of Philosophy, Aristotle University of Thessaloniki 54124 Thessaloniki, Greece

Michail Vavelidis
Department of Mineralogy, Petrology and Economic Geology, Faculty of Geology, Aristotle University of Thessaloniki, Thessaloniki 54124, Greece

Markos Vaxevanopoulos
Department of Mineralogy, Petrology and Economic Geology, Faculty of Geology, Aristotle University of Thessaloniki, Thessaloniki 54124, Greece

Panagiotis Voudouris
Department of Mineralogy and Petrology, Faculty of Geology & Geoenvironment, National and Kapodistrian University of Athens, Athens 15784, Greece

Irene Zananiri
Department of General Geology & Geological Mapping
Institute of Geology and Mineral Exploration, Athens, Greece

PREFACE

The papers in this volume in part stem from a conference that was conceived and organised by the Australian Centre for Ancient Numismatic Studies (Macquarie University) and the Epigraphical and Numismatic Museum, Athens. The conference, held at the Iliou Melathron in Athens from 20-22 April, 2015, was entitled 'Mines, Metals and Money in Attica and the Ancient World'. One of its goals was to survey the applications and current state of non-destructive metallurgical analyses in Greek numismatic study. In recent years, progress in these areas has been rapid; and as laboratory instrumentation and techniques have continued to multiply and expand, the topic could not be more timely. The other work that the conference and now this volume addresses is the renewed interest of geologists and archaeologists in further exploiting the evidence on the ground for reconstructing the silver mining and processing industries in Southeastern Attica and Northern Greece. Accompanying these studies are papers from the staff of the Numismatic Museum on the museum's program of testing new acquisitions and on the study of two hoards excavated in Athens.

Altogether, the articles trace precious metal in the Greek world from the extraction of ore in antiquity to museum artifacts of today. Expanding on previous volumes of the Royal Numismatic Society's *Metallurgy in Numismatics* series, the present contributions range from numismatic metallurgy in its traditional laboratory context to metallurgy in the broader, historical sense of ancient metal working in general. In what is probably the most significant achievement, a core of the papers present abundant, fresh evidence for the tremendous scale of long-distance trade in silver from a handful of sources in the Aegean to the great number of Greek city-states around the Mediterranean that began to coin in the late archaic period, including even the cities of Southern Italy and Sicily.

While this volume will be welcomed for its many such findings, its value rests also on the editors' foresight that by inviting these contributions and bringing them together in one place, the studies will become more accessible and prominent than if they had been published separately.

J. H. KROLL

FOREWORD

As Director of the Numismatic Museum at Athens, I am proud of our longstanding numismatic and scientific collaboration with the Australian Centre for Ancient Numismatic Studies (ACANS) at Macquarie University, Sydney. Many Australian researchers, including the two editors of this volume, have spent extensive periods researching at the museum over many years to our mutual benefit. Together we organised the major international conference entitled *Mines, Metal and Money in Attica and the Ancient World* hosted at the museum from 20-22 April, 2015 which formed the genesis of this volume.

The themes of the conference focused on archaic Greek coinage, methods of mining precious metals, and on the historical and institutional framework of the Archaic period in which the conventions for the organisation and control of mining were developed, and through which the commercial distribution of precious metals was carried out. The conference themes also embraced studies of coin production, and technological and research methods for the analysis and conservation of metals that reliably help authenticate ancient coins. In these themes the conference successfully brought together scientists from all over the world.

At the end of the Conference, the temporary exhibition, *When Silver was Born. Archaic Coinage of Athens, Mines, Metals and Coins*, was inaugurated. The exhibition was displayed in the Great Gallery of temporary exhibitions of the Iliou Melathron, the Library of Heinrich Schliemann, on 28 May 2015. It took as its subject the coinage of the Archaic period, an era during which profound changes occurred in politics, the arts, and in society more generally. The exhibition, which was the conclusion of the very fruitful co-operation of our Museum with our colleagues from Australia, exhibited 263 artifacts, most of them for the first time. The objects displayed included acquisitions by Museums and Ephorates of Antiquities, and objects from the Collection of the Alpha Bank. We thank and acknowledge the Alpha Bank for sponsoring the exhibition, and the Australian Research Council of the Australian Government for sponsoring the Conference.

GEORGE KAKAVAS

INTRODUCTION

Kenneth A. Sheedy and Gillan Davis

In a landmark 1970 symposium organised in London, later published as *Methods of Chemical and Metallurgical Investigation of Ancient Coinage* (Hall and Metcalf 1972), invited scientists were asked to suggest how modern scientific techniques could be applied to numismatic problems. In particular, they were asked to explain the capabilities of their instruments and analytical methods and to provide up-to-date bibliographies. Ironically, perhaps the most startling findings announced in the symposium came from a study of Merovingian coins in the Sutton Hoo hoard using specific gravity (Kent 1972), a technique which can be traced back to Archimedes. Not all the speakers were scientists; there were also numismatists and historians discussing the implications of using information gained from scientific analysis, and exploring in some cases what they saw as deficiencies. Perhaps the most important outcome of this symposium was the momentum which led the Royal Numismatic Society to form a standing committee to further the application of scientific methods in numismatics, and the creation of a publication series in which to present current research, *Metallurgy in Numismatics*.

It would be rash to suggest that the symposium and publication signalled a new era of 'critical self-consciousness' in numismatics echoing that which David Clarke (1973) believed had arrived in archaeology (his famous paper, 'Archaeology: The Loss of Innocence' was published in the very next year). But Clarke's claim that the changes were occurring in a new environment, in good part fostered by developments in World War II, characterised by a technical and social revolution ("new men, new methods and new equipment"; 1973, 86) does seem to (faintly) resonate in these numismatics proceedings. Archaeology and the natural sciences have been 'intertwinned' since their inception in the seventeenth century (Pollard and Bray 2015, 113). Chemical analysis has been applied as a technique in numismatics since 1798 (Ponting 2012). The engagement of numismatics with science goes back to the creation of archaeology as a discipline. It might be argued that the 1970 conference marked an attempt by numismatists to engage or at least catch up with archaeometry (a term apparently invented by Christopher Hawkes in the 1950s: Pollard and Bray 2015, 125), that is to say with advances in the physical sciences. Archaeology in the late 1960s and 1970s, under the banner of New Archaeology or Processual archaeology, consciously embraced a science agenda. The few science-based numismatic studies and projects that appeared (a good example is David Walker's *The Metrology of the Roman Silver Coinage* [1976–78] with its focus on establishing the silver content of these issues) were less concerned with models and paradigms. It is not immediately apparent that numismatics has succeeded in keeping up with advances in archaeological theory and with the current interest in material culture. But it is evident that numismatics then and now has remained strongly invested in the creation of data through scientific analysis that will advance "the quest for provenance" (Pollard and Bray 2015, 115), the search to identify the geological sources of the metal used to manufacture coins.

This volume of papers has its origins in the Conference, *Mines, Metals and Money in Attica and the Ancient World*, held at the Iliou Melathron, Athens between 20 and 22 April, 2015. The conference was a collaboration between the Australian Centre for Numismatic Studies at Macquarie University (director, K. A. Sheedy) and the (then) Epigraphic and Numismatic Museum, Athens (director, G. Kakavas). The event came as the culmination of a three-year research program, 'A Spring of Silver, a treasury in the earth: coinage and wealth in archaic Athens' (project members: K.A. Sheedy, D. Gore and G. Davis) financed by the Australian Research Council through the Discovery Project scheme (DP120103519).

The conference agenda and, in part, the contents of this book derive from the research interests of those involved in both the ARC Project and the Numismatic Museum, Athens. The ARC Project explores the thesis that locally mined silver had an important impact on the public revenues of the Athenian state throughout the years c.550 BC–c.480 BC. The research combines a comprehensive corpus and die study of archaic Athenian coinage with a statistically significant survey of the metal composition of these coins. It has employed non-destructive Energy Dispersive X-Ray Fluorescence (EDXRF) spectrometry, using a pioneering method to correct for differences between the surface and interior of the coin (Gore and Davis 2016). This study has sought to establish the elemental composition of silver coins from the Laurion in Attica. It makes use of comparanda from other silver producing regions in the Greek world to determine which suites of elements constitute useful diagnostic fingerprints. The Museum curates one of the most important numismatic collections in the world, and has significant holdings of Athenian coins from all periods. It undertakes and sponsors research into all aspects of numismatics. It is vitally concerned with the scientific analysis and conservation of the objects in the collection. The invitations which went out to scholars to attend the conference in Athens in April 2015 stressed the relevance of a wide range of interests and disciplines.

We should begin by noting that this volume is not strictly about numismatics, at least as it is usually narrowly defined in books addressed to historians and archaeologists as 'the study of coins and medals'. Nor does it subscribe to traditional views on numismatic research as expressed, for example, by Philip Grierson: "Coins are, of course, archaeological objects, and so cannot be expected to explain themselves in the way that written evidence often does" (Grierson 1975, 3). Rather, it is positioned within the interdisciplinary framework of what has been termed 'behavioural archaeology', here defined as "the relationships between human behaviour and material culture" (Hollenback and Schiffer 2010, 318), and with a particular focus on the interrelationships between technology and society (LaMotte and Schiffer 2001). A key heuristic tool in this approach is the life history framework, where the life history of a technology, such as the production of coinage, is conceived as "the sequence of activities occurring during a technology's entire existence, from the procurement of raw materials, through manufacture, use and reuse, to deposition and archaeological recovery and analysis" (Schiffer 2004, 580). The sequence of interactions and activities has also been described as the 'behavourial chain' (Hollenback and Schiffer 2010). The behavioural chain is obviously similar to the analytical method of the *chaîne opératoire*, associated with André Leroi-Gourhan and his followers (Coupaye 2015), which may be defined in terms of the "productive sequence(s) and decision-making strategies of raw material transformations, past and present" (Dobres 2010, 156). The life history of technologies, a slightly different concept, moves away from the more or less exclusive focus on material objects to the study of a technology within a specific environment "with contexts of development and use, and relevant communities of practice and interaction" (Hollenback and Schiffer 2010, 321). This approach invites us to reconfigure the design of numismatic research in order to incorporate "technology-specific narratives that fully account for historical contingency and social uniqueness" (Hollenback and Schiffer 2010, 321).

Traditionally, the prime vehicles for numismatic research in the classical world have been the mint study in the case of Greek states, and for the Roman Republic and Empire, the survey of minting activity at Rome itself in which there is chronological narrative that integrates iconography, inscriptions and links to historical events. Almost inevitably, the procedure has been to collect a large corpus of coins and then impose order. The discussion of context is usually limited, particularly in Greek numismatics. This is also true of those excavation reports devoted to coins. Mint studies and typologies are still crucial, but there is more to be gained from looking at the material in other ways. This has become apparent, for example, in Fleur Kemmer's 2006 study of the coins found at the legionary fortress at Nijmegen. Part of the problem could well be that numismatic projects are typically conducted by a single researcher. Numismatists have tended not to feature in multidisciplinary projects, or even to be part of the lead group in excavations.

Numismatists and scientists have a well-established tradition of collaboration. The publication *The Metallurgy of Roman Coinage* (2014) by Butcher and Ponting is exemplary (and their research is on-going). There are now a number of broad-based interdisciplinary projects underway. These include: 'Coinage and the dynamics of power: the Western Mediterranean 500-100 BC' (Kemmers, Birch *et al.*); a collaboration between Duyrat and Blet-Lamarquand for a study of the gold coinage of Lysimachus; the 'Silver Isotopes and the Rise of Money' project (Albarede *et al.*) identifying the sources and quantifying the use and movement of silver in ancient Mediterranean and Near Eastern societies; and 'A Spring of Silver Project' (Sheedy, Gore, Davis) which studies Archaic Athenian coinage. The benefits from discussions between these researchers seem obvious, and the conference forum is (arguably) the best way to begin the conversations.

Let us return to the life history approach. An artefact's life history runs from the procurement of the material from which it was made until its final abandonment and deposition (Hollenback and Schiffer 2010, 320). Lemonnier (1993, 26) argued that "by investigating technical choice, by taking material culture for what it is, a social production", we expand the range of cultural phenomena under consideration and improve our chances of understanding them. Anyone even remotely concerned with the study of ancient artefacts, especially through archaeological excavation, will quickly realise that complete behavioural chains are virtually impossible to construct; the best one can hope for is segments (Hollenback and Schiffer 2010, 321). How then should we conceive of the behavioural chain (or chain fragments) of a coin? It seems best to structure our approach by looking at the different technologies involved in the extraction of the raw materials, the refinement and smelting of the metal, and the minting of coins. But this only takes us part way. We cannot lose sight of the role(s) of precious metals in ancient societies and the peculiar institution of coinage. In addition, there are the mechanisms for coin distribution, and the factors which govern coin loss and their subsequent recovery and recording to become part of the archaeological record. Finally, there are questions of conservation and technologies which facilitate and govern our ability to adequately access and analyse the coins.

When numismatists engage with the sciences they typically work with scientists interested in the analysis of metals. The life history approach suggests we should start dialogues in a wider pool of studies or integrate a wider range of disciplines into the project design. It seems evident that a bridge is offered by archaeometallurgy. Here we might highlight two important European research clusters (both represented in chapters in this volume) which have embraced numismatics within archaeometry and have provided a special focus on the field of archeometallurgy. The first is the L'Institut de recherche sur les archéomatériaux, in Orléans which incorporates the Centre Ernest-Babelon (IRAMAT-CEB), le Laboratoire Métallurgie et Culture (LMC) in Belfort, and the Centre de Recherche sur la Physique Appliquée à l'Archéologie de Bordeaux. The Centre Ernest-Babelon, created in 1980, is well known to numismatists from the research of its founding director, Jean-Noël Barrandon, and especially for his collaborative studies in Attic coinage with H. Nicolet-Pierre. The second group of researchers interested in archaeometallurgy, the Deutsches Bergbau-Museum Bochum, has shown a greater emphasis on geophysical studies, and are renowned (especially through the volumes of *Der Anschnitt*) for their projects surveying ores, mines, and the evidence of metal processing (Wagner and Weisgerber 1985 and 1988). In Greece, a great deal of invaluable 'front-line' work has been carried out by the National Centre of Scientific Research ('Demokritos'); they have been active in studying ores, the evidence of mining and smelting, as well as the artefacts from innumerable excavations (including the Laurion and Siphnos). There has been a significant amount of work done on the geology of the Laurion region and on mapping the mines and refining facilities, but we are lacking a good modern survey which brings together all of the information which has accumulated, especially from the on-going work of Greek archaeologists in the regional *ephorias* and from the staff and students of the Technical University of Athens.

The role of this introduction is not to offer a review of the relationship between numismatics and the physical sciences. Rather, it is to position the chapters contained in this volume within a discussion about future numismatic research as a part of multidisciplinary archaeological projects. We want to bring together specialists in different areas not so much because of shared interests that might be collectively construed as interdisciplinary, but because it seems to us imperative that numismatists engage with other disciplines, expanding and changing the agenda of numismatic research in fundamental ways. In their thoughtful paper 'Rethinking Numismatics', Kemmers and Myrberg (2011) set out to "re-member coins into archaeological discourse". The particular discourse they had in mind was set within the theoretical framework of historical archaeology and material-culture studies. However, in his important survey and analysis, 'The Material-Culture Turn: event and effect', Dan Hicks (2010) noted that "critiques within material culture studies, especially relating to the limitations of the textual analogy of material culture, and arguments about the extension of 'agency' from humans to material things, have led to an unfolding of the idea of 'material culture'" (Hicks and Beaudry 2010, 5). For an even stronger attack on the idea of material culture see comments by Schiffer (Rathje *et al.* 2013, 26). Hicks and Beaudry in their introduction to the massive volume, *The Oxford Handbook of Material Culture Studies* (2010), with 774 pages and apparently not one mention of coins, currency or money, wearily plumped for "a return to disciplinarity" (we leave the reader to decide on the merits of "modernist models of disciplinary purity") but stress their "own deep sense...of the complexity, mess and diversity of practices from which our knowledge emerges" (2010, 20–21).

So what have we on offer here? Hopefully not 'The archaeological bazaar: scientific methods for sale?', the title of a Pollard and Bray paper in which they conclude, regarding working across the science-humanities divide in archaeology and more particularly in archaeometry, "at the practical level, however, beyond handwringing and saying we should work together more effectively, there has been little real movement in that direction" (2015, 16). Perhaps in the future this movement could be led by research in numismatics.

We have divided the volume into three parts. The first deals with geology and mining; the second with analysis, and the third with archaeology and museums. The traditional concern with questions of provenance is evident (Stos Gale and Davis; Birch and Kemmers, Sheedy *et al.*) but there is also a nuanced appreciation of the data and a more sophisticated understanding of what can and cannot be done with the advanced technologies now on offer. Other chapters focus on different concerns and contributions from the physical sciences, and here we highlight investigations of the processes and technology of flan preparation and coin striking using neutron diffraction (Luzin *et al.*) and neutron tomography (Salvemini *et al.*).

At this stage we should note that the volume seeks to introduce new research and researchers to an Anglophone audience; chapters by French, German and Greek authors (who provide some 15 of the 23 entries) come with extensive bibliographies.

We begin the volume with a survey of the geological context (Ross *et al.*), with comments and an extensive bibliography on the main deposits in Greece of precious metals. This is fundamental to any consideration of behavioural chains. The broader framework of life history studies relies heavily on contributions from archaeological fieldwork. Mining technologies as revealed by evidence from the Laurion mines are discussed by Morin *et al.*, while Lohmann narrows the focus on the remains of mining activity to one region within the Laurion with a report on finds from the survey at Ari. A broader view of the study of ancient mining and metallurgy in the Laurion, with some thoughts on recent finds, is offered by the Ephor for South-East Attica, E. Andrikou. These studies of the Laurion are rounded out with a discussion by Nomicos of Stöllner's theories of 'montanarchaeologie' and the 'imprinting process' (the transformation of a natural landscape into an industrial landscape) as a means of approaching mining activity in the Laurion during the poorly documented period of the sixth century BC. The section is brought to a close by Vaxavanopoulos *et al.* with a review of work on a four-year survey at the noted mining region of Mt. Pangaeon. Appropriately, this is a consideration of the 'metal production chain', combining studies of the region's geology and metallurgical sites.

The second section of the volume is primarily concerned with scientific methods of analysis as applied to the elemental composition of the ores and refined metals. Stos-Gale and Davis provide new interpretations of some 160 lead isotope analyses of archaic Greek coins from the OXALID database, notably the coins from the Asyut hoard, establishing a much broader range of ore sources for these coins than previously contemplated and looking at the relationship between minting and mining. Birch *et al.* introduce a large-scale sampling project which provides sound analytical protocols and standards as well as a case study exploring the silver sources for coins minted in the western Mediterranean 500–100 BC, with lead isotope analyses (LIA) but also EPMA (Electron probe micro-analyser Instrumentation). ED-XRF (a non-destructive technique in contrast to the drill sampling of LIA) was employed by the ARC Project, 'A Spring of Silver', to explore the elemental composition of silver coins and a unique gold drachm minted on Siphnos (Sheedy *et al.*). This study also includes data on Siphnian silver coins from Laser Ablation Inductively Coupled Plasma Mass Spectrometry (LA-ICP-MS). Craddock and Cahill turn our attention to Lydian electrum coins with new studies of Pactolus gold, and a renewed consideration of the excavated gold refinery at Sardis. Gold is also the theme of the extensive study of Lysimachi currently being conducted by Duyrat and Blet-Lamarquand using MS-ICP-MS; here the focus is on the identification of the gold sources for the lifetime and posthumous issues. Then we have a suit of studies which deal with the production of coinage by Athens. The first (Davis *et al.*) considers the physical characteristics and silver content of archaic Athenian coinage as well as suggesting a new rationale for the ancient practice of test-cutting. The next (Flament) summarises physical and chemical analyses performed on classical Athenian silver coins suggesting new areas of investigation. The third (Faucher) reports on the use of LA-ICP-MS to conduct a study into the composition of 79 coins previously identified as imitation Athenian owls but which he demonstrates are mostly minted from Attic silver. Two complementary papers by Luzin *et al.* and Salvemini *et al.* report on the application for numismatics of neutron diffraction texture analysis and then neutron imagining with a focus on data from the Incuse Coinage project.

The third and final section has numismatic studies which draw on the evidence of excavation. Hoards are critical in numismatics. In Tselekas' study of the famous Acropolis hoard found in a deposit in 1886 he reconsiders the evidence, coins and the context for associating the finds with the destruction of the Acropolis buildings by the Persians in 480 BC, as well as providing a catalogue of the coins. An enigmatic metal-working tool once thought to be a *Wappenmunzen* die is another find from an earlier excavation, again in an ancient *bothros* (pit), from Sounion in South-East Attica is subject to a fresh contextualised analysis by Theodoropoulou and Andreou. New finds, possibly from a hoard near the Koile Agora, are presented in an excavation report by Vogiatzoglou and Apostolou. We conclude with two studies from the staff of the Numismatic Museum in Athens (Kakavas *et al.* and Kakavas and Kontou) which highlight the role of museum conservation of coins and the procedures of museum researchers investigating the authenticity of doubtful coins.

In concluding we wish to thank the Australian Research Council for their support of research into the archaic coinage of Athens through the Discovery Project scheme (DP120103519) which made possible the 2015 Conference, Mines, Metals and Money in Attica and the Ancient World, held in collaboration with the Numismatic Museum, Athens and its strongly supportive director, Dr G. Kakavas. Similarly, we thank the Board of the Australian Centre of Ancient Numismatics Studies, Macquarie University, and its chairperson, Professor Martina Möllering, for their long-standing endorsement and encouragement of the research. This joint publication with the Royal Numismatic Society was made possible by its president, Dr Roger Bland, who also attended to the editing of the manuscript; we thank him for his timely assistance.

REFERENCES

Butcher, K. and Ponting, M. J. 2015. *The Metallurgy of Roman Silver Coinage: From the Reform of Nero to the Reform of Trajan* (Cambridge).
Clarke, D.L. 1973, 'Archaeology: The Loss of Innocence', *Antiquity* 47(1), 6–18.
Coupaye, L. 2015. 'Chaîne opératoire, transects et théories : quelques réflexions et suggestions sur le parcours d'une méthode Classique', in Soulier P. (ed.) André Leroi-Gourhan "l'homme, tout simplement", (Paris), 69–84.
Dobres, M.A. 2010. *Technology and Social Agency: Outlining a Practice Framework for Archaeology* (Oxford).
Gore, D.B. and Davis, G. 2016. 'Suitability of Transportable EDXRF for the On-site Assessment of Ancient Silver Coins and Other Silver Artifacts', *Applied Spectrometry* 70/5, 840–851.
Grierson, P. 1975. *Numismatics* (London).
Hall, E.T. and Metcalf, D.M. (eds) 1972. *Methods of chemical and metallurgical investigation of ancient coinage: a symposium held by the Royal Numismatic Society at Burlington House, London on 9-11 December 1970* (London).
Hicks, D. 2010. 'The Material-Cultural Turn: event and effect', in Hicks and Beaudry (eds) 2010, 25–98.
Hicks, D. and Beaudry, M.C. (eds.) 2010, *The Oxford Handbook of Material Culture Studies* (Oxford).
Hicks, D. and Beaudry, M.C. 2010. 'Introduction. Material culture studies: a reactionary view', in Hicks and Beaudry (eds) 2010, 1–21.
Hollenback, K, L. and Schiffer, M.B. 2010. 'Material Life and Technology', in Hicks and Beaudry (eds) 2010, 313–332.
Kemmers, F. 2006. *Coins for a legion: an analysis of the coin finds from Augustan Legionary Fortress and Flavian canabae legionis at Nijmegen*. (Studien zu Fundmünzen der Antike 21, Mainz).
Kemmers, F. and Myrberg, N. 2011. 'Rethinking Numismatics. The archaeology of coins', *Archaeological Dialogues* 18(1), 87–108.
Kent, J. P. C., 1972, 'Gold Standards of the Merovingian Coinage, A.D. 580–700', in *Hall* and *Metcalf* (eds) 1972, 69–74.
LaMotte, V.M. and Schiffer, M.B. 2001. 'Behavioral archaeology: toward a new synthesis', in Hodder, I. (ed.), *Archaeological Theory Today* (1st ed. Cambridge), 14–64.
Pollard, M. and Bray, P. 2015. 'The archaeological bazaar: scientific methods for sale? Or: 'putting the "arch-" back into archaeometry', in Chapman, R. and Wylie, A. (eds), *Material Evidence: Learning from Archaeological Practice* (London), 113–127.
Lemonnier, P. 1993. 'Introduction', in Lemonnier, P. (ed), *Technological choices: transformation in material cultures since the Neolithic* (London & New York), 1–35.
Ponting, M.J. 2012. 'The Substance of Coinage: The Role of Scientific Analysis in Ancient Numismatics', in Metcalf, W.E. (ed.), *The Oxford Handbook of Greek and Roman Coinage* (Oxford) 12–30.
Rathje, W. L., Shanks, M. and Witmore, C. 2013. *Archaeology in the Making: Conversations through a Discipline* (Abingdon).
Schiffer, M.B. 2004. 'Studying technological change: a behavourial perspective', *World Archaeology* 36, 579–585.
Wagner, G.A. and Weisgerber, G. (eds) 1985. *Silber, Blei und Gold auf Sifnos, Prähistorische und Antike Metal Produktion, Der Anschnitt* (Bochum).
Wagner, G.A. and Weisgerber, G. (eds) 1988. *Antike Edel- und Buntmetallgewinnung auf Thasos, Der Anschnitt* (Bochum).
Walker, D.R. 1976–78. *The Metrology of the Roman Silver Coinage* (British Archaeological Reports Suppl. 5, 22, and 30; Oxford).

Abbreviations: the abbreviations in this volume, for standard reference works and for journals and book series, follow those of the *American Journal of Archaeology* and can be accessed at: *https://www.ajaonline.org/submissions/abbreviations*

PART 1

GEOLOGY AND MINING

MINES, METALS AND MONEY IN ATTICA AND THE ANCIENT WORLD: THE GEOLOGICAL CONTEXT

James Ross, Panagiotis Voudouris, Vasilios Melfos & Markos Vaxevanopoulos

Abstract

Events associated with convergence of the African and Eurasian plates over the last 200 Ma, especially closure of the Tethyan ocean over the last ~100 Ma, led to the distinctive Hellenide orogen, a tectonic and geological entity which strongly influenced human history in Attica and the ancient world. This review focusses on tectonic events during the last 65 Ma, a period characterised by collisional and crustal-scale extensional tectonics accompanied by magmatic activity and precious and base metal mineralisation.

Hundreds of gold, silver and base metal deposits in Northern Greece, NW Anatolia, and within the Attic–Cycladic domain are closely associated with Oligocene to Pleistocene (33 to 1.5 Ma) igneous intrusions and volcanic activity. The distribution of these deposits is uneven and, whilst base metal mineralisation is common to most, Au deposits dominate in Northern Greece and NW Anatolia, and Ag is dominant in the south. This review is primarily concerned with mining during the period 600–100 BC and the more than 30 deposits and mineralised districts which are believed to have been exploited. Their diverse locations and characteristics resulted in a wide range of opportunities for substantial wealth creation, and the varying outcomes undoubtedly influenced the social, economic and political history of the broader Aegean region.

Introduction

Events over the last 100 million years (Ma), and principally the last 65 Ma, provide a geological and tectonic context for the principal themes of this volume. These events led to the distinctive Hellenide orogen[1] (Pe-Piper and Piper 2002; Schmid *et al.* 2008; Jolivet and Brun 2010; Ring *et al.* 2010; Jolivet *et al.* 2013) within the more extensive Tethyan-Alpine orogen (Figure 1).

The contemporary geography and attributes of this orogen are strongly influenced by its geology, tectonic history, intrusive and extrusive magmatic activity, associated mineralisation, contemporary sea levels, and palaeoclimate. It is a past which determined the spatial distribution of its islands and highly indented coastlines (Broodbank 2013); its elevated topography; its soils and vegetation; and the character and distribution of its precious and base metal deposits. Naturally these attributes influenced the maritime history of the Aegean and exploitation of its natural resources; outcomes central to the unfolding history of Archaic and Classical Greece and to the extension of Greek civilisation by Alexander the Great.

This contribution outlines the geological and tectonic history of the Hellenide orogen and its associated mineral deposits, with emphasis on the western Attic-Cycladic metamorphic complex which hosts the Lavrion Ag deposits (Skarpelis 2007; Voudouris *et al.* 2008a,b; Bonsall *et al.* 2011; Berger *et al.* 2013; Voudouris 2016; Melfos and Voudouris 2017; Scheffer

---

[1] An orogen is a belt or domain of deformed and metamorphosed rocks which formed within a convergent system (by subduction or collision), which were subject to increased pressure and temperature, formed a mountain range and may have been accompanied by intrusive igneous activity.

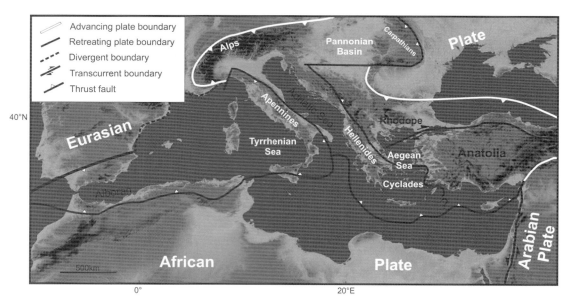

Figure 1. Simplified tectonic map of the Mediterranean plate boundary zone showing retreating, advancing, transcurrent and divergent boundaries, with teeth on overriding plate; modified after Ring et al. (2010).

et al. 2016, 2017). It then provides brief descriptions of the numerous Ag and Au districts and deposits in Greece and NW Anatolia likely to have been mined during the period from 600–100 BC (Figure 2).

Geological and Tectonic History

During the last 65Ma the Hellenide orogen has been dominated " the convergence of Africa and Eurasia leading to collision and subduction processes (Spakman, 1986; Menant et al. 2016). This complex tectonic process included accretion of new material to the European plate and slab retreat responsible for progressive exhumation of deeper rocks during and after orogenesis[2]. Slab retreat led to major crustal extension, emplacement of high-angle and low-angle detachment faults, and magmatism in the form of volcanics and intrusive bodies (Lister *et al.* 1984; Gautier *et al.* 1999; Vanderhaeghe and Teyssier 2001; Jolivet and Brun 2010; Scheffer *et al.* 2016). Periods of slower subduction are believed to have led to retreat of the descending slab within the earth's mantle (Brun and Faccenna 2008), crustal extension (Lister *et al.* 1984; Gautier *et al.* 1999), and ascent of fertile magmas with associated precious and base metal mineralisation in four periods: Oligocene (33–26 Ma), early Miocene (22–19 Ma), middle to late Miocene (14–7 Ma), and Pliocene-Pleistocene (3 to 1.5 Ma) (Blundell *et al.* 2005; Moritz *et al.* 2010; Bertrand *et al.* 2014; Menant *et al.* 2016; Melfos and Voudouris 2017). The resulting mineralisation occurs mostly within two areas across Greece and NW Anatolia: the Rhodope-Serbo-Macedonian-NW Anatolia belt (RSAB); and the Attic-Cycladic metamorphic complex (ACMC), shown in Figure 2.

Rhodope-Serbo-Macedonian-NW Anatolian Belt (RSAB)

The RSAB consists of fragments of continental crust accreted to the European plate ~185–100Ma (Ring *et al.* 2010) and subsequent tectonics determined its importance. Continued subduction conveyed oceanic crust (Vardar Suture Zone) and more crustal fragments (Pelagonian-Lycian Block) to its southern borders (Figure 2), before oceanic crust of the ancient Pindos ocean entered the subduction zone about 60Ma (Himmerkus *et al.* 2006;

---

[2] Orogenesis is the tectonic process leading to the formation of an orogen.

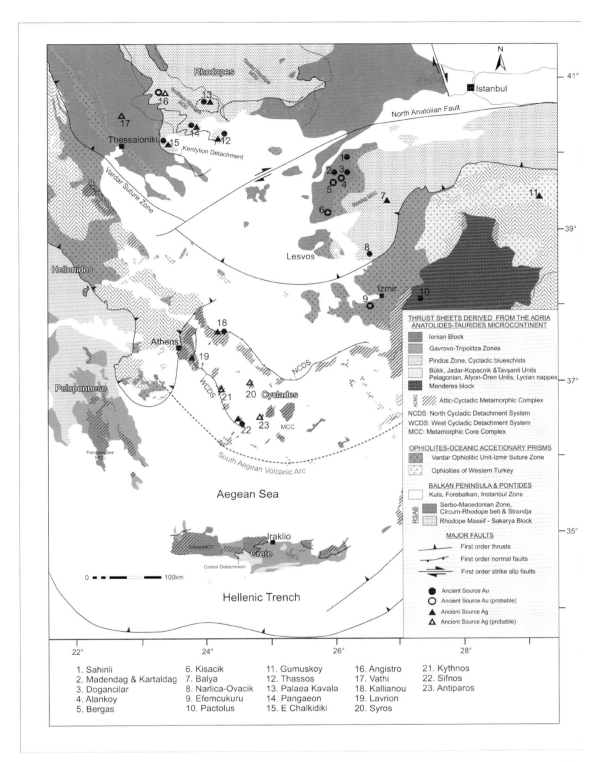

Figure 2. Simplified tectonic map of the Aegean region showing the main tectonic zones within the Hellenide orogen (modified after Schmid et al. 2008) together with the location of gold and silver deposits in Greece and NW Anatolia that were mined, or likely to have been mined, within the period 600-100BC.

Schmid *et al.* 2008; Ring *et al.* 2010; Burg 2012; Robertson *et al.* 2013; Kydonakis *et al.* 2015). Pindos oceanic crust appeared to trigger a change in subduction dynamics, from advancing or stationary, to retreat to the SSW (Brun and Faccenna 2008; Ring *et al.* 2010), accompanied by initiation of crustal scale extensional detachment faults which opened the Aegean ocean (Lister *et al.* 1984; Buick 1991; Gautier *et al.* 1999; Royden 1993) and facilitated magmatic activity.

The belt's structure reflects early compressional thrusting and syn-orogenic exhumation of deeper metamorphic rocks followed by post-orogenic exhumation during orogenic collapse accommodated by low-angle detachment and the formation of a Metamorphic Core Complex (Kilias *et al.* 1999; Bonev *et al.* 2006; Brun and Sokoutis 2007; Burg 2012; Kydonakis *et al.* 2015). Slab retreat is associated with progressive southward migration of magmatism in the back-arc domain, which commenced ~56Ma in northern Greece (Marchev *et al.* 2013) and ~52Ma in NW Anatolia (Yigit 2012), before migrating southward to today's Southern Aegean active volcanic arc (Fytikas et al. 1984).

The Attic-Cycladic Metamorphic Complex (ACMC)

This complex extends from the Attic peninsula and adjacent southern third of Evia island in the west, to Samos and Anatolia in the east (Figure 2). Its importance also results from a history of subduction and magmatism, combined with crustal scale extensional tectonics. The ACMC resulted from microcontinental collision following closure of the Pindos ocean, is characterised by multiple metamorphic events (Ring *et al.* 2010; Jolivet *et al.* 2013; Scheffer *et al.* 2016, 2017), and includes three major stratigraphic units, Basal, Middle ('Cycladic Blueschist unit' - CBU), and Upper (Katzir *et al.* 2007, Bröcker and Pidgeon 2007; Scheffer *et al.* 2016, 2017).

The Basal unit, which overlies a deep water sediments. It hosts most mineralisation at Lavrion and occurs on some Cycladic islands. This unit is in tectonic contact with the overlying CBU, and experienced the same metamorphic events described below .

The CBU consists of 360–300Ma basement gneiss tectonically overlain by a volcanic-sedimentary sequence that includes marbles, calc-schists, and mafic and felsic meta-igneous rocks (Parra *et al.* 2002, Bröcker and Pidgeon 2007). At ~50Ma it experienced high pressure-low temperature blueschist metamorphism when subducted (Pmax = 20 kbar, Tmax = 600°C, Avigad 1998), and higher temperature greenschist to amphibolite facies metamorphism (Pmax = 8 kbar, Tmax = 650–700 °C), during extension-related exhumation ~ 24Ma (Duchene *et al.* 2006; Martin *et al.* 2006, 2008; Seward *et al.* 2009).

The less extensive Upper Cycladic unit is a diverse array of metamorphosed and unmetamorphosed rocks (e.g. Zeffren *et al.* 2005) and overlies the Cycladic Blueschists along the North Cycladic Detachment System (Jolivet *et al.* 2010).

Extensional events, in response to slab retreat, persisted from ~23–5Ma and resulted in crustal scale detachments through the agency of low angle faults (Buick 1991, Gautier *et al.* 1999; Jolivet and Faccenna 2000; Vanderhaeghe *et al.* 2007; Jolivet *et al.* 2010). Extension and development of the ACMC was accompanied by formation of the Naxos migmatite dome as a metamorhic core complex in the central Cyclades from 24 to 16Ma (Vanderhaeghe 2004; Kruckenberg *et al.* 2010, 2011; Siebenaller *et al.* 2013), and by intrusion of various granitoids throughout the Cyclades between 15–7 Ma (Keay *et al.* 2001, Pe-Piper and Piper 2002; Skarpelis *et al.* 2008). These granitoids both crosscut, and are cut by, the detachment faults, suggesting that detachment and igneous activity are synchronous.

Current models indicate most crustal extension was accommodated by NE-dipping low-angle normal faults (Grasemann *et al.* 2012; Jolivet *et al.* 2013), such as the crustal-scale North Cycladic Detachment System (Jolivet *et al.* 2010) where NE-directed normal shear separates the CBU from the overlying Upper unit (Jolivet *et al.* 2010). Grasemann *et al.*

(2012) proposed another crustal-scale, low-angle normal fault system, the SW-dipping West Cycladic detachment system. It is exposed on Lavrion, Kea, Kythnos, and Serifos, extends at least 100 km, generally occurs between the Basal unit and the CBU, and may have continuously accommodated extension. These divergent, large-scale detachment systems could account for much of the crustal stretching in the Aegean.

The Mines and Metals

The RSAB and the ACMC are well documented regions of ancient metal exploitation within the Western Tethyan metallogenic belt (Heinrich and Neubauer 2002). Magmatism associated with slab retreat in the RSAB led to diverse styles of precious and base metal hydrothermal mineralization ranging from ~38–18Ma (Melfos *et al.* 2002; Voudouris 2006; Yigit 2009, 2012; Melfos and Voudouris 2012; Voudouris *et al.* 2013; Melfos and Voudouris 2017). Significant precious and base metal mineralisation also occurs in the ACMC in spatial association with volcanic, subvolcanic and plutonic rocks emplaced since 15Ma, in response to extension and exhumation of deeper rocks associated with the formation of metamorphic core complexes (Skarpelis 2002; Neubauer 2005; Voudouris *et al.* 2011; Alfieris *et al.* 2013; Melfos and Voudouris 2017).

Northern Greece

The Serbo-Macedonian and Rhodope metallogenic provinces include numerous, precious and base metal deposits related to magmatic processes (Melfos *et al.* 2002; Marchev *et al.* 2005; Voudouris 2006; Melfos and Voudouris 2012, 2017). Most mineralisation occurs in intrusion-hosted sheeted veins, skarns, carbonate replacements, porphyry-epithermal systems, and shear-zones. Placer Au occurrences and supergene Au-bearing iron oxides are associated with primary deposits and exploitation for precious metals dates back to ancient times.

The Au and Ag deposits of Pangaeon mountain feature prominently in ancient Greek writings (e.g. Herodotus and Thucydides – see Stos-Gale and Davis this volume) and mineralisation occurs in veins, carbonate replacements and shears within granodiorite, marbles, schists, gneisses, and amphibolites. Twenty five ancient adits and open casts with well-preserved tool marks have been identified (Vaxevanopoulos *et al.* 2018) which, together with archaeometric and archaeological research at twelve smelting sites (Vaxevanopoulos . 2017; Vaxevanopoulos *et al.* this volume), indicate intense mining activity from Hellenistic to Roman and Ottoman times.

Thasos was also a significant source of Au and Ag during antiquity, and the island provides evidence for extraction and working of metals since at least the early Bronze Age (Nerantzis and Papadopoulos 2013). Sources include Ag-rich Pb-Zn carbonate replacement and Au-rich Cu-Fe-Mn deposits (Vavelidis and Amstutz 1983) in veins and lenses of mostly oxidised massive and disseminated ore in marble and schists. Evidence for underground mining dates from at least the early Iron Age (Stos-Gale and Gale 1992; Nerantzis and Papadopoulos 2013). Workings of Classical and Roman age for Ag-rich Pb-Zn include Marlou, Sotiras, Vouves, Koumaria, Kourlou, whilst similar age workings for Au have been identified at Kynira and beneath the Acropolis at Thasos (Wagner and Weisgerber 1988).

Significant ancient mining activity was also clustered in an area of about 100 km^2 extending from ancient Philippoi to Palea Kavala (Figure 2) and Petropigi. It includes more than 150 ore occurrences rich in Fe, Mn, Pb, Zn, Cu, Ag, and Au, and numerous underground galleries are believed to have operated between 6th century BC and the Ottoman period (Vavelidis *et al.* 1996). Vavelidis equates this area with "Scapte Hyle" mentioned by Herodotus (6.46), Theophrastus (*On Stones* 17), Lucretius (*De rerum natura* 6.810) and Plutarch (*Cimon* 4.2) .

Mineralisation commonly occurs as carbonate replacement bodies and veins in marbles and schists.

Eastern Chalkidiki (Figure 2) is also a historical mining centre and the diverse mineralisation includes Cu-Au porphyry, Pb-Zn-Ag-Au carbonate replacement, Cu-skarn and oxidized Mn. Observations and metallurgical traces suggest mining since at least the 5th century BC, particularly at Metangitsi (Vavelidis 1989; Vavelidis and Andreou 2008), however, recent mining operations have obliterated much earlier evidence. Archaeological studies confirm mining in Roman times (2nd century BC in Skouries), continuing until the Middle Ages and the Ottoman period (Wagner *et al.* 1986; Vavelidis and Melfos 2012).

Two other mining areas may have contributed precious metals in ancient times, but evidence is incomplete. For example, a number of ancient surface and underground mining excavations and associated metallurgical slags have been recorded from the NE of Mt Orvilos to the SW of Mt Angistron, close to the Bulgarian border. Workings are focused on supergene Fe-oxides, enriched in Ag and Au, which formed from weathering of skarn, carbonate replacement and vein mineralisation in marbles, gneiss and schists (Nerantzis 2009), but they lack archaeological studies. In the area of Kilkis (Figure 2), several mining sites with ancient galleries have been identified in gold-rich deposits at Vathi, Gerakario, and Pontokerasia, but also without archaeological investigation. These gold-rich deposits are dominated by porphyry and epithermal styles of mineralisation in close association with subvolcanic rocks intruded into the dominantly gneissic metamorphic basement of the Serbo-Macedonian massif between about 25–18Ma (Frei 1992).

Finally, numerous occurrences of placer gold, sourced from both economic and low grade deposits, occur in rivers in northern Greece, including Aliakmon, Axios, Gallikos, Strymon and Evros (Davies, 1932; Vavelidis and Boboti-Tsitlakidou 1993). It is likely that these rivers made a significant contribution to the supply of Au accessed by Macedonians, Thracians and Greeks from 600–100 BC, however definitive archaeological and literary evidence is lacking.

North Western Anatolia

This sector of Anatolia is richly endowed with >100 precious and base metal deposits following numerous exploration discoveries during the last 25 years (Yigit 2009, 2012; Sánchez 2016). They include epithermal Au-Ag, porphyry Cu-Au and skarn and vein Pb-Zn-Ag-Au deposits and are associated with magmatic events (both volcanic and intrusive) from 52–18Ma during progressive exhumation, of metamorphic rocks, especially the Kazdag Metamorphic Core Complex (Sánchez *et al.* 2016).

Epithermal Au-Ag deposits (veins and breccias) are dominant and characterised by relatively high grades (up to 15g/t Au) and substantial Ag, with Ag:Au ranging from 1:1 up to >10:1. Base metal deposits contain up to 158g/t Ag, with lead bullion containing up to 2000g/t Ag and 7g/t Au (Kovenko 1940; Agdemir *et al.* 1994). Mining in the Archaic and Classical periods is confirmed at eight deposits and likely at another four (Figure 2). They include nine epithermal Au-Ag deposits (Narlica-Ovacik, Sahinli, Madendag, Kartaldag, Alankoy, Dagancilar, Bergas and Kisacik), two Pb-Zn-Ag deposits (Gumuskoy and Balya) and the Pactolus alluvial Au (Yigitguden 1984; Agdemir *et al.* 1994; Ramage 2000; Oyman *et al.* 2003; Begemann *et al.* 2003; Yilmaz *et al.* 2007, 2010; Yigit 2012; Imer *et al.* 2013). However, given the high relative values of gold and silver, and importance of mining in those periods, other deposits were probably also exploited for their near-surface enrichment zones.

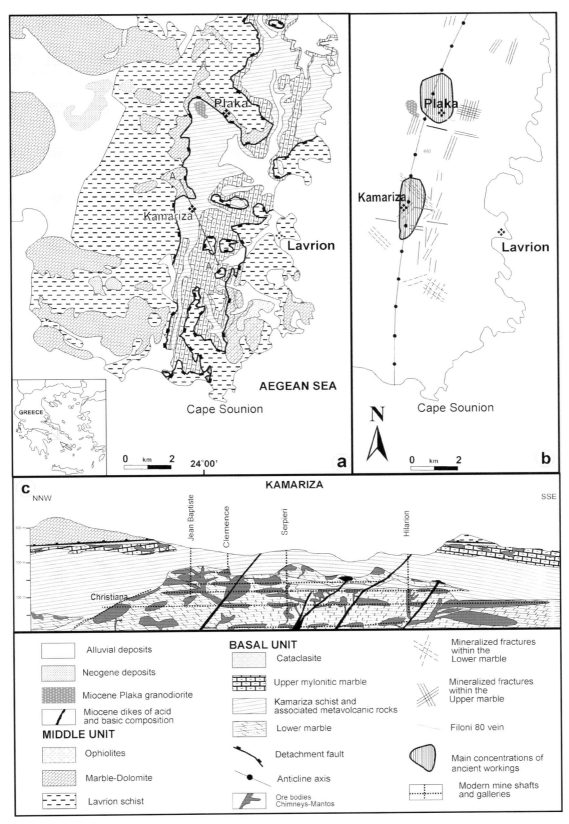

Figure 3a. Simplified geological map of the Lavrion district based on Voudouris et al. (2008b), updated according to Scheffer et al. (2016); 3b - simplified tectonic map after Voudouris et al. (2008b), showing concentrations of mineralisation at Kamariza (Lower marble) and Plaka (Upper marble and detachment) after Marinos and Petrascheck (1956); 3c - cross section A-A' of the Kamariza area, including some projected mineralisation.

Attic-Cycladic Region

Mineral deposits within the ACMC include: intrusion-related Ag, Au, and base metal-rich systems at Lavrion, Kallianou, Sifnos, Tinos, Kythnos, Serifos, Antiparos, Mykonos and Syros); and young (~2.7–1.5Ma) epithermal Au-Ag deposits along the South Aegean Active Volcanic Arc at Milos (Gale and Stos-Gale 1981; Pernicka 1987; Skarpelis 2002, 2007; Neubauer 2005; Voudouris *et al.* 2008a, b, 2011; Menant *et al.* 2013; Alfieris *et al.* 2013; Melfos and Voudouris 2017). Wide variation in mineralisation styles includes crosscutting veins in basement gneiss (Antiparos), schists (Kallianou, Platys Gialos on Sifnos, Tinos, Syros and Lavrion), marble (Tinos, Syros and Lavrion), and young volcanics (Milos). Other styles occur in marble host rocks, such as chimneys and conformable lenses at Lavrion (Skarpelis 2002, 2007; Voudouris *et al.* 2008b; Berger *et al.* 2013), disseminations in brecciated marble at Kallianou, and irregular lenses and layers at Syros and Sifnos.

The common theme to each of these occurrences is the presence of the CBU and evidence for close association of veins and other forms of mineralisation with extensional tectonics. Ancient mining has been confirmed at Lavrion, Sifnos (until its closure ~525 BC) and Kallianou, and is suggested by old workings and Ag-rich galena at Serifos, Syros and Antiparos (Gale and Stos-Gale 1981). Whilst Ag, and to a lesser extent Cu, were the main objectives, Sifnos, Kallianou and possibly Syros were also exploited for Au. Lead isotope data indicate that Lavrion and Sifnos were the principal sources of widely traded Cycladic Ag in ancient times (Gale and Stos-Gale 1981).

Lavrion Silver Deposits

The Lavrion Pb-Zn-Cu-Ag deposits were exploited by innumerable surface and shallow workings, >1000 ancient mine shafts up to >100m deep, and extensive underground workings (Ardaillon 1897; Morin *et al.* this volume) within an area 15km long (N-S) and up to 8km wide (Figure 3). Direct evidence of mining dates from the third millennium (Conophagos 1980) whereas indirect evidence, such as Pb isotopes and occurrences of litharge (Gale and Stos-Gale 1981; Kakavogianni et al, 2004), indicate commencement in the fourth millennium and continuation, at least intermittently, until about 100 BC. The resulting production is estimated at about 3,500 tonnes Ag and 1.4 million tonnes of Pb (Conophagos 1980) and was most intensive during 6th to 4th centuries BC.

In the Lavrion district all three units of the ACMC are present (Marinos and Petrascheck 1956; Photiades and Saccani 2006; Scheffer *et al.* 2016). The Basal unit includes two sequences of ~200Ma marble: the less competent Lower marble is up to ~300m thick, whilst the more competent Upper dolomitic marble varies from 5–150m thick and has been brecciated and milled by movement on the overlying West Cycladic detachment fault (Grasemann *et al.* 2012; Sheffer *et al.* 2017). These marble units are separated by up to 200m of Kamariza schists.

The structurally superimposed Middle unit also hosts mineralisation and contains ~50–30Ma high pressure-low temperature blueschists and marbles of the CBU (Altherr *et al.* 1982). In contrast, the Upper unit has limited exposure and is unmineralised. This tectonically stacked sequence is folded along a N-NW trending axis which is broadly coincident with the overall field of mineralisation and the two main areas where mining was concentrated, Plaka and Kamariza (Figure 3).

At Plaka, skarn, breccia, porphyry and vein mineralisation appears to be directly linked with the 7–10Ma Plaka granodiorite intrusion (Voudouris *et al.* 2008a,b; Bonsall *et al.* 2011). However, carbonate replacement mineralisation (veins, and lenses) is more extensive, and occurs within Upper marble of the Basal unit, the detachment zone and, to a lesser extent, within marble of the Middle unit, settings often exposed at the surface and in shallow workings. In contrast, at Kamariza and adjacent areas the more substantial occurrences of carbonate replacement mineralisation (veins, chimneys and conformable lenses) are mainly hosted by the Lower marble unit, or in overlying marble lenses within the Kamariza schists. These sites are rarely exposed at surface, can extend below sea level, and were the target of most mine shafts (Morin *et al.* 2012; Morin *et al.* this volume).

The history, geology, structure, mineralogy and deep supergene alteration of the Lavrion mineralisation has been adequately described elsewhere (Marinos and Petrascheck 1956; Photiades and Saccani 2006; Skarpelis 2007; Voudouris *et al.* 2008 a, b; Skarpelis and Argyraki 2009; Bonsall *et al.* 2011; Berger *et al.* 2013; Scheffer *et al.* 2016, 2017). Deposits are controlled by structure and lithology and were formed under extensional conditions, during development of the top-to-the-SSW West Cycladic detachment system. In this tectonic regime numerous igneous dykes and sills of Plaka granodiorite age intruded the Lower and Middle units and were emplaced along the detachment zone, indicating deeper links with igneous activity.

Silver was contained in primary galena, often as Ag-rich inclusions of sulphosalts (Voudouris *et al.* 2008b), and is believed to have been largely retained in the secondary minerals (cerussite, anglesite and plumbojarosite) during deep weathering, even though detailed mineral analyses and mass balances are unavailable. Wide variability in Ag content of Pb-bearing minerals is evident. For example, Conophagos (1980) reported 500–5000ppm in cerussite and Gale and Stos-Gale (1981) reported 504ppm–5920ppm Ag in Pb for 13 galena samples from the Upper and Lower marble units (average 2533ppm). Conophagos assumed 2000ppm of recovered Ag in Pb in his estimates of production.

Conclusions

Over the last 65Ma the geological and tectonic processes associated with convergence of the African plate with Eurasia within the Hellenide orogen have profoundly influenced human history in the broader Aegean region. Sustained periods of extensional tectonics since 33Ma have resulted in a range of intrusive and extrusive magmatic activity which appears to be closely associated in space and time with the formation of hundreds of precious and base metal deposits. Exploitation of these deposits helped shape the history of Attica and the ancient world during the Archaic, Classsical and Hellenistic periods.

The resulting precious metal endowment is focussed in Northern Greece and NW Anatolia within the RSAB and in the Attic-Cycladic domain of the ACMC. Whilst base metals occur throughout, Au mineralisation features more strongly in the RSAB deposits, whereas Ag mineralisation is dominant in the ACMC. The processes which gave rise to mineralisation also elevated and shaped topography, determined coastlines, and exposed many of these deposits at surface, where weathering often led to surface and near-surface metal enrichment. The ancient history of mineral exploitation, metallurgy and widespread use within these regions is therefore unsurprising.

Throughout history, exploitation of precious metal deposits has provided opportunities for substantial surges in wealth creation. Attica and the broader Aegean region were well endowed with such opportunities in the ancient world. However, geological history determined that these opportunities were unevenly distributed, as shown in Figure 2. Ancient history reflects this uneven distribution with more intensive exploitation of the remarkable silver deposits of Lavrion coinciding with the rise of Classical Athens. Similarly, the rise of the Macedonian Empire of Phillip II, and laying the foundation for the subsequent conquests of Alexander the Great, coincided with Philip's increasing control and exploitation of the numerous gold and silver deposits of Northern Greece (e.g. Herodotus. 5.17; Diodorus 16.8.6; cf. Hammond 1994). Whilst geological history does not determine destiny, it does provide opportunities to influence the course of history.

Acknowledgements

The authors wish to record appreciation to the editors of this special issue, Dr Gil Davis and Associate Professor Kenneth Sheedy, for their invitation to contribute this paper. In addition, we are grateful for the thoughtful and helpful contributions of the three anonymous reviewers.

References

Agdemir, N., Kirikoglu, M.S., Lehmann, B. and Tietze, J. 1994. 'Petrology and alteration geochemistry of the epithermal Balya Pb-Zn-Ag deposit', *Mineralium Deposita* 29, 366–71.

Alfieris, D., Voudouris, P. and Spry, P.G. 2013. 'Shallow submarine epithermal Pb-Zn-Cu-Au-Ag-Te-mineralization on western Milos Island, Aegean Volcanic Arc, Greece: Mineralogical, Geological and Geochemical constraints', *Ore Geology Reviews* 53, 159–80.

Altherr, R., Kreuzer, H., Wendt, I., Lenz, H., Wagner, G.A., Keller, J., Harre, W. and Hohndorf, A. 1982. 'A late Oligocene/early Miocene high temperature belt in the Attic–Cycladic crystalline complex (SE Pelagonian, Greece)', *Geologisches Jahrbuch* E23, 97–164.

Ardallion, E. 1897. *Les Mines du Laurium dans l'Antiquite* (Paris).

Avigad, D. 1998. 'High-pressure metamorphism and cooling on SE Naxos (Cyclades, Greece)', *European Journal of Mineralogy* 10/6, 1309–19.

Begemann, F., Schmitt-Strecker, S. and Pernicka, E. 2003. 'On the composition and provenance of metal finds from Besiktepe (Troia)', in Wagner, G.A., Pernicka, E. and Uerpmann, H.P. (eds.), *Ancient Troia and the Troad: scientific approaches* (Berlin), 173–201.

Berger, A., Schneider, D.A., Grasemann, B. and Stockli, D. 2013. 'Footwall mineralization during late Miocene extension along the west Cycladic detachment system, Lavrion, Greece', *Terra Nova* 25/3, 181–91.

Bertrand, G., Guillou-Frottier, L. and Loiselet, C. 2014. 'Distribution of porphyry copper deposits along the western Tethyan and Andean subduction zones: Insights from a paleotectonic approach', *Ore Geology Reviews* 60, 174–90.

Blundell, D., Arndt, N., Cobbold, P.R. and Heinrich, C. 2005. 'Processes of tectonism, magmatism and mineralization: Lessons from Europe', *Ore Geology Reviews* 27, 333–49.

Bonev, N., Burg, J.P. and Ivanov, Z. 2006. 'Mesozoic- Tertiary structural evolution of an extensional gneissdome - the Kesebir-Kardamos dome, E. Rhodopes, Bulgaria', *International Journal of Earth Sciences* 95, 318–40.

Bonsall,T.A., Spry, P.G., Voudouris, P., Tombros S., Seymour K. and Melfos, V. 2011. 'The Geochemistry of Carbonate-Replacement Pb-Zn-Ag Mineralization in the Lavrion District, Attica, Greece: Fluid Inclusion, Stable Isotope, and Rare Earth Element Studies', *Economic Geology* 106, 619–51.

Bröcker, M. and Pidgeon, R.T. 2007. 'Protolith ages of meta-igneous and metatuffaceous rocks from the Cycladic Blueschist Unit, Greece: results of a reconnaissance U-Pb zircon study', *Journal of Geology* 115, 83–98.

Broodbank, C. 2013. *The Making of the Middle Sea* (London).

Brun J.-P. and Faccenna C. 2008. 'Exhumation of high-pressure rocks driven by slab rollback', *Earth and Planetary Science Letters* 272, 1–7.

Brun, J.-P. and Sokoutis, D. 2007. 'Kinematics of the Southern Rhodope core complex (Northern Greece)', *International Journal of Earth Sciences* 96, 1079–99.

Buick, I.S. 1991. 'The late Alpine evolution of an extensional shear zone, Naxos, Greece', *Journal Geological Society London* 148, 93–101.

Burg, J.P. 2012. 'Rhodope: from Mesozoic convergence to Cenozoic extension. Review of petro-structural data in the geochronological frame', *Journal of the Virtual Explorer*, Electronic Edition, ISSN 1441–8142, Vol. 42, paper 1.

Conophagos, C.E. 1980. *Le Laurium antique: et la technique Grecque de la production de l'argent* (Athens).

Davies, O. 1932. 'Ancient Mines in Southern Macedonia', *Journal of the Royal Anthropological Institute* 62, 145–162.

Duchêne, S., Aissa, R. and Vanderhaeghe, O. 2006. 'Pressure-temperature-time evolution of metamorphic rocks from Naxos (Cyclades, Greece): constraints from thermobarometry and Rb/Sr dating', *Geodinamica Acta* 19, 301–21.

Frei, R. 1992. 'Isotope (Pb, Rb-Sr, S, O, C, U-Pb) geochemical investigations on Tertiary intrusives and related mineralizations in the Serbo-Macedonian Pb-Zn, Sb+Cu-Mo metallogenetic province in Northern Greece' (PhD dissertation, ETH, Zurich).

Fytikas, M., Innocenti, F., Manetti, P., Mazzuoli, R., Peccerillo, A. and Villari, L. 1984. 'Tertiary to Quaternary evolution of volcanism in the Aegean region', *Geological Society, London, Special Publications* 17, 687–99.

Gale, N.H. and Stos-Gale, Z.A. 1981. 'Cycladic lead and silver metallurgy', *The Annual of the British School at Athens* 76, 169–224.

Gautier, P. and Brun, J.-P. 1994. 'Ductile crust exhumation and extensional detachments in the central Aegean (Cyclades and Evvia Islands)', *Geodinamica Acta* 7/2, 57–85.

Gautier, P., Brun, J.P., Moriceau, R., Sokoutis, D., Martinod, J. and Jolivet, L. 1999. 'Timing, kinematics and cause of Aegean extension: a scenario based on a comparison with simple analogue experiments', *Tectonophysics* 315, 31–72.

Grasemann, B., Schneider, D.A., Stöckli, D.F. and Iglseder, C. 2012. 'Miocene bivergent crustal extension in the Aegean: Evidence from the western Cyclades (Greece)', *Lithosphere* 4, 23–39.

Hammond, N.G.L. 1994. *Philip of Macedon* (London).

Heinrich, C.A. and Neubauer, F. 2002. 'Cu-Au-Pb-Zn-Ag metallogeny of the Alpine-Balkan-Carpathian-Dinaride geodynamic province', *Mineralium Deposita* 37, 533–40.

Himmerkus, F., Reischmann, T. and Kostopoulos, D. 2006. 'Late Proterozoic and Silurian basement units within the Serbo-Macedonian Massif, northern Greece: the significance of terrane accretion in the Hellenides', *Geological Society, London, Special Publication* 260, 35–50.

Iglseder, C., Grasemann, B., Rice, A.H., Petrakakis, K. and Schneider, D. 2011. 'Miocene south directed low-angle normal fault evolution on Kea Island (West Cycladic Detachment System, Greece)', *Tectonics* 30, TC4013.

Imer, E.U., Gulec, N., Kuscu, I. and Fallick, A.I. 2013. 'Genetic investigations and comparison of Kartaldag and Madendag epithermal gold deposits in Cannakale, NW Turkey', *Ore Geology Reviews* 53, 204–22.

Jolivet, L. & Brun, J.P. 2010. 'Cenozoic geodynamic evolution of the Aegean region', *International Journal Earth Science* 99, 109–138.

Jolivet, L. and Faccenna, C. 2000. 'Mediterranean extension and the Africa-Eurasia collision', *Tectonics* 19, 1095–1106.

Jolivet, L., Faccenna, C., Huet, B., Labrousse, L., Le Pourhiet, L., Lacombe, O., Lecomte, E., Burov, E., Denèle, Y., Brun, J.-P., Philippon, M., Paul, A., Salaün, G., Karabulut, H., Piromallo, C., Monié, P., Gueydan, F., Okay, A.I., Oberhänsli, R., Pourteau, A., Augier, R., Gadenne, L. and Driussi, O. (2013). 'Aegean tectonics: Strain localization, slab tearing and trench retreat', *Tectonophysics* 597, 1–33.

Jolivet, L.E., Lecomte, B., Huet, Y., Denèle, O., Lacombe, L., Labrousse, L., Le Pourhiet, L. and. Mehl, C. 2010. 'The North Cycladic Detachment System', *Earth Planetary Science Letters* 289, 87–104.

Kakavogianni, O., Douni, K. and Nezeri, F. 2004. 'Silver metallurgical finds dating from the end of the final Neolithic Period until the Middle Bronge Age in the area of Mesogeia', in Tzachili, I. (ed.), *Aegean Metallurgy in the Bronze Age*.Proc. Of Int. Symposium, Crete, Rethymnon.

Katzir Y., Garfunkel Z., Avigad, D. and Matthews A. 2007. 'The geodynamic evolution of the Alpine orogen in the Cyclades (Aegean Sea, Greece): insights from diverse origins and modes of emplacement of ultramafic rocks', *Geological Society, London, Special Publications* 291, 17–40.

Keay, S., Lister, G. and Buick, I. 2001. 'The timing of partial melting, Barrovian metamorphism and granite intrusion in the Naxos metamorphic core complex, Cyclades, Aegean Sea, Greece', *Tectonophysics* 342, 275–312.

Kilias, A., Falalakis, G. and Mountrakis, D. 1999. 'Cretaceous–Tertiary structures and kinematics of the Serbomacedonian metamorphic rocks and their relation to exhumation of the Hellenic hinterland (Macedonia, Greece)', *International Journal of Earth Science* 88, 513–531.

Kovenko, V. 1940. 'Balya lead mines (Turkey)', *Bulletin Mineral Research Exploration Institute, Turkey* 4/21, 587–94.

Kruckenberg, S.C., Ferré, E.C., Teyssier, C., Vanderhaeghe, O., Whitney, D.L., Skord, J. and Seaton, N. 2010. 'Viscoplastic flow in migmatites deduced from fabric anisotropy: an example from Naxos dome, Greece', *Journal of Geophysical Research* 115, 9, B0940.

Kruckenberg, S.C., Vanderhaeghe, O., Ferré, E.C., Teyssier, C. and Whitney, D.L. 2011. 'Flow of partially molten crust and the internal dynamics of a migmatite dome, Naxos, Greece', *Tectonics* 30, TC3001.

Kydonakis, K., Brun, J-P., Sokoutis, D. and Gueydan, F. 2015. 'Kinematics of Cretaceous subduction and exhumation in the western Rhodope (Chalkidiki block)', *Tectonophysics* 665, 218–35.

Lister, G.S., Banga, G. and Feenstra, A. 1984. 'Metamorphic core complexes of Cordilleran type in the Cyclades, Aegean Sea, Greece', *Geology* 12/4, 221–25.

Marchev, P., Georgiev, S., Raicheva, R., Peytcheva, I., von Quadt, A., Ovtcharova, M. and Bonev, N. 2013. 'Adakitic magmatism in post-collisional setting: An example from the early–middle Eocene Magmatic Belt in Southern Bulgaria and Northern Greece', *Lithos* 180–181, 159–80.

Marchev, P., Kaiser-Rohrmeier, B., Heinrich, C., Ovtcharova, M., von Quadt, A. and Raicheva, R. 2005. 'Hydrothermal ore deposits related to post-orogenic extensional magmatism and core complex formation: The Rhodope Massif of Bulgaria and Greece', *Ore Geology Reviews* 27, 53–89.

Marinos, G. and Petrascheck W.E. 1956. 'Lavrion: geological and geophysical research', *Institute for Geology and Subsurface Research* 4, 1–246.

Martin, L., Duchêne, S., Deloule, E. and Vanderhaeghe, O. 2006. 'The isotopic composition of zircon and garnet: a record of the metamorphic history of Naxos, Greece', *Lithos* 87/3–4, 174–192.

Martin, L.A.J., Duchêne, S., Deloule, E. and Vanderhaeghe, O. 2008. 'Mobility of trace elements and oxygen in zircon during metamorphism: consequences for geochemical tracing', *Earth and Planetary Science Letters* 267/1–2, 161–74.

Melfos, V. and Voudouris, P. 2012. 'Geological, mineralogical and geochemical aspects for critical and rare metals in Greece', *Minerals* 2, 300–17.

Melfos, V. and Voudouris, P. 2017. 'Cenozoic metallogeny of Greece and potential for precious, critical and rare metals exploration', *Ore Geology Reviews* 59, 1030–1057.

Melfos, V., Vavelidis, M., Christofides, G. and Seidel, E. 2002. 'Origin and evolution of the Tertiary Maronia porphyry copper-molybdenum deposit, Thrace, Greece', *Mineralium Deposita* 37, 648–68

Menant, A., Jolivet, L. and Vrielynck, B. 2016. 'Kinematic reconstructions and magmatic evolution illuminating crustal and mantle dynamics of the eastern Mediterranean region since the late Cretaceous', *Tectonophysics* 675, 103–40.

Menant, A., Jolivet, L., Augier, R. and Skarpelis, N. 2013. 'The North Cycladic Detachment System and associated mineralization, Mykonos, Greece: Insights on the evolution of the Aegean domain', *Tectonics* 32, 433–52.

Morin, D., Herbach, R. and Rosenthal, P. 2012. 'The Laurion shafts, Greece: ventilation systems and mining technology in antiquity', *Historical Metallurgy* 46/1, 9–18.

Moritz, R., Márton, I., Ortelli, M., Marchev, P., Voudouris, P., Bonev, N., Spikings, R. and Cosca, M. 2010. 'A review of age constraints of epithermal precious and base metal deposits of the Tertiary Eastern Rhodopes: coincidence with Late Eocene-Early Oligocene tectonic plate reorganization along the Tethys', in Christofides, G., Kantiranis, N., Kostopoulos, D.S., & Chatzipetros. A.A. (eds.), *Proceedings of the XIX Congress of the Carpathian-Balkan Geological Association, Thessaloniki,* Special Publication 100 (Thessalonica), 351–358.

Nerantzis, N. and Papadopoulos, S. 2013. 'Reassessment and new data on the diachronic relationship of Thassos Island with its indigenous metal resources: a review', *Archaeological and Anthropological Sciences* 5/3, 183–96.

Nerantzis, N. 2009. 'Byzantine and Ottoman Mineral Exploration and Smelting in Eastern Macedonia, Greece and their Implications for Regional Economies' (PhD dissertation, University of Sheffield, UK).

Neubauer, F. 2005. 'Structural control of mineralization in metamorphic core complexes', in Mao J. Bierlein, F.P. (eds.), *Mineral deposit research: meeting the global challenge* (Berlin), 561–64.

Oyman, T., Minareci, F. and Piskin, O. 2003. 'Efemcukuru B-rich epithermal gold deposit (Izmir, Turkey)', *Ore Geology Reviews* 23, 35–53.

Parra T., Vidal O. and Jolivet, L. 2002. 'Relation between the intensity of deformation and retrogression in blueschist metapelites of Tinos Island (Greece) evidenced by chlorite-mica local equilibria', *Lithos* 63, 429–50.

Pe-Piper, G. & Piper, D.J. 2002. *The igneous rocks of Greece: The anatomy of an orogen* (Germany).

Pernicka, E. 1987. 'Erzlagerstätten in der Ägäis und ihre Ausbeutung im Altertum: geochemische Untersuchungen zur Herkunftsbestimmung archäologischer Metallobjekte', *Jahrbuch des römisch-germanischen Zentralmuseums Mainz* 34/2, 607–714.

Photiades, A. and Saccani, E. 2006. 'Geochemistry and tectono-magmatic significance of HP/LT metaophiolites of the Attic-Cycladic zone in the Lavrion area (Attica, Greece)', *Ofioliti* 31, 89–102.

Ramage, A. 2000. 'Golden Sardis', in Ramage, A. and Craddock, P. (eds.), *King Croesus' Gold: Excavations at Sardis and the History of Gold Refining* (Cambridge), 14–26.

Ring, U.J., Glodny, T., Will., T. and Thomson, S. 2010. 'The Hellenic subduction system: High-pressure metamorphism, exhumation, normal faulting, and large-scale extension', *Annual Review of Earth and Planetary Science* 38, 45–76.

Robertson, A.H., Trivić, B., Derić, N. and Bucurc, I.I. 2013. 'Tectonic development of the Vardar ocean and its margins: evidence from the Republic of Macedonia and Greek Macedonia', *Tectonophysics* 595–596, 25–54.

Royden, L.H. 1993. 'Evolution of retreating subduction boundaries formed during continental collision', *Tectonophysics* 12, 629–38.

Sánchez, M.G., McClay, K.R., King, A.R. and Wijbrams, J.R. 2016. 'Cenozoic crustal extension and its relationship to porphyry Cu-Au-(Mo) and epithermal Au-(Ag) mineralization in the Biga peninsula, northwestern Turkey. Tectonics and metallogeny of the Tethyan orogenic belt', *Society of Economic Geologists Special Publication* 19, 113–156.

Scheffer, C., Vanderhaeghe, O., Lanari, P., Tarantola, A., Ponthus, L., Photiades, A. and France, L. 2016. 'Syn- to post-orogenic exhumation of metamorphic nappes: Structure and thermobarometry of the western Attic-Cycladic metamorphic complex (Lavrion, Greece)', *Journal of Geodynamics* 96, 174–93.

Scheffer, C., Tarantola, A., Vanderhaeghe, O., Voudouris, P., Rigaudier, T., Photiades, A., Morin, D. and Alloucherie, A. 2017 'The Lavrion Pb-Zn-Fe-Cu-Ag detachment-related district (Attica, Greece): Structural control on hydrothermal flow and element remobilisation', *Tectonophysics* 717, 607–627.

Schmid, S.M., Bernoulli, D., Fügenschuh, B., Matenco, L., Schefer, S., Schuster, R., Tischler, M. and Ustaszewski, K. 2008. 'The Alpine-Carpathian-Dinaridic orogenic system: correlation and evolution of tectonic units', *Swiss Journal of Geosciences* 101, 139–83.

Seward, D., Seward, D., Vanderhaeghe, O., Siebenaller, L., Thomson, S., Hibsch, C., Zingg, A. and Holzner, P. 2009. 'Cenozoic tectonic evolution of Naxos Island through a multifaceted approach of fission-track analysis', *Geological Society of London Special Publications* 321, 179–96.

Siebenaller, L., Boiron, M. C., Vanderhaeghe, O., Hibsch, C., Jessell, M. W., Andre–Mayer, A. S., France-Lanord, C. and Photiades, A. 2013. 'Fluid record of rock exhumation across the brittle–ductile transition during formation of a Metamorphic Core Complex (Naxos Island, Cyclades, Greece)', *Journal of Metamorphic Geology* 31/3, 313–38.

Skarpelis, N. 2002. 'Geodynamics and evolution of the Miocene mineralization in the Cycladic-Pelagonian belt, Hellenides', *Bulletin of the Geological Society of Greece* 34, 2191–2206.

Skarpelis, N. 2007. 'The Lavrion deposit (SE Attika, Greece): geology, mineralogy and minor elements chemistry', *Neues Jahrbuch Mineralogie Abhandlungen* 183, 227–49.

Skarpelis, N. and Argyraki, A. 2009. 'Geology and Origin of Supergene Ore at the Lavrion Pb–Ag–Zn Deposit, Attica, Greece', *Resource Geology* 59/1, 1–14.

Skarpelis, N., Tsikouras, B. and Pe-Piper, G. 2008. 'The Miocene igneous rocks in the Basal unit of Lavrion (SE Attica, Greece): Petrology and geodynamic implications', *Geological Magazine* 145, 1–15.

Spakman, W. 1986. 'Subduction beneath Eurasia in connection with the Mesozoic Tethys', *Geologie en Mijnbouw* 65, 145–53.

Stos-Gale, Z. & Gale, N. 1992. 'Sources of copper used on Thasos in Late Bronze and Early Iron Age', in Koukouli-Chrysanthaki, Ch. (ed.), *Protohistoric Thasos: the cemeteries of the Kastri settlement. Archaeological Bulletin* 45, 782–93.

Vanderhaeghe O. 2004. 'Structural development of the Naxos migmatite dome', in Whitney, D.L., Teyssier C., and Siddoway C.S. (eds.), *Gneiss Domes in Orogeny. Geological Society of America Special Paper* 380, 211–27.

Vanderhaeghe, O., Hibsch, C., Siebenaller, L., Duchêne, S., de St Blanquat, M., Kruckenberg, S., Fotiadis, A. and Martin, L. 2007. 'Penrose conference-extending a continent-Naxos Field guide', *Journal of the Virtual Explorer* 28, 33.

Vanderhaeghe, O. and Teyssier, C. 2001. 'Partial melting and flow of orogens', *Tectonophysics* 342, 451–72.

Vavelidis, M. and Amstutz, G.C. 1983. 'New Genetic Investigations on the Pb-Zn Deposits of Thasos (Greece)', in Schneider H.J. (ed.), *Mineral Deposits of the Alps and of the Alpine Epoch in Europe* (Berlin-Heidelberg), 359–365.

Vavelidis, M. and Andreou, S. 2008. 'Gold and gold working in Late Bronze Age Northern Greece', *Naturwissenschaften* 95/4, 361–66.

Vavelidis, M. and Boboti-Tsitlakidou, I. 1993. 'Changes of the gold grains morphology during their downstream transport in the Gallikos placer example', *Bulletin of Geological Society of Greece* 28, 245–63.

Vavelidis, M. and Melfos, V. 2012. 'Study of the ancient metallurgical works in Kipouristra, Olympiada (Ancient Stageira), NE Chalkidiki', *Scientific Annals of the Faculty of Geology, School of Sciences, Aristotle University of Thessaloniki* 101, 9–16 (in Greek).

Vavelidis, M. 1989.' Das Au-Ag Vorkommen von Metagitsi, Chalkidiki (Nordgriechenland)', *Berichte der Deutschen Mineralogischen Gesellschaft. Beih. z. European Journal of Mineralogy* 1, 192.

Vavelidis, M., Gialoglou, G., Melfos, V. and Wagner, G.A. 1996. 'Goldgrube in Palaea Kavala Griechenland: Entdeckung von Skaptehyle', *Erzmetall* 49, 547–54

Vaxevanopoulos, M. 2017. Recording and study of ancient mining activity on Mount Pangaeon, E. Macedonia, Greece. Unpublished Doctoral dissertation, Thessaloniki, Greece, Aristotle University of Thessaloniki. 337 (in Greek).

Vaxevanopoulos, M., Vavelidis, M., Melfos, V., Malamidou, D. and Pavlides, S. 2018. 'Ancient Mining in Gold-Silver-Copper Deposits and Metallurgical Activity in Mavrokofi Area, Pangaeon Mount (NE Greece)', in Ben-Yosef, E. (ed.), *Mining for Ancient Copper: Essays in Memory of Beno Rothenberg.* Tel Aviv: The Institute of Archaeology of Tel Aviv University.

Voudouris, P. 2006. 'Comparative mineralogical study of Tertiary Te-rich epithermal and porphyry systems in northeastern Greece', *Mineralogy and Petrology* 87, 241–75.

Voudouris, P. 2016. A Field Guide on the Geology and Mineralogy of Lavrion, Attica, Greece, *National and Kapodistrian University of Athens*, 22p. DOI: 10.13140/RG.2.2.26582.86081

Voudouris, P., Melfos, V., Spry, P.G., Bonsall, T., Tarkian, M. and Economou-Eliopoulos M. 2008a. 'Mineralogical and fluid inclusion constraints on the evolution of the Plaka intrusion-related ore system, Lavrion, Greece', *Mineralogy and Petrology* 93, 79–110.

Voudouris, P., Melfos, V., Spry, P. G., Bonsall, T., Tarkian, M. and Solomos, Ch. 2008b. 'Carbonate-replacement Pb-Zn-Ag±Au mineralization in the Kamariza area, Lavrion, Greece: Mineralogy and thermochemical conditions of formation', *Mineralogy and Petrology* 94, 85–106.

Voudouris, P., Melfos, V., Spry, P.G., Bindi, L., Moritz, R., Ortelli, M. and Kartal, T. 2013. 'Extremely Re-Rich Molybdenite from Porphyry Cu-Mo-Au Prospects in Northeastern Greece: Mode of occurrence, causes of enrichment, and implications for gold exploration', *Minerals* 3, 165–91.

Voudouris, P., Spry, P.G., Sakellaris, G.A. and Mavrogonatos, C. 2011. 'A cervelleite-like mineral and other Ag-Cu-Te-S minerals [Ag_2CuTeS and $(Ag,Cu)_2TeS$] in gold-bearing veins in metamorphic rocks of the Cycladic Blueschist Unit, Kallianou, Evia Island, Greece', *Mineralogy and Petrology* 101, 169–83.

Wagner, G.A. and Weisgerber, G. 1988. 'Antike Edel- und Buntmetallgewinnung auf Thasos', *Der Anschnitt* 6, 279.

Wagner, G.A., Pernicka, E., Vavelidis, M., Baranyi, I. and Bassiakos, Y. 1986. 'Archäometallurgische Untersuchungen auf Chalkidiki', *Der Anschnitt* 38/5–6, 166–86.

Yigit, O. 2009. 'Mineral Deposits in Turkey in Relationship to Tethyan Metallogeny: Implications for Future Mineral Exploration', *Economic Geology* 104, 19–51.

Yigit, O. 2012. 'A prospective sector in the Tethyan Metallogenic Belt: Geology and Geochronology of mineral deposits in the Biga Peninsular, NW Turkey', *Ore Geology Reviews* 46, 118–48.

Yigitguden, H.Y. 1984. 'Silver ore deposit located in the vicinity of Kutahye, West Anatolia, Turkey', (PhD dissertation, Rheinland Westfalen Technical High School Mining and Metallurgy).

Yilmaz, H., Oyman, G., Arehart, G.B., Colakoglu, A.R. and Bulor, Z. 2007. 'Low sulfidation type Au-Ag mineralisation at Bergama, Izmir, Turkey', *Ore Geology Reviews* 32, 81–124.

Yilmaz, H., Oyman, G., Sonmez, F.N., Arehart, G.B. and Bulor, Z. 2010. 'Intermediate sulfidation epithermal gold-base metal deposits in Tertiary subaerial volcanic rocks, Sahinli/Tespih Dere (Lapeski/Western Turkey)', *Ore Geology Reviews* 37, 236–58.

Zeffren, S., Avigad, D., Heimann, A. and Gvirtzman, Z. 2005. 'Age resetting of hanging wall rocks above a low-angle detachment fault: Tinos Island (Aegean Sea)', *Tectonophysics* 400, 1–25.

3. AEGEAN MINING TECHNOLOGIES IN ANTIQUITY: A TRACEOLOGICAL APPROACH: THE LAURION MINES (GREECE)

Denis Morin, Patrick Rosenthal, Adonis Photiades, Serge Delpech, Denis Jacquemot

ABSTRACT

The Laurion district was one of the most important mining centres of ancient Greece during the fifth and fourth centuries BC, and the minerals extracted were a foundation of Athenian power. On the surface, remains associated with the whole mining process including adits, mineral processing and metallurgical workshops extend over tens of kilometers. The Laurion lead-silver mines are the only ones known from the ancient world where vertical shafts reach as far as 100m deep to connect underground networks dug to exploit ore deposits. These mines required sophisticated organisational, engineering and technological capabilities, and an excellent understanding of geology. Recently, field investigation has been carried out into these shafts and mines. Analysis of traces found on the walls of the ancient mining galleries and works is providing new information and insights about the structures and technology of the mining industry during antiquity.

INTRODUCTION

The Laurion district contains exceptionally rich mineral deposits covering a surface area of 17 x 6 kilometres along a NNE-SSW orientation in South East Attica, Greece (Figure 1). These silver mines were amongst the most important mines of ancient Greece in the fifth and fourth centuries BC. During the second half of the nineteenth century, the French Mining Company of Laurion (CFML) exploited three concessions with a total surface area of 3,171 hectares. The ancient works were visited by mining engineers who surveyed them, and reused some of the ancient shafts

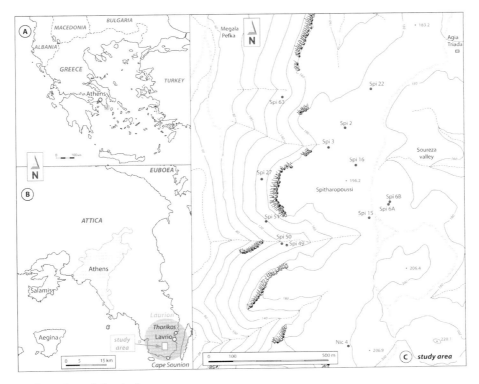

Figure 1. Laurion. Location of the study area

Figure 2. Laurion. Donning breathing apparatus (ARI-Fenzy) before a descent

Figure 3. Laurion. Exploring an ancient shaft (Spitharopoussi area – Shaft n° 15)

for ventilation. This was notably the case with the works in Mégala Pefka and the deepest shafts of the Spitharopoussi area.

In 2002, the first mission concentrated on the deepest shafts of the mining district (Morin *et al.* 2002). Several vertical shafts sounded out previously were explored using techniques developed by Alpine speleologists. Since then, there have been several successive missions under the auspices and permit of the French School at Athens (2002) and the Institute of Geology and Mineral Exploration (in the Department of General Geology and Geological Mapping known as IGME), conducted in order to survey the geology of this metalliferous district (Photiades *et al.* 2004; Photiades, *et al.* 2017), and also to understand how the ancient miners operated. Investigations were carried out into the shafts, with the deepest one discovered so far – the Persephone shaft - descending 109 m. These were exceptional structures for the ancient world (Figures 2 & 3).

This chapter summarises the authors' understandings of how ancient mining was conducted derived from their extensive physical investigations over the past 15 years.

THE COMPLEX NATURE OF THE DEEP DEPOSITS

The Laurion mining area consists mainly of metamorphic schists interposed with marble (Photiades and Carras 2001). The geological unit known as Kamariza comprises from the bottom up: lower marble approximately 100 m thick; Kamariza Schist varying between 15-40 m; and an upper marble layer which can exceed 80 m in places. In contrast to Kamariza, the Spitharopoussi geological area where exploration has been done comprises blue schist and metavolcanic material to the north-east and to the south of the studied area.

Geological surveys indicate that the upper and lower marbles derive from the same formation of marine carbonate from the Triassic/Jurassic periods. The doubling of the marble layers is explained by the tangential deformation into a marble/schist sequence by a bedded and eroded syncline, with the schist occupying the heart of the syncline.

The richest mineralisation is found at the greatest depth making it the most difficult to access. The ancient mine shafts in the area studied were mostly cut through into the upper marble layer, and/or across the schists of Kamariza, or even into the lower marble layer. Exploring them provides hitherto unknown information with each shaft being a veritable mine of information (Figures 4 and 21). The compilation of data from the surface and underground mining has allowed the creation of a geological section through the studied area. Four main layers of mineralisation have been plotted within the Kamariza formation. These are the so-called 'contacts' as described by Ardaillon (1897) and adopted by Conophagos (1980). This theory has been recently fully questioned based on recent geological field investigations and fluid mineral deposit analysis (Scheffer *et al.* 2019, 2017a, 2017b, 2016, 2015; Scheffer, 2016).

TRACES OF MINING ACTIVITY

Mining is a fully destructive and irreversible process; much evidence has been completely erased by later working both under and above ground. It is particularly difficult to date features such as shafts, galleries, stoping areas and toolmarks. Ancient mines usually still contain much evidence; the difficulties lie in interpretation and understanding of the processes used. Fortunately the underground environment preserves traces of mining activity rather well. Toolmarks, footprints in the soil, and tailings are signs of actual work which give indications about how the miners went about their business (Figure 5).

Anyone visiting the ancient mining works for the first time will be struck by the peculiar characteristics of the underground passages, with the regularity of the engineering works, and by the aesthetics of the shafts and galleries. But mostly seeing the mines gives rise to questions - how were the tunnels dug, and how to explain their sheer scale?

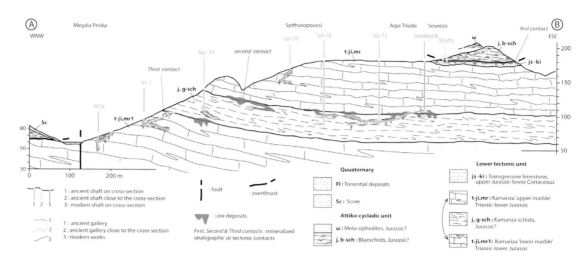

Figure 4.a Geological map of Spitharoupoussi area, Laurion district (Photiades et al., 2017) also showing the locations of the ancient shafts (Fadin 2011). **Figure 4.b** See pull out section.

Figure 5. Laurion. Mégala Pefka. Gallery and working face under examination. Point chisel (masonry tool) marks on the walls (Spi. 5)

MEASURING AND ANALYSING TOOLMARKS

Measuring requires discrimination of a range of semiotic traces which are directly observable:

- geological traces which are often tenuous, manifested from fluid circulation in the earth's crust
- traces directly connected to the act of extraction
- traces corresponding to secondary works
- toolmarks and signs of work, witness to the human presence in the galleries.

Macroscopic observation of rock and toolmarks permits a deeper understanding of both the morphology of the ore body and the nature of the mining techniques employed.

PARTICULAR UNDERGROUND ARCHITECTURE

Three types of works are to be found underground at Laurion: galleries, shafts and working areas. Drift galleries criss-cross the underground horizontally. They were the starting point for exploitation of a vein of minerals. They probed the mining area in terms of its potential for current and future exploitation. In the deepest parts, junction galleries connect shafts and mining areas. Influences on the architecture of the galleries include the flow of fracturing and density of marble, carbonisation or not of the rocks, the sloping of the vein, and type of mineralisation. Their morphology is generally very tidy, and form a pattern characteristic of these ancient networks. The size of junction, exploratory, and drift galleries and lanes can vary according to the template. The parameters of the sections are variable. The width at the base rarely exceeds an average of 80 cm, but these measurements are far from consistent. The geometric morphology of the works remains relatively constant, but variations are perceptible

Figure 6. Laurion. Spitharopoussi sector. Quadrangular section shafts. Grooves on walls: timber remains of ventilation system seen from the surface. (Spi 6)

on the interior of the same section. They probably correspond with the technique of the miner doing the work, who economised effort in the most difficult areas.

MEANS OF ACCESSING THE DEEP MINING WORKS - THE SHAFTS

To reach the mineralised areas, the ancient miners used vertical shafts. To bore them, and to traverse particularly hard ground, necessitated complex equipment and careful attention. The shafts on the Spitharopoussi plateau had a quadrangular shape, on average 1.35 x 1.65 m. Their depth was variable but could descend to over 100 m absolutely vertically (Figure 6).

Most of the shafts have grooves on their sides. This morphology was used to facilitate clamping the timber of the mine shaft installation onto the walls (Morin and Photiades 2012, 311-312). Studying the tunnels permits an understanding of timber techniques especially in relation to the problem of ventilation (Morin and Photiades 2005), a vital imperative of mining. Traces of many of these processes are in evidence at Laurion and have been the object of recent studies (Herbach *et al.* 2013).

EXTRACTION TECHNIQUES

Tool marks are the best way of identifying human activity, but these marks are often in complex patterns. They come from the nature of the tool used and from the edge, indicating the direction of the blow and the direction of the work. Most of the traces on the walls come from the use of the same type of cutting tool. The mallet and point chisel were the quintessential tools at Laurion. The point chisel, the so-called pointerolle (point chisel), is a small pointed metal chisel with a flattened head that was tapped with a mallet. Extraction in the marble zone was done manually with the point chisel, and probably with wedges inserted in cracks in more friable schists (Figure 7).

TECHNIQUES OF ROCK MINING

In the galleries, traces of mining are everywhere. They are evidenced by a multitude of almost parallel, curvilinear grooves equidistant on the walls. They indicate both the direction of mining and the position of the miner facing the rock. These marks, often very regular, mark the walls of the galleries and are one of the characteristics. Traces are still visible of the final removals intended to complete this task. What significance can be gleaned from this layout?

Repeated blows to the wall might erase all trace of the first part of the operation. The only alternative way of understanding the technique lies in observation and analysis of the 'front

Figure 7. Laurion. Research gallery in progress: miners at work. Reconstructed scene. The miner on the right is drilling through the rock with a hammer and a pointerolle (point chisel). This reconstruction is based on observations made underground. With permission of Bernard Nicolas, illustrator (www.danselombre.com)

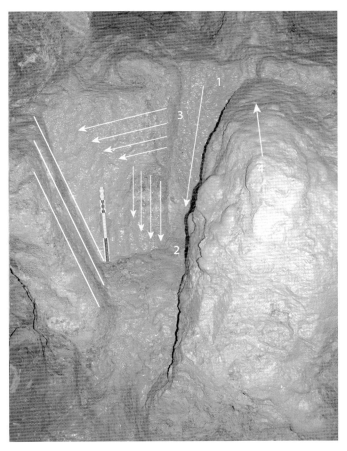

Figure 8. Laurion. Mégala Pefka sector. Spi 49 – a view of a typical working face showing traces of all faces of the process: 1) vertical lateral notch; 2 & 3) vertical lateral mining. Highlighted in white on the left: lateral remains of sections cut out successively

faces'. A front face is a surface at the limit of the working site in the direction of progress. In other words, it corresponds to the terminus of a gallery or work area. It is particularly interesting to observe and study the mining techniques when the work was abandoned for some unknown reason. The observation of front faces and topographical analysis shows that there were many variations to the basic technique which consisted of making a preliminary kerf or notch. The front faces bear the mark of this technique which was generally used in the trial galleries. The notch corresponds to about a third of the width of the face. Removal was carried out all along the operation with successive tiers removed down from the roof (Figure 8).

In larger works, whenever there was a perceptible incline, the miners tended to break up the working face into stopes. Splitting the working area into stopes allowed each to be more effectively exploited. In the networks of the Third Contact, it is not unusual to observe traces of 'underhand stoping' (Mi 7) (Figure 9).

FROM STOPING TO A COMPARTMENT: AN ORIGINAL MINING TECHNIQUE

The general aspect of numerous galleries resembles panels closely butted side by side, but in which their liaison was adjusted depending on the direction of the mining. Such works show a fairly regular succession of stopes. The volumetric standardised dimension of mining is a striking feature of the works. It seems the miners worked to a predetermined volume, defining in advance each compartment or panel to be excavated (Figure 10).

Figure 9. Laurion. Mégala Pefka sector. Mi 7 – Underhand stoping technique

Figure 10. Laurion. Spitharopoussi sector. Spi 15 – Upper marble gallery. Succession of panels

Figure 11. Laurion. Spitharopoussi sector. Spi 5 – Vertical sinking technique. Work in progress with well-preserved remains. The process was: Stages 1,2,3: successive benches; 4: Ongoing breaking of the upper bench. The arrows represent tool marks on the wall: finishing works

TECHNIQUE FOR VERTICAL SINKING: THE STACKING OF PANELS

It is, of course, easier to learn about the techniques of digging in well-preserved areas of the networks, but these examples are rare. The bottom of a shaft (Spi 5) sunk at the end of a network close to the surface permits a partial understanding. It reveals the presence of platform 0.4 m wide in a general section of the shaft measuring 1.02 x 0.96 m. The mining strategy employed here was similar to that in the galleries but progressed in a vertical fashion. Excavation was effected from a deep side notch of 0.56 m which was enlarged horizontally and continued in stopes. Here the progression of underhand stoping went in five successive, unidirectional steps. The final one involved equalising the sidewalls to an oblique position (Figure 11).

Mining carried out in the marble layers reveals a strong dexterity in achieving regularity in the geometry of the galleries. Beyond this aesthetic, the ancient mine indicates a particularly well-developed standard process with a hierarchically-based work flow. Mining at Laurion can be identified with a strong technical tradition in equipment and methods (Vernant 1965; Jockey 2003).

MINING TECHNIQUES AT DEEP LEVELS

The excavation technique differed according to the density or hardness of the rock. Extraction could be starting by scoring the rock, and then making a deep shearing following the horizontal strata (Spi 18) at floor level. This preparatory step, or undercut, was done to undermine the base of the stope, and thus weaken the rock to be extracted and decrease its resistance (Gruner 1921).

Most of the time, the front face progressed perpendicularly in the service gallery, and on each side in an irregular edge, creating a cavity. This could be as long as 15 m. Too great a length risked a roof collapse and was rarely justified, except occasionally by leaving supporting pillars. In the case of an oblique ore deposit, extraction was effected in an upwards

Figure 12. Laurion. Spitharopoussi plateau. Spi 18 – Deep works in the Third Contact. Mining technique process using a horizontal cut to the wall. 1: horizontal mining. 2. Vertical mining. 3. Pillar

Figure 13. Laurion. Spitharopoussi plateau. Spi 18 – Deep works in the Third Contact. Mining technique process using a horizontal cut to the roof. To the right, behind the working face, a cluster of mineralised blocks. 1. Horizontal mining. 2. Vertical mining

Figure 14. Laurion. Spitharopoussi sector – Spi 18. Deep works in the Third Contact. Ancient mining works around – 80m. Access lane and accumulation of waste (backfilling)

direction from a horizontal notch situated on the ceiling directly under a strata join. The disengaged front face was then cleared in a unidirectional fashion from top to bottom and progressed following the inclination (climbing face). (Figures 12 and 13).

The type of deposit in thin veins visible in the networks of Shaft Spi 18 was exploited with a partial or total backfilling of the work areas, and by installing waste deposit areas particularly along traffic lanes. Containing waste in a space avoided having to disperse it and facilitated the transport of materials and movement of workers, but waste deposits were never used to support the roof (Figure 14).

THE LAURION MINES – METHODS OF EXPLOITATION ADAPTED TO THE GEOLOGICAL CONTEXT

Two main scenarios are considered based on the location of the deposits:

1. Mineralisation close to the surface or outcropping was first exploited (Leleu 1966), starting with the outcrop, then underground by cuttings and extension galleries. As they advanced the cutting, the miners dug galleries of lesser size, horizontally and laterally to test the amount of mineralisation. Often the miners had recourse to this to gauge the extent of the deposit, and thus to decide the initial layout of the works.

The downward progress of the works was made by benching (Figure 15). Cuttings following the axis of the gallery were sunk from the floor. Traces of these levels are thus discernible in the roof, and bear witness to this original technique, the first phase of a general lateral exploitation. Certain works are peppered in places by the trial galleries which sometimes overlap, fuse, and can constitute a veritable labyrinth (Figure 16).

Figure 15. Laurion. Mégala Pefka sector. Mi 7 – Benching works: technique of downward stoping. The gallery is exploited along its length by taking off the material

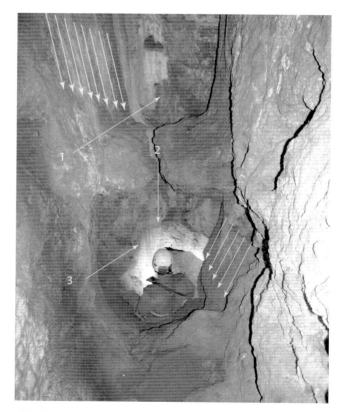

Figure 16. Spitharopoussi Plateau. Spi 15 – Nyphitsa network. Downward stoping process by benching (reboring) the original gallery. 1. Original 1st research gallery. 2. Remain of 1st gallery floor. 3. 2nd gallery

Figure 17. Laurion. Spitharopoussi sector: Spi 18. Deep works. Junction gallery between 2 work zones in the Third Contact

2. In deep mineralisations, it is possible to distinguish two methods of exploitation directly connected to the morphology and positioning of veins.

a) On top of the plateau, the deep works relied on shafts to the galleries of close to 30 m with quadrangular sections (Figure 17).

The excavations were developed following along thin, rangy axes. The miners then opened the cuttings or cavities, more or less equidistant, following in the direction of the vein. On each side of the leading gallery were openings of works. The layout this produced faithfully followed the morphological characteristics of this type of network served by deep vertical shafts which gave access to the Third Contact from around 80 m (Figure 18). In these cramped spaces, the miners looked for ways to progress efficiently and sought to minimise the quantity of sterile material excavated. They banked up the material they dug in order to obtain precisely what they needed to carry from the mine. In this way, only mineralised rock was extracted each day (Figure 19).

b) On the west side of the plateau, on the slope, the base of the shafts opened in schists often debouching into works. The principal axis of the exploratory galleries was parallel to the hillside. The plan of exploitation was mostly linear. The circulation route, uniquely, was sometimes cut into the block of the quadrangular section or laid out in the partly banked-up excavations.

Larger chambers can be found in the centre of particularly exiguous networks. They often correspond with the junction point of several veins or concentrated mineralisation. Mining was carried out on both sides of the galleries. These works evolved together and sometimes developed in terraces and more frequently in cells. With this scheme, the miners could control the progression from a security point of view. Ore was evacuated on a man's back or by dragging (Figure 20). Traces of the various stages of excavation are still visible.

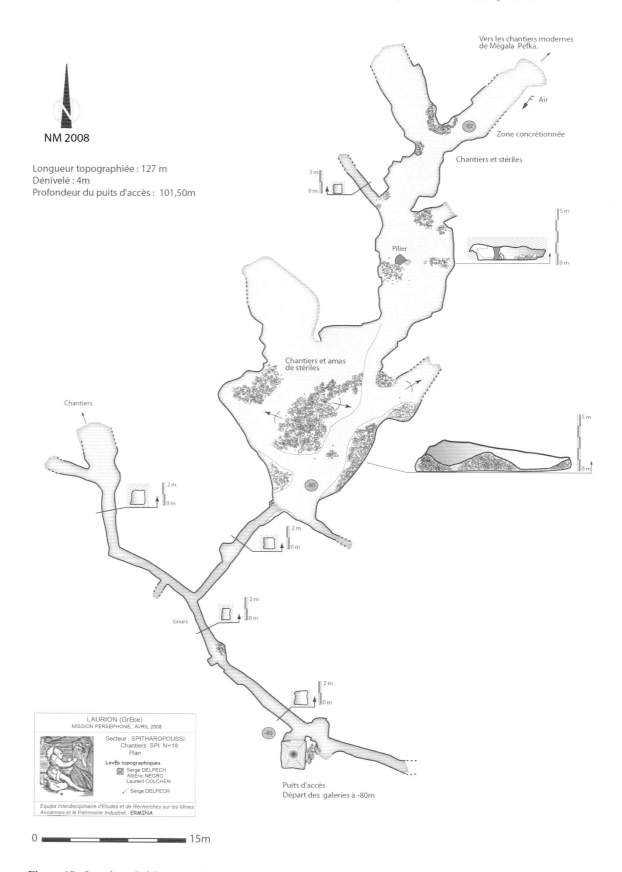

Figure 18. Laurion. Spitharoupoussi Plateau : Spi 18. (– 80 m) Topography of the works in the Third Contact. (Drawing: Serge Delpech)

Figure 19. Laurion. Sector Spitharopoussi : Spi 2. Deep works in the Third Contact. Ancient works around − 80m. Residual pillar

Figure 20. Laurion. Spitharopoussi Plateau. Spi 49 – Deep works in the Third Contact. Clear traces of dragging on the ground fossilized by the calcite. Junction gallery between two work zones

A RECURRENT PROBLEM: THE CHRONOLOGY OF THE PHASES OF EXCAVATION

The study of such a network of galleries raises the problem of identifying the chronology of mining operations. At first sight, the subterranean networks correspond with a single phase of exploitation. They do not seem to have undergone repeated phases of exploitation, with the exception of certain works in the lower marble layers, and the more easily accessed networks close to the surface. In these, the traces of ancient work are visible especially in the more recent re-workings undertaken for the most part during the fifth century AD. Oil lamp fragments are among the most characteristic markers of these subterranean networks.

CONCLUSION

Understanding the methods utilised by the ancient underground miners is a matter of reading the tiny clues they left. The demonstrated mining techniques are evidence of an art of mining which took on a real importance at Laurion. Regardless of the mode of exploitation, the miners devised processes to suit the mining conditions within the indispensable parameters for maintenance of mining: ventilation, movement of men and materials, extraction. It is also clear that there was a hierarchical structure because to conduct this work, it was necessary to plan the layout of the tunnels depending on the geology. This is attested in Xenophon (*Memorabilia* 2.5.2) who mentions how Nicias paid a small fortune for a slave capable of managing a mine.

In the course of making these investigations, more than 10 kms of underground workings were explored plus some topographic features. The mode of exploitation also frequently raises the central question of the geological and mineralogical knowledge of the miners of these gigantic mining operations. How did the ancient miners know where to locate the ore, and put in place the necessary organisation? The observation of certain mining activity on outcrops allows a partial answer to these questions.

Economic success and choice of method depended on the presence or otherwise or certain key factors: high-value minerals, available land, a workforce with the practical know-how and mastery of the necessary techniques, dynamism of the political elite, existence of a communication network, and availability of funds. These conditions were met at Laurion when mining operations were undertaken by the city-state of Athens (Davis 2014, 257-277). It was a quasi-industrial enterprise in the sense of being a concentration of technical means implemented to extract and process silver by a process unique in the ancient world at this scale.

Photographic credit

Except where otherwise stated, photos are by Denis Morin. Photographic enhancement – DAO: Hélène Morin-Hamon.

The research

Underground investigations were the result of a cross-disciplinary research team which combined to handle the important logistics. They have been conducted under the auspices and permit of the *French School at Athens* (2002) and of the *Institute of Geology and Mineral Exploration* (IGME). They were undertaken in a series of short forays under the aegis of the *Institute of Geology and Mineral Exploration of Athens – IGME*, and of the *TRACES* laboratory (*UMR CNRS* 5608) with the support of the *French School at Athens*. The exploration of the mines was undertaken by members of the *Equipe Interdisciplinaire d'Etudes et de Recherches Archéologiques sur les Mines Anciennes et le Patrimoine Industriel* (*ERMINA*):

Michel Aubert, Bernard Bohly, Patrice Cocuaud, Laurent Colchen, Maryse et Serge Delpech, Richard Herbach, Yves Imbert, Denis Jacquemot, Denis Morin, Hélène Morin-Hamon, Albéric Negro and Patrick Rosenthal.

Special thanks go to:

- Dr Gil Davis who translated and edited this paper and also for his corrections and wise advice.
- The *Institute of Geology and Mineral Exploration* in the *Department of General Geology & Geological Mapping of Athens* (*IGME* – Greece), in particular to the *Service of Geological Mapping at IGME*, responsible for the geological maps of Laurion (prepared by its Adjunct Director Dr Adonis Photiades and Dr Irene Zananiri).
- The *Ephorate of Attica* and its director, M.G. Steinhauer.
- M. Dimitris Loukas, Mayor of Lavrio.
- M.D. Mulliez, Director of the *French School at Athens*.
- Professor K. Panagopoulos, *National Technical University of Athens* (*NTUA*), and director of the *Laurion Technological and Cultural Park* (*LTCP*).
- Lionel Fadin, Surveyor at the *French School at Athens*
- The anonymous reviewers.

REFERENCES

Ardaillon, E. 1897. *Les mines du Laurion dans l'Antiquité*, Bibliothèque des Ecoles Françaises d'Athènes et de Rome, Fasc. 77 (Paris).

Conophagos, E.C. 1980. *Le Laurium antique et la technique grecque de la production de l'argent* (Athens).

Davis, G. 2014. 'Mining money in Late Archaic Athens', *Historia* 63/3, 257-277.

Fadin, L. (2011). Mission IGME - Laurion. Rapports d'activités topographiques. 30 mars et 08 avril 2010. 5 p. 7 plans, 1 tableau (CD Rom). Fadin L. 2011. 21 avril 2011. 4 p. 8 plans, 2 tableaux (CD Rom). *Ecole française d'Athènes*.

Gruner, L. 1921. *Cours d'exploitation des mines. Méthodes d'exploitation en carrière et souterraine* (Paris).

Herbach R., Morin D. and Rosenthal, P. 2013. 'La géométrie des puits du Laurion. Traces et indices des technologies minières de l'Antiquité'. *Actes du Colloque Indices et traces : la mémoire des gestes.* Nancy, juin 2011. PUN – Editions universitaires de Lorraine, coll. Archéologie, Espaces, Patrimoines, 171-185.

Jockey, Ph. 2003. 'L'artisan, l'objet et la société : à propos d'un éventuel blocage des techniques dans l'Antiquité, l'exemple de l'artisanat de la pierre', in Balansard, A. (ed.), *Le travail et la pensée technique dans l'Antiquité classique. Lecture et relectures d'une analyse de psychologie historique de Jean-Pierre Vernant* (Technologie/Idéologies/Pratiques, XV, 1), 57-81.

Leleu, M. 1966. 'Les gisements plombo-zincifères du Laurium (Grèce)', *Sciences de la Terre, Nancy,* XI/3, 293–343.

Morin, D. and Photiades, A. 2005. 'Nouvelles recherches sur les mines antiques du Laurion (Grèce). Mines et métallurgies dans l'Antiquité. Etat des recherches', *Pallas, revue d'Etudes Antiques* 67, 327-358.

Morin, D. and Photiades, A. 2012. 'L'exploitation des gisements métallifères profonds dans l'Antiquité. Les mines du Laurion (Grèce)', in Olshausen, E. and Sauer, V. (eds.), *Die Schätze der Erde – Natürliche Ressourcen in der antiken Welt. Stuttgarter Kolloquium zur Historischen. Geographie des Altertums* 10, 2008. (Stuttgart), 281-335.

Morin, D., Photiades, A., Jacquemot, D., Rosenthal, P. *et al.* 2002. 'Mission géologique et archéologique de reconnaissance au Laurion (Grèce). Les puits d'extraction antiques de Spitharopoussi : problématique générale de l'extraction des gîtes de contact. Campagne 2002. Avec une contribution de Domergue, Cl. sur les concessions', DVD - ROM, *Institute of Geology and Mineral Exploration, IGME - CNRS. Avec la participation de l'Ecole Française d'Athènes*.

Photiades, A. and Carras, N. 2001. 'Stratigraphy and geological structure of the Laurion area (Attica, Greece)', *Bull. Geol. Soc. Greece,* Vol. XXXIV/1, 103-109A.

Photiades, A., Mavridou, F. and Carras, N. 2004. 'Geological map of Greece in scale 1:50.000^e', *Laurion-Makronissos-Agios Georgios Islands* sheet. Edited by Institute of Geology and Mineral Exploration - IGME Athens.

Photiades, A., Rosenthal P., Zananiri, I. 2017. 'Geological map of Spitharopoussi Area (*Lavrion District*) in scale 1: 5000^e'. Edited by Institute of Geology and Mineral Exploration - IGME Athens.

Scheffer C., Tarantola A., Vanderhaeghe O., Rigaudier T. and Photiades A., 2017a. 'CO_2 flow during orogenic gravitational collapse: Syntectonic decarbonation and fluid mixing at the ductile-brittle transition (Lavrion, Greece)', *Chem. Geol.* 450, 248–263.

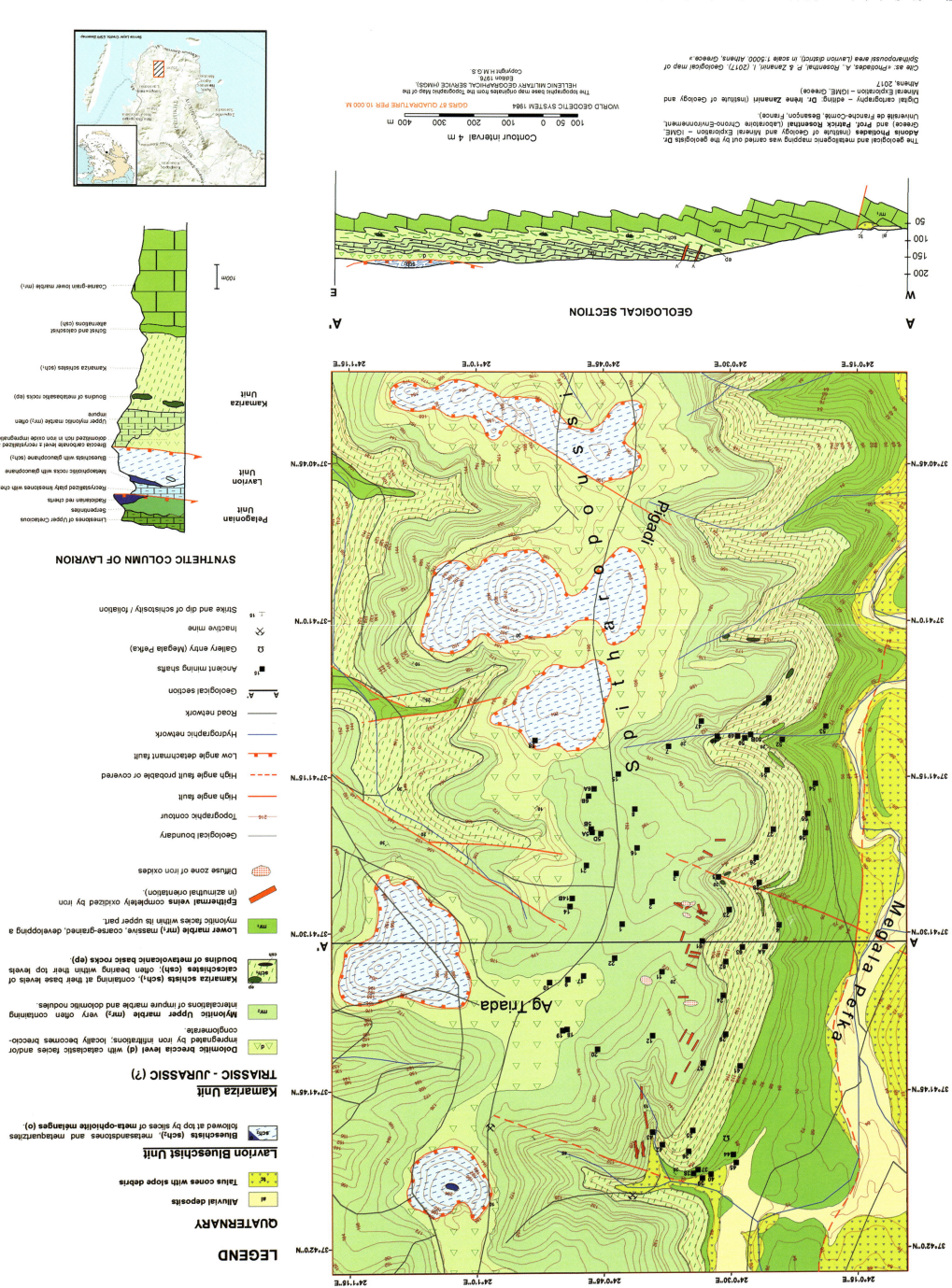

Figure 21. Geological map of Spitharopoussi area (Lavrion district) in scale 1:5,000. (Production by IGME; thanks to Adonis Photiades and Irene Zananiri)

Scheffer C., Tarantola A., Vanderhaeghe O., Voudouris P., Rigaudier T., Photiades A., Morin D. and Alloucherie A. 2017b. 'The Lavrion Pb-Zn-Fe-Cu-Ag detachment-related district (Attica, Greece): Structural control on hydrothermal flow and element transfer-deposition', *Tectonophysics* 717, 607–627.

Scheffer C., Tarantola A., Vanderhaeghe O., Voudouris P., Rigaudier T., Spry, P.G. and Photiades A. 2019. 'The Lavrion Pb-Zn-Ag-rich vein and breccia detachment related deposits (Greece): Involvement of evaporated seawater and meteoric fluids during postorogenic exhumation', *Economic Geology*. https://doi.org/10.5382/econgeo.4670

Scheffer C., Vanderhaeghe O., Lanari P., Tarantola A., Ponthus L., Photiades A. and France L., 2016. 'Syn- to post-orogenic exhumation of metamorphic nappes: Structure and thermobarometry of the western Attic-Cycladic metamorphic complex (Lavrion, Greece)', *J. Geodyn.* 96, 174–193.

Scheffer, C. 2016. 'Réservoirs fluides et transferts en contexte d'exhumation orogénique: Implications sur la position structurale des minéralisations Cu-Pb-Zn-Fe-Ag dans la région Laurion-Eubée (Grèce)' (PhD dissertation, Université de Lorraine, France).

Scheffer, C., Vanderhaeghe, O., Lanari, P., Tarantola, A., Ponthus, L., Photiades, A. and France, L. 2015. 'Syn-To Post Orogenic Exhumation Of Metamorphic Nappes: Structure and thermobarometry of the western Attic-Cycladic Metamorphic complex (Laurion, Greece)', *J. Geodynamics.*, http://dx.doi.org/10.1016/j.jog.2015.08.005

Vernant, J.-P. 1965. *Mythe et pensée chez les grecs. Etudes de psychologie historique*. Tome II (Paris).

Xenophon, *Mémorables*. Tome II. 2011. 1re partie. Livres II-III. Texte établi par Michèle Bandini, traduit et annoté par Louis-André Dorion. Collection des Universités de France, Série grecque.

4. ARI – A CLASSICAL MINING DISTRICT AT ANAVYSSOS (ATTICA)

Hans Lohmann

> Of silver they possess a veritable fountain,
> a treasure chest in their soil
> Aischlyos, *Persai* 322

ABSTRACT

The Laurion mining district in South East Attica was the largest and most important industrial complex of ancient Greece. It was intensively exploited for lead and silver from the late Archaic to the early Hellenistic period. After two hundred years of scholarly research, starting as early as 1815, several key questions concerning the workflow from the mine to the final product (mostly silver) remained unsolved. A new research project, started in 2014 as a joint venture with the Ephoria of East Attica, has been devoted to the small mining district of Ari which forms the westernmost ore deposit of the whole Laurion district. In a first step, substantial parts of Mt. Charvalo at Ari were cleaned, surveyed and mapped.

The Laurion district in South East Attica is not only the largest, but also the most important and best preserved mining district of ancient Greece. Its core area comprises no less than 80 km^2, stretching from Cape Sounion in the South to Plaka in the North and from Thorikos in the East to Ari near Anavyssos in the West (Curtius and Kaupert 1889, sheets 14 [Cap Sunion West], 15 [Cap Sunion Ost], 16 [Lavrion]; Papachatze 1974, 93, Fig. 22; Conophagos 1980, maps in folder; Goette 2000, maps). With its enormous wealth of ancient remains, including mines, workshops, smelting places, sanctuaries, towns, and farmsteads, it forms a unique fossilised industrial landscape of the Classical period deserving of listing UNESCO World Heritage Site.

The Laurion district is rich in polymetallic ore deposits; the main minerals are galena, cerussite, zincblende, and copper minerals (Morin and Photiades 2012). It is also rich in sulfidic iron ores. These were not, however, mined in antiquity because they are difficult to smelt. Iron was evidently imported in large quantities from elsewhere, most probably from Etruria (Gill 1994, 102; Corretti and Benvenuti 2004). Zincblende (Sphalerite, ZnS), which can still be found in Laurion (although in non-profitable quantities according to modern standards) was not utilisable before the eighteenth century AD. When in Roman times copper-zinc alloys (*i.e.* brass) came into use, calamine or zinc carbonate (ZnCO$_3$) was mined in large quantities in Sardinia. Even today the deposits of cerussite and galena at the Laurion are not totally exhausted. On entering the classical mines and galleries, however, it is often impossible to determine which minerals were mined at any particular point in time.

Academic research into Laurion mining started as early as 1815 with August Boeckh's *Über die laurischen Silberbergwerke in Attika*. This pioneering work in the new field of economic and social history relied exclusively on the extant literary sources, especially Xenophon's *Poroi*, written c.340 BC (Boeckh 1815; Boeckh 1842; for an appraisal of Boeckh's writings see Fischer 1992). Fieldwork was first undertaken in 1840 by Karl Fiedler, a German geologist who surveyed many parts of Greece looking for natural mineral deposits to enable the young Greek state to develop its resources (Fiedler 1840). Other important students were the Greek mining engineer Andrea Kordella, the Prussian officer Friedrich von Bernhardi who in 1882 mapped large parts of the Laurion district, the French historian, archaeologist and geographer Edouard Ardaillon, the former Greek industrial minister, Constantinos Conophagos, and Evangelos Kakavogiannis and his wife Olga (Cordella 1869; Curtius and Kaupert 1889, sheets 14 [Cap Sunion West], 15 [Cap Sunion Ost], 16 [Lavrion]; von Bernhardi 1927, 96–100; Ardaillon 1897; Conophagos 1980; Kakavogiannis 2005). A bibliography on the Laurion compiled by H. Kalcyk (Kalcyk 1982, 226–35), comprises no fewer than 200 entries. Since then, more than 180 new articles and books have appeared in print (Nomicos 2017).

On the other hand, much damage to archaeological evidence has occurred in the Laurion area, firstly by the reworking of the ancient slags since 1864, then by the reopening of the mines in 1870 (Kalcyk 1982, 214–9). During the last decades damage has also been caused by various building activities, such as roads, housing and industrialisation. In the 1980s the ammunition plant Elleneke

Biomechania Hoplon (EBO) was set up in the Botsari valley (Kakavogiannis 1983, 55–7, and 1984, 51–5; Lohmann 1993, 106–7; Goette 2000, 12). This led to the senseless devastation of the ancient mining district of Thrasymos, the largest and most important mining district within the deme of Sounion (Lohmann 1993, 106–7).

Although quantification of the output of silver from the Laurion mines during the sixth and fifth centuries BC is open to debate,[1] the contribution of the silver mines in the Laurion to the economy of Athens and her hegemonial role during the fifth and fourth centuries BC can hardly be overestimated. Astonishingly, however, it has been passed over in silence by several modern historians. The renowned historian Chr. Meier (1993, 48, and see 22 and 272 for the shipbuilding program of Themistokles) devoted a mere two lines out of 700 pages in his book on Athens to the silver mines at Laurion, stating that the mines were essential for the public finances of the polis. K.-W. Welwei (2011), another distinguished scholar, does not pay any attention at all to the Laurion and its contribution to the financial system of the polis of Athens (cf. Davis 2014).

As stated by Xenophon (*Poroi* 4.2), the very beginnings of mining activities in the Laurion area are lost. Neither the Kitsos cave nor the Final Neolithic settlement on Megalo Rimbari have provided any evidence for metallurgical processes (Lambert 1981; Lohmann *et al.* 2002). M. Nazou in her comprehensive dissertation on the findings from the famous mine 3 at Thorikos, concluded: "there is circumstantial evidence to associate the EBA II pottery [...] with the use of the mine. However, with the existing data, the unstratified LN-EBA II

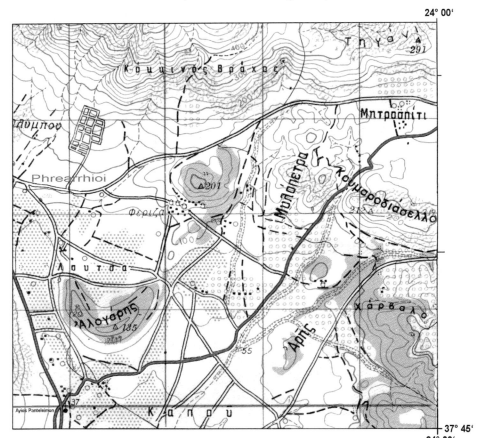

Figure 1. Map of district of Ari. From *Athenai-Koropion* 1 : 50 000, edited by the Geographiki Hyperessia Stratou (1976) (adjusted to a B/W image)

---

[1] The figure of 20,000 drachmas from a single die is often cited as a basis for quantification of output. Steel of high quality was available already in the archaic period (see Yalçın 1993), but it seems unlikely from a technical point of view that one could mint this many drachms. According to practical tests performed by D. G. Sellwood (1963), 4500 – 9000 coins (and no more) from one pair of dies should be considered as the norm. On this matter see also Wolters 1999, 107–14, esp. 108, 111.

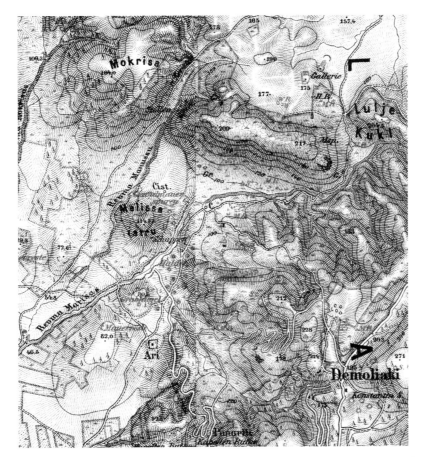

Figure 2. Map of Ari prepared by Friedrich von Bernhardi (1927) from survey in 1882 (adjusted to a B/W image)

pottery assemblage excavated throughout the area of the mine cannot be used to re-date the earliest mining activities at Thorikos" (Nazou 2013; Spitaels 1984; Waelkens 1990). We are still in need of firm evidence for the date of the very beginning of mining activities in the Laurion area.

A new research project was started in 2014 as a joint venture (*synergasia*) with the Ephoria of East Attica under Dr E. Andreikou and in close cooperation with Dr A. Kapetanios. It will hopefully contribute towards solving these key questions. The project is devoted to the small mining district of Ari, north of modern Anavyssos (ancient Anaphlystos) which forms the westernmost ore deposit of the whole Laurion district (Fig. 1) (Bultrighini 2015, 177–205).

The enormous density of mining galleries, shafts, workshops and associated structures at Ari, especially on the slopes of Mt. Charvalo, was already obvious from the map of Friedrich von Bernhardi who surveyed the area in 1882 (Fig. 2) when modern mining was in its early stages (Curtius and Kaupert 1889, sheets 16 [Lavrion], 17 [Olympos]; von Bernhardi 1927, 96–100). Since then, no better overall map of the ancient remains in the Laurion district has ever been made. For a new map of Mt. Spitharopoussi now see D. Morin *et.al.* in this volume.

Thanks to the discovery of several ancient *horoi* by M. Langdon and the author during the 1980s, it is possible to draw borderlines between at least some of the ancient demes in South Attica (for instance, between Sounion and Amphitrope, and between Amphitrope and Atene: Lohmann 1993, 109, fig. 12). According to a mining lease discussed below, the *rhevma* Ari at least partially formed the natural bounder between Anaphlystos and Phrearrhioi, a boundary which was also marked by *horoi*, including one which was found in 1979 (Traill 1986, 117 n. 7, pl. 16, 4; Bultrighini 2015, 146 n. 399).

Deme	Bouleutai	Mining leases
Atene	3	0
Amphitrope	3	8-9
Anaphlystos	10	5-6
Besa	2	24
Phrearrhioi	10	2-3
Sounion	4	16
- Nape		6
- Thrasymos		21
- Laureion		6-7
Thorikos	5	18
- Maroneia		6

Table 1. Statistic of bouleutai quota and number of mining leases pertaining to the six mining demes of Attica

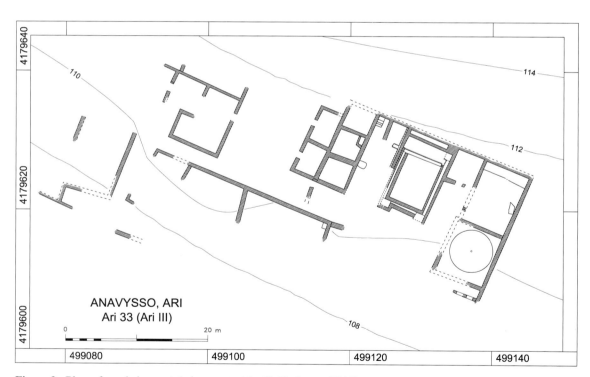

Figure 3. Plan of workshops at Ari excavated by K. Tsaïmou (2010)

Overall, some 289 mining leases have come down to us and of these 112 still preserve the location of the mine (Lohmann 2005, 118, n. 41). Although the demes of Anaphlystos and Phrearrhioi were evidently large and populous, mining played a minor role; only 5 or 6 leases out of these 112 are for mines at Anaphlystos, and even fewer belong to Phrearrhioi. The mines of these two demes are to be located to the north and northwest of modern Anavyssos at Ari, the name of which derives directly from Phrearrhioi (Lohmann 1993, 78; Goette 2014; Bultrighini 2015, 145–76).

A mining lease concerning the mine Phaneion at Anaphlystos mentions as its northern border ὁ λόφος [ὁ – 8 letters missing – ἐν] Φρεα (*IG* II² 1582 lines 12935; Langdon in Lalonde *et al.* 1991, 105–117 esp. 111 lines 297–299). ὁ λόφος (*lophos*) means 'crest of a hill', and since the abbreviation Φρεα clearly stands for Φρεαρροῖ (the locative of the deme Phrearrhioi) and the torrent Ari marked in blue in Fig. 2 once formed the borderline between the two demes of Phrearrhioi and Anaphlystos, it is evident that the hill mentioned is identical with today's Melissia Iatrou. Therefore, the workshops excavated by K. Tsaïmou between 2005 and 2008 on the western side of the torrent Ari (Fig. 3) are situated at Phrearrhioi, while those on the eastern side are at Anaphlystos (Tsaïmou 2010, 163–71).

On the hill called Mokriza (Fig. 4) to the west of the torrent Ari (and on the 'Phrearrhian' side), there are not only traces of a hilltop sanctuary and a settlement of the Classical period (first observed by H. Lauter) but also evidence of a large prehistoric site close to the ore deposits of Ari.² Did any prehistoric mining activities take place there? Are some of the hundreds of outcrops in the region datable to the prehistoric period? These questions will hopefully be solved within the near future. A. Kapetanios (*per. comm.*) holds that he has seen debris of metallurgical processes on Mokriza. In and around Mt. Charvalo east of the torrent Ari, an area which has undergone an intensive survey during 2015, neither prehistoric mining tools nor prehistoric pottery have come to light so far.³

Figure 4. Mokriza hill

² The name Mokriza derives from *arvanitic mókrëzë*, handmill, with the locative suffix *–iza*, evidently alluding to the shape of the hill. Lohmann 1993, 75, 505 (site no. AN 25) pl. 72, 1.2. A large rectangular building, excavated by M. Oikonomakou (1994, 66), was erroneously misplaced by Bultrighini (2015, 151, n. 417) on Mokriza.
³ For the typical fluted club as prehistoric mining tool see Rafel *et al.* 2016, 95–129.

Figure 5. Surface crushing tables, Ari

Since 2000, Denis Morin (Université de Lorraine) and his team have been studying the mines of Laurion with excellent results (Morin and Photiades 2005; Morin and Photiades 2008; Morin and Photiades 2012; Morin *et al.* in this volume). Unfortunately, shafts and galleries are often not precisely datable and we still do not know when the first shafts were sunk into the ground. For the mines at Ari investigated in 2016 by Morin and his team, there is sufficient evidence to date them to the Classical and early Hellenistic periods.

The step between mining the ore and smelting was enrichment. The age old question of how the ore was enriched has never been satisfactorily answered. Enriching the ore under pre-industrial conditions had to be performed in three steps: coarse crushing, fine crushing and beneficiation with the aid of water. The ore within the mines was not won mechanically (or by blasting) but with hammer and chisel. No large lumps of ore were brought up from the mines. Some initial sorting and crushing occurred underground; Morin (*per. comm.* and cf. Morin *et al.* this volume) has found crushing tables identical with those on the surface (Fig. 5).

After coarse crushing, the ore had to be fine crushed. Unpublished analyses on the surface of fragments of so-called 'Olynthian mills' (Fig. 6), made by Dr A. Hein (*pers. comm*), of the National Centre for Scientific Research *Demokritos* at Athens by means of an XRF analyser Niton XL3tGOLDD+, have not yet confirmed the theory of Conophagos (1980, 220, fig. 10-6 /10-10) that Olynthian mills were not only used for grinding grain but also for fine crushing the ore. The fragments of Olynthian mills tested by Dr Hein consist of basaltic lava, which is indeed harder than the fine crushed ore – mostly galena (PbS) or cerussite (also known as lead carbonate or white lead ore). On the grinding face of the mills so far tested, concentrations of lead up to 0.7% were measured, reflecting the overall lead pollution of the area.

The historian M.I. Finley and his school claimed that there was no substantial technological progress made during antiquity (*Greene 2000*). This claim is disproved by evidence of the invention of large mechanical mills during the second half of the fourth or the beginning of the third century BC (at the latest). Following Conophagos (1980, 248–52), these mechanical mills have been erroneously identified as helicoidal washeries. Quite a number of them have

Figure 6. An 'Olynthian mill' (Lavrion Museum). Photo: H. Lohmann

Figure 7. Mechanical mill (so-called 'helicoidal washery'), Ari

been found at Ari (Fig. 7). They are neither helicoidal nor washeries, but large *kollergangs* or pan grinders, as will be shown by S. Nomicos in 2 publications (Nomicos 2013; Nomicos forthcoming; for a similar installation at Daghbag [Egypt] see Klemm and Klemm 2014, 148). Her new interpretation has immediately gained much attention and approval (Papadimitriou forthcoming; see also available online https://ntua.academia.edu/george papadimitriou [Presentation 8 November 2015] accessed January 2017). But for what kind of material(s) were they used? Ore? Slags? Litharge? Why are they so abundant at Ari, where K. Tsaïmou found four of them (and the remains of a fifth were observed during our survey; Fig. 8), while they are rare in other parts of the Laurion?

The mechanisation of fine crushing by means of a *kollergang* would have brought about a substantial increase in productivity while additionally saving manpower. This fits well with the economic situation of the second half of the fourth century BC, when the output of the mines decreased and slave labour became more expensive. At the same time the *kollergang* for milling olives was also invented by the Athenian mathematician Aristaios (Lohmann 1993, 215).

A number of large limestone blocks have been discovered (Fig. 9), but we still do not know what they were used for, despite Conophagos' argument that they were crushing tables (Conophagos 1980, 220–21; against this view, see Lohmann 2005,113). Conophagos' proposal can easily be ruled out by the fact that the surfaces of all well-preserved examples are extremely smooth, with a slight circular depression. Most probably something has been ground on them in rotating movements with the addition of water. The grain size of the product which was ground up was probably very small. Seemingly, the ore was almost pulverised.

After fine crushing the ore had to be concentrated or enriched, which entailed removing the non-mineral parts with the aid of water. In the past, three different models have been suggested by Negris (1881), Conophagos (1980, 224–47) and Kakavogiannis (1992). The

Figure 8. Fragment from mechanical mill (so-called 'helicoidal washery'), Ari

Figure 9. Large limestone blocks from the Asklepiakon, Souriza

reconstruction of the operation of the so-called 'canonical' rectangular washeries by Conophagos has never convinced me. There is neither direct nor indirect evidence for the wooden sluices in which, according to him, the ore was enriched. The amazing standardisation of the rectangular washeries is not understandable if sluices were used. The jets in the front wall of the tank containing the water consistently measure between 18 and 20 mm (Fig. 10) in diameter. This would allow for 45 litres per minute! With four jets per tank, 180 litres per minute would have been needed, and correspondingly more for washeries with six or even more jets (Lohmann 2005, 114, 130). Since the washeries were not supplied with water by means of an aqueduct or tubes, but by manpower, nobody, not even the most athletic of slaves, would be able to replenish the tank of the washery in time to allow a constant flow of water. A simple mechanism to regulate the water flow was therefore indispensable.

In my opinion, Negris' reconstruction of the operation of the washeries is much closer to the truth. It is based on the work of Georgius Agricola, the Renaissance scholar and 'father of mineralogy', who described seven different types of washeries in *Bermannus sive de re metallica dialogus* (1530), and *de Re Metallica libri XII* (1556). The so-called 'short herd' (Fig. 11) is equivalent to the canonical rectangular washeries of Laurion in almost every detail. The tank has several adjustable jets, which can be regulated according to the amount of water needed. In front of them is a relatively short wooden box, in which the ore is enriched by agitating it by means of a brush or similar. In front of the box runs a channel, gathering the sandy debris. In the rectangular washeries of Laurion such a wooden box was not required, since the ore could be agitated on the slightly inclined area covered with hydraulic mortar in front of the tank. I have already mentioned the Classical workshops excavated by K.Tsaïmou at Ari between 2005 and 2008. In close cooperation with her, we mapped the site of Ari III in 2012. It consists of several large rooms, a rectangular washery and a *kollergang* (Fig. 3). It is significant that the pottery from the excavation of the site covers the same time span (from the early fifth to the early third centuries BC) as is evident in the pottery from the intensive surveys at Mt. Charvalo, and from the distant rural deme

Figure 10. Rear view of a jet in a water tank in one of the numerous washeries in the Agrileza valley. Photo. H. Lohmann

Figure 11. Agricola 1556 (H. Prescher ed Berlin 1974) 261 Figure 11

Figure 12. A large building on a western spur of Mt. Charvalo

of Atene (Lohmann 1993a).[4] In the publication of the survey at Atene I underestimated the impact of the need for oil in the Laurion area in relation to the sudden boom in oil production at Atene (Lohmann 1993a, 204, esp. 218–9, 294). This boom consequently led to enormous building activities, and the terracing of almost every available slope (Lohmann 1993a, 196–224, figs. 56–62, pls. 116–20, 1). With the loss of the Athenian empire, the Macedonian occupation of Athens, and the end of substantial mining at Laurion, the high levels of oil production also came to an abrupt end during the first third of the third century BC. While not directly related to each other, these combined events resulted in the depopulation and abandonment of the South Attic countryside.

During two first campaigns at Ari in 2014 and 2015 substantial parts of Mt. Charvalo were cleaned, intensively surveyed, and mapped. A large building on a western spur of Mt. Charvalo (Figs. 12 and 13) can be identified as a canonical rectangular washery because of two large cisterns (one to the north and the other to the south) which leave little doubt about the purpose of the building; they show no sign of modern plundering and looting. It is hoped that trial trenches might help us achieve a better understanding of the enrichment process and provide a precise dating of the activities at this site.

During the campaign of 2015 aerial photos were taken of Mt. Charvalo, thereby enabling it to be completely mapped. This work will enable us to make a complete map of all ancient and modern remains – buildings as well as mines and shafts. We expect the research work at Ari will provide a lively picture of the mining activities, and shed light on their duration. It

---

[4] In cooperation with K. Tsaïmou, the pottery was studied in 2012 at the museum at Lavrion by the author and his team. A joint publication with K. Tsaïmou is in preparation. Rescue excavations during the 1990s at several sites of the deme of Atene have shown that it was abandoned during the Chremonidean War (267/61 BC). See Lohmann 1993 and 1996.

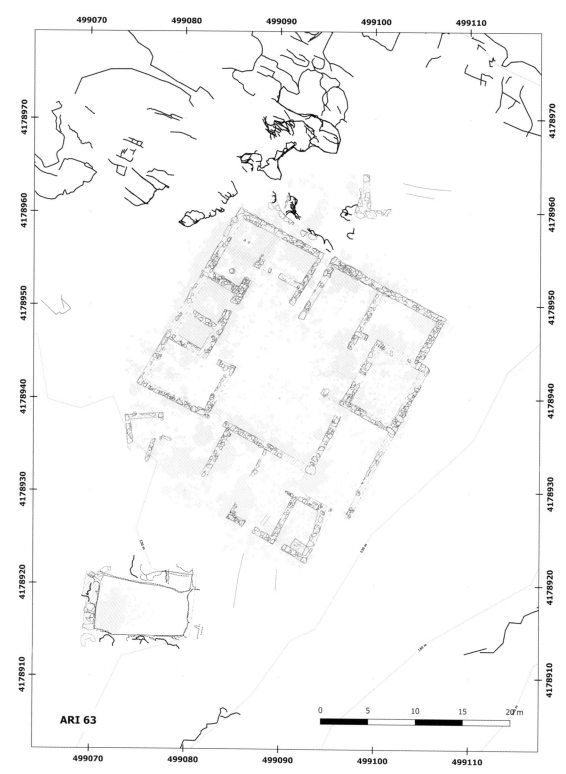

Figure 13. Plan of large building, Mt Charvalo

Figure 14. Smelting place found by K. Tsaïmou at the foot of Mt. Charvalo

might allow us to understand the workflow from the mine to the washeries and then to the smelting place (found by K. Tsaïmou at the foot of Mt. Charvalo; Fig. 14), and by this means present an overall picture of a Classical mining district of Attica.

ACKNOWLEDGMENTS

The project at Ari was enabled by the kind support of Prof Dr Katja Sporn and Prof Dr Reinhard Senff of the German Archaeological Institute at Athens. I wish to express my sincere thanks to the Greek Ministry of Culture for granting a permit for a joint venture (*synergasia*) with the Ephoria Anatolikis Attikis, represented by the Ephor Dr Eleni Andrikou and by Dr Andreas Kapetanios, whom I wish to thank for their constant help and support in almost every respect. The project started in 2012 with financial support from the MERCUR-Foundation (Essen) and has been funded by the Deutsche Forschungsgemeinschaft since 2014. A. Dombert, D. Gansera, J.-H. Hartung, F. Hulek, H.-P. Klossek, M. Korczynska, H. Marg, S. Nomicos, H. Wotruba, and Ü. Yalçın participated in the fieldwork with great enthusiasm. G. Kalaitzoglou kindly lent his support within the initial phase by providing the plans of the sites excavated by K. Tsaïmou and mapped by A. Dombert, F. Hulek, J.H. Hartung and myself in 2012. The mapping of Charvalo in 2015 by means of a drone was done by D. Gansera and H.P. Klossek, who also provided the plan reproduced here as Fig. 13. I thank Kenneth Sheedy for inviting me to the conference and for including this paper in its proceedings. Last but not least, I wish to thank Kenneth Sheedy, Gil Davis and Theresa Stewart for improving my English.

REFERENCES

Agricola, G. 1530. *Bermannus sive de re metallica dialogus*, H. Prescher ed. (Berlin 1955)
Agricola, G. 1556. *De re metallica libri XII* (Vom Bergbau und Hüttenwesen). H. Prescher ed. (Berlin 1974 ; reprint München 1977).

Ardaillon, E. 1897. *Les mines du Laurion dans l'antiquité* (Paris); reprint, Kounas, D.A. (ed.), *Studies on the Ancient Silver Mines at Laurion* (Lawrence, 1972).

Bernhardi, F. von. 1927. *Denkwürdigkeiten aus meinem Leben* (Berlin).

Bingen, J., Servais, J. and Spitaels P. (eds.) 1984. *Thorikos VIII 1972/76. Rapport préliminaire sur les 9ᵉ, 10ᵉ, 11ᵉ et 12ᵉ campagnes de fouilles* (Gent).

Boeckh, A. 1815. 'Über die laurischen Silberbergwerke in Attika', *AbhPreussAkdW* 1815 (Berlin, 1818), 85–140 = *Gesammelte kleine Schriften* (Leipzig, 1871; reprint Hildesheim 2005), vol. 5, 1–48).

Boeckh, A. 1842. 'A Dissertation on the Silver Mines of Laurion in Attica', in Boeckh, A., *The Public Economy of Athens* ² (London), 615–74; reprint Kounas D.A. (ed.), *Studies on the Ancient Silver Mines at Laurion* (Lawrence, 1972), 615–74.

Bultrighini, I. 2015. *Demi attici della paralia* (Lanciano).

Conophagos, C. 1980. *Le Laurium antique* (Athens).

Cordella, A. 1869. *Le Laurium* (Marseille).

Corretti, A. and Benvenuti, M. 2004. 'The Beginning of Iron Metallurgy in Tuscany, with Special Reference to Etruria Mineraria', *MeditArch* 14, 127–145.

Curtius, E. and Kaupert, J. A. (eds.) 1889. *Karten von Attika* (Berlin).

Davis, G. 2014. 'Mining money in late archaic Athens', *Historia - Zeitschrift für Alte Geschichte* 63:3, 257-277.

Fiedler, K.G. 1840. *Reise durch alle Theile des Königreiches Griechenland im Auftrag der Königlich-Griechischen Regierung in den Jahren 1834 bis 1837* (Leipzig), vol. 1, 36–79.

Fischer, W. 1992. 'Sozial- und Wirtschaftsgeschichte in Berlin', in Hansen R. and Ribber, W. (eds.), *Geschichtswissenschaft in Berlin im 19. und 20. Jahrhundert* (Berlin and New York), 489–92.

Gill, D.W.J. 1994. 'Positivism, pots and long-distance trade', in: Morris, I. (ed.), *Classical Greece: Ancient Histories and modern Archaeologies* (Cambridge), 99–107.

Goette, H. R. 2000. Ο αξιόλογος δήμος Σούνιον. *Landeskundliche Studien in Südost-Attika* (Rhaden i.W).

Goette, H.R. 2014. 'Zum Demos Phrearrhioi und seinem Thesmophorion', *AA* 2014, 19–36.

Greene, K. 2000. 'Technological innovation and Economic Progress in the ancient world: M.I. Finlay reconsidered', Economic History Review 53, 29–59.

Kakavogiannis, E. 1989a. 'Ελληνική Βιομηχανία Όπλων (ΕΒΟ)', *ADelt* 38, 1983 [1989] B1, 55-57.

Kakavogiannis, E. 1989b. 'Ελληνική Βιομηχανία Όπλων στην κοιλάδα Μπότσαρη'. *ADelt* 39, 1984 [1989] B, 51–55.

Kakavogiannis, E. 1992. 'Μια νέα υποψη για την λειτουργία των πλυντηρίων μεταλλεύματος της Λαυρεωτικής κατα τους κλασσικούς χρόνους', in: Α' Συμπόσιο Αρχαιομετρίας. Σύνδεση Αρχαιομετρίας και Αρχαιολογίας, Αθήναι 26–28 Ιανουάριου 1990 (Athens), 79–93.

Kakavogiannis, E. 2005. Μέταλλα εργάσιμα και συγκεχωρημένα. Η οργάνωση της εκμετάλλευσης του ορυκτού πλούτου της Λαυρεωτικής από την Αθηναϊκή δημοκρατία, Suppl. *Archaiologikon Deltion*.

Kalcyk, H. 1982. *Untersuchungen zum attischen Silberbergbau: Gebietsstruktur, Geschichte und Technik* (Frankfurt a.M.).

Klemm, R. and Klemm, D. 2014. 'Früher Goldbergbau in Ägypten und Nubien', in: Meller, H., Risch, R. and Pernicka, E. (eds.), *Metalle der Macht – Frühes Gold und Silber*. 6. Mitteldeutscher Archäologentag vom 17. bis 19. Oktober 2013 in Halle (Saale), Tagungen des Landesmuseums für Vorgeschichte in Halle 11,1 (Halle), 141-152.

Lambert, N. 1981. *La grotte préhistorique de Kitsos: missions, 1968-1978* (Paris).

Lalonde, G.V, Langdon, M.K. and Walbank, M.B., 1991. *Inscriptions: Horoi, Poletai Records, Leases of Public Lands. Agora XIX* (Princeton, N.J).

Lohmann, H. 1993a. *Atene – Forschungen zur Siedlungs- und Wirtschaftsstruktur des klassischen Attika* (Köln).

Lohmann, H. 1993b. 'Ein Turmgehöft klassischer Zeit in Thimari (Südattika)', *MDAI (A)* 108, 101–49.

Lohmann, H. 1996. 'Ein neuer Befund zum Chremonideïschen Krieg: Das sog. Atene Fort im Charaka-Tal (Attika)', *Boreas* 19, 5–68.

Lohmann, H. 2005.'Prähistorischer und antiker Blei-Silberbergbau im Laurion', in Yalçın, U. (ed.), *Anatolian Metal III* (Bochum).

Lohmann, H., Kalaitzoglou, G. and Weisgerber, G. 2002.'Ein endneolithisches Wehrdorf auf dem Megalo Rimbari (Attika) und verwandte Anlagen. Ein Beitrag zur Siedlungsarchäologie des endneolithischen Attika', *Boreas* 25, 1–48.

Meier, Chr. 1993. *Athen. Ein Neubeginn der Weltgeschichte* (Berlin).

Morin, D. and Photiades, A. 2005. 'Nouvelles recherches sur les mines antiques du Laurion (Grèce)', *Pallas* 67, 327–358.

Morin, D. and Photiades, A. 2008, 'Les techniques d'exploitation en gisements métallifères profonds dans l'Antiquité: approche géologique et technologique', in Olshausen, E. and Sauer, V. (eds.), *Die Schätze der Erde. Natürliche Ressourcen in der antiken Welt. Stuttgarter Kolloquium zur Historischen Geographie des Altertums* 10, 281–335;

Morin, D. and Photiades, A. 2012. 'Les mines antiques du Laurion: techniques minières et stratégies d'exploitation, recherches récentes', in Orejas, A. and Rico, C. (eds.), *Mineria y Metalurgia antiguas, visiones y revisiones* (Madrid), 9–26.

Nazou, M. 2013. 'Defining the Regional Characteristics of Final Neolithic and Early Bronze Age Pottery in Attica' (PhD dissertation, University of London, UK).

Negris, F. 1881. 'Laveries anciennes du Laurium', *Annales des Mines* 20, 160–64.

Nomicos, S. 2013. 'Laurion: Some remarks on the settlement pattern and the "helicoidal washeries" ', *Metalla* 20, 25–7.
Nomicos, S. 2017. 'Laurion. Montan- und siedlungsarchäologische Studien von der geometrischen Zeit bis in frühbyzantinische zeit' (PhD dissertation, Ruhr-Universität, Bochum).
Nomicos, S. forthcoming. 'The Helicoidal Washeries of Laurion Re-considered', in *Thorikos 50 Years.* 2013 Conference.
Oikonomakou, M. 1994. 'Λαυρεοτική', *ADelt* 49, Chr., 150–51.
Papachatze, N. D. 1974. Παυσανίου Ελλάδος Περιήγησις. Ἀττικα (Athens)
Papadimitriou, D. G. forthcoming. 'Ore Washeries and Water Cisterns in the Mines of Laurion-Attica', in: *16th International Conference Cura Aquarum in Greece, 28th of March – 6th of April 2015.*
Rafel, N., Montero, I., Ruiz, I., Soriano, I. and Delgado-Raack, S. 2016. 'L'activité minière préhistorique dans le Nord-Est de la péninsule Ibérique. Étude sur la Coveta de l'Heura et l'exploitation du cuivre à la Solana del Bepo (Tarragona, Espagne)', *Bulletin de la Société Préhistorique Française* (2016), 95–129.
Sellwood, D.G. 1963. 'Some Experiments in Greek Minting Technique', *NC* 1963, 217–31.
Spitaels, P. 1984. 'The Early Helladic period in Mine no. 3 (Theatre sector), in Mussche H.F., Bingen J., Servais J., Spitaels P. (eds.), *Thorikos VIII, 1972/1976. Rapport préliminaire sur les 9e, 10e, 11e et 12e campagnes de fouilles. Comité des Fouilles Belges en Grèce* (Gent), 151–174.
Traill, J.S. 1986. *Demos and Trittys. Epigraphical and topographical Studies on the Organization of Attica* (Toronto).
Tsaïmou, K. G. 2010. 'Αρχαία μεταλλουργική εγκατάσταση στην περιοχή Αρύ Λαυρεωτικής', in: Πρακτικά ΙΓ' 163–71.
Welwei, K.-W. 2011. *Athen. Von den Anfängen bis zum Beginn des Hellenismus* (Darmstadt).
Wolters, R. 1999. *Nummi signati* (Munich).
Yalcin, Ü. 1993. 'Archäometallurgie in Milet. Technologiestand der Eisenverarbeitung in archaischer Zeit', *IstMitt* 43, 361–70.

5. THE EXPLOITATION OF THE ARGENTIFEROUS ORES IN THE LAVREOTIKE PENINSULA, ATTICA, IN ANTIQUITY: SOME REMARKS ON RECENT EVIDENCE

Eleni Andrikou

To the memory of Evangelos Kakavogiannis

ABSTRACT

The Lavreotike peninsula, the southeastern part of Attica which is rich in argentiferous ores, evolved to a great mining area during the Classical period, enabling the city-state of Athens to become a leading power. The process of extracting ores and producing silver is summarized. Recent relevant finds from the Mesogeia area, dating to the Early Bronze Age (EBA), are emphasized. They demonstrate that mining and metallurgy started in Lavreotike as early as the beginning of the third millennium BC or the end of the fourth millennium BC. Some new interpretations concerning the metallurgical procedure during the Classical period are also discussed.

Understanding ancient mining and metallurgy needs a multifaceted approach, combining the study of the archaeological relics and inscriptions, the ancient literature, the geology of the area and the technology of metalworking. Ancient mining in Laurion area has been the object of study from the beginning of the nineteenth century (Fig. 1). Interest was intensified when the Hellenic State, after the mid-nineteenth century, explored the possibility of exploiting the ancient slags found all over the area. Within this framework, the mineralogist Andreas Kordellas in 1860 began walking through the area with a view to assessing the profitability of re-exploitation, but he also collected data related to the ancient mining and metallurgy (Kordellas 1894). Thus from the outset, the history of the modern town of Lavrion was connected to the reworking of the ancient slags. The work of E. Ardaillon, *Les mines du Laurium dans l' Antiquité* (1897), is of substantial importance because it treats various aspects of the subject and takes into account relevant previous research. The ancient technology of silver production was studied profoundly by a Professor of Metallurgy in the Polytechnic School,

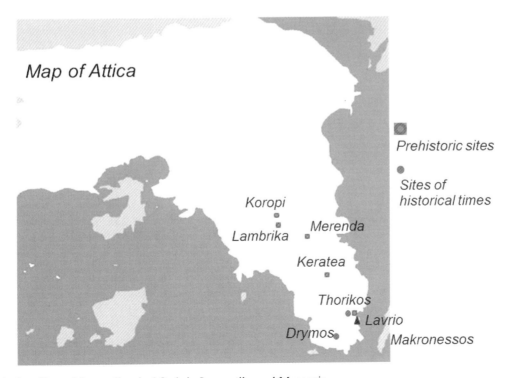

Figure 1. Attica. Sites with metallurgical finds in Lavreotike and Mesogeia

Constantinos Conophagos (Conophagos 1980). The organization of mining operations under the Athenian Democracy, as well as issues of topography and metallurgical technology in the Classical period, were also illuminated through the study of the archaeologist Dr Evangelos Kakavogiannis (Kakavogiannis 2005).

In this paper the results of the relevant research are summarised with an emphasis on the prehistoric mining and metallurgy in Lavreotike and Mesogeia, Attica, as revealed through the finds of the twenty-first century.

The Lavreotike peninsula, the southernmost part of Attica, has been continuously inhabited since prehistoric times (Andrikou 2020). Although human presence is attested in the Palaeolithic era at the Kitsos cave on the Megalo Rimbari mound, systematic habitation started in the Neolithic period after a gap of thousands of years, according to the finds (Lambert 1981, 710–716; Lohmann *et al.* 2002). Thorikos was already a significant centre in the second millennium BC, apparently due mainly to mining (Gill 2010), as the monumental Mycenaean tombs on Velatouri hill prove (Staes 1893; Laffineur 2010).

Following the state reorganization by Kleisthenes in 507 BC, seven demes were created in the Lavreotike (Whitehead 1986). The coastal deme of Anaphlystos (modern Anavyssos) and the mountainous deme of Phrearrioi (*phrear* = well, shaft) were more densely inhabited. From the Thorikos deme, part of the habitation *insulae*, the theatre, temples and cemeteries have come to light, as well as ore washeries and mining galleries on the west slope of Velatouri hill; the excavations of these sites are described in the reports of Belgian archaeologists (Mussche 1998). The deme of Sounion extended in the area north and north-east of the cape, where the fortress and village, the sanctuary of Poseidon as well as the nearby sanctuary of Athena were established (Oikonomakou-Salliora 2004, 41–127). This fortress was of crucial importance for the city-state of Athens, for it controlled the crossing to and from the Aegean Sea, as well as the hinterland with its argentiferous deposits. The famous Athenian tetradrachms were minted from Laurion silver. A hoard of 282 Athenian tetradrachms dating to the end of the fourth century BC was unearthed at Thorikos (Bingen 2010).

In the geological stratigraphy of Lavreotike, layers of schist (Kakavogiannis 2005, 92, fig. 2, S1, S2) alternate with layers of marble (M1, M2). Where these layers contact one another, the mineral deposits with metalliferous veins appear (Conophagus 1980, 156–160, fig. 9–1; Morin and Photiades 2005, 331–334). The upper 'first contact' lies near the soil surface and the lowest, the 'third contact', at a depth of nearly 100 m (Kakavogiannis 2005, 92).

Mining and metallurgical procedures for the production of silver comprised, at least from the sixth century BC onwards, the following stages:

- Extraction of the argentiferous ore.
- Cleansing of the ore through the removal of the barren elements, in order that the silver output is increased during the melting operation. The cleansing was achieved by washing the ore after crushing and grinding it.
- Smelting of the argentiferous ore to extract argentiferous lead.
- Smelting of the argentiferous lead (cupellation) to separate the silver from the lead. Lead oxide, called 'litharge' in antiquity (λιθάργυρος) comes as a by-product during cupellation.

The shape of the litharge ingots is the result of the method applied to remove the lead from the melted argentiferous lead in the cup, so that pure silver can be collected (Conophagus 1980, 305–330).

Exploitation of the metalliferous deposits pertaining to the first contact goes back to the prehistoric period (Gale *et al.* 2008; Kakavogianni *et al.* 2008; Gale and Stos-Gale 1982). Apparently, it continued and was intensified from the sixth century BC and into the Classical period (fifth–fourth centuries BC). Then it gradually declined and during the Roman and early Christian times (second BC–sixth AD centuries) mining became sporadic and of small scale (Oikonomakou-Salliora 2004, 143–144, Mussche 2006, 226).

Figure 2. Lambrika. The EH I metallurgical workshop (Archive: EphA East Attica)

Pottery found inside mine gallery 3 at Thorikos indicates that argentiferous ore was extracted in Early Helladic (EH) III phase (end of the third millennium BC), and perhaps already by the end of the previous phase, EH II (Spitaels 1984). Mining can reasonably be assumed to have started earlier, in the Final Neolithic (fourth millennium BC), by extracting the deposits of the first contact visible on the soil surface. This usually occurred on hills, such as Rimbari, Souvlero, Ovriokastro, where small mine galleries are observed (Kakavogiannis and Kakavogianni 2001, 56–57). Early ore extraction seems more probable since the EH I (3200–2800 BC) metallurgical workshop at Lambrika, Koropi (Fig. 2) was unearthed and published (in preliminary form) by Kakavogianni (Kakavogianni 2001–2004; Kakavogianni *et al.* 2009b, 241–244). The workshop consists of a large, nearly circular pit with five cavities (diam. 0.19 m and depth 0.10 m) on both sides, lined with a whitish material. In a second pit, immediately to the north-east, more than 1000 pieces of litharge ingots as well as a whole one had been discarded together with other objects, mostly pottery and millstones. The litharge ingots (Fig. 3) are bowl-shaped with 10 regular cavities arranged in rows of three – four – three on the upper surface. Chemical analysis has shown that they contain fluorine and copper, which characterise the argentiferous ores of Lavreotike (Kakavogianni *et al.* 2006). The ingots are not of pure lead oxide, since silica, aluminum oxide, calcium oxide and magnesium oxide were detected in amounts of 10–15% (Douni *et al.* forthcoming). A similar chemical synthesis was detected in the material used for the lining of the workshop cavities. The archaeological and archaeometric studies of the evidence have concluded that it is a cupellation workshop (Kakavogianni *et al.* 2008). Cupellation, the final stage of the metallurgical procedure for silver and lead production, requires advanced knowledge and experience in metallurgy. Although the exact procedure of cupellation at Lambrika remains unknown, it seems most probable that the litharge bowls were formed when lead oxide was absorbed by an aluminosilicate mass placed inside the cavities of the workshop (Kakavogianni *et al.* 2006, 81–82).

Figure 3. EH litharge ingots from Lambrika. (Archive: EphA East Attica)

Figure 4. Intact EH litharge bowl from Veniza-Zapani, Keratea. (Archive: EphA East Attica)

Similar litharge ingots but in smaller numbers have been found at various EH sites in the Lavreotike, such as Makronessos, Kalme hill, and Mokriza (Lambert 1972; Spitaels 1982a; Spitaels and Demolin 1993; Tsaravopoulos 1997; Parras 2010) and in the Mesogeia, at Merenda and Koropi (Kakavogianni and Douni, 2001–2004; Kakavogianni *et al.* 2009a, 165, 171, 172). However, in two adjacent sites in the Veniza–Zapani area of Keratea (Andrikou 2007) a significant number of litharge ingots, about 700 and 220 respectively (Fig. 4) were found. These quantities match those from the previously mentioned metallurgical workshop at Lambrika. Although remains of a workshop were not attested here, the particular features and dispersal of the litharge bowls suggest that they should be identified as material rejected after cupellation, as is the case at Lambrika. The fact that the intermediate stages of ore processing, from the extraction to the cupellation, are not detectable at Lambrika and Veniza–Zapani, leads to the conclusion that they took place near the mining area and that only argentiferous lead reached the workshops. The small number of litharge ingots at the other sites mentioned suggests secondary procedures, in order to produce lead. But such procedures are little known from the Early Bronze Age Aegean and this hypothesis is not supported by other finds, *e.g.* slags.

The litharge bowl with cavities on top, the main type in Attica, is apparently a local feature (Douni *et al.* forthcoming), since it is not found at other sites. At Limenaria on Thasos and Akrotiraki on Siphnos litharge bowls bear no cavities on top (Papadopoulos 2008); this type is rare in Attica. In any case, metallurgy was undoubtedly exercised at several EH settlements in E-SE Attica. At the extensive EH II settlement at Koropi, besides a few litharge ingots, lead masses were found, as well as evidence, such as clay moulds (Andrikou 2013, 179–180, fig. 17) for bronze metallurgy (Gale *et al.* 2008). Metallurgy of silver and lead continued in the Middle Helladic (MH) period, as is shown by the litharge ingots from Velatouri hill, Thorikos and from Velatouri hill, Keratea (Servais1967, 22–23; Kakavogianni and Douni 2010, 202). This is also true for the Late Helladic (LH) period, since silver and lead artifacts found in Athens, the Perate cemetery and at other sites, were manufactured from Lavrion metals (Gale and Stos-Gale 1982, 484–485), and as ore was mined in the mine gallery 3 at Thorikos in the LH IIIC phase (Spitaels 1982b; Mountjoy 1995).

The cupellation workshop at Lambrika and the great number of litharge bowls from layers securely dated to the EH and MH periods disprove the suggestion, based on two stray finds, that litharge bowls were minting cups (Conophagos *et al.* 1976, 12–16, figs 8–10; Conophagos 1980, 370f., fig. 16-4 and 5). The long-lasting ore extraction in the Laurion region resulted in the exhaustion of the first contact, but it also brought about the acquisition of knowledge and experience in searching for and mining argentiferous ores at a greater depth, including the successful handling of ventilation in vertical shafts and galleries (Kakavogiannis 2005, 100–103, pl. 3–4; Morin and Photiades 2005, 335–338; Morin *et al.* 2012). It is not possible to date the progression in detail, but it is believed that the miners reached the deepest third contact at the end of sixth or the beginning of fifth century BC, when the first ore washeries also appeared (Kakavogiannis 2005, 244–253).

But for all the improvements in mining technology noted above, the increase in the silver output could not have been realised unless the ore washery had been invented (Kakavogiannis 2001, 365–368). Ore cleansing was fundamental if a larger quantity of silver was to be smelted. It was accomplished by using water to remove the unwanted rock and earth that was lighter than the argentiferous ore (galenite or cerussite). Since the Lavreotike is an arid area, the washeries were installed in the valleys (characteristic of the terrain in the area) to benefit from the flow of streams which do not last the whole year. The unceasing activity of the workshops was secured by the washeries. Their operation relied on the gathering, use and recycling of rain water. The main parts of the washery (Fig.5) are the water tank (Δ) and an open conduit system of channels (A) alternating with basins (Φ). The water needed for the ore cleansing flowed from the water tank to the channels and the basins where the rock and earth could eventually

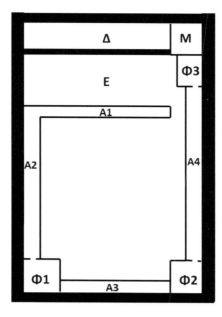

Figure 5. Schematic ground plan of rectangular ore washery, Type 1 (without scale). Classical period

settle on the bottom. The water thus cleaned could be transferred again to the tank and reused. In the Bertsekos valley, precursors of the washeries dating to the Archaic period (sixth century BC) have been revealed (Kakavogiannis 2005, 249–253, fig. 36–38). The arrangement of the main parts of the washeries at the Bertsekos valley indicates experimentation when compared to the standardised rectangular washeries of the Classical period.

The washery was supplied from big open cisterns lined with hydraulic cement (Papadimitriou and Kordatos 1995), where rain water was gathered (van Liefferinger *et al.* 2014) as, for example, at the *Asklepiakon* washery at Souriza valley, the washeries at Agia Triada (Drymos), Souriza valley and the washeries at Michalis mount, Agrileza (Conophagos 1980, 386 fig. 17–1; Jones 1984–85, 111, 123; Kakavogiannis 2001; Kakavogiannis 2005, 225–229, pl. 9–11). A cover of perishable materials protected the water from evaporation (*e.g.* Agia Triada (Drymos) and Souriza) (Kakavogiannis 2005, 226–227, pl. 10α).

Apart from the washery and the cistern the workshop for ore purification comprised the area for crushing the ores, the area for forming the cleaned ore into bricks, storage areas and residential buildings for the personnel and sometimes the owner (*e.g.* the *Asklepiakon* at Souriza valley: Conophagos 1980, 387–388; Oikonomakou-Salliora 2004, 106–108, fig. 95, 96.). The ore extracted from the mines was transferred to the workshop to be crushed on stone tables, grinded in mortars and mills and sieved in order to obtain uniform particle size before washing (*e.g.* Agia Triada (Drymos), Souriza: Kakavogiannis 2005, 220–224, pl. 6–8).

The water tank of the washery was closed in the front with big slabs, carrying a series of holes of a standard height above the floor. According to Conophagos (1980, 224ff), the ores once ground were put in wooden sluices placed in front of each hole and tilted downward to the first channel. As the water flowed through the hole it swept away the earth lighter than the argentiferous ore. However, neither excavation data nor any information from antiquity in texts or images indicates the existence of wooden sluices (Mussche 2006, 226–228; see Lohmann in this volume). Taking this into account as well as the fact that during the washery excavations a great many clay basins came to light (a number not compatible with everyday use), Kakavogiannis (2005, 233–242) suggested another interpretation. The worker put a small quantity of ground ore in the clay basin and filled it partially with water from the tank (which was full of water and had blocked front holes). Then, holding the basin by the two handles, he moved it cyclically causing the water to whirl. The heavy metalliferous grains settled to the bottom, while the lighter earth floated. The impure water was emptied back into the tank, for the earth to fall to the bottom. After this procedure had been performed several times and the water of the tank became cloudy, the holes were unblocked and the water flowed to the open conduit to be cleaned as described earlier. The mud which gathered gradually in the tank and in the conduit was scooped up with shovels and thrown away. Heaps of such mud, called *plynites* by Kordellas (1888, 27ff.), were found densely scattered all over the mining area of Lavreotike (Kakavogiannis 2005, 232–233, pl.14a). The washed ore, after draining off in the central rectangular area of the washery, was transported to another area to be formed into bricks and dried. 'Briquetting' was indispensable to allow the successful feeding of the ore into the furnace.

Only a few smelting workshops (such as found at Megala Pefka, Ary, Frangolimano and Oxygono at Thorikos, Ormos Asemake at Sounion, Pountazeza) are known in comparison to the number of those for cleansing (Kakavogiannis 2005, 261–264; Tsaimou 2013). At first, argentiferous lead was smelted in furnaces. Then, silver was smelted through the cupellation process in installations known today only from Kordellas' descriptions (1890, 77–78) before they were destroyed during modern exploitation. Cupellation was largely studied and illuminated by Conophagos (1980, 305–330). Pure silver was obtained after the lead oxide floating in the melting cup was poured into another vessel. When it cooled, it solidified and formed a flat litharge ingot. Later on litharge ingots were tubular, since iron rods were used to remove lead oxide from the cup (Kakavogiannis 2005, 273–279, pl. 23).

In the Classical period exploitation was intensified. The evidence of archaeology and especially epigraphy shows that relations between the Athenian state and entrepreneurs were now set out within a very detailed legal framework (Kakavogiannis 2005, 111–214).

The Lavreotike is densely covered with mining shafts and architectural relics of metallurgical workshops (mainly washeries in the valleys) and of residential and burial sites. Few washeries have been excavated and even fewer smelting workshops (which seem to concentrate at the coast). A detailed mapping of the vestiges will require extensive work to remove the vegetation and accumulated earth. Projects such as the mapping of Ari, a Collaboration of the Ephorate of Antiquities of East Attica and the German Archaeological Institute in Athens which has been in progress since 2014 (see Lohmann in this volume), will greatly contribute not only to a better understanding of mining and metallurgical procedures, but also to our knowledge of the spatial and social organisation of the people who lived at this site.

REFERENCES

Andrikou, E., 2007. "ΒΙΟΠΑ Κερατέας. Προϊστορικές θέσεις", *ADelt* 72 (B1), 206–207.
Andrikou, E., 2013. "Ο οικισμός της Πρώιμης Εποχής του Χαλκού στο Κορωπί. Η κεραμεική και τα άλλα κινητά ευρήματα", in Donka-Toli, M. and Oikonomou, S. (eds), Αρχαιολογικές Συμβολές. Τόμος Α: Αττική. ΚΣΤ΄ και Β΄ Εφορείες Προϊστορικών & Κλασικών Αρχαιοτήτων (Athens), 173–182.
Andrikou, E. 2020. 'Thorikos in Context: the Prehistory', in Papadimitriou N., Wright J.C., Fachard S., Polychronakou-Sgouritsa N., and Andrikou E. (eds), Athens and Attica in Prehistory. Proceedings of the International Conference Athens, 27–31 May 2015, Oxford. 19–28.
Bingen, J. 2010. 'The monetary hoard "Thorikos 1969": (IGCH 134)', in Iossif, P. (ed.), *All that glitters...', The Belgian Contribution to Greek Numismatics* (Athens), 62–67.
Conophagos, C. E., 1980. *Le Laurium antique et la technique grecque de la production de l'argent* (Athens).
Conophagos, C., Badecca, H. and Tsaimou, C. 1976. 'La technique Athénienne de la frappe des monnaies à l'époque classique', Νομισματικά Χρονικά 4, 4–33.
Douni, K., Georgakopoulou, M., Andrikou, E., and Kakavogianni, O. forthcoming. 'A regional approach to Early Helladic silver production in Southeastern Attica', in Bassiakos, Y. (ed.), *Prehistoric Metal Production in the Aegean: Material Evidence and Analysis*.
Gale, N.H. and Stos-Gale, Z.A. 1982. 'The sources of Mycenaean silver and lead.' *JFieldA* 9, 467–485.
Gale, N.H., Kayafa, M. and Stos-Gale, Z.A. 2008. 'Early Helladic Metallurgy at Raphina, Attica, and the Role of Lavrion', in Tzachili, I. (ed.), *Aegean Metallurgy in the Bronze Age: Recent Developments* (Athens), 87–104.
Gill, D.W.J., 2010. 'Amenhotep III, Mycenae, and the Laurion', in Sekunda, N. (ed.), *Ergasteria: Works Presented to John Ellis Jones on his 80th Birthday* (*Akanthina* 4) (Gdansk), 22–35.
Jones, J.E. 1984–85. 'Laurion: Agrileza 1977–1983: Excavations at a silver-mine site', *AR* 31, 106–123.
Kakavogianni O. 2001–2004. « Διαπλάτυνση λεωφόρου Βάρης–Κορωπίου. Λαμπρικά", *ADelt* 56–59, (B1), 343–344.

Kakavogianni, O., and Douni, K. 2001–2004. "Οικόπεδο Lidl και οδός Χατζή", *ADelt* 56–59 (Β1), 340 (Koropi).
Kakavogianni, O., Douni, K., Nezeri, F., Georgakopoulou, M. and Bassiakos, Y. 2006. "Απόπειρα τεχνολογικής προσέγγισης της παραγωγής αργύρου και μολύβδου κατά την Τελική Νεολιθική και Πρωτοελλαδική Ι περίοδο στα Μεσόγεια", ΕΜΑΕΤ 2005, in Kazazi, G. (ed.), Πρακτικά του 2ου Διεθνούς Συνεδρίου Αρχαίας Ελληνικής Τεχνολογίας, Αθήνα 17–21 Οκτωβρίου 2005 (Athens), 77–83.
Kakavogianni, O., Douni, K. and Nezeri, F. 2008. 'Silver Metallurgical Finds dating from the End of the Final Neolithic Period until the Middle Bronze Age in the Area of Mesogeia', in Tzachili, I. (ed.), *Aegean Metallurgy in the Bronze Age: Recent Developments* (Athens), 45–57.
Kakavogianni, O., Dimitriou, K., Koutsothanasis, Ch. and Petrou, A. 2009a. "Οικισμός της Πρωτοελλαδικής Εποχής και δύο μεμονωμένα κτίρια στη Μερέντα", in Vassilopoulou, V. and Katsarou-Tzeveleki, S. (eds), *Από τα Μεσόγεια στον Αργοσαρωνικό. Β΄ Εφορεία Προϊστορικών και Κλασικών Αρχαιοτήτων. Το έργο μιας δεκαετίας, 1994–2003. Πρακτικά Συνεδρίου, Αθήνα, 18–20 Δεκεμβρίου 2003* (Markopoulo, Mesogaias), 159–176.
Kakavogianni, O., Michaelidi, P., Nezeri, F. and Douni, K. 2009b. "Από τον πρωτοελλαδικό οικισμό στα Λαμπρικά Κορωπίου", in Vassilopoulou, V. and Katsarou-Tzeveleki, S. (eds), *Από τα Μεσόγεια στον Αργοσαρωνικό. Β΄ Εφορεία Προϊστορικών και Κλασικών Αρχαιοτήτων. Το έργο μιας δεκαετίας, 1994–2003. Πρακτικά Συνεδρίου, Αθήνα, 18–20 Δεκεμβρίου 2003* (Markopoulo, Mesogaias), 237–248.
Kakavogianni, O., and Douni, K. 2010. "Η Μεσοελλαδική Εποχή στη ΝΑ Αττική", in Phillipa-Touchais, A., Touchais, G., Voutsaki S. and Wright, J. (eds), *MESOHELLADIKA: La Grèce continentale au Bronze Moyen: actes du Colloque international, organize par l'* École française d' *Athènes, en collaboration avec l' American School of Classical Studies at Athens et le Netherlands Institute in Athens, Athènes, 8–12 mars 2006, BCH Suppl.* 52, 199–210.
Kakavogiannis, E. 2001. 'The Silver Ore-processing Workshops of the Lavrion Region', *BSA* 96, 365–380.
Kakavogiannis, E. 2005. ΜΕΤΑΛΛΑ ΕΡΓΑΣΙΜΑ ΚΑΙ ΣΥΓΚΕΧΩΡΗΜΕΝΑ. Η οργάνωση της εκμετάλλευσης του ορυκτού πλούτου από την Αθηναϊκή Δημοκρατία. (Athens).
Kakavogiannis, E., and Kakavogianni, O. 2001. "Τα μνημεία της περιοχής Οβριόκαστρο–Δάρδεζα – Ποτάμι – Σταθμός Δασκαλιού του Δήμου Κερατέας", Πρακτικά της Η΄ Επιστημονικής Συνάντησης ΝΑ. Αττικής, Κερατέα Αττικής *30/10–2/11/1997* (Keratea, Attikis), 55–66.
Kordellas, A., 1888. *Η Βιομηχανία της Εταιρίας των Μεταλλουργείων Λαυρίου και τα μεταλλευτικά και μεταλλουργικά αυτής προϊόντα εν τη Δ΄ Ολυμπιακή Εκθέσει, εν Αθήναις* (Athens).
Kordellas, A., 1890. "Το Λαύριον και ο Ελληνικός άργυρος', Παρνασσός ΙΓ'", 67–84.
Kordellas, A. 1894. "Λαυρεωτικαί αρχαιότητες", *AthMitt* 19, 238–244.
Laffineur, R., 2010. 'Thorikos rich in silver: the prehistoric periods', in Iossif, P. (ed.), *"All that glitters…" The Belgian Contribution to Greek Numismatics* (Athens), 26–40.
Lambert, N., 1972. 'Vestiges préhistoriques à Makronisos', *BCH* 96, 873–881.
Lambert N., 1981. *La grotte préhistorique de Kitsos (Attique)* (Paris).
Lohmann, H., Weisgerber, G. and Kalaitzoglou, G. 2002. 'Ein endneolithisches Wehrdorf auf dem Megalo Rimbari (Attika) und verwandte Anlagen. Ein Beitrag zur Seidlungs archaeologie des endneolithishen Attika', *Boreas* 25, 1–48.
Morin D. and Photiades, A. 2005. *Nouvelles recherches sur les mines antiques du Laurion (Grèce)* (Toulouse).
Morin, D., Herbach, R. and Rosenthal, P. 2012. 'The Laurion shafts, Greece: ventilation systems and mining technology in antiquity', *Historical Metallurgy* 46, 9–18.
Mountjoy, P. A. 1995. 'Thorikos Mine no 3. The Mycenaean Pottery', *BSA* 90, 195–227.
Mussche, H. 1998. *Thorikos: a mining town in Ancient Attica* (Gent).
Mussche, H. 2006. 'More about the Silver-rich Lead of Ancient Laurion', *L' Antiquité Classique* 75, 225–230.
Oikonomakou-Salliora, M., 2004. *Ο αρχαίος δήμος του Σουνίου. Ιστορική και τοπογραφική επισκόπηση,* (Koropi).
Papadimitriou, G., and Kordatos, J. 1995. 'The brown waterproofing plaster of the ancient cisterns in Laurion and its weathering and degradation', in Maniatis, Y., Herz, N. and Bassiakos, Y. (eds.), *The Study of Marble and other Stones Used in Antiquity* (London), 277–284.
Papadopoulos, St. 2008. 'Silver and Copper Production Practices in the Prehistoric Settlement at Limenaria, Thasos', in Tzachili, I. (ed.), *Aegean Metallurgy in the Bronze Age: Recent Developments* (Athens), 59–67.
Parras, D. 2010. "Λαυρεωτική: αρχαία τοπογραφία και νέες αρχαιολογικές έρευνες". Πρακτικά της ΙΓ΄ Επιστημονικής Συνάντησης ΝΑ. Αττικής, Παιανία 29–31/10 & 1–2/11/2008 (Kalyvia, Thorikou), 141–147.
Servais, J. 1967. 'Les fouilles sur le haut du Vélatouri', *Thorikos III–1965* (Bruxelles), 9–30.
Spitaels, P. 1982a. 'Provatsa on Makronisos', *AAA* 15, 155–158.
Spitaels, P. 1982b. 'An unstratified Late Mycenaean Deposit from Thorikos (Mine Gallery 3)–Attica', *Studies in South Attica I* (Ghent), 82–96.
Spitaels, P. 1984. 'The Early Helladic period in mine no 3', *Thorikos* VIII–1972/1976 (Ghent), 151–174.
Spitaels, P. and Demolin, I. 1993. "Θορικός, τα Προβάτσα και το Makronisos Project: τα μεταλλεία της Μακρονήσου", Πρακτικά της Δ΄ Επιστημονικής Συνάντησης ΝΑ. Αττικής, Καλύβια Αττικής *30/11 & 1–2/12/1989* (Kalyvia, Attikis), 557–565.
Staes, V., 1893. "Ανασκαφαί εν Θορικώ", *PAE* 1893, 12–17.
Tsaravopoulos, A., 1997. "Καλύβια Θορικού – Θέρμη", *ADelt* 52 (Β1), 84–85.
Van Liefferinger, K., van den Berg, M., Stal, C. Docter, R. F., de Wulf, A., and Verhoest, N. 2014. 'Reconsidering the role of Thorikos within the Laurion silver mining area (Attica, Greece) through hydrological analyses', *Journal of Archaeological Science* 41, 272–284.
Whitehead, D., 1986. *The Demes of Attica, 508/7–c.250 BC* (Princeton).

6. THE ROLE OF CHANGING SETTLEMENT STRUCTURES IN RECONSTRUCTING THE MINING HISTORY OF ARCHAIC LAURION

Sophia Nomicos

ABSTRACT

The purpose of this study was to look at the settlement history of sixth century BC Laurion in order to find evidence to support the theory of intensified Athenian mining. Changes in the settlement pattern can be plausibly explained by changes in the intensity of mining, not only because in the Laurion the natural preconditions are unfavourable for agricultural land use, but also because according to a theoretical model developed by T. R. Stöllner, intensive mining transforms a given landscape often in a distinctive way. These changes affect, among other things, the settlement structure and this is why, in principle, a correlation between mining and the settlement development is to be expected. In the Laurion an increase in settlement activity and a change in the settlement structure in the second half of the sixth century BC can be observed. In this paper, I have argued that this is due to the intensification of mining during this period, as indicated by the first appearance of the owl coinage.

Introduction

Reconstructing the economic history of an ancient mining region is complicated when crucial literary and archaeological sources are lacking. Identifying the starting point for a period of intensive exploitation can be particularly difficult when archaeological traces of the workings have been destroyed by later mining activities (Stöllner 2008, 77–78). In this paper I wish to explore the contribution that can be made in such difficult cases through a study of settlement history.

Despite the long history of research and the many important discoveries, the mining history of the Laurion has yet to be fully understood. The Laurion was the primary source of silver for the famous Athenian owl coinage (see Flament in this volume) and of critical importance for the Athenian economy during the Classical period of the fifth and fourth centuries BC. This boom phase of mining is not only well attested in the literary sources, it has also left an imprint on the landscape that has come down to us today. In contrast, the preceding sixth century in the Laurion remains shadowy, for the literary and archaeological evidence is meagre (Hopper 1961, 140; Mussche 1998, 62). Nonetheless, it is in the Archaic period that scholars (for example, Young 1942, 80; Picard 2001; van Liefferinge 2013, 111–112) place the beginning of the processes that led to the intensive exploitation of the fifth and especially the fourth centuries BC. The aim of this paper is to examine the largely unexplored contribution of settlement history to an understanding of the Laurion in the sixth century BC.

THE THEORETICAL BACKGROUND

The theoretical background of this study is provided by a model developed by T. Stöllner in regard to 'Montanarchäologie' which is based on the idea of specific development patterns characteristic of mining regions (Stöllner 2003; 2008; 2014). According to Stöllner (2014, 133), Montanarchaeologie – "a kind of 'raw material archaeology' whose main focus is on the entire chain of mineral resource production practices and its socio-economic consequences" – offers an advance on the traditional approaches of mining archaeology. This advancement comes with "the realization that mining archaeology is the study of systems used to describe long-term historical processes that have been influenced by other technologies, innovations and raw materials equally" (Stöllner 2014, 133). In particular, his research has focused on those development patterns characteristic of prehistoric mining landscapes (Stöllner 2008, 65–92).

According to Stöllner (2008, 76), a mining landscape is defined as "a specialized region whose primary economic structure is focused on the exploitation of (mineral) resources". It is the result of a socio-economic process which transforms a natural landscape into an industrial landscape

(Stöllner's term (2014, 139) is the 'imprinting process'). Intensive exploitation is usually preceded by a (long) period of extensive exploitation characterised by sporadic or seasonal activities and is therefore particularly difficult to verify in the archaeological record. Intensive exploitation typically destroys the traces of earlier activities – especially through the re-working of older mines/workplaces or the re-smelting of older slags (Stöllner 2008, 77–78). The imprinting process can be divided into several steps, each showing characteristic features. Stöllner recognised at first three (2008) then four phases (2014):

- An *initial or inventing phase* that is characterised by the introduction of a new concept or technology into a region as well as changes in settlement patterns (normally the emergence of permanent settlements close to the places of exploitation).
- An *establishing phase*, also called a phase of stabilisation or consolidation. This phase is characterised by the formation of successful working units that have a noticeable influence on the local society and environment.
- An *industrial phase* is characterised by the abundant and general usage of an exploitation concept in a regional context in combination with considerable effects on society, the natural environment, as well as the cultural landscape. Its main characteristic is frequent and standardised mass production.
- A *collapse and reorganization phase*: the collapse of an economic or ecological system as the result of over-exploitation or over-expenditure of technological or economic resources. There are also possible external reasons for collapse, such as changing demand, the influence of historical events, or a general economic crisis.

This model can serve as a useful tool for explaining certain phenomena and possibly illuminating periods of time for which historical and archaeological data are lacking. Since in the Laurion, the Classical period undoubtedly saw the most intensive pre-modern exploitation, it can be identified as the 'industrial phase'. According to the model, it was preceded by an 'initial phase' and an 'establishing phase'. These first phases, however, are not easily visible in the mining archaeological record of the Laurion. This is not surprising given the extent of the later phase of intense exploitation. They may be detected indirectly, however, through their impact on regional settlement patterns, an impact which Stöllner (2003) has illustrated in several case studies. In Early Bronze Age Feynan in Jordan, for example, intensified copper mining activities and new smelting techniques can be correlated with the appearance of permanent settlements in the vicinity of mines (Stöllner 2003, 433). This effect is equally obvious in the mediaeval Hartz mining region, where a shift in the settlement pattern from dispersed sites on the periphery of the mining area to the emergence of specialised towns in the previously uninhabited area of exploitation was observed (Stöllner 2003, 436).

Additionally, Stöllner identified several key factors which could determine if a deposit was to be exploited intensively. These include natural preconditions, such as the quality of the raw material. They also include the mode of production together with historical processes, such as changes in the supply-and-demand structure (Stöllner 2008, 75, table 2). It is possible, for example, to synchronise the intensification of mining in the Hartz mountains with the emergence of towns in mediaeval Germany, as well as with the Crusades. Both events ultimately led to an exponential increase in the demand for metal ores in order to meet the demand for building materials and weapons (Stöllner 2003, 436).

MINING IN ARCHAIC LAURION

The history of mining in the Laurion region in the Archaic period and indeed the general history of this important area, as noted above, is not well 'sign-posted' (Lohmann 2005; Nomicos 2017). But some understanding of the development of the region in these years is critical if we are to comprehend the later intensive exploitation of the Laurion mines. The evidence for south Attica has been presented in important surveys by J. H. Young (1942),

H. Lohmann (1993), H. R. Goette (2000) and most recently by M. Salliora Oikonomakou (2004). Before discussing the Laurion's settlement history I will briefly outline the key literary, archaeological and numismatic evidence to assist my discussion.

It is not until the fifth century BC that the Laurion was mentioned explicitly in the literary sources. One of the earliest reference to mining in the Laurion can be found in Aeschylus' *Persians* (238), in which the source of Athenian wealth is characterised as a "fountain of silver". It testifies to considerable mining activities during the 480s, but leaves room for speculation as to how long before this time the Athenians had been profiting from the mining revenues. Similarly, in the well-known passage from Herodotus (7.144; see also Plutarch, *Life of Themistocles* 4.1) in which it is reported that Themistocles persuaded the Athenians to invest in a fleet which was later key to victory at Salamis in 480 BC, we gain little sense of the early history of the mines. According to (pseudo) Aristotle (*Constitution of the Athenians* 22.7) the funds for the building of the ships were made possible in 483/2 BC through the revenues of mines at a place within the Laurion called Maroneia which yielded 100 talents of silver. Traditionally, this text is taken to refer to the discovery of the so-called third contact, a deep underground zone of rich mineralisations within the ore body (Marinos and Petraschek 1956, 231–236). Both the discovery of rich ores and the minting of coins from 100 talents of silver are unlikely to have happened within the same year of 483/2 BC (Picard 2001; Flament 2011). Firstly, the exact wording does not permit us to securely determine the date of the discovery of the third contact, and secondly, the process (Ardaillon 1897; Conophagos 1980) of obtaining 100 talents of silver from lead ore presupposes a considerable amount of time between these two events. Picard (2001, 8–10) concluded that the initial discovery of the third contact must have happened earlier, probably around 520/515 BC.

Other scholars (Kalcyk 1982, 99–106) have argued for a connection between Peisistratus and the intensification of mining in Laurion. This theory, too, is based on a passage in Herodotus (1.64), in which "substantial income for himself, partly from Attica, and partly from his estates on the River Strymon" is mentioned. However, since neither silver mines nor the Laurion are mentioned specifically, this account is not decisive (de Libero 1996, 50).

From a methodological point of view, archaeological findings from stratified contexts in a mine provide the most reliable evidence for an exploitation phase, but such findings from the Archaic period at Laurion have not yet been reported. The first indication of Late Archaic beneficiation activities in the region has possibly been discovered at Bertseko close to the modern mining town Hagios Konstantinos (Kamareza) by E. Kakavogiannis (1989; 2001; 2005, 245–253). In 1989, he excavated some peculiar cuttings in the bedrock that he concluded were early ore-washeries, because the cuttings looked like channels and basins, albeit in an unusual arrangement (Kakavogiannis 2001, 369). The discovery of surface pottery dating to the end of the sixth/first decades of the fifth century BC (Kakavogiannis 2001, 369) is the primary support for the early dating of this site. Nonetheless, the exact

Figure 1. Athenian tetradrachm (obverse). Fifth century BC. Ruhr-Universität Bochum, Collection of Coins, Inv. M 1310 (photo: M. Benecke). See Nomicos 2015.

Figure 2. Athenian tetradrachm (reverse). Fifth century BC. Ruhr-Universität Bochum, Collection of Coins, Inv. M 1310 (photo: M. Benecke). See Nomicos 2015.

interpretation of these structures seems problematic for neither walls nor foundations are visible. Moreover, tailings, which would attest to beneficiation activities, have not been reported, and the dating of the structures is apparently insecure due to the limited number of findings and their lack of stratification (Kakavogiannis 2001, 369; van Liefferinge 2013, 113).

The only solid indicator for measuring the intensity of pre-Classical Athenian mining is the city's archaic coinage, the *Wappenmünzen* and especially the silver tetradrachms with the Athena/owl types (Fig. 1–2; see Flament 2007 and in this volume). The numismatic evidence was presented by Seltman in 1924 but is now drastically in need of revision following the criticism of Kraay (1956; see also Cahn 1975; Kroll 1981; Sheedy, Gore and Davis 2009). The owl coins were linked to such an extent with the Laurion that Aristophanes called them γλαῦκες Λαυριωτικαί (*glaukes Lauriotikai*, "Laurion owls"—Aristoph. *Birds* 1106). The Attic origin of the silver used in these coins was confirmed not only by trace element analyses (Kraay 1958) but also by lead isotope studies (Gale, Gentner and Wagner 1980) which revealed that the isotopic fingerprints of a number archaic tetradrachms are consistent with that of ores from Laurion.

THE EVIDENCE FOR CHANGES IN THE SETTLEMENT STRUCTURE OF ARCHAIC LAURION

The prehistoric and iron age habitation of south-east Attica seems to have concentrated on the coastal area (Salliora-Oikonomakou 2004). Hardly any prehistoric or Geometric traces have been observed in the inner Laurion area, in contrast to the coast where not only the settlement on the Velatouri hill (see Mussche 1998, 61) is located, but also several small sites on the coast between Thorikos and Cape Sounion (Salliora-Oikonomakou 2004, 32–34). Although not all phases of occupation are equally visible archaeologically, this situation does not change until the Late Archaic period, when an increase in finds points to the habitation of inland sites. Settlement in the second half of the sixth century is attested through dispersed findings of rock-cut inscriptions (Langdon 1985, 145–148; Langdon 1991, 309–312) and sculptures (Karakasi 2001, 121, 124, 132, plate 124; Salliora-Oikonomakou 2004, 34–35, fig. 16; Mastrokostas 1974, 215–217, fig. 1). Young observed sixth century BC graves (Young 1942, 241–242) – a secure indicator of habitation (see Lohmann 2009, 36) – as well as dispersed archaic pottery in the vicinity of mines (Young 1942, 258–259). The large necropolis at Anemones in the heart of the mining area, with graves dating to the beginning of the fifth century BC (Salliora-Oikonomakou 1985), more clearly indicates the emergence of permanent off-coast habitation in close vicinity to the rich ore deposits (Salliora-Oikonomakou 2004, 34–37).

Intensified habitation activity during the Late Archaic period was also observed at Thorikos. According to the excavators, the archaic pottery found on the Velatouri hill shows a significant peak in the last quarter of the sixth and early fifth centuries BC (Mussche 1998, 62). This chronology has been confirmed by pottery findings from a recently excavated cistern in the industrial quarter (Docter, Monsieur and van de Put 2011, 119, fig. 42). The very limited amount of published material available makes such fine chronological distinctions impossible for other parts of the Laurion at the moment, but it could be argued that the situation in Thorikos reflects a general development in the whole region.

The occupation of off-coast sites is a phenomenon of the Late Archaic period that is not only limited to the Laurion, but has been observed in other parts of Attica as well (Houby-Nielsen 2009, 192, 206–210). In the case of the mining area, however, there seems to be a connection between the growing number and wider distribution of archaeological sites and the intensification of mining. Firstly, there is the chronological correlation between this phenomenon and the introduction of the owl coinage. Secondly, the natural landscape in this part of Attica offers only limited possibilities for land use by an agrarian society. Relatively fertile plains indeed exist in the eastern part of the Agrileza valley and the Adami plain (Marinos and Marinos 1981, 36, map), but central Laurion is very poor in water and arable soils (Philippson 1952, 836, 838). It is, therefore, reasonable to assume that the people who left traces in the Late Archaic period were initially attracted to this part of Attica by the silver ore.

If we are to adhere to Stöllner's model we need to accommodate the first two phases in the Archaic period, since the Classical period might be identified with the industrial, or third phase, in Stöllner's system. It is then necessary to explore the possible reasons for the early Athenian development of the Laurion mines. It has been convincingly suggested (Hopper 1961, 140; and recently van Liefferinge 2013, 111–112) that the initial motive was the growing demand for silver (cf. Stöllner 2008, 75, tab. 2) around 550 BC when it had become the main metal for coinage (Kroll 2012, 36–37). The date for the two phases of archaic Athenian coinage are still under consideration (Kraay 1975). Kroll (1981) has suggested that the *Wappenmünzen* commenced *c.* 546 BC and that the first owls appeared *c.* 517 BC. Consequently, the first phase, the 'invention phase' in which we see new technology and new strategies of exploiting the minerals could be placed around the mid-sixth century BC and the second phase perhaps be linked with the owl coinage. The increase in pottery found at the Velatouri could arguably point to the onset of the second phase, the 'establishing' phase (characterised by first successful applications and the formation of successful working units). This admittedly hypothetical division might be supported by the quantity of the late archaic finds in the Laurion. As argued above, they may be interpreted as a consequence of increasing exploitation of off-coast deposits, thus testifying to the "formation of successful working units" (Stöllner 2014), characteristic of the establishing phase.

CONCLUDING REMARKS

Having taken a brief look at the available evidence for Athenian mining in the Archaic period it is obvious that many aspects remain unclear. We do not know exactly when various key technological innovations, especially deep-shaft mining (see Ardaillon 1897; and Morin in this volume), large cisterns for water storage (van Liefferinge 2013) and the famous ore-washeries (Negris 1881; Conophagos 1980; Kakavogiannis 2005) were introduced into the Laurion. In line with Stöllner's theories, it might be argued that some of this might have happened during the initial phase during which new strategies of exploitation are introduced. Positive archaeological or historical evidence is, however, lacking. The possibility of the transfer of technological knowledge from other ancient Greek mining regions, such as the Pangaeum (as proposed for example by Kalcyk 1982, 109), Siphnos (see Wagner and Weisgerber 1985) or Thasos (see Wagner and Weisgerber 1988) remains for the moment a matter of speculation. Further excavation of these sites as well as in the Laurion are required to come to firmer conclusions. Nonetheless, there is evidence that during the second half of the sixth century BC the Laurion saw an intensification of habitation together with changes in the settlement pattern (from coastal habitation to both coastal and inland occupation), and they indicate that Stöllner's imprinting process, which saw the transformation of a natural landscape into an a mining landscape, had begun.

ACKNOWLEDGEMENTS

This article covers an aspect of my PhD thesis 'Laurion. Montan- und siedlungsarchäologische Studien von der geometrischen Zeit bis zur Spätantike' supervised by Prof. H. Lohmann (Bochum, Ruhr-University) whom I thank for his constant advice and support. I also thank my second supervisor, Prof. Th. R. Stöllner, for useful advice and for initiating the Bochum "RITaK" Graduate School; my PhD Dissertation was written with the scope of this School. Furthermore, I wish to warmly thank Associate Prof. K.A. Sheedy not only for the invitation to present some of my results in this volume, but also for corrections and numerous helpful comments on the first draft of this paper. This study as well as my PhD thesis draw upon published information only, and I am grateful for the kind permission of the Greek Department of Antiquities of East Attica to visit selected archaeological sites mentioned in this text.

REFERENCES

Ardaillon, E 1897. *Les Mines du Laurion dans l'antiquité* (Paris).
Cahn, H.A. 1975. 'Dating the Early Coinages of Athens', in Cahn. H.A. and Ackermann, H.C. (eds), *Kleine Schriften zur Münzkunde und Archäologie* (Basel), 81–97.
Conophagos, C. 1980. *Le Laurium antique et la technique Grecque de la Production de l'argent* (Athens).
de Libero, L. 1996, *Die archaische Tyrannis* (Stuttgart).
Docter, R., Monsieur, P. and van de Put, W. 2011. 'Late Archaic to Late Antique Finds from Cistern No. 1 at Thorikos (2010 Campaign)', *Thorikos* vol. 10, 75–128.
Flament, C. 2007. *Le Monnayage en argent d'Athènes. De l'époque archaïque à l'époque hellénistique (c 550–c 40 av. J.-C)* (Louvain-la-Neuve).
Flament, C. 2011. 'A Note on the Laurium Stratigraphy and the Early Coins of Athens: The Work of D. Morin and A. Photiades and its Impact on the Study of Athenian Coinage', *American Journal of Numismatics* 23, 1–6.
Gale, N.H., Gentner, W. and Wagner, G.A. 1980. 'Mineralogical and geographical silver sources of Archaic Greek Coinage', in *Metallurgy in Numismatics 1* (London), 3–49.
Goette, H.R. 2000. *Ὁ αξιόλογος δῆμος Σούνιον. Landeskundliche Studien in Südost-Attika* (Rahden).
Hopper, R.J. 2009. 'The Mines and Miners of Ancient Athens', *Greece & Rome* 8:2, 138–151.
Houby-Nielsen, S. 2013. 'Attica: A View from the Sea', in Raaflaub, K.A. and van Wees, H. (eds), *A Companion to Archaic Greece* (New York), 187–211.
Kakavogiannis, E. 1989. "Ἀρχαιολογικές έρευνες στην Λαυρεωτική για την ανακάλυψη μεταλλευτικών έργων και μεταλλουργικών εγκαταστασέων των προκλασικών χρωνών", *Ἀρχαιολογικά Ἀνάλεκτα εξ Ἀθηνών* 22, 71–88.
Kakavogiannis, E. 2001. 'The Silver Ore-Processing Workshops of the Lavrion Region', *Annual of the British School at Athens* 96, 369–374.
Kakavogiannis, E. 2005. *Μέταλλα Ἐργάσιμα και Συγκεχωρημένα. Η οργάνωση της εκμετάλλευσης του ορυκτού πλούτου της Λαυρεωτικής από την Αθηναϊκή Δημοκρατία* (Athens).
Kalcyk, H. 1982. *Untersuchungen zum attischen Silberbergbau. Gebietsstruktur, Geschichte und Technik* (Frankfurt am Main).
Karakasi, K. 2001. *Archaische Koren* (Munich).
Kraay, C.M. 1956. 'The archaic owls of Athens: classification and chronology', *Numismatic Chronicle* 16, 43–68.
Kraay, C.M. 1958. 'Gold and Copper Traces in Early Greek Silver', *Archaeometry* 1(1), 1–5.
Kraay, C.M. 1975. 'Archaic Owls of Athens. New Evidence for Chronology' in Mussche, H.F. and Spitaels, P. (eds.), *Thorikos and the Laurion in Archaic and Classical times, Papers and contributions of the colloquium held in march, 1973* (Ghent), 145–157.
Kroll, J.H. 1981. 'From Wappenmünzen to Gorgoneia to Owls', *American Numismatic Society Museum Notes* 26, 1–32.
Kroll, J.H. 2012. 'The Monetary Background of early coinage', in Metcalf, W.E. (ed.), *The Oxford Handbook of Greek and Roman Coinage* (Oxford), 33–42.
Langdon, M. 1985. 'The Grave of Posthon at Sounion', *Hesperia* 54, 145–148.
Langdon, M. 1991. 'Two Hoplite Runners at Sounion', *Hesperia* 60, 309–312.
Lohmann, H. 1993. *Atene. Forschungen zu Siedlungs- und Wirtschaftsstruktur des klassischen Attika* (Cologne).
Lohmann, H. 2005. 'Zum Forschungsstand des prähistorischen und antiken Blei-Silberbergbaus im Laurion', in Yalçın, Ü. (ed.), *Der Anschnitt 18, Anatolian Metal III* (Bochum), 105–136.
Lohmann, H. 2009. 'Quellen, Methoden und Ziele der Siedlungsarchäologie' in. Vött, A and Mattern, T. (eds), *Mensch und Umwelt im Spiegel der Zeit. Aspekte geoarchäologischer Forschungen im östlichen Mittelmeer* (Wiesbaden), 27–74.
Marinos, G.P. and Marinos, P.G. 1981, 'L'environnement géologique et quelques relations avec de grotte de Kitsos', in Lambert, N. (ed.), *La Grotte préhistorique de Kitsos (Attique). Missions 1968–1978, I,* (Paris), 35–40.
Marinos, G.P. and Petraschek, W.E. 1956, *Laurium* (Athens).
Mastrokoastas, E. I. 1974. 'Εις αναζήτησιν ελλειπόντων μελών επιτυμβίων αρχαϊκών γλυπτών παρά την Ανάβυσσον: το κλιμακωτόν βάθρον του κούρου Κροίσου', *Athens Annals of Archaeology* 7, 215–228.
Mussche, H.F. 1998. *Thorikos. A Mining Town in Ancient Attica* (Ghent).
Negris, F. 1881. 'Laveries anciennes du Laurium', *Annales des Mines* 20, 160–64.
Nomicos, S. 2015. 'Tetradrachme aus Athen', in Weber-Lehmann, C., Lichtenberger, A., and Berns, C. (eds.), *50 Jahre – 50 Antiken in den Kunstsammlungen der Ruhr-Universität Bochum* (Ruhpolding), 96–97.
Nomicos, S. 2017. 'Laurion. Montan- und siedlungsarchäologische Studien von der geometrischen Zeit bis zur Spätantike' (PhD dissertation, Ruhr-Universität Bochum).
Philippson, A. 1952. *Die griechischen Landschaften Band 1 Teil 3. Der Nordosten der griechischen Halbinsel Teil 3. Attika und Megaris* (Frankfurt).

Picard, O. 2001. 'La Découverte des Gisements du Laurion et les Débuts de la Chouette', *Revue Belge de Numismatique et de Sigillographie* 147, 1–10.

Salliora-Oikonomakou, M. 1985. "Αρχαίο Νεκροταφείο στην Περιοχή Λαυρίου", *Αρχαιολογικόν Δελτίον* 40 A, 90–132.

Salliora-Oikonomakou, M. 2004. *Ο αρχαίος δήμος του Σουνίου. Ιστορική και τοπογραφική επισκόπηση* (Koropi).

Seltman, C.T. 1924. *Athens: Its History and Coinage before the Persian Invasion* (Cambridge).

Sheedy, K.A., Gore, D. and Davis, G. 2009. 'A spring of silver, a Treasury in the Earth': Coinage and Wealth in Archaic Athens, *Australian Archaeological Fieldwork Abroad II. A special Issue of Ancient History: Resources for Teachers* 39:2, 248–257.

Stöllner, T. 2003. 'Mining and Economy. A Discussion of Spatial Organisations and Structures of Early Raw Material Exploitation' in Stöllner, T. and Weisgerber, G. (eds.), *Man and Mining. Studies in Honour of Gerd Weisgerber* (Bocchum), 415–446.

Stöllner, T. 2008. 'Mining Landscapes in Early Societies – Imprinting Processes in Pre- and Protohistoric Economies?' in Bartels C. and Küpper-Eichas, C. (eds.), *Cultural Heritage and Landscapes in Europe. Proceedings of the International Conference* (Bochum), 65–92.

Stöllner, T. 2014, 'Methods of Mining Archaeology' in Roberts, B.W. and Thornton C.P. (eds), *Archaeometallurgy in Global Perspective* (New York), 133–159.

van Liefferinge, K. 2013. 'Water use and management in the Classical and Early Hellenistic silver industry of Thorikos and the Laurion', *Babesch. Annual Papers on Mediterranean Archaeology* 88, 109–126.

Wagner, G.A. and Weisgerber, G. 1985. *Silber, Blei und Gold auf Sifnos. Prähistorische und antike Metallproduktion* (Bochum).

Wagner, G.A. and Weisgerber, G. 1988. *Antike Edel- und Buntmetallgewinnung auf Thasos* (Bochum).

Young, J.H. 1942. 'Sunium. An Historical Survey of an Attic Deme' (PhD dissertation, John Hopkins University).

7. METAL PRODUCTION CHAIN AT PANGAEON MOUNTAIN, EASTERN MACEDONIA, GREECE

Markos Vaxevanopoulos, Michalis Vavelidis, Dimitra Malamidou, Vasilios Melfos

ABSTRACT

Ancient writers mention Pangaeon Mountain in northeastern Greece as one of the richest gold and silver prospecting territories in antiquity. During a four year survey program, nine mining sites and eleven metallurgical locations from Hellenistic to Roman times were recorded and studied in Pangaeon. Findings dated since Byzantine and Ottoman times imply a diachronic mining activity. The mining and metallurgical operations are located mainly at the central and eastern parts of Pangaeon, where contemporary mining is recorded as well. The archaeological excavation at the Valtouda metallurgical site provides a useful tool for understanding the metal processing activities, especially during Roman times at the study area.

Mining in Pangaeon during antiquity focused on the oxidised ore following the main tectonic discontinuities and the schistosity of the marbles and the other metamorphic rocks (amphibolites, schists). Extracted ores rich in gold, silver, copper, lead and iron were transported to the adjacent metallurgical centers where enrichment and smelting were carried out. Gold, silver and copper were produced from smelting according to the analysis of the metallurgical slags. In some cases iron and lead were also extracted during these metallurgical workings.

INTRODUCTION

Mineral resources have played a key role in the Greek cultural evolution since prehistoric times. According to Herodotus (7.112), Thracian tribes exploited the gold and silver mines of Mount Pangaeon in Archaic and Classical times. During the seventh century BC, a Parian colony was

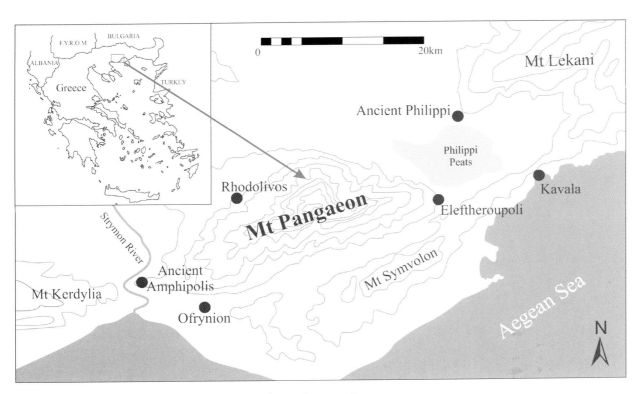

Figure 1. Geographical map of Mount Pangaeon in northeastern Greece

established on Thasos which expanded onto the opposite shores in order to control the metalliferous Pangaeon and Lekani mountains (Thucydides 4.104.4; Herodotus 6.46.2-3; Lazaridis 1971; Sanidas *et al.* 2018). Peisistratus the Athenian, who was in exile in this region around 550 BC, acquired sufficient riches and knowledge to pay mercenaries and return to Athens as a tyrant and exploit the Lavrion mines. Pangaeon was an apple of discord among Thasos, Athens and the Macedonian kingdom, until Philip II's conquest (Koukouli-Chrysanthaki 1990; Koukouli-Chrysanthaki 2014; Zannis 2014). Aristotle (*Athenaion Politeia* 15.2), Strabo (14.5.28), Titus Flavius Clemens (*Stromata* I.16.75.8) and other writers also refer to the fabulous richness of the gold and silver ores of the mountain.

Pangaeon is located in northeastern Greece, north of Mount Symvolon and southwest of Lekani Mountain (Fig. 1). During Classical and Hellenistic times two important cities, Amphipolis and Philippi (Krinides) were founded at the west and northeastern part of the mountain, respectively.

The present study is based on a survey of ancient mining and metallurgy in the broad region of Mount Pangaeon in northeastern Greece. The study area is extended from Kokkinochoma to Ofrynion and from Rhodolivos to the south foothills of Pangaeon near the modern Egnatia highway (Fig. 1). The research focuses on the geological features of the ore mineralisation, and the mining and metallurgical methods employed during antiquity aimed at achieving a better understanding of the metal production chain in a territory where research records mineral wealth (Maratos and Andronopoulos 1966; Unger and Schütz 1982; Zannis 2014).

The four year geological and archaeological survey conducted from 2009 to 2012 recorded 25 underground adits in nine discrete mining areas that were explored, mapped and studied. The exploitation in two sites is characterised by both underground and surface mining operations. In total, 11 metallurgical sites were surveyed and slags from these sites were sampled for a comparative analysis with the extracted material from the mines. Among the underground voids, seven recent adits at the central part of the mountain and nine natural caves were also recorded.

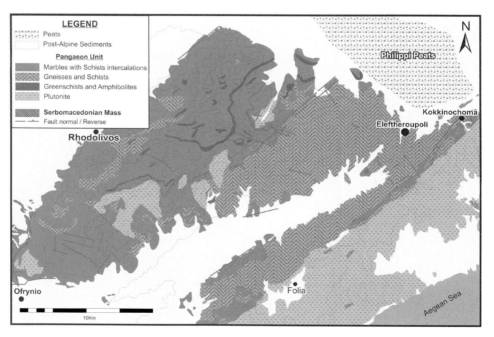

Figure 2. Geological map of Mount Pangaeon and surrounding area (modified after Kronberg 1972; Kronberg and Schenck 1974; Xidas 1978; Vaxevanopoulos 2017)

GEOLOGICAL SETTING

Mount Pangaeon belongs geotectonically in the Lower Tectonic Pangaeon Unit of the Rhodope massif (Fig. 2). It consists of marbles, amphibolites, schists and gneisses forming a dome like horst structure (Baker *et al.* 1992; 1993). These rocks are intruded by the pluton of Pangaeon which includes mainly tonalite, granodiorite, and granite (Eleftheriadis and Koroneos 2003). It has a hornblende $^{40}Ar/^{39}Ar$ age of 21 to 22 Ma (Eleftheriadis *et al.* 2001) and occupies the core of a large anticline.

A large number of small and large ore mineralisations occurs along veins filling fault systems and joints in metamorphic rocks, and as carbonate replacement ore bodies with elevated gold and/or silver content (Baker *et al.* 1993; Vaxevanopoulos 2017). Gold and silver are found in free state or in the crystal lattices of pyrite or the As-rich pyrite. Metallic minerals are also found along the schistosity of the marbles, schists or amphibolites and in quartz veins crosscutting the plutonite and the metamorphic rock. Oxidised mineralisation forming limonite gossans is hosted in carbonate rocks especially along fault and shear zones. Supergene oxidation expressed by the presence of Fe-oxides and also by malachite and azurite, was probably used as guide of mineralisation from the ancient prospectors. River sediments at the foothills of Pangaeon and surrounding areas are rich in gold placers (Baker *et al.* 1992).

Ore mineralisation found at the central-eastern part of Pangaeon contains mainly gold, silver, copper, lead and iron, as well as minor quantities of other metals (Bi, Te, W) related with various mineral assemblages. The ore at the western part of Pangaeon contains silver, iron, lead, zinc and minor barium, vanadium and antimony. Metallogenesis of Pangaeon is related with the magmatic-hydrothermal activity associated with the intrusion of the granodioritic magma during the Lower Miocene (Vaxevanopoulos 2017).

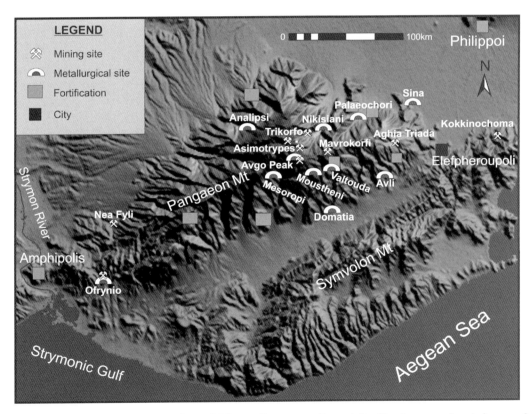

Figure 3. Mining and metallurgical sites of Mount Pangaeon. Several fortifications are located around the mountain including the ancient cities of Amphipolis and Philippi

MINING ACTIVITY

Nine mining sites were recorded with the main mining activity located at the central and eastern part of the mountain (Fig. 3). The archaeological survey revealed that the main mining activities were surrounded by eight strongly fortified establishments including the ancient cities of Amphipolis and Philippi.

The most important and extended mining area is 'Asimotrypes' at the central part of the mountain (Fig. 3). In a steep valley eight ancient and three modern (late twenthieth century) mining adits are found. The total volume of the extracted material is roughly estimated at >1450 m³ characterised by multileveled extraction of the ore. Exploitation followed mainly tectonic discontinuities with a NW-SE orientation. At the inner part of the mines, the ceiling is supported by columns consisting of gangue minerals or non-extracted ore. Two chronically different phases of exploitation and steps carved into the rock for accessing the second level of the mine were observed (Fig. 4a, b, c).

The primary mineralization is well exposed in the modern galleries of Asimotrypes area containing arsenopyrite and pyrite, with minor chalcopyrite, galena and sphalerite. However the ancient miners exploited the oxidised ore, consisting mainly of goethite, with high concentrations of Au and Ag, up to 51.2 mg/kg and 100 mg/kg respectively (Vaxevanopoulos 2017).

The Mavrokorfi mining site located 4 km southeast from Asimotrypes was also an important mining centre (Vaxevanopoulos *et al.* 2018). The Mavrokorfi-1 ancient mine comprises a gallery system with a total length of 120 m; it reveals two distinct phases of exploitation (Fig. 4d). The older phase is represented by narrow (around 120 cm high and 100 cm wide) galleries where Roman pottery was found. The second and later phase is dated to the early Ottoman period (fourtheenth to sixteenth century AD) based on pottery found

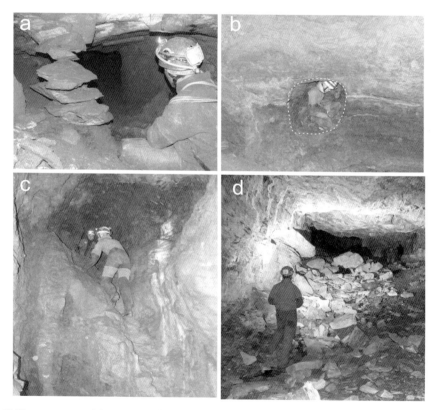

Figure 4. a) Ceiling support with gangue minerals in Asimotrypa-1 mine. **b)** Two distinct phases of exploitation in Asimotrypa-1 mine. **c)** Carved steps in the marble for accessing the second level of the Asimotrypa-1 mine. **d)** Enlarged chamber of exploitation in Mavrokorfi-1 mine

at places where the early phase gallery was enlarged, mainly at the entrance to the mine (Vaxevanopoulos *et al.* 2018).

At the southeastern margins of Pangaeon near the mountain Symvolon, the Kokkinochoma site comprises the most significant underground mine in this area. Based on the mapping of the galleries the total volume of the mine was roughly estimated at approximately 527 m^3. Traces on the gallery walls show that the main tools used for the ore extraction were chisels and hammers. It is also noteworthy that alluvial gold is found in streams adjacent to the mine (Baker *et al.* 1992).

The Aghia Triada mining site at the eastern part of the mountain is characterised by Au-Cu-rich mineralisation. The Aghia Triada-1 mine has an impressive underground gallery system.

At the western part of Pangaeon, three underground mines and one surface extraction are found in Ofrynion and Nea Fyli, respectively. The Ofrynion-3 mine was opened along tectonic faults and joints in hydrothermally altered marbles. Different levels of exploitation are clearly distinguished in the mine. At Nea-Fyli-1 mine surface exploitation with signs of previous underground mining was observed.

METALLURGICAL AREAS

Eleven metallurgical sites were recorded on Mount Pangaeon closely related with the mining works (Fig. 3). During the autumns of 2013 and 2014, an archaeometallurgical excavation was carried out by the School of Geology of the Aristotle University of Thessaloniki and the local Ephorate of Antiquities of Kavala-Thasos, Ministry of Culture in the Valtouda

Figure 5. a) The metallurgical site of Valtouda. **b)** Smelting furnace debris from Valtouda. **c)** Tapped slag from Sina metallurgical site

metallurgical site. This was located close to the Mavrokorfi mining area in the central part of Pangaeon (Fig. 5a).

At the eastern part of the site the research revealed a great quantity of ancient smelting furnace debris (Fig. 5b), consisting of cobbles of gneiss with clay matrix in a ground cavity with an average diameter of 150 cm (Vaxevanopoulos et al. 2018).

Tapped slags (Fig. 5c) found in Valtouda comprise copper prills inside a wustite-fayalite assemblage. Most of the pottery finds are fragments of small amphorae, jugs and bowls date to Roman times (second-fourth centuries AD). A number of grinding stones made of gneiss were found scattered in the area. They were possibly used for grinding and crushing the ore before smelting.

About 2.5 km northeast from the Nikisiani mining site is the homonym metallurgical area (Fig. 3). It constitutes the most extended metallurgical site in Mount Pangaeon covering an area over one km^2 with numerous slag heaps with compact, semi-compact and speiss slags. Surface pottery dates through Hellenistic, Roman, Byzantine and Ottoman times. Furnace remains and grinding stones are also found at the southern part of the site.

The Sina metallurgical area is located at the northeastern part of the mountain (Fig. 3). It comprises a hill covered with metallurgical slags, furnace remains and basalt grinding stones. Most of the metallurgical slags contain a significant quantity of lead prills, and a small number of slags includes copper prills. The slag minerals are wustite (FeO) and kirschsteinite (FeCaSiO$_4$) in a glassy matrix.

Table 1. Slag characteristics of Mount Pangaeon metallurgical areas, metallurgical remains and surface pottery datings. (Wus: wustite, Ki: kirschteinite, Fa: fayalite, Mo: monticellite, Mag: magnetite, Po: pyrrhotite, Me: melanotekite, Gal: galena, At: atakamite, Ilm: ilmenite, Ba: baryte)

Metallurgical Areas	Slag Types	Slag Minerals	Possible Metal Production	Metallurgical remains	Dating based on surface pottery
Valtouda	Compact, Semicompact, Spongy Speiss	Wus, Mn-Wus, Fa, Ki, Mo, Gal, At	Cu, Au, Ag	Furnace remain, Grinding Stones	Roman
Nikisiani	Compact, Semicompact, Speiss	Wus, Fa, Mo, Me	Au, Ag, Cu, Pb	Furnace remain, Grinding Stones	Hellenistic-Roman-Byzantine-Ottoman
Sina	Compact Speiss	Wus, Ki	Au, Ag, Cu, Pb	Furnace remains	Hellenistic-Roman-Ottoman
Chryssokastro	Compact Speiss	Wus, Ki, Fa	Au, Ag	–	Roman
Palaeochori	Compact, Semicompact, Speiss	Wus, Fa, Mo, Mag, Ki, Po	Ag	–	Ottoman
Moustheni	Compact, Semicompact, Speiss	Wus, Fa, Mo, Gal, At	Au, Ag	–	Roman
Pouliana (Mesoropi)	Compact, Semicompact, Spongy Speiss	Wus, Mn-Ki, Fa, Mo, Mag,	Au, Ag, Cu	Furnace remains	Roman
Avgo	Compact	Wus, Fa, Ki, Gal	Au, Ag	–	Roman
Analipsi	Compact, Semicompact, Spongy Speiss	Wus, Mo, Po	Ag	Furnace remains	Roman
Domatia	Compact, Semicompact, Spongy	Wus, Ilm, Ki	Fe	–	Ottoman
Ofrynion	Glassy	Ba	Ag	–	Roman

Metallurgical sites have also been recorded in Chryssokastro, Palaeochori, Mesoropi, Moustheni, Avgo Peak, Avli, Analipsi and Ofrynion (Fig.3) at the western part of the mountain probably exploited for precious metals and copper (Vaxevanopoulos 2017). In contrast, at the Domatia metallurgical site (Fig. 3), the studied slags demonstrated iron smelting.

Most of the metallurgical sites are dated from Hellenistic to Ottoman times based on the surface findings. The usual focus was on the extraction of precious metals (gold and silver), but in Valtouda the main extracted metal was copper (Vaxevanopoulos *et al.* 2018). Besides the Valtouda metallurgical area, copper was possibly produced in many other metallurgical sites as a byproduct (Sina, Avli, Nikisiani, Pouliana). The area of Eleftheroupoli city, named Pravi during the Ottoman period, was also an important metallurgical centre for iron production (Anhegger1943; Murphey 1980). Unfortunately the modern city was built over the metallurgical debris preventing research. Table 1 shows the metallurgical areas including the slag types and mineralogical composition, the metals extracted, the metallurgical activities remains and the dating of each process according to the surface pottery.

DISCUSSION – THE METAL PRODUCTION CHAIN

Using the archaeological and geological data gained during the four-year survey, a model of metal production for the Mount Pangaeon region can be proposed (Fig. 6). Prehistoric and early historic exploitation evidence is absent. This is possibly due to the destruction of evidence of same by the subsequent mining phases, or because during these periods, mineral extraction focused on the gold placers around Pangaeon and the adjacent areas. Based on our team's archaeometallurgical investigation, the main ore extraction phases are confirmed between Hellenistic and Ottoman times implying continuous mining activity on Pangaeon.

Oxidised ore rich in gold, silver, copper, lead and iron was extracted from all the studied mining sites. The enrichment process was commenced at the mining areas as evidenced by some findings of grinding stones in the mining sites. Gangue material was used for ceiling support in dry stone walls at inner part of the mines or in refilling the old galleries.

Ore was smelted after enrichment, producing three distinctive layers inside the furnace (Fig. 6). Slag comprised the upper layer, speiss the intermediate layer, and precious metals (Au, Ag) absorbed in lead in the bottom layer. The two upper layers have been studied mainly in the furnace remains of Valtouda metallurgical site, as well as in Nikisiani, Pouliana and Analipsi metallurgical areas (Vaxevanopoulos 2017). The lead was probably further processed by cupellation in order to extract gold and silver. Few traces of cupellation have been found at the metallurgical areas of the Mount Pangaeon. It is possible that cupellation, refining and resmelting were carried out at an administrative centre, as was proposed by Raber (1987), and not at the site. After cupellation litharge (PbO) and copper oxide (CuO) could be used for lead and copper extraction respectively.

During the main smelting process the upper layer of slag was tapped out, and the same was probably the case for the intermediate speiss layer. Gold and silver were then separated by refining, while lead and copper were probably produced from re-smelting.

On the basis of Valtouda metallurgical area findings, copper rich in gold and silver were probably extracted from the furnace bottom layer from the smelting procedure (Vaxevanopoulos 2017; 2018).

The metallurgical sites of Pangaeon are limited and dispersed in the mountain except the Nikisiani metallurgical area. Most of them are close to ore deposits and water sources. Two important centers, Amphipolis and Philippi were founded during Classical times probably to control the metal production of Pangaeon. Eleftheroupoli became an important city and probably an administrative center that controlled the metal production during the Ottoman period.

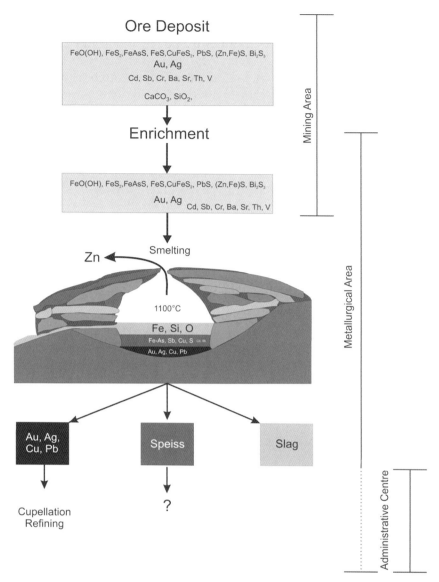

Figure 6. Proposed metal chain production scheme for Pangaeon mining and metallurgical activity (modified after Vaxevanopoulos 2017)

CONCLUSIONS

Mining and metallurgical activity is recorded in Mount Pangaeon from Hellenistic and Roman times through into the Byzantine and Ottoman periods. Earlier exploitation phases were not documented but they are not excluded. The main underground mining and metallurgical process is recorded during Roman times by archaeological finds. Intense activity is also documented during Byzantine and Ottoman times.

The extracted ores rich in gold, silver, copper, lead and iron were transferred to metallurgical sites where enrichment and smelting was carried out. The metal production chain was characterised by many dispersed and relatively small production centers located close to the ore deposits. Production centers were probably embedded within a larger productive system including the nearby mining centres. Amphipolis and Philippi are suggested as possible administration centres during Hellenistic and Roman times and Eleftheroupoli during the Ottoman period. Fortified establishments around Pangaeon protected an important area rich in precious metals and natural resources.

ACKNOWLEDGMENTS

This paper is based on research carried out as part of the doctorate thesis of the first author in the Department of Mineralogy, Petrology, Economic Geology, at the Faculty of Geology, of the Aristotle University of Thessaloniki, Greece. The research team thanks the 'Alexander S. Onassis' Public Benefit Foundation of Greece for financial support of the first author from 2009 to 2011 as well as for funding the chemical analyses of this project. Dr. Gil Davis is sincerely thanked for his valuable comments and suggestions. We also thank the Australian Centre for Ancient Numismatic Studies and the Epigraphic and Numismatic Museum of Athens for covering the first author's travel expenses for the attendance at the International Conference on Metallurgy, Mines, Numismatics and Archaeology 'Mines, Metals and Money in Attica and the Ancient World'.

BIBLIOGRAPHY

Anhegger, R. 1943. *Beiträge zur Geschichte des Bergbaus im Osmanischen Reich* (Istanbul).

Baker, J.H., Arvanitides, N., Eliopoulos, D. and De Groot, P. 1992. *Vein type mineralizations, N. Greece: Examples from Pangeon, Palea Kavala and Symvoulon. Internal progress report to IGME-Athens and DGXII* (Thessalonica).

Baker, J.H., Eliopoulos, D.G., Arvanitides, N.D., and Chatzipanagis, J., 1993. 'Carbonate-hosted precious and base metal mineralizations in northern Greece: Development of new exploration strategies. Fertile lineaments and regional variations of metallic elements.3.4 The Pangeon-Symvolon regions: Athens, Institute of Geology and Mineral Exploration, Final Report, EEC' Project *MA2M-CT-90-0015*, 42–48.

Eleftheriadis, G., Frank, W. and Petrakakis, K. 2001. '^{40}Ar/^{39}Ar geochronology of the Pangeon granitoids, Rhodope Unit (northern Greece)', *Beih. Z. Eur. J. Mineral* 11, 62.

Eleftheriadis, G. and Koroneos, A. 2003. 'Geochemistry and Petrogenesis of Post-Collision Pangeon Granitoids in Central Macedonia, northern Greece', *Chem. Erde* 63(4), 364-389.

Koukouli-Chrysanthaki, Ch. 1990. "Τα μέταλλα της Θασιακής Περαίας",in Lazaride, M.D. (ed.), Πόλις και Χώρα στην Αρχαία Μακεδονία και Θράκη, Πρακτικά Αρχαιολογικού Συνεδρίου (Thessalonica), 493–514.

Koukouli-Chrysanthaki, C. 1990. "Τα 'μέταλλα' της θασιακής Περαίας", in Koukouli-Chryssanthaki, Ch. and Picard, O. (eds.), Μνήμη Δ. Λαζαρίδη. Πόλις και Χώρα στην αρχαία Μακεδονία και Θράκη. Πρακτικά Αρχαιολογικού Συνεδρίου, Καβάλα, 9-11.493-514.

Koukouli-Chrysanthaki, Ch. 2014. "Η αρχαιολογική έρευνα στη Μακεδονία της Πρώιμης Εποχής του Σιδήρου. Απολογισμός και προοπτικές", in Stefani, E., Merousis, N. and Dimoula, A. (eds.), *A Century of Research in Prehistoric Macedonia 1912-2012* (Thessalonica), 153-180.

Kronberg, P. 1972. *Geological Map of Greece. Kavala Sheet. Scale 1:50.000* (National Institute of Geological and Mining Research, Athens).

Kronberg, P. and Schenck, P.F. 1974. *Geological Map of Greece. Nikisiani-Loutra Elevtheron Sheet. Scale 1:50.000* (National Institute of Geological and Mining Research, Athens).

Murphey, R. 1980. 'Silver Production in Rumelia according to an official Ottoman Reportcirca 1600', *Sudost-Forschungen* 33, 75–104.

Maratos, G. and Andronopoulos, V. 1966. *The Mineral Wealth of Northern Greece (Reconnaissance of the Area between Evros and Axios Rivers). Report 39a* (Athens).

Lazaridis, D. 1971. *Thasos and its Peraia (Ancient Greek Cities, 5)* (Athens).

Raber, P. 1987. 'Early Copper Production in the Polis Region, Western Cyprus', *J. Field A.* 14, 297–313.

Sanidas, G. M. Malamidou, D. and Nerantzis N. 2018. 'Paros, Thasos and the Question of Mining and Metal Production before and after Colonisation: Review and Perspectives. In: Katsonopoulou D. (ed.) Paros IV, Paros and its colonies, Proceedings of the Fourth International Conference on the Archaeology of Paros and the Cyclades, Paroikia, Paros, 11-14 June 2015. Athens: The Institute for archaeology of Paros and the Cyclades, pp. 251–265.

Unger, H.J. and Schütz, E. 1982. 'Pangaion - Ein Gebirge und sein Bergbau', in Geißlinger, H. (ed.), *Südosteuropa zwischen 1600 und 1000 v. Chr. (Berlin 1982)*, 145–172.

Vaxevanopoulos, M., Vavelidis, M, Melfos, V., Malamidou, D. and Pavlides, S. 2018. 'Ancient mining and metallurgical activity at the gold-silver-copper ore deposits in Mavrokorfi area, Mount Pangaeon (NE Greece)', in Ben-Yosef, E. (ed.) 2018. *Mining for Ancient Copper: Essays in Memory of Beno Rothenberg* (Tel Aviv), 385-98.

Vaxevanopoulos, M. 2017. 'Ancient mining and metallurgical activity on Mount Pangaon, E. Macedonia, Greece. Unpublished Doctoral dissertation, Thessaloniki, Greece, Aristotle Universtiy of Thessaloniki. 337 p. (in Greek).

Xidas, S. 1978. *Geological Map of Greece. Rhodolivos Sheet. Scale 1:50.000* (Institute of Geology and Mineral Exploration, Athens).

Zannis, A. G. 2014. *Le pays entre le Strymon et le Nestos: géographie et histoire (VIIe-IVe siècle avant J.-C.)* Μελετήματα *71* (Athens).

PART 2

ANALYSIS

8. THE MINTING/MINING NEXUS: NEW UNDERSTANDINGS OF ARCHAIC GREEK SILVER COINAGE FROM LEAD ISOTOPE ANALYSIS

Zofia Anna Stos-Gale and Gillan Davis

ABSTRACT

This paper presents fresh interpretations of 160 lead isotope analyses of Archaic Greek coins on the OXALID database based on new data for ore sources in Spain, Sardinia, Bulgaria, Romania, Greece, Turkey and Iran. It demonstrates that the earliest minters used far more diverse metal sources than the literary evidence suggests, and engaged in what could be described as opportunistic minting. Some currently held views on the importance of Siphnian silver, Peisistratid access to Thracian silver, the sources of Aiginetan, Thasian and Chian silver, the use of gold and tin as tracers for Siphnian and Lavrion silver, and the mixing of silver are challenged. Thoughts are offered on how archaic minting drove intensification of mining.

INTRODUCTION

The first large research project to use lead isotope and chemical analyses for the identification of ore sources of Archaic silver coins was begun in 1978 by Wolfgang Gentner, Otto Müller and Günther Wagner from the Max Planck Institute for Nuclear Physics in Heidelberg, in collaboration with Noel Gale from the Department of Geology, University of Oxford.[1] The main group of coins for analysis came from a large hoard discovered in 1969 in Asyut, southern Egypt, comprising 900 or so coins minted by many of the Archaic Greek cities from Sicily to Cyprus. The publishers of the Asyut Hoard suggested it was buried around 475 BC (Price and Waggoner 1975) which provides a useful *terminus ante quem* for silver sources and minting practices at the end of the Late Archaic Period.

The Stiftung Wolkswagenwerk purchased 120 severely damaged coins of low numismatic value for analysis, and a further 45 Aeginetan coins from the same hoard were contributed by Dr Leslie Beer. Altogether 99 coins and one silver ingot from the Asyut Hoard were analysed for their lead isotopes, and 89 of these also for their elemental compositions. The results were published in 1978 (Gentner *et al.* 1978) and in 1980 (Gale *et al.* 1980). They concluded that many coins were consistent with origins in the mines of Lavrion and Siphnos, but they had some doubts over interpretation of the data, mainly due to the lack of a database of lead isotope compositions from other ore deposits.

Over the next 20 years, two other research projects in the Isotrace Laboratory at the University of Oxford provided more lead isotope and chemical analyses of Archaic silver coins from Thasos (Gale *et al.* 1988) and Chios (Hardwick *et al.* 1998), summarised in Table 1. Since then, a great deal more lead isotope data and archaeometallurgical information have been published for ore sources in Spain, Sardinia, Bulgaria, Romania, Greece, Turkey and Iran.[2]

In this paper, the lead isotope data are re-evaluated in a numismatic context, endeavouring to understand the operations of the earliest Archaic Greek mints, and especially their sources of silver.

METHODOLOGY OF METAL PROVENANCE STUDIES

The lead isotope provenance method is based chiefly on comparisons of lead isotope and elemental compositions of ores and slags from known ore deposits and ancient artefacts. In the 1980s, the database of European and Middle-Eastern deposits of lead-silver and copper ores included only a few hundred lead isotope ratios. The current database used for interpretation of lead isotope data published on the Oxford Archaeological Lead Isotope Database (OXALID) and by other researchers

---

[1] We thank Professor Jack Kroll for reading and commenting on this paper as well as the anonymous reviewers.
[2] A preliminary re-evaluation of the possible origin of these coins was discussed at the RITaK Graduate seminar held in the Mining Museum Bochum in November 2014 (published in Stos-Gale 2017).

consists of over 6,000 lead isotope ratios for lead, silver and copper ores from the majority of important deposits in Europe, and some from the Middle East (Turkey, Israel, Jordan, Iran and Saudi Arabia), as well as several thousand data for prehistoric metals from the same regions. Furthermore, the methodology of comparing the data has been vastly improved due to advances in computer software over the last 30 years.

An ancient artefact is regarded as being fully consistent with originating from a given ore deposit if its three independent lead isotope ratios are identical (within ±0.1% analytical error for each ratio) with the lead isotope ratios obtained for the ores from this deposit. Finding the matching ore samples for each artefact is done using the TestEuclid procedure (Stos 2009). This three-step process involves first searching the database covering all ore data. Second, the lead isotope ratios of the artefacts are plotted on at least two lead isotope diagrams that include all three independent ratios, together with the data for all ore deposits that appear to show matching lead isotope ratios. In the third step of the interpretative process, a broader picture of the possible origin of metals is considered including:

i. Rejection of ore deposits that on geochemical or chronological ground could not have supplied silver or copper for these artefacts.
ii. Comparisons with lead isotope and elemental data for the artefact from various related archaeological sites.

It is important to stress that identical lead isotope characteristics of a group of metals do not guarantee that their elemental characteristics will also form a group and *vice versa* (Rychner and Stos-Gale 1998; Pernicka 1999). It is assumed that silver artefacts usually do not contain added lead since it is in most ores being cupellated, but only traces of lead remain after processing. Small amounts of copper that might have been added to silver do not usually contribute enough lead to change the lead isotope compositions of the original silver.

It is also necessary to consider the possibility that an artefact was made from melting together silver from different sources. The effect of this activity on lead isotope provenance studies has been discussed at length (summarised in Stos-Gale 2001; Ling *et al.* 2014). The problem of mixing can be assessed by examining the distribution of the data points on the lead isotope plots; each metal obtained from mixing two (or more) other sources will plot on a straight line between the data points representing these other sources. On lead isotope plots the 'mixing lines' run diagonally following the general trend of the radioactive decay lines.

POSSIBLE SOURCES OF SILVER FOR ARCHAIC GREEK COINS AND EVIDENCE OF THEIR EXPLOITATION

Silver was available in the Aegean from the Bronze Age (Gale and Stos-Gale 1981a and b; Pernicka *et al.* 1985; for dating cf. Wagner *et al.* 1986). Archaeometallurgical research has provided evidence that silver ores were mainly exploited on the Cycladic island of Siphnos in the Early Bronze Age (third Millennium BC) and in the first Millennium BC (Wagner and Weisgerber 1985), and more or less continuously in Lavrion, Attica, from the Early Bronze Age until the Roman period and later (Conophagos 1980; Gale *et al.* 2008).

Other main sources in the Archaic Period were in northern Greece in the Chalkidiki peninsula, the island of Thasos, and the Rhodope Mountains including Mt. Pangaion.[3] For Chalkidiki there seems to be no evidence of silver exploitation in the Bronze Age but quite possibly it was mined from the first millennium BC (Wagner *et al.* 1986).

---

[3] For the vexed question of the location the Mt Pangaion mines, see Wagner and Weisberger 1988.

Further afield to the east were the silver-bearing ores in the Troad Peninsula (Wagner *et al.* 1985), Taurus Mountains in southern Turkey (Yener *et al.* 1991) and Iran (Pernicka *et al.* 2011) where silver was exploited since the Early Bronze Age. The Phoenicians traded to the Western Mediterranean in the Archaic Period and eagerly sought Spanish silver which was exploited from the Argaric period in the third-second millennium BC (Kassianidou 1992; Rothenberg and Blanco Freijeiro 1981; Renzi *et al.* 2009 and 2012). There was also mining in Roman times in the south of France in Massif Central (Baron *et al.* 2006; Davis 1935), and on Sardinia (Valera *et al.* 2005), with some possibility they were exploited earlier in the Late Bronze Age.

A further potential source is to the north of Greece in present day Romania where there are rich mineral deposits. The Romans established a province of Dacia there at the beginning of the second century CE, and exploited gold and silver ores in the Apuseni Mountains in the south-east Carpathians (also known as the Transylvanian Metalliferous Mountains).[4] Some distance north in the Baia Mare part of the Eastern Carpathians there are also gold and silver ores (Kouzmanov *et al.* 2005b: Marcoux *et al.* 2002). It is quite possible these rich gold, silver and copper deposits were exploited before the Roman period by Thracian tribes back to the Bronze Age (Stos-Gale 2014).[5]

RE-EVALUATION OF THE RESULTS OF EARLIER LEAD ISOTOPE AND CHEMICAL ANALYSES OF ARCHAIC GREEK COINS

The OXALID database contains lead isotope data for 160 Archaic Greek coins analysed in Oxford and securely dated to sixth-fifth centuries BC (Table 1).[6]

Athens

A keen debate surrounds the source(s) of silver for the earliest Athenian coinage known as the *Wappenmünzen*, begun under the Peisistratids in the second half of the sixth century BC. [Aristotle] *Ath. Pol.* 15.2 claimed Peisistratos derived the *chrēmata* (literally 'resources' but usually understood in this context to mean 'money' in the form of bullion) to pay mercenaries to seize his tyranny of Athens from "the neighbourhood of Pangaion", though Herodotus said the inland mines were controlled by the local tribes (7.112). [Aristotle] *Ath. Pol.* 22.7 (cf. Hdt. 7.144) claimed the major strike of rich silver ore in Lavrion was in 483 BC, but the common scholarly opinion assumes the mines had been exploited somewhat earlier, spurred on by the loss of access to Thracian silver when Darius conquered the region in 512 BC (Hdt. 5.11; 5.23).[7] The expectation from literary evidence is thus that the *Wappenmünzen* were minted from Northern Greek silver, succeeded by Lavrion silver for the massive minting of 'owls' (Hdt. 1.64.1; cf. summary of evidence and arguments in Davis 2014a). Against this, there is clear evidence of Lavrion silver from lead isotope analyses of seventh century *Hacksilber* from Tel Miqne-Ekron in Southern Israel (Stos-Gale 2001 and OXALID).

Gale *et al.* (1980) analysed seven *Wappenmünzen* dating to the end of the sixth century BC from the British Museum and Ashmolean Museum (Oxford) collections (Fig. 1). Six of them show very varied lead isotope compositions which definitively exclude Lavrion, and reflect widely different origins of silver unknown to Gale *et al.* (1980, 30). Only one, a 'wheel' obol is fully consistent with Lavrion silver, supporting the independently derived conclusion

---

[4] This area covers about 900 km² and even today contains large quantities of epithermal Au-Ag, and porphyry Cu-Au ores (Neubauer *et al.* 2005; Kouzmanov *et al.* 2005a; Baron *et al.* 2011).
[5] The silver deposits in the Apuseni Mountains and Rosia Montana (to a lesser extend) are significant. Even in the second half of the 20th century over 30 tonnes a year of silver were extracted in Romania (Dunning *et al.* 1982, p. 287).
[6] The data are freely available at: http://oxalid.arch.ox.ac.uk. This includes information on where samples were collected.
[7] In fact, there are problems with this as Professor Kroll pointed out in correspondence. The Persians were not maritime traders, and collection of tribute did not amount to monopolisation. Trade in Aegean silver must have continued for Thracian coinage to show up in Egyptian and Levantine hoards.

Table 1. Lead isotope data for the 160 analysed coins from the OXALID database

Mint	Chronology	Number of analysed coins	Reference	Lead isotope based possible origin of silver
Acanthus	Before 475 BCE	3	Gale et al. 1980	2 Chalkidiki, 1 Pangeon
Aegina	6th-5th c. BCE	44	Gale et al. 1980	8 Chalkidiki, 8 Lavrion, 5 Pangeon, 10 Rhodope, 2 Romania, 6 Siphnos, 1 Thasos, 1 Troad, 1 South Spain, 2 unknown (1 South France, 1 Taurus Mts.)
Athens, 'Wappenmünzen'	6th c. BCE	7	Gale et al. 1980	1 Lavrion, 3 south Spain, 2 Rhodope, 1 Iran (Nakhlak)
Athens, 'Owls'	5th c. BCE	21	Gale et al. 1980	1 Chalkidiki or Thasos, 19 Lavrion, 1 Romania (Baia Mare)
Chios	6th-5th c. BCE	14	Hardwick et al. 1998	2 Chalkidiki or Thasos, 7 Lavrion, 2 Rhodope, 1 Romania (Rosia Montana), 2 south Spain
Corinth	Before 475 BCE	8	Gale et al. 1980	1 Chalkidiki, 5 Lavrion, 1 Siphnos, 1 Rhodope
Lesbos	Before 475 BCE	1	Gale et al. 1980	1 Chalkidiki or Thasos
Lycia	Before 475 BCE	2	Gale et al. 1980	2 Troad, Canakkale
Mallus or Caria	Before 475 BCE	5	Gale et al. 1980	3 Lavrion, 1 Iran (Pasar), 1 Rhodope or Thasos,
Messana, Sicily	Before 475 BCE	1	Gale et al. 1980	1 Lavrion
Orescii	Before 475 BCE	6	Gale et al. 1980	6 Chalkidiki
Persia	Before 475 BCE	3	Gale et al. 1980	1 Iran (Pasar), 2 Lavrion
Salamis, Cyprus	Before 475 BCE	1	Gale et al. 1980	1 Lavrion
Samos	Before 475 BCE	5	Gale et al. 1980	4 Lavrion, 1 Siphnos
Thasos	5th c. BCE	36	Gale et al. 1980 and Gale et al. 1988	9 Chalkidiki, 4 Lavrion, 1 Pangeon, 10 Rhodope, 2 Romania (Apuseni), 2 Siphnos, 5 Thasos, 1 south Spain, 2 unknown
Zankle, Sicily	Before 475 BCE	3	Gale et al. 1980	1 Lavrion, 1 Romania (Rosia Montana), 1 Thasos
		160		

that the wheel fractions do not belong with the early *Wappenmünzen* and date to the end of the sixth/beginning of the fifth century BC (Davis 2014b). A comparison of the previously unknown lead isotope ratios with the current database indicates that two of the analysed *Wappenmünzen* (BMC3 'amphora' and BMC 18 'gorgoneion') are indeed consistent with lead isotope ratios of ores from northern Greece (the southern Rhodope - Macedonia or Thrace). However, one (BMC 1[H] Histiaea) matches samples of ores from a silver mine at Nakhlak in Iran, and the three remaining coins have lead isotope compositions consistent with silver mines in Spain: BMC 17 with ores from Mazarrón in eastern Spain near Murcia, and BMC 1(D) (Diadus) and 9 with ores from Jaén in south-west Spain.

Gale et al. (1980, 28, Table 6) published analyses of fourteen Athenian unwreathed 'owl' tetradrachms dated to the early years of the fifth century BC and concluded that they all are consistent with an origin in the silver mines of Lavrion.[8] Another eight such coins have subsequently been analysed (from the Bibliothèque nationale de france and the Leslie Beer

---

[8] A fifteenth coin listed in their Table 6 as Athenian is in fact an Oresci coin - Price and Waggoner No. 65 = MPI 69.

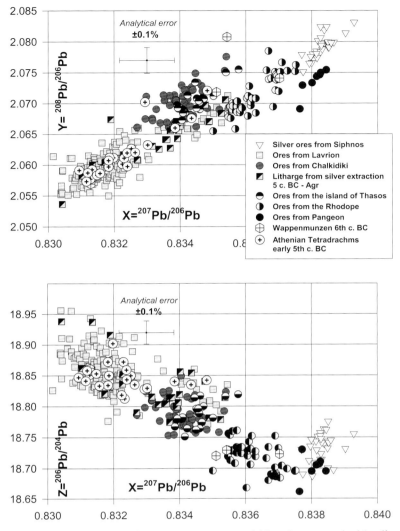

Figure 1. Lead isotope analysis of 7 Athenian *Wappenmünzen* and 12 early unwreathed 'owl' tetradrachms

collection) of which six are consistent with Lavrion. More specifically, two fit the lead isotope ratios of the litharge from the fifth century BC silver extraction site in Agrileza in Lavrion (Paris 289 and Paris 9; cf. Ellis Jones 1988) and the others are identical isotopically to the ores from the Lavrion mines of Kamareza, Plaka and Esperanza. One of the two non-Lavrion tetradrachms seems to be consistent with the ores from Chalkidiki or Thasos (MPI 38 (PW 407-417),[9] and the other with ores from Baia Mare in Romania (MPI X).

These data suggest the sixth century BC *Wappenmünzen* were minted from any silver that was to hand from Spain to Iran, and the early fifth century owls and wheel fractions from Lavrion silver with some admixture from silver coming into the system. For whatever reasons, silver mining at Lavrion must have (virtually) ceased in the sixth century BC only restarting towards the end of it (see discussion in Davis 2012; Davis 2014a).

Aegina

Aegina was one of the first Greek states to mint silver coinage, but the island does not have silver deposits. Lavrion might seem an unlikely direct source due to the political and com-

---

[9] These two sources cannot be distinguished on the grounds of lead isotope compositions of analysed ores.

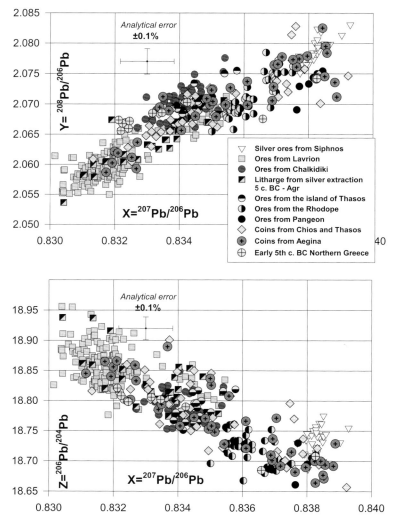

Figure 2. Lead isotope analysis of coins from Aegina, Chios, Thasos and other early fifth century coins from Northern Greece

mercial rivalry between Aegina and Athens dating back to the beginning of the sixth century BC (Hdt. 5.79-89; 6.49-51, 73, 85-94). The alternative is that silver was acquired through trade in which Aegina was a leader. The first attempt to find the origin of the silver was undertaken by Kraay and Emeleus (1962) using neutron activation for chemical analysis. They analysed 37 Aeginetan 'turtles' which provided them with good data on Ag, Au and Cu. In an oft-quoted finding, they concluded that the relatively high gold content of Aeginetan coins distinguished them clearly from Athenian 'owls' which they had analysed in parallel. Furthermore, they proposed that Aegina probably obtained its silver from Siphnos which Herodotus (3.57) stated had gold as well as silver mines.

Gale *et al.* (1980) analysed 44 coins from Aegina from the Asyut Hoard for their lead isotope compositions.[10] They concluded that nine were likely to be from Lavrion, and from their chemical testing they noted that eight had a low gold content which they contended indicated silver from Lavrion (p. 36). The ratios of the ninth coin (No. 540), and the chemical composition with high gold and low lead contents, were not completely consistent with Lavrion ores. Rechecking the data using the TestEuclid procedure confirms these eight coins

---

[10] Gale *et al.* (1980), Table 7 has 45 coins, but the last one is a fourth century BC coin from the Wells Hoard (LBT Ox) and thus not included here. This late coin has composition of ores from Romania.

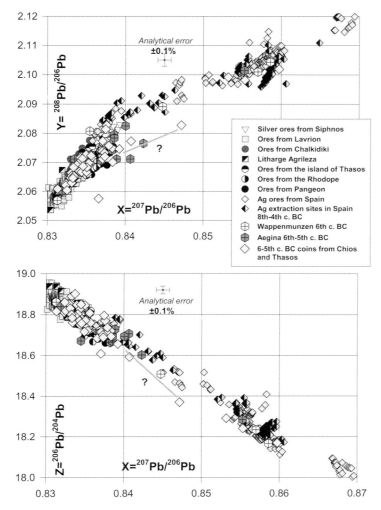

Figure 3. Lead isotope analysis showing diverse ore sources of Aeginetan coins

are fully consistent with Lavrion lead isotope compositions (Fig. 2). Their range of lead isotope ratios is nearly identical with the main group of *Hacksilber* from Tel Miqne-Ekron, indicating that the silver was from the same Lavrion mines used in the seventh century BC. However, only one of the eight coins is of the earlier type dated by Price and Waggoner to the end of the sixth century BC; the others are of the type dated to 495-485 BC. The ninth coin (No. 540) is slightly later still dated to 485/480 BC. It is fully consistent with the lead isotope ratios of the ores from northern Greek mines in Madem Lakkos and Olympias in the Chalkidiki.

Gale *et al.* claimed that 10 of the coins they analysed originated from Siphnos (1980, 36). In their discussion they combined the results of chemical and lead isotope analyses (1980, 33-43). They claimed that elemental compositions, in particular gold and tin content, are the main elements that can distinguish Siphnian ores on the bases that tin is often associated with gold ores, and, as mentioned previously, gold was mined on Siphnos. However, this is not convincing since the range of trace elements is quite varied. One difficulty is that Siphnos herself minted few coins and few of these have yet been subject to lead isotope analyses (cf. Sheedy *et al.* this volume). X-Ray Fluorescence spectrometry analyses of Siphnian coins (reproduced in Gale *et al.* (1980, 41, Table 12) show considerable differences in gold content. Using the much greater number of lead isotope analyses of Aegean lead/silver ores plotted on Figure 2, it seems that only six are fully consistent with lead isotope ratios of Siphnian ores and litharge (PW 514, PW 534, PW 542, PW 550, PW 435 and PW 436).[11] Unfortunately, Gale *et al.* (1980) did not identify all the coins which they interpreted as deriving from Siphnos, One (PW 512), perhaps originated from ores in the Apuseni Mountains in Romania (Rosia Montana: Baron *et al.* 2011), while another from Aegina has an isotopic composition more consistent with Transylvanian ores (PW 479 Windmill IVa). Crucially, five coins which it seems were identified as being from Siphnos, are tentatively consistent with the lead isotope compositions of the Pangaion region, noting that few samples have been analysed (PW 432, PW 433, PW 446, PW 471, PW 549; the data for the ores is also on the OXALID; cf. Vaxevanopoulos this volume).

However, there is a large group of Aeginetan coins for which the lead isotope compositions fall between the values for Lavrion and Siphnos, and which Gale *et al.* (1980, 42) suggested might have derived from Macedonian silver. Their hypothesis seems to be correct based on the currently available data for Greek silver/lead ores. Figure 2 shows a large group of coins which are fully consistent with lead isotope data for the ores from the Chalkidiki, Thasos and various ores from the southern Rhodope Mountains. An interesting detail given by Gale *et al.* (1980) concerns three coins from the same obverse die (511, 512, 513); two of them have lead isotope ratios consistent with Lavrion, and one is quite different, possibly from the Romanian mines in Rosia Montana (not Siphnos, as previously published).

Three of the Aeginetan coins have lead isotope compositions not consistent with any of the Aegean ore deposits (Fig. 3).[12] One coin (PW 444), has a lead isotope composition fully consistent with the mines of Jaén and the debris from the Phoenician site of La Fonteta near Alicante (Renzi *et al.* 2009) in southern Spain (as distinct from Rio Tinto). Another coin (PW 477) is consistent with the silver from the Massif Central in Southern France (Baron *et al.* 2006), and one is possibly from ores in the Taurus Mountains in southern Turkey. It is not known at present if these ores were exploited in the mid-first millennium BC, but they were mined in earlier periods (Yener *et al.* 1991).

Gale *et al.* (1980, 43) contemplated that Aegina derived silver for its coins from three main sources: Lavrion, Siphnos '...*and a third as yet unlocated source, perhaps in Macedonia, Lydia or even Euboea*' on the plausible basis that "silver was probably a normal item of export in exchange for goods" (p.34). This re-evaluation of the lead isotope data finds a different emphasis. Only eight of the 44 Aeginetan coins are consistent with Lavrion and six with Siphnos, while 24 are consistent with the northern Greek mines in Chalkidiki, Pangaion, southern Rhodope, and possibly Thasos. Single coins came from further away with origins in the east, west and north Aegean. This pattern suggests the main supply of silver was coming to Aegina from northern Greece, followed by Lavrion and Siphnos, the former especially in the fifth century, with a small trickle from various other places, possibly re-using existing bullion.

Thasos

36 Thasian coins are listed on the OXALID database, mostly also with elemental compositions (Figs. 2 and 3). This is a major advance on the four coins from the Asyut Hoard analysed solely for their lead isotope compositions by Gale *et al.* (1980). These additional analyses were performed on coins from the Ashmolean Museum in Oxford and from the Bibliothèque nationale de france in the Isotrace Laboratory (Gale *et al.* 1988). They published the results

---

[11] The seventh one (PW 537) seems to have the ratio of $^{206}Pb/^{204}Pb$ which is too high for Siphnos, but since there are no other silver ores that would have such sets of ratios it is most likely that the TIMS run of this coin was very poor and the ratios to ^{204}Pb were not accurately measured, such problems with TIMS measurements were not uncommon when lead extracted from samples was too low to run strong isotopic ion beams, and therefore it can be presumed that the silver in this coin is indeed of Siphnian origin.

[12] On Figure 3 these two coins are indicated with a '?'.

of 31 of these coins, (p.218) and concluded that 15 of them have lead isotope compositions consistent with Thasian silver ores, and three with Lavrion (1985, 1993 and J9). However, there are a maximum of five coins consistent with lead/silver ores from Thasos.

A major problem is that modern (mostly zinc) mining in Thasos has reprocessed the ancient galena slags making sampling difficult. As a result, there are currently only 22 lead isotope analyses of ores and slags. An added difficulty is that several groups of ores in the northern Aegean have a very similar range of lead isotope ratios; the data for ores from Chalkidiki and part of Thasos are isotopically indistinguishable (Fig. 2). However, on the present evidence it seems that there are many more coins consistent with lead isotope compositions from Chalkidiki and from several deposits in the Rhodope Mountains (Kirki, Virini, Madjarovo in Bulgaria, Iasmos and Farasinon in Thrace) than from Thasos. Overall, the data suggest the prolific mines of Thasos were those it controlled on the mainland, not the island itself, confirming Herodotus (6.46.2-3; cf. Gale *et al.* 1988, 221).[13]

Gale *et al.* (1988, 219) also concluded that five coins are consistent with a Siphnian origin. This again cannot be confirmed. Two coins (MPI 84 PW 123 and MPI 86 PW107) have lead isotope ratios within the analytical error of the group of the analysed Siphnian ores,[14] and do not fit with any other known silver ores, so they might be of Siphnian origin, but there are no other Thasian coins isotopically consistent with ores from Siphnos.

Chios

Chios like Aegina was an important minter with no local deposits of silver on the island. 19 coins from Chios (including two from its colony of Maronea) dating to the fifth century BC were analysed for their lead isotope and elemental compositions (Hardwick *et al.* 1998). The lead isotope ratios of the main group of coins from Chios are plotted on Figure 2. Three coins fall outside the range of lead isotope ratios on this diagram. Of these, number 1949-4-11.809 c. 510 BC is identified in Hardwick *et al.* (1998, 380) as of uncertain origin, but the reanalysis shows its lead isotope ratios to be fully consistent with the new data from the Rosia Montana in Romania. Another coin (BM 1841.3030) identified previously as from Balya is also consistent with the lead isotope ratios of the ores from this region (Baia Mare). Additionally, two coins are consistent with silver originating from the Iberian Peninsula, and in particular with the silver extraction site in Monte Romero in Huelva (Kassianidou 1992 and OXALID).

Others

The other small groups of coins analysed in the project published by Gale *et al.* (1980) were not mentioned in their paper but they seem to follow the same patterns of silver sources. The coins from other northern mints (Acanthus, Lesbos and Orescii) are mainly consistent with Chalkidiki (or Thasos) and Pangaion. Five of the eight coins from Corinth are consistent with Lavrion, while the other three are from the ores of Chalkidiki, Rhodope and (uncertain) Siphnos or Romania. Four of the five Samian coins are consistent with Lavrion ores, and the fifth with Siphnos. The two coins from Lycia are consistent with the Balya mines in the Çanakkale Peninsula (Wagner *et al.* 1985). The five coins from the Asyut Hoard described as 'Mallus or Caria' are partly from Aegean silver (3 Lavrion, 1 Rhodope) and one of them (PW 672) might be consistent with silver from Iran (Pasar). One of the Persian sigloi (PW 716) seems to be of the same origin, while the other three are consistent with Lavrion silver,

---

[13] Two coins (T2005 G16 and MPI83 PW82) are consistent with an origin in the Apuseni Mountains in Romania, and one (3664 J10) has lead isotope ratios of the silver mines in southern Spain. There are also two Thasian coins (T1999 and T777) which have lead isotope ratios not isotopically consistent with any known silver ore deposits. On Figure 3 they plot in the group marked with '?'.

[14] Two data points on Fig. 2 are above the value of 2.08 on the upper plot.

as is one coin from the Cypriot mint of Salamis. The four analysed coins from the Sicilian mints of Messana and Zankle represent silver from Lavrion (2), Thasos (1) and Romania, Rosia Montana (1).

The lead isotope data for the ores from Romania became available only in recent years (Baron *et al.* 2011; Marcoux *et al.* 2002) and therefore the possible origin of metals from there has not been raised in discussions about the prehistoric sources of metal in the Aegean. Out of 160 analysed Archaic Greek silver coins dated to the sixth-fifth centuries BC, seven have lead isotope compositions consistent with the ores from Rosia Montana (5) and Baia Mare (2) from several different mints: Athens (1), Aegina (2), Thasos (2), Chios (1), and Zankle (1).[15] These results suggest that a small quantity of silver from Transylvania circulated in the south of Europe in the first millennium BC, and possibly a small amount of silver may have been exploited at that time in the Massif Central in the south of France.[16]

COMMENTS ON THE ELEMENTAL ANALYSES OF THE ARCHAIC COINS

Out of the 160 coins dated to the sixth-fifth centuries BC discussed in this paper, 129 coins from the Asyut Hoard and Thasos have published analyses of Au, Cu and Pb with good accuracy and detection limits for the minor elements in silver. These published data show that the silver in these coins is very pure; nearly half of the analysed coins have silver content above 98%. The highest copper content was found in the coins from Thasos, with the average of 2.9%, highest of 11%, and for fourteen coins Cu is above 2%. The Cu values for coins from Aegina and Athens are much lower averaging at 1.1% and 0.65% respectively. The lead contents for Athens and Thasos coinage are just over 1%, while the Aeginetan coinage is quite low in lead at 0.47% average. For all the other early coins the contents of copper and lead are low, usually not exceeding 2% each. The chemically most interesting group of coins are the six Orescii coins from the Asyut Hoard. They are nearly identical isotopically, consistent with the ores from Chalkidiki, with very low gold contents (<0.01%), copper below 0.05% and lead around 2%. It seems that all these six coins were minted from the same batch of silver, most likely extracted from galena by cupellation that left around 2% of lead in silver.

As mentioned above, gold is one of the elements that during silver extraction is not separated from silver and therefore it has been often suggested that the Au/Ag values can be characteristic for the original silver ores. On Figure 4 the upper plot gives the values for contents of all three minor elements Au, Cu and Pb in the *Wappenmünzen* showing the variation of their content in relation to the origin of silver. The silver in the obol from the Ashmolean collection contains all three impurities below 0.1%. Two *Wappenmünzen* ('amphora' and 'gorgoneion') which have lead isotope compositions consistent with the ores from the Rhodope Mountains have very low Au content (0.04% and 0.17%), and copper and lead below 0.5%. It is interesting to note that apart from the coin consistent with an origin from Lavrion ores, all the other *Wappenmünzen* have lead contents close to 0.5%, indicating perhaps the common level of lead remaining from cupellation in experienced silver extraction regions.

The lower plot on Figure 4 shows the Au/Ag ratios for all coins with possible silver sources marked by different symbols. This plot demonstrates that even in Lavrion not all silver ore

---

[15] Also an ingot C with turtle stamp from the Selinus hoard found on Sicily (Beer-Tobey *et al.* 1998) has its lead isotope composition consistent with these ores.

[16] The information about the exploitation of the ores in this region is very fragmentary. The lead isotope ratios used in this paper for comparisons come from geological literature and the data from a paper about Mediaeval silver extraction in this area (Baron *et al.* 2006), but so far there is no scientific information about the production of silver in the south France in the first millennium BC, so the hypothesis of the origin of silver from this mines for the Archaic coins proposed here is very tentative. Davis in his book on Roman mining in Europe (1935, 77-78 and 81-83) mentions many ancient silver mines in southern Gaul, but much more information and lead isotope data is needed to confirm this hypothesis.

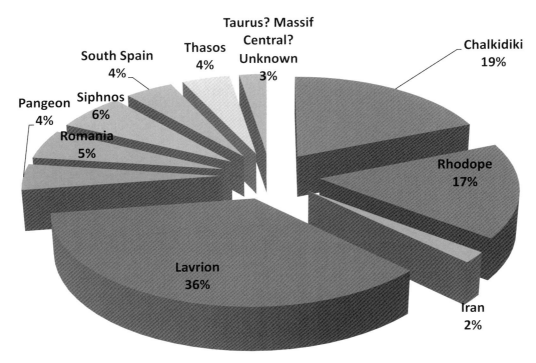

Figure 4. Pie chart representing fractions of silver from various sources

had the same low gold contents. In particular the coins consistent with the cupellation debris from Agrileza have generally higher gold content. On the other hand, the group of the Orescii coins while showing lead isotope ratios consistent with ores from Chalkidiki, have very low gold contents. Silver from Chalkidiki, Pangeon and Rhodope and Iran have a wide range of gold contents.

CONCLUSIONS

The lead isotope compositions of the analysed coins indicate that the majority of the silver used by the Archaic Greek mints was from Lavrion (36%), Chalkidiki (19%) and the deposits in the Rhodope Mountains (21% including 4% from Pangeon). Small quantities of silver seem to have originated in the West Mediterranean and perhaps the Carpathians. The fractions of silver from various sources are represented in Figure 4.

A key finding is that the percentages of silver in Archaic Greek coins originating in Siphnos (6%) and Thasos (4%) are considerably less than earlier evaluations would suggest. Further analyses of the earliest coins from different mints are required to confirm this hypothesis given the majority of coins analysed so far are from the Asyut Hoard and the north Aegean islands of Thasos and Chios.[17] Also, the interpretation of lead isotope data presented here relies on few analyses of ores from the mining regions of Pangaion, Thrace and Macedonia, which are known from the writings of Herodotus and other sources. More extensive archaeometallurgical research is required both in northern Greece and Bulgaria (northern Rhodope) where there are also large quantities of lead slags and known silver mines.

Having said this, the data are sufficient to challenge a number of current scholarly assumptions. Firstly, the Peisistratids did not derive the silver for the *Wappenmünzen* coinage principally from northern Greece, and thus probably did not control mines in the region.

---

[17] The predominance of silver from northern Greece can be related to the proximity of the islands to these mines.

Secondly, the Aeginetans did not derive more than a small proportion of their silver from Siphnos, but did make extensive use of Lavrion silver in the early fifth century BC. Thirdly, the Thasians derived substantially more silver from their control of mines on the mainland than from the island itself, which helps explain their later conflict with Athens. Fourthly, and perhaps surprisingly, there is little or no evidence for mixing of silver. It seems the mints struck silver from discrete sources, and more attention should be paid to the technical processes of producing coins in the light of this. The earliest mints were simple operations with low outputs. Silver is a relatively soft metal, and maybe it was easier to overstrike, trim, or fold to achieve the desired weight than to re-melt and create new flans.[18] Fifthly, gold and tin contents are not adequate chemical tracers by themselves for provenancing the ore sources of coins to either Siphnos or Lavrion.

Thought also needs to be given to the nexus between minting and mining. The data demonstrate that for all the early Archaic Period minters, minting was opportunistic. They minted when they had a supply of silver, and that supply could come from anywhere from Spain to Iran. With incipient monetisation of economies, as silver became money in the full sense of the word, and profit accrued to the state from minting, this lack of a secure supply would have been unsatisfactory. The demand drew in silver from further afield, and was the catalyst for an enormous expansion in mining. Any state lucky enough to possess silver mines could use it as an export commodity with no regard for the end user, which is why Aegina could apparently reliably access Lavrion silver despite their rivalry with Athens. In turn, minting practices changed, especially for export coinages such as Athens with the introduction of the new owl type and use of multiple dies.

REFERENCES

Baron, S., Carignan, J., Laurent, S. and Ploquin, A. 2006. 'Medieval lead making on Mont-Lozere Massif (Cevennes-France): Tracing ore sources using Pb isotopes', *Applied Geochemistry* 21, 241-252.

Baron, S. Tămaş, C.G., Cauuet, B. and Munoz, M. 2011. 'Lead isotope analyses of gold-silver ores from Roşia Montană (Romania). A first step of metal provenance study of Roman mining activity in Alburnus Maior (Roman Dacia)', *Journal of Archaeological Science* 38, 1090–1100.

Beer-Tobey, L., Gale, N.H., Kim, H. and Stos-Gale, Z.A. 1998. 'Lead isotope analyses of four late archaic silver ingots from the Selinus hoard', in Oddy, A. and Cowell, M. (eds.), *Metallurgy in Numismatics, Vol 4*. Royal Numismatic Society, Special Publication No. 30. (London), 385-393.

Conophagos, C.E. 1980. *Le Laurium Antique et la technique grecque de la production de l'argent* (Athens).

Davis, G. 2012. 'Dating the drachmas in Solon's laws', *Historia* 61, 1-30.

Davis, G. 2014a. 'Mining money in Late Archaic Athens', *Historia* 63, 257-277.

Davis, G. 2014b. 'Where are all the little owls?', in Matthaiou, A.P. and Pitt, R.K. (eds.), ΑΘΗΝΑΙΩΝ ΕΠΙΣΚΟΠΟΣ: Studies in honour of H. B. Mattingly (Greek Epigraphic Society, Athens), 339-47.

Davis, O. 1935. *Roman Mines in Europe* (Oxford).

Dunning, F.W., Mykura, W. and Slater, D. (eds.) 1982. *Mineral Deposits of Europe, Vol. 2: Southeast Europe*. The Mineralogical Society. The Institution of Mining and Metallurgy (London).

Ellis Jones, J. 1988. 'The Athenian silver mines of Laurion and the British School at Athens excavations at Agrileza', in Ellis Jones, J. (ed.) *Aspects of Ancient Mining and Metallurgy*. Acta of a British School of Athens Centenary Conference at Bangor (Bangor), 11–22.

Fischer-Bossert, W. 2015. 'Kyzikener Falzschrötlinge', *Mitteilungen der Österreichischen Numismatischen Gesellschaft* 55, 79-92.

Gale, N.H., Gentner, W. and Wagner, G.A. 1980a. 'Mineralogical and Geographical Silver Sources of Archaic Greek Coinage', in Metcalf, D. M. (ed.), *Royal Numismatic Society Special Publication No.13, Metallurgy in Numismatics*, Vol.1 (London), 3-50.

Gale, N. H. and Stos-Gale, Z. A. 1981. 'Lead and silver in the ancient Aegean', *Scientific American* 244/6, 176–192.

Gale, N. H. and Stos-Gale, Z. A. 1981b. 'Cycladic lead and silver metallurgy', *Annual of the British School at Athens* 76, 169–224.

Gale, N.H., Picard, O. and Barrandon, J.N. 1988. 'The Archaic Thasian silver coinage', in Wagner, G. A. and Weisgerber, G. (eds.), *Antike Edel- und Buntmetallgewinnung auf Thasos. Der Anschnitt*. Beiheft 6, (Bochum), 212-223.

---

[18] Professor Kroll has recently demonstrated the wide prevalence of folding and restriking coins in Archaic times – see Kroll 2017 for evidence from Athens, Elis, Thebes and Aegina, and an example from Cyzicus in Fischer-Bossert 2015.

Gale, N.H., Kayafa, M. and Stos-Gale, Z.A. 2008. 'Early Helladic Metallurgy at Raphina, Attica, and the Role of Lavrion', in Tzachili, I. (ed.), *Aegean Metallurgy in the Bronze Age*, University of Crete, Rethymnon (Athens), 87-104.

Gentner, W., Müller, O., Wagner, G.A. and Gale, N.H. 1978. 'Silver sources of Archaic Greek coinage', *Naturwissenschaften* 65, 273-284.

Hardwick, N., Stos-Gale, Z.A. and Cowell, M. 1998. 'Lead isotope analyses of Greek coins of Chios from the 6th - 4th centuries B.C', in Oddy, A. and Cowell, M. (eds.), *Metallurgy in Numismatics, Vol 4.*, Royal Numismatic Society, Special Publication No. 30. (London), 367-384.

Kassianidou, V. 1992. 'Monte Romero, a silver producing workshop of the 7th century BC in southwest Spain', *Institute for Archaeometallurgical Studies – IAMS 18*, (London), 7-10.

Kouzmanov, K., Ivăăcanu, P. and O'Connor, G. 2005a. 'Porphyry Cu-Au epithermal Au-Ag deposits in the southern Apuseni Mountains, Romania', in Blundell, D., Arndt, N., Cobbold, P. R. and Heinrich, C. (eds.), *Geodynamics and Ore Deposits Evolution in Europe. Ore Geol. Rev. 27*, 46–47.

Kouzmanov, K., Bailly, L., Tămaă, C. and Ivăăcanu, P. 2005b. 'Epithermal Pb_Zn-Cu (Au) deposits in the Baia Mare district, Eastern Carpathians, Romania', in Blundell, D., Arndt, N., Cobbold, P. R. and Heinrich, C. (eds.), *Geodynamics and Ore Deposits Evolution in Europe. Ore Geol. Rev. 27*, 48–49.

Kraay, C. M. and Emeleus, V.M. 1962. *The Composition of Greek Silver Coins. Analysis by Neutron Activation*, Ashmolean Museum (Oxford).

Kroll, J. H. 2017. 'Striking and Re-striking on Folded Flans: Evidence from Athens, Cyzicus, (?)Sinope, Elis, Thebes, and Aegina', in Caltabiano, M.C. (ed.), *XV International Numismatic Congress Taormina 2015 Proceedings*, Vol.1, 378-82.

Ling, J., Stos-Gale, Z.A., Grandin, L., Billström, K., Hjärthner-Holdar, E. and Persson, P.-O. 2014. 'Moving metals II: provenancing Scandinavian Bronze Age artefacts by lead isotope and elemental analyses', *Journal of Archaeological Science* 41, 106-132.

Marcoux, E, Grancea, L., Lupulescu, M and Milesi, J.-P. 2002. 'Lead isotope signatures of epithermal and porphyry-type ore deposits from Romanian Carpathian Mountains', *Mineralium Deposita* 37, 173−184.

Neubauer, F., Lips, A., Kouzmanov, K., Lexa, J. and Ivăşcanu, P. 2005. 'Subduction, slab detachment and mineralisation: the Neogene in the Apuseni Mountains and Carpathians', *Ore Geology Review* 27, 13–44.

Pernicka, E., Lutz, C., Bachmann, H.-G., Wagner, G. A., Elitsch, V. And Klein, E. 1985. 'Alte Blei-Silber-Verhüttung auf Sifnos', in Wagner, A. and Weisgerber, G. (eds.), *Silber Blei und Gold auf Sifnos*. Anschnitt Beih. 3 (Bochum), 185–199.

Pernicka, E. 1999. 'Trace element fingerprinting of ancient copper: A guide to technology or provenance?', in Young, S. M. M., Pollard, A. M., Budd, P. and Ixer, R. A. (eds.), *Metals in Antiquity*. BAR Internat. Ser. 792 (Oxford), 163–171.

Pernicka, E., Adam, K., Böhme, K., Hezarkhani, M., Nezafati, N., Schreiner, M., Winterholler, B. and Momenzadeh, M. 2011. 'Archaeometallurgical Research on the Western Central Iranian Plateau', in Vatandoust, A., Parzinger, H. and Helwing, B. (eds.), *Early Mining and Metallurgy on the Western Central Iranian Plateau. The first five years of work. Arch. Iran u. Turan 9* (Mainz), 631–688.

Price, M. and Waggoner, N. 1975. *Archaic Greek coinage – the Asyut Hoard* (London).

Renzi, M., Montero-Ruiz, I. and Bode, M. 2009. 'Non-ferrous metallurgy from the Phoenician site of La Fonteta (Alicante, Spain) a study of provenance', *Journal of Archaeological Science* 36, 2584−2596.

Renzi, M., Rovira-Llorens, S. and Montero Ruiz, I. 2012. 'Riflessioni sulla metallurgia fenicia dell'argento nella Penisola Iberica.' *Notizie Archeologiche Bergomensi* 20, 185-194.

Rothenberg, B. and Blanco Freijeiro, A. 1981. *Studies in ancient mining and metallurgy in south-west Spain. Institute for Archaeometallurgical Studies – IAMS*, (London).

Rychner, V. and Stos-Gale, Z. A. 1998. 'Compositions chimiques et isotopes du plomb: la production métallique l'Âge du Bronze moyen et final en Suisse', in Mordant, Cl., Pernot, M. and Rychner, V. (eds.), *L'Atelier du bronzier en Europe du XXe au VIIIe siècle avant notre ère : les analyses de composition du métal: leur apport à l'archéologie de l'Âge du Bronze*, vol I. Colloque int. Bronze (Neuchâtel et Dijon: session de Neuchâtel, 1996), Eds du CTHS, (Paris), 153–174.

Stos, Z.A. 2009. 'Across the wine dark seas. Sailor tinkers and royal cargoes in the Late Bronze Age eastern Mediterranean', in Shortland, A.J., Freestone, I.C. and Rehren, T. (eds.), *From Mine to Microscope – Advances in the Study of Ancient technology*', Oxbow Books (Oxford), 163-180.

Stos-Gale, Z.A. 2001. 'The impact of the natural sciences on studies of Hacksilber and early silver coinage', in Balmuth, M. (ed.), *Hacksilber to coinage: new insights into the monetary history of the Near East and Greece*. Numismatic Studies No. 24. The American Numismatic Society (New York), 53-76.

Stos-Gale, Z.A. 2014. 'Silver vessels in the Mycenaean Shaft Graves and their origin in the context of the metal supply in the Bronze Age Aegean', in Meller, H., Risch, R. and Pernicka, E. (eds.), *Metalle der Macht- Frühes Gold und Silber. 6. Mitteldeutscher Archäologentag vom 17. Bis 19 Oktober 2013 in Halle (Saale)*. Tagungen des Landesmuseums für Vorgeschichte Halle. Band 11/1, 183-208.

Stos-Gale, Z.A. 2017. 'The sources and supply of silver for Archaic Greek coinage: a re-evaluation of the lead isotope and chemical data', *The RITaK conferences 2013-2014*, (Mining Museum Bochum), Der Anschnitt, Beiheft 34, 201- 217.

Valera, R.G., Valera, P.G. and Rivoldini, A. 2005. 'Sardinian ore deposits and metals in the Bronze Age', in Lo Schiavo, F., Giumlia-Mair, A., Sanna, U. and Valera, R. (eds.), *Archaeometallurgy in Sardinia, from the origin to the Early Iron Age*. Monographies instrumentum 30. Editions Monique mergoil. (Montagnac), 43-88.

Wagner, G. A., Pernicka, E., Seeliger, T., Öztunali, Ö., Baranyi, I., Begemann, F. and Schmitt-Strecker, S. 1985. 'Geologische Untersuchungen zur frühen Metallurgie in NW-Anatolien', *Bulletin of the Mineral Research and Exploration Institute of Turkey* 101/102, 45–81; 100–101.

Wagner, G.A., Pernicka, E., Vavelidis, M., Baranyi, I. and Basiakos, I. 1986. *Archäeometallurgische Untersuchungen auf Chalkidiki.* Anschnitt 38, (Bochum), 166–186.

Wagner, G.A. and Weisgerber, G. (eds.). 1985. *Silber, Blei und Gold auf Siphnos, prähistorische und antike metallproduktion. Der Anschnitt,* Beiheft 3. Deutsches Bergbau Museum, (Bochum).

Wagner, G.A. and Weisgerber, G. (eds.). 1988. *Antike Edel- und Buntmetallgewinnung auf Thasos. Der Anschnitt,* Beiheft 6. Deutsches Bergbau Museum, (Bochum).

Yener, K.A., Sayre, E.V., Özbal, H., Joel, E.C., Barnes, I.L. and Brill, R.H. 1991. 'Stable lead isotope studies of central Taurus ore sources and related artefacts from eastern Mediterranean Chalcolithic and Bronze age sites', *Journal of Archaeological Science* 18, 541–577.

9. SILVER FOR THE GREEK COLONIES: ISSUES, ANALYSIS AND PRELIMINARY RESULTS FROM A LARGE-SCALE COIN SAMPLING PROJECT

Thomas Birch, Fleur Kemmers, Sabine Klein,
H.-Michael Seitz and Heidi E. Höfer

ABSTRACT

This paper introduces the large-scale coin sampling project, Coinage and the dynamics of power: the Western Mediterranean 500-100 BC, along with the results of the archaic coins analysed. The results demonstrate that multiple silver sources were accessible for minting archaic coinage, mostly consigned to the Aegean. In formulating a research design, it became apparent that long-standing and problematic issues remain with the archaeometric study of coinage (i.e. surface analyses, reference materials, data comparability). The principal purpose of this paper is to highlight the importance of a sound sampling protocol and analytical strategy for studying ancient coinage, to ensure the quality, reliability and comparability of future coin data. The paper also introduces a set of three new archaeological silver-alloy standards that can be used for studying coinage.

INTRODUCTION

The interdisciplinary research project aims to understand the development, function and use of coinage in the Western Mediterranean in the period 550-100 BC, studying the intervening process(es) from the earliest coinages to the unified currency system of the Roman world. The working hypothesis is that the adaptation and usage of coinage relates to the development of power relations.

Eight mints were selected for a diachronic study of their development, balancing historical interest with their sizeable output and possibility for sampling. These were Taras, Metapontum, Sybaris/Thurium, Syracuse, Emporion, Bruttium, Carthage and Rome. A map of the location of the mints presented in this study is shown in Figure 1. As well as sampling their chronological development,

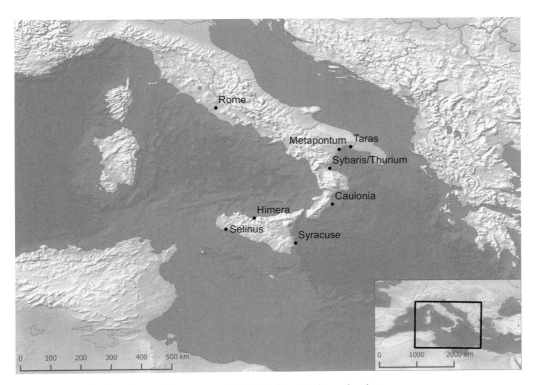

Figure 1. Map showing the locations of the seven mints (cities) under investigation.

two time slices are a particular focus of our analyses; the archaic period (representing the earliest coinage), and the period 218-201 BC (Second Punic War). This paper focuses on the results from 17 archaic coins, representing some of the earliest coinage from the Western Mediterranean, complementing Stos-Gale and Davis's review (this volume) of archaic Greek coinage, largely from the Eastern Mediterranean.

In embarking on this project, however, it was clear that long-standing issues associated with coin sampling and analysis needed to be tackled. After giving a background to the research project, the paper discusses the issues of data comparability, coin sampling, reference materials and data processing, which are all addressed in order to justify the analytical approach adopted.

ANALYSING SILVER FOR THE GREEK COLONIES: THE PROJECT

No coinage without metal. This is a very simple statement, but one rarely addressed when studying coin production in antiquity. Metal could be obtained by trade, through plunder, booty or tributes, or directly from mines. Direct access to mining districts was possible for a limited number of political entities only, as ores bearing silver are unevenly distributed across the Mediterranean and beyond. For the period circa 550-100 BC, silver mining activities at a substantial scale are attested in south-eastern Spain, the Laurion district in Attica, the island of Siphnos, Thrace and Macedonia. Other mining areas or potential ore sources include the Massif Central in France, central Italy, Egypt and the Near East.

From approximately 550 BC onwards, a considerable number of Greek poleis in Southern Italy and Sicily start issuing silver coinages on a large-scale. The question is whether these cities are embedded in a trading network with the Greek 'motherland', or with Punic groups exploiting Spanish or Sardinian ores. Does a polis' origin (e.g. Phocaean, Euboean, Spartan) influence access to trading networks, or does a panhellenic circulation of silver bullion exist? What are the consequences of the enormous increase in mining activity in Athens-controlled Laurion after 480 BC? Does the rise of Carthage as a hegemonic power, and slightly later Rome, disrupt existing networks? And how do these two superpowers obtain their metal? To put it succinctly, how far do alliances and animosities, on a political level, influence access to bullion?

From an historical-archaeological point of view, we were able to demonstrate that for Rome, in the third and early second centuries BC, booty and tribute were the main sources of precious metal. The Spanish mining zones, under their control from around 200 BC onwards, were only exploited on any scale beginning from the late second century BC (Rowan 2013). For the fifth and fourth centuries BC there is compelling historical and archaeological evidence that coins from Corinth, and to a lesser extent Athens, were traded as commodities with the poleis in Southern Italy and Sicily, probably in exchange for grain. The rise of the Hellenistic Kingdoms and Rome seems to have disturbed these networks (Rowan 2014). We aim to test and complement the historical-archaeological results empirically using archaeometallurgical data obtained from coin analyses.

COIN ANALYSIS: ISSUES AND SOLUTIONS

In reviewing the existing datasets of published coin analyses relevant to our research project, it became clear that individual datasets were not comparable, due to different analytical techniques and (or lack of) suitable reference materials. We therefore decided that a new comprehensive and comparable set of coin analyses and lead isotope compositions were needed for this project.

In order to promote and ensure comparability of our new coin dataset with future investigations we commissioned the manufacturing of a variety of certified archaeological silver standards. Moreover, in order to obtain uncontaminated and representative analyses that exclude surface alteration, each coin was sampled using the micro-drilling technique.

Data comparability

Over 4,000 coin compositions from the Western Mediterranean 500-100 BC have been published since the 1960's, summarised in Table 1. The data summarised in Table 1 is organised by cultural affiliation and region, representing the total Greek (Frey-Kupper and Barrandon 2003; Gale *et al.* 1980; Giovannelli *et al.* 2005; Kraay, 1962), Punic (Attanasio *et al.* 2001; Caro *et al.* 2002; Carradice and La Niece 1988; Frey-Kupper 2013; Frey-Kupper and Barrandon 2003; Ingo *et al.* 2000; Ripollès and Abascaö 1998; Sejas del Piñal 1993), Iberian (Chaves Tristán *et al.* 2005, 1999; Montero Ruiz *et al.* 2011; Rafel *et al.* 2010; Ripollès and Abascaö 1998), Italian (Burnett and Hook 1989; Craddock and Burnett 1998), Gaulish (Barrandon 1999; Barrandon and Nieto 2005) and Roman Republican (Burnett and Hook 1989; Hollstein 2000; Walker 1980; Zwicker 1993) coins analysed. Most published analyses are organised by coin series, though there are a few instances where this is not entirely clear, and in the case of the series total for the Roman Republican coins the figure represents the cumulative amount (representing combined totals from multiple studies with overlaps in the coin series studied).

The review here excludes some 400 analyses (40+ coin series) from the Eastern Mediterranean (Gale *et al.* 1980; Hardwick *et al.* 1998; Kraay 1962), including Romania (Constantinescu *et al.* 2009) and Macedonia (Lykiardopoulou-Petrou and Economou 1998). Also not included in this review are studies of Imperial Roman coinage (299 analyses, 41 coin series), which should also be considered relevant to this paper due to the analytical methodologies used (cf: Butcher and Ponting 2013, 2005; Chaves Tristán and Gómez-Tubío 1999; Kasztovszky *et al.* 2005; Klein *et al.* 2012, 2004; Ponting *et al.* 2003).

Despite the impressive number of analyses displayed in Table 1, most are inherently not comparable, hindered by the wide range of different analytical techniques and calibration standards (if any) used at different research institutions, covering both invasive and non-invasive sampling methods. The list of elements reported also varies across studies, producing detailed results for some coins (with minor and trace element data) and not others. Chemical compositions of coins can be incredibly insightful for characterising metal groups and informing on past technological choices, but the analytical results need to be comparable for an effective interpretation.

Provenancing silver coinage has only been made possible by using lead isotope analysis, and only seven of the 23 publications reviewed relevant to this project employed this method, constituting around 50% of the coin series analysed. Imperial Roman Coinage lends itself to chronological precision, hence being a principal focus of some lead isotope studies

Table 1. Summary of the cumulative number of coins analysed by cultural affiliation and region.

Group	Region	Series	Coins
Greek	Greece	33	317
	Sicily	13	108
	Southern Italy	18	61
	Northern Africa	1	3
Punic	Sicily	18	55
	Sardinia	50	109
	Northern Africa	16	65
Iberian	Spain	68	261
Italian	Italy	15	134
Gaulish	France	5	42
Roman Republic	Rome	669	3156
	Cumulative Total	906	4311

(Butcher and Ponting 2005; Klein et al. 2004; Ponting et al. 2003), though is unfortunately beyond our period of interest. The same is true of studies into electrum (Healy 1980; Keyser 2001; Pászthory 1980; Smekalova and Djukov 1999) and uncoined silver (Balmuth and Thompson 2000; Beer-Tobey et al. 1998; Stos-Gale 2001), which are noteworthy for their analytical methods. The most comprehensive study (Hollstein 2000) of Roman Republican coinage to date, encompassing both their chemical and lead isotope composition, may be subject to scrutiny as the majority of analyses conducted were minimally or non-invasive (coin surfaces). In summary, very few lead isotope studies have addressed the provenance of early silver coinage from the Western Mediterranean 550–100 BC.

The importance of reference materials

In many of the numismatic studies reviewed previously, it is unclear whether reference materials were used during analysis, to verify data quality. Reference materials (RM), or certified reference materials (CRMs), are used not only to calibrate analytical equipment and software, but to test how reliable an analytical technique is.

Accuracy and precision testing of instrumentation and analytical protocols is routine for most scientific studies, including archaeometry, which can only be achieved by repeated measurements of RM/CRM and reporting the results. Results need to be compared by analysing certified standards of known composition. Errors can be quantified, corrected and results then directly compared within and between studies. Without reporting accuracy and precision testing, it is difficult to establish the quality of a dataset, its reliability and repeatability. It is also important that appropriate standards are used that are the same material as that being analysed (matrix matched, i.e. silver, silver-alloy for silver artefacts). The use of international standards allows the comparability of coin compositions between different studies.

There are a number of different RM and CRM available for purchase. Amongst the main silver standards available are those from the London Bullion Metal Association (LBMA), The Institute of Non-Ferrous Metals in Poland (IMN), MBH Analytical in the UK (MBH) and Breitländer GmbH in Germany, part of LGC Standards (LGC). They range in their composition (purity to alloy), number of elements listed, usefulness (relevance to ancient coinage), certification (RM or CRM according to the International Organization for Standardization – ISO guidelines), as well as the reliability of element values listed (number of laboratories and analytical methods involved). Unfortunately, none of these standards contain elements in the concentrations relevant to the study of ancient silver coinage. Because of that, a new set of silver standards was thus commissioned via a collaborative effort (the institutions involved were: The University of Leicester, The University of Liverpool, The Metropolitan Museum, The British Museum, UCL, UCL Qatar and the host, Goethe-Universität Frankfurt am Main).

The three silver-alloy RM produced by MBH were independently verified by the Birmingham Assay Office via repeat inductively coupled plasma atomic emission spectrometry (ICP-AES) analyses. These silver-alloy standards are certified for 25 elements, with Cu being the main alloy component ranging from 5-20 wt%; they are 133X AGA1 ($\approx$20wt% Cu), 133X AGA2 (10wt% Cu) and 133XAGA3 ($\approx$5wt% Cu). The principal major and minor components that increase or decrease across the set are Pb, Au, Zn, Sn, Sb, Bi and Fe, elements all relevant to the study of ancient coinage. The remaining trace elements include transition metals and platinum group elements, which may be informative about the materials origin as well as for characterising artefact groups. It is hoped that such archaeologically relevant standards may be more commonly used as RM to promote the comparability of future silver coin analyses.

Sample representivity, reliability and coin drilling

A principal concern for conservators, numismatists and archaeologists is the degree of interference and visible damage a sampling (and/or analytical) method may impose on an artefact. The issue is commonly encompassed in the juxtaposition of invasive versus non-invasive sampling. The juxtaposition often emphasises the conservation aspects of an artefact and preserving its integrity. The choice of sampling, however, cannot simply be deemed an issue for conservation. It poses real complexities for analytical research, for producing reliable, representative and comparable information.

The sampling method should also be appreciated and understood in relation to sample integrity (i.e. what does the sample represent, surface or bulk material?) and data quality (reliability and comparability). This does not mean to justify invasive methods over minimally or non-invasive alternatives, but to weigh sampling against the value of the analytical results being generated, both in terms of their quality and representivity.

The problem with surface analyses is that they are unlikely to be representative of the original bulk coin composition. Studies have shown that lead isotope analysis of surface corrosion yields results that are indistinguishable from the metal core (Rehren and Prange 1998; Snoek et al. 1999). However, the surface may have been altered due to corrosion, natural or intentional surface depletion or enrichment (Beck et al. 2004; Condamin and Picon 1972; Guerra, 1995; Klockenkämper et al. 1999; Ponting 2012; Schweizer 1972), conservation treatment, contamination, plating (Cope 1972; Salvemini et al. 2016), or a combination of these reasons. Such surface alterations may result in the surface chemical composition being significantly different to that of the metal core. The depth to which a coin's surface may have been corrupted or affected can vary considerably; surface enrichment (where copper has leached away, artificially increasing the silver content) can sometimes be greater than 0.5 mm (Ponting 2012), severely undermining the reliability of chemical results obtained via surface analytical techniques.

Preparation for non-invasive surface analyses of a coin have sometimes involved routine cleaning prior to analysis, by physically abrading or chemically cleaning the surface to expose unadulterated heart metal beneath, which can visibly scar a coin. Without any cleaning, surface analytical methods, such as X-ray fluorescence spectrometry (XRF) or proton-induced X-ray emission spectrometry (PIXE), remain open to criticism due to the depth of beam penetration and surface issues outlined above, which has been aptly demonstrated when comparing drillings with surface analyses from the same coins (Ponting 2012). This is why most studies using drillings discard the first ≈1 mm obtained, corresponding to the zone potentially affected.

This does not mean to undermine surface analytical attempts to overcome the challenges of the surface, rather, that the quest for clean, representative, unadulterated samples remains important. Sample integrity is paramount. Neutron beam techniques such as prompt gamma activation analysis (PGAA) and neutron activation analysis (NAA) are exclusively non-invasive bulk chemical methods that have been used to study coins (Blet-Lemarquand et al. 2009; Kasztovszky et al. 2005; Sarah et al.2007). Even these techniques, however, are not free from criticism (Ponting, 2012) because the entire coin is analysed, yielding a bulk composition that disguises any internal variability, such as plating (cf. Padfield 1972), and includes corrosion phases.

More recently, laser ablation-inductively coupled plasma-mass spectrometry (LA-ICP-MS) has been used to analyse coins (Bendall et al. 2009; Blet-Lemarquand et al. 2009; Ponting et al. 2003; Sarah et al. 2007). The surface is sampled using a laser beam, drilling a crater up to around 100 microns in diameter (varying in depth) that is minimally invasive. When multiple analyses are performed, generating multiple craters or trenches (from line scans), it would be better to describe the technique as being minimally invasive (rather than microscopically invasive). It has been used to analyse the chemical composition of materials as well as being increasingly used in conjunction with a multi-collector ICP-MS to study isotopic ratios. The technique has successfully been used to analyse the chemical composition of Carolingian denarii (Sarah *et al.* 2007) and demonstrated to penetrate through their enriched surfaces. However, many ancient silver coins exhibit enriched surfaces thicker than 0.2 mm, sometimes greater than 0.5 mm as previously stated. Although results are promising, LA-ICP-MS also has analytical issues in need of consideration. Downhole elemental fractionation (Eggins *et al.* 1998; Gaboardi and Humayun 2009) resulting from continuous single-spot ablations (deep craters), as well as resampling of escaping material (increasingly problematic with increased crater depths), are issues that remain to be resolved. It is unclear 'how deep' is too deep with silver matrices, depending on the instrumental configuration (beam energy and pulse constraints) and laser beam diameter. The biggest constraint is its applicability; can this micro-invasive technique successfully penetrate the surface zone potentially affected, whilst also delivering reliable results?

The only sure means of obtaining a representative bulk sample of a coin is by fine drilling, penetrating the 'affected' surface in order to obtain unadulterated heart metal. The coin's imperfections can easily be exploited to further conceal a drilling by its deliberate placement in rim-cracks, indents, or targeting clean metal underneath corroded or discoloured parts, and drill holes can also be concealed by post-filling. Sampling via drilling has routinely been used to study ancient coinage (Beer-Tobey *et al.* 1998; Butcher and Ponting 2005; Carradice and La Niece 1988; Craddock and Burnett 1998; Hardwick *et al.* 1998; Klein *et al.* 2012, 2004; Stos-Gale 2001), where up to three drillings are made into the cylindrical edge of the coin, leaving the coin faces untouched. Previous studies (Butcher and Ponting 1995;

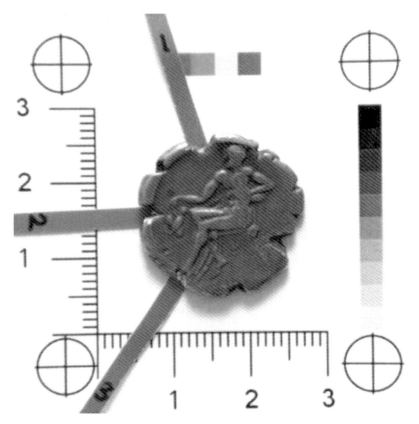

Figure 2. Example photograph of a silver coin being recorded after drilling, highlighting the location of the drillings.

Craddock and Burnett 1998; Hardwick *et al.* 1998; Klein *et al.* 2012, 2004) have obtained <10-20 mg of sample drillings using drill-bits ranging in diameter from 0.5-1.0 mm, roughly 10-15 mg sample after any surface corrosion (≈1 mm) has been discarded.

A standard metallographic block specimen (where the clean heart metal obtained via drilling is embedded in resin) can be subjected to different analytical methods, with multiple repeated analyses performed on different drill curls. The sample can be preserved for future studies/prosperity. Such sampling and preparation also provides an opportunity to gain insights into coin microstructure, as well as identifying any forgeries (i.e. identifying a different metal substrate to the surface).

The results yielded from sampling 'heart' metal have provided invaluable information about coin composition, their provenance, and ultimately an insight into past socio-political and economic processes. Such pioneering studies would not have been possible without the permission and co-operation of museum collections, such as The Museo Nazionale Romano (Klein *et al.* 2004), The Israel Museum (Stos-Gale 2001), The Jordan Museum, The British Museum (Carradice and La Niece 1988; Craddock and Burnett 1998; Hardwick *et al.* 1998), numerous other museums in Britain such as the Norwich Castle Museum, Doncaster Museum, Museum of London, Taunton Castle Museum and Colchester Castle Museum (Butcher and Ponting 2005), as well as directly from excavations (Stos-Gale and Gale 2009) and private collections. Uncoined metal has also been analysed from the Ashmolean Museum (Oxford).

Sampling protocol

For the reasons highlighted above the project team decided to pursue sampling via drilling. The project team has been sensitive to curatorial and conservation concerns, selecting coins where multiple specimens are known as well as spreading the burden of sampling across institutions. The number of coins sampled per collection so far have not exceeded one percent. At the time of writing this paper, the project collaborators include the Universities of Düsseldorf, Giessen, Heidelberg, and Tübingen as well as the LWL-Museum for Art and Culture at Münster, from which some 200 coins were sampled and analysed from their collections. Establishing such collaborations depended on extensive consultation, complete transparency

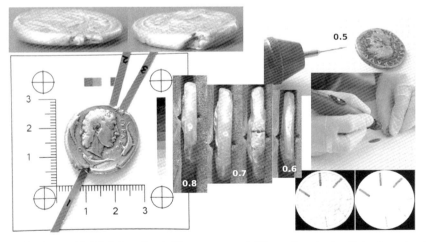

Figure 3. Composite image highlighting the drilling process: drillings disguised within the coin rims imperfections (top-left) corresponding to the coin displayed (bottom-left); drillings ranging in diameter width (centre, labelled) and an example of a forgery with a copper-core (0.7 mm diameter drilling, second from right); the smallest drill-bit used (0.5 mm diameter, top-right) and drilling in action (centre-right); an X-radiograph accompanied by a contrast-overlay of a Euro-cent coin (diameter=16.25 mm, thickness=1.67 mm) highlighting the depth of different drill bits used (0.5-0.8 mm diameter, bottom-right).

and education in understanding the sampling and analytical methods involved, the potential risks, as well as balancing the known issues with the quality of the results to be obtained.

Each coin was carefully documented prior to and post-drilling (Fig. 2). Each coin is documented with detailed photographs of the locations of proposed drillings. It is weighed before and after drilling. The coin is further photographed after drilling to record where it was sampled. Every effort is made to reduce the visible impact of sampling the coin, including selecting crevasses, cracks or areas of surface discolouration for drilling (see Fig. 3).

Each location is pre-drilled to a depth of ≈1 mm, from which the drillings are discarded (or collected for museum purposes). Having minimised the risk of surface contamination, each pre-drilled located is then drilled further using a 0.5-0.8 mm diameter drill bit to obtain unadulterated heart metal. Three drillings are made per coin to ensure a representative sample.

Analytical protocol

Three different samples were prepared from the drillings of each coin. A portion of the drillings were embedded in resin and prepared as standard metallographic blocks, which were carbon coated for electron microprobe analysis (EPMA) of the bulk composition, after which the carbon coating was removed and the blocks used for LA-ICP-MS analysis (with pre-ablation cleaning) for minor and trace element composition. LA-ICP-MS analyses are not reported in this paper but are forthcoming in a separate publication. Approximately 10 mg of sample was dissolved in acids and two solutions prepared for both lead isotope and copper isotope analysis by multiple collector-inductively coupled plasma-mass spectrometry (MC-ICP-MS), of which only the lead isotope results are reported here.

The bulk (major and minor element) composition of each silver coin was determined quantitatively using an electron probe microanalyser JEOL Superprobe JXA 8900-R1 equipped with four detectors, using a beam diameter of 6 µm, a beam current of 30 nA and operating at 20 kV. The analysis was conducted at the Institute for Geosciences (Goethe University, Frankfurt).

Approximately 10 mg of sample was treated and prepared for lead isotope analysis according to the procedure outlined in Klein *et al.* (2009). The 500 µg/L lead solution was spiked with 100 µg/L Tl standard NIST SRM997 and the 500 µg/L copper solution spiked with 1 mg/L Ni standard NIST SRM 986. Lead isotope analyses were performed with a ThermoFisher Scientific NEPTUNE multi collector ICP-MS at Goethe University Frankfurt, monitoring ^{202}Hg for the correction of isobaric interference of Hg on ^{204}Pb. Precision and accuracy testing was routinely performed throughout the daily campaign, using the standard bracketing methods, whereby the standard reference material (NIST 981) was repeatedly analysed after every five to eight samples.

Accuracy and precision testing

Accuracy and precision of the three RM 113X AGA1, 113X AGA2 and 113X AGA3 are reported in Appendix 1. The raw analytical totals are extremely accurate (99.9±1.3 wt%). The results for 113X AGA1 and 113X AGA3 are in good agreement with certified values, with the largest errors reported for 113X AGA2. The instrumentation and method are excellent for quantifying silver with an error of around 2 %. The high errors reported for elements in 113X AGA2 reflect the relative beam size used against the microstructural inhomogeneity of the standard.

The average of 46 measurements of the SRM 981 lead isotope standard during the course of this study of the ^{207}Pb/^{204}Pb ratio (certified as 15.49160) is 15.48774 ±0.002 (1σ), and for the ^{208}Pb/^{206}Pb (certified as 2.1681) is 2.1665 ±0.0002 (1σ), representing relative differences of δ=0.025% and δ=0.074% respectively. The measurements of the SRM 981 lead isotope standard are similar to those of Belshaw *et al.* (1998, 15.4830) and Todt *et al.* (1996, 15.4894). No bias corrections were made to the measurement data presented here. The long term reproducibility of the lead isotope analytical protocol and instrumentation at Frankfurt (Müller *et al.* 2015) dating into the late Roman Republican period, including two ore samples from Portman (Cartagena region), is comparable to other published (Baker *et al.* 2006) accuracy and precision values.

Lead isotope data treatment and evaluation

Two data treatments were utilised to assist in the interpretation of lead isotope data. The first method is the use of Kernel Density Estimates (KDE) in the form of density contours for plotting lead isotope reference data, a powerful exploratory tool (Lockyear 1999), and the second is to calculate the Euclidean distance between a given coin and all the reference data points (finding the nearest neighbours), similar to that of Stos-Gale's TestEuclid method (Stos-Gale and Gale 2009). The provenance of each coin based on on the KDE contour and the Euclidean distance is provided in Table 2, as if they were stand-alone independent methods. The 'suggested' provenance combines both methods for interpretation, which is why it may differ slightly to an individual provenance for one technique (KDE or Euclidean) alone. The suggested provenance takes into consideration the frequency of neighbouring data points from the lead isotope database also as a means of weighting the interpretation. Some caution is needed with this approach, however, as new data points from fresh lead isotope analyses of geological ores may invariably alter the interpretation. The overall approach is thus twofold, whereby the provenance of each coin is evaluated using a single method (KDE contour or Euclidean distance) before combining both methods together to suggest the provenance for a silver coin.

By measuring the Euclidean distance of an artefact to all known reference points, it is possible to calculate the closest neighbours in the 3D Euclidean space, making it possible to assess a provenance on a point by point basis. Point by point estimations are useful, but what is necessary is a holistic approach, to consider all points from a given group together.

Baxter *et al.* state that, "For bivariate data the case for regarding KDEs as a tool to be routinely used is a strong one. Even when an ordinary scatter plot could be used..." (1997, 353). Baxter *et al.* (2000) have demonstrated that three-dimensional contours can also be used in trivariate plots where all three lead isotope ratios are represented simultaneously. The choice here to pursue KDE contour plots for interpreting lead isotope data is because bivariate scatter-plots become increasingly difficult and problematic to construct, present and interpret, with an increase in the number of points plotted. The issues are graphically represented in Figure 4. Points are often overlapping due to over-plotting, and the order in which points are plotted is at the discretion of the plotter. This means that graphically, no appreciation of point density can be communicated where there are a cluster of points, and secondly, that some points are inadvertently hidden 'beneath' others. The issue can be improved on significantly by making points transparent, leading to a better appreciation of point density as well as illuminating all points in a plot.

The location of a lead isotope reference point is not fixed but exists within a 'cloud' of error, and whilst an artefact may directly overlie a single or few reference points, how representative are these reference points of a particular provenance field? When taken collectively, the distribution of reference points is by far more meaningful than any single point in isolation, representing the total variability of a provenance field. So a 100% KDE contour represents all points included within a particular provenance field and thus represents the total limits. It is then possible to visually assess the likelihood of a coin provenance hypothesis, based on where it resides in the KDE contour plot, such as the highest density contours.

Table 2. Coin identifications and summary of results from EPMA and lead isotope analyses accompanied by KDE contour and Euclidean distance provenance interpretations.

Sample ID	Mint	Denomination	Date	Date Reference	Type	Collection	Ag (wt%)	KDE-plot	Euclidean Distance	Suggested Provenance	Repeat Analysis
TB 022	Sybaris	Stater	550-510	(Rutter et al., 2001, p. 144)	HN 1729	Tübingen 475	96.9	Uncertain	Eastern Rhodopes	Eastern Rhodopes	similar
GE 043	Metapontum	Stater	510-440	(Rutter et al., 2001, p. 132)	HN 1482/1484	Giessen 42A3	96.9	Laurion	Laurion	Laurion	–
GE 010	Taras	Didrachm	500-480	(Rutter et al., 2001, p. 93)	HN 827	Giessen 38G3	95.5	Laurion	Laurion	Laurion	–
GE 018	Taras	Didrachm	500-480	(Rutter et al., 2001, p. 93)	HN 827	Giessen 39D1	99.4	Uncertain	Eastern Rhodopes/ Rhodopes/ SE Spain/	Eastern Rhodopes	repeat is E Rhodopes/ Siphnos
GE 032	Taras	Didrachm	500-480	(Rutter et al., 2001, p. 93)	HN 827	Giessen T13-1-rt-1	98.1	Uncertain	W Anatolia W Anatolia/ Attica/	Rhodopes Aegean/	–
GE 012	Taras	Didrachm	480-470	(Rutter et al., 2001, p. 93)	HN 833	Giessen 38H1	86.3	Aegean	Macedonia W Anatolia/ Rhodopes/	Macedonia	similar
TB 028	Caulonia	Stater	500-480	(Rutter et al., 2001, p. 164)	HN 2038	Tübingen 512	97.9	Aegean	Macedonia	Rhodopes (Xanthi)	similar
GE 004	Selinus	Didrachm	550-510	(Arnold-Biucchi, 1992, pp. 17–18)	Arnold-Biucchi 1	Giessen 31F2	95.3	Uncertain	Uncertain E Rhodopes/ W Anatolia/	Uncertain E Rhodopes (Xanthi)?!	similar
TB 031	Selinus	Didrachm	550-510	(Arnold-Biucchi, 1992, pp. 17–18)	Arnold-Biucchi 2	Tübingen 635	96.3	Uncertain	SE Spain Rhodopes/ Euboea/	W Anatolia	similar
TB 029	Himera	Didrachm	550-510	(Kraay, 1984, p. 16)	Kraay Himera II	Tübingen 583	98.1	Aegean	Siphnos	Rhodopes	similar
GE 003	Himera	Didrachm	515-500	(Kraay, 1984, p. 16)	Kraay Himera V–VI	Giessen 30F1	99.0	Laurion	Laurion	Laurion	–

Table 2. *Continued.*

Sample ID	Mint	Denomination	Date	Date Reference	Type	Collection	Ag (wt%)	KDE-plot	Euclidian Distance	Suggested Provenance	Repeat Analysis
TB 030	Himera	Didrachm	483-472	(Jenkins, 1971, p. 22)	Jenkins Himera II	Tübingen 586	97.1	Aegean	W Anatolia/ Macedonia/ Rhodopes	Macedonia	similar
TB 032	Syracuse	Tetradrachm	478-470	(Arnold-Biucchi, 1990, p. 44)	Boehringer series 9, 183	Tübingen 640	97.0	Aegean	W Anatolia/ Macedonia/ Attica/	Macedonia	similar
TB 033	Syracuse	Tetradrachm	478-470	(Arnold-Biucchi, 1990, p. 44)	Boehringer series 9, 203	Tübingen 641	97.5	Aegean	W Anatolia/ Macedonia	Attica/ Macedonia	similar
HE 002	Syracuse	Tetradrachm	478-470	(Arnold-Biucchi, 1990, p. 44)	Boehringer series 11 / SNG Cop 626	Heidelberg AN2001/1	96.7	Laurion	Laurion	Laurion	–
HE 001	Syracuse	Tetradrachm	478-470	(Arnold-Biucchi, 1990, p. 44)	Boehringer series 12 / SNG Cop 629	Heidelberg AN 2011/23	96.8	Laurion	Laurion	Laurion	–
GE 007	Syracuse	Tetradrachm	478-470	(Arnold-Biucchi, 1990, p. 44)	Boehringer series 12	Giessen 32G5	96.8	Aegean	W Anatolia/ Rhodopes/ Macedonia	Macedonia	similar

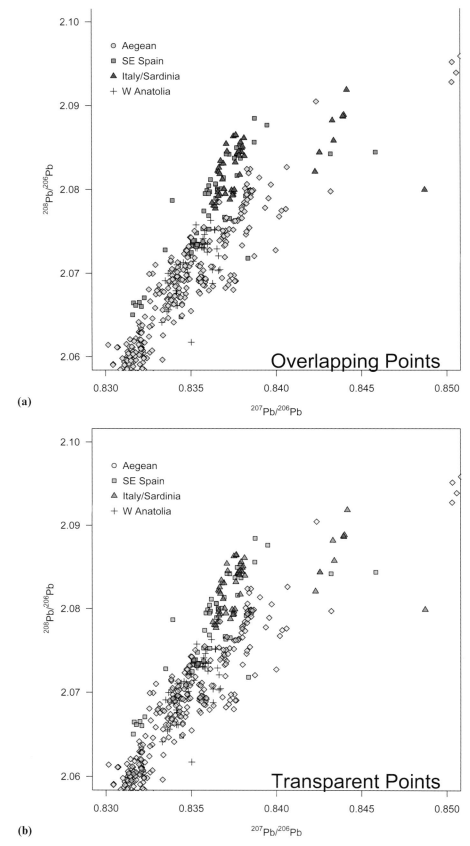

Figure 4. Composite image of different methods of plotting lead isotope reference data: overlapping points (a), transparent points (b), 100% KDE contour provenance field (c) and a contour-density plot using transparent KDE contours (d).

SILVER FOR THE GREEK COLONIES

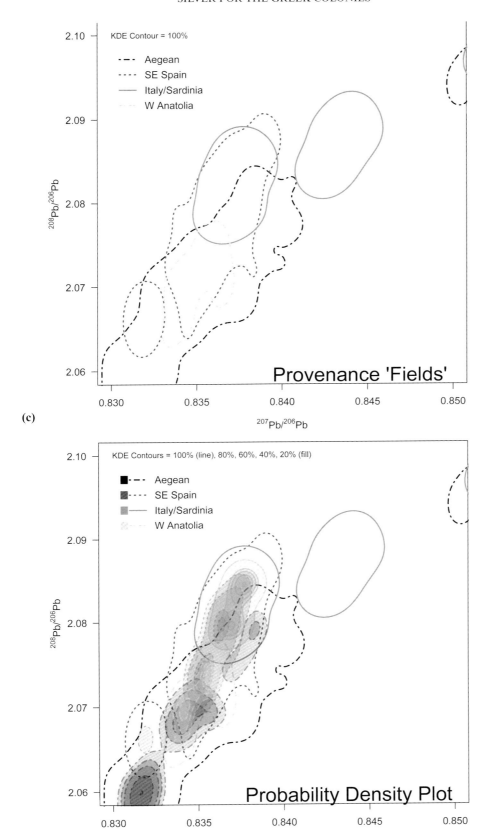

Interpolating the reference data in this fashion gives the dataset more value as a whole rather than finding connections between specific groups of points and their inherent error clouds. KDE contours may also prove useful where provenance fields overlap; instead of ruling out any hypothesis as impossible, the discussion instead becomes about probability.

Baxter has made strong arguments advocating the use of KDE contours for interpreting lead isotope data where the sample sizes are appropriate, but advised not to use it in isolation (Baxter 1999; Baxter *et al.* 2000, 1997). This is why the approach adopted here is a combination of methods (KDE contours, Euclidean distance, traditional plots) used to interpret lead isotope data.

CASE STUDY: ARCHAIC COINAGE FROM THE WESTERN MEDITERRANEAN

The summary results from the case study of 17 coins representing some of the earliest coinage from the Western Mediterranean are presented in Table 2. Seven mints from Southern Italy and Sicily are presented in total: Sybaris, Metapontum, Taras, Caulonia, Selinus, Himera and Syracuse, with coinage dating from 550-470 BC with one exception (440 BC). A number these coins can only be dated roughly to the period of *c.* 550-510 BC making precise chronological statements difficult. For the later part of Archaic period, after *c.* 510 BC, more precise dates are possible in most cases.

The EPMA results determining the bulk composition of each coin are presented in Appendix 2. With the exception of two coins from Syracuse (HE002 and HE001), the lead contents are all between 0.1-0.8 wt%, more often between 0.3-0.5 wt%, overall suggestive of cupelled silver from argentiferous lead-rich ores (particularly galena). This is also supported by the relatively clean composition of the coins, with gold contents between 0.2-0.5 wt% and minor to trace amounts of bismuth. These are all elements expected from cupelled silver (Gowland 1920).

Two of the archaic coins, one from Himera (GE003) and one from Taras (GE018) are extremely pure at 99-99.4 wt% Ag, and cupelled silver typically has a purity of 98.5-99.7 wt% Ag (Tylecote 1987, 140). If this is taken at face value, the remaining 15 archaic coins have varying copper contents that may reflect deliberate adulteration. However, it remains possible that the composition is reflective of silver that was not fully refined. The example from Taras (GE012) has a notably high copper content at 12.7 wt% as well as 0.8 wt% Sn, indicating the silver may have been debased with bronze (when the tin and copper contents are normalised, the composition is of a bronze containing 6 wt% Sn). The other possibility is that copper and tin were naturally integrated through the use of polymetallic or mixed copper-silver ores. Further caution is needed for the interpretation of lead isotope data with regard to bronze being added, as the bronze may have been leaded.

The general assumption is that copper contents above 0.5 wt% in silver are likely to have been added (Pernicka and Bachman 1983, 596). The cupellation process would remove most impurities including copper (Tylecote 1987, 88), and based on the two pure silver coins previously mentioned, it would appear that the contents above 0.4 wt% Cu in the other coins analysed would have deliberately been added. This appears to be the case for the remaining 14 archaic coins with 1.2-4 wt% Cu. The gold contents are relatively consistent (corresponding with analyses where bismuth is detected) as is the absence of other impurities, indicating that the copper being added was relatively pure. One coin from Syracuse (HE002) contains a high lead content at 2 wt% and it is unclear whether this represents a cupelled silver that was not fully refined, or a silver where lead was later intentionally added.

The lead isotope ratios of each coin are presented in Appendix 3, which also contains repeated independent sample analyses. Appendix 4 lists the top 20 nearest reference data points ('neighbours') to each coin based on their Euclidean distance, highlighting those points that are within the error range of the coin (and thus indistinguishable from it).

The lead isotope ratios for each coin were compared to reference data from the OXALID lead isotope database (Stos-Gale and Gale 2009, available online: http://oxalid.arch.ox.ac.uk) and other publications of archaeological and geographical relevance (Baron *et al.* 2006; Bartelheim *et al.* 2012; Brevart *et al.* 1982; Ceyhan 2003; Chalkias *et al.* 1988; Gale and Stos-Gale 1981; Graeser and Friedrich 1970; Hirao *et al.* 1995; Kalogeropoulos *et al.* 1989; Rafel *et al.* 2010; Sayre *et al.* 2001, 1992; Seeliger *et al.* 1985; Stos-Gale 1998; Velasco *et al.* 1996; Wagner *et al.* 2003, 1986, 1985; Yener *et al.* 1991). Only ores, slag, litharge and lead metal were used (all relevant to silver metal source ore, i.e. galena), excluding reference data from copper deposits (unless silver is indicated), totalling some 2,000 reference points. The lead isotope data used in the analysis here for reference includes the following mining areas listed below.

Domergue (2008) has summarised some of the key mining areas in antiquity, especially for argentiferous lead and silver ores (2008, 84–87). Those of relevance here include the famous mines in Laurion (Attica, Greece), the Rhodope Mountains (area of Xanthi for Eastern Rhodopes, Thasos and Pangaion for Western Rhodopes), Macedonia (Chalkidiki) and Siphnos, amongst others in the Aegean area, including sources from Western Anatolia (Balya). In Italy, there are metal ores in the Colline Metallifere (Islands of Giglio and Elba as well as the Tuscany area). It has been asserted that silver was mined in Calabria near "the modern San Marco Argentano... and in the Sila mountains near Longobucco", which are, "within the ancient territory of Sybaris" (Papadopoulos 2002, 38). Unfortunately, we have not been able to find any direct evidence for mining activity in this area, despite several references to twelfth and sixteenth century mining activity (Larocca and Breglia 2016;

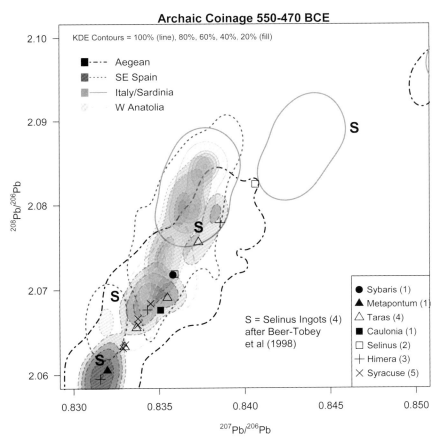

Figure 5. Lead isotope data for the 17 archaic coins analysed in this study, plotted in relation to the lead isotope reference data being used.

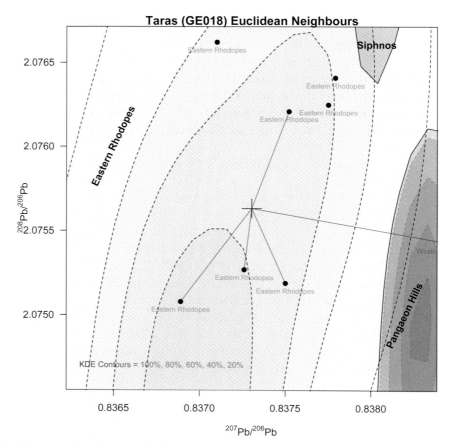

Figure 6. Lead isotope data for one coin from Taras highlighting the nearest five Euclidean neighbours (indicated by a connected line), in relation to the provenance fields for the East Rhodope Mountains and the Pangaeon Hills; coin provenanced to the 'Kirki' galena data from the Rhodope Mountains.

Papadopoulos 2002, 38). The area hosts polymetallic mineralisations, including galena, however the silver concentration is well below 100 mg/kg (Saccà et al. 2002) and the only lead isotope data that exists are of granitic rocks (Ayuso et al. 1994), which have been included in the analysis here for comparison. The Iberian Peninsula is also a potential source of silver, with mining in the Sierra Almagrera, Sierra Cartagene and Sierra del Cabo de Gata in Southeast Spain, whilst in the North there is exploitation in the Cantabrian Mountains (Basque Country).

The lead isotope ratios of the 17 coins are plotted in Figure 5, with a demonstration of utilising both KDE contour plots and Euclidean neighbours illustrated for a single coin in Figure 6. Repeat analyses are in excellent agreement with original analyses. The results reveal that multiple silver sources were being used to mint archaic coinage. Of the coins analysed, 13 appear to relate to the three mining zones within the Aegean, shown in Figure 7 (Laurion, Macedonia and the Eastern Rhodope Mountains).

Five coins have lead isotope ratios that are in excellent agreement with silver from the Laurion mines in Attica (GE043, GE010, GE003, HE002 and HE001), revealing that four different mints (Metapontum, Taras, Himera and Syracuse) in the Archaic period most likely had access to this silver in the closing decade of the sixth century BC (the earliest coin in the group, GE003 from Himera dates to 515–500 BC and the coin from Metapontum potentially dates between 510-470 BC) and most definitely so in the early years of the fifth century BC (the remaining coins fall in the years between 500 and 470 BC). Three coins (TB030, TB032, GE007) from two mints (Himera and Syracuse) have lead isotope ratios consistent with Macedonia (Chalkidiki), whilst a further five coins from four different mints (Sybaris, Taras, Selinus, Himera) are consistent with the Rhodope Mountains (TB022, GE018, GE032, TB031, TB029), in most cases reflective of the Eastern Rhodope Mountains. In the case of GE018, the second repeat analysis yielded Euclidean neighbours from Siphnos (not just the Eastern Rhodope Mountains), making this a potential source of silver.

The lead isotope analyses of three coins (GE012, TB028, TB033) from Taras, Caulonia, and Syracuse have Euclidean neighbours from different areas within the Aegean, reflecting an overlapping area in KDE contours, and so they should be considered in general terms as potentially originating from the Aegean, though more specific suggestions are provided in Table 2. The single coin from Selinus (GE004), based on both repeat analyses, could not be provenanced due to having Euclidean neighbours from the Iberian Peninsula, Aegean and Western Anatolia (though the first analysis is strongly in favour of the Cantabrian Mountains in the Basque country). Seven of the coins analysed have Euclidean neighbours from Western Anatolia (Balya), falling on overlapping KDE contours between Western Anatolia (Balya, Turkey) and other Aegean regions. Whilst points from the Greek mainland more often outnumber the Euclidean neighbours from Western Anatolia, it should, nonetheless, be considered a potential source of silver and cannot be excluded.

Pernicka and Bachman (1983, 596) have suggested that the high purity of the silver used for coinage in Athens may be because the metalworkers were able to cupel the silver to a higher extent at Laurion where the silver was produced. Therefore any measureable copper observed in these coins was likely added. However, the same impurities are the basis for the suggestion that the copper contents in coins from other mints might reflect the varying degree of success in cupellation, rather than deliberately being added. In this case, the same impurities provide the basis for interpreting, in one instance, Laurion's professional smelters producing high purity silver (impurities added), and other regions technically less capable of cupelling silver to a high purity (inherent impurities). It could be questioned why the metallurgists at Laurion were more seasoned in silver refining than their counterparts in Macedonia or elsewhere, and if so, why was there not any kind of technological exchange between Laurion and other parts of Greece? If one considers the ore processing practices at Laurion (Rehren et al. 2002), it may be that other smelters sorted their ores differently, or the original ores they mined were poorly sorted, giving rise to higher impurities in the cupelled silver.

For those coins that do not originate from Laurion, the higher copper contents are obviously added (i.e. 12.7 wt% Cu for GE012), but for the lower contents ranging from 1.3-2.3 wt% Cu and 0.1-0.5 wt% Pb (TB022, GE032, TB028, TB029, TB030, TB032 and TB033), it is possible that their composition reflects their cupelled state. At least with the silver from Laurion, if copper was intentionally added as Pernicka and Bachman (1983) suggest, then the consistency in composition (GE043, GE010, HE002, HE001) would indicate that it was added prior to minting and probably reflects the composition of the bullion available, otherwise one would expect greater variability between mints if they were debasing Laurion silver themselves.

Another two coins from different mints (and different silver sources), one from Taras (GE010) and the other from Selinus (GE004), have a very similar bulk composition of 95.3–95.5 wt% Ag and 3.9-4 wt% Cu, which may be an indication that some debasement recipes may have been consistent, even if the silver being used was not.

Although there are numerous silver sources being used for archaic coinage, they are mostly consigned to the Aegean and this is reflected even within individual mints. For instance, the silver sources of Taras include Laurion (GE010), the Rhodope Mountains (GE018) and probably Macedonia (GE012).

Two coins from Syracuse (TB033 and GE007), both dated to the years c. 478-470 BC, also appear to originate from Macedonia. Although the five coins analysed from Syracuse appear to originate from different sources, they are remarkably consistent in terms of their compo-

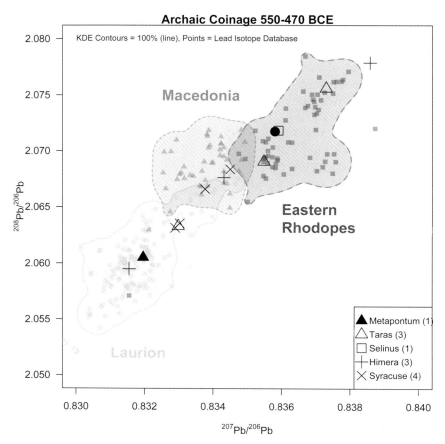

Figure 7. Lead isotope plot of the coins provenanced in this study to Laurion, Chalkidiki, Eastern Rhodope Mountains and Euboea, highlighting the 100% KDE contour field for each sub-region encompassing all reference data points (shown).

sition when compared internally, with 1.9-2.3 wt% Cu and 96.8-97 wt% Ag, indicating control over the composition of the coinage.

It is also interesting to note that two coins from different mints, one from Himera (TB030) and one from Syracuse (TB032) are remarkably similar in composition, being around 97 wt% Ag, 2.3 wt% Cu, 0.3 wt% Pb and 0.23 wt% Au; they also share very similar lead isotope signatures that are consistent with Macedonia (Chalkidiki), indicating that these two mints may have had access to the same bullion.

The most prevalent silver in the assemblage examined here is Laurion, which although is not surprising, does appear to reflect its importance as a source. However, it is clear that multiple different silver sources were being used with the incipience of silver coinage in the Western Mediterranean during the Archaic period. Even on a mint by mint basis, different sources of silver were being accessed. For instance, Syracuse and Taras both appear to be using silver from the mines at Laurion and Macedonia (Chalkidiki), as well as the Eastern Rhodope Mountains for Taras. The results align well with the idea that multiple silver sources were being utilised during the Archaic period, which is also supported by the different lead isotope ratios known from the Selinus hoard (Beer-Tobey *et al.* 1998). The findings complement the work also published in this volume for coinage from the Eastern Mediterranean (Stos-Gale and Davis), emphasising the plurality of silver sources used for archaic coinage.

SILVER SOURCES FOR ARCHAIC COINAGE FROM SOUTHERN ITALY AND SICILY

Neither Sicily nor Southern Italy have evidence of ancient exploitation of their ores, yet Greek poleis in these two regions were among the first Greek cities in the Mediterranean to start minting silver coins, around the middle of the sixth century BC. Little research has been done as to where and how they obtained the silver to do so. In the most recent survey of South Italian coinages by Rutter *et al.* (2001), the authors clearly stated, "It is probably safest to conclude that South Italy's silver either mined locally or obtained directly or indirectly from Carthaginian or Etruscan sources. Some Athenian silver may have arrived via Thurium…" (Rutter *et al.* 2001). With Carthaginian sources the famously rich silver mines in Southern Spain are implied. Local silver mining in Southern Italy is attested for the Mediaeval period (at Longobucco), but any concrete evidence for their exploitation in antiquity is lacking.

In the pioneering phase of lead isotope studies, a substantial number of Archaic Greek coins from mainland Greece and the Greek islands were investigated. In their paper (in this volume) Stos-Gale and Davis have reinterpreted the data in the light of the grown reference database for lead-isotope ratios. Their main conclusion is that in the formative phase of coin production cities in Greece used a wide array of silver sources, mainly from the Aegean, but also from regions further afield, such as Iran and Spain. Furthermore, no evidence was found for mixing of silver sources. The material used to mint coins seems to have come in as fresh bullion straight from the mines.

The data obtained for 17 silver coins from Magna Graecia and Sicily minted in the period 550-470 (440) BC allow us to both test Rutter's hypothesis and to compare analytical evidence from the East Mediterranean with the West Mediterranean. We could not pinpoint the provenance of the silver for each and every coin analysed, but even for those where an exact provenance could not be determined, it is very clear that neither silver from Italy nor from Spain was used (with one possible exception). Virtually all the silver used to mint coins in the Archaic period in the Western Mediterranean came from the Greek motherland and its immediate surroundings. Just like the material from the Eastern Mediterranean a wide variety of sources was used: silver from Laurion, the Rhodope Mountains and potentially Western Anatolia (Balya, Turkey). One polis could use multiple sources, even within a single emission, as testified by the coins from Taras. Silver from Laurion is most likely already being used in the final decade of the sixth century BC and Siphnos seems not to be as relevant a source as might be thought on the basis of historical sources. The importance of Laurion silver can be observed to increase in the course of time; whereas only one certainly late sixth century coin can be linked to this mining area, three certainly early-fifth century coins are made out of this material. Given the consistency of the coins made from Laurion silver, this material might have been obtained in a 'ready to mint' form. This does not seem to apply to the coins made out of non-Laurion silver. Based on the consistency of the silver-copper ratio for the coins from Syracuse, where different silver sources were being used, the copper was most likely added at the mint and not at the mines. It remains possible also that the copper contents are reflective of a poorer processing of the original ores than being intentionally added. Arnold-Biucchi (1990, 43-44) has suggested that the prolific coinage of Syracuse's group 3 (especially Boehringer (1993) series 8b-11) is related to the historically attested war indemnity of 2,000 talents of silver paid by Carthage to Syracuse. The consistent composition of the Syracusan coins analysed, all belonging to group 3, might be a testimony of a bulk of silver coming in and being prepared for minting in a consistent way. Nothing hints at Carthaginian-controlled Iberian silver being used for this potential indemnity though.

Thus, Greek poleis in Southern Italy and Sicily in the period up to approximately 470 BC were definitely not using locally mined silver, nor were they tapping into Carthaginian or Etruscan sources. Rather, they used their connections to the Aegean to obtain material to mint coins. Since their fellow Greek poleis in the Eastern Mediterranean used a wide variety of silver sources to mint their earliest coinages, it is unclear whether the poleis in the Western Mediterranean had direct access to silver through the cities controlling the mining of it. Potentially, they could have had indirect access through contacts with poleis with which they had a political and/or trading relationship.

ACKNOWLEDGEMENTS

This project was funded by the Volkswagen Foundation (2010 – present) under the Lichtenberg-scheme and more information can be found on the project webpage (http://www.uni-frankfurt.de/47219502/muenzen_dynamik_macht). The work was also supported by the Frankfurt Isotope and Element Research Center (FIERCE), Goethe-Universität Frankfurt, Frankurt am Main, Germany; FIERCE is financially supported by the Wilhelm and Else Heraeus Foundation and by the Deutsche Forschungsgemeinschaft (DFG, INST 161/921-1 FUGG and INST 161/923-1 FUGG), which is gratefully acknowledged. This is FIERCE contribution No. 38. The final write-up of this research was made possible by funding from the Danish National Research Foundation (DNRF 119). We wish to express our thanks to the curators and museum officials that gave us permission to sample their coin collections, as well as for their assistance, in particular Johannes Wienand (Henrich-Heine-Universität Düsseldorf), Matthias Recke and Anja Klöckner (Justus-Liebig-Universität Giessen), Susanne Börner (Ruprecht-Karls-Universität Heidelberg), Stefan Krmnicek and Thomas Schäfer (Eberhard Karls Universität Tübingen) and Stefan Kötz (LWL-Museum für Kunst und Kultur, Westfälisches Landesmuseum). Thanks are also due to Maria Bladt and Nils Prawitz at the Institute of Geosciences at Goethe Universiät for preparing metallographic blocks. We owe tremendous thanks to Katrin Westner and the two anonymous reviewers for their feedback and comments to help improve this paper. All errors and omissions are our own.

AUTHORS CONTRIBUTIONS

The coin sampling and analytical work was undertaken by Thomas Birch and the paper jointly drafted with Fleur Kemmers. Sabine Klein and H.-Michael Seitz setup the MC-ICP-MS analytical protocol for lead isotope analysis and Heidi Höfer established the EPMA method for analysing the silver coins, all assisting with sample preparation, measurements, and finalising this paper.

REFERENCES

Arnold-Biucchi, C., 1992. 'The Beginnings of Coinage in the West: Archaic Selinus', *Florilegium Numismaticum: Studia in Honorem U. Westermark Edita*, Stockholm, 13–19.

Arnold-Biucchi, C., 1990. *The Randazzo Hoard 1980 and Sicilian Chronology in the early fifth century BC* (Numismatic Studies 18; American Numismatic Society, New York).

Attanasio, D., Bultrini, G. and Ingo, G.M., 2001. 'The Possibility of Provenancing a Series of Bronze Punic Coins found at Tharros (Western Sardinia) using the Literature Lead Isotope Database', *Archaeometry* 43, 529–547.

Ayuso, R.A., Messina, A., Vivo, B.D., Russo, S., Woodruff, L.G., Sutter, J.F. and Belkin, H.E., 1994. 'Geochemistry and argon thermochronology of the Variscan Sila Batholith, southern Italy: source rocks and magma evolution', *Contrib. Mineral. Petrol.* 117, 87–109. doi:10.1007/BF00307732.

Baker, J., Stos, S. and Waight, T., 2006. 'Lead Isotope Analysis of Archaeological Metals by Multiple-Collector Inductively Coupled Plasma Mass Spectrometry', *Archaeometry* 48, 45–56. doi:10.1111/j.1475-4754.2006.00242.x.

Balmuth, M.S. and Thompson, C.M., 2000. 'Hacksilber: recent approaches to the study of hoards of uncoined silver. Laboratory analyses and geographical distribution', in Kluge, B. and Weisser, B. (eds.), *XII Internationaler Numismatischer Kongress Berlin 1997* (Berlin), 159–169.

Baron, S., Carignan, J., Laurent, S. and Ploquin, A., 2006. 'Medieval lead making on Mont-Lozère Massif (Cévennes-France): Tracing ore sources using Pb isotopes', *Appl. Geochem.* 21, 241–252. doi:10.1016/j.apgeochem.2005.09.005

Barrandon, J.-N., 1999. 'Le trésor de Tayac: apport analytique', *Pallas* 50, 287–296.

Barrandon, J.-N. and Nieto, S., 2005. 'L'apport des isotopes du plomb à l'étude des monnayages d'argent gaulois du centre de la Gaule', in Alfaro, C., Marcos, C. and Otero, P. (eds.), *XIII Congreso Internacional de Numismática Madrid 2003* (Madrid), 415–425.

Bartelheim, M., Contreras Cortés, F., Moreno Onorato, A., Murillo-Barroso, M. and Pernicka, E., 2012. 'The silver of the South Iberian El Argar Culture: A first look at production and distribution', *Trab. Prehist.* 69, 293–309.

Baxter, M.J., 1999. 'On the Multivariate Normality of Data Arising from Lead Isotope Fields', *J. Archaeol. Sci.* 26, 117–124. doi:10.1006/jasc.1998.0368.

Baxter, M.J., Beardah, C.C. and Westwood, S., 2000. 'Sample Size and Related Issues in the Analysis of Lead Isotope Data', *J. Archaeol. Sci.* 27, 973–980. doi:10.1006/jasc.1999.0546

Baxter, M.J., Beardah, C.C. and Wright, R.V.S., 1997. 'Some Archaeological Applications of Kernel Density Estimates', *J. Archaeol. Sci.* 24, 347–354. doi:10.1006/jasc.1996.0119.

Beck, L., Bosonnet, S., Réveillon, S., Eliot, D. and Pilon, F., 2004. 'Silver surface enrichment of silver–copper alloys: a limitation for the analysis of ancient silver coins by surface techniques', *Nucl. Instrum. Methods Phys. Res. Sect. B Beam Interact. Mater. At.* 226, 153–162. doi:10.1016/j.nimb.2004.06.044.

Beer-Tobey, L., Gale, N.H., Kim, H.S. and Stos-Gale, Z.A., 1998. 'Lead Isotope Analysis of Four Late Archaic Silver Ingots from the Selinus Hoard', in: Oddy, W.A. and Cowell, M.R. (eds.), *Metallurgy in Numismatics* Volume 4. (London), 385–392.

Belshaw, N.S., Freedman, P.A., O'Nions, R.K., Frank, M. and Guo, Y., 1998. 'A new variable dispersion double-focusing plasma mass spectrometer with performance illustrated for Pb isotopes', *Int. J. Mass Spectrom.* 181, 51–58. doi:10.1016/S1387-3806(98)14150-7.

Bendall, C., Wigg-Wolf, D., Lahaye, Y., von Kaenel, H.-M. and Brey, G.P., 2009. 'Detecting changes of celtic gold sources through the application of trace element and Pb isotope laser ablation analysis of celtic gold coins', *Archaeometry* 51, 598–625.

Blet-Lemarquand, M., Sarah, G., Gratuze, B. and Barrandon, J.-N., 2009. 'Nuclear methods and laser ablation inductively coupled plasma mass spectrometry: How can these methods contribute to the study of ancient coinage?', *Cercet. Numis.* 15, 43–56.

Boehringer, Chr. 1993. 'Die Münzprägung von Syrakus unter Dionysios: Geschichte und Stand der Numismatischen Forschung', *La monetazione dell'éta dionigiana* 8 (Kongreß des Internationalen Zentrums für numismatische Studien 1983). (Rome), 65–85.

Brevart, O., Dupre, B. and Allegre, C.J., 1982. 'Metallogenic provinces and the remobilization process studied by lead isotopes; lead-zinc ore deposits from the southern Massif Central, France', *Econ. Geol.* 77, 564–575. doi:10.2113/gsecongeo.77.3.564.

Burnett, A. and Hook, D., 1989. 'The Fineness of Silver Coins in Italy and Rome during the Late Fourth and Early Third Centuries BC', *Numis. E Antich. Class.* 18, 151–154.

Butcher, K. and Ponting, M.F., 2013. *The Metallurgy of Roman Silver Coinage: from the Reforms of Nero to the Reform of Trajan* (Cambridge).

Butcher, K. and Ponting, M.F., 2005. 'The Roman Denarius Under the Julio-Claudian Emperors: Mints, Metallurgy and Technology', *Oxf. J. Archaeol.* 24, 163–197. doi:10.1111/j.1468-0092.2005.00231.x.

Butcher, K. and Ponting, M.F., 1995. 'Rome and the East. Production of Roman Provincial Silver Coinage for Caesarea in Cappadocia Under Vespasian, Ad 69–79', *Oxf. J. Archaeol.* 14, 63–77. doi:10.1111/j.1468-0092.1995.tb00056.x.

Caro, T., Ingo, G.M. and Chiozzini, G., 2002. 'Composizione chimica, microstruttura e origine di alcuni manufatti punici in bronzo rinvenuti a Monte Sirai (Sardegna). Riv.', *Studi Fenici* 30, 107–119.

Carradice, I.A. and La Niece, S., 1988. 'The Libyan War and Coinage: A New Hoard and the Evidence of Metal Analysis', *Numis. Chron.* 148, 33–52.

Ceyhan, N., 2003. *Lead isotope geochemistry of Pb-Zn deposits from Eastern Taurides, Turkey (Masters)*, Middle East Technical University, Ankara, Turkey.

Chalkias, G., Vavelidis, M., Schmitt-Strecker, S. and Begemann, F., 1988. ‚Geologische Interpretation der Blei-Isotopen-Verhältnisse von Erzen der Insel Thasos, der Ägäis und Nordgriechenlands', in Wagner, G.A. and Weisgerber, G. (eds.), *Antike Edel- Und Buntmetallgewinnung Auf Thasos (59-74)*. Der Anschnitt: Beiheft 6. (Deutsches Bergbau-Museum, Bochum), 59–74.

Chaves Tristán, F. and Gómez-Tubío, B., 1999. ‚Nuevos datos acerca de la composición metálica de monedas hispanas: el caso de Gades', in Pailler, J.-M. and Moret, P. (eds.), *Pallas. Revue D'études Antiques, Mélanges C. Domergue* (Toulouse), 313–325.

Chaves Tristán, F., Otero Morán, P. and Gómez Tubío, B., 2005. 'Los hallazgos monetale del poblado minero de La Loba (Fuenteobejuna, Córdoba). Análisis metalográficos', in *Actas Del XIII Congreso Internacional de Numismática* (Madrid), 487–496.

Chaves Tristán, F., Pliego Vázquez, R., Gómez Tubío, B. and Respaldiza, M.Á., 1999. 'Análisis metalográficos de monedas procedentes de cecas púnicas del norte de África y del sur de la península Iberica', *Rev. Belge Numis.* 145, 199–214.

Condamin, J. and Picon, M., 1972. 'Changes Suffered by Coins in the Course of Time and the Influence of these on the Results of Different Methods of Analysis', in Hall, E.T. and Metcalf, D.M. (eds.), *Methods of Chemical and Metallurgical Investigation of Ancient Coinage* (Royal Numismatic Society, London), 49–66.

Constantinescu, B., Cojocaru, V., Bugoi, R. and Sasianu, A., 2009. 'Some metallurgical aspects of ancient silver coins discovered in Romania - originals and imitations', *Proc. 2nd Int. Conf. Archaeometall. Eur. Aquil. 17-21 June 2007*, 455–463.

Cope, L.H., 1972. 'Surface-silvered Ancient Coins', in Hall, E.T. and Metcalf, D.M. (eds.), *Methods of Chemical and Metallurgical Investigation of Ancient Coinage* (Royal Numismatic Society, London), 261–278.

Craddock, P.T. and Burnett, A.M., 1998. 'The composition of Etruscan and Umbrian copper alloy coinage', in Oddy, W.A. and Cowell, M.R. (eds.), *Metallurgy in Numismatics* Volume 4 (London), 262–275.

Domergue, C., 2008. *Les Mines Antiques. La production des métaux aux époques grecque et romaine* (Paris).

Eggins, S.M., Kinsley, L.P.J. and Shelley, J.M.G., 1998. 'Deposition and element fractionation processes during atmospheric pressure laser sampling for analysis by ICP-MS', *Appl. Surf. Sci.* 127–129, 278–286. doi:10.1016/S0169-4332(97)00643-0.

Frey-Kupper, S., 2013. *Die antiken Fundmünzen vom Monte Iato 1971-1990: Ein Beitrag zur Geldgeschichte Westsiziliens.* Vol. II, (Studia Ietina. Universität Zürich, Archäologisches Institut, Zurich).

Frey-Kupper, S. and Barrandon, J.-N., 2003. ,Analisi metallurgiche di monete antiche in bronzo circolanti nella sicilia occidentale', *Quarte Giornate Internazionali Studi Sullarea Elima Atti* 1, 507–536.

Gaboardi, M. and Humayun, M., 2009. 'Elemental fractionation during LA-ICP-MS analysis of silicate glasses: implications for matrix-independent standardization', *J. Anal. At. Spectrom.* 24, 1188. doi:10.1039/b900876d.

Gale, N.H., Gentner, W. and Wagner, G.A., 1980. 'Mineralogical and Geographical Silver Sources of Archaic Greek Coinage', in Metcalf, D.M. and Oddy, W.A. (eds.), *Metallurgy in Numismatics* Volume 1 (London), 3–49.

Gale, N.H. and Stos-Gale, Z.A., 1981. 'Cycladic lead and silver metallurgy', *Annu. Br. Sch. Athens* 76, 169–224.

Giovannelli, G., Natali, S., Bozzini, B., Siciliano, A., Sarcinelli, G. and Vitale, R., 2005. 'Microstructural Characterization of Early Western Greek Incuse Coins', *Archaeometry* 47, 817–833. doi:10.1111/j.1475-4754.2005.00234.x.

Gowland, W., 1920. 'VI.—Silver in Roman and Earlier Times: I. Pre-historic and Proto-historic Times', *Archaeol. Second Ser.* 69, 121–160.

Graeser, S. and Friedrich, G., 1970. ,Zur Frage der Altersstellung und Genese der Blei-Zink-Vorkommen der Sierra de Cartagena in Spanien', *Miner. Deposita* 5, 365–374. doi:10.1007/BF00206733.

Guerra, M.F., 1995. 'Elemental analysis of coins and glasses', *Appl. Radiat. Isot.* 46, 583–588. doi:10.1016/0969-8043(95)00095-X.

Hardwick, N., Stos-Gale, Z.A. and Cowell, M.R., 1998. 'Lead Isotope Analysis of Greek Coins of Chios from the Sixth to the Fourth Century BC', in Oddy, W.A. and Cowell, M.R. (eds.), *Metallurgy in Numismatics* Volume 4. (London), 367–384.

Healy, J.F., 1980. 'Greek white gold and electrum coin series', in Metcalf, D.M. and Oddy, W.A. (eds.), *Metallurgy in Numismatics* Volume 1. (London), 194–217.

Hirao, Y., Enomoto, J. and Tachikawa, H., 1995. 'Lead isotope ratios of copper, zinc and lead minerals in Turkey in relation to the provenance study of artefacts', in H. I. H. Prince Takahito Mikasa (ed.), *Essays on Ancient Anatolia and Its Surrounding Civilizations*, (Harassovitz Verlag, Wiesbaden), 89–114.

Hollstein, W. (ed.), 2000. *Metallanalytische Untersuchungen an Münzen der Römischen Republik*, (Gebr. Mann Verlag, Berlin).

Ingo, G.M., Manfredi, L.-I., Caroli, S., Bultrini, G. and Chiozzini, G., 2000. 'Chemical and metallurgical characterisation of a series of bronze Punic coins found at Tharros, Sardinia', in Kluge, B. and Weisser, B. (eds.), *XII Internationaler Kongress Berlin 1997* (Berlin), 306–315.

Jenkins, G.K., 1971. Himera: 'The Coins of the Akragantine Type', in *La Monetazione Arcaica Di Himera Fina Al 472 A.C.* (Atti Del II Convegno Del Centro Internazionale Di Studi Numismatici, Napoli 15-19 Aprile 1969), (Roma), 21–36.

Kalogeropoulos, S.I., Kilias, S.P., Bitzios, D.C., Nicolaou, M. and Both, R.A., 1989. 'Genesis of the Olympias carbonate-hosted Pb-Zn (Au, Ag) sulfide ore deposit, eastern Chalkidiki Peninsula, northern Greece', *Econ. Geol.* 84, 1210–1234. doi:10.2113/gsecongeo.84.5.1210.

Kasztovszky, Z., Panczyk, E., Fedorowicz, W., Révay, Z. and Sartowska, B., 2005. 'Comparative archaeometrical study of Roman silver coins by prompt gamma activation analysis and SEM-EDX', *J. Radioanal. Nucl. Chem.* 265, 193–199.

Keyser, P.T., 2001. 'Analysing and interpreting the metallurgy of early electrum coins', in Clark, D.D. (ed.), *Hacksilber to Coinage: New Insights into the Monetary History of the Near East and Greece* (New York), 105–126.

Klein, S., Domergue, C., Lahaye, Y., Brey, G.P. and Kaenel, H.-. V., 2009. 'The lead and copper isotopic composition of copper ores from the Sierra Morena (Spain)', *J. Iber. Geol.* 35, 59–68.

Klein, S., Lahaye, Y., Brey, G.P. and von Kaenel, H.-M., 2004. 'The early Roman imperial AES coinage II: Tracing the copper sources by analysis of lead and copper isotopes—copper coins of Augustus and Tiberius', *Archaeometry* 46, 469–480. doi:10.1111/j.1475-4754.2004.00168.x.

Klein, S., von Kaenel, H.-M., Lahaye, Y. and Brey, G.P., 2012. 'The Early Roman Imperial AES Coinage III: Chemical and Isotopic Characterisation of Augustan Copper Coins from the Mint of Lyons/Lugdunum', *Schweiz. Numis. Rundsch.* 91, 5–52.

Klockenkämper, R., Bubert, H. and Hasler, K., 1999. 'Detection of Near-Surface Silver Enrichment on Roman Imperial Silver Coins by X-Ray Spectral Analysis', *Archaeometry* 41, 311–320. doi:10.1111/j.1475-4754.1999.tb00985.x.

Kraay, C.M., 1984. *The archaic coinage of Himera* (Centro internazionale di studi numismatici , Napoli).
Kraay, C.M., 1962. *The Composition of Greek Silver Coins* (Ashmolean Museum, Oxford).
Larocca, F. and Breglia, F., 2016. 'Grooved stone tools from Calabria region (Italy): Archaeological evidence and research perspectives', *J. Lithic Stud.* 3, 301–312.
Lockyear, K. 1999. 'Coins, Copies and Kernels - a Note on the Potential of Kernel Density Estimates', in Dingwall, L., Exon, S., Gaffney, V., Laflin, S. and van Leusen, M. (eds.), *Computer Applications and Quantitative Methods in Archaeology* (British Archaeological Reports International Series 750), (Oxford), 85-90.
Lykiardopoulou-Petrou, M. and Economou, N.H., 1998. 'The debased silver coins of Amyntas III', in Oddy, W.A. and Cowell, M.R. (eds.), *Metallurgy in Numismatics* Volume 4. (London), 161–170.
Montero Ruiz, I., Santos Retolaza, M., Castanyer Masoliver, P., Hunt Ortiz, M., Pons Brun, E., Carmen Rovira Hortala, M. and Rovira Llorens, S., 2011. 'Estudio de procedencia del metal en monedas prerromanas', in: Mata-Perelló, J.M., Torro i Abat, L. and Fuentes Prieto, N. (eds.), *Libro En Homenaje a Claude Domergue. Actas Del Quinto Congreso Internacional Sobre Minería Y Metalurgia Históricas En El Se Europeo (León 2008)*, (Leon), 312–325.
Müller, R., Brey, G.P., Seitz, H.-M. and Klein, S., 2015. 'Lead isotope analyses on Late Republican sling bullets'. *Archaeol. Anthropol. Sci.* 7, 473–485. doi:10.1007/s12520-014-0209-0.
Padfield, J., 1972. 'Analysis of Byzantine Copper Coins by X-ray Methods', in Hall, E.T. and Metcalf, D.M. (eds.), *Methods of Chemical and Metallurgical Investigation of Ancient Coinage*, (Royal Numismatic Society, London), 219–236.
Papadopoulos, J.K., 2002. 'Minting Identity: Coinage, Ideology and the Economics of Colonization in Akhaian Magna Graecia', *Camb. Archaeol. J.* 12, 21–55.
Pászthory, E., 1980. 'Investigations of the early electrum coins of the Alyattes', in Metcalf, D.M. and Oddy, W.A. (eds.), *Metallurgy in Numismatics* Volume 1 (London), 151–156.
Pernicka, E. and Bachman, H.-G., 1983. ,Archäometallurgische Untersuchungen zur antiken Silbergewinning in Laurion - III', *Das Verhalten einiger Spurenelemente beim Abtreiben des Bleis. Erzmetall* 36, 592–597.
Ponting, M.F., 2012. 'The Substance of Coinage: The Role of Scientific Analysis in Ancient Numismatics', in: Metcalf, W.E. (ed.), *The Oxford Handbook of Greek and Roman Coinage* (Oxford University Press, Oxford), 12–30.
Ponting, M.F., Evans, J.A. and Pashley, V., 2003. 'Fingerprinting of Roman Mints Using Laser-Ablation MC–ICP–MS Lead Isotope Analysis', *Archaeometry* 45, 591–597. doi:10.1046/j.1475-4754.2003.00130.x.
Rafel, N., Montero-Ruiz, I., Castanyer, P., Aquilué, X., Armada, X., Belarte, M.C., Fairén, S., Gasull, P., Gener, M., Graells, R., Hunt, M., Martin, A., Mata, J.M., Morell, N., Pérez, A., Pons, E., Renzi, M., Rovira, M.C., Rovira, S., Santos, M., Tremoleda, J. and Villalba, P., 2010. 'New Approaches on the Archaic Trade in the North-Eastern Iberian Peninsula: Exploitation and Circulation of Lead and Silver', *Oxf. J. Archaeol.* 29, 175–202. doi:10.1111/j.1468-0092.2010.00344.x.
Rehren, T. and Prange, M., 1998. 'Lead metal and patina: a comparison', in Rehren, T., Hauptmann, A. and Muhly, J.D. (eds.), *Metallurgica Antiqua: In Honour of Hans-Gert Bachmann and Robert Maddin.*, Der Anschnitt, Beiheft 8, (Deutsches Bergbau-Museum, Bochum), 183–196.
Rehren, T., Vanhove, D. and Mussche, H., 2002. 'Ores from the ore washeries in the Lavriotiki', *Metalla* 9, 27–46.
Ripollès, P.P. and Abascaö, J.M., 1998. 'Varia metallica (II): anàlisis de moneges antigues', *Acta Numismàtica* 28, 33–52.
Rowan, C., 2014. 'The value of coinage in the Second Punic War and after', in Bokern, A. and Rowan, C. (Eds.), *Embodying Value: The Transformation of Objects in and from the Ancient World* (British Archaeological Reports, Archaeopress), 77–88.
Rowan, C., 2013. 'Coinage as commodity and bullion in the western Mediterranean, ca. 550–100 BCE', *Mediterr. Hist. Rev.* 28, 105–127. doi:10.1080/09518967.2013.837638.
Rutter, K., Burnett, A., Crawford, M., Johnston, A. and Price, M.J., 2001. *Historia Numorum Italy* (The British Museum Press, London).
Saccà, C., Saccà, D., Nucera, P. and D'Urso, D., 2002. 'Polymetalliferous mineralization in the Aspromonte Unit of the Southern Calabria (Italy)', *Atti Della Soc. Toscana Sci. Nat. - Mem. Ser. A* 108, 43–49.
Salvemini, F., Olsen, S.R., Luzin, V., Garbe, U., Davis, J., Knowles, T. and Sheedy, K., 2016. 'Neutron tomographic analysis: Material characterization of silver and electrum coins from the 6th and 5th centuries BCE', *Mater. Charact.* 118, 175–185. doi:10.1016/j.matchar.2016.05.018.
Sarah, G., Gratuze, B. and Barrandon, J.-N., 2007. 'Application of laser ablation inductively coupled plasma mass spectrometry (LA-ICP-MS) for the investigation of ancient silver coins', *J. Anal. At. Spectrom.* 22, 1163–1167. doi:10.1039/B704879C.
Sayre, E.V., Joel, E.C., Blackman, M.J., Yener, K.A. and Özbal, H., 2001. 'Stable Lead Isotope Studies of Black Sea Anatolian Ore Sources and Related Bronze Age and Phrygian Artefacts from Nearby Archaeological Sites. Appendix: New Central Taurus Ore Data', *Archaeometry* 43, 77–115. doi:10.1111/1475-4754.00006.
Sayre, E.V., Yener, K.A., Joel, E.C. and Barnes, I.L., 1992. 'Statistical Evaluation of the Presently Accumulated Lead Isotope Data from Anatolia and Surrounding Regions', *Archaeometry* 34, 73–105. doi:10.1111/j.1475-4754.1992.tb00479.x.
Schweizer, F., 1972. 'Analysis of Ancient Coins Using a Point Source Linear X-ray Spectrometer: A Critical Review', in Hall, E.T. and Metcalf, D.M. (eds.), *Methods of Chemical and Metallurgical Investigation of Ancient Coinage*. (Royal Numismatic Society, London), 153–169.

Seeliger, T.C., Pernicka, E., Wagner, G.A., Begemann, F., Schmitt-Strecker, S., Eibner, C., Öztunali, Ö. and Baranyi, I., 1985. ‚Archäometallurgische Untersuchungen in Nord- und Ostanatolien', *Jahrbuch des Romisch-Germanischen Zentralmuseums Mainz* 32, 597–659.

Sejas del Piñal, G., 1993. 'Consideraciones sobre la política monetaria bárquida a partir del análisis de sus monedas de plata. Riv.', *Studi Fenici* 21, 111–136.

Smekalova, T.N. and Djukov, R., 1999. 'The composition of the alloy of Cyzicene electrum coins', *Rev. Belge Numis.* 145, 21–35.

Snoek, W., Plimer, I.R. and Reeves, S., 1999. 'Application of Pb isotope geochemistry to the study of the corrosion products of archaeological artefacts to constrain provenance', *J. Geochem. Explor.* 66, 421–425. doi:10.1016/S0375-6742(99)80003-X.

Stos-Gale, Z.A., 2001. 'The impact of the natural sciences on studies of Hacksilber and early silver coinage', in Balmuth, M.S. (ed.), *Hacksilber to Coinage: New Insights into the Monetary History of the Near East and Greece* (New York), 53–76.

Stos-Gale, Z.A., 1998. 'The role of Kythnos and other Cycladic islands in the origins of Early Minoan metallurgy', in Mendoni, L. and Mazarakis, A. (eds.), *Meletimata 27, Kea-Kythnos: History and Archaeology: Proceeding of the Kea-Kythnos Conference, Kea June 1994* (Diffusion de Boccard, Paris & Athens), 717–736.

Stos-Gale, Z.A. and Gale, N.H., 2009. 'Metal provenancing using isotopes and the Oxford archaeological lead isotope database (OXALID)', *Archaeol. Anthropol. Sci.* 1, 195–213. doi:10.1007/s12520-009-0011-6.

Todt, W., Cliff, R. A., Hanser, A. and Hofmann, A.W., 1996. 'Evaluation of a 202Pb–205Pb Double Spike for High - Precision Lead Isotope Analysis', in Basu, A. and Hart, S. (eds.), *Earth Processes: Reading the Isotopic Code*. American Geophysical Union, 429–437. doi:10.1029/GM095p0429.

Tylecote, R.F., 1987. *The early history of metallurgy in Europe* (Longman, London and New York).

Velasco, F., Pesquera, A., Herrero, J.M., 1996. 'Lead isotope study of Zn-Pb ore deposits associated with the Basque-Cantabrian basin and Paleozoic basement, Northern Spain', *Miner. Deposita* 31, 84–92. doi:10.1007/BF00225398.

Wagner, G.A., Pernicka, E., Seeliger, T.C., Lorenz, I.B., Begemann, F., Schmitt-Strecker, S., Eibner, C., Öztunali, Ö., 1986. *Geochemische und isotopische Charakteristika früher Rohstoffquellen für Kupfer, Blei, Silber und Gold in der Türkei.* (Jahrb. Röm.-Ger. Zentralmuseum Mainz), 723–752.

Wagner, G.A., Pernicka, E., Seeliger, T.C., Öztunali, Ö., Baranyi, I., Begemann, F., Schmitt-Strecker, S., 1985. ‚Geologische Untersuchungen zur fruhen Metallurgie in NW-Anatolien', *Bull. Miner. Res. Explor. Inst. Turk.* 101, 45–81.

Wagner, G.A., Wanger, I., Öztunali, Ö., Schmitt-Strecker, S., Begemann, F., 2003. ‚Archäometallurgischer Bericht über Feldforschung in Anatolien und bleiisotopische Studien an Erzen und Schlacken', in Stöllner, T., Körlin, G., Steffens, G., Cierny, J. (eds.), *Man and Mining: Studies in Honour of Gerd Weißgerber.* (Der Anschnitt, Beiheft 16. Deutsches Bergbau-Museum, Bochum),. 475–494.

Walker, D.R., 1980. 'The Silver Content of the Roman Republican Coinage', in Metcalf, D.M. and Oddy, W.A. (eds.), *Metallurgy in Numismatics* Volume 1 (London), 55–72.

Yener, K.A., Sayre, E.V., Joel, E.C., Özbal, H., Barnes, I.L., Brill, R.H., 1991. 'Stable lead isotope studies of central taurus ore sources and related artifacts from eastern mediterranean chalcolithic and bronze age sites', *J. Archaeol. Sci.* 18, 541–577. doi:10.1016/0305-4403(91)90053-R.

Zwicker, U., 1993. 'Metallographic and analytical investigation of Silver- and Aes- Coinage of the Roman Republic', in *Proceedings of the XIth International Numismatic Congess. Louvain-la-Neuve*, 73–93.

APPENDICES

Appendix 1. Results from accuracy and precision testing (EPMA) of silver-alloy reference materials: n = number of analyses, δ rel (%) = relative difference (expressed as a percentage), STDev = standard deviation (expressed as the absolute value), < = detection limit. Reference and analysed values are presented as element wt%.

Standard	*n=58*	*Ag*	*Cu*	*Pb*	*Au*	*Zn*	*Sn*	*Sb*	*Bi*	*Total*
113X AGA1	Analysed	79.53	17.99	0.213	1.39	0.198	0.314	0.05	0.132	100.3
	Reference	77.37	19.95	0.207	1.48	0.211	0.291	0.05	0.194	
	δ rel (%)	2.8	9.8	2.8	6.4	6.0	8.0	3.4	32.1	
	STDev	9.0	8.8	0.1	0.2	0.1	0.1	0.0	0.1	1.3
113X AGA2	Analysed	88.95	8	1.18	0.369	0.482	0.59	0.169	0.142	99.6
	Reference	86.97	10	1.02	0.507	0.502	0.52	0.192	0.113	
	δ rel (%)	2.3	19.4	15.8	27.2	4.1	12.9	11.8	25.7	
	STDev	3.1	3.1	0.1	0.1	0.1	0.1	0.0	0.0	1.1
113X AGA3	Analysed	90.76	4.87	1.90	0.190	0.773	0.991	0.401	<0.075	99.7
	Reference	90.10	4.91	1.89	0.258	0.816	0.921	0.459	0.048	
	δ rel (%)	0.7	0.9	0.6	26.2	5.2	7.7	12.7		
	STDev	1.0	0.3	0.5	0.0	0.2	0.2	0.1		1.2

Appendix 2. EPMA results from coins analysed, normalised to a total of 100%: n = number of analyses, ± = absolute standard deviation of analyses (σ). Total column represents the raw analytical totals prior to normalisation. Values are presented as element wt%. Results below detection limits are represented as missing values.

Sample ID	Mint	Date	Ag	σ (abs)	Cu	σ (abs)	Pb	σ (abs)	Au	σ (abs)	Bi	σ (abs)	Sn	σ (abs)	Sb	σ (abs)	Total	σ (abs)
TB 022	Sybaris	550-510	96.925	±0.48	2.287	±0.45	0.128	±0.05	0.501	±0.05							98.244	±0.34
GE 043	Metapontum	510-440	96.931	±1.24	2.100	±0.90	0.692	±0.29			0.128	±0.05					101.210	±0.32
GE 010	Taras	500-480	95.477	±0.82	3.858	±0.73	0.464	±0.09	0.153								99.999	±0.34
GE 018	Taras	500-480	99.406	±0.24	0.398	±0.24	0.069	±0.02									99.196	±0.75
GE 032	Taras	500-480	98.085	±0.38	1.357	±0.36	0.210	±0.03	0.155	±0.03	0.143	±0.03					101.395	±0.48
GE 012	Taras	480-470	86.271	±3.76	12.704	±3.68	0.576	±0.03	0.211	±0.03			0.790	±0.00			100.350	±0.80
TB 028	Caulonia	500-480	97.858	±0.13	1.677	±0.13	0.133	±0.02	0.203	±0.04							97.229	±0.25
GE 004	Selinus	550-510	95.305	±0.89	3.966	±0.84	0.097	±0.02	0.411	±0.04	0.144	±0.04					100.410	±0.39
TB 031	Selinus	510-500	96.290	±1.01	2.881	±0.80	0.334	±0.15	0.303	±0.05	0.174	±0.13					97.410	±0.33
TB 029	Himera	530-520	98.093	±0.13	1.429	±0.08	0.105	±0.03	0.234	±0.05							97.958	±0.45
GE 003	Himera	515-500	99.000	±0.23	0.088	±0.03	0.779	±0.22									100.707	±0.45
TB 030	Himera	483-472	97.090	±0.15	2.250	±0.12	0.311	±0.05	0.227	±0.05							97.574	±0.28
TB 032	Syracuse	478-470	97.011	±0.20	2.324	±0.17	0.300	±0.08	0.211	±0.03			0.099		0.074	±0.00	97.353	±0.25
TB 033	Syracuse	478-470	97.489	±0.16	1.726	±0.10	0.519	±0.05	0.157	±0.01							97.437	±0.24
HE 002	Syracuse	478-470	96.721	±0.19	1.198	±0.08	1.946	±0.11									101.843	±0.32
HE 001	Syracuse	478-470	96.751	±0.77	1.907	±0.32	1.197	±0.48			0.348	±0.06					101.631	±0.19
GE 007	Syracuse	478-470	96.753	±0.26	2.533	±0.20	0.235	±0.03									100.909	±0.23

Appendix 3. Lead isotope ratio results from coins analysed with the absolute standard deviation (σ) reported of the signals acquired. Repeated analyses are indicated (rep) to provide an indication of precision.

Sample ID	Mint	Date	Sample	206Pb/204Pb	σ (abs)	207Pb/204Pb	σ (abs)	208Pb/204Pb	σ (abs)	207Pb/206Pb	σ (abs)	208Pb/206Pb	σ (abs)
TB 022	Sybaris	550-510	TB022	18.720	0.009	15.647	0.008	38.784	0.022	0.836	0.000	2.072	0.000
			TB022 rep	18.726	0.006	15.652	0.006	38.800	0.014	0.836	0.000	2.072	0.000
GE 043	Metapontum	510-440	GE043	18.854	0.007	15.686	0.006	38.850	0.017	0.832	0.000	2.061	0.000
GE 010	Taras	500-480	GE010	18.833	0.008	15.687	0.007	38.857	0.018	0.833	0.000	2.063	0.000
GE 018	Taras	500-480	GE018	18.698	0.021	15.655	0.015	38.810	0.042	0.837	0.000	2.076	0.000
			GE018 rep	18.713	0.009	15.675	0.008	38.877	0.022	0.838	0.000	2.077	0.000
GE 032	Taras	500-480	GE032	18.654	0.146	15.586	0.123	38.598	0.316	0.835	0.001	2.069	0.003
GE 012	Taras	480-470	GE012	18.805	0.018	15.677	0.015	38.841	0.039	0.834	0.000	2.066	0.000
			GE012 rep	18.811	0.007	15.683	0.007	38.861	0.019	0.834	0.000	2.066	0.000
TB 028	Caulonia	500-480	TB028	18.756	0.011	15.663	0.009	38.780	0.025	0.835	0.000	2.068	0.000
			TB028 rep	18.759	0.009	15.669	0.008	38.803	0.021	0.835	0.000	2.068	0.000
GE 004	Selinus	550-510	GE004	18.626	0.026	15.657	0.020	38.787	0.054	0.841	0.000	2.082	0.000
			GE004 rep	18.640	0.009	15.674	0.008	38.842	0.020	0.841	0.000	2.084	0.000
TB 031	Selinus	510-500	TB031	18.750	0.020	15.674	0.014	38.846	0.038	0.836	0.000	2.072	0.000
			TB031 rep	18.754	0.009	15.677	0.008	38.861	0.020	0.836	0.000	2.072	0.000
TB 029	Himera	530-520	TB029	18.679	0.011	15.664	0.009	38.813	0.025	0.839	0.000	2.078	0.000
			TB029 rep	18.682	0.010	15.665	0.008	38.811	0.023	0.839	0.000	2.078	0.000
GE 003	Himera	515-500	GE003	18.866	0.008	15.687	0.008	38.853	0.020	0.832	0.000	2.059	0.000
TB 030	Himera	483-472	TB030	18.792	0.010	15.679	0.008	38.857	0.027	0.834	0.000	2.068	0.001
TB 032	Syracuse	478-470	TB032	18.792	0.009	15.682	0.007	38.869	0.021	0.834	0.000	2.068	0.000
			TB032 rep	18.788	0.009	15.678	0.008	38.853	0.023	0.834	0.000	2.068	0.000
			TB032 rep	18.760	0.008	15.670	0.008	38.844	0.020	0.835	0.000	2.071	0.000
TB 033	Syracuse	478-470	TB033	18.811	0.013	15.684	0.011	38.862	0.031	0.834	0.000	2.066	0.000
			TB033 rep	18.808	0.010	15.680	0.009	38.845	0.023	0.834	0.000	2.065	0.000
HE 002	Syracuse	478-470	HE002	18.832	0.007	15.688	0.006	38.862	0.017	0.833	0.000	2.064	0.000
HE 001	Syracuse	478-470	HE001	18.836	0.008	15.689	0.007	38.862	0.021	0.833	0.000	2.063	0.000
GE 007	Syracuse	478-470	GE007	18.798	0.008	15.673	0.007	38.847	0.020	0.834	0.000	2.067	0.000
			GE007 rep	18.799	0.009	15.674	0.008	38.851	0.022	0.834	0.000	2.067	0.000

Appendix 4. Table of the top 20 nearest neighbours (lead isotope reference points) for each coin based on their Euclidean distance. The maximum error (Max. Err=) for each coin is provided, based on the standard deviation of the $^{208}Pb/^{204}Pb$ value; any Euclidean distance within this error range can be considered indistinguishable from the coin (these neighbours are highlighted in bold). Euclidean distances of coins from repeat analyses are indicated (rep).

Coin	Euclidean Neighbour	Euclidean Distance	Type	Metals	Sample ID	Region	Sub-Region	Area	Site
TB022 Max. Err = 0.0217717	**1**	**0.016**	**Ore**	**Pb-Ag**	**ER1**	**Greece**	**Eastern Rhodopes**		**Essimi**
	2	**0.017**	**Ore**	**Pb-Ag**	**ER17**	**Greece**	**Eastern Rhodopes**		**Kirki**
	3	0.022	Ore	Pb-Ag	BS25	Turkey	Black Sea region	Merzifon	Gümüşhaci Köy, Deligözler Köyü
	4	0.027	Ore	Pb-Ag	ER83	Bulgaria	Eastern Rhodopes	Kardzhali	Zvezdel
	5	0.027	Ore	Pb-Ag	ER5	Greece	Eastern Rhodopes		Essimi
	6	0.029	Ore	Pb-Ag	ER26	Greece	Eastern Rhodopes		Kirki
	7	0.030	Ore	Pb-Ag	ER24	Greece	Eastern Rhodopes		Kirki
	8	0.031	Ore	Pb-Ag	ER15	Greece	Eastern Rhodopes		Kirki
	9	0.031	Ore	Pb-Ag	WR8	Greece	Western Rhodopes	Thasos	Agios Eleftherios
	10	0.032	Heavy slag	Pb-Ag	TG53 A/2	Greece	Cyclades	Kea	Nikoleri/Platy Yalos
	11	0.033	Ore	Pb-Ag	ER21	Greece	Eastern Rhodopes		Kirki, King Arthur Mine
	12	0.034	Ore	Pb-Ag	ER4	Greece	Eastern Rhodopes		Essimi
	13	0.036	Ore	Pb-Ag	ER9	Greece	Eastern Rhodopes		Essimi
	14	0.036	Ore	Pb-Ag	WA15	Turkey	Western Anatolia	Balikesir	Karaaydin-Biçkayeri
	15	0.037	Ore	Pb-Ag	ER6	Greece	Eastern Rhodopes		Essimi
	16	0.037	Ore	Pb-Ag	ER23	Greece	Eastern Rhodopes		Kirki
	17	0.037	Ore	Pb-Ag	ER25	Greece	Eastern Rhodopes		Kirki
	18	0.038	Ore	Pb-Ag	ER22	Greece	Eastern Rhodopes		Kirki, King Arthur Mine
	19	0.039	Slag	Pb-Ag	35 (CP311)	Turkey	Central Anatolia	Kayseri	Kültepe
	20	0.039	Ore	Pb-Ag	ER8	Greece	Eastern Rhodopes		Essimi
TB022 rep Max. Err = 0.0141634	1	0.016	Ore	Pb-Ag	ER83	Bulgaria	Eastern Rhodopes	Kardzhali	Zvezdel
	2	0.021	Ore	Pb-Ag	WA15	Turkey	Western Anatolia	Balikesir	Karaaydin-Biçkayeri
	3	0.022	Ore	Pb-Ag	ER1	Greece	Eastern Rhodopes		Essimi
	4	0.025	Ore	Pb-Ag	ER26	Greece	Eastern Rhodopes		Kirki
	5	0.027	Ore	Pb-Ag	ER15	Greece	Eastern Rhodopes		Kirki
	6	0.029	Ore	Pb-Ag	ER84	Bulgaria	Eastern Rhodopes	Kardzhali	Zvezdel
	7	0.030	Ore	Pb-Ag	ER3	Greece	Eastern Rhodopes		Essimi
	8	0.031	Ore	Pb-Ag	ER17	Greece	Eastern Rhodopes		Kirki
	9	0.031	Ore	Pb-Ag	BS25	Turkey	Black Sea region	Merzifon	Gümüşhaci Köy, Deligözler Köyü
	10	0.031	Ore	Pb-Ag	WR8	Greece	Western Rhodopes	Thasos	Agios Eleftherios
	11	0.031	Ore	Pb-Ag	ER24	Greece	Eastern Rhodopes		Kirki
	12	0.031	Ore	Pb-Ag	WA6	Turkey	Western Anatolia	Balikesir	Altinoluk

Appendix 4. *Continued.*

Coin	Euclidean Neighbour	Euclidean Distance	Type	Metals	Sample ID	Region	Sub-Region	Area	Site
	13	0.034	Ore	Pb-Ag	BC24	Iberian Peninsula	Betic Cordillera	Sierra del Cabo de Gata	Minas del Monsu
	14	0.034	Ore	Pb-Ag	ER33	Greece	Eastern Rhodopes		Ayios Demetrios
	15	0.034	Ore	Pb-Ag	ER18	Greece	Eastern Rhodopes		Kirki
	16	0.035	Ore	Pb-Ag	M13	Greece	Macedonia	Chalkidiki	Madem Lakos
	17	0.035	Ore	Pb-Ag	M34	Greece	Macedonia	Chalkidiki	Olympias
	18	0.036	Ore	Pb-Ag	WR4	Greece	Western Rhodopes		Pangeo, Nikisiani Valley
	19	0.037	Ore	Pb-Ag	ER32	Greece	Eastern Rhodopes		Ayios Demetrios
	20	0.037	Ore	Pb-Ag	M15	Greece	Macedonia	Chalkidiki	Madem Lakos
GE043	**1**	**0.006**	**Ore**	**Pb-Ag**	**L37**	**Greece**	**Attica**	**Lavrion**	**Megala Pefka**
Max. Err =	**2**	**0.007**	**Ore**	**Pb-Ag**	**L86**	**Greece**	**Attica**	**Lavrion**	**Plaka**
0.0165417	**3**	**0.007**	**Ore**	**Pb-Ag**	**L85**	**Greece**	**Attica**	**Lavrion**	**Plaka**
	4	**0.007**	**Ore**	**Pb-Ag**	**L97**	**Greece**	**Attica**	**Lavrion**	**Plaka**
	5	**0.008**	**Ore**	**Pb-Ag**	**L71**	**Greece**	**Attica**	**Lavrion**	**Plaka**
	6	**0.009**	**Ore**	**Pb-Ag**	**L107**	**Greece**	**Attica**	**Lavrion**	**Thorikos**
	7	**0.009**	**Ore**	**Pb-Ag**	**L108**	**Greece**	**Attica**	**Lavrion**	**Thorikos**
	8	**0.009**	**Ore**	**Pb-Ag**	**L70**	**Greece**	**Attica**	**Lavrion**	**Plaka**
	9	**0.009**	**Ore**	**Pb-Ag**	**L74**	**Greece**	**Attica**	**Lavrion**	**Plaka**
	10	**0.011**	**Pb metal**	**Pb-Ag**	**TM65.4**	**Greece**	**Attica**	**Lavrion**	**Thorikos**
	11	**0.011**	**Ore**	**Pb-Ag**	**L87**	**Greece**	**Attica**	**Lavrion**	**Plaka**
	12	**0.011**	**Slag**	**Pb-Ag**	**ET281**	**Greece**	**Attica**	**Lavrion**	**Thorikos**
	13	**0.011**	**Pb metal**	**Pb-Ag**	**TM68.4**	**Greece**	**Attica**	**Lavrion**	**Thorikos**
	14	**0.013**	**Ore**	**Pb-Ag**	**L58**	**Greece**	**Attica**	**Lavrion**	**Plaka**
	15	**0.013**	**litharge**	**Pb-Ag**	**ZO350**	**Greece**	**Attica**	**Lavrion**	**Thorikos**
	16	**0.013**	**Ore**	**Pb-Ag**	**L64**	**Greece**	**Attica**	**Lavrion**	**Plaka**
	17	0.017	Ore	Pb-Ag	L6	Greece	Attica	Lavrion	Esperance
	18	0.017	Ore	Pb-Ag	L82	Greece	Attica	Lavrion	Plaka
	19	0.017	Pb metal	Pb-Ag	AGR10	Greece	Attica	Lavrion	Agrileza
	20	0.017	Ore	Pb-Ag	L89	Greece	Attica	Lavrion	Plaka
GE010	**1**	**0.013**	**Pb metal**	**Pb-Ag**	**TC69.471**	**Greece**	**Attica**	**Lavrion**	**Thorikos**
Max. Err =	**2**	**0.016**	**Ore**	**Pb-Ag**	**L85**	**Greece**	**Attica**	**Lavrion**	**Plaka**
0.018236	**3**	**0.016**	**Ore**	**Pb-Ag**	**L97**	**Greece**	**Attica**	**Lavrion**	**Plaka**
	4	0.019	Slag	Pb-Ag	ET281	Greece	Attica	Lavrion	Thorikos
	5	0.019	Pb metal	Pb-Ag	TM68.4	Greece	Attica	Lavrion	Thorikos
	6	0.019	Pb metal	Pb-Ag	K716	Greece	Attica	Lavrion	Thorikos
	7	0.020	Pb metal	Pb-Ag	B338	Greece	Attica	Lavrion	Thorikos

Appendix 4. *Continued*.

Coin	Euclidean Neighbour	Euclidean Distance	Type	Metals	Sample ID	Region	Sub-Region	Area	Site
	8	0.020	Ore	Pb-Ag	L74	Greece	Attica	Lavrion	Plaka
	9	0.020	Ore	Pb-Ag	L81	Greece	Attica	Lavrion	Plaka
	10	0.021	Pb metal	Pb-Ag	AGR10	Greece	Attica	Lavrion	Agrileza
	11	0.021	Ore	Pb-Ag	L70	Greece	Attica	Lavrion	Plaka
	12	0.022	litharge	Pb-Ag	ZO350	Greece	Attica	Lavrion	Thorikos
	13	0.023	Ore	Pb-Ag	L71	Greece	Attica	Lavrion	Plaka
	14	0.023	Ore	Pb-Ag	L64	Greece	Attica	Lavrion	Lavrion Thorikos
	15	0.023	Cerussite/litharge		Pb-Ag	C4.i.2	Greece	Attica	Megala Pefka
	16	0.023	Ore	Pb-Ag	L37	Greece	Attica	Lavrion	Hacibekirler-Maden Deresi
	17	0.025	Ore	Pb-Ag	WA43	Turkey	Western Anatolia	Çanakkale	
	18	0.026	Ore	Pb-Ag	C67	Greece	Cyclades	Kea	Faros
	19	0.026	Pb metal	Pb-Ag	TM65.4	Greece	Attica	Lavrion	Thorikos
	20	0.027	Ore	Pb-Ag	L86	Greece	Attica	Lavrion	Plaka
GE018	1	0.005	Ore	Pb-Ag	ER15	Greece	Eastern Rhodopes		Kirki
Max. Err =	2	0.007	Ore	Pb-Ag	ER26	Greece	Eastern Rhodopes		Kirki
0.0416171	3	0.008	Ore	Pb-Ag	ER18	Greece	Eastern Rhodopes		Kirki
	4	0.014	Ore	Pb-Ag	ER24	Greece	Eastern Rhodopes		Kirki
	5	0.022	Ore	Pb-Ag	ER83	Bulgaria	Eastern Rhodopes	Kardzhali	Zvezdel
	6	0.022	Ore	Pb-Ag	WR3	Greece	Western Rhodopes		Pangeo, Nikisiani Valley
	7	0.024	Ore	Pb-Ag	C211	Greece	Cyclades	Siphnos	Agios Ioannis
	8	0.027	Heavy slag	Pb-Ag	TG53A/2	Greece	Cyclades	Kea	Nikoleri/Platy Yalos
	9	0.027	Ore	Pb-Ag	WR4	Greece	Western Rhodopes		Pangeo, Nikisiani Valley
	10	0.028	Ore	Pb-Ag	ER82	Bulgaria	Eastern Rhodopes	Kardzhali	Zvezdel
	11	0.031	Ore	Pb-Ag	ER84	Bulgaria	Eastern Rhodopes	Kardzhali	Zvezdel
	12	0.032	Ore	Pb-Ag	ER27	Greece	Eastern Rhodopes		Kirki
	13	0.034	Ore	Pb-Ag	ER79	Bulgaria	Eastern Rhodopes	Kardzhali	Zvezdel
	14	0.035	Ore	Pb-Ag	WR6	Greece	Western Rhodopes		Pangeo, Nikisiani Valley
	15	0.035	Ore	Pb-Ag	WA15	Turkey	Western Anatolia	Balikesir	Karaaydin-Biçkayeri
	16	0.036	Ore	Pb-Ag	ER30	Greece	Eastern Rhodopes		Farasino
	17	0.036	Ore	Pb-Ag	EB3	Greece	Euboea	South	Kallianou
	18	0.037	Ore	Pb-Ag	BS15	Turkey	Black Sea region	Giresun	Tirebolu, Maden Tetkik Arama Genel Müdürlüğü
	19	0.037	Ore	Pb-Ag	ER31	Greece	Eastern Rhodopes		Iasmos
	20	0.039	Ore	Pb-Ag	BS18	Turkey	Black Sea region	Giresun	Tirebolu

Appendix 4. *Continued*.

Coin	Euclidean Neighbour	Euclidean Distance	Type	Metals	Sample ID	Region	Sub-Region	Area	Site
GE018 rep	**1**	**0.007**	**Litharge**	**Pb-Ag**	**TG53B/2**	**Greece**	**Cyclades**	**Kea**	**Nikoleri/Platy Yalos**
Max. Err =	**2**	**0.010**	**Ore**	**Pb-Ag**	**CA2**	**Turkey**	**Central Anatolia**	**Ankara**	**Kızılcahamam, Işık Dağ**
0.0215986	**3**	**0.020**	**Ore**	**Pb-Ag**	**ER85**	**Bulgaria**	**Eastern Rhodopes**	**Kardzhali**	**Zvezdel**
	4	**0.020**	**Litharge**	**Pb-Ag**	**TG43/7**	**Greece**	**Cyclades**	**Siphnos**	**Agios Sostis**
	5	**0.021**	**Ore**	**Pb-Ag**	**ER81**	**Bulgaria**	**Eastern Rhodopes**	**Kardzhali**	**Zvezdel**
	6	**0.021**	**Litharge**	**Pb-Ag**	**TG43/6**	**Greece**	**Cyclades**	**Siphnos**	**Agios Sostis**
	7	0.022	Heavy slag	Pb-Ag	TG53A/1	Greece	Cyclades	Kea	Nikoleri/Platy Yalos
	8	0.023	Litharge	Pb-Ag	TG43/4	Greece	Cyclades	Siphnos	Agios Sostis
	9	0.025	Ore	Pb-Ag	BC12	Iberian Peninsula	Betic Cordillera	Sierra Almagrera	Guzmana Mine
	10	0.027	Pb droplet	Pb	SJ-1006-278	Iberian Peninsula	NE Spain		Sant Jaume
	11	0.029	Slag	Pb-Ag	HDM 1114	Turkey	Black Sea region	Samsun	Besiktepe
	12	0.029	Ore	Pb-Ag	CA12	Turkey	Central Anatolia	Kayseri	Near Aladağ/Delikkaya deposit
	13	0.030	Ore	Pb-Ag	ER80	Bulgaria	Eastern Rhodopes	Kardzhali	Zvezdel
	14	0.031	Ore	Pb-Ag	BC14	Iberian Peninsula	Betic Cordillera	Sierra Almagrera	Las Herrerías
	15	0.031	Ore	Pb-Ag	WA22	Turkey	Western Anatolia	Bursa	Madenbelenitepe-Soğukpınar
	16	0.032	Ore	Pb-Ag	BC23	Iberian Peninsula	Betic Cordillera	Sierra del Cabo de Gata	Minas del Monsu
	17	0.032	Ore	Pb-Ag	ER39	Greece	Eastern Rhodopes		Pefka
	18	0.035	Slag	Pb-Ag	ASN17 104	Turkey	Black Sea region	Gümüşhane	
	19	0.035	Ore	Pb-Ag	BC62	Iberian Peninsula	Betic Cordillera	Sierra Cartagena	Mina Piedra Almarilla
	20	0.036	Ore	Pb-Ag	WA46	Turkey	Western Anatolia	Çanakkale	Kurttaşı
GE032	1	0.035	Ore	Pb-Ag	BS29	Turkey	Black Sea region	Ordu	Ünye/Kumarlı, Karadere region
Max. Err =	2	0.037	Ore	Pb-Ag	BC60	Iberian Peninsula	Betic Cordillera	Sierra Cartagena	Mazarrón
0.315509	3	0.047	Ore	Pb-Ag	WR5	Greece	Western Rhodopes		Pangeo, Nikisiani Valley
	4	0.052	Ore	Pb-Ag	ER29	Greece	Eastern Rhodopes		Virini
	5	0.052	Ore	Pb-Ag	CA77	Turkey	Central Anatolia	Sivas	Sisorta
	6	0.054	Ore	Pb-Ag	ER12	Greece	Eastern Rhodopes		Essimi
	7	0.062	Ore	Pb-Ag	BC46	Iberian Peninsula	Betic Cordillera	Sierra del Cabo de Gata	Minas del Cerro de los Guardias (Sol Mine)
	8	0.070	Ore	Pb-Ag	BS6	Turkey	Black Sea region	Giresun	Buluncak, Yukarıtekmezar
	9	0.072	Ore	Pb-Ag	CT9	Greece	Crete	South, Gortyn	Miamou, Lenta A

Appendix 4. *Continued.*

Coin	Euclidean Neighbour	Euclidean Distance	Type	Metals	Sample ID	Region	Sub-Region	Area	Site
	10	0.080	Ore	Pb-Ag	CT7	Greece	Crete	South, Gortyn	Miamou
	11	0.081	Ore	Pb-Ag	BS12	Turkey	Black Sea region	Giresun	Şebinkarahisar/Kavala Mine
	12	0.095	Ore	Pb-Ag	ER14	Greece	Eastern Rhodopes		Kirki
	13	0.098	Slag	Pb-Ag	ASN18 765	Turkey	Black Sea region	Merzifon	Gümüşhaci
	14	0.099	Ore	Pb-Ag	CT6	Greece	Crete	South, Gortyn	Miamou
	15	0.100	Ore	Pb-Ag	MC19	France	Massif Central	Cévennes	La Bleymard
	16	0.102	Ore	Pb-Ag	CM1	Iberian Peninsula	Cantabrian Mountains	Basque-Cantabrian basin, central district	Jugo
	17	0.104	Ore	Pb-Ag	MC16	France	Massif Central	Cévennes	Causses
	18	0.106	Ore	Pb-Ag	ER44	Bulgaria	Eastern Rhodopes	Kardzhali	Bakadzhik
	19	0.108	Ore	Pb-Ag	BS14	Turkey	Black Sea region	Giresun	Tirebolu-Harşit Köprübaşi
	20	0.113	Ore	Pb-Ag	BS19	Turkey	Black Sea region	Gümüşhane	Gümüşhane-Hazine Mağara
GE012	**1**	**0.011**	**Ore**	**Pb-Ag**	**WA43**	**Turkey**	**Western Anatolia**	**Çanakkale**	**Hacibekirler-Maden Deresi**
Max. Err =	2	0.016	Pb metal	Pb-Ag	K716	Greece	Attica	Lavrion	Thorikos
0.0386135	**3**	**0.021**	**Ore**	**Pb-Ag**	**WA34**	**Turkey**	**Western Anatolia**	**Çanakkale**	**Balya**
	4	0.022	Ore	Pb-Ag	L2	Greece	Attica	Lavrion	Agrileza
	5	**0.023**	**Pb slag**	**Pb-Ag**	**STAG 2**	**Greece**	**Macedonia**	**Chalkidiki**	**Stagira**
	6	**0.026**	**Ore**	**Pb-Ag**	**WR15**	**Greece**	**Western Rhodopes**	**Thasos**	**Sotiros**
	7	0.028	Pb metal	Pb-Ag	TC69.471	Greece	Attica	Lavrion	Thorikos
	8	**0.028**	**Pb slag**	**Pb-Ag**	**STAG 3**	**Greece**	**Macedonia**	**Chalkidiki**	**Stagira**
	9	0.031	Ore	Pb-Ag	M4	Greece	Macedonia	Chalkidiki	Madem Lakos
	10	**0.031**	**Ore**	**Pb-Ag**	**ER53**	**Bulgaria**	**Eastern Rhodopes**	**Kardzhali**	**Madjarovo**
	11	0.031	Ore	Pb-Ag	WA1	Turkey	Western Anatolia	Balikesir	Alibey Adasi (near Lesbos)
	12	**0.032**	**Ore**	**Pb-Ag**	**WR12**	**Greece**	**Western Rhodopes**	**Thasos**	**Kourlou**
	13	**0.032**	**Ore**	**Pb-Ag**	**M28**	**Greece**	**Macedonia**	**Chalkidiki**	**Olympias**
	14	**0.032**	**Ore**	**Pb-Ag**	**M16**	**Greece**	**Macedonia**	**Chalkidiki**	**Madem Lakos**
	15	**0.033**	**Ore**	**Pb-Ag**	**M33**	**Greece**	**Macedonia**	**Chalkidiki**	**Olympias**
	16	**0.033**	**Ore**	**Pb-Ag**	**WR13**	**Greece**	**Western Rhodopes**	**Thasos**	**Marlou**
	17	**0.033**	**Ore**	**Pb-Ag**	**M17**	**Greece**	**Macedonia**	**Chalkidiki**	**Madem Lakos**
	18	**0.034**	**Ore**	**Pb-Ag**	**M5**	**Greece**	**Macedonia**	**Chalkidiki**	**Madem Lakos**
	19	**0.036**	**Ore**	**Pb-Ag**	**WR17**	**Greece**	**Western Rhodopes**	**Thasos**	**Vouves**
	20	**0.037**	**Ore**	**Pb-Ag**	**L81**	**Greece**	**Attica**	**Lavrion**	**Plaka**

Appendix 4. Continued.

Coin	Euclidean Neighbour	Euclidean Distance	Type	Metals	Sample ID	Region	Sub-Region	Area	Site
GE012 rep	**1**	**0.011**	**Ore**	**Pb-Ag**	**WA43**	**Turkey**	**Western Anatolia**	**Çanakkale**	**Hacibekirler-Maden Deresi**
Max. Err =	**2**	**0.013**	**Pb metal**	**Pb-Ag**	**TC69.471**	**Greece**	**Attica**	**Lavrion**	**Thorikos**
0.0191448	**3**	**0.014**	**Ore**	**Pb-Ag**	**M5**	**Greece**	**Macedonia**	**Chalkidiki**	**Madem Lakos**
	4	**0.015**	**Ore**	**Pb-Ag**	**WA1**	**Turkey**	**Western Anatolia**	**Balikesir**	**Alibey Adasi (near Lesbos)**
	5	**0.015**	**Ore**	**Pb-Ag**	**L2**	**Greece**	**Attica**	**Lavrion**	**Agrileza**
	6	**0.015**	**Pb metal**	**Pb-Ag**	**K716**	**Greece**	**Attica**	**Lavrion**	**Thorikos**
	7	0.024	Ore	Pb-Ag	M17	Greece	Macedonia	Chalkidiki	Madem Lakos
	8	0.026	Ore	Pb-Ag	L81	Greece	Attica	Lavrion	Plaka
	9	0.026	Ore	Pb-Ag	WA34	Turkey	Western Anatolia	Çanakkale	Balya
	10	0.028	Ore	Pb-Ag	M4	Greece	Macedonia	Chalkidiki	Madem Lakos
	11	0.028	Ore	Pb-Ag	L1	Greece	Attica	Lavrion	Agrileza
	12	0.029	Litharge	Pb-Ag	AGR2	Greece	Attica	Lavrion	Agrileza
	13	0.030	Pb metal	Pb-Ag	B338	Greece	Attica	Lavrion	Thorikos
	14	0.030	Pb slag	Pb-Ag	MADL1	Greece	Macedonia	Chalkidiki	Madem Lakkos
	15	0.030	Ore	Pb-Ag	TH9	Greece	Thessaly	Pelion	Bourboulithres
	16	0.032	Ore	Pb-Ag	M20	Greece	Macedonia	Chalkidiki	Mavres Petres
	17	0.032	Ore	Pb-Ag	M25	Greece	Macedonia	Chalkidiki	Mavres Petres
	18	0.033	Ore	Pb-Ag	M28	Greece	Macedonia	Chalkidiki	Olympias
	19	0.034	Ore	Pb-Ag	C67	Greece	Cyclades	Kea	Faros
	20	0.035	Ore	Pb-Ag	ER55	Bulgaria	Eastern Rhodopes	Kardzhali	Madjarovo
TB028	**1**	**0.019**	**Ore**	**Pb-Ag**	**WA40**	**Turkey**	**Western Anatolia**	**Çanakkale**	**Dağoba-Taşağıl Sirt**
Max. Err =	**2**	**0.019**	**Ore**	**Pb-Ag**	**WR14**	**Greece**	**Western Rhodopes**	**Thasos**	**Marlou**
0.0250895	3	0.021	Ore	Pb-Ag	M34	Greece	Macedonia	Chalkidiki	Olympias
	4	0.024	Ore	Pb-Ag	WR8	Greece	Western Rhodopes	Thasos	Agios Eleftherios
	5	0.024	Ore	Pb-Ag	WA18	Turkey	Western Anatolia	Balikesir	Maden Adasi
	6	0.025	Ore	Pb-Ag	M30	Greece	Macedonia	Chalkidiki	Olympias
	7	0.027	Ore	Pb-Ag	M26	Greece	Macedonia	Chalkidiki	Olympias
	8	0.027	Ore	Pb-Ag	CM8	Iberian Peninsula	Cantabrian Mountains	Basque-Cantabrian basin, Santander district	Reocin
	9	0.028	Ore	Pb-Ag	ER5	Greece	Eastern Rhodopes		Essimi
	10	0.029	Ore	Pb-Ag	ER1	Greece	Eastern Rhodopes		Essimi
	11	0.031	Ore	Pb-Ag	ER33	Greece	Eastern Rhodopes		Ayios Demetrios
	12	0.031	Ore	Pb-Ag	M19	Greece	Macedonia	Chalkidiki	Mavres Petres
	13	0.031	Ore	Pb-Ag	WA6	Turkey	Western Anatolia	Balikesir	Altinoluk
	14	0.031	Pb slag	Pb-Ag	TG 130A-4.1	Turkey	Western Anatolia	Balikesir	Güre

Appendix 4. *Continued.*

Coin	Euclidean Neighbour	Euclidean Distance	Type	Metals	Sample ID	Region	Sub-Region	Area	Site
	15	0.032	Ore	Pb-Ag	ER17	Greece	Eastern Rhodopes		Kirki
	16	0.032	Ore	Pb-Ag	CM11	Iberian Peninsula	Cantabrian Mountains	Basque-Cantabrian basin, Santander district	Udias
	17	0.033	Ore	Pb-Ag	ER32	Greece	Eastern Rhodopes		Ayios Demetrios
	18	0.034	Ore	Pb-Ag	ER40	Greece	Eastern Rhodopes		Viper
	19	0.035	Ore	Pb-Ag	ER9	Greece	Eastern Rhodopes		Essimi
	20	0.036	Ore	Pb-Ag	M13	Greece	Macedonia	Chalkidiki	Madem Lakos
TB028 rep Max. Err = 0.0212417	**1**	**0.009**	**Ore**	**Pb-Ag**	**ER33**	**Greece**	**Eastern Rhodopes**		**Ayios Demetrios**
	2	**0.009**	**Ore**	**Pb-Ag**	**M34**	**Greece**	**Macedonia**	**Chalkidiki**	**Olympias**
	3	**0.010**	**Ore**	**Pb-Ag**	**ER32**	**Greece**	**Eastern Rhodopes**		**Ayios Demetrios**
	4	**0.011**	**Ore**	**Pb-Ag**	**ER40**	**Greece**	**Eastern Rhodopes**		**Viper**
	5	**0.014**	**Pb slag**	**Pb-Ag**	**TG 130A-4.1**	**Turkey**	**Western Anatolia**	**Balikesir**	**Güre**
	6	**0.014**	**Ore**	**Pb-Ag**	**M30**	**Greece**	**Macedonia**	**Chalkidiki**	**Olympias**
	7	**0.020**	**Ore**	**Pb-Ag**	**M27**	**Greece**	**Macedonia**	**Chalkidiki**	**Olympias**
	8	0.022	Ore	Pb-Ag	WA6	Turkey	Western Anatolia	Balikesir	Altinoluk
	9	0.022	Ore	Pb-Ag	M29	Greece	Macedonia	Chalkidiki	Olympias
	10	0.023	Ore	Pb-Ag	WA5	Turkey	Western Anatolia	Balikesir	Altinoluk
	11	0.023	Ore	Pb-Ag	WA3	Turkey	Western Anatolia	Balikesir	Altinoluk
	12	0.023	Ore	Pb-Ag	WR11	Greece	Western Rhodopes	Thasos	Koumaria
	13	0.024	Ore	Pb-Ag	ER37	Greece	Eastern Rhodopes		Kommaros
	14	0.024	Ore	Pb-Ag	WR18	Greece	Western Rhodopes		Vouves
	15	0.026	Ore	Pb-Ag	M13	Greece	Macedonia	Chalkidiki	Madem Lakos
	16	0.026	Ore	Pb-Ag	M15	Greece	Macedonia	Chalkidiki	Madem Lakos
	17	0.026	Ore	Pb-Ag	WR14	Greece	Western Rhodopes	Thasos	Marlou
	18	0.027	Ore	Pb-Ag	M33	Greece	Macedonia	Chalkidiki	Olympias
	19	0.028	Ore	Pb-Ag	CM11	Iberian Peninsula	Cantabrian Mountains	Basque-Cantabrian basin, Santander district	Udias
	20	0.030	Ore	Pb-Ag	WR13	Greece	Western Rhodopes	Thasos	Marlou
GE004 Max. Err = 0.053574	**1**	**0.011**	**Ore**	**Pb-Ag**	**CM18**	**Iberian Peninsula**	**Cantabrian Mountains**	**Basque-Cantabrian basin, Troya-Legorreta district**	**Legorreta**

Appendix 4. *Continued.*

Coin	Euclidean Neighbour	Euclidean Distance	Type	Metals	Sample ID	Region	Sub-Region	Area	Site
	2	0.028	Ore	Pb-Ag	CM16	Iberian Peninsula	Cantabrian Mountains	Basque-Cantabrian basin, Troya-Legorreta district	Troya
	3	0.031	Ore	Pb-Ag	CM23	Iberian Peninsula	Cantabrian Mountains	Basque-Cantabrian basin, Western Vizcaya district	Siete Puertas
	4	0.036	Ore	Pb-Ag	CM26	Iberian Peninsula	Cantabrian Mountains	Basque-Cantabrian basin, Western Vizcaya district	La Rasa
	5	0.037	Ore	Pb-Ag	CM15	Iberian Peninsula	Cantabrian Mountains	Basque-Cantabrian basin, Troya-Legorreta district	Troya
	6	0.039	Ore	Pb-Ag	SARD12	Italy	Sardinia	Mid	Capo Marargiu
	7	0.041	Ore	Pb-Ag	CA45	Turkey	Central Anatolia	Kayseri	Near Yoncaliseki Zn-Pb-Fe showing
	8	0.043	Ore	Pb-Ag	CR1	Greece	Central Rhodopes		Kaloticho
	9	0.043	Ore	Pb-Ag	MC17	France	Massif Central	Cévennes	Causses
	10	0.043	Ore	Pb-Ag	MC20	France	Massif Central	Cévennes	La Croix de Pallieres
	11	0.044	Ore	Pb-Ag	EB5	Greece	Euboea	South	Kallianou
	12	0.044	Ore	Pb-Ag	SARD14	Italy	Sardinia	Mid	Capo Marargiu
	13	0.045	Ore	Pb-Ag	MC90	France	Massif Central	Cévennes	Mont-Lozère
	14	0.045	Ore	Pb-Ag	CM13	Iberian Peninsula	Cantabrian Mountains	Basque-Cantabrian basin, Troya-Legorreta district	Troya
	15	0.046	Ore	Pb-Ag	EB3	Greece	Euboea	South	Kallianou

Appendix 4. *Continued.*

Coin	Euclidean Neighbour	Euclidean Distance	Type	Metals	Sample ID	Region	Sub-Region	Area	Site
	16	0.048	Ore	Pb-Ag	BS15	Turkey	Black Sea region	Giresun	**Tirebolu, Maden Tetkik Arama Genel Müdürlüğü**
	17	0.050	Ore	Pb-Ag	BS16	Turkey	Black Sea region	Giresun	**Tirebolu (İnköy)**
	18	0.055	Ore	Pb-Ag	SARD17	Italy	Sardinia	Mid	Capo Marargiu
	19	0.056	Ore	Pb-Ag	SARD19	Italy	Sardinia	Mid	Capo Marargiu
	20	0.056	Ore	Pb-Ag	SARD18	Italy	Sardinia	Mid	Capo Marargiu
GE004 rep	**1**	**0.020**	**Ore**	**Pb-Ag**	**EB4**	**Greece**	**Euboea**	**South**	**Kallianou**
Max. Err = 0.0203011	2	0.028	Ore	Pb-Ag	EB6	Greece	Euboea	South	Kallianou
	3	0.031	Ore	Pb-Ag	CR1	Greece	Central Rhodopes		Kaloticho
	4	0.036	Ore	Pb-Ag	CA24	Turkey	Central Anatolia	Kayseri	Aladağ/Yahyali
	5	0.037	Ore	Pb-Ag	CA29	Turkey	Central Anatolia	Kayseri	Ayvan (Sultankuyu Fe showing)
	6	0.043	Ore	Pb-Ag	CA27	Turkey	Central Anatolia	Kayseri	Aladağ Yahyali Kay
	7	0.045	Ore	Pb-Ag	EB3	Greece	Euboea	South	Kallianou
	8	0.049	Ore	Pb-Ag	CA86	Turkey	Central Anatolia	Kayseri	Cakilpinar Develi
	9	0.050	Ore	Pb-Ag	CA26	Turkey	Central Anatolia	Kayseri	Aladağ Yahyali Kay
	10	0.051	Ore	Pb-Ag	C211	Greece	Cyclades	Siphnos	Agios Ioannis
	11	0.053	Ore	Pb-Ag	CA34	Turkey	Central Anatolia	Kayseri	Denizovasi
	12	0.056	Ore	Pb-Ag	CM23	Iberian Peninsula	Cantabrian Mountains	Basque-Cantabrian basin, Western Vizcaya district	Siete Puertas
	13	0.056	Ore	Pb-Ag	CA32	Turkey	Central Anatolia	Kayseri	Çakılpınar deposit
	14	0.056	Ore	Pb-Ag	CA33	Turkey	Central Anatolia	Kayseri	Celaldagi
	15	0.060	Ore	Pb-Ag	CA7	Turkey	Central Anatolia	Kayseri	Aladağ/Delikkaya, mine
	16	0.061	Ore	Pb-Ag	EB5	Greece	Euboea	South	Kallianou
	17	0.062	Ore	Pb-Ag	CA45	Turkey	Central Anatolia	Kayseri	Near Yoncaliseki Zn-Pb-Fe showing
	18	0.063	Ore	Pb-Ag	ER30	Greece	Eastern Rhodopes		Farasino
	19	0.064	Litharge	Pb-Ag	TG43/4	Greece	Cyclades	Siphnos	Agios Sostis
	20	0.064	Ore	Pb-Ag	ER18	Greece	Eastern Rhodopes		Kirki

Appendix 4. *Continued.*

Coin	Euclidean Neighbour	Euclidean Distance	Type	Metals	Sample ID	Region	Sub-Region	Area	Site
TB031	1	0.008	Ore	Pb-Ag	ER50	Bulgaria	Eastern Rhodopes	Kardzhali	Madjarovo
Max. Err =	2	0.008	Ore	Pb-Ag	ER38	Greece	Eastern Rhodopes		Pefka
0.0381675	3	0.009	Ore	Pb-Ag	WA49	Turkey	Western Anatolia	Çanakkale	Sofular
	4	0.013	Ore	Pb-Ag	ER41	Greece	Eastern Rhodopes		Viper
	5	0.016	Ore	Pb-Ag	ER11	Greece	Eastern Rhodopes		Essimi
	6	0.016	Ore	Pb-Ag	ER54	Bulgaria	Eastern Rhodopes	Kardzhali	Madjarovo
	7	0.017	Ore	Pb-Ag	ER39	Greece	Eastern Rhodopes		Pefka
	8	0.017	Ore	Pb-Ag	WA24	Turkey	Western Anatolia	Çanakkale	Bağırkaç
	9	0.019	Ore	Pb-Ag	BC30	Iberian Peninsula	Betic Cordillera	Sierra del Cabo de Gata	Minas de la Paniza
	10	0.023	Ore	Pb-Ag	BC27	Iberian Peninsula	Betic Cordillera	Sierra del Cabo de Gata	Minas del Monsu
	11	0.023	Ore	Pb-Ag	BC25	Iberian Peninsula	Betic Cordillera	Sierra del Cabo de Gata	Minas del Monsu
	12	0.023	Ore	Pb-Ag	ER37	Greece	Eastern Rhodopes	Kommaros	Minas de la Paniza
	13	0.024	Ore	Pb-Ag	BC28	Iberian Peninsula	Betic Cordillera	Sierra del Cabo de Gata	Minas del Monsu
	14	0.024	Ore	Pb-Ag	BC22	Iberian Peninsula	Betic Cordillera	Sierra del Cabo de Gata	Minas del Monsu
	15	0.024	Ore	Pb-Ag	BC26	Iberian Peninsula	Betic Cordillera	Sierra del Cabo de Gata	Minas del Monsu
	16	0.024	Ore	Pb-Ag	WA44	Turkey	Western Anatolia	Çanakkale	Kıraçoba-Deliktaş
	17	0.024	Ore	Pb-Ag	WA52	Turkey	Western Anatolia	Çanakkale	Sofular
	18	0.027	Ore	Pb-Ag	WA5	Turkey	Western Anatolia	Balıkesir	Altınoluk
	19	0.027	Ore	Pb-Ag	ER53	Bulgaria	Eastern Rhodopes	Kardzhali	Madjarovo
	20	0.027	Ore	Pb-Ag	ER86	Bulgaria	Eastern Rhodopes	Kardzhali	Zvezdel
TB031 rep	1	0.010	Ore	Pb-Ag	ER54	Bulgaria	Eastern Rhodopes	Kardzhali	Madjarovo
Max. Err =	2	0.012	Ore	Pb-Ag	WA44	Turkey	Western Anatolia	Çanakkale	Kıraçoba-Deliktaş
0.0204419	3	0.012	Ore	Pb-Ag	WA52	Turkey	Western Anatolia	Çanakkale	Sofular
	4	0.017	Ore	Pb-Ag	ER38	Greece	Eastern Rhodopes		Pefka

Appendix 4. *Continued.*

Coin	Euclidean Neighbour	Euclidean Distance	Type	Metals	Sample ID	Region	Sub-Region	Area	Site
	5	0.017	Ore	Pb-Ag	WA46	Turkey	Western Anatolia	Çanakkale	Kurttaşi
	6	0.018	Ore	Pb-Ag	WA50	Turkey	Western Anatolia	Çanakkale	Sofular
	7	0.018	Ore	Pb-Ag	ER50	Bulgaria	Eastern Rhodopes	Kardzhali	Madjarovo
	8	0.018	Ore	Pb-Ag	BC34	Iberian Peninsula	Betic Cordillera	Sierra del Cabo de Gata	Minas de la Paniza
	9	0.018	Ore	Pb-Ag	BC28	Iberian Peninsula	Betic Cordillera	Sierra del Cabo de Gata	Minas de la Paniza
	10	0.019	Ore	Pb-Ag	M12	Greece	Macedonia	Chalkidiki	Madem Lakos
	11	0.021	Ore	Pb-Ag	ER51	Bulgaria	Eastern Rhodopes	Kardzhali	Madjarovo
	12	0.021	Ore	Pb-Ag	ER41	Greece	Eastern Rhodopes		Viper
	13	0.021	Ore	Pb-Ag	WA49	Turkey	Western Anatolia	Çanakkale	Sofular
	14	0.021	Slag	Pb-Ag	ASN17 104	Turkey	Black Sea region	Gümüşhane	
	15	0.022	Ore	Pb-Ag	ER39	Greece	Eastern Rhodopes		Pefka
	16	0.023	Ore	Pb-Ag	WA53	Turkey	Anatolien, West	Çanakkale	Sofular
	17	0.023	Ore	Pb-Ag	BC30	Iberian Peninsula	Betic Cordillera	Sierra del Cabo de Gata	Minas de la Paniza
	18	0.023	Ore	Pb-Ag	ER53	Bulgaria	Eastern Rhodopes	Kardzhali	Madjarovo
	19	0.023	Ore	Pb-Ag	M7	Greece	Macedonia	Chalkidiki	Madem Lakos
	20	0.023	Ore	Pb-Ag	BC27	Iberian Peninsula	Betic Cordillera	Sierra del Cabo de Gata	Minas del Monsu
TB029	1	0.017	Ore	Pb-Ag	EB3	Greece	Euboea	South	Kallianou
Max. Err =	2	0.018	Ore	Pb-Ag	ER18	Greece	Eastern Rhodopes		Kirki
0.0251362	3	0.020	Ore	Pb-Ag	C211	Greece	Cyclades	Siphnos	Agios Ioannis
	4	0.023	Ore	Pb-Ag	ER15	Greece	Eastern Rhodopes		Kirki
	5	0.023	Ore	Pb-Ag	WR3	Greece	Western Rhodopes		Pangeo, Nikisiani Valley
	6	0.024	Ore	Pb-Ag	ER24	Greece	Eastern Rhodopes		Kirki
	7	0.026	Ore	Pb-Ag	ER26	Greece	Eastern Rhodopes		Kirki
	8	0.028	Ore	Pb-Ag	EB5	Greece	Euboea	South	Kallianou
	9	0.029	Ore	Pb-Ag	EB6	Greece	Euboea	South	Kallianou
	10	0.030	Ore	Pb-Ag	CA27	Turkey	Central Anatolia	Kayseri	Aladağ Yahyali Kay

Appendix 4. *Continued.*

Coin	Euclidean Neighbour	Euclidean Distance	Type	Metals	Sample ID	Region	Sub-Region	Area	Site
	11	0.031	Ore	Pb-Ag	CA26	Turkey	Central Anatolia	Kayseri	Aladağ Yahyali Kay
	12	0.032	Heavy slag	Pb-Ag	TG53A/2	Greece	Cyclades	Kea	Nikoleri/Platy Yalos
	13	0.032	Ore	Pb-Ag	CR1	Greece	Central Rhodopes		Kaloticho
	14	0.033	Ore	Pb-Ag	ER82	Bulgaria	Eastern Rhodopes	Kardzhali	Zvezdel
	15	0.033	Ore	Pb-Ag	WR4	Greece	Western Rhodopes		Pangeo, Nikisiani Valley
	16	0.033	Ore	Pb-Ag	BS15	Turkey	Black Sea region	Giresun	Tirebolu, Maden Tetkik Arama Genel Müdürlü?ü
	17	0.037	Ore	Pb-Ag	ER79	Bulgaria	Eastern Rhodopes	Kardzhali	Zvezdel
	18	0.037	Ore	Pb-Ag	ER30	Greece	Eastern Rhodopes		Farasino
	19	0.038	Ore	Pb-Ag	ER27	Greece	Eastern Rhodopes		Kirki
	20	0.038	Ore	Pb-Ag	ER83	Bulgaria	Eastern Rhodopes	Kardzhali	Zvezdel
TB029 rep	**1**	**0.017**	**Ore**	**Pb-Ag**	**ER18**	**Greece**	**Eastern Rhodopes**		**Kirki**
Max. Err =	**2**	**0.018**	**Ore**	**Pb-Ag**	**EB3**	**Greece**	**Euboea**	**South**	**Kallianou**
0.0229769	**3**	**0.020**	**Ore**	**Pb-Ag**	**WR3**	**Greece**	**Western Rhodopes**		**Pangeo, Nikisiani Valley**
	4	**0.021**	**Ore**	**Pb-Ag**	**ER15**	**Greece**	**Eastern Rhodopes**		**Kirki**
	5	**0.021**	**Ore**	**Pb-Ag**	**C211**	**Greece**	**Cyclades**	**Siphnos**	**Agios Ioannis**
	6	**0.022**	**Ore**	**Pb-Ag**	**ER24**	**Greece**	**Eastern Rhodopes**		**Kirki**
	7	0.025	Ore	Pb-Ag	ER26	Greece	Eastern Rhodopes		Kirki
	8	0.027	Ore	Pb-Ag	EB5	Greece	Euboea	South	Kallianou
	9	0.030	Ore	Pb-Ag	CA27	Turkey	Central Anatolia	Kayseri	Aladağ Yahyali Kay
	10	0.030	Ore	Pb-Ag	WR4	Greece	Western Rhodopes		Pangeo, Nikisiani Valley
	11	0.030	Heavy slag	Pb-Ag	TG53A/2	Greece	Cyclades	Kea	Nikoleri/Platy Yalos
	12	0.031	Ore	Pb-Ag	CA26	Turkey	Central Anatolia	Kayseri	Aladağ Yahyali Kay
	13	0.031	Ore	Pb-Ag	EB6	Greece	Euboea	South	Kallianou
	14	0.032	Ore	Pb-Ag	ER82	Bulgaria	Eastern Rhodopes	Kardzhali	Zvezdel
	15	0.032	Ore	Pb-Ag	BS15	Turkey	Black Sea region	Giresun	Tirebolu, Maden Tetkik Arama Genel Müdürlüğü
	16	0.035	Ore	Pb-Ag	ER83	Bulgaria	Eastern Rhodopes	Kardzhali	Zvezdel
	17	0.036	Ore	Pb-Ag	CR1	Greece	Central Rhodopes		Kaloticho

Appendix 4. *Continued.*

Coin	Euclidean Neighbour	Euclidean Distance	Type	Metals	Sample ID	Region	Sub-Region	Area	Site
	18	0.037	Ore	Pb-Ag	ER79	Bulgaria	Eastern Rhodopes	Kardzhali	Zvezdel
	19	0.037	Ore	Pb-Ag	WR6	Greece	Western Rhodopes		Pangeo, Nikisiani Valley
	20	0.038	Ore	Pb-Ag	ER27	Greece	Eastern Rhodopes		Kirki
GE003	**1**	**0.009**	**Ore**	**Pb-Ag**	**L14**	**Greece**	**Attica**	**Lavrion**	**Kamariza**
Max. Err =	**2**	**0.009**	**Ore**	**Pb-Ag**	**L107**	**Greece**	**Attica**	**Lavrion**	**Thorikos**
0.0201567	**3**	**0.009**	**Ore**	**Pb-Ag**	**L108**	**Greece**	**Attica**	**Lavrion**	**Thorikos**
	4	**0.011**	**Ore**	**Pb-Ag**	**L52**	**Greece**	**Attica**	**Lavrion**	**Plaka**
	5	**0.013**	**Ore**	**Pb-Ag**	**L58**	**Greece**	**Attica**	**Lavrion**	**Plaka**
	6	**0.014**	**Ore**	**Pb-Ag**	**L37**	**Greece**	**Attica**	**Lavrion**	**Megala Pefka**
	7	**0.014**	**Ore**	**Pb-Ag**	**L89**	**Greece**	**Attica**	**Lavrion**	**Plaka**
	8	**0.014**	**Ore**	**Pb-Ag**	**L86**	**Greece**	**Attica**	**Lavrion**	**Plaka**
	9	**0.016**	**Ore**	**Pb-Ag**	**L73**	**Greece**	**Attica**	**Lavrion**	**Plaka**
	10	**0.017**	**Ore**	**Pb-Ag**	**L9**	**Greece**	**Attica**	**Lavrion**	**Kamariza**
	11	**0.017**	**Slag**	**Pb-Ag**	**ET281**	**Greece**	**Attica**	**Lavrion**	**Thorikos**
	12	**0.017**	**Pb metal**	**Pb-Ag**	**TM68.4**	**Greece**	**Attica**	**Lavrion**	**Thorikos**
	13	**0.017**	**Ore**	**Pb-Ag**	**L87**	**Greece**	**Attica**	**Lavrion**	**Plaka**
	14	**0.017**	**Ore**	**Pb-Ag**	**L31**	**Greece**	**Attica**	**Lavrion**	**Kamariza**
	15	**0.017**	**Ore**	**Pb-Ag**	**L85**	**Greece**	**Attica**	**Lavrion**	**Plaka**
	16	**0.017**	**Ore**	**Pb-Ag**	**L97**	**Greece**	**Attica**	**Lavrion**	**Plaka**
	17	**0.018**	**litharge**	**Pb-Ag**	**ZO350**	**Greece**	**Attica**	**Lavrion**	**Thorikos**
	18	**0.018**	**Ore**	**Pb-Ag**	**AI6**	**Greece**	**Aegean Islands**	**Samos**	**Zestos**
	19	**0.018**	**Ore**	**Pb-Ag**	**L91**	**Greece**	**Attica**	**Lavrion**	**Plaka**
	20	**0.018**	**Ore**	**Pb-Ag**	**L72**	**Greece**	**Attica**	**Lavrion**	**Plaka**
TB030	**1**	**0.010**	**Ore**	**Pb-Ag**	**WA34**	**Turkey**	**Western Anatolia**	**Çanakkale**	**Balya**
Max. Err =	**2**	**0.012**	**Ore**	**Pb-Ag**	**L2**	**Greece**	**Attica**	**Lavrion**	**Agrileza**
0.02205	**3**	**0.016**	**Ore**	**Pb-Ag**	**WA1**	**Turkey**	**Western Anatolia**	**Balikesir**	**Alibey Adasi (near Lesbos)**
	4	**0.016**	**Ore**	**Pb-Ag**	**M28**	**Greece**	**Macedonia**	**Chalkidiki**	**Olympias**
	5	**0.017**	**Ore**	**Pb-Ag**	**ER53**	**Bulgaria**	**Eastern Rhodopes**	**Kardzhali**	**Madjarovo**

Appendix 4. *Continued.*

Coin	Euclidean Neighbour	Euclidean Distance	Type	Metals	Sample ID	Region	Sub-Region	Area	Site
	6	0.019	Ore	Pb-Ag	WA43	Turkey	Western Anatolia	Çanakkale	Hacibekirler-Maden Deresi
	7	0.019	Ore	Pb-Ag	WR15	Greece	Western Rhodopes	Thasos	Sotiros
	8	0.021	Ore	Pb-Ag	M17	Greece	Macedonia	Chalkidiki	Madem Lakos
	9	0.022	Ore	Pb-Ag	WR12	Greece	Western Rhodopes	Thasos	Kourlou
	10	0.023	Ore	Pb-Ag	M5	Greece	Macedonia	Chalkidiki	Madem Lakos
	11	0.023	Ore	Pb-Ag	WR17	Greece	Western Rhodopes	Thasos	Vouves
	12	0.023	Pb slag	Pb-Ag	STAG 3	Greece	Macedonia	Chalkidiki	Stagira
	13	0.023	Ore	Pb-Ag	M4	Greece	Macedonia	Chalkidiki	Madem Lakos
	14	0.024	Ore	Pb-Ag	M20	Greece	Macedonia	Chalkidiki	Mavres Petres
	15	0.026	Pb slag	Pb-Ag	STAG 2	Greece	Macedonia	Chalkidiki	Stagira
	16	0.027	Ore	Pb-Ag	WR16	Greece	Western Rhodopes	Thasos	Sotiros
	17	0.027	Ore	Pb-Ag	TH9	Greece	Thessaly	Pelion	Bourboulithres
	18	0.027	Pb metal	Pb-Ag	K716	Greece	Attica	Lavrion	Thorikos
	19	0.029	Ore	Pb-Ag	ER51	Bulgaria	Eastern Rhodopes	Kardzhali	Madjarovo
	20	0.030	Ore	Pb-Ag	BC34	Iberian Peninsula	Betic Cordillera	Sierra del Cabo de Gata	Minas de la Paniza
TB030 rep	1	0.009	Ore	Pb-Ag	WA34	Turkey	Western Anatolia	Çanakkale	Balya
Max. Err =	2	0.013	Ore	Pb-Ag	L2	Greece	Attica	Lavrion	Agrileza
0.0272748	3	0.016	Ore	Pb-Ag	M28	Greece	Macedonia	Chalkidiki	Olympias
	4	0.017	Ore	Pb-Ag	WA1	Turkey	Western Anatolia	Balikesir	Alibey Adasi (near Lesbos)
	5	0.017	Ore	Pb-Ag	ER53	Bulgaria	Eastern Rhodopes	Kardzhali	Madjarovo
	6	0.018	Ore	Pb-Ag	WR15	Greece	Western Rhodopes	Thasos	Sotiros
	7	0.019	Ore	Pb-Ag	WA43	Turkey	Western Anatolia	Çanakkale	Hacibekirler-Maden Deresi
	8	0.021	Ore	Pb-Ag	M17	Greece	Macedonia	Chalkidiki	Madem Lakos
	9	0.021	Ore	Pb-Ag	WR12	Greece	Western Rhodopes	Thasos	Kourlou
	10	0.022	Ore	Pb-Ag	WR17	Greece	Western Rhodopes	Thasos	Vouves
	11	0.022	Pb slag	Pb-Ag	STAG 3	Greece	Macedonia	Chalkidiki	Stagira
	12	0.023	Ore	Pb-Ag	M4	Greece	Macedonia	Chalkidiki	Madem Lakos
	13	0.023	Ore	Pb-Ag	M5	Greece	Macedonia	Chalkidiki	Madem Lakos

Appendix 4. *Continued.*

Coin	Euclidean Neighbour	Euclidean Distance	Type	Metals	Sample ID	Region	Sub-Region	Area	Site
	14	**0.024**	**Ore**	**Pb-Ag**	**M20**	**Greece**	**Macedonia**	**Chalkidiki**	**Mavres Petres**
	15	**0.025**	**Pb slag**	**Pb-Ag**	**STAG 2**	**Greece**	**Macedonia**	**Chalkidiki**	**Stagira**
	16	**0.026**	**Ore**	**Pb-Ag**	**WR16**	**Greece**	**Western Rhodopes**	**Thasos**	**Sotiros**
	17	0.027	Ore	Pb-Ag	TH9	Greece	Thessaly	Pelion	Bourboulithres
	18	0.027	Pb metal	Pb-Ag	K716	Greece	Attica	Lavrion	Thorikos
	19	0.029	Ore	Pb-Ag	BC34	Iberian Peninsula	Betic Cordillera	Sierra del Cabo de Gata	Minas de la Paniza
	20	0.029	Ore	Pb-Ag	ER51	Bulgaria	Eastern Rhodopes	Kardzhali	Madjarovo
TB032 Max. Err = 0.0211739	**1**	**0.008**	**Ore**	**Pb-Ag**	**WA1**	**Turkey**	**Western Anatolia**	**Balikesir**	**Alibey Adasi (near Lesbos)**
	2	**0.015**	**Ore**	**Pb-Ag**	**M20**	**Greece**	**Macedonia**	**Chalkidiki**	**Mavres Petres**
	3	**0.015**	**Ore**	**Pb-Ag**	**L2**	**Greece**	**Attica**	**Lavrion**	**Agrileza**
	4	**0.017**	**Ore**	**Pb-Ag**	**M5**	**Greece**	**Macedonia**	**Chalkidiki**	**Madem Lakos**
	5	**0.018**	**Ore**	**Pb-Ag**	**M17**	**Greece**	**Macedonia**	**Chalkidiki**	**Madem Lakos**
	6	**0.019**	**Ore**	**Pb-Ag**	**TH9**	**Greece**	**Thessaly**	**Pelion**	**Bourboulithres**
	7	**0.019**	**Ore**	**Pb-Ag**	**M28**	**Greece**	**Macedonia**	**Chalkidiki**	**Olympias**
	8	**0.019**	**Ore**	**Pb-Ag**	**ER55**	**Bulgaria**	**Eastern Rhodopes**	**Kardzhali**	**Madjarovo**
	9	**0.020**	**Ore**	**Pb-Ag**	**WA34**	**Turkey**	**Western Anatolia**	**Çanakkale**	**Balya**
	10	0.021	Ore	Pb-Ag	WA35	Turkey	Western Anatolia	Çanakkale	Balya
	11	0.023	Ore	Pb-Ag	ER53	Bulgaria	Eastern Rhodopes	Kardzhali	Madjarovo
	12	0.023	Ore	Pb-Ag	ER51	Bulgaria	Eastern Rhodopes	Kardzhali	Madjarovo
	13	0.024	Ore	Pb-Ag	WR9	Greece	Western Rhodopes	Thasos	Koumaria
	14	0.025	Ore	Pb-Ag	M31	Greece	Macedonia	Chalkidiki	Olympias
	15	0.025	Ore	Pb-Ag	M4	Greece	Macedonia	Chalkidiki	Madem Lakos
	16	0.025	Ore	Pb-Ag	WR17	Greece	Western Rhodopes	Thasos	Vouves
	17	0.026	Ore	Pb-Ag	WA53	Turkey	Anatolien, West	Çanakkale	Sofular
	18	0.026	Ore	Pb-Ag	WA43	Turkey	Western Anatolia	Çanakkale	Hacibekirler-Maden Deresi
	19	0.026	Ore	Pb-Ag	WA51	Turkey	Western Anatolia	Çanakkale	Sofular
	20	0.027	Ore	Pb-Ag	WR16	Greece	Western Rhodopes	Thasos	Sotiros

Appendix 4. Continued.

Coin	Euclidean Neighbour	Euclidean Distance	Type	Metals	Sample ID	Region	Sub-Region	Area	Site
TB032 rep	1	0.006	Ore	Pb-Ag	WA34	Turkey	Western Anatolia	Çanakkale	Balya
Max. Err = 0.0231189	2	0.012	Ore	Pb-Ag	ER53	Bulgaria	Eastern Rhodopes	Kardzhali	Madjarovo
	3	0.013	Ore	Pb-Ag	M28	Greece	Macedonia	Chalkidiki	Olympias
	4	0.014	Ore	Pb-Ag	WR15	Greece	Western Rhodopes	Thasos	Sotiros
	5	0.016	Ore	Pb-Ag	L2	Greece	Attica	Lavrion	Agrileza
	6	0.017	Ore	Pb-Ag	WR12	Greece	Western Rhodopes	Thasos	Kourlou
	7	0.019	Pb slag	Pb-Ag	STAG 3	Greece	Macedonia	Chalkidiki	Stagira
	8	0.020	Ore	Pb-Ag	WR17	Greece	Western Rhodopes	Thasos	Vouves
	9	0.021	Pb slag	Pb-Ag	STAG 2	Greece	Macedonia	Chalkidiki	Stagira
	10	0.022	Ore	Pb-Ag	WA1	Turkey	Western Anatolia	Balikesir	Alibey Adasi (near Lesbos)
	11	0.022	Ore	Pb-Ag	WA43	Turkey	Western Anatolia	Çanakkale	Hacibekirler-Maden Deresi
	12	0.024	Ore	Pb-Ag	M17	Greece	Macedonia	Chalkidiki	Madem Lakos
	13	0.024	Ore	Pb-Ag	BC30	Iberian Peninsula	Betic Cordillera	Sierra del Cabo de Gata	Minas de la Paniza
	14	0.025	Ore	Pb-Ag	M4	Greece	Macedonia	Chalkidiki	Madem Lakos
	15	0.025	Ore	Pb-Ag	WR16	Greece	Western Rhodopes	Thasos	Sotiros
	16	0.025	Ore	Pb-Ag	ER54	Bulgaria	Eastern Rhodopes	Kardzhali	Madjarovo
	17	0.026	Ore	Pb-Ag	BC28	Iberian Peninsula	Betic Cordillera	Sierra del Cabo de Gata	Minas de la Paniza
	18	0.026	Ore	Pb-Ag	M7	Greece	Macedonia	Chalkidiki	Madem Lakos
	19	0.027	Ore	Pb-Ag	BC34	Iberian Peninsula	Betic Cordillera	Sierra del Cabo de Gata	Minas de la Paniza
	20	0.027	Ore	Pb-Ag	M20	Greece	Macedonia	Chalkidiki	Mavres Petres
TB032 rep-2	1	0.003	Ore	Pb-Ag	ER50	Bulgaria	Eastern Rhodopes	Kardzhali	Madjarovo
Max. Err = 0.0199572	2	0.009	Ore	Pb-Ag	BC30	Iberian Peninsula	Betic Cordillera	Sierra del Cabo de Gata	Minas de la Paniza
	3	0.010	Ore	Pb-Ag	ER41	Greece	Eastern Rhodopes	Kardzhali	Viper
	4	0.013	Ore	Pb-Ag	ER54	Bulgaria	Eastern Rhodopes	Kardzhali	Madjarovo
	5	0.017	Ore	Pb-Ag	WA49	Turkey	Western Anatolia	Çanakkale	Sofular
	6	0.018	Ore	Pb-Ag	ER38	Greece	Eastern Rhodopes	Chalkidiki	Pefka

SILVER FOR THE GREEK COLONIES 143

Appendix 4. *Continued.*

Coin	Euclidean Neighbour	Euclidean Distance	Type	Metals	Sample ID	Region	Sub-Region	Area	Site
	7	0.018	Ore	Pb-Ag	ER11	Greece	Eastern Rhodopes		Essimi
	8	0.018	Ore	Pb-Ag	BC28	Iberian Peninsula	Betic Cordillera	Sierra del Cabo de Gata	Minas de la Paniza
	9	0.020	Ore	Pb-Ag	ER53	Bulgaria	Eastern Rhodopes	Kardzhali	Madjarovo
	10	0.020	Ore	Pb-Ag	ER37	Greece	Eastern Rhodopes		Kommaros
	11	0.021	Ore	Pb-Ag	M7	Greece	Macedonia	Chalkidiki	Madem Lakos
	12	0.022	Ore	Pb-Ag	WR12	Greece	Western Rhodopes	Thasos	Kourlou
	13	0.022	Ore	Pb-Ag	WR11	Greece	Western Rhodopes	Thasos	Koumaria
	14	0.023	Ore	Pb-Ag	M14	Greece	Macedonia	Chalkidiki	Madem Lakos
	15	0.023	Ore	Pb-Ag	WR15	Greece	Western Rhodopes	Thasos	Sotiros
	16	0.023	Ore	Pb-Ag	WA24	Turkey	Western Anatolia	Çanakkale	Bağırkaç
	17	0.023	Ore	Pb-Ag	M1	Greece	Macedonia	Chalkidiki	Madem Lakos
	18	0.023	Ore	Pb-Ag	M6	Greece	Macedonia	Chalkidiki	Madem Lakos
	19	0.024	Ore	Pb-Ag	M27	Greece	Macedonia	Chalkidiki	Olympias
	20	0.025	Ore	Pb-Ag	WR18	Greece	Western Rhodopes	Thasos	Vouves
TB033	1	0.012	Pb metal	Pb-Ag	TC69,471	Greece	Attica	Lavrion	Thorikos
Max. Err = 0.0305591	2	0.013	Ore	Pb-Ag	WA43	Turkey	Western Anatolia	Çanakkale	Hacibekirler-Maden Deresi
	3	0.014	Ore	Pb-Ag	M5	Greece	Macedonia	Chalkidiki	Madem Lakos
	4	0.015	Ore	Pb-Ag	WA1	Turkey	Western Anatolia	Balikesir	Alibey Adasi (near Lesbos)
	5	0.015	Ore	Pb-Ag	L2	Greece	Attica	Lavrion	Agrileza
	6	0.016	Pb metal	Pb-Ag	K716	Greece	Attica	Lavrion	Thorikos
	7	0.025	Ore	Pb-Ag	M17	Greece	Macedonia	Chalkidiki	Madem Lakos
	8	0.026	Ore	Pb-Ag	L81	Greece	Attica	Lavrion	Plaka
	9	0.026	Ore	Pb-Ag	L1	Greece	Attica	Lavrion	Agrileza
	10	0.027	Litharge	Pb-Ag	AGR2	Greece	Attica	Lavrion	Agrileza
	11	0.028	Pb metal	Pb-Ag	B338	Greece	Attica	Lavrion	Thorikos
	12	0.028	Ore	Pb-Ag	WA34	Turkey	Western Anatolia	Çanakkale	Balya
	13	0.029	Ore	Pb-Ag	M4	Greece	Macedonia	Chalkidiki	Madem Lakos
	14	0.030	Pb slag	Pb-Ag	MADL1	Greece	Macedonia	Chalkidiki	Madem Lakkos

Appendix 4. *Continued.*

Coin	Euclidean Neighbour	Euclidean Distance	Type	Metals	Sample ID	Region	Sub-Region	Area	Site
	15	0.031	Ore	Pb-Ag	TH9	Greece	Thessaly	Pelion	Bourboulithres
	16	0.032	Ore	Pb-Ag	M20	Greece	Macedonia	Chalkidiki	Mavres Petres
	17	0.032	Ore	Pb-Ag	M25	Greece	Macedonia	Chalkidiki	Mavres Petres
	18	0.034	Ore	Pb-Ag	C67	Greece	Cyclades	Kea	Faros
	19	0.034	Ore	Pb-Ag	ER55	Bulgaria	Eastern Rhodopes	Kardzhali	Madjarovo
	20	0.035	Ore	Pb-Ag	M28	Greece	Macedonia	Chalkidiki	Olympias
TB033 rep	**1**	**0.005**	**Ore**	**Pb-Ag**	**WA43**	**Turkey**	**Western Anatolia**	**Çanakkale**	**Hacibekirler-Maden Deresi**
Max. Err =	**2**	**0.011**	**Pb metal**	**Pb-Ag**	**K716**	**Greece**	**Attica**	**Lavrion**	**Thorikos**
0.0230467	**3**	**0.019**	**Ore**	**Pb-Ag**	**L2**	**Greece**	**Attica**	**Lavrion**	**Agrileza**
	4	**0.022**	**Pb metal**	**Pb-Ag**	**TC69.471**	**Greece**	**Attica**	**Lavrion**	**Thorikos**
	5	**0.023**	**Ore**	**Pb-Ag**	**WA34**	**Turkey**	**Western Anatolia**	**Çanakkale**	**Balya**
	6	0.027	Ore	Pb-Ag	WA1	Turkey	Western Anatolia	Balikesir	Alibey Adasi (near Lesbos)
	7	0.028	Pb slag	Pb-Ag	STAG 2	Greece	Macedonia	Chalkidiki	Stagira
	8	0.029	Ore	Pb-Ag	M5	Greece	Macedonia	Chalkidiki	Madem Lakos
	9	0.030	Ore	Pb-Ag	WR15	Greece	Western Rhodopes	Thasos	Sotiros
	10	0.031	Ore	Pb-Ag	M4	Greece	Macedonia	Chalkidiki	Madem Lakos
	11	0.032	Pb slag	Pb-Ag	STAG 3	Greece	Macedonia	Chalkidiki	Stagira
	12	0.032	Ore	Pb-Ag	M17	Greece	Macedonia	Chalkidiki	Madem Lakos
	13	0.033	Ore	Pb-Ag	L81	Greece	Attica	Lavrion	Plaka
	14	0.033	Ore	Pb-Ag	ER53	Bulgaria	Eastern Rhodopes	Kardzhali	Madjarovo
	15	0.033	Ore	Pb-Ag	M28	Greece	Macedonia	Chalkidiki	Olympias
	16	0.034	Ore	Pb-Ag	WR12	Greece	Western Rhodopes	Thasos	Kourlou
	17	0.037	Ore	Pb-Ag	WR17	Greece	Western Rhodopes	Thasos	Vouves
	18	0.038	Ore	Pb-Ag	L59	Greece	Attica	Lavrion	Plaka
	19	0.039	Ore	Pb-Ag	M16	Greece	Macedonia	Chalkidiki	Madem Lakos
	20	0.039	Ore	Pb-Ag	L4	Greece	Attica	Lavrion	Esperance
HE002	**1**	**0.012**	**Pb metal**	**Pb-Ag**	**TC69.471**	**Greece**	**Attica**	**Lavrion**	**Thorikos**
Max. Err =	**2**	**0.017**	**Pb metal**	**Pb-Ag**	**B338**	**Greece**	**Attica**	**Lavrion**	**Thorikos**
0.0170531	3	0.019	Ore	Pb-Ag	L85	Greece	Attica	Lavrion	Plaka

Appendix 4. *Continued.*

Coin	Euclidean Neighbour	Euclidean Distance	Type	Metals	Sample ID	Region	Sub-Region	Area	Site
	4	0.019	Ore	Pb-Ag	L97	Greece	Attica	Lavrion	Plaka
	5	0.019	Slag	Pb-Ag	ET281	Greece	Attica	Lavrion	Thorikos
	6	0.019	Pb metal	Pb-Ag	TM68.4	Greece	Attica	Lavrion	Thorikos
	7	0.020	Ore	Pb-Ag	L81	Greece	Attica	Lavrion	Plaka
	8	0.020	Pb metal	Pb-Ag	AGR10	Greece	Attica	Lavrion	Agrileza
	9	0.021	Pb metal	Pb-Ag	K716	Greece	Attica	Lavrion	Thorikos
	10	0.024	litharge	Pb-Ag	ZO350	Greece	Attica	Lavrion	Thorikos
	11	0.024	Ore	Pb-Ag	C67	Greece	Cyclades	Kea	Faros
	12	0.024	Ore	Pb-Ag	L74	Greece	Attica	Lavrion	Plaka
	13	0.025	Cerussite/litharge	Pb-Ag	C4.i.2	Greece	Attica	Lavrion	Thorikos
	14	0.025	Ore	Pb-Ag	L70	Greece	Attica	Lavrion	Plaka
	15	0.026	Ore	Pb-Ag	L64	Greece	Attica	Lavrion	Plaka
	16	0.026	Ore	Pb-Ag	L73	Greece	Attica	Lavrion	Plaka
	17	0.026	Ore	Pb-Ag	L37	Greece	Attica	Lavrion	Megala Pefka
	18	0.027	Ore	Pb-Ag	WA43	Turkey	Western Anatolia	Çanakkale	Hacibekirler-Maden Deresi
	19	0.027	Ore	Pb-Ag	L71	Greece	Attica	Lavrion	Plaka
	20	0.027	Litharge	Pb-Ag	AGR2	Greece	Attica	Lavrion	Agrileza
HE001	**1**	**0.015**	**Ore**	**Pb-Ag**	**L85**	**Greece**	**Attica**	**Lavrion**	**Plaka**
Max. Err =	**2**	**0.015**	**Ore**	**Pb-Ag**	**L97**	**Greece**	**Attica**	**Lavrion**	**Plaka**
0.0210113	**3**	**0.016**	**Slag**	**Pb-Ag**	**ET281**	**Greece**	**Attica**	**Lavrion**	**Thorikos**
	4	**0.016**	**Pb metal**	**Pb-Ag**	**TM68.4**	**Greece**	**Attica**	**Lavrion**	**Thorikos**
	5	**0.016**	**Pb metal**	**Pb-Ag**	**TC69.471**	**Greece**	**Attica**	**Lavrion**	**Thorikos**
	6	**0.016**	**Pb metal**	**Pb-Ag**	**AGR10**	**Greece**	**Attica**	**Lavrion**	**Agrileza**
	7	**0.017**	**Pb metal**	**Pb-Ag**	**B338**	**Greece**	**Attica**	**Lavrion**	**Thorikos**
	8	**0.021**	**litharge**	**Pb-Ag**	**ZO350**	**Greece**	**Attica**	**Lavrion**	**Thorikos**
	9	0.022	Ore	Pb-Ag	L81	Greece	Attica	Lavrion	Plaka
	10	0.022	Ore	Pb-Ag	L74	Greece	Attica	Lavrion	Plaka
	11	0.022	Ore	Pb-Ag	L73	Greece	Attica	Lavrion	Plaka

Appendix 4. *Continued.*

Coin	Euclidean Neighbour	Euclidean Distance	Type	Metals	Sample ID	Region	Sub-Region	Area	Site
	12	0.023	Ore	Pb-Ag	L70	Greece	Attica	Lavrion	Plaka
	13	0.023	Ore	Pb-Ag	L64	Greece	Attica	Lavrion	Plaka
	14	0.023	Ore	Pb-Ag	L37	Greece	Attica	Lavrion	Megala Pefka
	15	0.024	Ore	Pb-Ag	L71	Greece	Attica	Lavrion	Plaka
	16	0.024	Cerussite/ litharge	Pb-Ag	C4.i.2	Greece	Attica	Lavrion	Thorikos
	17	0.024	Pb metal	Pb-Ag	K716	Greece	Attica	Lavrion	Thorikos
	18	0.024	Ore	Pb-Ag	C67	Greece	Cyclades	Kea	Faros
	19	0.025	Ore	Pb-Ag	C71	Greece	Cyclades	Kea	Faros
	20	0.027	Ore	Pb-Ag	L107	Greece	Attica	Lavrion	Thorikos
GE007	**1**	**0.011**	**Ore**	**Pb-Ag**	**WA34**	**Turkey**	**Western Anatolia**	**Çanakkale**	**Balya**
Max. Err = 0.0200387	**2**	**0.015**	**Ore**	**Pb-Ag**	**WA43**	**Turkey**	**Western Anatolia**	**Çanakkale**	**Hacibekirler-Maden Deresi**
	3	**0.017**	**Ore**	**Pb-Ag**	**WR15**	**Greece**	**Western Rhodopes**	**Thasos**	**Sotiros**
	4	**0.018**	**Pb slag**	**Pb-Ag**	**STAG 2**	**Greece**	**Macedonia**	**Chalkidiki**	**Stagira**
	5	**0.019**	**Pb slag**	**Pb-Ag**	**STAG 3**	**Greece**	**Macedonia**	**Chalkidiki**	**Stagira**
	6	**0.020**	**Ore**	**Pb-Ag**	**L2**	**Greece**	**Attica**	**Lavrion**	**Agrileza**
	7	0.022	Ore	Pb-Ag	WR12	Greece	Western Rhodopes	Thasos	Kourlou
	8	0.022	Ore	Pb-Ag	M28	Greece	Macedonia	Chalkidiki	Olympias
	9	0.022	Pb metal	Pb-Ag	K716	Greece	Attica	Lavrion	Thorikos
	10	0.023	Ore	Pb-Ag	M4	Greece	Macedonia	Chalkidiki	Madem Lakos
	11	0.023	Ore	Pb-Ag	ER53	Bulgaria	Eastern Rhodopes	Kardzhali	Madjarovo
	12	0.025	Ore	Pb-Ag	M17	Greece	Macedonia	Chalkidiki	Madem Lakos
	13	0.025	Ore	Pb-Ag	WR17	Greece	Western Rhodopes	Thasos	Vouves
	14	0.026	Ore	Pb-Ag	WA1	Turkey	Western Anatolia	Balikesir	Alibey Adasi (near Lesbos)
	15	0.029	Ore	Pb-Ag	M5	Greece	Macedonia	Chalkidiki	Madem Lakos
	16	0.030	Ore	Pb-Ag	BC30	Iberian Peninsula	Betic Cordillera	Sierra del Cabo de Gata	Minas de la Paniza
	17	0.031	Ore	Pb-Ag	WR16	Greece	Western Rhodopes	Thasos	Sotiros
	18	0.031	Ore	Pb-Ag	M16	Greece	Macedonia	Chalkidiki	Madem Lakos

Appendix 4. *Continued.*

Coin	Euclidean Neighbour	Euclidean Distance	Type	Metals	Sample ID	Region	Sub-Region	Area	Site
	19	0.031	Ore	Pb-Ag	WR13	Greece	Western Rhodopes	Thasos	Marlou
	20	0.031	Pb metal	Pb-Ag	TC69.471	Greece	Attica	Lavrion	Thorikos
GE007 rep	**1**	**0.011**	**Ore**	**Pb-Ag**	**WA34**	**Turkey**	**Western Anatolia**	**Çanakkale**	**Balya**
Max. Err =	**2**	**0.013**	**Ore**	**Pb-Ag**	**WA43**	**Turkey**	**Western Anatolia**	**Çanakkale**	**Hacibekirler-Maden Deresi**
0.0223367	**3**	**0.017**	**Ore**	**Pb-Ag**	**L2**	**Greece**	**Attica**	**Lavrion**	**Agrileza**
	4	**0.019**	**Ore**	**Pb-Ag**	**WR15**	**Greece**	**Western Rhodopes**	**Thasos**	**Sotiros**
	5	**0.021**	**Ore**	**Pb-Ag**	**M4**	**Greece**	**Macedonia**	**Chalkidiki**	**Madem Lakos**
	6	**0.021**	**Pb slag**	**Pb-Ag**	**STAG 3**	**Greece**	**Macedonia**	**Chalkidiki**	**Stagira**
	7	**0.021**	**Pb metal**	**Pb-Ag**	**K716**	**Greece**	**Attica**	**Lavrion**	**Thorikos**
	8	**0.021**	**Ore**	**Pb-Ag**	**M28**	**Greece**	**Macedonia**	**Chalkidiki**	**Olympias**
	9	**0.021**	**Ore**	**Pb-Ag**	**WA1**	**Turkey**	**Western Anatolia**	**Balikesir**	**Alibey Adasi (near Lesbos)**
	10	**0.022**	**Pb slag**	**Pb-Ag**	**STAG 2**	**Greece**	**Macedonia**	**Chalkidiki**	**Stagira**
	11	**0.022**	**Ore**	**Pb-Ag**	**M17**	**Greece**	**Macedonia**	**Chalkidiki**	**Madem Lakos**
	12	0.023	Ore	Pb-Ag	WR12	Greece	Western Rhodopes	Thasos	Kourlou
	13	0.023	Ore	Pb-Ag	ER53	Bulgaria	Eastern Rhodopes	Kardzhali	Madjarovo
	14	0.025	Ore	Pb-Ag	M5	Greece	Macedonia	Chalkidiki	Madem Lakos
	15	0.025	Ore	Pb-Ag	WR17	Greece	Western Rhodopes	Thasos	Vouves
	16	0.028	Pb metal	Pb-Ag	TC69.471	Greece	Attica	Lavrion	Thorikos
	17	0.030	Ore	Pb-Ag	WR16	Greece	Western Rhodopes	Thasos	Sotiros
	18	0.031	Ore	Pb-Ag	M20	Greece	Macedonia	Chalkidiki	Mavres Petres
	19	0.032	Ore	Pb-Ag	TH9	Greece	Thessaly	Pelion	Bourboulithres
	20	0.032	Ore	Pb-Ag	BC30	Iberian Peninsula	Betic Cordillera Cabo de Gata	Sierra del	Minas de la Paniza

10. ELEMENTAL COMPOSITION OF GOLD AND SILVER COINS OF SIPHNOS

Kenneth A. Sheedy, Damian B. Gore, Maryse Blet-Lemarquand and Gillan Davis

ABSTRACT

Three areas in mainland and Aegean Greece are known to have been important sources of silver during antiquity: Laurion in south-east Attica, the Thraco-Macedonian region of northern Greece, and the Cycladic island of Siphnos. The mines of Siphnos are thought to have been a major source of silver for archaic Greece coinage, especially that of Aegina. Lead isotope and elemental analyses have been used in published studies of ores, slag and litharge (lead oxide; PbO) found on Siphnos, and elemental analyses on 12 coins. Here we present elemental analyses of one gold and 29 silver coins from Siphnos. This data leads us to reconsider the claim made by Gale et al. 1980 that the levels of bismuth in Siphnian silver are higher than those recorded levels for Laurion silver. Finally, the evidence of the analyses is considered in relation to the history of minting on Siphnos.

INTRODUCTION: 'WEALTHY' SIPHNOS

During the sixth century BC, the inhabitants of Cycladic Siphnos were held to be 'the richest of the islanders' (Herodotus 3.57) (Wagner *et al.* 1980, 17–58; Sheedy 2000; 2006, 41–57).[1] This rocky island in the western chain of islands in the Aegean covers only 73 km^2, and has little arable land. Its early wealth came from gold and silver mines (Sheedy 2006, 41–57). Revenue from this source was paid out to the citizens (Herodotus 3.57.2). In thanks for this good fortune the Siphnians paid a tithe to Apollo at Delphi and built an ostentatious treasury, the first in marble at this sanctuary, to house their offerings (Sheedy 2000). Just before 525 BC (around the time their treasury was completed), the islanders received an oracle from Apollo, recorded by Herodotus (3.57), that the source of their wealth would be taken from them when their *prytanaion* (town hall) and *agora* (market place) were faced with white marble. They were also warned of "a wooden trap" – which proved to have been set by Samian pirates; although the city walls were not breached they were forced to pay a ransom of 100 talents to free those citizens caught outside the town (Herodotus 3.58). The Siphnians were evidently unable to recover from the loss of these 100 talents so we can infer that the island's mines were already failing. Pausanias (10.11.2) tells another story: the Siphnians continued to pay the tithe to Apollo until through greed they stopped and as a consequence the sea flooded the mines. In the fifth century BC the island was no longer considered wealthy; it paid only three talents to the Delian League (Sheedy 2006, 52). They had evidently slipped from being among the rich, but Brun (2000) has argued that the island was still comparatively prosperous (cf. Isocrates *Aeginetica* 30). By the time of Strabo (10.5.1) it was a by-word for worthlessness.

Siphnos is part of the Attic-Cycladic crystalline complex within the Hellenides (Vavelidis *et al.* 1985; Roche *et al.* 2016); the same is true of the Laurion area. The island features Cycladic Blueschist overlain by a nappe consisting of marble, schist and gneiss. Silver-bearing lead-antimony sulfides and sulfates occur in a near-surface zone of oxidised and strongly weathered rock (Gale *et al.* 1980, 4). Silver occurs on Siphnos in association with the minerals galena (PbS), cerussite ($PbCO_3$) and jarosite ($KFe^{3+}_3(OH)_6(SO_4)_2$) (Vavelidis *et al.* 1985, 63–66, fig. 42).

An interdisciplinary project on prehistoric and ancient metal production on Siphnos, organized by the Bergbau-Museum, Bochum and the Max-Planck-Institut für Kernphysik (Wagner and Weisgerber 1985a), recorded in detail the evidence for mines and metal-rich ores (for summaries see Wagner 2000; Birkett-Smith 2000). Ore deposits occur in the middle and south of the island (Vavelidis *et al.* 1985). There are five deposits of silver-bearing ores (mostly galena dominated) in the island's centre, forming a line between the known mining sites of Agios Sostis, Agios Silvestros, Vorini,

---

[1] We wish to warmly thank Prof Bernhard Weisser, director of the Münzkabinett der Staatlichen Museen zu Berlin, for his invaluable support of the project 'A Spring of Silver', undertaken by Sheedy, Gore and Davis, to study the composition of the metal used to mint archaic Athenian coinage. The XRF analyses of Athenian and Siphnian coins in the Berlin collection were essential for the writing of this study of Siphnian silver.

Kapsalos and Xeroxylon (Matthaus 1985, 19, fig. 2). Of these, the mine at Agios Sostis on the coast (often linked to the story in Pausanias 10.11.2 that Apollo flooded the mines) is the most famous and the most carefully studied (Weisgerber 1985). To the south, at Agios Ioannis, Apokofto and Aspro Prygos, are deposits of gold (see also Vavelidis 1997). Ancient mines at these sites, however, have suffered badly from the extraction of iron ore in nineteenth and twentieth century (Vavelidis *et al.* 1985, 65; Birkett-Smith 2006).

The working of silver and gold surface deposits on the island dates back at least to Early Bronze Age II (Keros-Syros culture) which began *c.* 2,700 BC (Pernicka and Wagner 1985a, 200; Pernicka and Wagner 1985b). But after the evidence of intensive activity during the third millennium the Bochum/Heidelberg survey found little until a second period of activity in the sixth and fifth centuries BC (Pernicka and Wagner 1985a, 205). The more substantial evidence for prehistoric mining and metalwork has continued to dominate recent research on Siphnos (Bassiakos *et al.* 2013).

In his account of a visit to Siphnos in 1884, before the advent of modern mining on the island, J. Theodore Bent (1885) colourfully describes two mines that were still known to the local people (Aghios Sostis and Kapsalos). He noted (1885, 197) that local potters pick up "bits of vitrified lead, which they use for mixing with their clay to prevent it expanding." He also mentioned seeing (1885, 197) "quantities of scoriae, which the ancient smelters have used and cast on one side." Nonetheless, a paucity of slag dumps was reported by the Bochum/Heidelberg survey, despite evidence for intensive mining (Pernicka *et al.* 1985). There are traces of slag-covered pit furnaces (e.g. Ayios Sostis: Pernicka *et al.* 1985, 186–7), and lead oxide mineral litharge (PbO) has been found at three sites (Platy Gialos, Agios Sostis and Kapsalos), indicating that at least some extraction of silver from lead did take place on Siphnos (Pernicka *et al.* 1985). However, even if ancient slag heaps were recycled in the Roman and Byzantine periods, more evidence of slag should be visible. Numerous tuyeres survive (Pernicka *et al.* 1985, 185–6) but none exhibit a slag coating. Should we then conclude (as did Pernicka *et al.* 1985, 197) that their absence can only mean that most Siphnian ores were smelted somewhere else?

Wagner and Wiesgerber Analyses of Siphnian Coinage

Compositional analyses of Siphnian coinage arguably began with Gale *et al.* (1980), who focused on the evidence of the then recently found Asyut Hoard (*IGCH* 1644; Price and Waggoner 1975; see Beer 1980 for a history of the analytical research project). Compositional data for coins in the Asyut hoard derived from neutron activation analysis (NAA) and lead isotope analysis (LIA) (Gale *et al.* 1980). No coins from Siphnos were included in this sample, but LIA of Siphnian ores, slags and litharge (Gale *et al.*, 1980, 10, n. 31 with references to earlier publications; Wagner *et al.* 1980) was used to identify a distinct Siphnian lead isotope field.

45 Aeginetan coins from the Asyut hoard (plus one more Aeginetan tortoise from the 'Wells Hoard') were analysed, with LIA leading to the identification of 10 Aeginetan coins from the Siphnian lead isotope field, with a further four near the edge (Gale *et al.* 1980, 28, fig. 8). The 14 coins in or near the Siphnian field (over 30 % of the sample) typologically extended down to the small skew variety (Price and Waggoner 1975, 73, Group VIIb) which was believed to have concluded *c.*485 BC. Aeginetan coins which fit the Laurion lead isotope field represent 17 % of the sample (9 coins within the field; Gale *et al.* 1980, 36). These Laurion silver Aeginetan coins all carry later reverse patterns (with the exception of one Union Jack variety) which begin *c.*495 BC (Gale *et al.* 1980, 28, 35). This suggested that the Siphnos-derived silver coins of Aegina are earlier, and that *c.*495 BC the mint began to rely on silver from Laurion. The sample was too small to have any confidence in this division but it would then seem that a significant part of the archaic output of the Aeginetan mint was

made from the silver of Siphnos. In a review of these data, and a proposed revision of the conclusions, Stos-Gale and Davis (this volume) now argue in contrast that the role of silver from Siphnos in the production of Aeginetan coinage was minor.

The earliest study quantifying elemental compositions to help determine the provenance of silver in Greek coins used NAA on a similarly large sample of Aeginetan coins, focusing on copper, silver and gold (Kraay and Emeleus, in Kraay 1962). They contrasted the relatively low concentrations of copper (<0.25 %) and gold (<0.04 %) in Athenian owls with the greater copper and gold concentrations in 37 Aeginetan staters (Kraay 1962, 12–14). On the basis of the NAA analyses, three clusters of Aeginetan coins were apparent to Kraay and Emeleus, and they concluded that there were three silver sources: Laurion, Siphnos and a third uncertain source, possibly the Thraco-Macedonian mines (see Stos-Gale and Davis in this volume on the question of silver sources). There were no Siphnian coins in the sample, and none from the Thraco-Macedonian region.

Elemental analyses of Siphnian ores and slag showed a greater silver content in ores from the main area of mineralisation (typically more than 500 g/ton but ranging up to 7,000 g/ton) than was present in Laurion ores (Gale *et al.* 1980, 38). The gold content in Siphnian ores was said to be 'chiefly' in the range of 0.005 % to 0.05 % in the extracted silver (Gale *et al.* 1980, 39) and with all data taken into account they concluded that a gold content in Siphnian silver "from 0.01 to 0.2 and even, rarely, up to 1%" could be expected. These findings supported the theory of Kraay and Emeleus that Siphnian silver typically had more gold than Laurion silver.

Gale *et al.* (1980, 41, table 12) incorporated elemental analyses of Siphnian coins carried out by M. Cowell at the British Museum (nine coins using X-ray Fluorescence spectrometry (XRF)) and by Ch. Lahanier at the Bibliothèque nationale de France, Paris (three coins using XRF). The gold content of these 12 coins was 0.2–0.6 % for sixth century BC coins and 0.02–0.2 % for early fifth century BC coins (Gale *et al.* 1980, 40) (now see Table 1). They did not explain why the gold content decreased over this short period. The XRF data (Gale *et al.* 1980, 41, table 12) showed that (a) the purity of Siphnian silver coins is very high (nearly all >97 %; with 7 coins >98 %); (b) the gold content is relatively high (8 coins >0.1 %); (c) Cu concentrations are 0.1–2.0 % (11 coins) and (d) lead concentrations are as high as 0.3–2.0 %, but with most <1 %.

GOLD COINS OF SIPHNOS

Siphnos is the only Cycladic island known to have certainly produced a gold coinage, though this is seldom recognized (Sheedy 2006, 48; the existence of a gold coinage of Tenos seems

Figure 1. Gold drachm (4.295g). Siphnos, *c.*375–357 BC. Berlin inv.18207419. Image courtesy of the Staatliche Museen zu Berlin, Münzkabinett

Figure 2. Silver tetrobol (3.72g). Siphnos, fourth century BC. British Museum inv. 1887,1003.5. Image courtesy of the trustees of the British Museum

unlikely, but see Étienne 1990, 235, cat. 201). The presence of gold mines on Siphnos has been confirmed by the Bochum/Heidelberg survey. A tiny (0.11 g) unpublished electrum fraction in New York (ANS 1944.100.27956) has been attributed to Siphnos without good reason (see Sheedy 2006, 48, pl. 18), and it seems more likely that the coin belongs to an unknown mint in Asia Minor (as suggested by Waggoner 1983, cat 315). The gold coins of Siphnos are confined to one issue that today is represented by a single drachm now in Berlin (inv.18207419; Dressel 1898, 216–7, cat. 1411, pl. 5, 4; ex Photiades Coll.1411). This rather beautiful coin (Fig. 1) depicts the head of Apollo wearing a tainia and, on the reverse, an eagle in flight (the traditional coin types of the island) combined with the inscription ΣΙΦ. At 4.295 g, it is a drachm or hemi-stater on the Attic weight standard (Dressel 1898, 217). The fourth century BC coinage of Siphnos has yet to be studied. Nonetheless, it is possible to see that the reverse die employed for the gold drachm in Berlin was also used to mint the well preserved fourth century silver tetrobol in London (inv. 1887,1003.5; Fig. 2). This gold issue was then contemporary with the last known phase of silver coins from Siphnos.

The first known analysis of the Berlin drachm, which was reported by H-D Schultz, was undertaken with an electron microprobe (Pernicka and Wagner 1985a, 207-8, table 3; the measurements were of the obverse). The gold content was given as ~92 % and the sum of calcium, iron, copper, zinc and silver was estimated at <8 %. Our XRF analysis of the gold drachm (with the data normalized to 100%) has now revealed a gold content of 96.4 %, with 2.92 % silver and 0.677 % copper (Table 1, cat. 29).

A more precise dating for the fourth century BC coinage of Siphnos is suggested by comparisons with Euboean League issues produced between 375 and 357 BC (for earlier attempts at dating these Siphnian coins see Gardner 1913). Depictions of the nymph Euboea maintain formalised hair strand patterns (Wallace 1956, cat. 1–13) until a change to a naturalistic hair rendering c. 357 BC (Wallace 1956, cat. 14–19). The depictions of Apollo on Siphnian coins (e.g. Figs 1, 2) show a similar formal pattern with clearly delineated hair strands but the more naturalistic hair rendering is unknown. The eagle on the Siphnian gold drachm is set within a shallow round incuse, and not in a square frame. The change from a square to a round incuse can also be seen in the coinage of the Euboean League where it occurs in the period c. 375-357 BC (Wallace 1956, cat. 1–13).

Siphnian silver staters were traditionally minted on the Aeginetan standard. After c. 475 BC, however, Siphnos began minting tetrobols around 3.80 g. Sheedy (2006, 49–50) suggested that Siphnos had adjusted the weights of these issues so that they might pass on either the Aeginetan standard common in the Cyclades during the archaic period, or on the Attic standard – perhaps reflecting the importance of Athens in fifth century Aegean trade.

It seems likely, however, that Siphnos simply reduced the average weight of its fractions at this time because it had less silver (and in this study we have identified the various fractions according to the Aeginetan standard rather than the Attic). The practice of reduced weight fractions continued into the fourth century. The Berlin gold coin is the first example of a Siphnian issue that is clearly on the Attic standard.

There were very few gold coinages minted in Greece in the first half of the fourth century BC. Athens had minted an emergency gold coinage c. 407–404 BC (which included drachms) but then ceased (Robinson 1960), and would not produce another gold issue until 295 BC.

Is there an historical context that might explain this surprising gold issue? In 376 BC, after the battle of Naxos, most of the Cycladic city-states joined the Second Athenian Confederacy (Rutishauser 2012, 160–1). The Confederacy was not formally dissolved until 338 BC. There was no 'Cycladic coinage alliance' and nothing similar to the Ionian coinage alliance suggested by the ΣYN issues (Rutishauser 2012, 152). If Siphnos paid its *syntaxeis* (contributions; see Rutishauser 2012, 168–9) in coin then perhaps this gold drachm was part of the supposedly voluntary contributions of the island towards supporting the Athenian navy.

SILVER COINS OF SIPHNOS

Discussion of the chemical composition of Siphnian silver coins was initially determined by XRF analyses of nine examples in London (from M. Cowell) and a further three in Paris (Ch. Lahanier), first published in Gale *et al.* (1980). The data were confined to copper, silver, gold and lead, and there were no certified reference materials reported in the analytical suite, so the accuracy of these measurements is unconstrained. These data were re-published in Pernicka and Wagner (1985a, 207), which appears to offer a larger range of coins; however, although the weights of five additional coins are recorded, there are no new elemental analyses, and furthermore the silver concentrations of the coins from Paris are omitted. This small sample size with unconstrained analytical accuracy is the context and justification for our new measurement program.

This research reports new elemental analyses (Table 1) for a range of Siphnian silver coins with two aims. First, we re-analyse 11 of the 12 coins reported in Gale *et al.* (1980), in order to check the veracity of those older measurements. Second, we increase the number of analysed silver coins from Siphnos to a total of 29 coins. We then discuss these new data in the context of the typology and analysis of Siphnian coinage established by Sheedy (2006, 41–57).

METHODS

Twelve legacy analyses (Gale *et al.* 1980) were tabulated and 11 of these coins were re-located and re-measured (Table 1). Elemental compositions of 24 coins were measured on each side using a PANalytical Epsilon 3 energy dispersive XRF, with a 15 W, rhodium anode tube operated at 50 kV for the elements reported (Table 2). Data were corrected for the presence of the patina by subtraction of environmental contaminants, with the remaining data normalised to 100 % (following Gore and Davis 2016), thereby approximating the interior composition of the coin metal. Compositional values (Table 1) are the arithmetic mean of a single measurement from each of the obverse and reverse. Analytical inaccuracy of the XRF was constrained by measurement of 12 certified reference materials (MBH, UK: 131XAGP2A, 131XAGP3A, 131XAGP4A, 131XPAG1, 131XPAG2, 132X925Zn1, 132X925Zn3, 132XAGB87, 132XAGB92, 132XAGB94, 133XAGQ2, 133XAGQ3; summarised in Fig. 3). In general, elements with concentrations of <0.1 wt% have relative errors of 10-100 %, and elements present at >1 wt% have relative errors of <10 % (Fig. 3).

LA-ICP-MS (Laser Ablation Inductively Coupled Plasma Mass Spectrometry) was also carried out on six Siphnian coins held in the collection of the Département des Monnaies,

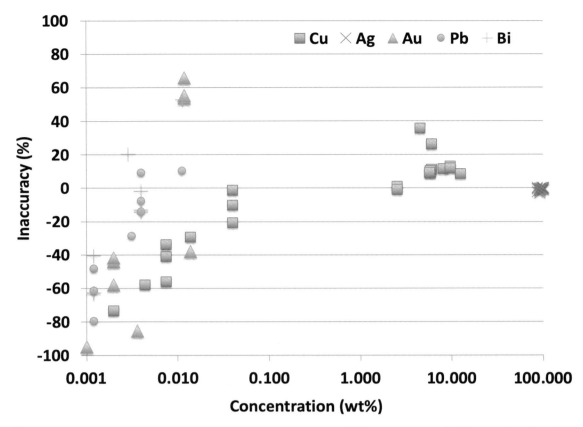

Figure 3. Analytical inaccuracy for the new measurements using XRF spectrometry (PANalytical Epsilon 3)

médailles et antiques in the Bibliothèque nationale de France to give a complementary characterisation of this set of coins. LA-ICP-MS permits a rapid and almost non-destructive determination of the concentration of many elements in silver coins (Sarah *et al.* 2007; Sarah and Gratuze 2016) and gold coins (Blet-Lemarquand *et al.*, this volume) with very low detection limits (less than 1 mg/kg). Micro-sampling was conducted with a laser ablation device. The ablated matter is ionised in a plasma torch, and the extracted ions were analysed using a mass spectrometer. Traces of sampling on the coin are virtually invisible to the naked eye. Single spot analysis is used in order to reach deep into the coin being analysed. Depth profile mode was chosen to measure continuously the composition of all the elements, starting at the surface of the coin. This mode makes it possible to remove the surface layer (that can be enriched with elements such as Zn and Pb) from the calculations and to characterise the underlying unaffected alloy. Two to three different samples are generally taken from each coin. The relative error of this method is <2% for silver content >90% and <10% for minor elements in most cases.

In this study of the Siphnos coins in Paris, however, two examples (FG 387 and FG 389) which the data obtained by Lahanier (see Table 1) suggested were plated, required another method of analysis. Fast Neutron Activation Analysis (FNAA) was performed to obtain the mean composition of these coins for 10 elements (Guerra and Barrandon 1998).

Some 43 measurements from our XRF study (Table 1, source 4) are presented from one gold and 29 silver coins (Table 1). Data were analysed using one-way analysis of variance (ANOVA) using Minitab v.17 for Windows (Minitab Inc.). α=0.05 was used for all analyses. Where the ANOVA showed a significant interaction, a Tukey's post-hoc test for differences of means was performed. Since Series III consisted of one coin only, it is not discussed as a separate group in these data analyses. Elemental data were analysed raw, and also expressed as a ratio to Ag concentrations to remove the constant sum effect, and then $\log_{10}$ transformed to avoid spurious negative correlations (Aitchison's solution; Aitchison 1986, Rollinson 1992). However, because log-transformed ratios are not intuitive for most readers, the raw compositional data will be discussed throughout the manuscript.

RESULTS

The following analysis pertains to the recent XRF data (Table 1, source 4). The data from LA-ICP-MS and FNAA is in agreement with the XRF results. Concentrations of copper ranged from 0.04 to 4.3 %, with an arithmetic mean of 0.80 % and a geometric mean of 0.38 %. ANOVA of both untransformed and transformed data showed a significant difference between the groups (ANOVA; d.f.=23, F=5.68, P=0.0056), and a Tukey's test (T=4.06, P=0.0032) revealed that Series IV coins have a significantly greater copper content than Series II coins. Concentrations of silver ranged from 94.0 to 99.3 %, with an arithmetic and geometric means of 97.5 %. An ANOVA of the untransformed data showed that there were no significant differences (ANOVA; d.f.=23, F=1.77, P=0.1847) between the Series. Concentrations of gold ranged from 0.007 to 0.58 %, with an arithmetic mean of 0.19 % and a geometric mean of 0.081 %. An ANOVA of both untransformed and transformed data revealed a strong, significant interaction (ANOVA; d.f.=23, F=12.83, P <0.0001), and a Tukey's test revealed that both Series I (T=4.83, P=0.0006) and Series IV (T=5.18, P=0.0003) have more gold than Series II coins. Concentrations of lead ranged from 0.006 to 1.56 %, with an arithmetic mean of 0.39 % and a geometric mean of 0.172 %. ANOVA of both untransformed and transformed data showed a weak, but significant difference between the groups (ANOVA; d.f.=23, F=3.37, P=0.0388), and a Tukey's test revealed that Series I has significantly less lead than Series II (T=3.05, P=0.0295). Concentrations of bismuth ranged from 0.001 to 0.086 %, with an arithmetic mean of 0.027 % and a geometric mean of 0.016 %. ANOVA of both untransformed and transformed data revealed no significant interactions at the 5 % level, although in general the concentration of bismuth decreased monotonically from Series I to Series IV.

DISCUSSION

Our first aim was to compare our XRF data with those obtained by Cowell and Lahanier over 27 years ago. Table 1 shows that there is a reasonably close match in both the estimates of the amount of silver and in the minor and trace elements. The second aim was to re-examine the earlier chemical characterisation of Siphnian silver coins. In general, the purity of the silver remains high (97.6 to 99.5 %) as does gold (0.01 to 0.6 %) relative to concentrations in Athenian silver coins (Gale et al. 1980, 12: in Athenian owl coins "gold content varies chiefly between 0.02 and 0.05 %").

We have reported bismuth concentrations (<0.15 %), which are thought to be a diagnostic element for silver sources (L'Héritier et al. 2015). Concentrations of gold are directly linked to the ores from which the silver was extracted and are not altered by smelting and refining (see for instance Gale et al. 1980; Meyers 2003 and quoted references). Bismuth is only slightly altered by these processes (Gitler et al. 2009, 34; L'Héritier et al. 2015). It is important to note that our study has shown bismuth concentrations which are usually lower than those reported by Gale et al. 1980 as typical of Laurion silver (1980, 33: in Athenian owls "bismuth lies chiefly between 0.05 and 0.25%"). Gale et al. (1980, 40, fig. 10) had observed that ten Aeginetan coins believed to have been manufactured from Siphnian silver "are relatively higher in bismuth than Laurion silver". These different conclusions must underline the dangers of inferring typical levels for trace elements from coins only suspected of being made of Siphnian silver. We (Sheedy, Gore and Davis) are currently studying XRF data from over 1,000 archaic Attic coins. Our impression is that the concentrations of bismuth in Laurion silver typically sit between 0.01 and 0.04 % and are comparable to concentrations in Siphnian silver.

Copper and lead concentrations change with smelting and are a reflection of technology and practices. Curiously, Siphnian silver coins typically have slightly lower concentrations of lead in comparison with Athenian coins. It now seems highly probable that where copper concentrations exceed 0.5 %, as often happens in Attic silver coins, copper had been deliberately added (this is noted, for example, by Gitler *et al.* 2009, 38).

At least three plated silver coins of Siphnos have been detected (Sheedy 2006, cat. 9, 13 and 27) (see Table 1, cat. 30, 31 for analyses of Paris FG 387 and FG 389) – a significant number within the sample from this fairly small range of issues. We believe that these plated coins were minted by the Siphnian state; the style of the engraved types is extremely close to contemporary dies used by the Siphnians. The practice of official mints producing plated coins was not uncommon (van Alfen 2005), but it is extremely rare to find a fourrée from the Cyclades (we are aware of only one example from another Cycladic mint, a plated archaic stater from Thera: Classical Numismatic Group (CNG) Sale 317 (2013) 58). The production of plated coins by the Siphnian mint should be viewed as a response to falling stocks of silver.

Our discussion of the data employs a typological and chronological framework for Siphnian coinage established by Sheedy (2006). In Series I, there is a noticeably wide distribution of stater weights (Table 3) but it is clear that the mint is adhering to the Aeginetan weight standard. As noted above, in Series II the fractions show an evident reduction from the Aeginetan weight standard. In the 4th century BC the tetrobols continued to be issued at a reduced weight (Table 3).

The first issues of Siphnos, Series I (Fig. 4), belong to the years *c.* 540–525 BC (Sheedy 2006, 177–178). This is the era of the largest output of staters but the low number of surviving examples is surprising; the 17 didrachms recorded were minted from six obverse and six reverse dies. The XRF data of Lahanier and our project (Table 1, cat. 30) and our FNAA analyses concur that the stater Paris FG 387 is plated. The concentrations of Ag among the coins sampled are very high – between 96.6 % and 99.3 % with an average of 98 %. There is a range in copper concentrations from 0.04–1.69 % but most analyses are greater than 0.5 %, suggesting deliberate addition. Lead concentrations seem surprisingly low, from 0.006 % to 0.10 % but with the earlier data suggesting slightly higher concentrations.

The unusual drachm in New York (00.999.42388; Fig. 5) with a reverse incuse diagonal cross was probably minted in the years after Series I (though for convenience we have placed it in this series). The diagonal cross was adopted by other island mints in the western Cycladic chain after *c.* 480 BC (see Sheedy 2006, Koressos Series III; Melos Series III). This denomination is otherwise unknown at the mint (weight 5.54 g), but the composition of this one example (Table 1, cat. 6) is consistent with Siphnian silver coins.

Series II (*c.* 475–460 BC; Sheedy 2006, 178–180) began after a break in minting of roughly half a century. The eight surviving didrachm staters (Fig. 6) were minted with four obverse and five reverse dies. The mint in this series showed a greater interest in tetrobols and a range of smaller fractions. FNAA data and previous Specific Gravity (SG) analysis demonstrate that the tetrobol Paris FG 389 is plated (Table 1).[2] The average weight of the staters is slightly lighter than Series I coins (Table 3). This includes the three staters in Sheedy (2006, cat. 19) (Fig. 6) which are all of low weight (and are worn). The concentrations of silver and

---

[2] Analyses of FG 389 by XRF and FNAA have produced data showing very different concentrations of copper (around 15 % and 7 % respectively for XRF and FNAA). Lahanier had measured the specific gravity of this coin using a pycnometer (stated in a report held by the BnF) and he proved that it is around 9.4 kg/m^3. This datum tallies with a 30 % copper concentration if it is hypothesised that FG 389 is made of a binary silver-copper alloy. The discrepancy between the FNAA and the specific gravity may be due to porosities inside the coin as a result of copper corrosion phases leached from the coin. Moreover, the surface of this coin was highly scratched, probably to get rid of corrosion products. These indications lead us to think that FG 389 is a plated coin.

Figure 4. Silver stater (12.35g). Siphnos, c.540-525 BC. New York 1967.152.287. Photo courtesy of the American Numismatic Society

Figure 5. Silver drachm (5.54g). Siphnos, c.525-500 BC (?). New York 0000.999.42399. Photo courtesy of the American Numismatic Society

Figure 6. Silver stater (11.44g). Siphnos, c.475-460 BC. Cambridge, McClean Collection 7286. Photo K.A. Sheedy

trace elements conform to the results for Series I. Series III (c. 460–455 BC; Sheedy 2006, 181) is a brief extension of Series II, and is known only from a small group of obols and hemiobols. The one hemiobol analysed is 97.5 % silver.

The Siphnian silver issues of the fourth century belong to a brief phase of minting c. 375–357 BC (Fig. 2). A small hoard found on Siphnos (*IGCH* 91), dated c. 320–300 BC (and thus well after the minting of silver on the island may have ceased), contained one didrachm (Fig. 7) on the Aeginetan standard (11.02 g) and three tetrobols from Siphnos (Newell 1934; 3, cat. 1–4), all of relatively low weight (Table 3, cf. Table 1, cat. 24–27). Analyses of two

Figure 7. Silver stater (11.09g). Siphnos, late fifth or fourth century BC. New York 1944.100.27959. Photo courtesy of the American Numismatic Society

hoard tetrobols show a change from earlier concentrations as a result of smelting (the gold and bismuth concentrations are as expected): 1944.100.27960 (Newell 1934, cat. 3) has only 94.0 % silver but 4.29 % copper (Table 1, cat. 25) while 1944.100.27961 (Newell 1934, cat. 2) has 95.4 % silver and 3.28 % copper (Table 1, cat. 26). But these are exceptional. In general, slightly higher concentrations of copper exist in all fourth century coins from Siphnos.

CONCLUSIONS

This chapter presents the first comprehensive survey of the composition of the silver issues from Siphnos. These data had been noticeably absent from earlier discussions of the composition of archaic Greek coinage and Greek silver sources in which, paradoxically, there is already widespread speculation regarding the importance of Siphnos. These new analyses have introduced data on elements, mostly notably bismuth, which need to be considered in any discussion of the characteristics of Siphnian silver. Importantly, we have presented the coin analyses within a clearly defined chronology, and provided examples from each phase of minting (of precious metals) on the island. This will facilitate further study of changing practices which altered the purity of the metal.

The gold and silver mines of Siphnos began failing around 525 BC and the island's inhabitants lost their reputation for riches. We might then have expected a decrease in the purity of their silver coins after 525 BC. We can see a progressive lowering of the average weight of the different denominations during the fifth and fourth centuries BC, but the purity of their coins was never really compromised. They preferred to reduce the weights of the issues and to strike plated coins if the silver supplies did not support the intended volume of coinage.

Characterisation of Siphnian silver by Gale *et al.* (1980, 41), on the basis of XRF analyses of 12 Siphnian coins and earlier, by Kraay and Emeleus (1962) using NAA analyses of Aeginetan coins thought to be of Siphnian silver, can be confirmed in most aspects with the notable exception of bismuth. The gold concentration was chiefly 0.005 % to 0.05 % in the extracted silver of Siphnos (Gale *et al.* 1980, 39). The new analyses of the coins, however, consistently showed higher gold concentrations (the great majority fall between 0.01–0.60 %). There is no evidence to support the suggestion of Gale *et al.* (1980, 40) that the concentration of gold falls among coins of the early fifth century BC (or even in later issues). Concentrations of bismuth found in Aeginetan coins believed to be of Siphnian silver were reported to be "relatively higher" than in Laurion silver (Gale *et al.* 1980, 40). We can now see that bismuth in the Siphnian coins we have analysed occurs at approximately the same concentrations reported by Gale *et al.* for the silver of Laurion. Concentrations of copper and lead, as noted above, change with smelting and are a reflection of technology. Copper

ELEMENTAL COMPOSITION OF GOLD AND SILVER COINS OF SIPHNOS

Table 1. Elemental compositions of silver coins. n.r. = element not reported. The column 'Ref' refers to the data sources: (1) Source: M. Cowell, in Gale et al. (1980). Method: XRF spectrometry. (2) Source: Ch. Lahanier, in Gale et al. (1980). Method: XRF spectrometry. (3) Source: Ch. Lahanier, in Pernicka and Wagner 1985a, table 3, 207. Method: XRF spectrometry. (4) Source: this study. Method: XRF spectrometry. (5) Source: this study. Method: LA-ICP-MS. (6) Source: this study. Method: FNAA

Cat.	Denomination/Weight (g)	Ref	Sheedy 2006	Cu (%)	Ag (%)	Au (%)	Pb (%)	Bi (%)
	SERIES I c.540–525 BC							
	Obv.Eaglel Rev. Incuse.							
1	New York 1967.152.287	4	1a	1.43	97.3	0.461	0.121	0.037
2	London RPK.p101A.1. Ses. (BMC1)	4	2a	0.796	98.3	0.385	0.006	0.024
2	London RPK.p101A.1.Ses. (BMC1)	1	2a	1.1	98.4	0.2	0.3	n.r.
3	Cambridge McClean 7285	4	2b	1.18	97.5	0.389	0.017	0.082
4	Paris Delepierre 2457	2	4	1.1	98.2	0.61	0.1	n.r.
4	Paris Delepierre 2457	5	4	1.3	98.2	0.2718	0.0542	0.1457
5	London G.4269. (BMC2)	4	8	1.69	96.6	0.577	0.105	0.072
5	London G.4269. (BMC2)	1	8	2.5	96.6	0.55	0.3	n.r.
6	New York 0000.999.42399	4	—	0.271	99.3	0.067	0.137	0.037
7	New York 1944.100.27957	4	10	0.355	98.0	0.281	0.066	0.015
8	London 1878-0301.230. (BMC3)	4	11	0.107	98.8	0.077	0.025	0.002
8	London 1878-0301.230. (BMC3)	1	11	1.3	98.0	0.37	0.3	n.r.
	SERIES II c.475–460 BC							
	Obv.Head of Apollol							
	Rev. Eagle.							
9	Paris FG 388	4	14	0.135	98.0	0.007	0.123	0.001
9	Paris FG 388	2	14	0.32	99.1	0.18	0.39	n.r.
9	Paris FG 388	5	14	0.02	99.5	0.0072	0.4309	0.0003
10	London 1845,0109.7. (BM 4)	4	16	0.040	97.8	0.013	1.35	0.016
10	London 1845,0109.7. (BM 4)	1	16	0.1	97.9	0.02	2.0	n.r.
11	Paris de Luynes 2381	2	17	0.43	97.7	0.1	1.8	n.r.
11	Paris de Luynes 2381	5	17	0.15	98.5	0.0591	1.2280	0.0947
12	Cambridge McClean 7286	4	19b	0.719	98.4	0.022	0.090	0.086
13	Athens (Kambanis)	4	19c	0.494	94.3	0.035	0.064	0.062
14	London 1950,0401.8.	4	20	0.051	98.8	0.012	0.443	0.038
14	London 1950,0401.8.	1	20	0.2	98.5	0.06	1.3	n.r.
15	London 1841.B.2173. (BM 6)	4	21	0.058	98.5	0.021	0.573	0.037
15	London 1841.B.2173. (BM 6)	1	21	0.2	98.6	0.08	1.1	n.r.
16	New York 1944.100.27958	4	22e	0.412	95.7	0.023	0.856	0.017
17	London EH.p471.Sic. (BM 5)	4	25	0.522	98.5	0.131	0.100	0.002
17	London EH.p471.Sic. (BM 5)	1	25	0.25	99.3	0.07	0.4	n.r.
18	London 1949,0411.707	4	28	0.096	98.2	0.058	0.619	0.031
19	Paris FG 390	4	29iv	0.116	97.5	0.025	1.56	0.022

Cat.	Denomination/Weight (g)
1	Stater, 12.35
2	Stater, 12.77
2	Stater, 12.77
3	Stater, 12.07
4	Stater, 11.45
4	Stater, 11.45
5	Stater, 11.12
5	Stater, 11.12
6	Drachm, 5.54
7	Hemidrachm, 2.95
8	Hemidrachm, 2.88
8	Hemidrachm, 2.88
9	Stater, 11.90
9	Stater, 11.90
9	Stater, 11.90
10	Stater, 12.08
10	Stater, 12.08
11	Stater, 12.05
11	Stater, 12.05
12	Stater, 11.44
13	Stater, 11.19
14	Tetrobol, 3.66
14	Tetrobol, 3.66
15	Tetrobol, 3.71
15	Tetrobol, 3.71
16	Tetrobol, 3.82
17	Tetrobol, 3.97
17	Tetrobol, 3.97
18	Trihemiobol; 1.43
19	Hemiobol; 0.52

Table 1. *Continued.*

Cat.		Denomination/Weight (g)	Ref	Sheedy 2006	Cu (%)	Ag (%)	Au (%)	Pb (%)	Bi (%)
20	New York 1967.152.288	Tetartemorion; 0.30	4	31i	0.076	97.8	0.012	0.933	0.013
21	Oxford	Tetartemorion; 0.31	4	31iii	0.184	97.6	0.024	1.13	0.015
	SERIES III c.460-455 BC								
	Obv. Head of Artemis/								
	Rev. Eagle.								
22	Paris FG 391	Obol, 0.84	4	32	0.190	99.1	0.049	0.206	0.009
22	Paris FG 391	Obol, 0.84	5	32	0.1	99.35	0.0409	0.3694	0.0125
	SERIES IV 4th CENTURY BC								
	Obv. Head of Apollo/Rev. Eagle.								
23	London 1887,1003.5	Tetrobol; 3.72	4		1.35	97.6	0.431	0.056	0.008
23	London 1887,1003.5	Tetrobol; 3.72	1		1.5	97.9	0.35	0.3	n.r.
24	New York 1944.100.27959 (Hoard)	Stater, 11.09	4		0.485	97.8	0.580	0.060	0.003
25	New York 1944.100.27960 (Hoard)	Tetrobol; 3.47	4		4.30	94.0	0.306	0.304	0.012
26	New York 1944.100.27961 (Hoard)	Tetrobol; 3.34	4		3.28	95.4	0.210	0.352	0.013
27	New York 1944.100.27962 (Hoard)	Tetrobol; 3.68	4		0.907	97.6	0.356	0.597	0.013
28	London 1949,0411.706	Tetrobol; 3.52	1		2.0	97.8	0.5	0.3	n.r.
	GOLD ISSUE								
	c.375-357 BC								
29	Berlin 18207419	Drachm, 4.295	4		0.677	2.29	96.4	<0.001	0.013
	PLATED COINS								
30	Paris FG 387	Stater, 11.65	3	9	20.5	n.r.	0.22	0.1	n.r.
30	Paris FG 387	Stater, 11.65	6	9	80.3	19.3	0.053	0.05	n.r.
31	Paris FG 389	Tetrobol; 2.95	3	27a	15.1	n.r.	0.1	1.24	n.r.
31	Paris FG 389	Tetrobol; 2.95	6	27a	6.8	92.3	<0.01	0.59	n.r.

Table 2. XRF measurement conditions. Current was set automatically, increasing until the instrument could not count further X-rays (typically around 100,000 counts per second); typical currents are shown. "Time" is the period the spectrometer counted X-rays (also known as "live time"). Filter compositions and thicknesses (μm) are given

Elements	Voltage (kV)	Current (μA)	Time (s)	Filter (μm)	Detector mode
Ag	50	266	120	Cu 300	Normal
Cu, Au, Pb, Bi	50	300	120	Ag 100	Normal

Table 3. Weights (g) of Siphnian coins (Sheedy 2006)

Coin weights (g)	Series I	Series II	Series III	4th century BC
Staters				
Above 12.40	xx			
12.31-40	xxxx			
12.21-30	xx			
12.11-20	x			
12.01-10	x	xxx		
11.91-12.00	x	x		
11.81-90				
11.71-80				
11.61-70	x			
11.51-60	xx	x		
Below 11.50	xxx	xxx		x (11.02)
Tetrobols				
3.91-4.00		xxx		
3.81-90		xxxx		
3.71-80		x		X
3.61-70		xx		X
3.51-60		xxx		
Below 3.50		x (plated)		XX
Hemidrachms				
2.90-3.00	xx			
2.80-90	x			
Obols				
0.81-90			xxx	
Hemiobols				
0.61-70		xxx		
0.51-0.60		xxxx		
Below 0.50			x	
Tetartemoria				
0.31-40		x		
0.21-30		xx		

was evidently added, perhaps from the start, but it is worth repeating that the purity of the island's silver coinage was maintained.

It has been pointed out that the scale of minting on Siphnos does not seem to match the island's reputed wealth (at least in the sixth century BC) from its mines (Price 1980, 51: "the coinage of the island is insignificant"). It is likely that the Siphnians only minted coin when there were local payments (distribution of profits?) to be made in coin and that otherwise precious metal was exported as bullion (Sheedy 2006, 54–57). Part of the mined ores was crushed and refined on Siphnos and it was here that it was smelted. This metal was used, among other purposes, for the production of local coinage. The absence of slags, however, appears to suggest that Siphnos exported the greater part of its gold and silver rich ores, after beneficiation, to be refined elsewhere.

REFERENCES

Aitchison, J. 1986. *The statistical analysis of compositional data.* (New York).
Bassiakos, I., Georgakopoulou, M. and Wagner G.A. 2013. Οι νέες αρχαιομεταλλουργικές μελέτες στη Σίφνο, *Πρακτικά Δ΄ Διεθνούς Σιφναϊκού Συμποσίου, Σίφνος, 25–26 Ιουνίου 2010* (Athens), 45–64.
Bent, J.T. 1885. 'On the Gold and Silver Mines of Siphnos', *JHS* 6, 195–198.
Beer, L. 1980. 'Analysis of Coins from the Asyut Hoard. An introduction', in Metcalf, D.M. and Oddy, W.A. (eds.), *Metallurgy in Numismatics*, vol. 1 (London), 1–2.
Birkett-Smith, J. 2000. 'On the Towers and Mines of Siphnos', in *Πρακτικά Α΄ Διεθνούς Σιφναϊκού Συμποσίου, Σίφνος, 25–28 Ιουνίου 1998*, vol. 1 (Athens), 279–294.
Birkett-Smith, J. 2006. 'The Modern Mines of Sifnos', In *Πρακτικά Β΄ Διεθνούς Σιφναϊκού Συμποσίου, Σίφνος, 27–30 Ιουνίου 2002*, vol. 3 (Athens), 173–188.
Brun, P. 2000. 'La prospérité après la richesse: Siphnos classique et hellénistique (V-II siècles Av. J.C.)', in *Πρακτικά Α΄ Διεθνούς Σιφναϊκού Συμποσίου, Σίφνος, 25–28 Ιουνίου 1998*, vol. 1 (Athens), 227–238.
Dressel, H. 1898. 'Fortsetzung des Erwerbungsberichts', *ZfN* 21, 210–249.
Étienne, R. 1990. *Ténos II: Ténos et les Cyclades du milieu du IVe siècle av J.-C. au milieu du IIIe siècle ap. J.-C.* (Bibliothèques des Ecoles françaises d'Athènes et de Rome 263 bis. Athens and Paris).
Gale, N.H., Gentner, W. and Wagner, G.A. 1980. 'Mineralogical and geographical silver sources of archaic Greek coinage', in Metcalf, D.M. and Oddy, W.A. (eds.), *Metallurgy in Numismatics*, vol. 1 (London), 3–49.
Gardner, P. 1913. 'Coinage of the Athenian Empire', *JHS* 33, 147–188.
Gitler, H., Ponting, M. and Tal, O. 2009. 'Athenian Tetradrachms from Tel Mikhal (Israel): A Metallurgical Perspective', *AJN* 21, 29–49.
Gore, D.B. and Davis, G. 2016. 'Suitability of transportable EDXRF for the on-site assessment of ancient silver coins and other silver artifacts', *Applied Spectroscopy* 70(5), 840–851.
Guerra, M. F., and Barrandon, J.-N. 1998. 'Ion Beam Activation Analysis with a Cyclotron', in Oddy, W.A., and Cowell, M.R. (eds.), *Metallurgy in Numismatics*. Vol. 4 (London), 15–34.
Kraay, C.M. 1962. *The Composition of Greek Silver Coins: analysis by neutron activation.* With a chapter by V.M. Emeleus (Oxford).
L'Héritier, M., Baron, S., Cassayre, L. and Téreygeol, F. 2015. 'Bismuth behaviour during ancient processes of silver–lead production', *Journal of Archaeological Science* 57, 56–68.
Matthäus, H. 1985. 'Sifnos im Altertum', in Wagner and Weisgerber (eds.) 1985, 17–58.
Newell, E.T. 1934. *A Hoard from Siphnos. NNM 64* (New York).
Meyers, P. 2003. 'Production of Silver in Antiquity: Ore Types Identified Based upon Elemental Compositions of Ancient Silver Artifacts', in Van Zelst, L. (ed.), *Patterns and Process: A Festschrift in Honor of Dr. Edward V. Sayre* (Suitland), 271–288.
Pernicka, E., Lutz, C., Bachmann, H.-G., Wagner, G.A., Elitzsch, C. and Klein, E. 1985, 'Alte Blei-Silber-Verhüttung auf Sifnos', in Wagner and Weisgerber 1985a, 185-199.
Pernicka, E. and Wagner, G.A. 1985a. 'Die metallurgische Bedeutung von Sifnos im Altertum', in Wagner and Weisgerber 1985a, 200–211.
Pernicka, E. and Wagner, G.A. 1985b. 'Alte Goldgruben auf Sifnos', in Wagner and Weisgerber 1985a, 174–184.
Price, M.J. 1980. 'The Uses of Metal Analyses in the Study of Archaic Greek Coinage: Some Comments' in Metcalf, D.M. and Oddy, W.A. (eds.), *Metallurgy in Numismatics* vol. 1 (London), 3–49.
Price, M. and Waggoner, N. 1975. *Archaic Greek Silver Coinage. The 'Asyut' Hoard* (London).
Robinson, E.S.G. 1960. 'Some Problems in the Later Fifth Century Coinage of Athens', *ANSMN* 9, 1–15.
Roche, V., Laurent, V., Cardello, G.L., Jolivet, L. and Scaillet, S. 2016. 'Anatomy of the Cycladic Blueschist Unit on Sifnos Island (Cyclades, Greece)', *Journal of Geodynamics* 97, 62–87.
Rollinson, H.R. 1992. 'Another look at the constant sum problem in geochemistry.' *Mineral Magazine* 56, 469–475.
Rutishauser, B. 2012. *Athens and the Cyclades: economic strategies 540-314 BC* (Oxford).
Sarah, G., and Gratuze, B. 2016. 'LA-ICP-MS Analysis of Ancient Silver Coins Using Concentration Profiles', in Dussubieux, L., Golitko, M., and Gratuze, B. (eds.), *Recent Advances in Laser Ablation ICP-MS for Archaeology* (Berlin Heidelberg), 73–87.
Sarah, G., Gratuze, B., and Barrandon, J.-N. 2007. 'Application of Laser Ablation Inductively Coupled Plasma Mass Spectrometry (LA-ICP-MS) for the Investigation of Ancient Silver Coins', *Journal of Analytical Atomic Spectrometry* 22(9), 1163–1167.
Sheedy, K.A. 2000. 'The Richest of the Islanders', in *Πρακτικά Α΄ Διεθνούς Σιφναϊκού Συμποσίου, Σίφνος, 25–28 Ιουνίου 1998*, vol. 1 (Athens), 219–226.
Sheedy, K.A. 2006. *The Archaic and Early Classical Coinages of the Cyclades. Special Publications No. 40* (London).

van Alfen, P.G. 2005. 'Problems in ancient imitative and counterfeit coinage', in Archibald, Z.H. Davies, J.K. and Gabrielsen, V. (eds.) *Making, Moving and Managing: the new world of ancient economies* (Oxford), 322–354.

Vavelidis, M. 1997. 'Au-bearing quartz veins and placer gold on Sifnos island, Aegean Sea, Greece', in Papunen, H. (ed.), *Mineral Deposits: Research and Exploration.* (Rotterdam), 335–338.

Vavelidis, M., Bassiakos, I., Begemann, F., Patriacheas, K., Pernika, E., Schmidt-Strecker, S. and Wagner, G.A., 'Geologie und Erzvorkommen', in Wagner and Weisgerber 1985a, 59–80.

Waggoner, N. 1983. *Early Greek coins from the collection of Jonathan P. Rosen. Ancient coins in North American collections* (New York).

Wagner, G.A. 2000. 'Ancient Gold and Silver Mines of Sifnos', in Πρακτικά Α´ Διεθνούς Σιφναϊκού Συμποσίου, Σίφνος, 25–28 Ιουνίου 1998, vol. 1 (Athens), 147–164.

Wagner, G.A., Gentner, N., Gropengiesser, H. and Gale, N.H. 1980. 'Early Bronze Age lead-silver mining and metallurgy in the Aegean: The ancient workings on Siphnos', in Craddock, P.T. (ed.), *Scientific Studies in Early Mining and Extractive Metallurgy. Occasional Paper No. 20.* (London), 63–86.

Wagner, G.A. and Weisgerber, G. (eds.) 1985a. *Silber, Blei und Gold auf Siphnos. Prähistorische und antike Metallproduktion. Der Anschnitt Beih.3* (Bochum).

Wagner, G.A. and Weisgerber, G. 1985b. 'Andere Blei-Silbergruben auf Sifnos', in Wagner and Weisgerber 1985a, 159–173.

Wallace, W.P. 1956. *The Euboian League and its Coinage* (Numismatic Notes and Monographs 134. New York).

Weisgerber, G. 1985. 'Die Blei- und Silbergruben von Agios Sostis', in Wagner and Weisgerber 1985a, 113–158.

11. THE GOLD OF THE LYDIANS

Paul Craddock and Nicholas Cahill

ABSTRACT

Continuing archaeological and survey work at Sardis have radically changed our perception of the nature of the production of the first coinage and of the famous gold refinery situated there. Geological survey work has shown that the Pactolus gold was almost pure and thus initially would have required no refining. In fact, when the local gold source was exhausted it would have made the development of a refining technique to deal with gold from elsewhere, including scrap gold, imperative. The process of exposing finely divided gold to acid salts was not very different from the existing practice of the surface treatment of gold artefacts. When applied to thin gold foils this would have completely removed the silver and copper, being in effect a refining process. The Lydian achievement was to turn an enhancement technique into an industrial refining process. Recent archaeological work has also required a radical reassessment of the refinery itself. It is now known that in fact it lay outside the city walls and is likely to have been operational for only a short period in the second quarter of the sixth century BC (probably as a private enterprise, principally refining recalled coins and other scrap gold).

INTRODUCTION

The publication of *King Croesus' Gold* (Ramage and Craddock 2000) on the refining of gold at Sardis and the introduction of coinage left some important questions unresolved. In particular, the question of whether the gold in the Electrum series of coins had been refined prior to alloying with silver remained uncertain. Further research and discoveries have not only suggested answers to some of these questions but have also led to a substantial revision of many of our assumptions and perceptions. These concern not only the nature of the Sardis gold itself but also the very function, date and position of the Lydian refinery at Sardis.

THE PROCESS OF REFINING GOLD

The understanding of the actual technology of the gold refining process as practised at the refinery is unchanged from the original publication (Figs. 1 and 2) (Craddock 2000a; Geçkinli 2000 *et al*) Kleber 2020 discusses Mesopotamian antecedents to the technology. Silver-rich gold including, perhaps, both freshly mined gold dust and granules as well as scrap gold and electrum coins beaten into foils would have been placed in earthenware pots, together with salt and powdered brick or clay to act both as a support for keeping the gold dispersed and to provide a source of iron oxides necessary for the process to proceed (Fig. 3). Some of the chloride ions in the vapour would react with the iron oxides in the clay to produce the volatile and highly astringent ferric chloride ($FeCl_3$), which was probably the major reagent in the refining process, attacking the silver in the gold. A wood fire burned in the furnace and the flames would have been able to lick all around the pot sat on its pedestal ensuring even heating from all sides (Fig. 3). For parting to succeed it was essential that the gold and the salt were as hot as possible in order for the salt to vaporise but not so hot that the gold melted and coagulated into a puddle at the base of the pot which would have left only a small surface exposed to the salt vapours. The pots never exceeded 800°C and the process may well have been somewhat cooler. Periodically foils would have been removed from the pots and tested to ascertain the progress of the parting. This would have been done by touchstone (Craddock 2000b). In mediaeval and later times the parting process was carried on for several hours at least, a process going on through the course of a night was not uncommon. Modern reconstruction experiments confirm that several hours are required. At the conclusion of the process the gold was physically removed from the pot and melted in separate crucibles (the gold could not be melted in the parting vessel, the fabric of which was laden with silver salts which would have re-entered the gold).

The chemistry of the process can be reconstructed from the excavated remains (Craddock 2000a). The burning wood created a hot damp atmosphere which was able to permeate the earthenware vessels. There it was able to react with the salt and iron salts in the brick dust and earthenware creating an extremely astringent vapour of hydrogen chloride, chlorine and ferric chloride (Craddock 2000c).

Figure 1. The bases of two typical brick-built parting furnaces at the Sardis refinery with openings and central plinths.

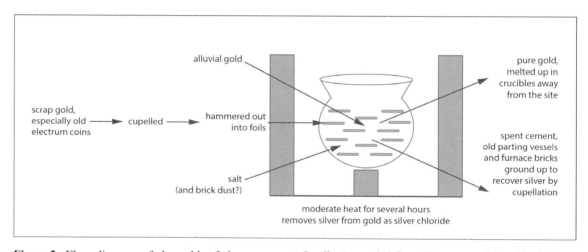

Figure 2. Flow diagram of the gold refining process at Sardis. (amended from Ramage and Craddock 2000, Fig. 10.2)

THE CONTEXT

Our research into the nature of the refining process originally assumed that the Pactolus gold would have contained appreciable quantities of silver as is usual in gold deposits around the world (Wise 1964, 20; Hannington *et al.* 2016). This assumption was supported by existing analyses of gold flakes that were thought to have been panned from the Pactolus, and found to contain appreciable quantities of silver. The samples were analysed by neutron activation at the Cekmece Nuclear Research Center, Istanbul in 1968 who reported that "ore from the Pactolus has been found to have a silver content of 17–24%". This information is

Figure 3. Section through a typical Lydian earthenware cooking pot used as a parting vessel with layers of gold and the parting cement. (from Ramage and Craddock 2000, Fig. 4.31)

Figure 4. Reconstruction: A typical Lydian earthenware cooking pot similar to the type that would have been used for the gold cementation set on the central plinth of one of the parting furnaces at Sardis. (from Ramage and Craddock 2000, 5.3)

from an unpublished report by S. M. Goldstein, quoted by J.C. Waldbaum (1983, 186). Furthermore, a large granule (Sample 30A) found at the refinery and assumed by us, almost certainly wrongly as it turns out, to have come from the Pactolus, was found to actually be two granules (the larger containing 29.8% of silver, and the other 16.2%). However, the original packet of gold flakes was found at the Manisa Museum twenty years later and they were found to be almost pure gold (Geçkinli *et al.* 2001; Geçkinli 2008). It was concluded that there had been a muddling of samples and these must be flakes of refined gold. Another disquieting discovery was a flake of pure gold, this time actually imbedded within one of the crucible fragments (sherd 45676T: Ramage and Craddock 2000, 114, fig. 5.19). It was argued that this crucible must have been made at the refinery and a refined flake had become accidentally incorporated.

As it was believed that the Pactolus gold had a considerable but variable silver content, the next question was how had the constant alloy of the electrum coins been achieved? The electrum series coins typically contain approximately 55% of gold and 45% of silver together with minor amounts of copper (Cowell *et al* 1998; Cowell and Hyne 2000). This could be achieved in two ways: by determining the silver content of each batch of freshly mined gold with a touchstone and then adding additional silver in sufficient quantities to bring the content up to the required 45% or, alternatively, by purifying the gold and then adding 45% of silver. There was a potential method of checking this. The intrinsic silver in the natural gold is not accompanied by lead, but silver smelted from its ores invariably contains substantial traces of lead (Craddock 1995, 211-14; Konuk 2016). Thus, if all of the silver had been added to the gold then the lead content should be markedly higher than if only a proportion had been added. At the time of the original analytical work for the 2000 publication, non-destructive analysis was done by X-ray fluorescence which was not capable of quantifying small traces of lead. Subsequently, a small selection of both the electrum and Croeseid coins from the Cabinet de Médailles, Bibliothèque Nationale de France were analysed at the Laboratoire des Musées de France at the Palais de Louvre by proton induced X-ray emission (PIXE; see Table 1; cf. Craddock *et al.* 2005). This showed the lead content was sufficiently high to indicate that all of the silver must have been added, which was taken at the time as an indication that the gold had been refined prior to alloying. Further analyses have shown that the lead content of Lydian coins varies more widely from low to high (Blet-Lemarquand and Duyrat 2020).

There was another possibility that had been briefly considered but rejected - that the gold had been intrinsically pure. However, over the past decades geological sampling of deposits in the Sardis area has produced many flakes of gold. One sample was panned from the Pactolus river, while others came from streambeds within 3.5-5 km of the site, and from excavation into the slopes of the Necropolis hill east of the site. In addition, the Pomza Export mining company is currently extracting gold and other minerals from the conglomerate of the site; they and other Turkish geologists report that there is gold but no silver. A selection of these samples have been analysed by scanning electron microscopy with energy dispersive x-ray micro-analytical facilities (SEM/EDS) and by laser-ablated induced coupled plasma mass spectrometry (LA-ICP-MS), showing that the gold is substantially pure (Table 2; Cahill *et al.* 2020).

This has important implications for the origins of gold refining generally, but also more specifically for the genesis of the first coinage and for the role and function of the Lydian gold refinery at Sardis. Clearly, all the original assumptions were incorrect. Extraordinary though it seems, the Lydian refinery was not treating the gold from the Pactolus that flows alongside (Craddock 2016). In fact, as discussed below, it is likely that the Pactolus North refinery was a small-scale operation mainly treating scrap gold.

There are a number of possible interpretations now for the inception of coinage and refining. It could be argued that the pure local Sardis gold was the Lydian's easy route to coinage. The concept of coins guarantees both the weight and purity of the precious metal. Most gold deposits have variable but significant silver contents, which the coin-issuing authority must be able to control by refining to remove the silver, or by adding silver to achieve a consistent composition. At Sardis, at least initially, this was not the case. Their natural gold was pure and could be alloyed straight away to produce the electrum coins. Continuing this somewhat simplistic line of thought, the later Croeseid coins of pure gold should just have been of untreated Sardis gold, but this seems not to have been the case.

Table 1. PIXIE analyses of electrum and Croeseid coins now in the Cabinet de Médailles, Paris. Note the high concentration of platinum and ruthenium but the low concentration of mercury. Figures in ppm (from Craddock et al. 2005)

BNF Ref.	%Au	%Ag	%Cu	As	Cr	Fe	Hg	Pd	Pb	Pt	Ru	Sb	Sn	Ti	Zn
Electrum Issues															
22	51.0	46.2	2.4	15	<1	377	<1	1106	9	41	<1	12	1860	6	11
23	55.6	42.1	2.0	16	<1	600	876	1139	9	255	<1	10	529	3	16
24	57.0	40.9	1.9	8	<1	324	<1	1202	6	43	<1	10	203	19	26
25	77.1	19.9	1.1	26	<1	829	<1	2042	34	1860	12933	6	1009	12	1
26	55.8	42.3	1.8	9	9	428	9	675	<1	84	<1	5	269	7	9
Electrum Issues															
526	99.3	0.3	<0.03	1	2	327	<1	66	62	2592	292	0.2	<1	4	15
527	98.0	1.6	0.03	3	5	247	<1	156	55	2858	562	1	23	5	78
528	99.2	0.5	0.04	<1	<1	460	<1	104	<1	204	802	<1	65	13	26
529	98.1	1.0	0.10	4	16	261	<1	49	36	2865	4499	<1	25	5	16
532	99.4	0.3	0.20	<1	<1	287	18	27	<1	446	38	3	65	7	11
533	99.2	0.5	0.30	6	3	123	<1	157	<0.4	<1	<1	1	18	3	13
537	98.3	1.2	0.20	<1	<1	255	<1	74	<1	1229	1148	<1	37	6	47

Table 2. LA-ICP-MS analysis of a selection of gold flakes from the Sardis area. A) bulk elements in %. (from Cahill et al. 2020)

	Sample	Au	Ag	Cu	Fe
Emiroğlu	1	98.70%	0.27%	0.07%	0.83%
	2	98.58%	0.73%	0.02%	0.60%
	3	99.00%	0.57%	0.01%	0.37%
	4	99.25%	0.20%	0.00%	0.52%
	5	98.61%	0.73%	0.00%	0.58%
	Avg.	98.83%	0.50%	0.02%	0.58%
	Std. Dev.	0.29%	0.25%	0.03%	0.17%
Tirebolu	6	98.66%	0.64%	0.08%	0.03%
	7	97.16%	1.38%	0.92%	0.14%
	8	96.00%	0.95%	0.64%	0.05%
	9	94.87%	4.34%	0.03%	0.10%
	10	98.08%	1.55%	0.02%	0.17%
	Avg.	96.95%	1.77%	0.34%	0.10%
	Std. Dev.	1.54%	1.48%	0.42%	0.06%
Ventilation Gallery	12	99.18%	0.20%	0.01%	0.44%
	13	97.89%	1.64%	0.01%	0.18%
	14	98.77%	0.65%	0.01%	0.34%
	15	97.49%	1.51%	0.19%	0.56%
	16	98.43%	0.58%	0.01%	0.40%
	17	98.76%	0.48%	0.00%	0.65%
	Avg.	98.27%	0.97%	0.05%	0.43%
	Std. Dev.	0.56%	0.56%	0.08%	0.19%

Comparing the trace element content of the admittedly very small number of electrum and Croeseid coins from the Louvre (Table 1) with the trace elements found in the flakes (Table 3) is instructive. Both the electrum coins and the flakes are comparatively pure, although certainly not identical. The trace element content of the Croeseids is much higher, especially in the platinum group elements, which even on the very small sample of coins strongly suggests a different source of gold. The traces of mercury found in some of the recently panned flakes would have been largely reduced or removed in the refining processes. Thus the scenario could be that the Sardis gold was used to make the electrum coins by simple dilution. This source soon proved inadequate to meet the demand and gold from other sources and scrap gold had to be used. This gold all contained varying amounts of silver necessitating the urgent development of gold refining techniques on an industrial scale.

There are other possibilities. It does seem perverse that at the outset the first coins are of an alloy of gold and silver if the gold that was used for them was pure – surely the first coinage would have been of pure gold. If, instead, other sources of gold had been used then they would have required refining. Much has been made of gold refining as a major breakthrough; conceptually it was, but the technology was already largely in place.

Almost from the inception of the use of gold, the surfaces of gold artefacts had been treated to remove the silver naturally occurring in gold (Craddock 2000d; Kleber 2020), as exemplified by much of the gold work from Ur in the third millennium BC (La Niece 1995). There is no direct evidence of how this was done in antiquity, but in the recent past, gold artefacts were coated with a poultice of wet clay mixed with the salts of mineral acids, such as alum (potassium aluminium sulphate), saltpetre (potassium nitrate) or common salt (sodium chloride). This was gently heated for some time and the anion, be it sulphate, nitrate or chloride would preferentially attack the silver to form the soluble silver salt which would be absorbed by the poultice. The removal of the silver would leave the surface pure but rather matt and porous such that burnishing and polishing would be required to create a

Table 3. LA-ICP-MS analysis of a selection of gold flakes from the Sardis area. Trace elements in parts per million. Note the high concentration of mercury but the low concentration of platinum group elements (from Cahill *et al.* 2020)

	Sample	Ti	Cr	Mn	Co	(Ni)	Zn	As	Se	(Ru)	Rh
Emiroğlu	1	75.87	6.03	731.07	11.94	(3.71)	133.65	11.76	20.75	(0.01)	0.01
	2	238.11	7.03	224.80	3.08	(3.60)	27.33	6.05	0.00	(0.00)	0.01
	3	30.03	2.33	45.42	1.89	(0.97)	8.70	21.36	0.00	(0.01)	0.00
	4	67.65	2.81	103.85	2.34	(1.12)	6.22	11.49	0.00	(0.00)	0.01
	5	45.89	176.13	282.82	3.24	(4.00)	8.11	6.45	0.00	(0.00)	0.00
	AVG	91.51	38.87	277.59	4.50	(2.68)	36.80	11.42	4.15	(0.01)	0.01
	Std. Dev.	83.91	76.76	270.44	4.20	(1.50)	54.81	6.18	9.28	(0.00)	0.00
Tirebolu	6	6.24	1.11	3.14	0.09	(0.14)	7.34	0.00	8.31	(0.13)	0.09
	7	232.91	4.32	7.75	0.41	(0.37)	26.99	7.44	6.19	(0.16)	0.20
	8	17.66	1.40	4.17	0.28	(0.18)	10.66	1.07	0.00	(0.06)	0.10
	9	26.54	1.73	4.37	0.34	(0.42)	14.58	0.00	0.00	(0.10)	0.08
	10	74.86	3.64	33.72	0.86	(0.48)	37.41	0.87	0.00	(0.03)	0.05
	AVG	71.64	2.44	10.63	0.40	(0.32)	19.40	1.88	2.90	(0.10)	0.10
	Std. Dev.	93.87	1.44	13.02	0.29	(0.15)	12.52	3.15	4.04	(0.05)	0.06
Vent. Gallery	12	123.32	3.91	52.68	7.36	(1.21)	39.33	467.90	0.00	(0.04)	0.05
	13	68.95	2.24	465.65	9.27	(0.88)	17.49	0.00	0.00	(0.02)	0.03
	14	223.15	8.25	640.62	17.90	(1.44)	33.71	6.87	5.22	(0.03)	0.03
	15	571.71	4.43	341.39	5.64	(1.15)	41.60	5.09	2.07	(0.00)	0.02
	16	3021.06	10.52	984.13	18.84	(1.30)	59.95	0.00	2.97	(0.03)	0.02
	17	125.13	3.36	83.40	2.91	(0.69)	104.74	4.01	0.00	(0.01)	0.01
	AVG	802.00	5.76	503.04	10.91	(1.09)	51.50	3.19	2.05	(0.02)	0.02
	Std. Dev.	1255.77	3.49	336.90	7.18	(0.31)	33.46	3.09	2.20	(0.01)	0.01
	Sample	Pd	In	Sn	Sb	Os	Ir	Pt	Hg	Pb	Bi
Emiroğlu	1	0.30	(169.14)	1.60	4.03	(0.00)	(0.04)	0.08	173.14	33.00	0.13
	2	0.07	(20.46)	2.05	2.51	(0.00)	(0.01)	0.03	143.53	46.92	0.09
	3	0.06	(5.05)	1.04	0.86	(0.00)	(0.01)	0.03	366.98	22.31	0.03
	4	0.17	(1.28)	0.80	1.19	(0.00)	(0.00)	0.05	104.89	15.97	0.02
	5	0.10	(1.45)	0.57	1.34	(0.00)	(0.00)	0.02	265.89	17.89	0.17
	AVG	0.14	(39.48)	1.21	1.99	(0.00)	(0.01)	0.04	210.89	27.22	0.09
	Std. Dev.	0.10	(72.91)	0.60	1.30	(0.00)	(0.02)	0.02	105.58	12.84	0.07
Tirebolu	6	0.40	(1.38)	0.14	0.81	(1.91)	(0.15)	0.19	5400.71	487.94	0.19
	7	0.81	(0.13)	0.27	2.67	(9.46)	(0.38)	0.36	2794.15	924.02	0.92
	8	1.22	(0.09)	0.21	1.17	(1.22)	(0.16)	0.27	22686.62	753.62	0.41
	9	0.08	(0.38)	0.17	1.61	(0.55)	(0.00)	0.14	5495.20	1070.60	6.51
	10	0.18	(0.00)	0.65	2.89	(0.59)	(0.00)	0.17	980.39	671.36	0.79
	AVG	0.54	(0.40)	0.29	1.83	(2.75)	(0.14)	0.22	7471.41	781.51	1.77
	Std. Dev.	0.47	(0.57)	0.21	0.91	(3.79)	(0.16)	0.09	8713.58	225.27	2.67
Vent. Gallery	12	0.53	(0.34)	0.19	45.64	(1.87)	(0.06)	0.31	439.81	458.67	0.29
	13	8.70	(0.12)	0.23	11.33	(0.58)	(0.20)	0.28	1307.91	881.45	0.07
	14	0.30	(0.14)	0.46	6.86	(0.15)	(0.11)	0.07	966.31	425.64	0.30
	15	0.43	(0.04)	0.43	3.50	(0.00)	(0.00)	0.02	1094.44	380.49	0.23
	16	0.33	(0.14)	1.97	6.43	(0.46)	(0.05)	0.17	692.37	1033.70	0.31
	17	0.12	(0.12)	0.15	2.27	(0.00)	(0.01)	0.03	339.58	376.97	0.41
	AVG	1.98	(0.11)	0.65	6.08	(0.24)	(0.07)	0.11	880.12	619.65	0.26
	Std. Dev.	3.76	(0.04)	0.75	3.52	(0.27)	(0.08)	0.11	375.43	313.73	0.13

surface of pure shining gold. Recent work on some Egyptian statuary of the Third Intermediate Period (900-600 BC) has shown that the gold foils which frequently cover the surfaces are often of pure gold (Craddock forthcoming). Egypt had ample gold resources, and as these all contain substantial quantities of silver it is very likely that the gold of the foils must have been treated to remove it. Probably this was not intended as a true refining to create a foil of pure gold, but rather this was the standard surface enhancement treatment. When carried out on a thin foil (typical thickness about 2–3 microns, 0.002–0.003 mm) it had the effect of actually removing all the silver throughout the thickness. The surface enhancement by removing all of the silver from the foil had actually refined it. The Lydian achievement was to turn an enhancement technique into an industrial refining process.

The Pactolus is certainly the most famous source of gold, not least because the river flowed through the centre of the Lydian capital, and the association of the gold's origin with the Midas legend, but there were other sources within the boundaries of the Lydian Empire. The first Lydian king, Gyges, who reigned from about 680–644 BC, was famous for his gold, made great dedications at Delphi and elsewhere. He also controlled the Troad, where the famous gold mines of Astyra and Cremaste (mentioned by both Xenophon and Strabo) were located. The city of Daskyleion is rich in Lydian pottery of this period, and was apparently named after Gyges' father. Croesus was governor of Adramytteion, another Lydian city in the Troad, and the Lydians worked gold mines between Pergamon and Atarneus. Northwest Anatolia was of primary strategic importance to the Lydians throughout their history, and many modern gold mines are located in this region, particularly at Narlıca, Ovacık, Kartaldağ and Madendağ and other sites near Balikesir. These mines contain substantial quantities of silver. The grains of gold from Ovacık, for example, contain about 72% gold and 25% silver.

Alternatively, we suggest, therefore, that the electrum for the earliest Lydian coins came not from Sardis, but from northwest Anatolia, and that the early Lydian kings wanted to control that area because of its gold mines. Coinage is a result of Lydian imperialism, and it was invented in the seventh century BC because that is the first time in history that western Anatolia was subject to a single imperial powers, as argued in Cahill *et al.* 2020.

This is not to say that gold from the Pactolus was unimportant. But at this early stage it may not have been used for coins, since it *could* be used in that traditional economy of weighed metals (Balmuth 2001). If pure gold were not struck into coins at this stage, but only electrum, we would not find or recognize the gold from the Pactolus in the archaeological record, except possibly by trace element analysis.

THE LYDIAN GOLD REFINERY AT PACTOLUS NORTH (PN)

As already discussed, our current perception of the function of the Sardis refinery has changed since its initial excavation in the 1960s. At that time, Lydian Sardis was thought to be a city ranged along the Pactolus River, where Herodotus describes the lower city in 499 at the time of the Ionian Revolt. In the last decades, however, it has become clear that the Pactolus stream, and sector PN, were never within the fortification walls of Lydian Sardis, but were always extramural; and that PN was a mixed extramural neighbourhood, with houses, an altar of Cybele, and evidence for other activity such as jewellery manufacture (Cahill 2008 and 2019; Bruce 2015).

Occupation continued up and down the Pactolus river for at least two kilometres, but the fortified city centre always lay to the east, along the northern slopes of the acropolis. It would seem anomalous for an important refinery involved with the production of state-controlled coinage to be left in an unfortified region of the city.

Moreover, the refinery seems small in scale and informal, and embedded in a domestic neighbourhood, not what one might expect had this been one of the centres for the production of gold for coinage on a large scale. Finally, recent work on the chronology of the refinery at PN concludes that it was used for only a very short period of time, perhaps only five to ten years, in the second quarter of the sixth century BC (Bruce 2015). It thus does not span the period of production of electrum coinage, nor of gold and silver croeseids or later, Persian coins.

If this installation was certainly not created to separate natural silver-rich gold or electrum from the Pactolus into pure gold and silver, and if it was most probably not involved with the production of the new bimetallic coinage of Croesus, as was originally suggested, what was it used for?

The discovery of electrum jewellery and chunks of cut electrum, perhaps from coins, among the debris from the refinery suggest the source of the raw materials that were refined here: not just natural gold but also damaged jewellery and particularly electrum coins that were now out of circulation (Ramage 2000, samples 14, 21a, 216-7; Geçkinli 2008). The Lydian state must have had some way of recalling and re-minting existing electrum coins into the new gold and silver issues; the relatively quick change from a heavy gold standard to the later, lighter gold standard may reflect this deliberate shift (Kroll and Cahill 2005, 612-13). But there may have been opportunities for private individuals and families to convert old electrum coins, which had lost their value, to pure gold and silver, to be used in jewellery and other materials. The discovery of a jewellery mould, rock crystal, and other artefacts related to the manufacture of jewellery among the household detritus from PN suggest that this installation was part of a larger complex including both domestic and household industry, a common situation in the ancient world. Comparison may be made with the installations at Thorikos, similarly in a domestic quarter (Mussche 1998) and at Sardis itself (Cahill 2004).

Rather than interpreting this refinery as part of the production of Lydian coinage, which was controlled, at least in a broad sense, by the state, we suggest that it was a private enterprise, primarily a sort of recycling facility for electrum artefacts including coins, and that it arose in part as a result of the change from electrum to pure gold and silver coinage and the consequent reduction in value of electrum. The gold produced may have made its way into the new Croeseid bimetallic coinage. We hope that further analyses will help to support or modify the hypotheses proposed here.

REFERENCES

Balmuth, M.S. (ed.) 2001. *Hacksilber to Coinage: New Insights into the Monetary History of the Near East and Greece. Numismatic Studies* 24 (New York).

Blet-Lemarquand, M. and Duyrat, F. 2020. 'Elemental Analysis of the Lydo-Milesian Electrum Coins of the Bibliothèque Nationale de France Using LA-ICP-MS', in van Alfen, P., Wartenberg, U., Gitler, H. and Konuk, K. (eds.), *White Gold: Studies in Early Electrum Coinage* (New York), 337–378.

Bruce, W., 2015. 'Industry, Community, and the Sacred: Life Outside the Walls at Sardis', (PhD thesis, University of Wisconsin-Madison).

Cahill, N. 2004. 'Household Industry in Greece and Anatolia', in Ault, B.A. and Nevett, L.C. (eds.), *Ancient Greek Houses and Households: Chronological, Regional, and Social Diversity*, (Philadelphia), 54–66.

Cahill, N., 2008. 'Mapping Sardis', in Cahill, N.D. (ed.), *Love For Lydia: A Sardis Anniversary Volume Presented to Crawford H. Greenewalt, Jr. Sardis Report 4*, (Cambridge, MA), 111-124.

Cahill, N.D. 2019. "Inside Out: Sardis in the Achaemenid and Lysimachean Periods." In *Spear-Won Land: Sardis, from the King's Peace to the Peace of Apamea*, edited by A. Berlin and P. Kosmin, 11–36. Madison, WI: University of Wisconsin Press.

Cahill, N., Hari, J., Önay, B., and Dokumacı, E. 2020. 'Depletion Gilding of Lydian Electrum Coins and the Sources of Lydian Gold,' in van Alfen, P., Wartenberg, U.; Gitler, H. and Konuk, K. (eds.), *White Gold: Studies in Early Electrum Coinage* (New York), 291–335.

Cowell, M.R., Hyne, K., Meeks, N.D. and Craddock, P.T. 1998. 'Analyses of the Lydian electrum, gold and silver coins', in Oddy, W.A. and Cowell, M.R. (eds.), *Metallurgy in Numismatics* 4 (London), 526–38.

Cowell, M.R. and Hyne, K. 2000. 'Scientific Examination of the Lydian Precious Metal Coinages', in Ramage, A. and Craddock, P.T. (eds.), *King Croesus' Gold* (London), 167-74.

Craddock, P.T. 1995. *Early Metal Mining and Production* (Edinburgh).

Craddock, P.T. 2000a. 'Reconstruction of the Salt Cementation Process at the Sardis Refinery', in Ramage, A. and Craddock, P.T. (eds.), *King Croesus' Gold* (London), 200-11.

Craddock, P.T. 2000b. 'Assaying in Antiquity', in Ramage, A. and Craddock, P.T. (eds.), *King Croesus' Gold* (London), 245-50.

Craddock, P.T. 2000c. 'Replication Experiments and the Chemistry of Gold Refining', in Ramage, A. and Craddock, P.T. (eds.), *King Croesus' Gold* (London), 175-83.

Craddock, P.T. 2000d. 'Historical Survey of Gold Refining (1): Surface treatments and refining worldwide and in Europe prior to AD 1500', in Ramage, A. and Craddock, P.T. (eds.), *King Croesus' Gold* (London), 27–53.

Craddock, P.T. 2016. 'The refining of gold at Sardis', in *Lidya "Altin Ülke" Proceedings of conference held 9-11th October Salihli* (Salihli), 55–60.

Craddock, P.T. forthcoming. 'Unpublished data based on examination and analysis of Egyptian golded statuary of the Third Intermediate period in the British Museum'.

Craddock, P.T., Cowell, M.R. and Guerra, M.-F. 2005. 'Controlling the composition and the invention of gold refining in Lydian Anatolia', in Yalçin, Ü. (ed.), *Anatolian Metal III, Der Anschnitt 18* (Bochum), 67–77.

Geçkinli, A.E., Özbal, H, Meeks, N.D. and Craddock, P.T. 2000. 'Examination of the Sardis Gold and the Replication Experiments', in Ramage, A. and Craddock, P.T. (eds.), *King Croesus' Gold* (London), 175–84.

Geçkinli, A.E., Meeks, N.D. and Craddock, P.T. 2001. 'The examination of the gold samples from Pactolus North at Sardis, Turkey', in Mihok, L. (ed.), *Archaeometallurgy in Central Europe III: Acta Metallurgica Slovaca* 7, 20–26.

Geçkinli, A.E. 2008. 'On the Pactolus alluvial gold grains of Sardis, Turkey', in Yalçin, Ü. (ed), *Ancient Mining in Turkey and the Eastern Mediterranean* (Bochum), 119–132.

Hannington, M., Haröadóttir, V., Garbe-Schönberg, D. and Brown, K. 2016. 'Gold enrichment in active geothermal systems by accumulating colloidal suspansions', *Nature Geoscience* 9, 299–302.

Kleber, K. forthcoming. 'As Skillful as Croesus. Evidence for the Parting of Gold and Silver by Cementation from Second and First Millennium Mesopotamia,' in van Alfen, P., Wartenberg, U.; Gitler, H. and Konuk, K. (eds.), *White Gold: Studies in Early Electrum Coinage* (New York).

Konuk, K. 2016. 'The electrum coinage of Samos in the light of a recent hoard', in Schwertungen, E. and Winter, E. (eds.), *Neue Forschungen zu Ionien. Asia Minor Studien* 54, 43–55.

Kroll, J.H. and Cahill, N. 2005. 'New Archaic Coin Finds at Sardis', *American Journal of Archaeology* 109, 589–617.

La Niece, S. 1995. 'Depletion gilding from third millennium BC Ur', *Iraq* 57, 41–47.

Mussche, H. 1998. *Thorikos. A mining town in ancient Attika. Fouilles de Thorikos*, 2 (Gent).

Ramage, A. 2000. 'Inventory and Descriptions of the Gold Samples', Appendix in Ramage, A. and Craddock, P.T. (eds.), *King Croesus' Gold* (London), 215–220.

Ramage, A. and Craddock, P.T. (eds.) 2000. *King Croesus' Gold* (London).

Waldbaum, J.C. 1983. *Metalwork from Sardis: The Finds Through 1974* (Cambridge, MA).

Wise, E.M. 1964. 'Gold alloy systems', in Wise, E.M. (ed.). *Gold: Recovery, Properties and Applications* (Princeton, NJ), 97–153.

12. THE GOLD OF LYSIMACHUS. ELEMENTAL ANALYSIS OF THE COLLECTION OF THE BIBLIOTHÈQUE NATIONALE DE FRANCE USING LA-ICP-MS

Frédérique Duyrat and Maryse Blet-Lemarquand

ABSTRACT

The collection of the department of Coins, Medals and Antiques of the Bibliothèque nationale de France contains 56 lifetime and posthumous gold staters and fractions with the types of Lysimachus. They were struck between the beginning of the third and the beginning of the first century BC. Most mints issuing this type of coinage are represented. The coins have all been analysed using the Laser Ablation Inductively Coupled Plasma Mass Spectrometry (LA-ICP-MS) method to determine the content of major and trace elements. The purpose of this study was two-fold. First, we wanted to see if there were elemental differences between the mints and the periods of production (lifetime and posthumous issues). Second, since there is a clear discrepancy between the trace elements in Eastern and Western gold revealed in the results obtained by the IRAMAT – Centre Ernest-Babelon during the last twenty years, we wanted to evaluate the case of the Lysimachi in the light of this discrepancy. The results show that, on the one hand, the fractions analysed are probably forgeries. On the other hand, if the lifetime and the third and second centuries issues share the same characteristics, the Mithridatic Wars Lysimachi can be distinguished and seem to be closer in composition to some of the Republican gold coins.

INTRODUCTION

Lysimachus, as satrap and then king of Thrace, ruled that area from Alexander's death in 323 BC until his own death at the battle of Corupedium in 281 BC. As a close friend of Cassander, he benefitted from the support of Macedonia throughout his reign. Our knowledge of his coinage remains incomplete; the only attempt of a complete catalogue is by Müller written back in 1858 and the classification it offers is largely superseded. The classification of the lifetime issues is still under discussion, but the posthumous ones have benefitted from two corpora based on die studies (Marinescu 1996 and Callataÿ 1997) helping to secure their identification. Thrace had not received a royal mint during the reign of Alexander; Pella and Amphipolis supplied the region with Philips and Alexanders. This observation led Newell, whose conclusions were published by Thompson (1968), to propose that Lysimachus did not issue any coinage before the foundation of his new capital, Lysimachia, in 309 BC. These were small silver and bronze coins with the types of Philip II and Lysimachus' initials and his personal mark: the forepart of a lion (Thompson 1968, 164–165, 168-169; Price 1991, 130–131 attributes these issues to Amphipolis c. 310-301 BC and suggests that the issues of Alexanders may also refer to Lysimachus). But Arnold-Biucchi has concluded that these coins were minted before 309 BC (Arnold-Biucchi forthcoming). Newell and Thompson dated the first issues in the name of Lysimachus with the types of Alexander to the period after the battle of Ipsus (Price 1991, 197 follows this dating). Lysimachus retained the same denominations: gold staters, silver tetradrachms and drachms. According to Thompson (1968, 165 in agreement with Newell), it is only after Cassander's death in 297 BC, that Lysimachus began a coinage with his own types: a head of Alexander deified with Ammon horn, and Athena seated on a throne. Arnold-Biucchi (forthcoming) has recently challenged this statement, arguing that a date before 301 BC would better conform to the monetary behaviour of the other successors. The issues with the name and types of Lysimachus are predominantly tetradrachms, and are accompanied by gold staters, and drachms at the Anatolian mints. The royal mints of Lysimachus (Thompson 1968, 164–166) opened and closed following his victories and defeats in Asia Minor and in Macedonia (see Lund 1992 on these military campaigns). After his death, certain authorities, among them cities, continued sporadically to produce posthumous coinage with Lysimachus' types for another two centuries (see Franco 1993, 230–236 for a short overview).

The royal and then later civic gold coinages with the name and types of Lysimachus were missing from an earlier program of elemental analyses of ancient eastern gold coinages performed at the IRAMAT–Centre Ernest-Babelon (Institut de recherche sur les Archéomatériaux, CNRS–University of Orléans). To fill this gap the Paris collection was analysed in 2010–2011 by Damien Pujol, a Masters student at the University of Orleans (Pujol 2011).[1] The broader purpose of the study was to situate the gold coins struck by Alexander's successors in the Northern Aegean region within the general landscape of gold analyses of ancient coins already available in the IRAMAT–Centre Ernest-Babelon database (Duyrat and Olivier 2010; Suspène *et al.* 2011; Blet-Lemarquand *et al.* 2015 with an updated graph in Fig. 8). The laboratory has been analysing ancient gold for more than twenty years and has developed the LA-ICP-MS method which has proved to be particularly efficient for nearly pure metal (Dussubieux and van Zelst 2004; Gratuze *et al.* 2004; Blet-Lemarquand *et al.* 2009; Blet-Lemarquand *et al.* in this volume).

THE PARIS COLLECTION OF LYSIMACHUS GOLD COINS

The Paris collection of Lysimachus gold coins can be separated into three groups: 48 staters and imitations, 3 fractions and 6 coins classified as forgeries. 34 coins entered the collection before the beginning of the twentieth century. The oldest identified was part of Joseph Pellerin's collection from the eighteenth century (Fonds général 62, Pellerin 1763, pl. II) but it is possible that some of the coins of the Fonds général are older. Most of the twentieth century acquisitions are gifts (Armand-Valton, Beistegui, Smith-Lesouëf) or part of the collection of Henri Seyrig bought by the Bibliothèque nationale in 1973. Thus the collection has many different origins. None of the coins come from an identified hoard.

The general arrangement of the coins adopted here follows the classification by E.T. Newell, summarised by M. Thompson, for lifetime Lysimachi (Thompson 1968 and 1986). Newell's criteria for distinguishing the lifetime mints remain quite obscure since the same monograms, and sometimes the same dies (see Arnold-Biucchi forthcoming), are shared by different mints. The style of Alexander's head on the obverse has been carefully studied by H.A. Cahn (1991) who distinguished two main groups (A and B) in Thompson's catalogues. Here he emphasised the peculiarities in the style of each of the mints. From the complexity of this coinage, we must conclude that the principles of classification used by Newell (1923) for the Alexanders cannot be easily applied to the Lysimachus coinage. This led Thompson to the conclusion that there were probably several central workshops issuing the coins for different mints (Thompson 1968, 166-167). In the absence of a corpus of Lysimachus gold coins, the classification remains under discussion. That explains why nine staters in the Paris collection remain of uncertain origin, if we follow the bibliography currently available (Fonds général 62, Fonds général 68, Fonds général 71, Fonds général 73, Beistegui 28, Luynes 1812, 1973.1.9, 1973.1.13, 1973.1.14, 1973.1.16).

The Paris collection does not reflect the general output of Lysimachus. For the lifetime Lysimachi, Thompson's article (1968) is a type catalogue and gives no information regarding dies, so that it is impossible to make a precise evaluation of the importance of the collection. Thompson gives a long list of control-marks that are not represented in Paris. However, the unpublished manuscript of Newell that her article summarises seems not to have included some of the Paris coins that could be lifetime issues.

For posthumous issues, the reference works used are the PhD thesis and publications of Constantin Marinescu (1996) on the mint of Byzantium and Chalcedon and of François de Callataÿ (1997) on the Mithridatic Wars. They are based on die-studies that permit an evaluation of the representativeness of the Paris collection. This provides some opportunity to

---

[1] We are very grateful to Damien Pujol for authorising us to use his results to write this article. His research also included the Flamininus stater and the seven Antigonid gold coins kept at the BnF.

evaluate the output of posthumous Lysimachi from the third to the first century BC. However, this is a partial overview since the third and second century BC issues and mints other than Byzantium and Chalcedon have never been thoroughly studied (but note Fonds général 79 is attributed to Istros during the second century BC by Callataÿ 1997, 146, n. 12). Nonetheless, they give a general idea of what this incomplete landscape might be. Only one coin in Paris drifts from lifetime to posthumous issues in the Marinescu thesis: the stater, Fonds général 69, that he dates to $c.$230-220 BC and attributes to Chalcedon instead of Pella $c.$286/5-282/1 BC (as Thompson 1968). The reasons for this attribution are the closeness of the obverse style with two other obverse dies of his group III and a nearly identical monogram on a tetradrachm of the same group (Marinescu 1996, 222). The Paris coins in the catalogue of these two mints provided by Marinescu (1996) is as follows (Table 1):

Table. 1. Representativeness of the Paris collection of gold staters of Lysimachus (Byzantium and Chalcedon) in Marinescu (1996).

	Total	*Staters*	*Paris*
Byzantium	1,166	333	7 (2.1%)
Chalcedon	258	40	4 (10%)

Moreover, the chronological spread of the Paris collection is not regular: only one stater of Byzantium of the second century has been analysed although that period is the most productive (Table 1). On the contrary, the Paris collection represents 10% of the corpus of Chalcedon staters in Marinescu's study. The concentration of this relatively limited output between $c.$260 and the 190s makes the Paris collection a good sample. Callataÿ's 1997 book on the Mithridatic Wars gathers the issues of four mints active between $c.$150 and 72 BC: Byzantium, Callatis, Istros and Tomis. The share of Paris coins in Callataÿ's study is respectively 20% for Byzantium (note that two staters are missing in the latter study: Fonds général 89 and 1973.1.12, which means three coins in a catalogue of fifteen), 14.3% for Istros, 8.3% for Callatis and 3.5% for Tomis.

Callataÿ (1997, 139, no. D1-R1d) re-examined the coins in the Paris collection, and reclassified two supposed forgeries as genuine (Rothschild 921 and 922). By contrast, he noticed that the stater 1973.1.16, previously considered genuine, has an unusual style and control-marks, which suggest it may be modern.[2] Finally, we must note that the Paris collection contains three fractions that are completely unknown within the whole literature on the Lysimachus gold coinage (Fonds général 572; Fonds général 95; M 4901–Fonds général 1115 a). This obviously raises the question of their authenticity.

To summarise, the collection of Paris is a small but relatively well-distributed sample of the gold of Lysimachus, with several dubious coins requiring verification of their authenticity. It can be divided into five groups: the lifetime staters, the third and second century posthumous staters (mainly Byzantium and Chalcedon), the Mithridatic Wars staters and the uncertain staters. The three fractions form a sixth and separate group. The analyses performed were intended to improve the classification and our knowledge of these coinages.

GOLD FINENESS, MINOR AND TRACE ELEMENTS CONCENTRATIONS OF LYSIMACHUS' GOLD COINS

LA-ICP-MS analyses were performed on all the Lysimachus gold coins to determine the contents of the major, minor and trace elements. This method requires several micro samplings using a laser. The hole created on the surface of the coin is so small that it is

---

[2] We are grateful to F. de Callataÿ who kindly gave us his opinion of this doubtful coin. However, the metal of this coin is consistent with the characteristics of the Hellenistic Eastern gold. If it is a modern fake, it may have been produced with ancient gold.

Figure 1. Gold fineness of the Paris Lysimachi

virtually invisible to the naked eye (see Blet-Lemarquand *et al.* 2009 and in this volume). The elemental contents that are discussed in the next pages can be found in Table 2. They shed light on the monetary choices of the issuer, on the manufacture of the gold alloy and on the provenance of the minted gold.

In Figure 1, the lifetime Lysimachi have the highest gold contents, ranging from 97.5% to 99.7% and with an average of 98.7%. There appears to be a slight decrease in the gold content for the third century posthumous Lysimachi which contain an average of 97.8% gold. The second century BC coins are too few to suggest a meaningful trend. Most of all, there is a clear drop in the gold content for the Mithridatic Wars Lysimachi staters, for their average fineness decreases to 95.3% and they show a higher dispersion than the previous series (as noted by Vîlcu *et al.* 2011, 507 from XRF analyses carried out on around 50 lifetime and early posthumous Lysimachus type staters). The standard deviation of this group reaches almost 3%; in contrast, this parameter is less than 1.5% for the other groups. The corpus of these coins is not sufficient to try to interpret separately the monetary policy of each of the four mints of Byzantium, Istros, Tomis and Callatis. Nevertheless the data show that the mints of Byzantium and Callatis did not strike gold at a fixed fineness, and further analyses of coins from Istros or Tomis are likely to lead to similar conclusions.

The three fractions give a contrasting picture: one of them contains 99.6% gold, whereas the other two present an anomalously low gold content of 92%.

The gold contents of lifetime, third and second century BC Lysimachi are consistent with the fineness measured for late fourth century BC gold coins and other series of Hellenistic gold coins, which are usually over 96% (Duyrat and Olivier 2010, 75). The Mithridatic Wars Lysimachi are, by contrast, clearly separated from the bulk of these classical and Hellenistic royal issues.

As usual in Roman or Greek gold coins, silver is the main minor element of all the analysed coins, fractions included. The silver contents range from 0.07% to almost 9%. The silver amounts in ancient gold either come from gold ore which has not been completely purified or testify that gold was deliberately alloyed with silver. The copper and lead concentrations can help to interpret these silver contents because gold ores are generally poor in

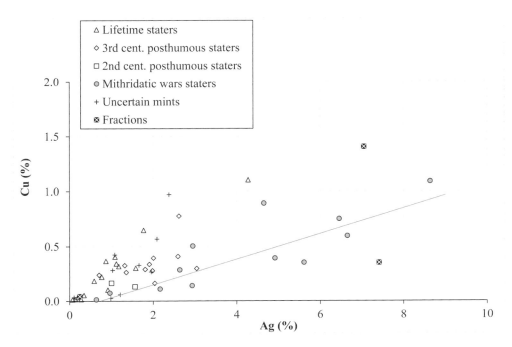

Figure 2. Silver and copper in gold

both these elements. The copper contents are between 0.01% and 1.4% (Fig. 2 and Table 2). There appears to be a linear correlation between the copper and silver contents for almost all the Mithridatic Wars Lysimachi and this is marked by the grey straight line on the graph (Fig. 2). As copper is an impurity of silver, the correlation between the two metals might suggest that some silver was added to purified gold when preparing the bullion. The silver used in the Black Sea mints in the context of the Mithridatic Wars would have contained ten times more silver than copper. On the contrary, no clear trend can be noticed between the copper and silver contents measured for the lifetime or the other posthumous staters. The small silver and copper amounts contained in these latter coins can be understood as remaining from purification of the gold.

The highest lead contents (mainly up to 250 ppm but even as high as 600 ppm) were measured in the coins containing 2 % or less silver, that is to say most of the lifetime and third and second century posthumous staters (Table 2). These lead amounts surely did not enter gold as an impurity of silver. One wonders if they could be pollution from the purification process of gold.[3]

Platinum and palladium are gold impurities which follow gold when it is melted down and purified by cupellation or cementation (Blet-Lemarquand *et al.* 2014). The platinum to gold and palladium to gold ratios are relevant and reliable to tackle the question of the characterisation of gold. These parameters are plotted on a graph to determine if the Lysimachi coins present a similar chemical fingerprint in platinum and palladium, or if they were manufactured from different gold bullions, and also to discuss the authenticity of the three fractions (Fig. 3). Most of the lifetime Lysimachi and the third and second century posthumous coins can be grouped into a rectangle characterised with a platinum/palladium ratio around 23. The corresponding contents generally span from 240 to 450 ppm for platinum and from 10 to 24 ppm for palladium. The Lysimachi issued during the Mithridatic Wars can be

---

[3] A cementation process of gold is described by Diodorus Siculus who quotes, in the first century BC, Agatharchides of Cnidus (*fl.* second century BC). This recipe reports a problematic use of lead and tin to purify Egyptian ground gold ore (Craddock 2000, 34 see also Halleux 1985, 50).

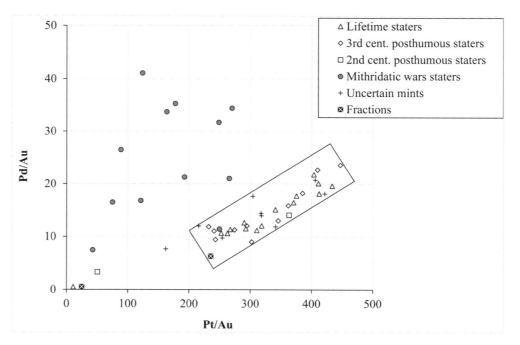

Figure 3. Platinum and palladium normalized to gold. A fraction isn't plotted on the chart because its Pt/Au and Pd/Au ratios are out of the scale (FG 95; Pt/Au 698 and Pd/Au 546)

clearly distinguished because they contain more palladium and less platinum than the previous coins and are spread on the graph (the platinum/palladium ratios are ranging between 3 and 13). The gold from which they are made is different from the gold used for the lifetime or posthumous Lysimachi.

One of the fractions, Fonds général 95, lies outside the boundaries of Figure 3. It contains 99.6% gold and has very high platinum and palladium levels (Pt 695 ppm and Pd 544 ppm), which are unusual for ancient gold as far as we know. These ratios can be compared with the contents of certain eighteenth century gold coins for instance (cf. Morrison and Barrandon 1999); nevertheless, these modern coins were struck with a lower gold ratio of about 90% gold. The two other fractions cannot be separated from genuine coins on the basis of their platinum to gold and palladium to gold ratios. However, one of them (M 4901–Fonds général 1115 a) has a gold ring soldered on it showing that it was part of a jewellery piece. As the ring has exactly the same composition as the coin, it can be deduced that the coin was actually conceived to be jewellery.

LYSIMACHUS GOLD IN THE CONTEXT OF CLASSICAL AND HELLENISTIC ROYAL GOLD COINAGE

The laboratory of Orléans has been working on Hellenistic gold for 20 years, mostly on the collections of the Bibliothèque nationale de France. The aim of these studies is to complete regional or chronological studies by combining the research of a physicist and an historian and by constantly using the same method for elemental analysis. At present (2017) the results of the analyses of about 300 Greek and Roman gold coins can be compared. They have been performed with the same machines and method or with methods that prove to be comparable for seeking the same information. They allow us to situate the gold Lysimachi in a global metal context.

The coins with types of Philip II and Alexander the Great, issued after 323 BC commonly show marked levels of platinum and palladium, whereas the Macedonian coins struck before

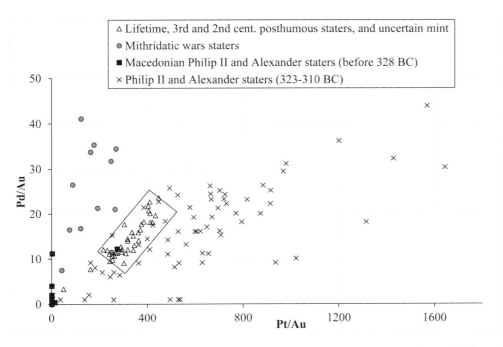

Figure 4. Platinum and palladium normalized to gold. Comparison between the gold Lysimachi (this study) and the gold coinages of Philip II and Alexander the Great (from Gondonneau 2001)

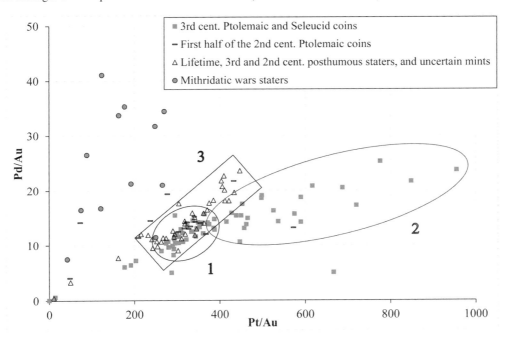

Figure 5. Comparison between the gold Lysimachi and the gold coinage of the Ptolemies and the Seleucids (from Duyrat and Olivier 2010; Olivier and Lorber 2013)

328 BC have low levels in both platinum and palladium (Gondonneau and Guerra 2000). None of the Lysimachi has this peculiar Macedonian chemical 'fingerprint' (Fig. 4).

Previous works made it possible to discriminate between the coins minted in the Eastern part of the Seleucid kingdom (Fig. 5, ellipse 2), and most of the coins from Alexandria and from the western Seleucid mints (ellipse 1) (Duyrat and Olivier 2010; Olivier and Lorber 2013). The rectangle 3 in Figure 5 draws the limits of the lifetime to second century BC gold Lysimachi. It is remarkable that it includes the ellipse 1, gathering the Western Seleucid

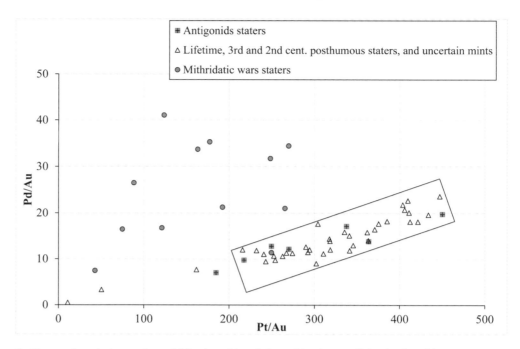

Figure 6. Comparison between the gold Lysimachi and the gold coinage of the Antigonids

mints and Alexandria, but does not overlap the group of the Eastern Seleucid mints (ellipse 2). The lifetime and the third and second century posthumous Lysimachi are generally consistent with coins minted in the Western mints of the Seleucids and especially by the Ptolemies during the third century BC. In contrast, the Mithridatic Wars coins were manufactured from a gold bullion that appears to be completely different from the other royal Hellenistic coins. Another provenance must be hypothesised the characteristics of which are not easily recognised.

Seven rare Antigonid gold coins (Fig. 6) from the Hellenistic kings of Macedonia have been analysed (Pujol 2011). These coins (four from Demetrius Poliorcetes (294–288), one of Antigonus Gonatas (277–239), one of Philip V (221–179) and one of Philip VI Androniscus (149–148) all date to the third century BC and the first half of the second century BC. They have a platinum-palladium 'fingerprint' that perfectly matches the gold of the Lysimachi issued before the Mithridatic Wars. The strong links between Cassander and Lysimachus have already been emphasised but the relationships between Macedonia and Thrace, especially from a monetary point of view, were constant. It seems that the gold supply was common to the whole area.

CONCLUSION

The analyses of gold Lysimachi in the collection of the Bibliothèque nationale de France allow us to characterise the three different groups according to their elemental composition. Our first conclusion is that the lifetime, third and second century posthumous Lysimachi share the same general characteristics. They have a high ratio of gold of over 96%. Their levels of platinum and palladium attach them to the group of 'Eastern gold', in contrast to the 'Western gold' used to strike Philips and Alexanders before 328 BC (Fig. 4). More precisely, these Lysimachi share the same characteristics with coins from the Western Seleucid mints and Alexandria group. The closeness to the few Antigonid gold coins analysed is not a surprise. The interesting point is that the very low levels of platinum and palladium discovered in the issues of Philip II and Alexander the Great in Macedonia before 328 BC are no

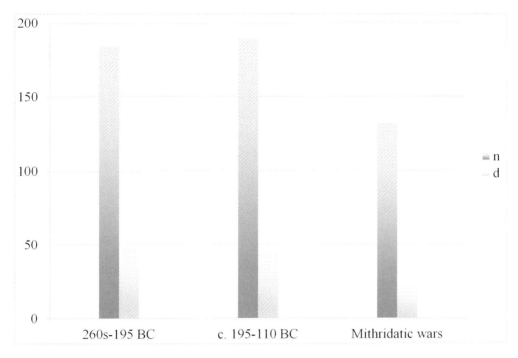

Figure 7. Global output of gold Lysimachi according to Marinescu's (1996) and Callataÿ's (1997) die-studies (n: number of coins and d: number of obverse dies)

longer a characteristic of Macedonian and Thracian coinage after 323 (Gondonneau and Guerra 2000). They are closer to the characteristics of coinages probably minted with the metal seized by Alexander in the Persian treasuries and then re-struck by his successors.

Thanks to Marinescu's PhD (1996), we have a detailed die-study of the issues of Chalcedon and Byzantium. Marinescu determined that Byzantium increased its gold production during the second century BC, when the relatively limited issues of Chalcedon were interrupted (Fig. 7). The importance of this observation for our study is that we can see the continuity of production and use of staters with the types of Lysimachus down to the beginning of the Mithridatic Wars. This explains why the cities of the northern shore of the Pontus Euxine began minting Lysimachi due to the pressures of war (Callataÿ 1997, 150). But it also underlines changes in the source of the metal. While Byzantium used gold with the 'Eastern' characteristics described above, the Lysimachi from the period of the Mithridatic Wars are different in composition. Their gold content is lower on average (from 90.2 to 99.3%). Moreover, their lead, copper, platinum and palladium levels put them in a completely different category. It is unfortunate that the collection of Paris has so few staters of Byzantium of the second century BC. However, the one specimen analysed does not show any change from the third century issues. It is interesting to add the gold Lysimachi to the general graph of ancient gold presented at the beginning of this article (Fig. 8). This clearly shows that the lifetime of second century Lysimachi are part of the more general 'Eastern' group of gold coins with relatively high levels of platinum and paladium. In contrast, the Mithridatic Wars Lysimachi are spread across the gap that separates the Classical and Hellenistic coinages from the beginning of the first century AD Roman coinage (black triangles). It is not possible to draw detailed conclusions from this observation. But it is clear that from the end of the second century and during the first century BC, major changes occurred in the supply of gold in the Mediterranean (Suspène *et al.* 201, Suspène et. al. 2018.

Finally, the existence of three fractions in the Paris collection can now be explained: these coins are forgeries of different kinds. Two have a low gold content and one has abnormally

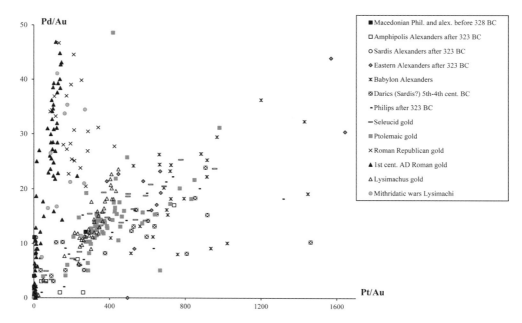

Figure 8. The Lysimachi in the LA-ICP-MS analyses landscape of ancient gold coins (4th century BC to the beginning of the 1st century AD) (from Duyrat and Olivier 2010; Suspène *et al.* 2011)

high contents of platinum and palladium. The remaining example was mounted as jewellery and has the same composition as the ring.

REFERENCES

Arnold-Biucchi, C. forthcoming. 'Attributing and Dating the Lifetime Lysimachi', in Peter, U. and Weisser, B. (eds.), *Thrace–Local Coinage and Regional Identity: Numismatic Research in the Digital Age, Berlin, April 15th to 17th, 2015*.

Blet-Lemarquand, M., Sarah, G., Gratuze, B. and Barrandon, J.-N. 2009. 'Nuclear Methods and Laser Ablation Inductively Coupled Plasma Mass Spectrometry: How Can these Methods Contribute to the Study of Ancient Coinage?', *Cercetări numismatice* 15, 43–56.

Blet-Lemarquand, M., Nieto-Pelletier, S. and Téreygeol, F. 2014. ''Tracer' l'or monnayé : le comportement des éléments traces de l'or au cours des opérations de refonte et d'affinage. Application à la numismatique antique', *Bulletin de la Société Française de Numismatique* 69(4), 90–95.

Blet-Lemarquand, M., Suspène, S. and Amandry, M. 2015. 'Augustus' Gold Coinage: Investigating Mints and Provenance through Trace Element Concentrations', in Hauptmann, A. and Modaressi-Tehrani, D. (eds.), *Archaeometallurgy in Europe III, Proceedings of the 3rd International Conference Deutsches Bergbau-Museum Bochum, June 29–July 1 2011* (Bochum), 107–113.

Cahn, H.A. 1991. 'Zum Alexanderbildnis der Lysimachos-Prägungen,' in Noeske, H.-C. and Alföldi, M.R. (eds.), *Die Münze, Bild-Botschaft-Bedeutung. Festschrift für Maria R.-Alföldi* (Frankfurt am Main/New York), 84–98.

Craddock, P.T. 2000. 'Historical Survey of Gold Refining. 1. Surface Treatments and Refining Worldwide, and in Europe prior to AD 1500', in Ramage, A. and Craddock, P.T. (eds.), *King Croesus' Gold: Excavations at Sardis and the History of Gold Refining* (Cambridge), 27–53.

Callataÿ, F. 1997. *L'histoire des guerres mithridatiques vue par les monnaies* (Louvain-la-Neuve).

Dussubieux, L. and van Zelst, L. 2004. 'LA-ICP-MS Analysis of Platinum-Group Elements and other Elements of Interest in Ancient Gold', *Applied Physics A: Materials Science & Processing* 79(2), 353–356.

Duyrat, F. and Olivier, J. 2010. 'Deux politiques de l'or. Séleucides et Lagides au IIIe siècle avant J.-C.', *RN* 166, 71–93.

Franco, C. 1993. *Il regno di Lisimaco: strutture amministrative e rapporti con le città* (Studi ellenistici 6, Pisa).

Gondonneau, A. 2001. *Développement et application des techniques ICP-MS et LA-ICP-MS à la caractérisation de l'or : circulation monétaire entre Orient et Occident dans l'Antiquité et au Moyen Age* (PhD dissertation, University of Orléans).

Gondonneau, A. and Guerra, M.F. 2000. 'Les statères au type d'Alexandre : apport analytique', *Bulletin de la Société Française de Numismatique* 55(6), 97–101.

Gratuze, B., Blet-Lemarquand, M. and Barrandon, J.-N. 2004. 'Caractérisation des alliages monétaires à base d'or par LA-ICP-MS', *Bulletin de la Société Française de Numismatique*, 59(6), 163–169.

Halleux, R. 1985. 'Méthodes d'essai et d'affinage des alliages aurifères dans l'Antiquité et au Moyen Age', in Morrisson, C., Brenot, C., Callu, J.-P., Barrandon, J.-N., Poirier, J. and Halleux, R. (eds.), *L'or monnayé I. Purification et altérations de Rome à Byzance* (Cahiers Ernest-Babelon 2, Paris), 39-77.

Lund, H.S. 1992. *Lysimachus: A Study in Early Hellenistic Kingship* (London).

Marinescu, C. 1996. 'Making and Spending Money along the Bosporus: The Lysimachi Coinages Minted by Byzantium and Chalcedon' (PhD dissertation, Columbia University).

Marinescu, C. 2014. 'Byzantium's Early Coinage in the Name of King Lysimachus: Problems and New Attributions', *First International Congress of the Anatolian monetary history and numismatics, 25-28 February 2014* (Suna), 383–395.

Marinescu, C. forthcoming. *The Lysimachi Coinage of the Bosporus Strait – The Coordinated Emissions of Byzantium and Chalcedon, ca. 260-120 BC* (New York).

Morrisson, C. and Barrandon, J.-N. 1999. *Or du Brésil, monnaie et croissance en France au XVIIIe siècle* (Paris).

Müller, L. 1858. *Die Münzen des thracischen Königs Lysimachus* (Copenhagen).

Newell, E.T. 1923. *Alexander Hoards: II. Demanhur, 1905* (New York).

Olivier, J. and Lorber, C. 2013. 'Three Gold Coinages of Third-Century Ptolemaic Egypt', *RBN* 159, 49–150.

Pellerin, J. 1763. *Recueil de médailles de peuples et de villes, qui n'ont point encore été publiées, ou qui sont peu connues* (Paris).

Price, M.J. 1991. *The Coinage in the Name of Alexander the Great and Philip Arrhideus. A British Museum Catalogue* (Zurich and London).

Pujol, D. 2011. 'L'or monnayé dans l'espace nord-égéen, IIIe-Ier siècles avant J.-C' (Masters dissertation, University of Orléans).

Suspène, A., Blet-Lemarquand, M. and Amandry, M. 2011. 'Les monnaies d'or d'Auguste: l'apport des analyses élémentaires et le problème de l'atelier de Nîmes', in Holmes, N. (ed.), *Proceedings of the XIVth International Numismatic Congress, Glasgow 2009* (London), 1073–1081.

Suspène, A., Blet-Lemarquand, M., Hochard, P.-O., Flament, J., Gehres, B. 'Un exemple d'enquête numismatique et archéométrique : les aurei des Libérateurs Brutus et Cassius dans le cadre du projet Aureus', *Bulletin de la Société française de numismatique*, 73, 6, 210-217.

Thompson, M. 1968. 'The Mints of Lysimachus', in Kraay, C.M. and Jenkins, G.K. (eds.), *Essays in Greek Coinage Presented to Stanley Robinson* (Oxford), 163–82, pls. 16–22.

Thompson, M. 1986. 'The Armenak Hoard (*IGCH* 1423)', *American Numismatic Society. Museum Notes* 31, 63–106.

Vîlcu, A., Petac, E., Constantinescu, B., Chiojdeanu, C., Stan, D. and Niculescu, G. 2011. 'Considerations regarding the Greek gold coins struck during the 4th to the 1st centuries BC', *Peuce Serie Nouă* 9, 501–512.

Since the 2015 conference where this article was presented, the IRAMAT-Centre Ernest-Babelon performed several hundreds of new analyses thanks to a reasearch program funded by the Région Centre: Aureus. The conclusions of this new research are to be published in the final conference proceedings: Arnaud Suspène, Frédérique Duyrat, Sylvia Nieto-Pelletier, Maryse Blet-Lemarquand (eds.), Aureus. Le pouvoir de l'or - The Power of Gold. Actes du colloque d'Orléans, 13-14 novembre 2018, Bordeaux.

Table 2. LA-ICP-MS results in percentage or ppm

The pictures of all these coins are available online.[1] They all bear the types of Lysimachus and his name:

Obverse: Laureate head of Alexander with horn of Ammon r.

Reverse: Athena seated l. on a throne, Nike in her outstretched r., resting l. elbow on a shield, a spear behind her.

Only the coin Fonds général 62 has Alexander types and Lysimachus' royal title.

Acquisition number and link to image	Mint	Date	Bibliographical ref.	Au%	Ag%	Cu%	Pb	Pd	Pt
Lifetime staters									
Armand-Valton 284 http://gallica.bnf.fr/ark:/12148/btv1b8480744v	Lysimachia	297/6 – 282/1	Thompson 1968, 8 var (nothing in exergue)	98.7	0.87	0.37	21	17	370
FG 67 http://gallica.bnf.fr/ark:/12148/btv1b8576561h	Lysimachia	297/6 – 282/1	Thompson 1968, 8 var (nothing in exergue)	98.7	0.87	0.37	21	17	370
Beistegui 26 http://gallica.bnf.fr/ark:/12148/btv1b8576567o	Pella or Byzantium	286/5 – 282 or c. 270	Thompson 1968, 241 (Pella); Marinescu 2014 (Byzantium)	99.0	0.77	0.22	205	11	264
Beistegui 27 http://gallica.bnf.fr/ark:/12148/btv1b8576568d	Pella	286/5 – 282	Thompson 1968, 241	99.2	0.58	0.18	48	12	316
FG 78 http://gallica.bnf.fr/ark:/12148/btv1b8576566k	Pella	286/5 – 282	Thompson 1968, 253 (tetradrachm)	99.5	0.34	0.054	23	15	340
FG 64 http://gallica.bnf.fr/ark:/12148/btv1b8576559f	Pella	286/5 – 282/1	Thompson 1968, 247 (tetradrachm)	98.5	1.1	0.34	58	10	259

Table 2. *Continued.*

Acquisition number and link to image	Mint	Date	Bibliographical ref.	Au%	Ag%	Cu%	Pb	Pd	Pt
FG 66 http://gallica.bnf.fr/ark:/12148/btv1b85765603	Pella?	286/5 – 282/1	Thompson 1968, 241, 252-5 var. tetradrachm	98.4	1.1	0.41	98	18	406
Beistegui 28 http://gallica.bnf.fr/ark:/12148/btv1b8576569t	Pella	?	Thompson 1968, 244 var. (tetradrachm with other monogram), Thompson Armenak 931 var.	98.0	1.6	0.30	12	16	363
Luynes 1808 https://gallica.bnf.fr/ark:/12148/btv1b11316927g	Pella	286/5 – 282/1	Thompson 1968, 247 (tetradrachm)	98.4	1.2	0.32	18	19	427
FG 69 http://gallica.bnf.fr/ark:/12148/btv1b8576563b	Pella or Chalcedon	286/5-282/1 or c. 230-225	Thompson 1968, 240 (Pella) / Marinescu 1996, 73.1 (Chalcedon) = Marinescu Forthcoming C120	98.8	0.91	0.10	9	11	307
FG 63 http://gallica.bnf.fr/ark:/12148/btv1b85765581	Alexandria Troas	297/6 – 282	Thompson 1968, 146 or 157?	99.7	0.27	0.016	30	0.5	11
FG 74 http://gallica.bnf.fr/ark:/12148/btv1b85765655	Lampsacus	297/6 – 282/1	Thompson 1968, 57 (tetradrachm)	94.6	4.3	1.1	61	11	277
Luynes 1809 https://gallica.bnf.fr/ark:/12148/btv1b11316928x	Amphipolis?	288/7 – 282/1	Thompson 1968, 190 var. (tetradrachm)	99.7	0.14	0.017	54	22	403

Table 2. *Continued.*

Acquisition number and link to image	Mint	Date	Bibliographical ref.	Au%	Ag%	Cu%	Pb	Pd	Pt
HS 1973.1.11 http://gallica.bnf.fr/ark:/12148/btv1b8576593g	Ephesus	c. 294 – 287	Thompson 1968, 166 var. (tetradrachm)	99.6	0.19	0.036	125	20	410
HS 1973.1.10 http://gallica.bnf.fr/ark:/12148/btv1b85765922	Ephesus	c. 294 – 287	Thompson 1968, 164	99.8	0.070	0.015	608	13	289
3rd century posthumous staters									
FG 76 http://gallica.bnf.fr/ark:/12148/btv1b8576586b	Byzantium	c. 260 – 245	Marinescu 1996, 63.1 Issue 25 = Marinescu forthcoming B104	99.6	0.29	0.062	25	16	334
Smith Lesouëf 22 – Y 28912.22 http://gallica.bnf.fr/ark:/12148/btv1b8479032r	Byzantium	c. 260 – 245	Marinescu 1996, 84.3 Issue 35 = Marinescu forthcoming B136	96.5	2.6	0.78	104	9	235
1968.1183 http://gallica.bnf.fr/ark:/12148/btv1b85765796	Byzantium	c. 245 – beginning of the 220s	Marinescu 1996, 122.2 Issue 47 = Marinescu forthcoming B182	96.6	3.0	0.30	9	13	334
FG 85 http://gallica.bnf.fr/ark:/12148/btv1b8576577c	Byzantium	c. 245 – beginning of the 220s	Marinescu 1996, 145.1 Issue 62 = Marinescu forthcoming B200	98.3	1.3	0.33	103	11	270
FG 86 http://gallica.bnf.fr/ark:/12148/btv1b8576580v	Byzantium	c. 245 – beginning of the 220s	Marinescu 1996, 148.1 Issue 65 = Marinescu forthcoming B213	98.3	1.4	0.26	45	23	439

Table 2. *Continued.*

Acquisition number and link to image	Mint	Date	Bibliographical ref.	Au%	Ag%	Cu%	Pb	Pd	Pt
FG 90 http://gallica.bnf.fr/ark:/12148/btv1b8576578s	Byzantium	c. 245 – beginning of the 220s	Marinescu 1996, 102.1 Issue 41 = Marinescu forthcoming B157	99.0	0.71	0.24	69	11	238
Luynes 1810 https://gallica.bnf.fr/ark:/12148/btv1b11316929c	Byzantium	c. 210 – 195	Marinescu 1996, 213.1 Issue 90 = Marinescu forthcoming B293	97.7	1.9	0.34	53	22	400
R 2977 http://gallica.bnf.fr/ark:/12148/btv1b8576576z	Chalcedon	c. 260 – 230	Marinescu 1996, 47.1 Issue 20 = Marinescu forthcoming C85	96.9	2.6	0.41	197	12	285
FG 75 http://gallica.bnf.fr/ark:/12148/btv1b8576585x	Chalcedon	230s – c. 225	Marinescu 1996, 78.1 Issue 35 = Marinescu forthcoming C127	97.5	2.0	0.39	162	15	353
FG 91 http://gallica.bnf.fr/ark:/12148/btv1b8576587r	Chalcedon	230s – c. 225	Marinescu 1996, group III, 79, 81, 84, 85, 97, 92 var; other monogram = Marinescu forthcoming C203	97.7	2.0	0.28	52	18	376
HS 1973.1.15 http://gallica.bnf.fr/ark:/12148/btv1b85765885	Chalcedon	c. 225 – 190	Marinescu forthcoming C203	97.8	1.8	0.29	239	12	227
FG 77 http://gallica.bnf.fr/ark:/12148/btv1b8576596q	Odessos	c. 255-240 ? or 230 ?	Marinescu 1996, p. 420	97.7	2.0	0.16	48	9	295

Table 2. *Continued.*

Acquisition number and link to image	Mint	Date	Bibliographical ref.	Au%	Ag%	Cu%	Pb	Pd	Pt
2nd century posthumous staters									
FG 79 http://gallica.bnf.fr/ark:/12148/btv1b8576594w	Istros	2nd century	Callataÿ 1997, p. 146, n. 12	98.8	1.00	0.17	44	14	359
FG 87 http://gallica.bnf.fr/ark:/12148/btv1b85765818	Byzantium	c. 195 – 110	Marinescu 1996, 509.1 Issue 150 = Marinescu forthcoming	98.3	1.6	0.13	70	3	49
Mithridatic wars									
HS 1973.1.12 http://gallica.bnf.fr/ark:/12148/btv1b8576582p	Byzantium	105-96	Callataÿ 1997, D2 R1	94.3	4.7	0.89	83	11	235
FG 88 http://gallica.bnf.fr/ark:/12148/btv1b85765833	Byzantium	105-96	Callataÿ 1997, D7 R1a	97.7	2.2	0.11	169	7	42
FG 89 http://gallica.bnf.fr/ark:/12148/btv1b8576584h	Byzantium	105-96	Callataÿ 1997, D2 R1	90.2	8.6	1.1	70	31	243
FG 80 http://gallica.bnf.fr/ark:/12148/btv1b8576589k	Callatis	110-90	Callataÿ 1997, D4 R2a	92.7	6.7	0.60	163	20	178
FG 81 http://gallica.bnf.fr/ark:/12148/btv1b85765907	Callatis	110-90	Callataÿ 1997, D6 R1a	99.3	0.64	0.014	0.3	35	176

Table 2. *Continued.*

Acquisition number and link to image	Mint	Date	Bibliographical ref.	Au%	Ag%	Cu%	Pb	Pd	Pt
2015.24 https://gallica.bnf.fr/ark:/12148/btv1b113536782	Callatis	110-90	Müller 1858, 260; Callataÿ 1997, D3 R-	96.5	2.9	0.50	77	31	240
Rothschild 921 http://gallica.bnf.fr/ark:/12148/btv1b10316657b	Callatis	110-90	Callataÿ 1997, D6 R1a	94.7	4.9	0.39	60	16	71
Luynes 1811 https://gallica.bnf.fr/ark:/12148/btv1b11316930r	Callatis	110-90	Callataÿ 1997, D6 R2b	98.9	0.96	0.075	7	26	87
FG 82 http://gallica.bnf.fr/ark:/12148/btv1b85765959	Istros	150-72?	Callataÿ 1997, D1 R1c	97.0	2.6	0.28	13	33	158
Rothschild 922 http://gallica.bnf.fr/ark:/12148/btv1b10316656w	Istros	150-72?	Callataÿ 1997, D1 R1d	96.9	2.9	0.14	9	40	120
FG 83 http://gallica.bnf.fr/ark:/12148/btv1b85765974	Tomis	Beginning of the 1st century BC	Callataÿ 1997, D4 R1a	92.7	6.5	0.75	49	19	246
FG 84 http://gallica.bnf.fr/ark:/12148/btv1b8576598j	Tomis BC	Beginning of the 1st century	Callataÿ 1997, D2 R1a	94.0	5.6	0.35	34	16	114

Table 2. *Continued.*

Acquisition number and link to image	Mint	Date	Bibliographical ref.	Au%	Ag%	Cu%	Pb	Pd	Pt
Uncertain mints									
HS 1973.1.13 http://gallica.bnf.fr/ark:/12148/btv1b85765744	?	?	Müller 1858, 341 (Aphytis)	98.6	1.0	0.28	82	18	416
HS 1973.1.14 http://gallica.bnf.fr/ark:/12148/btv1b8576575j	?	?	Close to Thompson 1968, 113 and 115 (Magnesia) but with different obverse style	98.9	0.98	0.025	14	12	213
HS 1973.1.16 http://gallica.bnf.fr/ark:/12148/btv1b8576570g	?	?	Fake?	97.7	2.0	0.27	21	14	311
FG 71 http://gallica.bnf.fr/ark:/12148/btv1b103037168	?	?	No control-mark	96.6	2.4	0.97	90	17	294
FG 62 http://gallica.bnf.fr/ark:/12148/btv1b8576557m	?	?	Müller 1858, 29	98.5	1.1	0.42	33	8	159
FG 68 http://gallica.bnf.fr/ark:/12148/btv1b8576562x	?	?	Marinescu 1996, 79 (without the bull)	99.7	0.11	0.033	73	14	317
FG 73 http://gallica.bnf.fr/ark:/12148/btv1b8576564r	?	?	Müller 1858, 464	97.3	2.1	0.57	247	12	332

Table 2. Continued.

Acquisition number and link to image	Mint	Date	Bibliographical ref.	Au%	Ag%	Cu%	Pb	Pd	Pt
Luynes 1812 https://gallica.bnf.fr/ark:/12148/btv1b113169316	Rhodes?	?	Müller 1858, 451 (Rhodes)	98.7	1.2	0.059	27	20	401
HS 1973.1.9 http://gallica.bnf.fr/ark:/12148/btv1b8576591n	Kios?	?	Thompson 1968, 179 – 185, (tetradrachm), with ear of corn	97.9	1.7	0.33	168	10	249
Fractions									
FG 572	?			92.2	7.4	0.35	4	0.5	23
FG 95 http://gallica.bnf.fr/ark:/12148/btv1b8576573q	?			99.6	0.24	0.044	0.6	544	695
M 4901 – FG 1115 a http://gallica.bnf.fr/ark:/12148/btv1b85765729	?			91.5	7.0	1.4	44	6	215

13. DEPTH PROFILE LA-ICP-MS ANALYSIS OF ANCIENT GOLD COINS

Maryse Blet-Lemarquand, Sylvia Nieto-Pelletier, Bernard Gratuze

ABSTRACT

This paper presents use of the Depth Profile mode coupled with LA-ICP-MS for analysing ancient gold coins. It explains how this mode can improve the characterisation of coins for the following difficult analytical problems: surface gold enrichment, low fineness gold alloys, localised enrichments in platinum and palladium and inclusions of platinum group elements.

INTRODUCTION

LA-ICP-MS (Laser Ablation Inductively coupled Plasma Mass Spectrometry)[1] is an elemental analytical method which has proved its worth for analysis of silver and gold coins.[2] Two or more micro-samplings are taken starting from the surface of the coin using the laser ablation process with diameters so small as to be practically invisible to the naked eye. The elemental composition of these samples is assumed to be representative of the metal worked in the mint, an hypothesis which has to be demonstrated for each alloy.

The Depth Profiling (DP) mode enables determination of the depth composition from the surface to the interior of the coin, and is particularly useful for artefacts that show composition gradients from their surface to their core. It has been studied for multi-layered industrial samples and for depth-heterogeneous minerals (Mason and Mank 2001; Woodhead *et al.* 2008). Its application to cultural heritage artefacts was first tested and validated for silver-copper alloy coins which often present significant silver enrichment on their surface due to a depletion of the copper (Sarah *et al.* 2007; Sarah and Gratuze 2016).[3]

Gold alloy artefacts, including coins, may be enriched in gold on their surface as a result of depletion-gilding processes by goldsmiths done to enhance the gold colour, and also from corrosion developed post deposition.[4] More generally, ancient gold artefacts can sometimes appear to be 'heterogeneous' at the scale of the tiny laser micro-sampling. Our article assesses, from various case studies, how the DP mode can contribute to improve the characterisation of gold coins. It aims to describe the consequences for numismatic studies of the following analytical problems: surface gold enrichment of coins, low fineness gold alloys, localised enrichments in platinum and palladium and inclusions of platinum group elements.

THE DP-LA-ICP-MS METHODOLOGY

LA-ICP-MS presents many advantages for analysing ancient gold coins in order to discuss archaeological, numismatic and historical questions (Dussubieux and van Zelst 2004; Gratuze *et al.* 2004; Blet-Lemarquand *et al.* 2009).[5] The damage left by the laser ablation is virtually invisible to the naked eye as the diameter of the crater is usually tuned to around 80 micrometres (Fig. 1). The contents of a very large number of elements are determined with detection limits reaching the sub-ppm level: gold, silver, copper and the whole set of the trace elements that could characterise these metals can be studied (notably Pb, Bi, Sn, Pt, Pd, etc.). More than 10 coins can be analysed per day and the compositions determined in the course of the analytical session.

---

[1] For a recent general presentation: Fricker and Günther 2016.
[2] See for instance studies quoted in the last editions of the *Survey of Numismatics Research* (Blet-Lemarquand and Ponting 2009; Blet-Lemarquand and Nieto-Pelletier 2015).
[3] The question of the surface enrichment of ancient silver-copper alloy coins and the impacts of this phenomenon for metallurgical analysis have been much discussed. See especially Ponting 2012; Sarah and Gratuze 2016.
[4] Examples of depletion gildings: Blakelock *et al.* 2016; Bray 1993. On the corrosion of gold alloys: Scott 1983.
[5] Recent review of the constraints when analysing precious metal coins in Blet-Lemarquand *et al* 2014a; recent summary of the difficulties faced when provenance studies of gold objects in Pernicka 2014, 260.

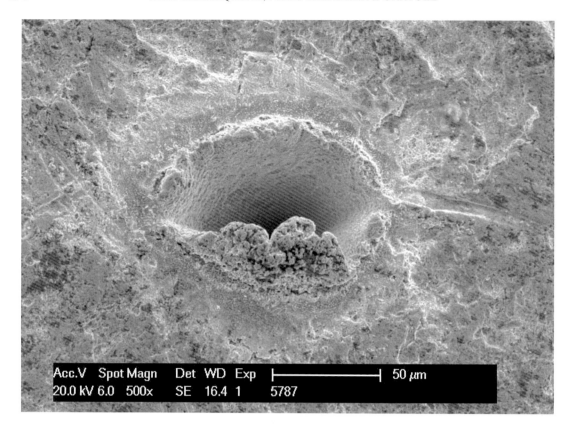
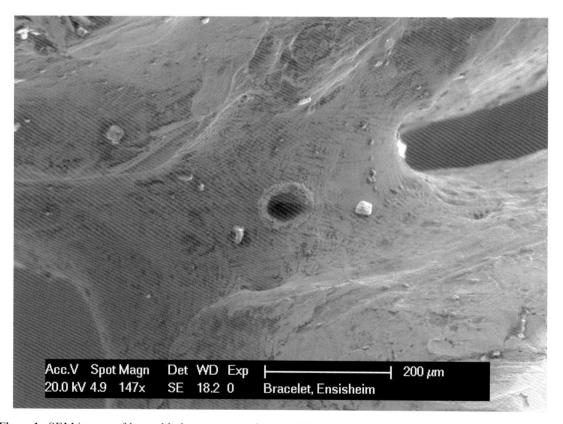

Figure 1. SEM images of laser ablation craters made on prehistoric gold artefacts using the two laser equipment available in the IRAMAT-CEB: (a) Nd:YAG; (b) ArF-excimer. © CNRS IRAMAT-CEB

However, there are challenges to solve that are specific to the analysis of archeomaterials and to the use of LA-ICP-MS on metals. Gold alloy coins and artefacts in general cannot be systematically regarded as homogeneous materials at the scale of micro-sampling mainly because of possible surface enrichment in gold. However, it seems that above 50 atomic percent gold corrosion will be very limited (Scott 1983); this level corresponds to 76 weight% and 65 weight% respectively in binary gold-silver or gold-copper alloys. To solve the problem of corrosion, the gold artefacts are analysed with LA-ICP-MS using the Depth Profiling (DP) mode with a procedure that directly derives from the investigations carried out on silver coins (Sarah et al. 2007; Sarah and Gratuze 2016). With this procedure, the transient signal generated from the LA-ICP-MS is recorded each time slice the laser drills down into the sample at one spot. Thus, it is possible to determine variations in the elemental concentration starting at the surface of the coin (see for example Figs. 3, 4 and 6). When the signals plateau, it indicates that intact material is being sampled. This metal, that has neither been deliberately enriched in gold, corroded nor contaminated, reflects the metal worked in the mint to produce the blank, and for which composition is meaningful. Two to three laser ablations are generally carried out on each coin and the compositions are averaged.

The depth of the crater is around 200-250 micrometres after 3,000 laser shots in the operating conditions fixed for the ArF-excimer (Table 1, diameter 80 μm, laser energy 6 mJ, irradiance 0.4 GW.cm^{-2}).[6] The crater is cylindrical near the surface and ends with a conical shape at its bottom (Eggins et al. 1998). This geometry is consistent with the evolution of the ablation efficiency with depth. It is maximum at first when the laser is started because ablation takes place at the focus point of the laser, and then there is a drop in efficiency with depth as ablation proceeds further away from the focus (Mason and Mank 2001, 1384). The raw transient signal obtained for a gold standard shows a similar evolution (Fig. 2); it is reduced by a factor of five after 3,000 laser shots for the considered analysis. Its decrease with depth has different consequences for the analysis; as the sensitivity decreases with time, the error made on the calculation of the contents increases and finally the detection limits increase. However, this loss of sensitivity does not limit the detection of trace element in ancient gold artefacts. In fact, at the end of this analysis, after 200 or 300 seconds of laser

Table 1. Instrumental parameters for the laser devices and the ICP-MS available at the IRAMAT-CEB.
*usual operating conditions

Laser System	1	2
Laser Type	VG UV Microprobe (*VG Elemental*)	Resolution M-50-E (*Resonetics*)
Lasing source	Nd:YAG	ArF-excimer
Wavelength (nm)	266	193
Output energy (mJ)	4	240
Ablation rate (Hz)	1-10; 6-8*	1-300; 6-8*
Pulse duration (ns)	3-5	6-8
Laser spot diameter (μm)	About 30; 60; 90; 200	2-100; 80*
Ablation cells	VG cell + in-house cells designed for big objects	S-155 (*Laurin Technic*) + in-house cells designed for big objects
Carrier gas	Ar	Mixing of Ar and He or Ar
ICP-MS type	Element XR (*Thermo Fisher*)	
RF forward power (W)	1,350	
Sampling cone (mm)	1.0 Ni	
Skimmer cone (mm)	0.7 Ni	
Detector	Faraday Cup + Secondary Electron Multiplier	

[6] The laser ablation efficiency depends on many parameters (composition and microstructure of the metal, focus of the laser beam, power density...) that can change in the course of the ablation realized at one spot and from an analytical session to another. The rate of ablation per laser pulse is ranging from 0.1 to 2 micrometres (Mason and Mank 2001).

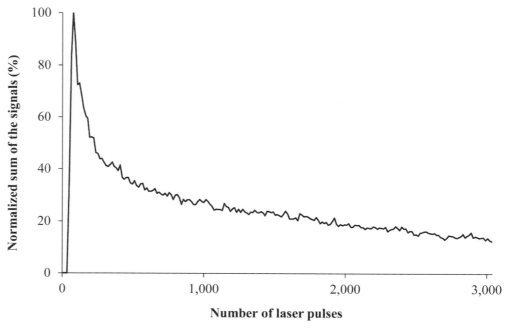

Figure 2. Normalised LA-ICP-MS response of laser ablation of the certified reference gold material RAuP7. Average of 4 analyses carried out in the course of an analytical session. Normalisation to the highest signal. ArF-excimer laser. Laser spot diameter fixed at 80 micrometres.

Table 2. Sensitivity of the DP-LA-ICP-MS calculated for the main trace elements in ancient gold from the analysis of the certified reference gold material RAuP7.

Isotope	Zn66	Rh103	Pd108	Sb121	Pt195	Pb208	Bi209
Isotopic abundance	28%	100%	27%	57%	34%	52%	100%
Element	**Zn**	**Rh**	**Pd**	**Sb**	**Pt**	**Pb**	**Bi**
Background (counts rates)	180	52	20	214	0	305	134

Time of laser ablation (s) / Number of laser pulses for 1 ppm of element	**Net intensity counts rates corrected for isotopic abundance**						
	Zn	**Rh**	**Pd**	**Sb**	**Pt**	**Pb**	**Bi**
3 / 29	20,219	5,814	6,955	7,008	6,221	14,343	10,603
50 / 505	2,441	2,457	2,872	2,907	2,329	3,724	3,800
100 / 996	1,898	2,236	2,411	2,457	1,774	3,138	3,385
201 / 2,006	1,221	1,794	1,798	1,772	1,432	2,488	2,026
297 / 2,972	890	1,128	920	1,038	908	1,402	1,435

ablation (shots), the net intensity counts rates for 1 ppm are ranging from 1,000 to 1,500 for the main trace elements, and the corresponding background intensities are less than 300 counts (Table 2).

Previous studies have investigated different parameters in order to achieve maximum depth resolution (Mason and Mank 2001). They came to the conclusion that a small depth/diameter ratio for the ablation crater was the best for determining the composition of thick layers in multi-layered samples. In other words this would correspond to a wide but shallow ablation crater. However, other parameters have to be taken into account for analysing ancient gold artefacts. We have on the one hand to limit the diameter of the crater ablation for conservation purposes, and on the other hand we wish to reach the deepest zone possible when analysing low gold content coins (see below application on Late Celtic coins). A compromise has to be made between all these constraints. The depth resolution reached with 80 micrometre wide craters that are as deep as possible seems sufficient for our studies. It allows in nearly all the cases to reach a plateau of stable composition showing good reproducibility for a minimum of two micro-samplings carried out at different places on the artefacts.

Elemental fractionation is a problem ruled by many parameters peculiar to metals (Cromwell and Arrowsmith 1995; Russo *et al.* 2002; Dussubieux 2016). It concerns metals having a low melting point (e.g. Pb and Zn) when they are present in large quantities. This may cause their preferential volatilisation during ablation, leading to non-representative subsampling. Standardisation with matrix-matched standards is an efficient solution to correct this problem in brass (Flament 2017). Elemental fractionation does not happen for ancient gold artefacts analysed with our analytical conditions (table 1) mainly because both lead and zinc are only present at low levels.[7]

The signals yielded by the LA-ICP-MS are standardised using matrix-matched standards that are analysed several times during each analytical session. Some of these standards are certified reference materials: high purity gold doped with trace elements at the 100-200 ppm or 15-30 ppm concentration levels (RAuP3 and RAuP7, Rand Refinery Ltd, South Africa) and standards made for XRF analysis (Comptoir Lyon-Alemand, Louyot et Cie, France). Others are in-house standards: Au-Ag-Cu alloys doped or not with tin and lead which were manufactured at our request, or ancient gold coins previously analysed by other methods.[8] The calculation procedure normalises the sum of the elemental contents to 100 weight%, and derives from the procedure previously developed for archaeological glass samples (Gratuze 2016). This standardisation procedure and the LA-ICP-MS analysis of gold as a whole were validated comparing the results obtained for different types of gold coins with their compositions obtained performing PAA (Blet-Lemarquand *et al.* 2009; Blet-Lemarquand *et al.* 2014a; Blet-Lemarquand *et al.* 2015).

HETEROGENEITIES IN ANTIQUE GOLD COINS

Gold enrichment of the surface

Some coins made of gold-silver binary alloys show strong enrichment of gold on their surface.[9] An antique Greek coin from Boeotia provides a typical example (Fig. 3).[10] Its worn reliefs are whitish while the rest of the surface is golden. The DP-LA-ICP-MS analysis shows that the surface is heavily enriched in gold to the detriment of silver and copper compared with the alloy beneath the surface. The gold content is about 90 % at the surface of the coin, then it decreases rapidly and stabilises at about 61 % after 40 seconds of laser shots. It is assumed that the composition is then representative of the inner part of the coin. In parallel, the silver concentration increases from the surface to about 37 % in the original alloy. The thin golden layer[11] of this coin results from metallurgical treatments carried out to disguise the low fineness of the gold alloy. The DP mode informs us about the enrichment and yields the compositions in major, minor and trace elements of the original alloy.

---

[7] Elemental analysis carried out for years on gold coins dating back from the antiquity to the modern period at the IRAMAT-CEB gives us an overview of the compositions. 0.1 % appears to be a maximum for the zinc contents in gold coins (see especially Merovingian gold coins: Blet-Lemarquand *et al.* 2010). Lead concentrations depend mostly on the proportion of silver added to debase gold. They can reach 0.3 % (see Celtic coins: Barrandon *et al.* 1994 and Byzantine coins: Morrisson *et al.* 1985).
[8] ICP-MS in liquid mode: Dussubieux and van Zelst 2004; PAA (Proton activation analysis): Gratuze *et al.* 2004; cupellation, ICP-OES.
[9] Examples of surface gold-enriched coins: Lehrberger and Raub 1995; Gruel *et al.* 2010; Araújo *et al.* 1993; Beck *et al.* 1991; Travaini 1998; Blet-Lemarquand *et al.* 2010; Artru 2015.
[10] FG 635, MMA BnF http://catalogue.bnf.fr/ark:/12148/cb418141891. This coin has been analysed in the framework of the AUREUS research project funded by the French Région Centre-Val de Loire. We owe a special thanks to Arnaud Suspène and Benjamin Gehres for allowing us to use this analysis.
[11] Fig. 3 shows that it took 44 seconds (352 laser shots) for the Au signal to decrease from 61 % to 30 %. This delay depends not only on the thickness of the golden layer but also on the aerosol washout time. This parameter is about 20 seconds for the S-155 cell used to analyse this coin.

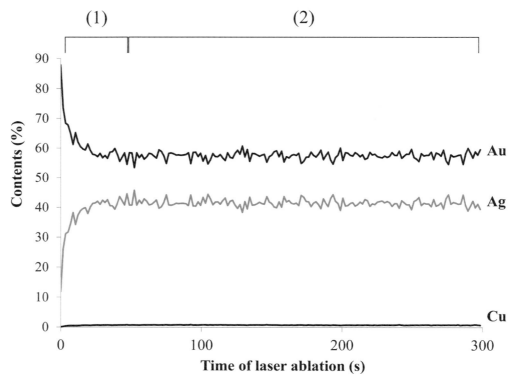

Figure 3. Concentrations profiles for gold, silver and copper versus the time of laser ablation obtained by DP-LA-ICP-MS for a Greek gold coin (FG 635, MMA BnF). (1) Gold enriched surface; (2) original alloy.

Ternary gold-based alloy coins[12]

LA-ICP-MS analyses were made on Celtic coins some years ago when the DP mode could not be performed with the available instrumentation (Blet-Lemarquand *et al.* 2009; 2014a). Before starting the analysis, a 20 second pre-ablation was first performed to remove potential corrosion and contamination, and then the transient signal obtained from 40 seconds of ablation was integrated to calculate elemental concentrations. For some coins noticeable variations could be obtained for the copper contents between the three micro-samplings (Blet-Lemarquand *et al.* 2009; 2014a). Could the DP mode improve the quality of analysis and reduce these variations?

An analytical program using the DP mode was undertaken on a representative set of 150 Late Celtic gold coins from the Laniscat hoard and providing the opportunity to test this question (Nieto-Pelletier *et al.* 2011).[13] Three types of depth-profiles were obtained (Fig. 4). For a minority of coins, gold, silver and copper signals are relatively constant from the surface to the core of the coins (Fig. 4a). Certain coins have a surface layer mainly enriched in gold but also slightly in silver to the detriment of copper (Fig. 4b). Other coins gave very irregular signals which eventually stabilized (Fig. 4c). However, in some cases the alloy appeared to be too heterogeneous to calculate a reliable composition. These fluctuations could be due to corrosion phases. Generally speaking, the elemental analyses showed that the coins contain about 18 % gold, 5-35 % silver and 42-78 % copper. The DP mode appeared to be the only way of producing reliable composition data using the LA-ICP-MS method.

---

[12] It has already been shown that DP-LA-ICP-MS was suitable for analysis of binary gold-silver alloy coins like the early electrum coins made from weakly homogenised alloys (Blet-Lemarquand and Duyrat 2020).
[13] All the coins contained in this hoard are attributed to the *Osismii*.

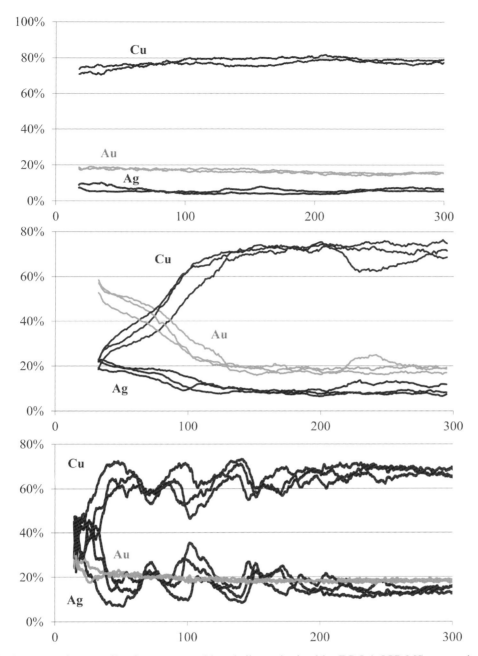

Figure 4. Concentrations profiles for copper, gold and silver, obtained by DP-LA-ICP-MS versus the time of analysis in seconds, for three different Late Celtic coins from the Laniscat hoard. Two or three different laser micro-samplings were made per coin. From top to bottom: (a), (b), (c).

Localised enrichments in platinum and palladium

Platinum and palladium are impurities of gold that are of prime importance for provenance studies (Blet-Lemarquand *et al.* 2014b; Blet-Lemarquand *et al.* 2017; Duyrat and Blet-Lemarquand this volume). These elements are soluble in gold (Ogden 1977) and most of the time, using LA-ICP-MS, their contents are indeed uniform all over a coin. This is the case for a set of 12 Augustus' gold coins (Table 3). The relative standard deviations calculated for the three laser micro-samplings are usually below 10 %. It should be noted that the Pt/Pd ratios are always less variable than the platinum and palladium contents with the exception of coin BNC 330 for which palladium level is near the detection limit (Table 3).

Table 3. Partial results of the LA-ICP-MS analysis of 12 Augustus' gold coins for platinum and palladium (contents and ratios). The arithmetic means (AM) and relative standard deviations (RSD) are calculated from three laser micro-samplings. The contents are expressed in ppm. From Blet-Lemarquand *et al.* 2015.

		BNC 83	*BNC 86*	*BNC 106*	*BNC 107*	*BNC 108*	*BNC 109*	*BNC 110*	*BNC 111*	*BNC 220*	*BNC 330*	*BNC 531*	*BNC 1281*
Pt	AM (ppm)	103	138	150	114	113	99	138	105	77	1.8	125	5.5
	RSD	3%	2%	10%	7%	2%	1%	17%	12%	18%	3%	3%	4%
Pd	AM (ppm)	35	45	14	27	22	27	40	25	23	0.7	38	5.9
	RSD	5%	5%	4%	5%	7%	5%	21%	16%	21%	23%	6%	3%
Pt/Pd	AM	2.9	3.1	10.4	4.2	5.2	3.6	3.4	4.2	3.4	2.7	3.3	0.9
	RSD	3%	3%	7%	4%	5%	1%	5%	4%	3%	26%	4%	2%

Table 4. Platinum and palladium concentrations and platinum to palladium ratios determined for a Lysimachus gold coin (MMA BnF, Luynes 1808).[14] Four laser micro-samplings were carried out. AM: arithmetic mean; SD: standard deviation; RSD relative standard deviation.

	No. 1	*No. 2*	*No. 3*	*No. 4*	*AM*	*SD*	*RSD*
Pt (ppm)	503	502	276	95	344	197	57%
Pd (ppm)	23	23	12	3.4	15	10	62%
Pt/Pd	21	22	23	28	24	3.1	13%

Sometimes significant variations in platinum and palladium can be observed among the micro-samplings. Table 4 presents the contents in both these elements obtained for a Lysimachus coin with four laser micro-samplings that led to three different concentrations. Despite these variations, the Pt/Pd ratio is essentially the same. Localised enrichments in platinum and palladium can be shown in the gold with the DP-LA-ICP-MS analysis. They are likely the result of platinum elements inclusions associated with gold flakes in the gold placer.

What are the consequences of these variations in the platinum and palladium contents? The Pd/Au and Pt/Au ratios of seven different Lysimachus gold coins classified into different groups are plotted on a binary graph (Fig. 5). The relative standard deviations for each element are reported as errors. This graph can be compared with the one showing all the available data for Lysimachus gold (Duyrat and Blet-Lemarquand this volume; Fig. 3). Moreover, it leads to the same conclusions between two groups of coins: the Mithridatic Wars Lysimachi can be distinguished from the other groups of Lysimachus coins. This means that the gold they are made of is different from the gold used for the lifetime or posthumous Lysimachi. Thus, the micro-sampling does not limit the provenance studies on gold coinages.

The PGE inclusions

Platinum group elements (PGE) inclusions can be observed at the surface of certain ancient gold coins. Most of these inclusions are made of osmium-iridium-ruthenium alloy (Meeks and Tite 1980; Ogden 1977) but noticeable contents of platinum were sometimes reported for some of them (Blet-Lemarquand and Duyrat 2020; Lemasson *et al.* 2015) and could perhaps account for the platinum content of the gold.

---

[14] See Duyrat and Blet-Lemarquand this volume. Values from No. 4 micro-sampling were discarded from the calculations because they were too low.

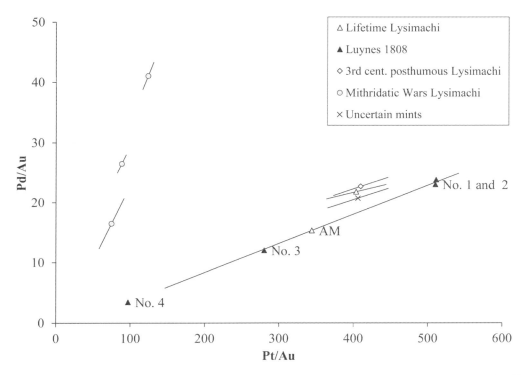

Figure 5. Scatterplot of the ratios of palladium and platinum to gold for seven Lysimachus gold coins.[15] The errors derive from the standard deviations calculated from the three (or four) different laser micro-samplings made per coin and take into account the fact that the platinum to palladium ratios remain constant for a coin. The four results obtained for Luynes 1808 (MMA, BnF) are made distinctive (see Table 4).

An inclusion was fortuitously analysed in the course of the LA-ICP-MS analysis of an early electrum coin (Fig. 6). The osmium, iridium and ruthenium contents dramatically increase from 100 seconds onwards whereas the platinum and palladium concentrations remain stable during the sampling. The profile graph clearly establishes that a PGE inclusion has been sampled and that it is of no consequence on the platinum and palladium content of the gold. As gold and PGE inclusions are only very rarely associated in primary deposits (Ogden 1977), it can be hypothesised that this coin was very likely manufactured from gold coming from a placer deposit containing both gold particles and PGE inclusions.

Conclusions

Depth profile analysis mode represents a real improvement compared with average quantitative analysis for gold coins. Different microstructural data can be obtained such as PGE inclusions, enrichment or depletion phenomena and so forth. It enables the researcher to characterise the alloy beyond enrichment and contamination layers leaving minor damage almost invisible to the naked eye. However, it seems that DP-LA-ICP-MS is not suitable for certain coins made of highly debased and corroded gold. Some elements may appear to be inhomogeneous at the scale of the micro-sampling (e.g. Pt, Pd and Pb). As a consequence, their contents have a higher degree of uncertainty than other elements. These limitations do not adversely impact the conclusions concerning the manufacture of coins or the provenance of metals.

[15] For explanations on the different groups, see Duyrat and Blet-Lemarquand this volume.

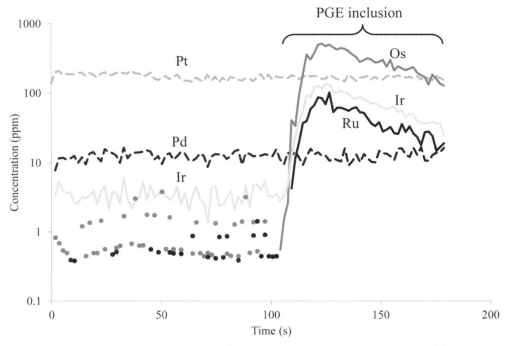

Figure 6. Concentrations profile for the main platinum elements versus the time of laser ablation obtained by DP-LA-ICP-MS for an early electrum coin (Luynes 2625, MMA BnF).[16]

Acknowledgments

We are grateful to F. Duyrat, to J. Olivier and to D. Hollard (Bibliothèque nationale de France, département des Monnaies, médailles et antiques), and to Y. Menez (SRA Bretagne), for allowing us to carry out analysis on their coinages.

Bibliography

Araújo, M.F., Alves, L.C. and Cabrai, J.M.P. 1993. 'Comparison of EDXRF and PIXE in the analysis of ancient gold coins', *Nuclear Instruments and Methods in Physics Research Section B: Beam Interactions with Materials and Atoms* 75, 450–453.

Artru, J. 2015. 'Carthage : monnaie et histoire, des origines à la troisième guerre punique' (Master II dissertation, University of Orléans).

Barrandon, J.-N., Aubin, G., Benusiglio, J, Hiernard, J., Nony, D. and Scheers, S. 1994. *L'or Gaulois. Le trésor de Chevanceaux et les monnayages de la façade atlantique*. Cahiers Ernest-Babelon 6 (Paris). Ed. du CNRS.

Beck, L., Barrandon, J.-N. and Gratuze, B. 1991. 'A non destructive method of the characterization of plating: depth profiles using the PIGE technique', in Pernicka, E. and Wagner, G.A. (eds), *Archaeometry '90* (Berlin,), 1–10.

Blakelock, E., La Niece, S. and Fern, C. 2016. 'Secrets of the Anglo-Saxon goldsmiths: Analysis of gold objects from the Staffordshire Hoard', *Journal of Archaeological Science* 72, 44–56.

Blet-Lemarquand, M. and Duyrat, F. 2020. 'Elemental analysis of the Lydo-Milesian electrum coins of the Bibliothèque nationale de France using LA-ICP-MS', in van Alfen, P., Wartenberg, U., Fischer-Bossert, W., Gitler, H., Konuk, K. and Lorber, C. (eds.), White Gold. Studies in early electrum coinage (New York, Jerusalem). 337–378.

Blet-Lemarquand, M. and Nieto-Pelletier, S. 2015. 'Analyses élémentaires, métallographiques et isotopiques', in Arnold-Biucchi, C. and Caccamo Caltabiano, M. (eds.), *Survey of Numismatic Research 2008-2013* (Taormina), 743–750.

Blet-Lemarquand, M. and Ponting, M. 2009. 'Scientific and Technical Examinations', in Amandry, M. and Bateson, D. (eds.), *Survey of Numismatic Research 2002-2007* (Glasgow), 714–719.

Blet-Lemarquand, M., Sarah, G., Gratuze, B. and Barrandon, J.-N. 2009. 'Nuclear methods and Laser Ablation Inductively Coupled Plasma Mass Spectrometry: how can these methods contribute to the study of ancient coinage?', *Cercetări numismatice* XV, 43–56.

---

[16] From Blet-Lemarquand and Duyrat 2020.

Blet-Lemarquand, M., Bompaire, M. and Morrisson, C. 2010. 'Platine et plomb dans les monnaies d'or mérovingiennes : nouvelles perspectives analytiques', *Revue numismatique* 166, 175–198.

Blet-Lemarquand, M., Gratuze, B. and Barrandon, J.-N. 2014a. 'L'analyse élémentaire des monnaies : adéquation entre les problématiques envisagées, les alliages étudiés et les méthodes utilisées', in Derschka, H.R. *et al.* (eds.), *Selbstwahrnehmung und Fremdwahrnehmung in der Fundmünzenbearbeitung. Bilanz und Perspektiven am Beginn des 21. Jahrhunderts. II* (Lausanne), 121–146.

Blet-Lemarquand, M., Nieto-Pelletier, S. and Sarah, G. 2014b. 'Chapitre 7 L'or et l'argent monnayés', in Dillmann, Ph. and Bellot-Gurlet, L. (eds.), *Circulation et provenance des matériaux dans les sociétés anciennes* (Paris), 133–159.

Blet-Lemarquand, M., Suspène, A. and Amandry, M. 2015. 'Augustus' gold coinage: investigating mints and provenance through trace element concentrations', in Hauptmann, A. and Modaressi-Tehrani, D. (eds.), *Archaeometallurgy in Europe III, Proceedings of the 3rd International Conference Deutsches Bergbau-Museum Bochum, June 29 - July 1 2011* (Bochum), 107–113.

Blet-Lemarquand, M., Nieto-Pelletier, S., Suspène, A. and Téreygeol, F. 2017. 'Are Platinum and Palladium Relevant Tracers for Ancient Gold Coins? Archaeometallurgical and Archaeometric Data to Study an Antique Numismatic Problem', in Montero-Ruiz, I. and Perea Caveda, A. (eds.), *Archaeometallurgy in Europe IV*, Bibliotheca Praehistorica Hispana, Vol XXXIII (Madrid), 19–28.

Blet-Lemarquand, M., Da Mota, H., Gratuze, B., Schwab, R. and Leusch, V. 2018. 'Material sciences applied to West Hallstatt Gold', in Schwab, R., Armbruster, B., Milcent, P.-Y. and Pernicka E., (eds.), *Iron Age Gold in Celtic Europe*, Society, Technology and Archaeometry. Proceedings of the International Congress held in Toulouse, France, 11–14 March 2015 [Forschungen zur Archäometrie und Altertumswissenschaft 6,1] (Rahden/Westf.), 101–132.

Bray, W. 1993. 'The Techniques of Gilding and Surface-Enrichment in Pre-Hispanic American Metallurgy', in La Niece, S., Craddock, P. T. and Terence, P. (eds), *Metal Plating and Patination* (Oxford), 182–192.

Cromwell, E. F. and Arrowsmith, P. 1995. 'Fractionation Effects in Laser Ablation Inductively Coupled Plasma Mass Spectrometry', *Applied Spectroscopy* 49, 11, 1652–1660.

Dussubieux, L, Golitko, M. and Gratuze, B. (eds.) 2016. *Recent Advances in Laser Ablation ICP-MS for Archaeology* (Berlin, Heidelberg).

Dussubieux, L. 2016. 'Analysis of Non-Siliceous Archaeological Materials by LA-ICP-MS', in Dussubieux, Golitko and Gratuze 2016, 91–93.

Dussubieux, L. and van Zelst, L. 2004. 'LA-ICP-MS analysis of platinum-group elements and other elements of interest in ancient gold', *Applied Physics A: Materials Science & Processing* 79, 353–356.

Eggins, S.M., Kinsley, L.P.J. and Shelley, J.M.G. 1998. 'Deposition and element fractionation processes during atmospheric pressure laser sampling for analysis by ICP-MS', *Applied Surface Science* 127–129, 278–286.

Flament, J. 2017. 'Les métallurgies associées de la fin du XIIIᵉ siècle au XVᵉ siècle. L'argent, les cuivres et le plomb à Castel-Minier (Ariège, France)', (PhD dissertation, University of Orléans).

Fricker, M. B. and Günther, D. 2016. 'Instrumentation, Fundamentals, and application of Laser Ablation-Inductively Coupled Plasma-Mass Spectrometry', in Dussubieux, Golitko and Gratuze 2016, 1–19.

Gratuze, B. 2016, 'Glass Characterization Using Laser Ablation-Inductively Coupled Plasma-Mass Spectrometry Methods', in Dussubieux, Golitko and Gratuze 2016, 179–196.

Gratuze, B., Blet-Lemarquand, M. and Barrandon, J.-N. 2004. 'Caractérisation des alliages monétaires à base d'or par LA-ICP-MS', *BSFN* 59, 163–169.

Gruel, K., Leclerc, G., Nieto-Pelletier, S., avec la collab. de Barrandon, J.-N., Blet-Lemarquand, M. and Gratuze, B. 2010. 'Les monnaies gauloises de l'Orne, de la Mayenne et de la Sarthe, approches typologique, analytique et territoriale', in Barral, P., Dedet, B., Delrieu, F., Giraud, P., Le Goff, I., Marion, S. and Villard-Le Tiec, A. (eds.), *L'Âge du fer en Basse-Normandie. Gestes funéraires en Gaule au Second Âge du fer. Actes du XXXIIIe colloque international de l'AFEAF* (Besançon), 247–260.

Lehrberger, G. and Raub, C. 1995. 'A look into the interior of Celtic gold coins', in Morteani, G. and Northover, J. P. (eds.), *Prehistoric gold in Europe: mines, metallurgy and manufacture* (Dordrecht), 341–355.

Lemasson, Q., Moignard, B., Pacheco, C., Pichon, L. and Guerra, M. F. 2015. 'Fast mapping of gold jewellery from ancient Egypt with PIXE: Searching for hard-solders and PGE inclusions', *Talanta* 143, 279–286.

Mason, P.R.D. and Mank, A.J.G. 2001. 'Depth-resolved analysis in multi-layered glass and metal materials using laser ablation inductively coupled plasma mass spectrometry (LA-ICP-MS)', *Journal of Analytical Atomic Spectrometry* 16, 1381–1388.

Meeks, N.D. and Tite, M.S. 1980. 'The Analysis of Platinum-group Element Inclusions in Gold Antiquities', *Journal of Archaeological Science* 7, 267–275.

Morrisson, C., Brenot, C., Callu, J.-P., Barrandon, J.-N., Poirier, J. and Halleux, R. 1985. *L'or monnayé I*, Cahiers Ernest-Babelon 2 (Paris), éditions du CNRS.

Nieto-Pelletier, S., Gratuze, B. and Aubin, G. 2011. 'Le dépôt monétaire gaulois de Laniscat (Côtes-d'Armor) : 547 monnaies de bas titre. Étude préliminaire', in Holmes, N. (ed.), *Proceedings of the XIVth International Numismatic Congress Glasgow 2009* (London), 1217–1225.

Ogden, J.M. 1977. 'Platinum group metal inclusions in ancient gold artefacts', *Historical metallurgy* 11, 53–72.

Pernicka, E. 2014. 'Provenance Determination of Archaeological Metal Objects', in Roberts, B. W. and Thornton, C. P. (eds.), *Archaeometallurgy in Global Perspective* (New York), 239–268.

Ponting, M. J. 2012. The Substance of Coinage: The Role of Scientific Analysis in Ancient Numismatics, in Metcalf, W. E. (ed.), *The Oxford Handbook of Greek and Roman Coinage* (Oxford), 12–30.

Russo, R. E., Mao, X., Liu, H., Gonzalez, J. and Mao, S. S. 2002, 'Laser Ablation in analytical chemistry—a review', *Talanta* 57, 425–451.

Sarah, G., Gratuze, B. and Barrandon, J.-N. 2007. 'Application of laser ablation inductively coupled plasma mass spectrometry (LA-ICP-MS) for the investigation of ancient silver coins', *Journal of Analytical Atomic Spectrometry* 22, 1163–1167.

Sarah, G. and Gratuze, B. 2016. 'LA-ICP-MS analysis of ancient silver coins using depth profile analysis', in Dussubieux, Golitko and Gratuze 2016, 73–87.

Scott, D.A. 1983. 'The deterioration of gold alloys and some aspects of their conservation', *Studies in Conservation* 28, 194–203.

Travaini, L. 1998. 'The fineness of Sicilian Taris, and of those of Amalfi and Salerno (11th to 13th centuries)', in Oddy, A. and Cowell, M.R. (eds.), *Metallurgy in Numismatics Volume 4* (London), 504–517.

Woodhead, J., Hellstrom, J., Paton, C., Hergt, J., Greig, A. and Maas, R. 2008. 'A guide to depth profiling and imaging applications of LA-ICP-MS', in Sylvester, P.J. (ed.), *Laser-Ablation-ICP-MS in the Earth Sciences: Current Practices and Outstanding Issues* (Vancouver), 135–145.

14. STUDIES IN ATHENIAN SILVER COINAGE: ANALYSIS OF ARCHAIC 'OWL' TETRADRACHMS

Gillan Davis, Kenneth A. Sheedy and Damian B. Gore

ABSTRACT

Archaic owl tetradrachms form an important subset of our research into Early Attic coinage. This paper analyses their physical characteristics and silver content based on measurements of 424 owl tetradrachms and 81 owl obols for comparison with fractional coinage. The paper proposes that the tetradrachms were deliberately minted at their ideal standard weight and with a consistently high purity of silver to make them acceptable as an export coinage. This stood in contrast to the preceding 'Wappenmünzen' and contemporary fractional coinage both of which were minted primarily for use in the domestic market place. Test-cutting in antiquity appears to have been carried out as a matter of routine checking primarily by overseas end-users, rather than on suspicion of individual coins.

INTRODUCTION

Towards the end of the sixth century BC, the Athenians changed their coinage from the so-called *Wappenmünzen* ('heraldic' coinage) series with its variety of state-sanctioned types, to the 'owl' type series.[1] The former was primarily a fractional (small denominational) coinage for domestic use in the marketplace (Davis 2014b), but it has been argued that the latter was developed as an export coinage seeking to capitalise on geopolitical factors which enabled substantially increased exploitation of the Lavrion silver mines (Davis 2014a). The doubling of the largest denomination *Wappenmünze* of the latest 'gorgon' type from a didrachm (stater) to a tetradrachm (distater) foreshadowed the change of series. Even after the introduction of the owl tetradrachms, the fractional *Wappenmünzen* coins continued to be used domestically alongside a lesser number of owl fractions until *c*. 479 BC which marked the defeat of the Persian invasion (Davis 2014b). Thereafter, a new owl type was clearly differentiated by the addition of a wreath to the helmet of Athena on the obverse to mark the victory (Starr 1970, 16-19), and all coins including fractions were struck as owls.

Somewhat neglected in earlier studies of Archaic Athenian owls is the important fact that they constituted a transitional phase between the *Wappenmünzen* and post-479 BC coinages. *Wappenmünzen* didrachms were struck approximately 4.3% under their theoretical weight standard on pre-cast, flattened flans (Davis 2011, 241),[2] presumably to generate a profit for the minting authority, but making such money fiduciary. A state could get away with this in areas under its direct control where it could mandate acceptance, but it could not have been the practice for an export coinage or the coins would not have been accepted at face value. Similarly, the purity of silver would have needed to be consistently high for an export coinage. The fabric of Archaic owl tetradrachms changed part way through the series with the introduction of striking from dumpy flans (Price and Waggoner 1975, 64), and this seems to have affected the regularity of their shape. There was continual experimentation in design leading to many variations in type. A proportion of coins were test-cut in antiquity, presumably on suspicion that they were not made from pure silver,[3] but this assumption needs to be tested.

The foregoing led to several research questions being posed about the Archaic owl tetradrachms which could be answered by physical measurements and chemical analyses. Firstly, what is the shape of the coins and can any deductions be made from this about their manufacture? Secondly, how

---

[1] This study forms part of combined research by the authors pursuant to Australian Research Council grant DP 120103519 (details in Sheedy, Gore and Davis 2009). *Wappenmünzen* is a poor descriptor popularised by Seltman 1924 based on the mistaken belief that the types represented the personal devices of aristocrats operating as mint magistrates. The date of the transition is likely to be *c*. 520-510 BC. Sheedy and Davis are preparing a full corpus of Archaic Athenian coins, die study, and discussion for publication.
[2] The *Wappenmünzen* didrachms consistently across all types had a weight of *c*. 8.36 g against a theoretical weight of 8.72 g. Although some allowance must be made for wear and corrosion, only 2 of the 145 known coins were over the ideal weight.
[3] Cf. *Hesperia* 1974, 157-88, lines 10-13 = Melville Jones 2009 number 91: "But if it (the coin being tested by the Certifier) is bronze beneath or lead beneath or counterfeit, let him cut across it at once, and let it be sacred to the Mother of the Gods and let it be deposited with the Council".

closely were the coins minted to the theoretical weight standard and how did this compare with contemporary obols? Thirdly, what is the purity of silver and is it related to the weight of the coin and the practice of test-cutting?

MATERIALS AND METHODS

This study forms part of a larger analytical program testing the extent to which Archaic Athenian *Wappenmünzen* and owl coins were derived from Lavrion (Attic) ores, together with comparanda from the other ore-producing areas in the ancient Aegean of Siphnos and Northern Greece. 2,516 elemental analyses have been undertaken of the obverse and reverse of 1,258 coins in seven major museum collections in Europe and the United States.[4] Of these, 424 coins (848 analyses) are Archaic owl tetradrachms. To put this in perspective, only a total of 110 Archaic owls have previously been reported in the literature analysed in six studies by a variety of methods over the last 50 plus years.[5]

The coins comprised every available specimen in the museums. They were measured for weight (424 coins), and orthogonal *a-axis* length (410 coins), *b-axis* width (338 coins) and *c-axis* thickness (176 coins). Weights were measured with a HA-Series 'Pocket Balance' portable diamond scale with a minimum increment of 0.01 g. Scale accuracy was checked against a 50.0 g calibration weight at least twice daily. Coin a, b and c axes were measured using a Measumax 0-25 mm Digital disc micrometer. The micrometer zero point was checked before every measurement, and repeated measurement of a stainless steel feeler gauge showed that the measurements were repeatable and accurate to 0.01 mm. Coins were photographed on both sides and in some cases on the edge, and all known details were recorded in a FileMaker (FileMaker Inc) database.

Elemental analyses were conducted on-site using transportable benchtop energy dispersive X-ray fluorescence spectrometry (EDXRF). Epsilon 3 spectrometers were supplied by PANalytical with 50 kV Mo or Rh anode tubes, and samples were measured on obverse and reverse, in air, for 600 s with spinner at 1 hz. Software was used in automatic mode with standardless quantification whereby automated qualitative spectrum analysis software ('Omnian') supplied by the instrument manufacturer was combined with a fundamental parameters matrix model. The automated deconvolution of every spectrum was checked manually. Certified reference materials were added to refine the Omnian calibration, and several ancient Greek silver coins were measured at least twice daily to check for instrumental drift.

Advantages of using EDXRF for coin analysis are that it is non-destructive and the instruments can be taken to the museums. This made it possible to gain permission from museum curators to analyse the coins. However, EDXRF is a near surface technique and a simple mathematical correction was adopted to correct for differences between near surface and bulk compositions (Sheedy, Gore and Ponting 2015; Gore & Davis 2016).[6]

---

[4] Museums: ANS New York; ANM Athens; Ashmolean Oxford; BnF Paris; BM London; Fitzwilliam Cambridge; SMB Berlin. We thank these institutions and their curators for facilitating the research.

[5] Data presented by Davis, G. in a paper delivered to the 14th International Numismatic Conference held in Glasgow, 30 Aug-4 Sep 2008. Methods include neutron activation analysis, ICP-MS with lead isotope analysis, X-ray fluorescence spectrometry and proton activation analysis. Problems with comparing these data include the analytical capabilities of the older equipment (such as poor mass resolution of ICP MS), analytical volume, elements reported, normalisation of results, and concerns about how representative the small sample of selected coins are of the chemistry.

[6] Differences arise from surface enrichment or depletion of certain elements in the patina. The correction works best for analysis of gold, electrum, or relatively pure silver coins or artifacts with thin patinas. It may not work for plated coins where the plating is sufficiently thick, but when the plating is even slightly damaged, EDXRF with the spinner on will detect elements from the coin core allowing the numismatist to treat it as suspicious.

Figure 1. SMB 18227651 – one of the earliest owl tetradrachms. a) obverse; b) reverse

Figure 2. BM 1896,0703.971 – an elongated owl tetradrachm. a) obverse; b) reverse

RESULTS AND DISCUSSION

Shape

The first question concerns the shape of the coins and whether or not deductions can be made about their manufacture. If the coins were struck from flans made in moulds, it might be expected they would be round. This is often the case, especially the earliest owls which were minted on deliberately flattened flans (Fig. 1).

However, a proportion are elongated (e.g. Fig. 2). This correlates with later coins in the series when the rate of striking dramatically increased to fund the war effort against Persia, and the technique of manufacture changed to using dumpy flans.

Some coins are almost triangular and appear to show signs of layers on part of their edges (Fig. 3). Professor Kroll's recent suggestion that some archaic coins were minted by re-striking through a process of adjusting for weight, folding twice, and striking is plausible for this series (Kroll 2017).

To test the variability in shape more accurately, the length (a-axis), width (b-axis) and thickness (c-axis) of coins were measured. The histogram of the a-axis lengths show some coins are very long, up to 30 mm (Fig. 4). However their maximum width is 26 mm (Fig. 5). The a/b ratio plots show most coins are slightly elliptical, with some coins being very elongate, with ratios >1.40 (Fig. 6).

The plot of a/b ratio vs a-axis shows that the very elongate coins (ratio >1.4) have similar a-axis lengths to other tetradrachms (Fig. 7). It follows that the elongation must be due to narrower widths. A plot of a/b ratio vs b-axis (Fig. 8) shows this to be the case, with all elongated coins (ratio >1.4) having substantially narrower widths (12-16 mm vs an average of 20.8 mm for the 338 coins whose b-axes were measured).

The thickness (c-axis) of the coins is extremely variable, ranging from 6 to 9 mm (Fig. 9). The a/c ratio shows that there is a population of owl tetradrachms with ratio >3.3, that are

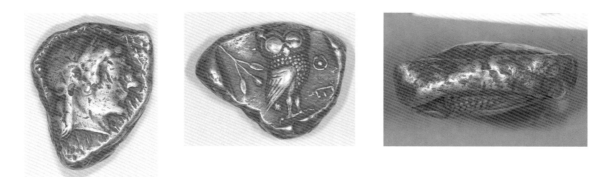

Figure 3. ANM Empedocles 35. a) obverse; b) reverse; c) edge - note probable evidence of folding on the third photograph

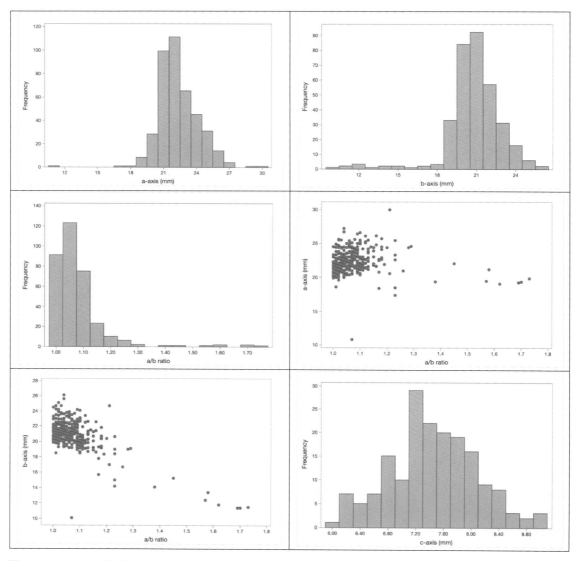

Figure 4. (upper left). Length of a-axis of owl tetradrachms (n=424 coins). Coins <19 mm are fragments.
Figure 5. (upper right). Length of b-axis of owl tetradrachms (n=338 coins). Coins <19 mm are fragments.
Figure 6. (middle left). a/b ratio of owl tetradrachms (n=338 coins).
Figure 7. (middle right). a/b ratio vs a-axis of owl tetradrachms (n=338 coins).
Figure 8. (lower left). a/b ratio vs b-axis of owl tetradrachms (n=338 coins).
Figure 9. (lower right). Length of c-axis of owl tetradrachms (n=176 coins)

thinner than the mode of 2.7-3.1 (Fig. 10). These are the early owl tetradrachms minted on the pre-flattened flans. Thereafter, and in marked contrast to the earlier *Wappenmünzen*, regularity of flans does not appear to have been a concern for the minting authority.

Weight

The second research question asks how closely the coins were minted to the theoretical weight standard to test whether they were fiduciary or intended for export, and how closely manufacture was controlled. The results of weighing the tetradrachms are presented in Figures 11 and 12.

The ideal weight of a tetradrachm on the Attic standard was 17.44 g. The average weight of the analysed coins is 16.91 g and median 16.95 g.[7] Some allowance should be made for the loss of metal mass through wear, corrosion and cleaning, and conversely for the extra mass gained from oxidation and accumulation of grime, but even without such allowance, the histogram demonstrates how closely the coins cluster around the ideal weight. 27 coins (6.9%) weigh more than the ideal weight with the heaviest weight being 18.45 g. This suggests that the output of mint production was averaged by the batch.

A contrast can be drawn with fractional coinage. Athenian owl obols in the same period had an ideal weight of 0.73 g but an average weight of only 0.60 ± 0.08 g (n=81 coins; Fig. 13), some 18% less. Small coins suffered wear by being frequently handled in everyday transactions, whereas tetradrachms (each worth roughly 4 day's pay for a skilled worker) were used less and mainly held as a store of worth or for trade. Nevertheless, it is likely the obols were deliberately minted under standard to defray minting expenses and perhaps to make a profit for the state.

There is a lighter weight tail in both the tetradrachms and obols, and there is also an elongated tail in the a/b ratio distribution. This elongation (greater a/b ratio) could be due to manufacture, wear or fragmentation. If from manufacture, elongate coins would have weights typical for their denomination; however, if the elongated shape was due to wear, then their weights would necessarily be less than what is typical for that denomination. Examination of the coin weight versus a/b ratios for the tetradrachms (Fig. 14) shows that all elongate coins (ratio >1.3; n=8) are lighter, consistent with loss of mass through fragmentation post-manufacture. There is also a population of lighter coins that are not elongated (ratio <1.3; n=8). This could be due either to wear or lack of purity (cf. section 3.3). In contrast, the obols (Fig. 15) do not cluster tightly in their weights and apart from two outliers (ratio>1.3) there appears to be no clear relationship with elongation and weight.

The percentage of silver

The third question considers the percentage of silver and its relationship to the weights of the coins and the ancient practice of test-cutting suspect coins. Figure 16 shows that owl tetradrachms were mostly composed of very pure silver, including almost all the fragments. The same holds true for the obols notwithstanding the spread of weights (Fig. 17).

Table 1 summarises the silver content of the owl tetradrachms. Over three-quarters of the coins have at least 98% silver, and ~95% of the coins have at least 95% silver. This confirms the ancient belief that Attic coins were minted from reasonably pure silver (for instance, Aristophanes *Frogs* 719-724). However, 20 coins (5.1%) have less than 95% silver. In antiquity, suspect coins were often test cut to check the interior. This was a matter of considerable concern with the death penalty attested in the fourth century at Athens for debasing the currency (Demosthenes 20.167). The ancient sources tell of testing by feel or suspicion;

---

[7] All specimens under 15 g were fragments of coins or severely damaged and were excluded from the calculations of average and median. The figure for all tetradrachms = 16.46+/-1.96, n=424.

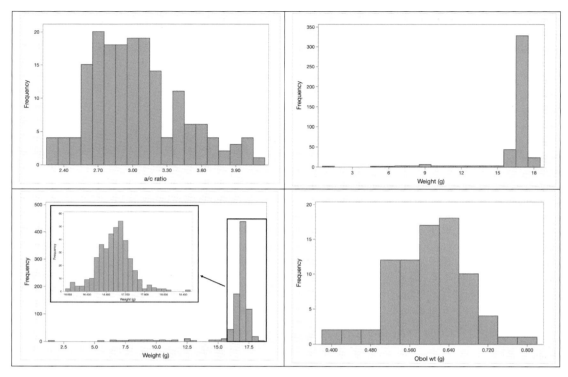

Figure 10. (upper left). The a/c ratio of owl tetradrachms (a/c ratio >3.3; n=176 coins).
Figure 11. (upper right). Weight of owl tetradrachms (n=424 coins).
Figure 12. (lower left). Detail of Fig. 11.
Figure 13. (lower right). Weight of owl obols (n=81 coins)

the physical evidence of the coins attests to chisel-cutting.[8] Intriguingly, the Early Attic coin database reveals that 5% of the tetradrachms were tested in this way (Sheedy and Davis forthcoming – see n.1). However, a check of the composition of the test-cut coins among our sample (n=18) reveals that only one has less than 95% silver, and 31 (86%) have greater than 98% silver. In other words, they follow the normal distribution, and suspicion of debasement cannot have been the reason for testing them. A likely explanation is that a proportion of coins were routinely tested by test-cutting, especially when they travelled to destinations abroad such as Egypt where they were valued primarily as bullion.[9] The coins officially tested at Athens (cf. n.3) were taken out of circulation.

Some of the 20 debased coins are ancient imitations or forgeries and are often distinguished by very high iron content (>10%; Sheedy and Davis forthcoming – see n.1). It is clear from the scatterplots that there is no relationship between the weight of the coins and the percentage of silver.

Table 1. Percentage of silver

Ag content (%)	No of coins	% of coins
> 98	315	76.5
> 97	366	87.7
> 96	386	93.7
> 95	391	94.9

[8] Aristophanes *Frogs* 723 spoke of coins made from pure metal "ringing true". Later [Arrian], *Discourses of Epictetus* 1.20.7-9 expanded on the "many means the silver tester uses to test it – sight, touch, smell and finally hearing; he throws the denarius down and listens closely to the sound, and is not satisfied with ringing it once, but becomes a sort of musician because of the great attention he pays to this" (= Melville Jones 2009, number 560 with translation, slightly adapted).
[9] Although the publication of the Asyut hoard does not identify which coins were test-cut, a scan of the plates clearly shows how regularly coins were test-cut (Price and Waggoner 1975, Plates I-XXXII).

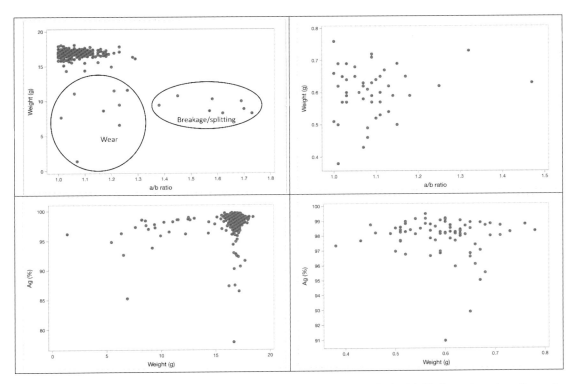

Figure 14. (upper left). a/b ratio vs weight of owl tetradrachms (n=338 coins) with likely explanations for underweight coins.
Figure 15. (upper right). a/b ratio vs weight of owl obols (n=81 coins).
Figure 16. (lower left). Weight versus percentage of silver for owl tetradrachms. Coins <15 g are fragments (n=424 coins).
Figure 17. (lower right). Weight versus percentage of silver for owl obols (n=81 coins)

CONCLUSIONS

1,258 silver coins have been measured including 424 owl tetradrachms which are the focus of this presentation and 81 owl obols used for comparison. Most coins are slightly elliptical and vary in thickness, probably as a result of hurried minting when production was massively ramped up before and during the Persian Wars. Analysis of the weights reveals that the coins were minted to their ideal standard. This is in contrast to both the *Wappenmünzen* which preceded them and the contemporary obols as an example of the fractional coinage minted for use in the local market place. 95% of the owl tetradrachms were minted from over 95% pure silver. It is proposed that these data demonstrate the owls were specifically intended as an export coinage from the outset. Approximately 5% of coins were test-cut in antiquity, but this appears to be routine practice, and not on suspicion that individual coins were debased.

BIBLIOGRAPHY

Davis, G. 2011. 'Law, Money, and the Transformation of Athens in the Sixth Century B.C.E.' (PhD dissertation, Macquarie University, Australia).
Davis, G. 2014a. 'Mining Money in Late Archaic Athens', *Historia* 63(3), 257-77.
Davis, G. 2014b. 'Where are all the Little Owls?', in Matthaiou, A. and Pitt, R. (eds.), *ΑΘΗΝΑΙΩΝ ΕΠΙΣΚΟΠΟΣ: Studies in Honour of Harold Mattingly* (Athens), 339-47.
Gore, D.B. and Davis, G. 2016. 'Suitability of Transportable EDXRF for the On-site Assessment of Ancient Silver Coins and Other Silver Artifacts', *Applied Spectroscopy* 70(5), 840-51.
Kroll, J.H. 2017. 'Striking and Re-striking on Folded Flans: Evidence from Athens, Cyzicus, (?)Sinope, Elis, Thebes, and Aegina', *Proceedings of the XVth International Numismatic Congress Taormina 2015*, 378-82.

Melville-Jones, J.R. 2009. *Testimonia Numaria: Greek and Latin Texts concerning Ancient Greek Coinage*, Vol.1 (London).

Price, M. and Waggoner, N. 1975. *Archaic Greek Coinage: the Asyut Hoard* (London).

Seltman, C. 1924. *Athens, its History and Coinage before the Persian Invasion* (Cambridge).

Sheedy, K., Gore, D.B., and Davis, G. 2009. ' "A Spring of Silver, a Treasury in the Earth": Coinage and Wealth in Archaic Athens', in Burness, J. and Hillard, T. (eds.), *Australian Archaeological Fieldwork Abroad II* 39(2), 248-57.

Sheedy, K., Gore, D.B., and Ponting, M. 2015. 'The Bronze Issues of the Athenian General Timotheus: evaluating the evidence of Polyaenus's *Stratagemata*', *American Journal of Numismatics* 27, 1-20.

Starr, C. 1970. *Athenian Coinage 480-449 B.C.* (Oxford).

15. THE SILVER OF THE OWLS: ASSESSMENT OF AVAILABLE ANALYSES PERFORMED ON ATHENIAN SILVER COINAGE (FIFTH – THIRD CENTURIES BC)

Christophe Flament

ABSTRACT

This paper proposes a critical and qualified assessment of the available physical and chemical analyses performed on the Athenian 'owl' coinage issued between c.475 and the early third century BC, discussing results and suggesting new issues and questions for future investigation.

INTRODUCTION

Many kinds of analytical methods have been applied to Athenian coins from as early as the eighteenth century. These include: chemical analyses (Barthelemy 1757, 154–8; Beulé 1858, 103–4; Hussey 1836, 45; Hultsch 1882, 233; Christomanos 1905, 115–20; Imhoof-Blumer 1972, 472; Bibra 1873, 40; Elam 1931, 57–6),[1] specific gravity analyses (Weber 1979, 975),[2] optical emission spectroscopy (Allin and Wallace 1954; Wallace 1962; Starr 1970, 91–3), neutron activation analyses (Kraay 1958, 1–2; Emeleus and Kraay 1962; Diebolt and Nicolet-Pierre 1977; Gale, Gentler and Wagner 1980), proton activation analyses (Nicolet-Pierre 1985; Nicolet-Pierre and Kroll 1990; Nicolet-Pierre 1998), X-ray fluorescence (Conophagos, Badecca and Tsaimou 1976; Pászthory and Hurter 1981; Pászthory 1982; Gore and Davis 2016; see also Davis, Sheedy and Gore in this volume), particle induced X-ray emission (Flament 2007b), inductively-coupled plasma atomic emission spectrometry (Gitler, Ponting and Tal 2009; Ponting, Gitler and Tal 2011; see also Faucher in this volume), lead isotope analyses (Gale, Gentner and Wagner 1980; Nicolet-Pierre 1998; Gitler, Ponting and Tal 2009; Ponting, Gitler and Tal 2011), and ToF-SIMS (Marjo *et al.* forthcoming).

Using these analyses, numismatists have tried to obtain information chiefly in two domains: the silver content of the coins and the determination of the provenance of the metal.

SILVER PROVENANCE OF THE OWLS – THE CHALLENGES

There are two ways of determining the provenance of the silver minted. The first is the respective proportions of the trace elements in silver. According to Gale, Gentner and Wagner (1980, 12), Athenian silver extracted from Laurion is characterised by a low gold (*c.* 0.016–0.33 %) and copper (*c.* 0.09 %) content, but by a relative high content of lead (*c.* 0.32–2.99 %).[3] The second method is lead isotope analysis, considered as one of the most accurate methods of identifying the original ore (Gale, Gentner and Wagner 1980, 9–10).

To question the provenance of the metal might seem at first sight superfluous in the case of Athenian coinage of the classical period, because it is well known that the silver of the owls came from the mining district of Laurion. The Athenian coins were nicknamed 'laureotic owls' (γλαῦκες Λαυρειωτικαί) during antiquity, as Aristophanes attests in his *Birds* 1105–8 (trans. Melville-Jones 1993, no. 58):

> First of all, which every judge longs for most of all, Laureotic owls will never leave you, but will dwell within (your city), and will nest in your purses, and hatch out little (deposit of) small change.

But there could have been several instances during the sixth-third centuries BC when the Athenian mint used foreign silver bullion. Identifying those instances, and the coins that were then minted,

---

[1] However, the results of most of these chemical analyses are difficult to exploit, if not totally unusable, because very few of the coins analysed were illustrated or accurately described.
[2] Specific gravity is accurate only for a binary alloy of gold and silver: Schmitt-Korte & Cowel 1989, 35.
[3] According to Stos-Gale and Davis (this volume), the Cu values average 0.65% and Pb just over 1%.

would provide the classification of Athenian coinage with chronological indications that are currently lacking.[4]

The determination of the metal provenance of the owls is also crucial because of the questions surrounding the so-called 'imitations' of Athenian coins. These are coins of correct weight and purity for Athenian monetary types which were issued by foreign rulers or states, especially Egypt where they were found in huge quantities (Robinson 1937, 189; Buttrey 1982). The principal criterion by which numismatists have identified several categories of Athenian coins as imitations is the poor style of their dies.[5] Determining the provenance of the silver of the coins identified as imitations may act as a crucial check of these attributions.

SILVER PROVENANCE OF THE OWLS – THE RESULTS

As far as the writer knows, none of the Athenian owl-type coins submitted to lead isotope analyses has ever proved to be indisputably made of non-Attic silver, even the most famous class of imitations known as Buttey's Styles M, B and X. Nine exemplars were analysed in 2009 with other coins from the Tel Mikhal hoard by Gitler, Ponting and Tal (2009). They concluded that "the majority of these coins are thought to be Eastern imitations based on style, but the analysis suggests that all these coins may actually be authentic Athenian issues" (Gitler, Ponting and Tal 2009, 29). The writer came to the same conclusion by way of the traditional methods of numismatics (die-links, hoard studies, etc.), underlining that arguments based solely on stylistic criteria are highly subjective and inconclusive (Flament 2005). Die-study indisputably reveals that talented and mediocre engravers worked together in the official Athenian mint (Flament 2012).

However, it is important to note that the number of Athenian coins submitted to lead isotope analyses is insignificant compared with the huge quantities minted by Athens during classical antiquity. Accordingly, information procured by elemental analyses cannot be neglected. Using elemental analysis, Pázthory and Hunter (1981; Pázthory 1982) claimed that Athenian coinage was partly made of Thracian silver until 512 BC, and Starr (1970 91–3) alleged that the coins of his Group II.C (to which the famous decadrachms belong) were made from the Eurymedon booty.[6] But those interpretations (Nicolet-Pierre 1998, 297 as concerns the decadrachms) as well as the accuracy of the analyses on which they were based (see Stos-Gale 1986, 987) were later discredited.

More reliable XRF, PIXE or NAA analyses (amongst others Gale, Gentler, Wagner 1980) have revealed several coins with chemical compositions that differ from the Laurion standard defined by Gale, Gentner and Wagner (see above), most of them belonging to Buttrey's Style X (Nicolet-Pierre 1985, Flament 2007b) and to the 'Quadridigité' Style (Nicolet-Pierre, Kroll 1990). Are those coins made of foreign silver? It is a high probability, but they should not to be automatically considered as foreign imitations on this account.

The results for Style X are mixed. The composition of several coins differs from those of Athenian coins, whereas other specimens match Laurion characteristics (Flament 2007a, 95). Furthermore, it was noted above that the lead isotope composition of the Style X coins analysed by Gitler, Ponting and Tal is not incompatible with a Laurion origin for their silver. According to the writer, Style X tetradrachms are not imitations, but Athenian coins struck partly with non-Attic silver. If they were issued at the beginning of the fourth century BC, historical events may provide a ready explanation.[7] At the end of the fifth century, mining operations were disrupted in Laurion by the Spartan permanent occupation of Dekelia and

---

[4] The recent interpretation of the lead isotopes analyses of the OXALID database by Stos-Gale and Davis (this volume) confirms the expectation from literary sources that non-Attic silver was used to issue the *Wappenmünzen*, but not all from Northern Greece.
[5] Several dies with Athenian types were actually found in Egypt: cf. Dattari 1905, and Meadows 2011.
[6] The precise date of this famous event is far from being well established: see Briant 2004, 38.
[7] The reader will find another interpretation of the Style X owls in Kroll 2011.

the Athenians opted to strike silver plated coins (Flament 2007c, 118–120). At the beginning of the fourth century, however, after Konon's victory over the Spartan fleet in 393, Athens received payments from the Persian Great King (Xen. *Hell*. IV, 8, 8–10; Paus. III, 9, 8; Diod. 14, 85, 3; Nepos *Conon* 4).[8] If Style X owls are among the first Athenian coins struck during the fourth century, it is not surprising that some of them were made from foreign metal.

The silver of the QD Style owls could also have come from a foreign gift to Athens. Nicolet-Pierre and Kroll (1990) considered that they were made of the 200 talents of silver (= 1,200,000 drachms) given by Hellenistic kings in 286/5 (Plut. *Moralia*, 851 D-F).[9] If those coins were not made of Laurion silver – noting that QD exemplars have still to be submitted to lead isotope analyse – it is simply because mining operations definitely collapsed in Laurion at the end of the 4th century B.C. (Flament 2007d, 79–80).[10]

To summarise, the two instances for which we have strong indications that Athens made use of foreign metal are each to be connected with a disruption of mining activities in Laurion. This perfectly illustrates the strong link between the mining industry and coinage in Athens, with lessees of the mines being definitely the main suppliers of the Athenian mint. The writer has argued elsewhere (Flament 2007d, 240–50) that probably almost all of the silver produced was minted, not just the sole part received by the State (such as the 100 talents[?] in 483/2).[11] This implies that the lessees had access to the Athenian mint to convert to coins the silver extracted from the ore.[12] Under those conditions, perhaps the Thorikos hoard (*IGCH 134*) is the deposit of such a lessee whose silver production was freshly minted. At closer sight, this solution actually accounts for many of the particularities of this hoard recorded by Bingen: "dans le cas du trésor de *Thorikos* 1969, ces trois caractéristiques (proportions des " fleurs-de-coin ", nombre de *die-links*, et homogénéité du style de la majorité des pièces) apparaissent avec une intensité que je ne connais pas pour d'autres ensembles de cette importance numérique, une intensité tellement exceptionnelle que, sur le plan de l'espace, le fait que Thorikos est en Attique ne suffit pas à l'expliquer" (Bingen 1973, 10).[13] The writer has also proposed that the Athenian mint was readily accessible to any private individuals wishing to convert silver objects (vessels, foreign coins, etc) to Athenian coins (Flament 2010a, 12–29)[14]; if this were the case, we would have then to conclude that the use of foreign silver by the Athenian mint is not necessarily to be associated with specific historical events, but could have occurred anytime.

DEBASED COINS

The majority of elemental analyses have confirmed the very high percentage of silver in Athenian coinage (more than 95% usually; cf. Davis, Sheedy and Gore in this volume), which probably explains why the owls were considered as the first international currency in the ancient world, as Aristophanes proudly wrote in his *Frogs* 718–725 (trans. J.R. Melville Jones 1993, no. 86):

---

[8] Maybe 400 talents: Asmonti 2015, 159–160.
[9] But the present writer (Flament 2010b) suggested that QD Style is earlier than Bingen believed, and thus made the assumption that the silver used was granted by Demetrios in 307/6. Against this proposal, see Kroll 2013.
[10] Even if some activities – which consisted essentially of resmelting of slags (Strabo IX, 1,23) – are attested until the Proto-Byzantine Period (Rehren, Vanhove and Mussche 2002, 28).
[11] [Aristotle] *Athenaion Politeia*, XXII, 7. See Flament 2014, and Davis 2014.
[12] Same opinion in Bissa 2009, 59.
[13] "In the case of the treasure of Thorikos 1969, the three characteristics (proportion of coins in mint condition, number of die-links, and homogeneity of style for the majority of pieces) appear with an intensity that I have not seen with any other numerically comparable assemblage, an intensity so exceptional that, in terms of space, the fact that Thorikos is in Attica is an insufficient explanation." (trans. G. Davis).
[14] Picard (2000, 83) made this proposal for the New Style tetradrachms.

We have often thought that the same thing has happened to the city, in respect of the good and fine men among its citizens, as happened with the old coinage and the new gold. We do not make use of these coins, not counterfeit but the fairest, as it seems, of all, and the only one struck well and ringing true among the Greeks and the barbarians everywhere.

Table 1. Selection of coins with unusually high levels of copper and/or lead

Abnormal amounts of copper:

Period	References	No. of coins	Cu %
Archaic	Emeleus and Kraay 1962	C38	2.8
	Pászthory and Hurter 1981	26	3
		28	1
		29	1.5
	Nicolet 1985	CA 263	4.03
5th century	Allin and Wallace 1954	9	1.3
	Conophagos, Badecca and Tsaimou 1976	10 (decadrachm)	2.5
	Gale, Gentner and Wagner 1980	17	2.48
	Flament 2007b	289 (group II.34)	2.12
	"	365 (group III.31)	3.19
4th century	Gale, Gentner and Wagner 1980	14	4.31

Abnormal amounts of lead:

Period	References	No. of coins	Pb %
Last third of the 5th century	Flament 2007b	291 (group II.?)	3.44
	"	297 (group III.7),	5.43
	"	394 (group III.9)	5.3
	"	395 (group III.9)	4.08
	"	421 (group III.13)	3.01

But some of those analyses also revealed Athenian coins whose silver may have been debased since they show unusually high levels of copper and/or lead.[15] They are listed in Table 1. This table lists a selection of coins with a far higher copper content than appears to have been standard at Laurion (see Gale, Gentner and Wagner above),[16] but also those with a high lead content (more than 3%), because lead, available in huge quantities in Athens at a very low price,[17] was used to debase silver. This can be deduced from Demosthenes regarding the falsification of coins (*Against Timocrates*, 214, trans. J. H. Vince, Loeb Classical Library):

> By way of proof that it is a more heinous crime to debase laws than silver coinage, he added that many states that use without concealment silver alloyed with copper and lead (πρὸς χαλκὸν καὶ μόλυβδον κεκραμένῳ) are safe and sound and suffer no harm thereby; but that no nation that uses bad laws or permits the debasement of existing laws has ever escaped the consequence.

Several questions arise when dealing with debased coins. First, who was responsible: private counterfeiters or the Athenian officials? Second, was the debasement intentional? As far as Athenian coinage is concerned, it is currently impossible to get firm answers to those crucial questions, but some lines of thought can be suggested.

As suspicious coins are few in number and scattered among different typological and chronological groups, it seems hazardous to link them with specific historical events. But it is worth noting that most of the exemplars with high lead content belong to groups issued

---

[15] G. Davis suggested to me that some of them may actually have been plated coins (pers. comm.).

[16] It is of course extremely difficult to draw a line between what is intentional and what is not. Gitler, Ponting, and Tal (2011, 119) proposed that a percentage of copper above 0.5–1% is intentional.

[17] 2 to 4 kg of lead had to be cupelled to produce a silver drachma of 4 g. according to Rehren, Vanhove and Mussche 2002. We learn from [Aristotle], *Econ.* II, 37 that a talent of lead cost 2 silver drachmas. So every percent of lead substituted into a talent of silver (that is to say the equivalent of a weight of 60 drachmas), 'saved' almost 60 silver drachmas, the equivalent of two months of pay for a soldier.

during the last third of the fifth century, and are specimens of the group III defined in Flament 2007c (see Table 1). Since the Athenian *Ekklesia* resolved to issue plated coins at the end of this century (see above), it is possible that Athens did not change from coins made of pure silver to plated coins without any transition, and hence that coins made of debased silver were struck before plated coins were issued in 407/6. But the concentration of coins with high lead content in those specific groups may have also resulted from a less efficient refining method (see below).

Prior to issuing plated owls, Athenians melted down silver offerings from their temples to strike coins, especially *phialai* (libation bowls - Flament 2007d, 101–2).[18] Such reuse may perhaps explain the higher copper content in some of the Athenian coins (especially Flament 2007b, nos. 289, 365). Picard (2010, 35–36 [writing about Euboean coins]; cf. Emeleus and Kraay 1962, 7; Panagopoulou 2007, 315) explained that copper might have been deliberately added to make the silver of the vessel more durable; the copper concentration in the coins made from the *phialai* would therefore be higher than usual. However, the melting down of vessels or offerings may not have been characteristic of the end of the Peloponnesian War. The following quotation from Demosthenes (*Against Androtion*, 48–9, trans. J. H. Vince, Loeb Classical Library) clearly suggests that during the fourth century this always remained an option when public funds were lacking:

> He delivered sundry harangues on the subject, telling you that you had a choice of three courses, either to break up the sacred plate, or to impose a fresh tax, or to squeeze the money out of the defaulters; and you naturally chose the last.

It should be borne in mind that debasement is not always intentional; the abnormalities in the composition of silver may also result from various incidents that occurred during the refining of the ore or the minting of the coins. For example, when the smelting pot is heated above the melting point of copper (which is higher than silver), some portion of the copper may alloy with the silver (Thompson 1960, 11). Such incidents may occur at anytime.

EVOLUTIONS IN THE CHEMICAL COMPOSITION OF THE OWLS

In 2007, the writer submitted all the results then available to a test of the equality of the statistical 'means' used to detect evolutions in the chemical composition of the owls between the fifth and third centuries (Flament 2007b, 18–21). One of the results is that the mean percentage of gold is higher in archaic owls than in the coins of the other periods. As the gold/silver *ratio* is not constant in the Laurion district (Thompson 1960, 10–5; Conophagos, Badecca and Tsaimou 1976, 12; Rehren, Vanhove and Mussche 2002, 27–46), this difference in composition may result from progressive spreading of the mining activities during the Classical period (see Morin *et al.* in this volume), or because the extraction shafts became deeper and deeper. But this high percentage of gold may also reflect the less efficient refining technique practised during the Archaic period (Picard 2001, 4), or the use of different sources of metal (cf. Stos-Gale and Davis in this volume).

Another important finding highlighted in the 2007 above-mentioned study is that the lead content of the fifth century owls proved to be higher and more variable than in the coins of the later centuries. The equality test applied in this study may have been distorted by the possible presence of debased coins issued at the end of the Peloponnesian War (mentioned above). But as the percentage of lead in silver is generally taken as an indicator of the efficiency of the refining technology (Clay 1988, 342), and as the output of the Athenian mint reached its zenith during the fifth century, another solution is that the high level of coin production led to less efficient refining. Perhaps to economise fuel, the cupellation was not

---

[18] It is worth noting that *IG* I³ 379 (ll. 28, 40, 72) mentions *epistatai* who, according to Ferguson 1932, 77f. were probably those of the Athenian mint.

totally completed. Transformation of ore required huge quantities of fuel: to produce a drachma of 4 g., about 1 kg of charcoal was needed for which 7 kg of wood had to be felled, chopped, stacked and burnt. In such conditions, the trees at Laurion would have been quickly denuded.[19]

Conversely, the lead content of fourth century owls is lower and more uniform, probably because refining methods were then optimised. It would be interesting to determine if this improvement is reflected archaeologically. The furnaces of Megala Pevka were reconstructed during the fourth century (Domergue 2008, 158), replacing previous ones dating from the fifth century. Was this rebuilding necessary because the former installations were dilapidated or required by technical improvements?

CONCLUSIONS

The contribution of metallurgical analyses has been crucial to the proposed re-attribution to Athens of most of the 'imitation owls'. This does not mean that imitations of Athenian coins were never minted during antiquity - the famous clause of the Nikophon Law (Rhodes and Osborne 2003, no. 25) testifies that they existed at the beginning of the fourth century, but many such previous identifications were not well founded. Furthermore, up until now, results of analyses have provided the classification of 'genuine' classical Athenian coinage with very few fixed points. For example, which owls were made from the melting down of the treasury of the Delian League after its transfer to Athens in 454 B.C. (Diod. XII, 38. 1–3), or from the recasting of the currencies of the members of the League ordered by the famous *IG* I^3 1453 decree enforcing uniformity of coinage, weights and measures to the allies?[20]

It would also be profitable to perform future investigation into two other important topics: first, the functioning and organisation of the Greek mints; and second, the refining operations practised in Laurion, and above all, their evolution.

BIBLIOGRAPHY

Allin, E.J. and Wallace, W.P. 1954. 'Impurities in Euboean Monetary Silver', *ANSMN* 6, 35–67.
Asmonti, L. 2015. *Conon the Athenian. Warfare and Politics in the Aegean, 414–386 B.C.* (Stuttgart).
Barthelemy, J.-J. 1757. *Voyage du Jeune Anacharsis en Grèce vers le milieu du quatrième siècle avant l'ère vulgaire* (Paris).
Beulé, C.-E. 1858. *Les monnaies d'Athènes* (Paris).
Bibra, E. 1873. *Ueber alte Eisen- und Silber-Funde, archaeologisch-chemische Skizze* (Nürnberg-Leipzig).
Bingen, J. 1973. 'Le trésor monétaire de Thorikos 1969', in Bingen, J., De Geyter, J. and Deraymaeker, D. (eds.), *Thorikos 1969. Rapport préliminaire sur la 6e campagne de fouilles*, vol. 6 (Bruxelles), 7–60.
Bissa, E.M.A. 2009. *Governmental Intervention in Foreign Trade in Archaic and Classical Greece* (Leiden).
Briant, P. 2004. 'La guerre et la paix', in *Le monde grec aux temps classiques. I. Le Ve siècle* (La nouvelle Clio. L'histoire et ses problèmes) (Paris), 17–131.
Buttrey, T.V. 1982. 'Pharaonic Imitations of Athenian Tetradrachms', in Hackens, T. and Weiler, R. (eds.), *Proceedings of the 9th International Congress of Numismatics, Berne, September 1979*, vol. 1 (Louvain-la-Neuve), 137–140.
Christomanos, A.K. 1905. 'Ἀναλύσεις ἀρχαίων νομισμάτων', *JIAN* 8, 115–120.
Clay, T. 1988. 'Metallurgy and Metallography in Numismatics', *NAC* 17, 341–352.
Conophagos, C.E. 1980. *Le Laurium antique* (Athens).
Conophagos, C.E., Badecca, H. and Tsaimou, C. 1976. 'La technique athénienne de la frappe des monnaies à l'époque classique', *NomChron* 4, 4–33.
Dattari, G. 1905. 'Comments on a Hoard of Athenian Tetradrachms Found in Egypt', *JIAN* 8, 103–111.
Davis, G. 2014. 'Mining Money in Late Archaic Athens', *Historia* 63(3), 257–277.

---

[19] According to Mussche e.a. 1967, 71, this phenomenon explains why mining activities during the late fifth century moved to Thorikos, a coastal site where import of wood from Euboea was easier. *Contra* Conophagos 1980, 300.

[20] The date and political significance of this decree are still a matter of dispute See Mattingly 1972, 324. One provision of this decree (section V) seems to order the melting down of a huge quantity of coins. See on *IG* I^3 1453: T. Figueira 1998; 2006; Flament 2010a, 12–20.

Diebolt, J. and Nicolet-Pierre, H. 1977. 'Recherches sur le métal de tétradrachmes à types athéniens', *RSN* 56, 79–91.
Domergue, C. 2008. *Les mines antiques. La production des métaux aux époques grecques et romaines* (Paris).
Elam, C.F. 1931. 'An Investigation of the Microstructures of Fifteen Silver Greek Coins (500–300 B.C.) and some Forgeries', *Journal of the Institute of Metal* 45, 57–69.
Emeleus, V. and Kraay, C.M. 1962. *The Composition of Greek Silver Coins. Analysis by Neutron Activation* (Oxford).
Ferguson, W.S. 1932. *The Treasurers of Athena* (Cambridge).
Figueira, T. 1998. *The Power of Money. Coinage and Politics in the Athenian Empire* (Philadelphia).
Figueira, T. 2006. 'Reconsidering the Athenian Coinage Decree', *AIIN* 52, 9–44.
Flament, C. 2005. 'Un trésor de tétradrachmes athéniens dispersé suivi de considérations relatives au classement, à la frappe et à l'attribution des chouettes à des ateliers étrangers', *RBN* 151, 29–38.
Flament, C. 2007a. 'Quelques considérations sur les monnaies athéniennes émises au IVe s.', *NAC* 36, 91–110.
Flament, C. 2007b. 'L'argent des chouettes. Bilan de l'application des méthodes de laboratoire au monnayage athénien tirant parti de nouvelles analyses réalisées au moyen de la méthode *PIXE*', *RBN* 153, 9–30.
Flament, C. 2007c. *Le monnayage en argent d'Athènes. De l'époque archaïque à l'époque hellénistique (c. 550 – c. 40 av. J.-C.)* (Louvain-la-Neuve).
Flament, C. 2007d. *Une économie monétarisée : Athènes à l'époque classique (440–338). Contribution à l'étude du phénomène monétaire en Grèce ancienne* (Namur).
Flament, C. 2010a. *Contribution à l'étude des ateliers monétaires grecs. Étude comparée des conditions de fabrication de la monnaie à Athènes, dans le Péloponnèse et dans le royaume de Macédoine à l'époque classique* (Louvain-la-Neuve).
Flament, C. 2010b. 'Le monnayage en argent d'Athènes au IIIe siècle avant notre ère', *RBN* 156, 35–71.
Flament, C. 2012. 'Ἀπόδοτε οὖν τὰ νομίσματα Ἀθηναίων Ἀθηναίοις. Retour sur les critères qui définissent habituellement les «imitations» athéniennes', in Holmes, N. (ed.), *Proceedings of the XIVth International Numismatic Congress, Glasgow 2009 vol. 1* (London), 170–177.
Flament, C. 2014. 'Études sur la « loi navale » de Thémistocle. II. Montant et gestion des revenus miniers', *LEC* 82, 247–265.
Gale, N.H., Gentler, W. and Wagner, G.A 1980. 'Mineralogical and Geographical Silver Sources of Archaic Greek Coinage', in Metcalf, D.M. and Oddy, W.A. (eds.), *Metallurgy in Numismatics*, vol. 1 (London), 3–49.
Gitler, H., Ponting, M. and Tal, O. 2009. 'Athenian Tetradrachms from Tel Mikhal (Israel): A Metallurgical Perspective', *AJN2* 21, 29–49.
Gore, D.B., G. Davis 2016. 'Suitability of Transportable EDXRF for the On-site Assessment of Ancient Silver Coins and Other Silver Artifacts', *Applied Spectrometry* 70/5, 840–851.
Hultsch, F. 1882. *Griechische und Römische Metrologie* (Berlin).
Hussey, R. 1836. *Essay on the Ancient Weights and Money* (Oxford).
Imhoof-Blumer, F. 1972. *Griechische Münzen: Neue Beiträge und Untersuchungen* (Graz).
Kraay, C.M. 1958. 'Gold and Copper Traces in Early Greek Silver', *Archaeometry* 1, 1–2.
Kroll, J.H. 2011. 'Athenian Tetradrachm Coinage of the First Half of the Fourth Century BC', *RBN* 157, 12–15.
Kroll, J.H. 2013. 'On the Chronology of Third-Century BC Athenian Silver Coins', *RBN* 159, 33–44.
Marjo, C., Davis, G., Gong, B. and Gore, D.B. Forthcoming. 'Spatial variability of elements in ancient Greek (ca. 600–250 BC) silver coins using scanning electron microscopy with energy dispersive spectrometry (SEM-EDS) and time of flight-secondary ion mass spectrometry (TOF-SIMS)', *Powder Diffraction* 32 (S2).
Mattingly, H.B. 1972. 'A Summing-up from the Point of View of the Numismatist', in Hall, E.T. and Metcalf, D.M. (eds.), *Methods and Metallurgical Investigation of Ancient Coinage. A Symposium Held by the Royal Numismatic Society at Burlington House, London 9–11 Dec. 1970* (London), 321–6.
Meadows, A. 2011. 'Athenian Coins Dies from Egypt: a New Discovery at Herakleion', *RBN* 157, 95–116.
Melville Jones, J.R. 1993. *Testimonia Numaria: Greek and Latin Texts Concerning Ancient Greek Coinage. Volume I* (London).
Mussche, H., Servais, J., Bingen, J., De Geyter, J., Donnay, G., and Hackens, T. 1967. *Thorikos 1965. Rapport préliminaire sur la troisième campagne de fouilles* (Bruxelles).
Nicolet-Pierre, H. 1985. 'Monnaies archaïques d'Athènes sous Pisistrate et les Pisistratides (c. 545 - c. 510). II Recherches sur la composition métallique des *Wappenmünzen*, en collaboration avec Jean-Noël Barrandon et Jean-Yves Calvez', *RSN6* 27, 23–44.
Nicolet-Pierre, H. 1998. 'Autour du décadrachme athénien conservé à Paris', in Ashton, R. and Hurter, S. (eds.), *Studies in Greek Numismatics in Memory of Martin Jessop Price* (London), 293–299.
Nicolet-Pierre, H. and Kroll, J.H. 1990. 'Athenian Tetradrachm Coinage of the Third Century B.C.', *AJN2* 2, 1–35.
Panagopoulou, K. 2007. 'Between Necessity and Extravagance: Silver as Commodity in the Hellenistic Period', *ABSA* 102, 315–43.
Pászthory, E. 1982. 'Archäometrische Untersuchungen an archaïschen Münzen Athens', *Gazette numismatique suisse* 126, 30–36.
Pászthory, E. and Hurter, S. 1981. 'Metallurgische Untersuchungen an archaischen Münzen aus Athen', *Gazette numismatique suisse* 124, 77–86.
Picard, O. 2000. 'Le contre-exemple du monnayage stéphanéphore d'Athènes', *RN* 155, 79–85.
Picard, O. 2001: 'La découverte des gisements du Laurion et les débuts de la chouette', *RBN* 147, 1–10.

Picard, O. 2010. 'Vingt-cinq ans de recherches sur les monnaies grecques avec Jean-Noël Barrandon', *RN* 166, 35–39.

Ponting, M., Gitler, H. and Tal, O. 2011. 'Who Minted those Owls? Metallurgical Analyses of Athenian-Styled Tetradrachms Found in Israel', *RBN* 157, 117–134.

Rehren, T., Vanhove, D. and. Mussche, H. 2002. 'Ores from the Ore Washeries in the Lavriotiki', *Metalla* 9/1, 27–46.

Rhodes, P.J. and Osborne, R. 2003. *Greek Historical Inscriptions 404–323 BC* (Oxford).

Robinson, E.S.G. 1937. 'Coins from the Excavations at El-Mina (1936)' *NC*5 17, 182–190.

Schmitt-Korte, K. and Cowell, M. 1989. 'Nabataean Coinage – Part I. The Silver Content Measured by X-Ray Fluorescence Analysis', *NC* 149, p. 33–58.

Starr, C.G. 1970. *Athenian Coinage 480–449 B.C.* (Oxford).

Thompson, M. 1960. 'Gold and Copper Traces in Late Athenian Silver', *Archaeometry* 3, 10–15.

Wallace, W.P. 1962: 'The Early Coinages of Athens and Euboia', *NC* 2, 23–42.

Weber, C.E. 1979: 'Gravimetric Characteristics of Greek Silver Coins: A Survey', *The Numismatist* 92/5, 971–981.

Stos-Gale, Z. 1986. 'X-Ray Fluorescence and Lead Isotope Analysis', in Price, M., Besley, E., Macdowall, D., Jones, M. and Oddy, A. (eds.) *A Survey of Numismatic Research 1978–1984* (London), 978–1003.

16. METALLIC COMPOSITION OF ANCIENT IMITATIVE OWLS – PRELIMINARY ANALYSES

Thomas Faucher

ABSTRACT

The IRAMAT-CEB in Orleans has a long tradition in the study of Athenian coins. One might note in particular the work done by H. Nicolet on the metallic composition of Athenian and Athenian style coinages. More recent studies have followed, employing various analytical techniques. Analyses by LA-ICP-MS in the IRAMAT-CEB offer more accurate results. The main aim of these new studies has been to provide new information on long debated questions regarding the Athenian owl coinage and their Eastern imitations (especially those from Egypt) by analysing coins from Eastern and Egyptian hoards. The results of the analyses of 79 coins by LA-ICP-MS show clearly that only those coins bearing a distinctive imitative feature (type, legend, or excessive crude style) have a different composition to coins known to have been minted in Athens. It is likely that all of the owls found in Egypt and previously thought to be Egyptian imitations, but without these distinct imitative features, were in fact minted with silver from the Laurion in Attica.

This study of the metal of silver tetradrachms identified as 'imitations' of Athenian coins came about not so much from an interest in the Laurion mines but rather in the coinage of Egypt. My curiosity was aroused by the huge number of tetradrachms with the characteristic Athenian types (head of Athena/owl) found in Egypt in the past. The archives of Giovanni Dattàri, an Italian antiquities dealer living in Cairo at the end of nineteenth and beginning of the twentieth centuries, reveal just how common these 'owls' were on the Egyptian market at the time. In 1904 or 1905, the Numismatic Museum in Athens received a donation from Dattàri of some 84 of these coins from the Tell Athrib hoard (*IGCH* 1663) together with the famous die (inv. 1904/5, no. IQ) with the same provenance (Dattàri 1905, 103–114). However, since the second half of the twentieth century, only two hoards containing owls have been reported as found in Egypt (van Alfen forthcoming). The same scarcity is also evident in reports from excavations. The only owl tetradrachm that I have seen in recent years was unearthed in the courtyard of the 10th pylon in the temple of Karnak in 2015 by the team of the Centre franco-égyptien d'étude des temples de Karnak (my thanks to G. Charloux for showing me this find).

The great quantities of silver tetradrachms with Athenian types found in Egypt persuaded a number of scholars that Egypt was a center for the mass production of imitative owls (see most notably Buttrey 1979, 1981 and 1982; Nicolet-Pierre 1998, and 2005). Clearly, Egypt was a center of production of imitative owls since some of the coins also carry the names of Artaxerxes, Sabaces and Mazaces (van Alfen 2002, 24–32). Furthermore, the discovery of dies for striking Athenian owls, such as that from Tel Athrib and the square shaped die found (underwater) at Herakleion and published by Andrew Meadows (2011), leaves no doubt that the production of imitations did occur in Egypt. Die-links between coins from hoards buried in Egypt also support this conclusion.

Nonetheless, in recent years, there was a tendency, especially as the result of the significant amount of work done by Christophe Flament, to give back to Athens many owls previously classified as imitative largely because of their crude style (Flament 2001; 2003; 2005; 2007a; see Flament this volume). We know that style can be misleading. However, if not by style, how can we separate genuine Athenian tetradrachms from imitations? Is it possible that an analysis of a coin's metal may provide answers? This approach is not new. Studies of the composition of ancient coins had begun as early as the eighteenth century; Flament (2007b) has reviewed the historiography of these analyses (see also Flament *et al.* 2008; Flament and Marchetti 2004).

In this chapter, I propose to explore the metallic signature of owls found in Egypt and the Near East. Although the question might be debated, I would argue that the silver of imitative coins does not come from the Laurion mines of Attica because there is no reason for any authority to melt down genuine owls to struck imitative ones. It is certain that the silver did not come from Egypt itself, as there are only rare occurrences of galena in the country, and analyses of Egyptian silver artifacts have yet to show the use of native Egyptian silver (Stos-Fernter and Gale 1979).

The coins in this sample have been analysed by LA-ICP-MS in the IRAMAT–Centre Ernest Babelon (for a presentation of the method see Sarah *et al.* 2007). This technique employs micro-sampling, virtually invisible to the naked eye (80μ), that goes through the surface of the coin and offers the quantification of 25 elements with very low detection limits (often under one part per million). The coins were chosen for two reasons. Firstly, they were available for analysis and secondly they all had a known provenance. All coins come from the Département des Monnaies, médailles et antiques (MMA) of the Bibliothèque nationale de France (we would like to thank F. Duyrat, director of the MMA of the BnF and J. Olivier, in charge of the Greek coins collection for their help and support). In the development of the MMA there has been a special interest in Athenian owls; the collection now has around 400 examples (Archaic and Classical periods). Furthermore, the Département holds a number of hoards of these coins from Egypt, Turkey, Syria and Iraq. Some 79 coins were chosen. They fall into six groups (see table 1 and plates): three groups are from Egypt and three are from outside Egypt. The Egyptian coins belong firstly to the Tell el Maskhuta hoard (*IGCH* 1649), and then secondly to the Delepierre collection (*SNG France* 1) where several coins (Table 1, no. 15–31) are said to come from a hoard of 200 coins unearthed in Egypt. The third Egyptian grouping consists of coins in the names of Artaxerxes, Sabaces and Mazaces (surely minted in Egypt) as well as two obols with a hieroglyph on the reverse (Table 1, no. 46–47). The other coins come from different finds in Turkey and Near East. These hoards are first, the hoard of Hillah 1953 (*IGCH* 1752), a city 10km south of the Ancient Babylon; second, the hoards of Baghdad 1954 (*IGCH* 1753) and 1957 (we have no information on this hoard); and third, the hoard of Marache (*IGCH* 1243) found in northeastern Syria (Modern Turkey) in 1947 or 1948 (Seyrig 1972). There is one coin from the hoard of Karaman, central Anatolia (*IGCH* 1243). In addition, a few imitations from Gaza were analysed. Finally, we included two coins from the excavations at Susa in modern Iran (Göbl *et al.* 1960)

Many different methods have been used to characterise the metallic content of silver tetradrachms with Athenian types, including nuclear (both neutron and proton activation), Pixe, XRF and chemical analyses (Flament 2007b). I leave aside isotopic analysis as this has not been conducted on the coins in our sample. Isotopic analysis is a complex topic with many problems that still need to be resolved (see Blet-Lemarquand *et al.* and Stos-Gale and Davis in this volume). On reviewing the results from the various methods listed above we can see that a number of studies (see Flament 2007b) simply provide the basic elements present in the metal, often only copper and gold. This does not permit the study of the trace elements that can be detected through LA-ICP-MS. Furthermore, it is difficult to compare analyses done on different coins by different methods. It is easier to compare results when different methods are applied on the same coins. Finally, it would appear that some of the data provided by earlier studies is doubtful at best, as we shall see below.

The owl coins in the collection of the BnF are ideal for the present study for there is a large number of specimens and some information regarding provenance. The first analyses were conducted by Nicolet and Diebolt (1977); here neutron activation analysis was performed by Diebolt at Grenoble, France. In this project coins from three different hoards were analysed: Bagdad, Marache and Cilicia (see references above). Eight of these coins have been analysed again by LA-ICP-MS within the framework of this chapter. As is apparent from the data and diagrams I present here, the results are completely different, especially in relation to the amount of copper and gold. One might contrast the recorded levels of less than 0.1% in the coins analysed by ICP-MS on the one hand, and levels of several percent from the nuclear neutron activation analysis of the same coins. However, analyses made by neutron activation are supposed to derive from the entire coin and therefore to be more accurate than methods where only the upper layer is analysed (which is the case for LA-ICP-MS). In the publication of the NAA results (Nicolet and Diebolt 1977), Hélène Nicolet made a clear separation between coins that she believed were of a crude style, and thus apparently imitations in her view, and genuine coins which contained less gold and less copper. Nicolet was nevertheless sceptical about the results obtained by Kraay and Emeleus (1962), which showed much lower levels of gold and copper: "On constate donc aisément que les mesures effectuées à Grenoble après irradiation de la totalité de chaque pièce par une source de Californium–252 se situent dans un ordre de grandeur différent de toutes celles que nous venons d'énumérer" ("It is therefore easy to see that the measurements made in Grenoble after irradiation of all the samples by Californium–52 are of a different order of magnitude than the others we have mentioned." Nicolet and Diebolt 1977, 90). But the results obtained in Grenoble clearly do not suit other sets of data ; therefore, the results from these analyses from 1977 need to be discarded.

The most interesting comparisons prove to come from coins found in the Tell el Maskhuta hoard and analysed by Flament (2007b; Flament and Marchetti 2004). We will leave aside the question of style and the distinctions between imitative and genuine coins proposed by Buttrey (Buttrey 1982). Here we compare analyses made by PIXE for Flament (2007b) and those by LA-ICP-MS for the present study. The analyses were performed on coins from the same hoard, Tell el Maskhuta, but not on the same coins. Those studied by Flament are part of the Koninklijke Bibliotheek van België (KBR) collection in Brussels while the coins analysed here are part of the collection of the BnF in Paris. I have selected coins in accordance with those previously studied; they were taken from the same series in order to be able to make comparisons (my thanks go to C. Flament for help in this matter). Comparing the graphs, we can see that the analyses done by LA-ICP-MS provide slightly different results overall. For some coins the results are similar but for most of them the copper content in coins analysed by PIXE is far higher (three of 69 have over 0.1% copper) than in coins analysed by LA-ICP-MS (only six of 15 coins contain more than 0.1% copper). We have found less copper but also less gold in coins analysed by LA-ICP-MS (Figure 1). The gold

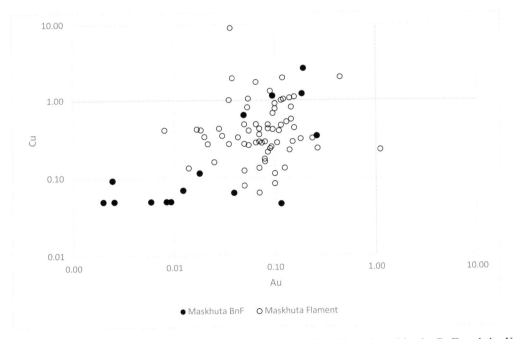

Figure 1. Copper and gold content of the coins from the Tell el Maskhuta hoard in the BnF and the KBR by PIXE and LA-ICP-MS

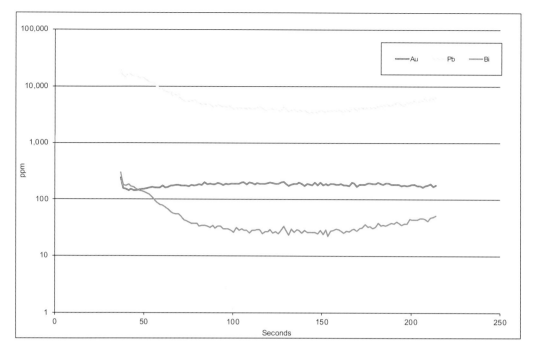

Figure 2. Profile spectrum showing correlation between lead and bismuth

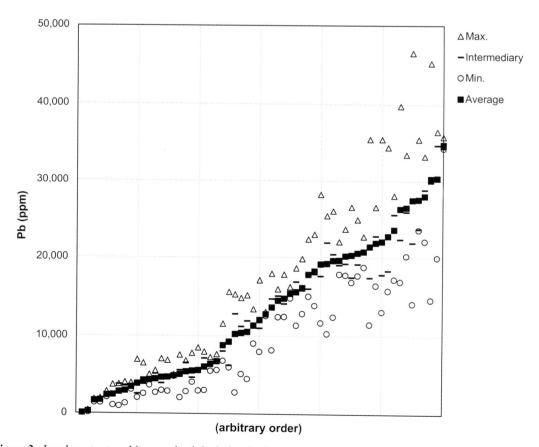

Figure 3. Lead content and its standard deviation in the analysed sample

content measured by LA-ICP-MS for these coins is always higher than the detection limit (which is equivalent to 0.12 ppm; Sarah and Gratuze 2016, 82).

One of the important features of the results of LA-ICP-MS analysis is the data for numerous trace elements. It is necessary, however, to determine which elements are related if we are going to use this data to investigate the provenance of the ores. Significant attention has been given to bismuth. Bismuth is known to be one of the elements linked to silver and lead and it has been argued that it can be used to determine the origins of silver ores (L'Heritier *et al.* 2015). The LA-ICP-MS profile spectrum (Fig. 2) shows the relationship between bismuth content and the level of lead in coins (Sarah *et al.* 2007) when, at the same time, the level of gold stays constant. Most of the time the quantity of lead is greater than the quantity of bismuth, with bismuth being only a trace element. The ratio can vary quite significantly (from 1–5 ppm to 2000 ppm). In the case of one coin from the Marache hoard (sample R 2693), the bismuth content is 10 times larger than lead, the coin showing in this case very low levels of lead (about 300 ppm).

Figure 3 shows the different amounts of lead inside the coins and the deviation within each coin. In general, three analyses were performed on the coin, sometimes four, when the spectrum or the results revealed something unusual. The range is on average 35.4%. If we consider the three coins with the most lead content (3% and 3.5% and 3.8%) (table 1: 56, 58 and 33), the standard deviation for the first is of 50%, only 2.5% for the second and 20% for the third. It shows that the standard deviation can be very high but it also differs greatly from coin to coin.

So what about the imitative owls? Figure 4 shows gold and bismuth (with the size of the 'bubble' being related to the amount of copper). It is possible to identify two groups. The first has a relatively low amount of gold; the amount of bismuth increases when there is more gold. It also has low quantities of copper. The second group is richer in gold and generally has more copper. The first group consists mainly of coins from the tell el Maskhuta

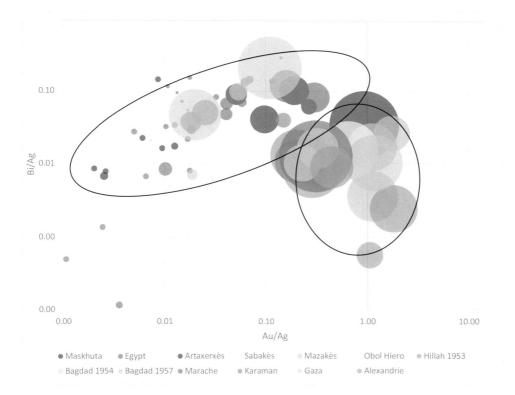

Figure 4. Gold and bismuth content in the analysed sample

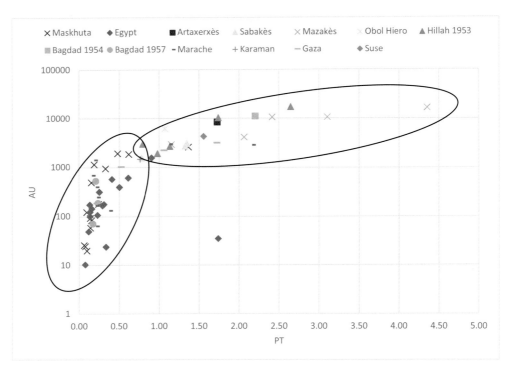

Figure 5. Platinum and gold content in the analysed sample

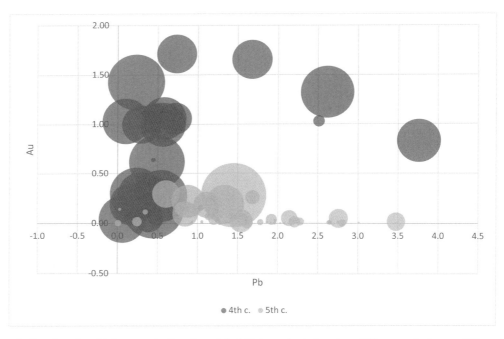

Figure 6. Lead and gold (copper is the size of bubble) content showing differences between fifth and fourth century coins

hoard, the Marache hoard (except one, but this has a very clear sign on the cheek of Athena that it is an imitation) and the Bagdad hoard. The second group is mainly composed of coins minted by Sabaces and Mazaces, and coins from the Hillah hoard. The coins from Gaza are mainly in the second group but two are part of the first group (even if their content in copper is a lot higher).

The amount of gold contained in these silver tetradrachms produces similar groupings. The coins from the Delepierre collection, and from the Tell el Maskhuta and Marache hoards are clearly distinct (Fig. 5). Coins struck in Egypt and the East studied in this project show different levels of gold and platinum, two elements that are connected (Blet-Lemarquand *et al.* 2014, 135).

Of course, these results need confirmation from other analyses. Julien Olivier (2012) has now completed the analysis of the first Ptolemaic silver coins issued in Alexandria, all from the end of fourth century; these results will be published in his forthcoming volume of *Etudes Alexandrines*. The lower levels of lead and copper in these Ptolemaic coins distinguish them from the silver issues of Mazaces (for an overview of the Egyptian coinage elementary composition see Olivier and Faucher forthcoming). This leads us to consider the consequences of the dissemination of the silver captured by Alexander from the Persian treasuries.

A final question. Is there any difference between the silver of the fifth and the fourth century BC tetradrachms that we have examined in this study? We can see that for most of the coins the levels of lead are higher in coins of the fifth century BC (Fig. 6). On the other hand, the levels of gold are much higher in coins of the fourth century BC. Are these differences the product of the deliberate addition of lead, or even the result of changes in the thoroughness of the smelting processes (as suggested most recently by Gitler *et al.* 2009, 34)? These questions will need to be answered in the future.

These analyses of silver tetradrachms with Athenian types, found mostly in Egypt and the Near East, were undertaken to explore the possibility that they might offer a means to distinguish the products of the Egyptian mint from genuine Attic productions. The question of the characterisation of the Attic silver is a complex one and this chapter does not intend to give an answer to this specific point. The analyses show that coins with no clear imitative features and which we believed to have been minted by Athens appear on the graphs (Fig. 4) as a large 'cloud'. Studies of a larger sample will be needed to determine the origin of the metallic stocks used by Athens to strike its owls. These metal analyses would have to be coupled with die analyses and hoard studies. The main focus of the present study is the possibility of distinguishing Oriental and Egyptian imitations. The results of the analyses show that when coins are clearly imitations (an obvious crude style, a corrupted legend or a change in the typology), the composition in major metallic elements and/or traces elements will be different. There is no reason to believe that coins sometimes identified as imitations (such as Buttrey 1982, group X), but showing the exact same features as genuine Attic coins, are local products. If they were, it is very likely that they would show the same elemental characteristics as coins which are obvious imitations (because of inscriptions *etc.*).

I wish to conclude by proposing that the production of local Egyptian imitations, even if they existed, has been largely overestimated in the past. I note in this regard that Ponting *et al.* (2011, 44) have concluded from the analysis of Athenian-type tetradrachms and Philistian and Edomite coinages that much of the silver used for their production "probably originated in the Greek world, especially Athens". They find (2011, 44–47) that their metallurgical analyses suggest that coins typically identified as eastern imitations are in fact genuine Athenian issues. The larger, more representative, sample published here adds weight to this evidence. Furthermore, the present study also supports the broader claim by Flament that large numbers of coins found in eastern hoards, sometimes believed to be imitations, were in fact minted in Athens.

Table 1. Sample Analyses

Catalogue	BnF Number	Ruler/Provenance	Denomination	Ag (%)	Cu (%)	Pb (%)	Au (%)	Bi (%)	Co (ppm)	Zn (ppm)	As (ppm)	Pd (ppm)	Sn (ppm)	Sb (ppm)	Pt (ppm)	Au (ppm)
1	Y28001	Maskhuta	Tetradrachm	97.9	1.13	0.85	0.09	0.040	0.04	4.0	1.5	1.9	12.7	0.8	0.3	950
2	Y28005	Maskhuta	Tetradrachm	98.0	<0.05	1.96	0.00	0.008	0.08	5.6	4.3	1.9	3.4	0.6	0.1	26
3	Y28006	Maskhuta	Tetradrachm	96.5	0.64	2.76	0.05	0.087	0.60	4.2	10.0	2.7	40.6	1.5	0.2	495
4	Y28007	Maskhuta	Tetradrachm	97.1	0.09	2.81	0.00	0.007	0.26	9.0	4.7	2.3	37.4	0.8	0.1	25
5	Y28008	Maskhuta	Tetradrachm	99.4	0.05	0.35	0.12	0.137	0.01	3.1	0.1	1.3	0.3	0.1	0.2	1153
6	Y28009	Maskhuta	Tetradrachm	97.6	0.12	2.28	0.02	0.028	0.04	1.0	0.1	2.1	1.9	0.1	0.1	179
7	Y28010	Maskhuta	Tetradrachm	98.6	<0.05	1.36	0.01	0.016	0.05	3.7	0.4	1.9	3.2	0.7	0.1	93
8	Y28011	Maskhuta	Tetradrachm	97.0	<0.05	2.64	0.01	0.100	0.04	5.3	3.5	1.8	4.4	0.5	0.1	96
9	Y28012	Maskhuta	Tetradrachm	98.1	0.07	1.78	0.01	0.017	0.09	10.6	6.3	1.9	5.8	1.4	0.1	123
10	Y28013	Maskhuta	Tetradrachm	98.0	<0.05	1.92	0.01	0.022	0.05	5.0	0.5	1.8	0.6	0.2	0.1	59
11	Y28014	Maskhuta	Tetradrachm	98.5	<0.05	1.48	0.002	0.008	0.05	2.4	0.6	1.9	0.5	0.2	0.1	20
12	Y28015	Maskhuta	Tetradrachm	95.8	2.61	1.34	0.19	0.010	0.35	1.2	14.4	0.9	127.0	35.4	0.5	1920
13	Y28153	Maskhuta	Tetradrachm	97.4	1.21	1.11	0.19	0.100	0.09	5.1	2.8	0.8	27.4	1.2	0.6	1861
14	Y28154	Maskhuta	Tetradrachm	97.6	0.35	1.69	0.26	0.060	0.05	14.7	1.0	1.9	3.5	0.4	1.4	2606
15	Y23432	Maskhuta	Tetradrachm	97.5	0.06	0.06	0.04	0.004	1.63	20046.4	1.4	0.8	30.9	1.6	0.5	393
16	1442	Egypt	Tetradrachm	97.1	0.02	2.75	0.01	0.069	0.04	1.3	0.5	0.6	0.2	0.2	0.2	145
17	1452	Egypt	Tetradrachm	97.3	0.04	2.65	0.01	0.031	0.03	3.9	0.3	0.6	9.7	0.3	0.1	100
18	1455	Egypt	Tetradrachm	98.1	0.12	1.56	0.06	0.132	0.02	3.8	0.2	0.8	0.5	0.1	0.6	615
19	1460	Egypt	Drachm	98.9	<0.05	1.05	0.02	0.008	0.01	0.7	0.1	0.4	1.0	0.0	0.1	175
20	1461	Egypt	Drachm	98.1	<0.05	1.86	0.01	0.033	0.05	1.8	0.1	0.6	6.0	0.1	0.1	124
21	1462	Egypt	Drachm	97.9	<0.05	1.97	0.03	0.081	0.01	3.1	0.5	0.4	0.4	1.8	0.3	317
22	1463	Egypt	Drachm	98.5	0.21	1.20	0.04	0.047	0.07	4.6	6.6	0.6	1.5	0.9	0.5	400
23	1464	Egypt	Trihemiobol	99.9	0.07	0.01	0.004	0.000	0.02	0.1	0.1	0.5	0.1	0.0	1.7	35
24	1466	Egypt	Hemiobol	98.0	<0.05	2.03	0.002	0.001	0.01	7.8	0.5	1.7	2.9	0.3	0.3	24
25	1467	Egypt	Hemiobol	97.9	<0.05	2.08	0.001	0.000	0.02	4.2	0.1	0.5	0.2	0.0	0.1	10
26	1468	Egypt	Hemiobol	98.7	<0.05	1.28	0.005	0.027		6.5	0.5	0.5	1.8	0.1	0.1	49
27	1472	Egypt	Tetradrachm	97.2	1.50	1.04	0.16	0.115	0.31	2.4	4.0	1.1	41.0	1.6	0.9	1561
28	1475	Egypt	Tetradrachm	99.4	0.13	0.39	0.06	0.070	0.04	2.1	0.5	0.7	28.1	0.1	0.4	578
29	1478	Egypt	Tetradrachm	99.3	0.03	0.51	0.01	0.116	0.02	0.6	0.2	0.5	23.9	0.0	0.2	107
30	1481	Egypt	Tetradrachm	99.5	<0.05	0.43	0.02	0.021	0.03	2.0	0.1	0.6	0.2	0.1	0.3	168
31	1482	Egypt	Tetradrachm	99.2	0.03	0.56	0.02	0.153	0.02	1.9	0.4	0.6	0.9	0.1	0.3	177
32	1968-940	Found in Egypt	Tetradrachm	95.5	3.33	0.45	0.64	0.055	0.19	7.5	1.9	2.5	19.6	2.5	1.9	6390
33	2002-143	Artaxerxes	Tetradrachm	88.7	6.63	3.76	0.83	0.031	8.13	154.9	162.1	2.6	182.5	33.0	1.7	8295
34	R2716	Sabaces	Tetradrachm	99.2	0.15	0.45	0.16	0.014	0.04	9.4	0.2	2.6	2.3	0.1	0.8	1563
35	SdeR 322A	Sabaces	Tetradrachm	99.1	0.10	0.55	0.27	0.007	0.06	9.8	1.4	2.8	23.4	0.2	1.3	2728
36	3045	Sabaces	Tetradrachm	98.8	0.23	0.64	0.31	0.000	0.03	0.5	0.0	0.8	0.4	0.0	1.3	3059
37	R2713	Mazaces	Tetradrachm	91.4	4.92	2.51	1.03	0.021	0.21	2.7	11.4	4.0	682.3	13.6	2.7	10285
38	R2714	Mazaces	Tetradrachm	90.3	5.66	2.62	1.32	0.016	0.58	3.2	20.8	2.7	494.3	51.1	2.4	13242
39	R2715	Mazaces (Hillah)	Tetradrachm	95.6	2.64	0.23	1.43	0.007	0.13	5.3	25.7	4.3	433.5	19.9	3.0	14264
40	R2717	Mazaces (Bagdad 1954)	Tetradrachm	95.2	3.40	0.30	1.00	0.007	1.58	5.5	12.9	3.0	373.9	19.4	2.4	9982
41	1973-1-190	Mazaces	Tetradrachm	99.2	0.13	0.28	0.29	0.008	0.03	1.8	1.8	2.2	373.7	1.3	1.2	2942

Table 1. *Continued.*

Catalogue	BnF Number	Ruler/Provenance	Denomination	Ag (%)	Cu (%)	Pb (%)	Au (%)	Bi (%)	Co (ppm)	Zn (ppm)	As (ppm)	Pd (ppm)	Sn (ppm)	Sb (ppm)	Pt (ppm)	Au (ppm)
42	M4967	Mazaces	Tetradrachm	96.3	2.80	0.47	0.41	0.013	0.21	1.6	7.3	3.1	366.3	8.0	2.1	4136
43	1987-164	Mazaces	Tetradrachm	94.8	1.84	1.68	1.66	0.025	0.20	3.0	3.7	4.7	226.5	12.1	4.4	16553
44	1972-1340-67	Mazaces	Tetradrachm	94.6	3.31	0.72	1.06	0.016	0.96	6.8	92.7	4.0	2235.4	36.4	2.4	10595
45	1970-91	Mazaces	Drachm	94.8	3.56	0.58	1.06	0.003	0.37	5.6	13.2	3.4	218.7	9.1	3.1	10602
46	3043	Obol Hieroglyph	Obol	93.0	5.38	0.57	1.00	0.016	0.03	2.2	5.4	1.3	4.9	3.0	1.7	9967
47	3044	Obol Hieroglyph	Obol	94.0	4.81	0.49	0.62	0.014	2.83	3.9	39.8	1.1	114.0	10.9	1.1	6170
48	R2708	Hillah 1953	Tetradrachm	94.3	4.89	0.54	0.28	0.009	1.76	5.7	28.3	2.2	275.2	15.6	1.1	2687
49	R2709	Hillah 1953	Tetradrachm	96.7	2.75	0.24	0.30	0.010	0.82	8.5	14.3	1.8	19.8	6.9	0.8	2987
50	R2710	Hillah 1953	Tetradrachm	94.4	3.13	0.74	1.71	0.002	0.22	5.9	7.0	1.5	47.2	8.3	2.6	17132
51	R2711	Hillah 1953	Tetradrachm	95.8	3.79	0.17	0.19	0.012	1.45	9.2	13.2	1.6	7.4	11.3	1.0	1919
52	R2712	Hillah 1953	Tetradrachm	97.9	0.98	0.10	1.03	0.001	0.02	5.8	1.9	1.9	6.9	1.0	1.7	10315
53	R2718	Bagdad 1954	Tetradrachm	93.9	4.44	0.45	1.10	0.010	0.18	16.8	13.2	2.0	227.7	9.1	2.2	11001
54	R2719	Bagdad 1957	Tetradrachm	97.2	0.46	2.14	0.05	0.096	0.12	5.2	5.2	2.9	10.7	1.7	0.2	522
55	R2720	Bagdad 1957	Tetradrachm	99.6	0.16	0.24	0.02	0.007	0.36	7.5	2.5	1.6	16.1	1.7	0.2	186
56	R2721	Bagdad 1957	Tetradrachm	96.9	0.01	3.01	0.01	0.020		4.2	5.5	2.1	2.5	0.2	0.2	71
57	1973-1-105	Marache	Tetradrachm	90.9	7.35	1.45	0.28	0.012	0.01	0.8	131.6	3.4	18.7	59.5	2.2	2820
58	R2684	Marache	Tetradrachm	95.9	0.60	3.48	0.02	0.036	0.01	3.8	2.5	3.2	43.5	0.9	0.2	175
59	R2685	Marache	Tetradrachm	98.9	0.01	0.93	0.01	0.093		6.2	0.2	1.7	6.2	0.1	0.4	132
60	R2686	Marache	Tetradrachm	97.4	0.93	1.54	0.02	0.049	0.18	5.7	4.8	2.8	25.1	8.1	0.2	247
61	R2687	Marache	Tetradrachm	97.7	0.01	2.19	0.02	0.053	0.01	3.7	0.3	1.7	1.8	0.1	0.2	167
62	R2688	Marache	Tetradrachm	97.8	0.22	1.92	0.04	0.065	0.005	6.0	2.3	2.5	18.8	2.9	0.2	400
63	R2689	Marache	Tetradrachm	98.6	0.09	1.13	0.07	0.143	0.02	4.0	0.3	1.9	70.3	0.5	0.2	685
64	R2690	Marache	Tetradrachm	97.5	<0.05	2.21	0.01	0.035	0.03	3.3	1.4	2.3	4.0	0.8	0.2	152
65	R2691	Marache	Tetradrachm	98.1	0.26	1.62	0.02	0.008	0.01	4.0	0.7	2.4	1.8	0.7	0.1	100
66	R2692	Marache	Tetradrachm	97.6	1.32	0.61	0.29	0.081	0.10	6.9	2.6	4.0	458.4	1.7	1.1	2943
67	R2693	Marache	Tetradrachm	99.5	0.02	0.03	0.14	0.292	0.13	12.5	5.4	1.0	2.1	0.2	0.2	1413
68	R1760	Karaman	Tetradrachm	98.7	0.33	0.80	0.15	0.039	0.17	6.4	1.3	2.0	17.0	1.1	0.8	1471
69	R2778	Gaza	Obol	98.2	1.19	0.17	0.39	0.018	0.08	14.1	19.5	3.1	11.8	6.5	1.8	3937
70	1986-234	Gaza	Drachm	93.7	3.82	2.36	0.02	0.044	0.05	20.9	2.5	9.8	7.6	5.7	0.2	187
71	FG 326	Gaza	Drachm	97.0	2.39	0.30	0.31	0.016	0.07	2.8	2.9	3.6	6.5	0.5	1.7	3140
72	FG 327	Gaza	Drachm	97.0	1.90	0.88	0.22	0.010	0.08	2.1	2.2	5.8	10.0	7.4	1.1	2210
73	FG 330	Gaza	Drachm	92.0	5.64	2.02	0.10	0.195	0.02	2.0	3.2	10.2	7.9	12.5	0.5	1011
74	2014-25	Gaza	Drachm	95.6	3.68	0.17	0.54	0.001	0.09	0.2	0.4	1.2	0.5	5.9	2.0	5373
75	Suse642	Suse	Tetradrachm	97.7	<0.05	1.52	0.18	0.022	6.14	42.6	47.4	1.6	8.8	1.1	0.04	1796
76	Suse644	Suse	Tetradrachm fourré	96.9	2.53	0.17	0.43	0.009	0.10	0.5	5.5	2.4	0.5	0.3	1.6	4306
77	R3681-12	Bought in Afghanistan	Tetradrachm fourré	85.6	13.25	0.46	0.50	0.077	31.31	3.7	534.4	2.2	1.6	90.2	1.3	5037
78	R2722	Bought in Syria	Tetradrachm	97.8	0.08	1.94	0.10	0.023	0.06	4.4	0.4	2.9	0.9	0.4	0.7	1019
79	1973-1-447	Bought in Beyrut	Tetradrachm	92.7	4.97	1.33	0.92	0.017	2.91	2.0	65.3	2.2	52.6	20.7	2.2	9192

ACKNOWLEDGEMENTS

Plates, photo credits: Gallica.bnf.fr / Bibliothèque nationale de France

I would like to warmly thank M. Blet-Lemarquand for her help in reviewing the manuscript and for her help in discussing the results. I would also like to thank the editors for their help in improving the language and their constructive remarks. Errors that remain are the unique responsibility of the author.

Abbreviations

IGCH
Haut du formulaire
Thompson, M., Kraay, C. M., and Morkholm, O. 1973. *An inventory of Greek coin hoards.* (New York).
Bas du formulaire

References

Blet-Lemarquand, M., Nieto-Pelletier, S. and Sarah, G. 2014. 'L'or et l'argent monnayés', in Dillmann, Ph. and Bellot-Gurlet, L. (eds.), *Circulation et provenance des matériaux dans les sociétés anciennes* (Paris), 133–159.
Buttrey, T.V. 1979. 'The Athenian Currency Law of 375/4', in Mørkholm, O. and Waggoner, N.M. (eds.), *Greek Numismatics and Archaeology: Essays in Honor of Margaret Thompson* (Wetteren), 33–45.
Buttrey, T.V. 1981. 'More on the Athenian Coinage Law of 375/4 B.C.', *Quaderni ticinesi di Numismatica e Antichità Classiche* X, 78–79.
Buttrey, T.V. 1982. 'Pharaonic Imitations of Athenian tetradrachms', in Hackens T. and Weiller R. (eds.), *Proceedings of the Ninth International Congress of Numismatics* (Louvain-la-Neuve), 137–140.
Dattàri, G. 1905. 'Comments on a Hoard of Athenian Tetradrachms Found in Egypt', *Journal International d'Archéologie Numismatique* 8, 103–11.
Faucher, Th. and Olivier, J. 2020. 'From Owls to Eagles. Metallic composition of Egyptian coinage (5th – 1st c. BC)', in Butcher K. (ed.), *Debasement Manipulation of Coin Standards in Pre-Modern Monetary Systems* (London), 97–109.
Flament, Chr. 2001. 'A propos des styles d'imitations athéniennes définis par T.V. Buttrey', *RBN* CXLVII, 39–50.
Flament, Chr. 2003. 'Imitations athéniennes ou monnaies authentiques? Nouvelles considérations sur quelques chouettes athéniennes habituellement identifiées comme imitations', *RBN* CXLIX, 1–10.
Flament, Chr. 2005. 'Un trésor de tétradrachmes athéniens dispersé suivi de considérations relatives au classement, à la frappe et à l'attribution des chouettes à des ateliers étrangers', *RBN* CLI, 29–38.
Flament, Chr. 2007a. '*Le monnayage en argent d'Athènes: de l'époque archaïque à l'époque hellénistique', c. 550-c. 40 av. J.-C.* (Louvain-la-Neuve).
Flament, Chr. 2007b. 'L'argent des chouettes. Bilan de l'application des méthodes de laboratoire au monnayage athénien tirant parti de nouvelles analyses réalisées au moyen de la méthode PIXE', *RBN* CLIII, 9–30.
Flament, Chr. and Marchetti, P. 2004. 'Analysis of Ancient Silver Coins', *Nuclear Instruments & Methods in Physics Research* CCXXVI/1–2, 179–184.
Flament, Chr. Lateano, O. and Demortier, G. 2008. 'Quantitative Analysis of Athenian Coinage by PIXE', in Facorellis, Y.,Zacharias, N. and Polikreti, K. (eds.), *Proceedings of the 4th Symposium of the Hellenic Society of Archaeometry. National Hellenic Research Foundation, Athens, 28–31 May 2003*, BAR International Series 1746 (Oxford), 445–450.
Gitler, H. Ponting, M. and Tal, O. 2009. 'Athenian tetradrachms from Tel Mikham (Israel): A metallurgical perspective', *AJN* 21, 29–49.
Göbl, R. Le Rider, G. Miles, G.C. and Walker, J. 1960. *Numismatique susienne: Monnaies trouvées à Suse de 1946 à 1956, Mémoires de la mission archéologique en Iran* 37 (Paris).
Kraay, C.M. and Emeleus V. 1962. 'The Composition of Greek Silver Coins: Analysis by *Neutron Activation*' (Oxford).
L'Héritier, M., Baron, S., Cassayre, L. and Téreygeol, F. 2015. 'Bismuth behaviour during ancient processes of silver-lead production', *Journal of Archaeological Science* 57, 56–68.
Meadows, A. 2011. 'Athenian coin dies from Egypt: the new discovery at Herakleion', *RBN* CLVII, 95–116.
Nicolet-Pierre, H. 1998. 'Autour du décadrachme athénien conservé à Paris', in Ashton, R. and Hurter, S. (eds.), *Studies in Greek Numismatics in memory of Martin Jessop Price*
(London), 293–299.
Nicolet-Pierre, H. 2005. 'Les imitations égyptiennes des tétradrachmes athéniens d'époque classique (v^e–ive s. av. J.-C.)', *Arch. Eph.* 142, 139–154.
Nicolet-Pierre, H. and Diebolt, J. 1977. 'Recherches sur le métal de tétradrachmes à types athéniens', *RSN* 56, 79–91.

Ponting, M., Gitler, H. and Tal, O. 2011. 'Who minted those owls? Metallurgical analyses of Athenian-styled tetradrachms found in Israel', *RBN* 157, 117–134.

Sarah, G. and Gratuze, B. 2016. 'LA-ICP-MS Analysis of Ancient Silver Coins Using Concentration Profiles', in Dussubieux, L.,Golitko, M. and Gratuze, B. (eds.), *Recent Advances in Laser Ablation ICP-MS for Archaeology, Natural Science in Archaeology* (Berlin, Heidelberg), 73–87.

Sarah, G., Gratuze, B. and Barrandon, J.-N. 2007. 'Application of laser ablation inductively coupled plasma mass spectrometry (LA-ICP-MS) for the investigation of ancient silver coins', *Journal of Analytical Atomic Spectrometry* 22–9, 1163–1167.

SNG Delepierre= Nicolet, H. and Dalaison J. 1983. *Sylloge Nummorum Graecorum, France, Bibliothèque National, Collection Jean et Marie Delepierre* (Paris).

Seyrig, H. 1972. 'Une question de numismatique gréco-arabe', *Bulletin d'études orientales* 25, 1–4.

Stos-Fertner, Z. and Gale N.H. 1979. 'Chemical and lead isotope analysis of ancient Egyptian gold, silver and lead', *Archeo-Physika* 10, 299–314.

van Alfen, P. 2002. 'The 'owls' from the 1989 Syria hoard, with a review of pre-Macedonian coinage in Egypt', *American Journal of Numismatics* 14, 1–57.

van Alfen, P. 2020. 'The Role of Coinage in Archaic Aegean-Egyptian Overseas Trade: Another Look at TAD C.3.7', in Faucher, T. (ed.), *Money Rules! The monetary economy of Egypt, from Persians until the beginning of Islam* (Cairo), 43–67.

Plates on following pages Photo credits: Gallica.bnf.fr / Bibliothèque nationale de France

PLATES

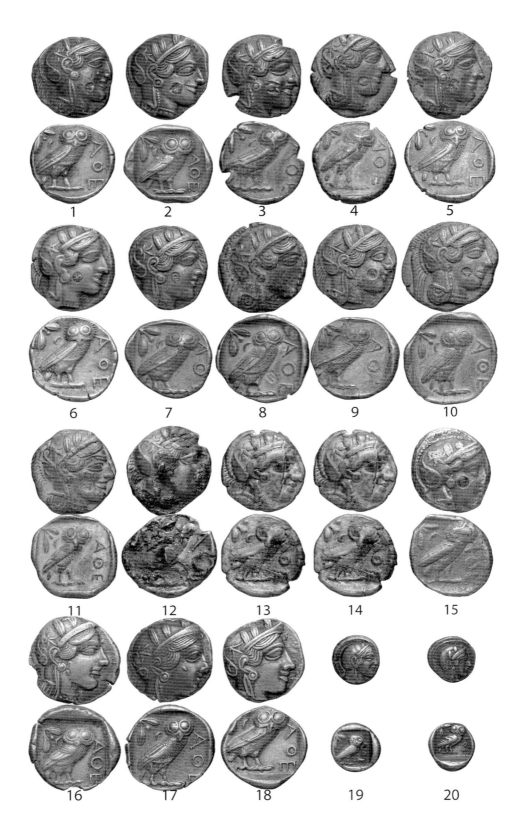

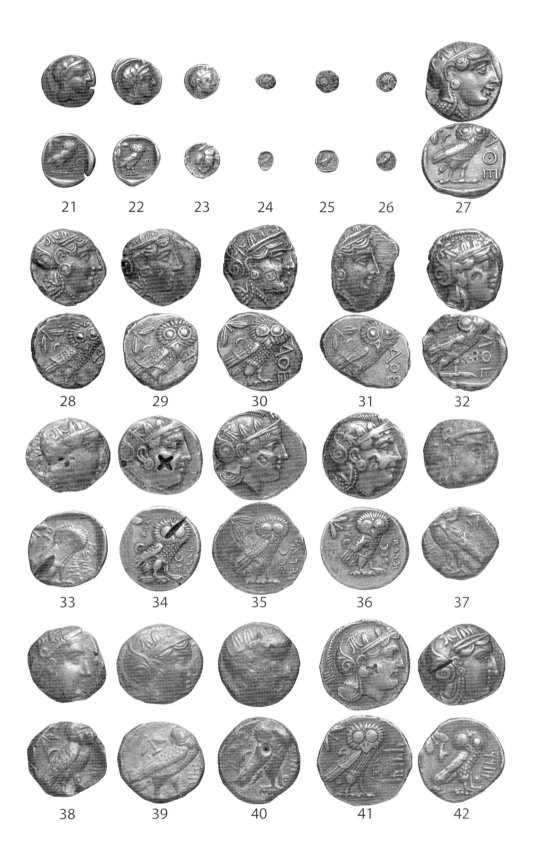

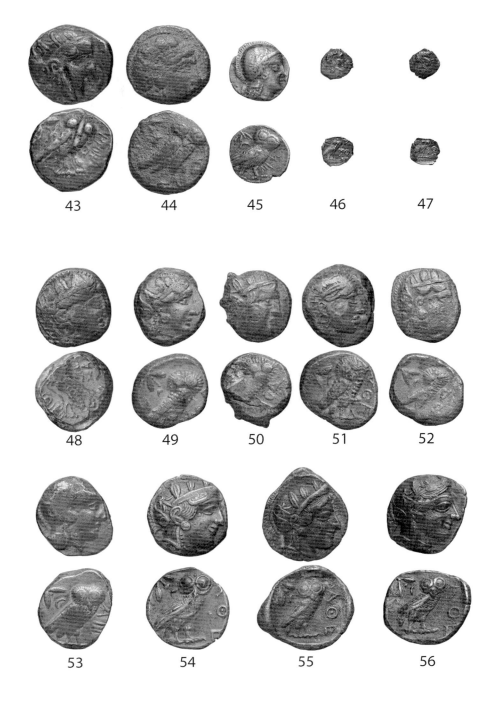

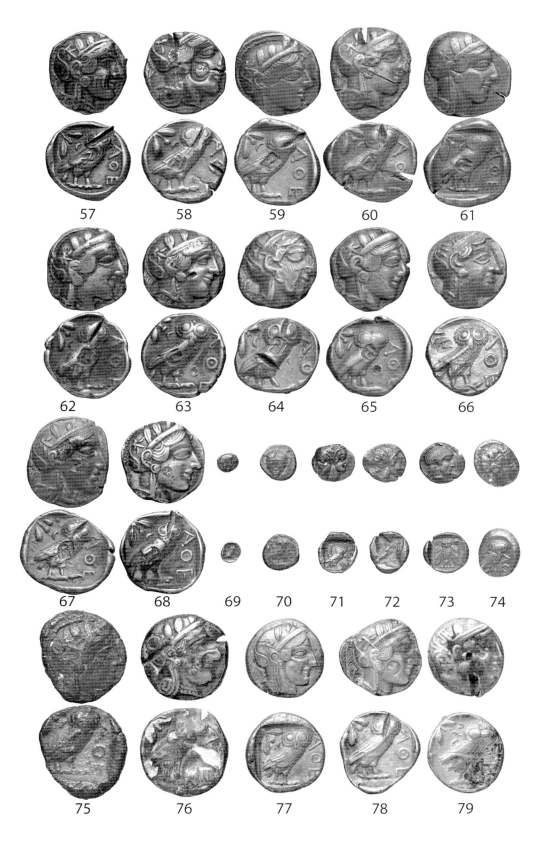

17. NEUTRON DIFFRACTION TEXTURE ANALYSIS FOR NUMISMATICS

Vladimir Luzin, Kenneth A. Sheedy, Scott R. Olsen, Filomena Salvemini and Max Avdeev

ABSTRACT

Neutron diffraction analysis has emerged as a powerful, non-invasive, non-destructive method in the field of numismatics. In this chapter we report on some preliminary results from the Incuse Coinage Project which explores methods employed by city-states in South Italy to produce a very distinctive regional form of silver currency, incuse coinage, during the sixth and fifth centuries BC. In order to understand what makes these minting procedures unique it is necessary to obtain data from incuse as well as non-incuse coinages, and we report on studies of twelve coins from mints in different cities and from different eras. Neutron texture and phase analyses can provide an insight into the processing of the metal during the production of coinage.

NEUTRON RADIATION TECHNIQUES: AN INTRODUCTION

Neutron radiation techniques are a relatively well-known and important means in archaeology for the investigation of the cultural heritage objects (Rinaldi *et al.* 2002; Kockelmann *et al.* 2004). The most critical advantage of employing neutrons is their high penetration: in contrast to other elementary particle probes or types of radiation (such as X-rays, electron beams), neutrons are only weakly absorbed by matter and thus have a greater penetration depth in millimetres (e.g. 6 mm half-attenuation depth into steel and 60 mm into aluminium) in comparison with <0.1 mm for laboratory X-ray radiation (http://henke.lbl.gov/optical_constants/atten2.html). Since the modules of ancient coins are also usually many millimetres in thickness, the advantages of neutron radiation techniques are evident: (1) the interior of coins can be investigated non-destructively and non-invasively using neutron beams, (2) a much larger sample volume can be surveyed than alternative radiation methods and (3) since neutron diffraction takes measurements from the bulk of the coin rather than from the surface (that can be easily altered and might not be representative of the bulk) the data are statistically more reliable.

Many neutron beam techniques are available to numismatists (Liang *et al.* 2009). Neutron resonance analysis and prompt-γ neutron activation analysis are useful for determining elemental/isotope composition (Postma *et al.* 2007). Neutron radiography, tomography and imaging are used for determining inner material structure and morphology (Anderson *et al.* 2009; Salvemini *et al.* in this volume). Neutron diffraction techniques are typically employed to study the crystal structure of metals as well as other substances (Liang *et al.* 2009). They can provide qualitative and quantitative data about 1) phase identification and composition; 2) crystal and magnetic structures of each constituent phase; 3) crystallographic preferred orientation (crystallographic texture) and 4) residual micro- and macro-stress.

Full pattern analysis involves measurement in a single orientation (though sample spinning can be involved for some statistical reasons) in a wide angular range, e.g. 10–160°, with multiple reflections being measured, from a few to hundreds depending on the crystal structure of the material. Through the full analysis, information related to crystal structure can be obtained, such as a lattice parameter values (Liang *et al.* 2009). Information on the preferred orientation can also be extracted but it is not as extensive as the data from a specialized texture analysis experiment.

While the use of neutron diffraction for phase and structural analysis is more or less common, neutron diffraction texture analysis of coins is less traditional and we will therefore provide some details. When metals are worked (rolled, cast, hammered, annealed, etc.) these actions cause crystallographic preferred orientations in the alignment of the atomic lattice of metal grains (Bunge 1989). The texture of a polycrystalline material, such as a metal, is defined in the most rigorous way through the orientation distribution function (ODF) of its crystallites (Bunge 1989), a three-dimensional distribution of the probability density in the orientational space. Using neutron diffraction, pole figures are measured, which are two-dimensional projections of the ODF for certain crystal lattice planes (hkl - the three integers, h, k, and l, also known as the Miller indices, form a notation system for planes in crystal (Bravais) lattices), and they are most commonly used for the graphical representation of the texture in a material. Colouring accordingly to density indicates the intensity of the diffraction - which relates to the proportion (probability density distribution) of crystallites oriented in a specific way. The pole figures are normalised to 1 and density is measured in units of m.r.d. (multiples of random distribution), since random distribution is equal to 1.

NEUTRON DIFFRACTION STUDIES IN ARCHAEOMETRY AND NUMISMATICS

Neutron diffraction full pattern analysis is a relatively standard technique for cultural heritage object research (Rinaldi *et al.* 2002) including numismatics. Kirfel *et al.* (2011) used neutron diffraction full pattern analysis to study the silver-copper alloy of Southern Arabian coins (fourth - third centuries BC). Together with a successful phase analysis, they were able to distinguish between coins that had been cast, and those that had been free-poured and struck. Siouris, Katsavounis and Kockelmann (2012) employed neutron diffraction profile analysis to measure the silver-copper composition of ten Greek (Thasian) coins from the fifth century BC, including three plated coins. Canovaro *et al.* (2013) studied 12 bronze coins with neutron diffraction to determine the amount of tin in the bronze through full neutron diffraction pattern analysis. Corsi *et al.* (2016) used neutron diffraction analysis on a group of 30 coins from varying Celtic settlements in Northern Italy from the fifth - fourth centuries BC to correlate the time frame and probable minting history through the measurement of the relative silver-copper content; here they were able to demonstrate a general debasement in silver content from >95% to around 70% over three centuries.

Neutron diffraction texture analysis is a highly appropriate means to investigate questions regarding the technology of production for cultural heritage objects (Artiolo 2007). Its application to numismatics, however, is relatively uncommon. Xie, Lutterotti and Wenk (2004) used neutron diffraction for the comparative analysis of two Thracian bronze coins (c.450–350 BC) in an attempt to assess their authenticity. The experimentally determined crystallographic texture, which showed axial compression, suggested the same production process for both (i.e. the metal flan was struck between two dies). Kockelmann *et al.* (2006) published texture analyses of six silver Thalers from the sixteenth century which confirmed the historically documented evolution of the Thaler fabrication technique (from hammer striking to the machine minting of coins from rolled metal sheets). Neutron texture analysis was extended into experimental archaeometry by Siano *et al.* (2006) with the texture measurement of a series of test pieces produced in controlled conditions and compared to the texture measurements of a Roman bronze coin.

THE INCUSE COINAGE PROJECT

In 2014 the ACANS and ANSTO (Australian Nuclear Science and Technology Organisation) launched a joint project to explore the techniques for manufacturing incuse coinage by cities in South Italy during the sixth and fifth centuries BC (Gorini 1975; Rutter 2001). Incuse coinage, which was invented at Sybaris or perhaps Metapontum c.550 BC, contrasts markedly with contemporary coinages from Asia Minor and the Greek mainland in a number of key features: 1) *Reverse type*. A proper reverse type is in use from the very beginning of minting incuse coinage. The reverse type is the same as that on the obverse but is rendered as a 'negative' image sunk into the flan; 2) *Alignment of the types*. The types are centred with great precision on both sides of the coin; 3) *Border*. Integral to their design is a prominent border (beaded, cable, dots between two lines); and 4) *Module*. A distinct feature of these flans is their regularity. Unlike the coins of the mainland these flans are evenly circular.

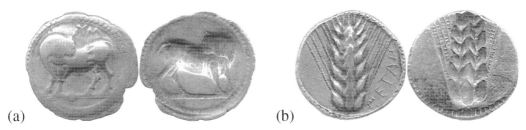

Figure 1. (a) Incuse stater, ACANS inv.07GS730 (Sybaris *c*. 550-510 BC, 7.73 g; 31mm) and (b) ACANS inv.07GS526 (Metapontum *c*.540-510 BC, 7.98 g; 23mm).

The technology and means by which these incuse coinages were manufactured remain an enigma (Scavino 2011), though a recently published study of incuse coin minting experiments by Williams and Lock (Williams 2016) sheds light on many features (notably the production of wide, thin flans). The Incuse Coinage Project began with the hypothesis that these coins were minted from flans that had received extensive treatment (hammering and annealing) prior to being struck with the coin dies. We are currently exploring the evidence that the flan was made to shape before minting and that when the flan was eventually struck with the dies the metal was at a relatively low temperature. Neutron imaging (Salvemini *et al.* 2016 and in this volume) have highlighted the extreme pressure which the striking of the dies placed on these thin flans. Neutron diffraction analysis, providing qualitative and quantitative data on topics such as the phase composition of coins, micro and macro (residual) strains within the metal, offers the chance to explore the deformation history of the coin flan, and thus offers the means of reconstructing working processes. Studies of a rare incuse silver coin of the sixth century BC, jointly issued by the South Italian states of Sirinos and Pyxoes, exemplify our interdisciplinary approach to the exploration of this material (Sheedy *et al.* 2015; most coins sampled in the project are from ACANS: Sheedy 2008). We have broadened our sample base to include coins from later periods and different regions (we have analysed, for example, a silver English penny from the reign of Edward I minted in 1270 A.D.) in order to permit a comparative study of pole figures from coins produced using the better documented manufacturing techniques of pre-industrial societies. All selected coins in our study are silver, though some proved to be silver plated.

THE NEUTRON BEAM INSTRUMENTATION AND MEASUREMENT PROCEDURE

The sample coins were studied using three neutron beam instruments at ANSTO that have each been 'named': ECHIDNA, a high-resolution powder diffractometer (Liss *et al.* 2006), KOWARI, a residual stress and texture diffractometer (Kirstein *et al.* 2009), and DINGO, a radiography and tomography instrument (Garbe *et al.* 2011). The studies using neutron tomography are reported separately (Salvemini *et al.* in this volume), and here we will focus on neutron diffraction texture analysis with subsidiary full pattern analysis.

In the texture experiments, the sample was mounted in non-invasive manner onto a manipulator (usually a goniometer or a robotic arm) that provided a sample rotation that can cover at least a hemisphere of scattering directions. During measurements the whole coin volume was fully irradiated by choosing an appropriate primary neutron beam aperture, somewhat bigger than the sample size. At each sample orientation a diffraction pattern/signal covering approximately 15° (the size of the KOWARI detector) was measured by the neutron 2D position sensitive detector. Overall, some 1200 individual positions were measured; these correspond approximately to a 5°×5° equi-angular grid on a hemisphere. With the experimental constant wavelength of 1.5 Å all diffraction reflections of interest were available within the instrumental range of the scattering angles. The prime index pole figures of Ag (a face-centered cubic (fcc) metal) – Ag(111), Ag(200), Ag(220) and Ag(311)

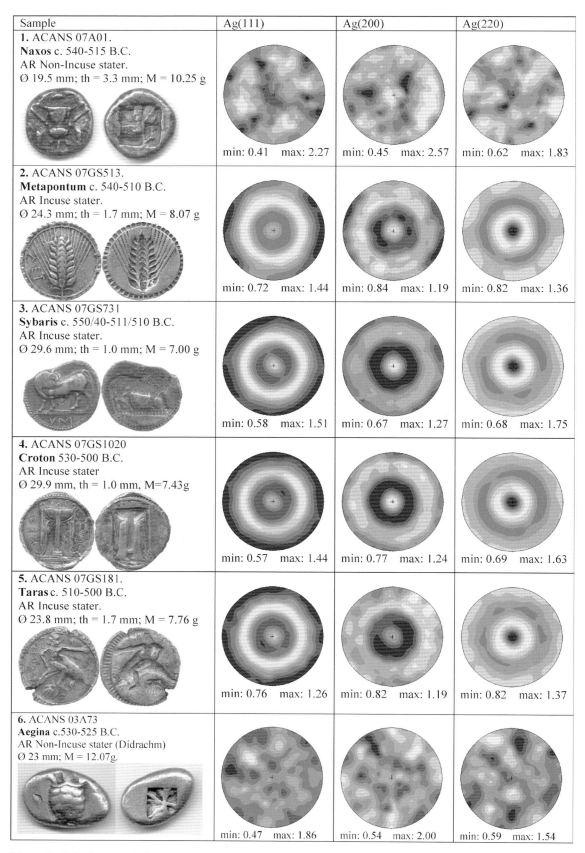

Figure 2. Pole figures of the samples. The minimum and maximum values are given for each individual pole figure.

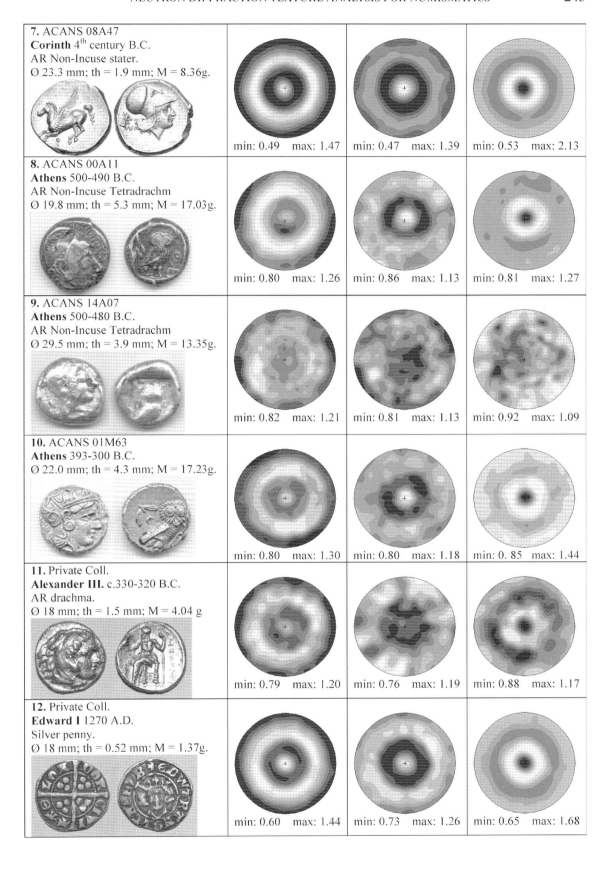

were collected through the detection of the intensity of the diffraction peak of the corresponding (hkl) reflection. Although measurement time varied accordingly to the size of different coins, typically 4–5 coins were measured in a day.

The shape of the object to be studied can present a problem in texture analysis. Neutrons are attenuated differently by different orientations of a coin, and this can result in severe attenuation effects. For disk-like objects, such as coins, depending on orientation, the anisotropic neutron attenuation effect (a ratio between highest to lowest attenuation value) can reach a factor of greater than 20 (this factor also depends on the coin's exact dimensions). This problem can be resolved through applying corrections. These corrections can be calculated theoretically from the geometrical characteristics (shape, thickness and diameter) and attenuation properties of coins. Alternatively, these corrections can be determined empirically through the analysis of self-consistency to the set of pole figures, and can be evaluated by means of the ODF analysis. The latter approached was used in our study and the corrected pole figures are reported in this work.

SOME PRELIMINARY RESULTS

The results of the texture analysis for twelve coins are shown in Figure 2. The common feature of all textures is the presence of the texture (110)-fiber component (Xie *et al.* 2004). In the data sets for some coins this presence is not obvious; the pole figures of sample 6, for example, look 'spotty' due to the large grain microstructure, but statistically even in this case a weak (110)-fiber component is present. The (110)-fiber component manifests itself in the most evident way in the Ag(110), or the crystallographically equivalent Ag(220) pole figure, as a peak intensity in the centre of the pole figure. Therefore, the degree of the preferred orientation can be judged easily by comparing the minimum/maximum values of the Ag(220) pole figure. For easy quantification of the fiber component in the analysed coins, the averaged over azimuth angle of Ag(220) pole densities are plotted in Figure 3 (assuming cylindrical symmetry of the pole figures). Within our sample selection the strongest texture is exhibited by a Corinthian coin (sample 7) with maximum value ~ 2 m.r.d. The coin with almost no preferred orientation (the density is 1 everywhere, meaning a random texture) is the Athens tetradrachm (sample 9). The data from the remainder of the coins fall into the range between 1 and 2 m.r.d. The degree of the preferred orientation is linked to the deformation history of each individual coin and it is this information which allows us to discuss possible techniques of manufacture.

Another feature of the pole figures, especially visible in the two staters Aegina (sample 6) and Naxos (sample 1), is 'spottiness' which can be associated with large grain size and which is most evident for cast coins. Usually these spots are random density oscillations with no preferred orientation (though upon averaging, in addition, they reveal some typical fiber pattern). In this case, the minimum/maximum values on pole figures do not represent the degree of deformation but rather the degree of the grain growth.

DISCUSSION

Neutron diffraction analysis of the samples in this study demonstrates a variety of textures within the metal (silver) that can be attributed to different techniques of production. We have been particularly interested to see how the pole figures for the mediaeval English coin would compare with those from the much earlier ancient coins (and have been fascinated by the resemblance to the poles figures from the incuse coin of Croton, sample 4). Our core research, the Incuse Coinage Project, is still in progress but for the purposes of the current paper we can make some observations which reflect on the usefulness of neutron diffraction analysis for numismatics. Differences in pole patterns reflect variation in the amount of

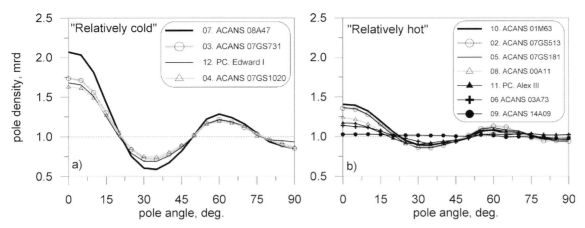

Figure 3. Average Ag(220) pole figure density for the coins with different strengths of texture. Two groups are differentiated: a) 'relatively cold' and 'relatively hot' based on the average minimum/maximum values.

plastic deformation (hammering, annealing, striking) applied to coins as well as the temperature of the flans when minting occurred. Samples 1 and 6 are without clear patterning and apparently have an almost random distribution of large grains; they are typical of flans that have not been worked but where the metal has been poured into a mould and then, when still hot, struck with dies to produce the coin. Still, they exhibit some very weak (110)-fiber texture in a statistical sense (Fig. 3), most likely from being struck with the coin dies when the metal was still very hot. Those pole figures with a 'spotty' appearance indicate slow cooling after casting, with grain growth and the formation of dominant large grains (dendrites) which appear as in the pole figures as bright spots.

Samples 2, 5 8, and 10 indicate rather hot working at close to the temperature at which silver melts (~960 °C). Samples 9 and 11 demonstrate the least amount of working, for the pole figures are much closer to a uniform distribution. While sample 11 was most likely struck when very hot, producing the pole figure pattern with (110)-fiber typical from working of the metal, sample 9 (an Athenian tetradrachm) exhibits a very small degree of deformation (a very weak compression-like texture) most likely created from shaping the metal in an almost molten condition. The sample with the strongest preferred orientation is 7, a Corinthian stater, with the highest maximum values on pole figures. It should be noted that this coin was minted in the fourth century and is significantly later than the archaic issues.

All incuse coins (samples 2–6) have a very similar and well defined patterning of the (110)-fiber texture component, though with a certain variation in the strength of texture, suggesting the extensive working of the metal. Two of the incuse coins (samples 3 and 4) show strong indication of cold working with a higher degree of the preferred orientation of the crystallites (Fig. 3). Their pole figures resemble that of the hammered silver penny (sample 12), as noted above, suggesting some possible similarities in the treatment of the metal (similar deformation-temperature conditions). But in what way could the methods of treating the metal have been similar? And how were they different to those employed, for example, by archaic mints on the Greek mainland? There seems little doubt that the evidence from neutron diffraction analysis provides important insights into the techniques of manufacturing incuse coinage, but at the same time the data poses new questions.

REFERENCES

Anderson, I.S., McGreevy, R.L., and Bilheux, H.Z. 2009. *Neutron imaging and applications*. Springer Science+Business Media, 200, 987–990.

Artiolo, G. 2007. 'Crystallographic Texture Analysis of Archaeological Metals: Interpretation of Manufacturing Techniques', *Applied Physics A* 89, 899–908.

Bunge, H. J. 1989. 'Advantages of Neutron Diffraction in Texture Analysis', *Textures and Microstructures* 10, 265–307.

Canovaro, C., Calliari, I., Asolati, F., Grazzi, F. and Scherillo, A. 2013. 'Characterization of Bronze Roman Coins of The Fifth Century Called Nummi Through Different Analytical Techniques', *Applied Physics A* 113 4, 1019–1028.

Corsi, J., Grazzi, F., Lo Giudice, A., Re, A., Scherillo, A., Angelici, D., Allegretti, S. and Barello, F. 2016. 'Compositional and microstructural characterization of Celtic silver coins from northern Italy using neutron diffraction analysis', *Microchemical Journal* 126, 501–508.

Garbe, U., Hughes, C. and Randall T. 2011. 'The new neutron radiography /tomography / imaging station DINGO at OPAL', *Journal of Nuclear Instruments And Methods in Physical Research* 651(1), 42–46.

Gorini, G. 1975. *La monetazione incusa della Magna Grecia*. Milan.

Kirfel, A., Kockelmann, W. and Yule, P. 2011. 'Non-destructive Chemical Analysis of Old South Arabian Coins, Fourth Century BCE to Third Century CE', *Archaeometry* 53, 930–949.

Kirstein, O., Luzin, V. and Garbe, U. 2009. 'The Strain-Scanning Diffractometer Kowari', *Neutron News* 20(4), 34–36.

Kockelmann, W., Kirfel, A., Siano, S., Fros, C.D., 2004. 'Illuminating the past: the neutron as a tool in archaeology.' *Phys. Educ.* 39 (2), 155–165.

Kockelmann, W., Siano, S., Bartoli, L., Visser, D., Hallebeek, P., Traum, R., Linke, R., Schreiner, M. and Kirfel, A. 2006. 'Applications of TOF Neutron Diffraction in Archaeometry', *Applied Physics A* 83(2), 175–182.

Kockelmann, W., Siano, S., Bartoli, L., Visser, D., Hallebeek, P.,

Liang, L., Rinaldi, R., and Schober, H. (eds.) 2009. Neutron Applications in Earth, Energy and Environmental Sciences, Neutron Scattering Applications and Techniques, DOI 10.1007/978-0-387-09416-8_2, Springer Science+Business Media.

Liss, K.-D., Hunter, B., Hagen, M., Noakes, T. and Kennedy, S. 2006. 'Echidna—the new high-resolution powder diffractometer being built at OPAL', *Physica B: Condensed Matter* 385–386(2), 1010–1012.

Postma, H., Perego, R.C., Schillebeeckx, P., Siegler, P. and Borella, A. 2007. 'Neutron resonance capture analysis and applications', *Journal of Radioanalytical and Nuclear Chemistry* 271(1), 95–99

Rinaldi, R., Artioli, G., Kockelmann, W., Kirfel, A. and Siano, S. 2002. 'The contribution of neutron scattering to cultural heritage research', *Notiziario neutroni e luce di sincrotrone* 7(2), 30–37.

Rutter, N.K. (ed) 2001. *Historia Numorum. Italy*, (London).

Salvemini, F., Olsen, S.R, Luzin, V., Garbe, U., Davis, J., Knowles, T. and Sheedy, K.A. 2016. 'Neutron Tomographic Analysis: Material Characterisation of Silver and Electrum coins from the 6th and 5th Centuries B.C.', *Materials Characterization* 118, 175–185.

Scavino, R. 2011. 'Monetzione Incusa Magnogreca: destinazione e funzioni', in Holmes, N. (ed.) *Proceedings of the XIVth International Numismatic Congress, Glasgow 2009*, (Glasgow), 382–392.

Sheedy, K. A. 2008. *Sylloge Nummorum Graecorum Australia I. The Gale Collection of South Italian Coins*. (Adelaide: Numismatic Association of Australia).

Sheedy, K.A., Munroe, P., Salvemini, F., Luzin, V., Garbe, U. and Olsen S. 2015. 'An incuse stater from the series 'Sirinos/Pyxoes'', *Journal of the Numismatic Association of Australia* 26, 36–52.

Siano, S., Bartolio, L., Santisteban, J. R., Kockelmann, W., Daymond, M. R., Miccio, M. and De Marinis, G. 2006. 'Non-destructive Investigation of Bronze Artifacts From The Marches National Museum of Archaeology Using Neutron Diffraction', *Archaeometry* 48(1), 77–96.

Siouris, I. M., Katsavounis ,S. and Kockelmann, W. 2012. 'Characterization of Ancient Greek Coins Using Non-destructive TOF Neutron Diffraction', *Journal of Physics: Conference Series* 340, 1–8.

Williams, R. 2016. 'An Experiment in Manufacturing Blanks and Striking Coins', *Antichthon* 50, 17–32.

Xie, Y., Lutterotti, L. and Wenk, H. R. 2004. 'Texture Analysis of Ancient Coins with TOF Neutron Diffraction', *Journal of Materials Science* 39, 3329–3337.

18. NEUTRON IMAGING FOR NUMISMATICS

F. Salvemini, K. Sheedy, S.R. Olsen, V. Luzin, U. Garbe

ABSTRACT

The rapid development of large scale scientific facilities providing neutron and synchrotron radiation sources offers important opportunities for the study of cultural materials. Here we highlight the application of neutron imaging as a powerful non-destructive method in numismatics. Neutron tomograms facilitate the investigation of coin morphology, porosity, inclusions and the presence of composite structures. This information can be vital for an understanding of minting techniques. In this chapter we present studies of Greek coins that substantiate arguments for the existence of diverse approaches to producing coins in antiquity.

INTRODUCTION: NEUTRONS FOR CONTEMPORARY NUMISMATICS RESEARCH

Over the last decades there has been a rapid development of large scale scientific facilities which feature reactor based and pulsed neutron, and synchrotron (X-ray) radiation sources. There is now considerable literature on the application of analytical techniques which employ these sources (Lehmann *et al.* 2005; Nguyen *et al.* 2011; Salvemini *et al.* 2016; Treimer, 2017). Neutron scattering, for example, has emerged as a powerful non-destructive analytical tool for the investigation of artefacts with an archaeological, historical, cultural and artistic interest (Anderson *et al.* 2009; Kockelmann *et al.* 2006). The application of neutron imaging to the discipline of numismatics, however, is fairly new (Kardjilov *et al.* 2007). Here we propose to show how neutron tomography can be a remarkably effective means to explore the presence of defects, voids and inclusions (Griesser *et al.* 2016; Salvemini *et al.* 2016). We also wish to highlight the information it can provide about the different techniques utilised in the actual shaping of the coin flan.

The advantages of employing neutrons, in contrast to other elementary particle probes, have been discussed in detail elsewhere (Liyuan *et al.* 2008; Kardjilov *et al.* 2017) and may be briefly summarized.

1. Neutrons are weakly absorbed by matter and thus have greater penetration into the bulk (as deep as ~50 mm into iron for thermal neutron in comparison with ~0.1mm for laboratory X-ray radiation) (Sears 2006; Hubbell and Seltzer 1996). As a result, the neutron beam can survey a much larger sample volume than, for example, an X-ray beam.

2. A beam of neutrons interacts with the atomic nuclei of the object under examination. In fact, since neutrons don't interact with the electron cloud around the nuclei, the probability for interaction with the atom as a whole is quite low. Only a small fraction of the neutrons act upon atoms – being scattered or captured – for most simply pass through the subject. This makes neutrons particularly suitable for imaging methods i.e. radiography and tomography. On the other hand, the high flux of modern neutron sources (neutron flux can be defined as the number of neutrons travelling through a unit area in unit time) provide an intensity of scattered neutrons that permits various types of quantitative analysis i.e. neutron powder diffraction, reflectometry, small angle scattering (Kardjilov *et al.* 2007). The signal transmitted through the sample is attenuated via both absorption and scattering. In advanced imaging applications, the fraction of neutrons elastically and coherently scattered, fulfilling the well-known Bragg condition, can be detected to obtain information about the crystalline structure of the sample. Beside these contributions, incoherent scattering also occur and can sum over the intensity from individual atoms. When this effect is not negligible, e.g. hydrogen, an increase of the transmission can be recorded leading to an underestimation of the attenuation coefficient. This artefact, which depends also on the size of the object and on the distance between sample and detector, can be corrected using appropriate strategies.

3. X-rays interact with the electron cloud; the greater the atomic number and thus number of electrons, the greater the interaction and thus the higher X-ray attenuation. Neutrons interact with the nucleus, thus isotopes of the same element, or elements of slight different atomic number can be discerned. A peculiarity of neutrons is their ability to more easily interact with light elements, (hydrogen, carbon, oxygen) than X-rays.

As with X-rays, neutron imaging (neutron radiography and tomography) measures the degree to which an object attenuates (scatters or absorbs) the probing neutron beam. This attenuation depends on the elemental composition and density within its volume (Anderson *et al.* 2009). The result of the interaction between the probe and the sample is a shadow image of the object yielding information on its inner structure. The image is called a radiograph. Neutron tomography involves the collection of radiographic projections while the object is rotated around its vertical axis over a range of (at least) 180°. These projections are then used to create an image stack representing a virtual three-dimensional model of the object (Hounsfeld 1980).

Both X-ray (Nguyen *et al.* 2011; Bozini *et al.* 2014) and neutron tomography have been applied to the study of coins (Kockelmann *et al.* 2006). An interesting comparative study of the two techniques is offered, for example, in a study by Gerald Eisenblätter *et al.* (2013) in which neutron tomography of Roman copper coins revealed information about the coins' internal composition that could not be obtained by X-ray tomography. Neutron tomograms showed areas of brass distinct from spots consisting of copper alone where, due to weathering processes, the zinc had been leached out of the alloy.

EXPERIMENTAL SET-UP AND DATA RECONSTRUCTION

At the 20MW Open-Pool Australian Lightwater (OPAL) nuclear research reactor (ANSTO, Sydney) the neutron radiography and tomography instrument is called DINGO (Garbe *et al.* 2015). The high spatial resolution configuration of DINGO corresponds to a pixel size range between 16 - 27 μm (Mays *et al.* 2017). During the measurement, projections were obtained by rotating the sample around its vertical axis for 1439 steps spaced *equiangular* from 0° to 360°. At each step the coins were exposed to the neutron beam for a period of 60s, for an overall measuring time of 24 hours. The ANDOR iKon CCD camera - 2048 x 2048, 16-bit was coupled with a 100 mm optical lens and a 100 mm thick ^{6}LiF/ZnS scintillation plate. The size of the acquisition window at the utilised high spatial resolution configuration of 27 μm is 50x50 mm^2. This permits four coins to be studied at one time by stacking the samples vertically and by separating them with aluminium foil (aluminium is nearly transparent to neutrons and does not appear in the tomographic images). With a 24 hour scan time for each set of 4 coins and a 1 hour change over to the next set, there was no need to automate the sample changing process, though this is available on instruments at OPAL (Olsen *et al.* 2010). In fact, the DINGO sample stage has a vertical translation range of ~36 cm and stacking of sample sets is often utilised.

Appropriate corrections were applied during data-set reconstruction by using the Octopus package (Dierick *et al.* 2004). In addition to conventional flat-filed and dark current corrections and spot filtering, due to the nature of the sample, also beam hardening effect was taken into account. In fact, when a polychromatic neutron beam interacts with matters, low energy neutrons are more easily attenuated or even completely adsorbed when traveling through a dense part. A decrease in the measured attenuation towards the centre through a homogenous object is observed if the image is reconstructed assuming that the beam attenuation is linear. This artefact is called beam-hardening, or cupping artefact that can give false information about the sample's composition/density. Therefore a polynomial correction to the logarithmic projection values, increasing the weight of longer attenuation paths, was applied during reconstruction of our samples.

Finally, AVIZO software (https://www.fei.com/software/amira-avizo/) was used for visualization and quantification.

THE INCUSE COINAGE PROJECT

In 2014 researchers from the Australian Centre for Ancient Numismatic Studies (ACANS) at Macquarie University, in collaboration with staff at the Australian Nuclear Science and Technology Organisation (ANSTO) in Sydney initiated a program to study the techniques of minting the 'incuse coinages' struck by Greek cities in Southern Italy during the 6th and 5th centuries BC (Rutter 2001). Our work combines neutron tomographic analysis of coins with texture analysis performed on the neutron strain scanner KOWARI (Kirstein et al. 2009) at OPAL, together with data from the High Resolution Powder Diffractometer ECHIDNA (Liss et al. 2006). As noted above, here we will focus on neutron tomography; the reader is referred to an accompanying study in this volume on neutron diffraction studies from the same project (Luzin et al.). To date we have analysed some twenty-five incuse coins from South Italy together with seventeen non-incuse coins from a range of mints, mostly on the Greek mainland (Sheedy et al. 2015; Salvemini et al. 2016). We are aware that the techniques for producing Attic coins are now coming under increasing scrutiny as the result of Professor Kroll's claims (Kroll 2011) that the flan of Attic tetradrachms during the 4th century BC were bent double before the types were struck (see Davis, Sheedy and Gore in this volume). Given that on-going research into both the incuse coinages and the coins of Athens points to diverse manufacturing practices, it seems appropriate to present our data on Attic coins now (Table 1).

We begin, by way of introduction, with some very brief notes on coin minting. Coinage was invented in the Lydian empire (Kraay 1976, 20–30); the first (electrum) issues were minted at the capital Sardis in the last quarter of the 7th century BC. It is accepted with little discussion that the technology and practices of minting first devised by the Lydians, who were accomplished metal workers, were then copied by the Greeks without change (Moesta and Franke 1995, 11–46). The processes for striking coins in antiquity have been largely reconstructed from studies of surviving coins (Moesta and Franke 1995). It is assumed that the mints of Asia Minor and the Greek mainland (and indeed through-out the Greek world) employed the same techniques of coin manufacture. A piece of metal of predetermined weight (a 'blank' or flan) was held by pliers between two engraved dies made of hardened bronze, and the reverse or punch die was then struck in order to imprint the types on both sides of the flan (Conophagus et al. 1976). In order to create blanks it was the typical practice of archaic mints, we believe, to pour molten metal on to a flat surface or into an open mould, so as to produce a roughly circular or 'bun'-shape flan that could at times be quite irregular. In the 5th century mould-made flans of very even shape became common (Mørkholm 1991). We know very little, however, about the secondary treatment of blanks (hammering, annealing etc.) in early minting.

POROSITY

Before examining the various samples we wish to add a brief note on the study of coin porosity using neutron imagining as a means of exploring techniques of manufacture. In an

Table 1. Sample number and details for each coin presented in this study.

Sample No.	ACANS	Mint	Date	Denomination	Weight [g]	Diameter [mm]
1	07GS729	Sirinos-Pyxoes	540–510 BC	Stater	6.73	29.6
2	07GS731	Sybaris	550/540 BC	Stater	6.99	28.9
3	00A11	Athens	500–490 BC	Tetradrachm	17.06	22
4	03A07	Aegina	550–530 BC	Didrachm	12.09	23
5	14A07	Athens	500–480 BC	Tetradrachm	17.03	22.4
6	01M63	Athens	393–300 BC	Tetradrachm	17.23	23

Table 2. This table lists different parameters for porosities in samples 03A07, 00A11, 14A07 and 01M63. The volume refers to the % of pores detected within the whole coin volume; the equivalent diameter is the diameter of a sphere having the same volume as the feature; the aspect ratio is the ratio of the average width to the average length of voids, and provides an indication of their average shape; the max and average volume of the pores.

Sample No.	ACANS	Volume [%]	Equivalent [mm³]		Aspect	Volume 3D	
	diameter	ratio [mm]	min	max		max	average
3	00A11	0.02	0.075	0.631	0.529	0.132	0.032
4	03A07	0.09	0.072	0.552	0.581	0.088	0.002
5	14A07	6.09	0.065	1.691	0.601	2.530	0.047
6	01M63	0.67	0.057	1.194	0.463	0.890	0.038

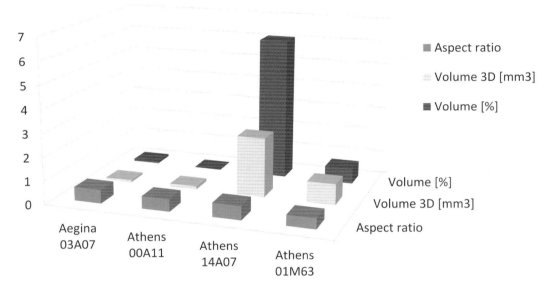

Figure 1. Volume percent, maximim volume and aspect ratio of porosities evaluated for samples 03A07, 00A11, 14A07 and 01M63.

earlier article (Salvemini *etc al*. 2016) we explored distinctions between copper inclusions and pores. Porosity is an umbrella term covering micro- and meso-pore agglomerates and large macro-voids. The morphology of pores can be an important indicator of the reasons for their existence. Casting voids, for example, are often the result of gas formation or solidification shrinkage while the metal is still in a liquid form. They can be eliminated or significantly reduced through hammering and annealing. Geometry, pore size, orientation, location and type of connectivity are related to the manufacturing process of a metal.

SAMPLES 1–2

The incuse coinage of South Italy, which begin at Sybaris and Metapontum c.550 BC, contrast markedly with contemporary coinages from Asia Minor and the Greek mainland (Rutter 2001). Early technical studies supervised by Williams over 30 years ago have remained unpublished until recently (Williams 2016). The defining attribute of this coinage is the fact that it employs a proper reverse type which is the same as that on the obverse but is rendered as a 'negative' image sunk into the flan. In our investigation of the minting process we looked at flan design and the pressure of dies. Tomography of a silver incuse stater (ACANS 07GS729; sample 1; Fig. 2) with the inscription 'Sirinos/Pyxoes', minted

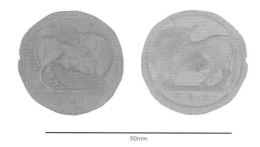

Figure 2. Sirinos/Pyxoes, stater, c.540–510 BC. ACANS inv. 07GS729.Weight: 6.73g. Diameter: 29.6mm. Scale 3:1. Photo© ACANS.

Figure 3. Sample 1. Neutron tomography 3D model of the Sirinos/Pyxoes stater, ACANS inv. 07GS729.

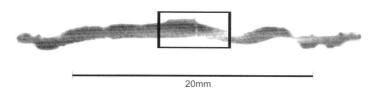

Figure 4. Sample 1. Neutron tomography cross section of the Sirinos/Pyxis stater; orthogonal cross section showing crack. The obverse surface of the coin is shown on top.

c.540–510 BC, highlighted two major cracks (one running diagonally from above the head of the bull joins a second crack passing across the coin from side to side) which are more visible on the reverse. They are also apparent in Fig. 3 (3D model of the reverse and obverse) and in Fig. 4 (cross section). These cracks developed on the surface and spread from 0.10mm up to 1.20mm into the bulk of the flan. It is unlikely that the coin was released from the mint if the cracks were visible.

Sybaris, which struck coins between 550/540 BC and its destruction in 511/ 510 BC, and only produced incuse coins, may have been the originator of the incuse coinage technique (Spagnoli 2013). ACANS 07GS731 (sample 2; Fig. 5) is dated 525–514 BC (Spagnoli 2013, cat. 124c). Two cross-sections serve to underline the thinness of the flan (Fig. 6b-c). A significant fragment of the coin, from the upper left of the flan (when seen from the obverse) has broken away. As a result, the coin weighs only 6.99 g and not the expected 8.1 g (the Achaean weight for staters of the incuse coinage mints). These orthogonal cross sections of 07GS729 (Sirinos/Pyxeos) and 07GS731 (Sybaris), which vividly demonstrate the thinness of the metal, show how closely the obverse relief and reverse incuse types are aligned. They also reveal that the design of these dies placed considerable pressure on the flan when it was struck.

Figure 5a–b. Sample 2. ACANS 07GS731 (Sybaris).

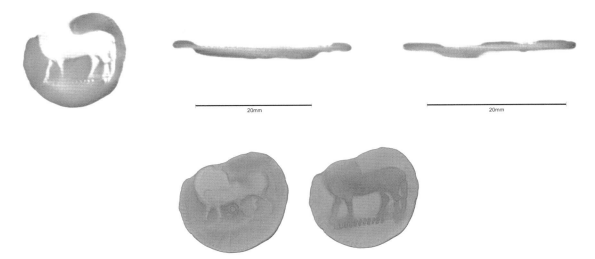

Figure 6a–d. Sample 2. ACANS 07GS731 (Sybaris). Neutron tomography.

This tomographic data highlights the great strain placed on the very thin flans of incuse coinage through this technique of minting. It explains why incuse coins are often found in a broken state (and very often chipped) – in contrast to the coins minted by techniques common to the Greek mainland. We suggest that many of these incuse coins had hidden cracks after minting which did not initially come to the surface and which caused the coin to break up after they had entered circulation. We point out that these cross-sections (esp. Fig 5a-c) highlight another feature of the incuse technique; the pressure placed on the circumference of the flan, in which the decorated border is contained, which pushes up this band of metal around the type.

SAMPLE 3

ACANS 00A11 (Fig. 7) is an archaic Athenian coin from the decade 500–490 BC (17.06g) and was not minted using the incuse technique. The tomographic image shows the noticeably thick, rather dumpy flan (diam. 22mm) that was typical of Athenian tetradrachms until the New Style period (beginning in the 160s BC). An interesting feature is the side lug on the outer surface of the flan below the claws of the owl suggesting that the flan was originally circular before being struck. The diameter of the flan is relatively small and the pressure of the hammer when applied to the reverse punch die was calculated not to spread the metal to any great extent (so part of the image is typically missing). The contrast with incuse coinage

Figure 7 a-b. Sample 3. ACANS 00A11 (Athens); 7c. ACANS 00A11 with the unusual area noted in the tomography (Fig 7a) highlighted in black. A possible explanation is the coin was folded along the white line prior to being struck.

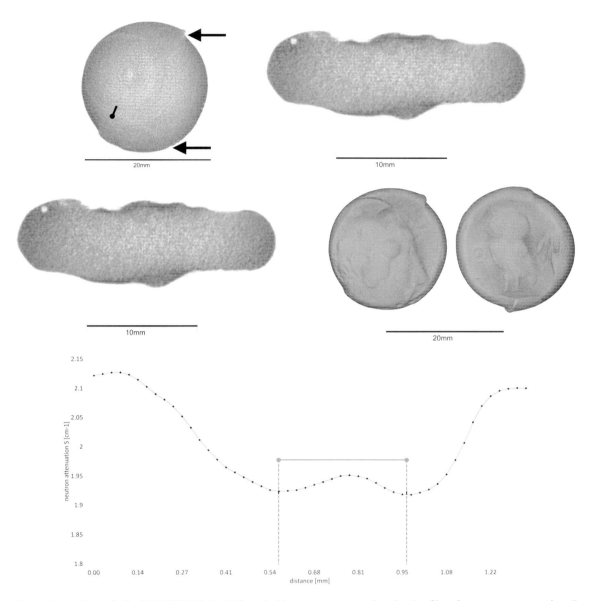

Figure 8a-e. Sample 3. ACANS 00A11 (Athens). Neutron tomography; 8e. Profile of neutron attenuation S plotted across an area of the folding highlighted by a black line in cross section Fig. 8e. A dip in attenuation of ~0.4 mm is visible between the dotted lines..

could not be more evident. Tomography (Figs. 8, 9) reveals signs of light porosity (only 0.02% of the total mass). Another interesting feature revealed by neutron tomography is a line of low density crossing the bulk of the coin (Fig. 8a – black arrows show the start and finish of this line), perhaps due to a more porous area. A possible explanation might be that the flan was folded along this line and then struck. As shown in Fig. 7c, the porous line also fits the morphology of the sample. If this can be accepted then this is the first evidence that the practice of folding the flan, which Kroll detected in Athenian tetradrachms of the 4th century BC (Kroll 2011), began in the archaic period.

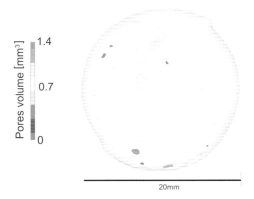

Figure 9. Sample 3. ACANS 00A11 (Athens). 3D map of the porosities. The chart on the left side indicates the grey-colour code adopted to render the volume of the detected pores.

SAMPLE 4

Sample 4 (ACANS 03A07) is a didrachm stater from Aegina (12.09g) which belongs to the island's earliest phase of minting (c.550–530 BC) and thus from the earliest phase of minting among Greek states (Sheedy, 2012). In Fig. 10 we see a dumpy flan (diam 23mm). In comparing this stater with the Attic tetradrachm (00A11; Fig. 7) we note a similarity in the profile of the flan. While there was relatively little porosity in the Attic tetradrachm, there is slightly more to be seen in the Aegina stater (0.09% of the total mass) (Fig. 12).

SAMPLE 5

ACANS 14A07 (Fig. 13) is also an archaic Athenian tetradrachm that belongs to the years between 500 and 490 (or 480 BC). Its diameter and flan shape are not unexpected – 19.8mm is typical of the thick lumpy flans of this coinage. Its weight (17.03g) is also typical of Attic tetradrachms (on the theoretical weight of an Athenian tetradrachm see Davis, Sheedy and Gore, this volume). Nonetheless, the surface of the coin is very worn (the result of excessive cleaning?). This coin was purchased as 'plated' – and thus quite a rarity as there are very few plated archaic owls recorded. The evidence of plating was a small blister over the nose of Athena on the obverse. The tomographic reconstruction, shown in Fig. 14, demonstrated, however, that the coin was not plated, but was very largely composed of silver. The pit over the nose harbours a plug, a repair to the coin, perhaps modern, that was made after it had been holed, probably to allow it to be worn as jewellery.

Figure 10a-b. Sample 4. ACANS 03A07 (Aegina).

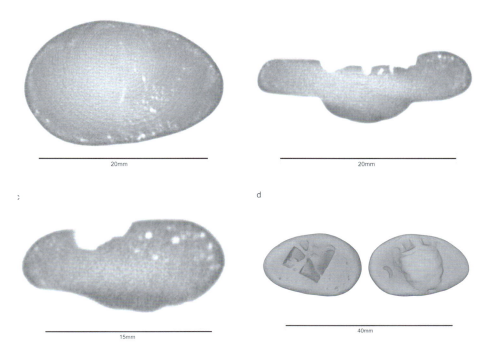

Figure 11 a-d. Sample 4. ACANS 03A07 (Aegina). Neutron tomography.

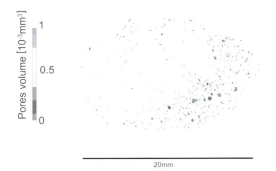

Figure 12. Sample 4. ACANS 03A07 (Aegina). 3D map of the porosities.

Figure 13. Sample 5. ACANS 14A07 (Athens).

The important scientific data to emerge from the analysis of this coin is the high porosity which has been detected within the mass of the coin. Remarkably, 6.09% of the total coin volume consists of voids (Fig. 15). In fact, cast metals often display characteristic spherical holes or porosity that can be caused by gases dissolved in the melt (Scott, 1991).

The presence of diffuse porosities is apparent in the tomographic analyses of 14A07 and the Aeginetan stater 03A07. The existence of these large voids, up to a volume of 3 mm^3, within the silver of this very small sample of coins in the current study can be linked to different factors of the casting process, i.e. the type of mould, the melt temperature, solidification rate, solubility and internal pressure of the gas, etc. (tab. 2; Fig. 6) (Gupta *et al.*, 1992). Since many variables can influence the properties of the final product, robust conclusions cannot be made yet due to the lack of robust evidence supported by complementary analyses (i.e. investigation of replica produced under controlled and known conditions).

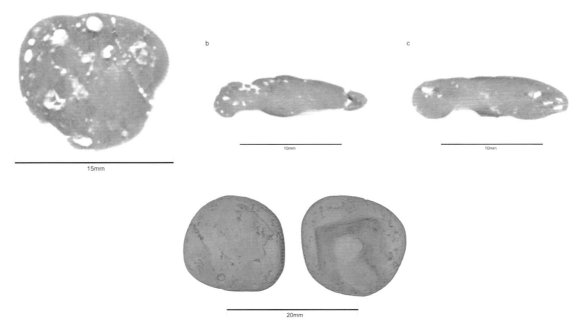

Figure 14. Sample 5. ACANS 14A07 (Athens). Neutron tomography.

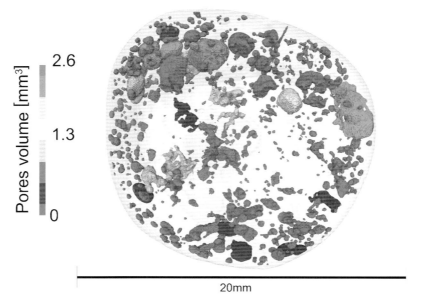

Figure 15. Sample 5. ACANS 14A07 (Athens). 3D map of the porosities. The largest pores are over 2mm³ in volume.

SAMPLE 6

This Athenian tetradrachm from the 4th century BC shows a crease in the profile wall (indicated by a black arrow in fig. 16 suggesting that the flan had been bent double before being struck with dies – and this crease is also evident in Fig. 17 b. The thick flan has a light scattering of voids – 0.67% (Fig. 18). A strongly elongated void highlighted in Fig. 18, running at 45° with respect to the coin's flat surface, might reflect the means of making the flan. However, this feature might also be formed during solidification of the melt due to the interplay of several phenomena that can influence the shape of porosity-related defects (Carlson *et al.*, 2002).

Figure 16. Sample 6. ACANS 01M63 (Athens). The black arrow indicates a crease in the profile wall.

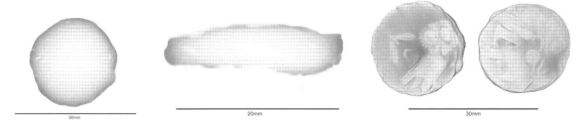

Figure 17 a-c. Sample 6. ACANS 01M63 (Athens). Neutron tomography.

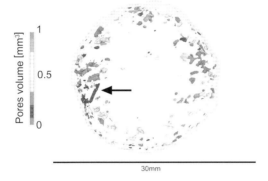

Figure 18. Sample 6. ACANS 01M63 (Athens). The black arrow points to a feature, an area in this coin of unusually uniform sized small pores that line up. A possible explanation is that this is a fold line in this coin.

CONCLUSION

The overall aim of the Incuse Coinage Project is to explore the methods by which one of the earliest silver coinages in the Greek world was produced. The thesis that mints striking incuse coins worked in a different manner to other producers (such as Athens and Aegina) has required that we also explore the evidence for what are held to be traditional minting practices. Neutron tomography has been employed in our project as a means of investigating coin morphology. In particular, we have examined the question of porosity. In this short chapter we have presented the evidence for unusually high porosity in two coins of the archaic period from Athens and Aegina (samples 5 and 6). It can be argued that the voids we have detected were largely caused by gases dissolved in the melt. No working of the metal subsequently reduced these voids (in contrast to the evidence for a substantial working of the thin flans of incuse coins). We have also discovered evidence to support claims that the mint of Athens folded over a metal strip to create the flan before striking. The technique has been recognized from the exterior appearance of 4th century BC coins. Remarkably, the Attic coin we have examined is archaic (500–480 BC), and we might then hypothesize that the practice of folded flans may have been introduced at around the same time as Athens began minting her famous owl coinage (in the decade 530–520 BC).

REFERENCES

Anderson, I.S., McGreevy, R.L., and Bilheux, H.Z. 2009. *Neutron imaging and applications*. Springer Science+Business Media, 200, 987–990.

Bozzini, B., Gianoncelli, A., Mele, C., Siciliano, A. and Mancini, L. 2014. 'Electrochemical reconstruction of a heavily corroded Tarentum hemiobolus silver coin: a study based on microfocus X-ray computed microtomography', *Journal of Archaeological Science* 52, 24–30.

Carlson, K. D., Lin, Z., Hardin, R. A. and Beckermann, C. 2002. 'Modelling of porosity formation and feeding flow in steel casting'. *Proceeding of the 54th SFSA Technical and Operating Conference, Paper 4.4, AFS - American Foundry Society, Chicago, IL*.

Conophagus, C., Badecca, E., and Tsaimou, C. 1976, 'La technique Athenienne de la frappe des monnaies à l'Epoque Classique', *Nomismatika Khronika* 4, 4–33.

Eisenblätter, G., Franz, A.; Kardjilov, N., Kloess G. 2013. 'Anwendung von Röntgen- und Neutronencomputertomographie – ein Blick in das Innere antiker römischer Kupfermünzen', *Metalla*, Sonderheft 6, 89.

Dierick, M., Masschaele, B., Van Hoorebeke, L. 2004. 'Octopus, a fast and user-friendly tomographic reconstruction package developed in LabView®', *Measurement Science & Technology* 15:7, 1366–1370.

Garbe, U., Randall, T., Hughes, C., Davidson, G., Pangelis, S. and Kennedy, S.J. 2015. 'A new neutron radiography/tomography/imaging station DINGO at OPAL', *Physics Procedia* 69, 27–32.

Griesser, M., Kockelmann, W., Hradil, K. and Traum, R. 2016. 'New insights into the manufacturing technique and corrosion of high leaded antique bronze coins', *Microchemical Journal* 126, 181–193.

Gupta, A. K., Saxena, B. K., Tiwari, S. N., Malhotra, S. L. 1992, 'Review - Pore formation in cast metals and alloys', *Journal of Materials Science* 27, 853–862.

Hounsfield, G.N. 1980. 'Computed medical imaging', *Medical physics* 7:4, 283–290.

Hubbell, J. H. and Seltzer, S. M. 1996. *X-Ray Mass Attenuation Coefficients, NIST Standard Reference Database 126* (U.S. Secretary of Commerce on behalf of the United States of America).

Kardjilov, N., Lehmann, E., Strobl, M., Woracek, R. and Manke, I. 2017. 'Neutron Imaging', in Kardjilov, N. and Festa, G. (eds), *Neutron Methods for Archaeology and Cultural Heritage* (Springer, Berlin).

Kardjilov, N., Lo Celso, F., Donato, D.I., Hilger, A. and Triolo, R. 2007. 'Applied neutron tomography in modern archaeology', *Nuovo Cimento C Geophysics Space Physics C* 30, 79–83.

Kirstein, O., Luzin, V. and Garbe, U. 2009. 'The strain-scanning diffractometer Kowari', *Neutron News* 20:4, 34–36.

Kockelmann, W., Siano, S., Bartoli, L., Visser, D., Hallebeek, P., Traum, R., Linke, R., Schreiner, M. and Kirfel, A. 2006. 'Applications of TOF neutron diffraction in archaeometry', *Applied Physics A: Materials Science & Processing*, 83:2, 175–182.

Kraay, C.M. 1976. *Archaic and Classical Greek Coin* (London).

Kroll, J.H. 2011. 'The reminting of Athenian Silver Coinage', *Hesperia* 80, 229–256.

Liyuan, L., Rinaldi, R. and Schober, H. (eds). 2008. *Neutron applications in earth, energy and environmental sciences* (Springer Science & Business Media).

Lehmann, E.H., Vontobel, P., Deschler-Erb, E. and Soares, M. 2005. 'Non-invasive studies of objects from cultural heritage', *Nuclear Instruments and Methods in Physics Research Section A: Accelerators, Spectrometers, Detectors and Associated Equipment*, 542:1, 68–75.

Lehmann, E.H., Vontobel, P. and Wiezel, L. 2001. 'Properties of the radiography facility NEUTRA at SINQ and its potential for use as European reference facility', *Nondestructive Testing and Evaluation* 16:2–6, 191–202.

Liss, K.D., Hunter, B., Hagen, M., Noakes, T. and Kennedy, S. 2006. 'Echidna—the new high-resolution powder diffractometer being built at OPAL', *Physica B: Condensed Matter* 385, 1010–1012.

Mays, C., Bevitt, J.J. and Stilwell, J. 2017. 'Pushing the limits of neutron tomography in palaeontology: Three-dimensional modelling of in situ resin within fossil plants', *Palaeontologia Electronica*, 20.3.57A.

Moesta H., Franke P. R. 1995. *Herstellung von Muenzen Antike Metallurgie und Muenzpraegung. Ein Beitrag zur Technikgeschichte (Basel)*.

Mørkholm, O. 1991. *Early Hellenistic Coinage* (Cambridge).

Nguyen, H.Y., Keating, S., Bevan, G., Gabov, A., Daymond, M., Schillinger, B. and Murray, A. 2011. 'Seeing through Corrosion: Using Micro-focus X-ray Computed Tomography and Neutron Computed Tomography to Digitally "Clean" Ancient Bronze Coins', *MRS Online Proceedings Library Archive 1319*.

Olsen, S.R., Pullen, S.A. and Avdeev, M., 2010. 'A 100-position robotic sample changer for powder diffraction with low-background vacuum chamber', *Journal of Applied Crystallography* 43:2, 377–379.

Rutter, K. (ed). 2001. *Historia Numorum. Italy* (London).

Salvemini, F., Grazzi, F., Kardjilov, N., Manke, I., Civita, F. and Zoppi, M. 2015. 'Neutron computed laminography on ancient metal artefacts', *Analytical Methods* 7:1, 271–278.

Salvemini, F., Olsen, S.R., Luzin, V., Garbe, U., Davis, J., Knowles, T. and Sheedy, K. 2016. 'Neutron tomographic analysis: Material characterization of silver and electrum coins from the 6th and 5th centuries BC', *Materials Characterization* 118, 175–185.

Scott, D. A. 1991. *Metallography and Microstructure in Ancient and Historic Metals* (Los Angeles).

Sears, V. F. 2006. 'Neutron scattering lengths and cross sections', *Neutron News* 3:1, 26–37.

Sheedy, K. A. 2012. 'Aegina, the Cyclades and Crete', in Metcalf, W.E. (ed.), *Oxford Handbook of Greek and Roman Coinage* (Oxford), 105–127.

Sheedy, K.A., Munroe, P., Salvemini, F., Luzin, V., Garbe, U. and Olsen, S., 2015. 'An incuse stater from the series 'Sirinos/Pyxoes', *Journal of the Numismatic Association of Australia* 26, 36–52.

Spagnoli, E. 2013. *La prima moneta in Magna Grecia: il caso di Sibari* (Campbasso).

Treimer, W. 2017. 'Neutron Tomography', in Kardjilov, N. and Festa G. (eds), *Neutron Methods for Archaeology and Cultural Heritage* (Berlin), 81–108. DOI: 10.1007/978-0-387-78693-3_6.

Williams, R. 2016. 'An Experiment in Manufacturing Blanks and Striking Coins', *Antichthon* 50, 17–32.

PART 3

ARCHAEOLOGY AND MUSEUMS

19. THE ACROPOLIS, 1886 HOARD (*IGCH* 12) REVISITED

Panagiotis Tselekas

ABSTRACT

The Acropolis, 1886 hoard (IGCH 12) was revealed during excavations of a deposit between the northwest side of the Erechtheum and the north wall of the Acropolis that has been part of the debris made up from various damaged artefacts associated with the Persian destruction of the site in 480 BC. The hoard consists of Athenian silver coins, both Wappenmünzen and the archaic 'owl' series. Because of its connection with the Persian destruction of 480 BC (Perserschutt) it has been regarded as crucial for the study of Athenian coinage. This chapter presents the circumstances in which the hoard was found, and surveys its interpretation by various scholars in the context of studying the early owl coinage of Athens. Furthermore, in light of the evidence provided by a reexamination of these coins, the significance of the hoard in dating the conclusion of archaic Athenian coinage is evaluated. In addition, coin production and coin use in late Archaic and early Classical Athens is also considered.

INTRODUCTION

The Acropolis, 1886 hoard (*IGCH* 12) was discovered in February 1886 during the large-scale excavations on the Acropolis conducted under the direction of P. Kavvadias (1886a; 1886b). It was revealed inside a deposit in the area between the northwest side of the Erechtheum and the north wall of the Acropolis. This deposit had been part of the debris made up from various damaged artefacts (sculpture, inscriptions and pottery) associated with the Persian destruction of the site in 480 BC.[1]

The hoard was briefly reported by Kavvadias, who noted that 35 Attic tetradrachms, 2 drachms and 23 obols (60 coins in total) were discovered in the uppermost level of the deposit, not scattered but all together at the same spot (Kavvadias 1886a, 78 n. 1; Kavvadias 1886b, 19 n. 1; Kavvadias 1906, 29–30). The coins were kept at the National Archaeological Museum and in the academic year 1904–5 reached the Athens Numismatic Museum, then housed at the Academy of Athens (Svoronos 1898, 368).

The hoard was first published by I. Svoronos in 1898, who provided a list of 63 coins kept at the National Archaeological Museum with some commentary and illustration of 21 specimens (Svoronos 1898). The 63 coins comprise one drachm (Cat. 1), thirteen obols (Cat. 2–14) and three hemiobols (Cat. 15–17) of the wheel type in the *Wappenmünzen* series, 36 tetradrachms (Cat. 18–53), one drachm (Cat. 54) and eight obols (Cat. 55–62) of the Owl series without a wreath, and one tetradrachm (Cat. 63) of the Owl series with a wreath. Fifty-four coins of the hoard were further published and illustrated by Svoronos in 1926 (Svoronos 1923–6, pl. 3). Additionally, some of the tetradrachms were later reproduced by E. Babelon (1905), M.L. Kambanis (1906), C.T. Seltman (1924) and C. Starr (1970) (individual references can be found in the catalogue).

STUDYING AND INTERPRETING THE HOARD

One major theme regarding the Acropolis, 1886 hoard is the discrepancy between the 1886 and 1906 reports of Kavvadias and the 1898 publication of Svoronos, since the latter included three more items (two tetradrachms and one fraction, either an obol or hemiobol) (Svoronos 1898, 375). When

---

[1] The Acropolis, 1886 hoard caught the author's attention in early 2000's. At the time, the hoard was one of the important exhibits at the Museum on the first floor of the *Iliou Melathron* (see Galani-Krikou 1996, 93; Tselekas 2008, 34–35). In 2009, in accordance with a decision of the Hellenic Ministry of Culture, the hoard was transferred to the Acropolis Museum, where it has been exhibited in the Archaic Gallery in a case also containing some of the fragmented korai from the *Perserschutt*. Sincere thanks are extended to Professor Emeritus D. Pantermalis, President of the Acropolis Museum, and Dr G. Kakavas, Director of the Athens Numismatic Museum, for the provision of the photographs of the coins of the Acropolis, 1886 hoard and the permission to use them; to Mss E. Kontou and N. Katsikosta, conservators at the Athens Numismatic Museum, for assisting in the description of the condition of the coins and providing the relevant bibliography. Acknowledgements should also offered to the two anonymous reviewers for their helpful comments.

Svoronos examined the coins, he noted that all except two tetradrachms and most of the smaller denominations had been badly damaged in a great fire (Svoronos 1898, 374). Svoronos interpreted the hoard as a monetary dedication in one of the sanctuaries on the Archaic Acropolis before the Persian Wars and connected the burning of the coins with the fire caused by the Persian looting of the site in 480 BC (Svoronos 1898, 377). He rejected the wreathed owl tetradrachm (Cat. 64) because firstly, it showed no traces of fire and secondly, it was of a different and later style than the other tetradrachms. He suggested that this coin might have come from other contemporary excavations on the Acropolis although, as he admitted, none of those who had been in charge could give him any information on this matter (Svoronos 1898, 375).

The hoard was poorly exploited by Seltman in his 1924 study of the Athenian mint before the Persian Invasion (Seltman 1924, 147). After "a careful examination" he confirmed Svoronos' observations that the coins of the hoard had been through fire (Seltman 1924, 59 n. 6), and he too rejected the wreathed owl tetradrachm as being part of this find. He also excluded the unwreathed owl drachm (Cat. 54) since it also, according to him, did not bear any marks of fire (Seltman 1924, 58 n. 1 and 147 n. 1).

The description provided by Svoronos, and confirmed by Seltman, of coins bearing the marks of fire and therefore associated with the Persian destruction of the site has been repeatedly adopted by scholars (see, for example, Starr 1970, 4; Kroll 1981, 18 n. 51; Kroll and Waggoner 1984, 329; Galani-Krikou 1996, 93; Theodorou 1996, 58–9; Stewart 2008, 384–5; Stoyas 2008; Davis 2014, 344, though in recent years the coins have been unavailable for physical inspection). This narrative is found yet again on the packaging of the Acropolis Museum medal struck in 2012 to commemorate International Museum Day; it depicts the obverse of a tetradrachm from the Acropolis, 1886 hoard (Cat. 51).[2]

The dating of the hoard to the time of, or shortly after, the Persian destruction of the Acropolis in 480/79 BC, and the exclusion of the wreathed owl tetradrachm, proved of vital importance for the classification and the chronology of the owl coinage of Athens. The hoard has been treated as a firm chronological anchor, with many scholars claiming that the addition of the diadem of olive leaves to Athena's helmet on the obverse of the coins should be dated after 479/8, when Athens emerged victorious from the Persian wars. Lermann (1900, 24–6), Kambanis (1906, 90), Kraay (1962, 418–9), Starr (1970, 4), and Price and Waggoner (1975, 20 and 62), who all argued for a post–479/8 BC date for the inauguration of the wreathed owls, followed Svoronos in excluding the wreathed owl tetradrachm from the hoard. On the other hand, Babelon (1905, 44–5;1907, 767–8) and Wallace (1962, 34–5 n. 4) favoured a date around 490 BC for the introduction of the wreathed owls; although they admitted some uncertainty about the presence of this tetradrachm in the hoard they concluded that, even if it was not part of the find, the coin must inevitably have belonged to another section of the *Perserschutt* excavated by Kavvadias.

Moreover, the hoard proved useful for the classification of the unwreathed owl coinage. Kraay, in his rearrangement of Seltman's work on the early owl coinage, concluded that the groups represented in the Acropolis hoard were the last and not the first to be produced (Kraay 1956, 53; Kraay 1975, 146 and 153). His view was accepted by Starr (1970, 4–6), Price and Waggoner (1975, 20 and 62), Kagan (1987, 21–2) and Flament (2007, 36–41).

Apart from the inclusion of the wreathed owl tetradrachm in the find, much has been made of the composition of the hoard as a whole. The questioning of the accuracy of Kavvadias' excavations and reports, the implication that some coins might have been found elsewhere, led scholars such as Hopper, Kroll and Waggoner to suggest that the remaining

---

[2] The Acropolis Museum, in cooperation with the National Mint of the Bank of Greece, has since 2012 produced a series of medals to commemorate International Museum Day. The first medal depicts a tetradrachm. See, http://www.marblesreunited.org.uk/2012/05/the-acropolis-museum-shares-visitor-survey-results-and-announces-production-of-replicas-and-commemorative-coin/; http://www.archaiologia.gr/blog/2012/05/17/45-εκατ-είδαν-τους-θησαυρούς/.

62 specimens may have formed two separate groups of coins (Hopper 1968, 25–6 n. 2; Kraay 1975, 158 with Hopper's remarks; Kroll 1981, 18 n. 51; Kroll and Waggoner 1984, 327 n. 16). Moreover, the inclusion of only 54 specimens – among them the wreathed owl tetradrachm – in the 1924 publication of Svoronos led to the mistaken belief that the hoard comprised 54 coins (Wallace 1962, 24 n. 3 and 34–5 n. 4; Stewart 2008, 383–4; Davis 2014, 344).

Despite the ambiguity regarding the excavation procedures of Kavvadias (Svoronos 1898, 377–8; Bundgaard 1974, 11–14), it could not be denied that the Acropolis, 1886 hoard was found in a post-Persian context, since the pit where the coins and the other artefacts were buried was created after the Persian Wars (Kavvadias 1906, 29–30). The rubble and statues were used as a fill behind the North Wall of the Acropolis, which consequently had been built before the material could be placed there (Vickers 1985, 25; Vickers 1986, 256, commenting on the section drawing of the area excavated in 1886; for the latter see Kavvadias 1886a, 78, fig. 2 [reproduced in Svoronos 1898, 369]; Kavvadias 1906, 23–4, fig. 1; Bundgaard 1974, 13). The construction of the North Wall coincided with the extensive efforts to reshape the landscape of the Acropolis, as terracing helped to produce a more level and larger surface area. Special care was taken in the working of blocks. Architectural members from buildings badly damaged by the Persians were incorporated to serve as a kind of memorial of the destruction (Lambrinoudakis 1986, 44; Kousser 2009, 271). The crucial question is when was the North Wall of the Acropolis, or at least the section near the Erechtheum, constructed? According to some scholars, this wall was built at the time of Themistocles as part of the rushed fortification of Athens in 479/8 (Lindenlauf 1997, 72–3; Korres 2002; Stewart 2008, 385 n. 31). However, strong arguments have been expressed in support of dating the wall later, around the time of the building activity on the south side of the Acropolis associated with Kimon (Vickers 1985, 25–6; Vickers 1986, 257; Lambrinoudakis 1986, 44–5; Steskal 2004, 161–2 and 251). The literary evidence is not conclusive. Thucydides (1.90.3 and 1.93.1–2) in his account of the fortification of Athens refers only to the building of the Athens circuit wall. On the other hand, Pausanias (1.28.3) in reference to the Acropolis wall only mentions that part of the wall constructed at the time of Kimon in relation to that of the Mycenaean period, without any reference to the intervening building phases. The deposit where the hoard was unearthed seems to have been stratified in three levels and sealed by a layer of clay and stones. All the material unearthed from here is archaic (Stewart 2008, 381–5). Although the damage to these artefacts may well be the result of the Persian sack of the Acropolis, their careful burial and the subsequent levelling of this area of the site should not necessarily be dated immediately after the return of the Athenians (contrary to Stewart 2008, 385). Building and backfilling the North Wall was a huge task that required clearing operations, the importation of at least 10,000 m^3 of fill, and the commitment of labour and time (Stewart 2008, 389 and 390 fig. 18).

The Acropolis 1886 hoard might provide a *terminus post quem* for the deposit and, along with it, for the wall as well. If the wreathed owl tetradrachm did not belong to the hoard, the hoard might date the whole construction to the early 470s (Stewart 2008, 383–5; Kousser 2009, 271); but if it does belong, the date of the wall should be lowered to the 460s (Lindenlauf 1997, 71 n. 193; Ferrari 2002, 23).

An entirely different picture emerged in the spring of 2009, when the hoard was taken out from its exhibition case in the Athens Numismatic Museum to be handed over to the Acropolis Museum. Baffled by the rather good appearance of the coins, the author asked Ms E. Kontou and Ms N. Katsikosta of the Numismatic Museum's laboratory to examine and confirm that the coins had been actually passed through fire. Their inspection of the coins revealed that their moderate-poor condition was the result of severe corrosion, and certainly not of fire.

Examination under a stereomicroscope Leica MZ 9.5 in magnification of 25x–60x, revealed that the unwreathed owl tetradrachms (Cat.18–53) and the drachm (Cat. 54) had undergone chemical cleaning in the past (Svoronos 1898, 370). This process had not only removed corrosion to reveal the pitted surfaces of the coins (Cronyn 1990, 233), it had also decreased their original weight. The coins are now coated with a greyish-black patina, possibly as a consequence of atmospheric corrosion following the cleaning process (Stambolov 1985, 184). Another possibility is that the chemicals used to clean the coins were not thoroughly removed so further erosion of the surface has occured (Argyropoulos 2008, 56). The *Wappenmünzen* drachm (Cat. 1), obols (Cat. 2–14) and hemiobols (Cat. 15–17) as well as the unwreathed owl obols (Cat. 55–62) have not been cleaned; they have retained corrosion on their surface and bear no traces of burning. Furthermore, the wreathed owl tetradrachm also bore signs of corrosion. The theory that metal corrosion is an irreversible physical-chemical phenomenon only occurring locally seems to be proven by these silver coins (Bertholon and Relier 1990, 171). At certain points, or even on one of the two sides of the coin, the corrosion is severe (a thick layer of substances) and unstable, while elsewhere it simply forms a film (Cronyn 1990, 230–32).

The argument that the coins bear traces of fire from the Persian occupation is evidently false. It had originated in Svoronos' misinterpretation of the appearance of the coins as having been through fire because they came from the *Perserschutt*. This account, supported by Seltman after his examination of the hoard, was often repeated by scholars who relied on Svoronos' interpretation without looking closely at his initial text (but see Kraay 1975 with comments by Hopper). According to Svoronos, the details of these coin types from the Acropolis find (eyes, noses, lips, hair, earrings etc.) were bloated from the melting process during the fire and as a result looked quite 'barbaric' (Svoronos 1898, 374). However, the appearance of the coins was not the result of the damage caused by the high temperatures; rather, it was due to the shabby dies employed as well as clumsy striking (with insufficient hammer blows). Following the interpretation of Svoronos, J.P. Six, who had received casts of one or two of the tetradrachms not long after the discovery of the Acropolis, 1886 hoard, speculated that the 'barbaric' look of the coins may have resulted from their fabrication by the Persians when they were in control of Athens (Svoronos 1898, 374). This theory was supported by Holloway (1999, 14–5). Others have argued that the use of dies of 'low' or 'barbaric' artistic quality and the crude striking process can be attributed to the urgency to turn bullion into coin in the late 480s (Kraay 1956, 58; Kraay 1976, 62; Kroll and Waggoner 1984, 329).

THE IMPORTANCE OF THE HOARD

Despite the problems surrounding the composition of the Acropolis, 1886 hoard, it nevertheless remains important for the chronology of archaic Athenian coinage (and for the dating of pottery and sculpture linked to the *Perserschutt*). Nonetheless, I have tried to demonstrate that there is no evidence that the coins were damaged by fire and thus nothing to link them directly to the destruction of buildings on the Acropolis in 480 BC (see Steskal 2004, 64–5 who disassociates the hoard from the *Perserschutt* on the grounds of the uncertainty regarding their exact number and finding). Thus it seems to me that the interpretation of the hoard as belonging to one of the defenders of the Acropolis who perished during the Persian attack, or even in the possession of the Persians who looted the site (Lermann 1900, 27; Price and Waggoner 1975, 21; Theodorou 1996, 59), cannot be valid. Similarly, Holloway's interpretation of the hoard as an accumulation of barbarian owls struck by a Persian military mint that was not acceptable currency is rather unconvincing; Holloway believed these issues were removed from circulation and deposited on the Acropolis in the aftermath of the Persian invasion (Holloway 1999, 14–15). In his view, the *Wappenmünzen* were long superseded. But if this was the case, why were the unwanted coins not used as bullion for the striking of wreathed owls? In fact, it is difficult to argue with certainty that the hoard was a dedication to one of the sanctuaries on the Acropolis (Svoronos 1898, 377; Babelon 1907, 739–40 n. 2; Seltman 1924, 58; Kraay 1956, 53; Kroll 1981, 18 n. 51; Kroll and Waggoner 1984, 327 n. 16; Galani-Krikou 1996, 93; Tselekas 2008, 34). It could just as easily be associated with the variety of activities that involved the use of coins within the boundaries of a sanctuary (see Knapp 2005, 32–6 on coin-using activities in sanctuaries).

A die study of the hoard specimens has revealed that these coins were produced from a significant number of unlinked pairs of dies (Table 1). This suggests that the coinage had a low survival rate. It may also indicate that several pairs of dies were in use at the same time. This evidence can be used to examine arguments about the output of the Athenian mint during the late Archaic period, both in relation to the fractions of the *Wappenmünzen* coinage and especially the wheel series (Davis 2014, 341–2; Davis 2015, 4) as well as claims for the mass production of unwreathed owl tetradrachms (Kraay 1976, 62; Kroll and Waggoner 1984, 329; Kroll 2009, 196). If we accept that the Acropolis, 1886 hoard consisted of the 63 coins listed by Svoronos in 1898, then the hoard appears to contain local issues struck in the late sixth century (the *Wappenmünzen*), 480s (the unwreathed owls), and 460s (the wreathed owl). The inclusion of coins that cover more than 60 years suggests that older and new issues were in use at the same time. It has been argued that this was a feature of local circulation in the last decades of the sixth and the first decades of the fifth centuries BC. Kroll, following Kraay (1956), proposed that during the transition period from *Wappenmünzen* to owls, the small change of Attica continued to consist of *Wappenmünzen* and that these fractions remained in circulation even after the production of owl coins (Kroll 1981, 18–20). Davis has further argued that the *Wappenmünzen* wheel type fractions continued to be the main fractional coinage of Athens in the first decades of the fifth century since the production of owl fractions was not as plentiful as that of the tetradrachms (Davis 2014, 343–5). Davis largely based his arguments on the conclusion that the Acropolis, 1886 hoard did not contain the wreathed owl tetradrachm. However, if this coin was part of the hoard, it is reasonable to assume that the use of *Wappenmünzen* fractions, unwreathed owl tetradrachms and smaller denominations continued well after the Persian wars, when Athens was producing the first phase of its wreathed owl coinage.

The production of the wreathed owls dated to the period 478–449 BC by Starr (1970, 8–63), or more plausibly to the 470s and 460s as proposed by Kagan (1987, 22–4) and supported by Kroll (1993, 5–6) and Flament (2007, 47–54), might not have driven out earlier issues from circulation. After all, they were Athenian silver of good quality and struck on the same weight standard. Others hoards found in Attica (such as Attica, before 1906: *IGCH* 16; Starr 1970, 87; Flament 2007, 177–8), or hoards found in Egypt (such as Zagazig, 1901: *IGCH* 1645; Starr 1970, 90; Flament 2007, 209–210), and in the Levant (such as Elmali, 1984: *CH* 8, 48; Flament 2007, 194–5, Massyaf, 1961: *IGCH* 1483; Flament 2007, 200 and Jordan, 1967: *IGCH* 1482; Starr 1970, 87; Flament 2007, 198–9) contain both unwreathed and wreathed owls (see Table 2). The composition of these hoards then probably reflects the various series of Athenian coinage in circulation in Athens during the second quarter of the fifth century BC, coins which were arguably exported together, possibly in the course of trade and/or military operations.

The limited occurrence of unwreathed owls in Attic hoards of the early Classical period might suggest they had been called in and reminted as wreathed owls. Demonetising and restriking larger-denomination silver coinage in Athens in 353 resulted in the disappearance of nearly all earlier fourth century tetradrachms from circulation in Attica and their survival mainly in hoards that were buried abroad (Kroll 2011, 240–1). However, it should be stressed that the surviving hoard evidence with regards to Attica is scant not only for the unwreathed but for the early wreathed owls as well.

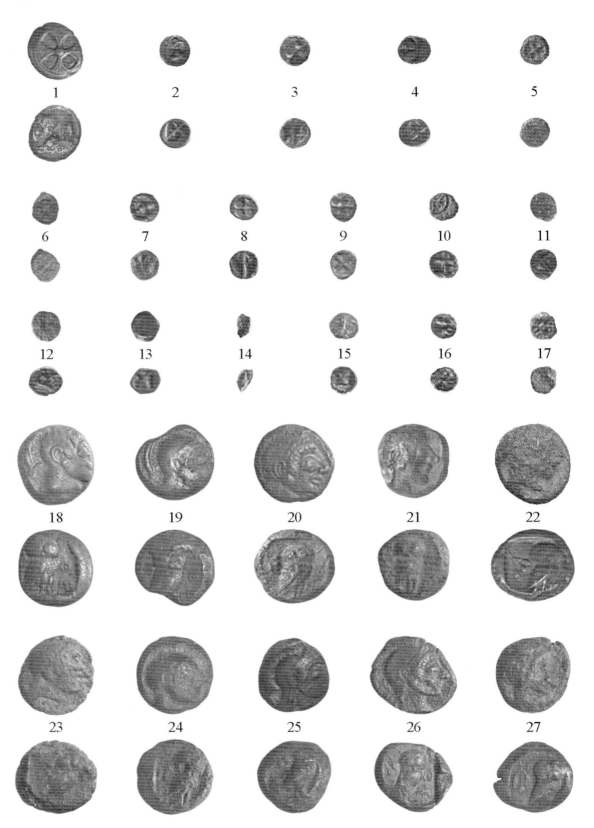

Plates 1–3. Acropolis Hoard

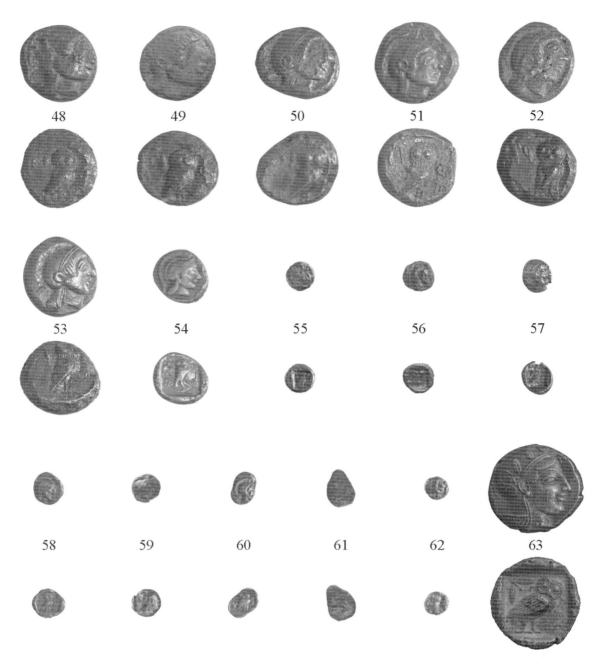

The coexistence of *Wappenmünzen* wheel fractions with owls in the Acropolis hoard does not necessarily indicate that *Wappenmünzen* fractions continued to be minted well after the introduction of the owl coinage as has been suggested by Kroll (1981, 19), Flament (2007, 22), H. van Wees (2013, 127) and Davis (2014, 343; 2015, 3). This matter remains to be decided. The comprehensive die study and the metallurgical analysis of the early Athenian coinage undertaken by Sheedy, Gore and Davis (2009) for the *Early Attic Coinage Project* may help decide this question. A die study will provide evidence for the patterns as well as the scale of production of the various phases of the coinage. The metal analyses will show whether the same sources of bullion were used for the production of the *Wappenmünzen* wheel fractions and the unwreathed owls.

Table 1. Number of obverse and reverse dies detected in the Acropolis, 1886 hoard

	Wappenmünzen (wheel)			Owls (unwreathed)			Owls (wreathed)
	Drachms	*Obols*	*1/2obols*	*4drachms*	*Drachms*	*obols*	*4drachms*
Specimens	1	13	3	36	1	8	1
Obv. Dies	1	13	3	30	1	8	1
Rev. Dies	1	13	3	31	1	8	1

Table 2. Hoards containing late Archaic and early Classical Athenian coins

Coin Hoards	*Burial (BC)*	*Athenian content*	*Wappenmünzen*	*Owls (unwreathed)*	*Owls (wreathed)*
Acropolis, 1886 (*IGCH* 12)	460's	63	17	45	1
Attica, b. 1906 (*IGCH* 16)	465	9	–	1	8
Elmali, 1984 (*CH* 8, 48)	460	187	–	12	175
Zagazig, 1901 (*IGCH* 1645)	450's	34	–	16	18
Massyaf, 1961 (*IGCH* 1483)	450	35	–	1	34
Jordan, 1967 (*IGCH* 1482)	445	31	1	23	7

CATALOGUE[3]

Athens

Obv. Wheel with four spokes and struts.
Rev. Quadripartite incuse square divided diagonally in four triangles.
Drachm
01. O1-R1; 4.00g; --h. Svoronos 1898, 372, no. 47; Svoronos 1923–6, pl. 3.1.

Obv. Wheel with four spokes and struts.
Rev. Quadripartite incuse square divided diagonally in four triangles.
Obols
02. O1-R1; 0.71g; --h. Svoronos 1898, 372, no. 48; Svoronos 1923–6, pl. 3.4.
03. O2-R2; 0.58g; --h. Svoronos 1898, 372, no. 50; Svoronos 1923–6, pl. 3.5.
04. O3-R3; 0.62g; --h. Svoronos 1898, 372, no. 49; Svoronos 1923–6, pl. 3.3.
05. O4-R4; 0.56g; --h. Svoronos 1898, 372, no. 51.
06. O5-R5; 0.53g; --h. Svoronos 1898, 372, no. 52; Svoronos 1923–6, pl. 3.2.
07. O6-R6; 0.44g; --h. Svoronos 1898, 373, no. 55; Svoronos 1923–6, pl. 3.8.
08. O7-R7; 0.46g; --h. Svoronos 1898, 373, no. 56; Svoronos 1923–6, pl. 3.9.
09. O8-R8; 0.40g; --h. Svoronos 1898, 373, no. 60; Svoronos 1923–6, pl. 3.7.
10. O9-R9; 0.43g; --h. Svoronos 1898, 373, no. 58; Svoronos 1923–6, pl. 3.6.
11. O10-R10; 0.49g; --h. Svoronos 1898, 372, no. 53.
12. O11-R11; 0.43g; --h. Svoronos 1898, 373, no. 59.
13. O12-R12; 0.45g; --h. Svoronos 1898, 373, no. 54.
14. O13-R13; 0.16g broken; --h. Svoronos 1898, 373, no. 57.

Obv. Wheel with four spokes and struts.
Rev. Quadripartite incuse square divided diagonally in four triangles.
Hemiobols
15. O1-R1; 0.38g; --h. Svoronos 1898, 373, no. 61; Svoronos 1923–6, pl. 3.10.
16. O2-R2; 0.35g; --h. Svoronos 1898, 373, no. 62; Svoronos 1923–6, pl. 3.11.
17. O3-R3; 0.31g; --h. Svoronos 1898, 373, no. 63.

---

[3] Individual coin listings consist of the obverse and reverse dies used, weight, die-axis, and bibliographical references. The weight measurements were taken in the spring of 2009 at the Laboratory of the Athens Numismatic Museum. The weight of nos. 18, 21, 36, 38, 41, 47, 48, 49 and 63 is notably different from that given in Svoronos 1898 and repeated in Svoronos 1923–6. Svoronos provided information on the weight of the tetradrachms before and after their cleaning since this process reduced their overall weight.

Obv. Head of Athena right, wearing crested Attic helmet and round earring.
Rev. Owl standing right with head facing and closed wings; in left field, olive spring; in right field, ΑΘΕ. All within incuse square.

Tetradrachms

18. O1-R1; 16.59g; 06h. Svoronos 1898, 371, no. 29; Svoronos 1923–6, pl. 3.40; Seltman 1924, 172, no. 132b.
19. O2-R2; 16.79g; 06h. Svoronos 1898, 370, no. 4; Svoronos 1923–6, pl. 3.44; Seltman 1924, 173, no. 137a.
20. O2-R3; 15.19g; 10h. Svoronos 1898, 371, no. 31; Babelon 1905, 12, fig. 5; Kambanis 1906, pl. II.10; Babelon 1907, pl. XXXIV.10; Svoronos 1923–6, pl. 3.33; Seltman 1924, 173, no. 138a.
21. O3-R3; 15.95g; 12h. Svoronos 1898, 371, no. 28; Svoronos 1923–6, pl. 3.30; Seltman 1924, 173, no. 139a.
22. O4-R4; 15.78g; 10h. Svoronos 1898, 370, no. 1; Svoronos 1923–6, pl. 3.26.
23. O5-R5; 15.39g; 09h. Svoronos 1898, 371, no. 26; Svoronos 1923–6, pl. 3.46.
24. O6-R6; 15.93g; 09h. Svoronos 1898, 371, no. 21; Svoronos 1923–6, pl. 3.22.
25. O7-R7; 16.20g; 10h. Svoronos 1898, 371, no. 16; Svoronos 1923–6, pl. 3.43; Seltman 1924, 175, no. 149b.
26. O8-R8; 15.35g; 09h. Svoronos 1898, 370, no. 9; Babelon 1907, pl. XXXIV.13; Svoronos 1923–6, pl. 3.47; Seltman 1924, 176, no. 161a.
27. O9-R9; 16.20g; 02h. Svoronos 1898, 371, no. 12; Babelon 1905, 12, fig. 4 (rev.); Kambanis 1906, pl. II.9 (rev.); Svoronos 1923–6, pl. 3.42.
28. O10-R10; 16.30g; 09h. Svoronos 1898, 371, no. 20; Svoronos 1923–6, pl. 3.21; Seltman 1924, 168, no. 93b.
29. O11-R11; 15.99g; 03h. Svoronos 1898, 370, no. 7; Svoronos 1923–6, pl. 3.32.
30. O12-R12; 16.27g; 09h. Svoronos 1898, 370, no. 3; Svoronos 1923–6, pl. 3.41; Seltman 1924, 170, no. 112a.
31. O13-R13; 16.28g; 04h. Svoronos 1898, 371, no. 13; Svoronos 1923–6, pl. 3.23.
32. O14-R14; 16.49g; 03h. Svoronos 1898, 371, no. 25; Svoronos 1923–6, pl. 3.24; Babelon 1907, pl. XXXIV.6; Seltman 1924, 168, no. 94a.
33. O15-R15; 15.96g; 09h. Svoronos 1898, 371, no. 14; Babelon 1905, 12, fig. 3; Babelon 1907, pl. XXXIV.3; Svoronos 1923–6, pl. 3.15; Seltman 1924, 168, no. 95a.
34 19. O15-R15; 16.07g; 00h. Svoronos 1898, 371, no. 30; Babelon 1905, 12, fig. 4 (obv.); Kambanis 1906, pl. II.9 (obv.); Babelon 1907, pl. XXXIV.4; Svoronos 1923–6, pl. 3.14; Seltman 1924, 168, no. 95b.
35. O16-R16; 16.14g; 10h. Svoronos 1898, 371, no. 33; Svoronos 1923–6, pl. 3.25.
36. O17-R17; 15.93g; 06h. Svoronos 1898, 371, no. 27; Svoronos 1923–6, pl. 3.28.
37. O18-R18; 16.23g; 02h. Svoronos 1898, 370, no. 2; Svoronos 1923–6, pl. 3.27; Seltman 1924, 169, no. 100a.
38. O18-R18; 17.04g; 07h. Svoronos 1898, 371, no. 22; Babelon 1907, pl. XXXIV.8; Svoronos 1923–6, pl. 3.16; Seltman 1924, 169, no. 100b.
39. O19-R19; 15.55g; 09h. Svoronos 1898, 371, no. 15; Svoronos 1923–6, pl. 3.20.
40. O20-R20; 16.33g; 04h. Svoronos 1898, 371, no. 23; Svoronos 1923–6, pl. 3.17; Seltman 1924, 169, no. 107a.
41. O21-R21; 16.53 g; 07h. Svoronos 1898, 370, no. 5; Svoronos 1923–6, pl. 3.38; Seltman 1924, 170, no. 115b.
42. O22-R22; 16.48g; 01h. Svoronos 1898, 371, no. 36; Svoronos 1923–6, pl. 3.35.
43. O23-R23; 15.85g; 11h. Svoronos 1898, 371, no. 19; Svoronos 1923–6, pl. 3.34.
44. O24-R24; 14.93g; 12h. Svoronos 1898, 370, no. 8; Svoronos 1923–6, pl. 3.39.
45. O25-R25; 16.54g; 06h. Svoronos 1898, 371, no. 11; Svoronos 1923–6, pl. 3.31.
46. O26-R26; 15.66g; 06h. Svoronos 1898, 371, no. 32; Svoronos 1923–6, pl. 3.12; Seltman 1924, 169, no. 102a.
47. O26-R27; 15.77g; 09h. Svoronos 1898, 371, no. 18; Svoronos 1923–6, pl. 3.36; Seltman 1924, 169, no. 103a.
48. O26-R28; 16.39g; 08h. Svoronos 1898, 371, no. 35; Svoronos 1923–6, pl. 3.37; Seltman 1924, 169, no. 104a.
49. O26-R28; 16.82g; 07h. Svoronos 1898, 371, no. 34; Svoronos 1923–6, pl. 3.29; Seltman 1924, 169, no. 104b.
50. O27-R28; 16.10g; 07h. Svoronos 1898, 371, no. 17; Babelon 1907, pl. XXXIV.7; Svoronos 1923–6, pl. 3.18; Seltman 1924, 169, no. 105a.

51. O28-R29; 16.34g; 07h. Svoronos 1898, 370, no. 10; Babelon 1907, pl. XXXIV.11; Svoronos 1923–6, pl. 3.19; Seltman 1924, 168, no. 96a.
52. O29-R30; 16.23g; 02h. Svoronos 1898, 371, no. 24; Svoronos 1923–6, pl. 3.13; Seltman 1924, 170, no. 118a.
53. O30-R31; 17.08g; 09h. Svoronos 1898, 170, 6; Babelon 1905, 12, fig. 2; Kambanis 1906, pl. II.8; Babelon 1907, pl. XXXIV.5; Svoronos 1923–6, pl. 3.45; Seltman 1924, 170, no. 119a.

Obv. Head of Athena right, wearing crested Attic helmet and round earring.
Rev. Owl standing right on a floral branch with head facing and closed wings; in left field, olive spring; in right field, [AΘ]E. All within incuse square.
Drachm
54. O1-R1; 4.02g; 03h. Svoronos 1898, 371, no. 37; Svoronos 1923–6, pl. 3.48.

Obv. Head of Athena right, wearing crested Attic helmet and round earring.
Rev. Owl standing right with head facing and closed wings; in left field, olive spring; in right field, AΘE. All within incuse square.
Obols
55. O1-R1; 0.73g; 09h. Svoronos 1898, 372, no. 38.
56. O2-R2; 0.71g; 08h. Svoronos 1898, 372, no. 39 Svoronos 1923–6, pl. 3.50 (obv.) and 3.49 (rev.).
57. O3-R3; 0.60g; 03h. Svoronos 1898, 372, no. 40.
58. O4-R4; 0.59g; 09h. Svoronos 1898, 372, no. 41; Svoronos 1923–6, pl. 3.49 (obv.).
59. O5-R5; 0.51g; 09h. Svoronos 1898, 372, no. 42; Svoronos 1923–6, pl. 3.51.
60. O6-R6; 0.45g; 03h. Svoronos 1898, 372, no. 43; Svoronos 1923–6, pl. 3.52.
61. O7-R7; 0.43g; 06h. Svoronos 1898, 372, no. 44.
62. O8-R8; 0.42g; 06h. Svoronos 1898, 372, no. 45.

Obv. Head of Athena right, wearing crested Attic helmet ornamented with three olive leaves above visor, round earring and necklace.
Rev. Owl standing right with head facing and closed wings; in left field, olive sprig and crescent moon; in right field, AΘE. All within incuse square.
Tetradrachm
63. O1-R1; 16.70g; 03h. Svoronos 1898, 372, no. 46; Babelon 1905, 45, fig. 13; Kambanis 1906, pl. II.6; Babelon 1907, pl. XXXV.16; Svoronos 1923–6, pl. 3.54; Starr 1970, 59, no. 181.

REFERENCES

Argyropoulos, V. 2008. 'Past and current conservation practices: The need of innovative and integrated approaches', in Argyropoulos, V. (ed.) *Metals and Museums in the Mediterranean: Protecting, Preserving and Interpreting* (Athens), 55–75.
Babelon, E. 1905. 'Les origines de la monnaie à Athènes', *JIAN* 8, 7–52.
Babelon, E. 1907. *Traité des monnaies grecques et romaines* II: *Description historique*, vol. 1 (Paris).
Bertholon, R. and Relier, C. 1990. 'Les métaux archéologiques', in Berducou, M.C. (ed.), *La conservation en archéologie; méthodes et pratique de la conservation-restauration des vestiges archéologiques* (Paris / Milan / Barcelona), 163–221.
Bundgaard, J.A. 1974. *The Excavation of the Athenian Acropolis 1882–1890* (Copenhagen).
Cronyn, J.M. 1990. *The Elements of Archaeological Conservation* (London / New York).
Davis, G. 2014. 'Where are the little owls?', in Matthaiou, A.P. and Pitt, R.K. (eds), *AΘHNAIΩN EΠIΣKOΠOΣ. Studies in Honour of Harold B. Mattingly* (Athens), 339–47.
Davis, G. 2015. 'Athenian electrum coinage reconsidered: types, standard, value, and dating', *NC* 175, 1–9.
Ferrari, G. 2002. 'The ancient temple of the Acropolis at Athens', *AJA* 106, 11–35.
Flament, C. 2007. *Le monnayage en argent d'Athènes. De l'époque archaïque à l'époque hellénistique (c. 550-c. 40 av. J.-C.)* (Louvain-la-Neuve).
Galani-Krikou, M. 1996. 'Ancient Greek coin hoards', in *Coins and Numismatics. Hellenic Ministry of Culture - Numismatic Museum, Athens* (Athens), 91–103.
Holloway, R. 1999. 'The early owls of Athens and the Persians', *RBN* 145, 5–15.
Hopper, R.J. 1968. 'Observations on the *Wappenmünzen*', in Kraay, C.M. and Jenkins, G.K. (eds.), *Essays in Greek Coinage Presented to Stanley Robinson* (Oxford), 16–39.
Kagan, J.H. 1987. 'The decadrachm hoard: Chronology and consequences', in Carradice, I. (ed.), *Coinage and Administration in the Athenian and Persian Empires. The Ninth Oxford Symposium on Coinage and Monetary History* (*BAR International Series* 343) (Oxford), 21–28.
Kambanis, M.L. 1906. 'Περί της χρονολογικής κατατάξεως αθηναϊκών τινών νομισμάτων', *BCH* 30, 58–91.
Kavvadias, P. 1886a. 'Ανασκαφαί εν τη Ακροπόλει', *AE*, 74–82.

Kavvadias, P. 1886b. 'Ανασκαφαί εν τη Ακροπόλει', *AD* 2, 15–22.
Kavvadias, P. 1906. 'Ιστορική έκθεσις περί των ανασκαφών / Historischer Bericht über die Ausgrabungen', in Kavvadias, P. and Kawerau, G., *Η ανασκαφή της Ακροπόλεως από του 1885 μέχρι του 1890 / Die Ausgrabung der Akropolis vom Jahre 1885 bis zum Jahre 1890* (Athens), 1–54.
Knapp, R.C. 2005. 'The Classical, Hellenistic, Roman Provincial and Roman coins', in Knapp, R.C. and Mac Isaac, J.D., *Excavations at Nemea* III: *The Coins* (Berkeley / Los Angeles / London), 1–179.
Korres, M. 2002. 'On the North Akropolis wall', in Stamatopoulou, M. and Yeroulanou, M. (eds.), *Excavating Classical Culture: Recent Archaeological Discoveries in Greece* (*BAR International Series* 1031) (Oxford), 179–86.
Kousser, R. 2009. 'Destruction and memory on the Athenian Acropolis', *Art Bull* 91.3, 263–82.
Kraay, C.M. 1956. 'The Archaic owls of Athens: Classification and chronology', *NC* 6th series 16, 43–68.
Kraay, C.M. 1962. 'The early coinage of Athens: a reply', *NC* 7th series 2, 417–23.
Kraay, C.M. 1975. 'Archaic owls of Athens: New evidence for chronology', in Mussche, H., Spitaels, P. and Goemaere-De Poerck, F. (eds.), *Thorikos and the Laurion in Archaic and Classical Times. Papers and Contributions of the Colloquium Held in March, 1973, at the State University of Ghent* (Ghent), 145–160.
Kraay, C.M. 1976, *Archaic and Classical Greek Coins* (London).
Kroll, J.H. 1981. 'From *Wappenmünzen* to gorgoneia to owls', *ANSMN* 26, 1–32.
Kroll, J.H. 1993. *The Athenian Agora*, vol. XXVI: *The Greek Coins* (Princeton).
Kroll, J.H. 2009. 'What about coinage?', in Ma, J., Papazarkadas, N. and Parker, R. (eds.), *Interpreting the Athenian Empire* (London), 195–209.
Kroll, J.H. 2011. 'The reminting of Athenian silver coinage, 453 BC', *Hesperia* 80, 229–59.
Kroll, J.H. and Waggoner, N.M. 1984. 'Dating the earliest coins of Athens, Corinth and Aegina', *AJA* 88, 325–40.
Lambrinoudakis, V.K. 1986. *Οικοδομικά προγράμματα στην αρχαία Αθήνα, 479–431 π.Χ.* (Athens).
Lermann, W. 1900. *Athenatypen auf griechischen Münzen: Beiträge zur Geschichte der Athena in der Kunst* (Munich).
Lindenlauf, A. 1997. 'Der Perscherschutt der athener Akropolis', in Hoepfner, W. (ed.), *Kult und Kulltbauten auf der Akropolis. Internationales Symposion von 7. bis 9 Juli 1995 in Berlin* (Berlin), 46–115.
Price, M.J. and Waggoner, N.M. 1975. *Archaic Greek Coinage. The Asyut Hoard* (London).
Seltman, C.T. 1924. *Athens. Its History and Coinage before the Persian Invasion* (Cambridge).
Sheedy, K.A., Gore, D. and Davis, G. 2009. '"A spring of silver, a treasury in the earth": Coinage and wealth in Archaic Athens', in Beness, J. and Hillard, T. (eds.), *Australian Archaeological Fieldwork Abroad II, Ancient History: Resources for Teachers* 39:2, 248–57.
Stambolov, T. 1985. *The Corrosion and Conservation of Metallic Antiquities and Works of Art* (Amsterdam).
Starr, C.G. 1970. *Athenian Coinage, 480–449 B.C.* (Oxford).
Steskal, M. 2004. *Der Zerstörungsbefund 480/79 der Athener Akropolis. Eine Fallstudie zum etablierten Chronologiegerüst* (*Antiquitates* 30) (Hamburg).
Stewart, A. 2008. 'The Persian and Carthaginian invasions of 480 B.C.E. and the beginning of the Classical style. Part 1: The stratigraphy, chronology, and significance of the Acropolis deposits', *AJA* 112, 377–412.
Stoyas, Y. 2008. 'The coinages of Athens', in Moschonas, N.G. (ed.), *Archaeology of the City of Athens* (Athens) [Available online <http://www.eie.gr/archaeologia/En/chapter_more_7.aspx> accessed July 2017).
Svoronos, J.N. 1898. 'Νομισματικά ευρήματα. Α΄. Εκ των ανασκαφών της Ακροπόλεως Αθηνών', *JIAN* 1, 367–378.
Svoronos, J.N. 1923–6. *Les monnaies d'Athènes*, edited by B. Pick (Munich).
Theodorou, J. 1996. 'Athenian silver coins: 6th–3rd centuries BC. The current interpretation', in Tzamalis, A.P. (ed.), *Μνήμη Martin J. Price* (*Βιβλιοθήκη της Ελληνικής Νομισματικής Εταιρείας* 5) (Athens), 51–81.
Tselekas, P. 2008. 'Use and circulation of coins in the ancient Greek world', in *The History of Coinage* (Athens), 34–37.
van Wees, H. 2013. *Ships and Silver, Taxes and Tribute: A Fiscal History of Archaic Athens*. (London / New York).
Vickers, M. 1985. 'Early Greek coinage, a reassessment', *NC* 145, 1–44.
Vickers, M. 1986. 'Persepolis, Athènes et Sybaris: questions de monnayage et de chronologie', *REG* 99, 239–270.
Wallace, W.P. 1962. 'The early coinages of Athens and Euboia', *NC* 7th series 2, 23–42.

20. A SMALL NUMISMATIC GROUP FROM THE ANCIENT ROAD OF KOILE

Olga Dakoura-Vogiatzoglou and Eva Apostolou

ABSTRACT

This chapter examines a group of 24 silver and bronze coins (Athenian and non-Athenian) and 20 lead tokens, recovered from a rock-cut oval basin found in recent excavations at the ancient Koile road, Athens. Chronologically, these coins range from the second half of the sixth century BC down to the first half of the first century BC. It is proposed that this material was a hoard buried alongside the Koile road and perhaps close to the agora of the deme of Koile.

The group of coins presented in this paper was discovered in December 2000 during excavations to uncover the ancient Koile road, as part of the 'Global Promotion of the Hills of the Muses–Pnyx–Nymphs' program and the plan of the 'Unification of Archaeological Sites of Athens' (1997–2004) (Dakoura-Vogiatzoglou 2013, 193–212; Lazaridou and Dakoura-Vogiatzoglou, 2004). The 'Koile road' (Fig. 1) (Ficuciello 2008, 99–102; Dakoura-Vogiatzoglou 2009, 220–235) was mentioned, for example, by Herodotus (6.103), who reported that Kimon had been buried in front of the city of Athens and across from the road known as that which went to Koile (πέρην τῆς διὰ Κοίλης καλεομένης ὁδοῦ).

Figure 1. General view of Koile Road from the east. (Archive of the Athens Ephorate of Antiquities)

This road ran through the urban deme of Koile, which lay in the deep gorge between the hills of Pnyx and the Muses leading from Athens to Piraeus, and was protected along its course by the Long Walls (Dakoura-Vogiatzoglou, 2009). As a protected supra-local axis, it played a vital role for the transport of goods and supplies for the city during periods of siege, as in the Peloponnesian War, when it was also used as a safe-place for refugees. During the Classical period the deme of Koile experienced considerable growth, protected as it was to the west by the Themistoclean Wall. However, at the end of the fourth century BC, as the city's boundaries were redefined by a new internal cross wall within the city fortifications, the Diateichisma (Thompson and Scranton 1943, 297–301; Thompson, 1982, 133–147; Rotroff and Camp, 1996, 263–65), a significant part of the deme was left outside the walls and gradually fell into decline. From the late Hellenistic period to the late Roman period an extensive cemetery developed on either side of the historic road, where there were abandoned buildings from the once densely populated settlement (Dakoura-Vogiatzoglou, 2008, 257).

The recent excavations of the Koile road has brought to light a number of coins (which have yet to be fully examined) that offer insight into the periods the road was in operation, and which demonstrate that the road was still being maintained until the fourth century AD (Dakoura-Vogiatzoglou 2008, 258).

The decision to present this specific group of coins was made because of the conditions under which they were discovered and the period of time they cover. The coins were found in one location, which led us to characterise it (for convenience) as the 'Koile Hoard'. They cover an extensive chronological period and thus in some ways present a chronological overview of the settlement from the archaic period down to the first decade of the first century BC, a time in which the Koile cemetery developed along the length of the road.

The finds we will examine were discovered to the north-east of the road while we were searching for the boundaries of the Agora of the deme of Koile cited in historical sources (Lauter 1982, 45, fig. 2; Lampert 1997, 96, n. 24; Dakoura-Vogiatzoglou 2009, 229; Consoli 2011, 349–350). The agora (Fig. 2) lies on a flat area created at the junction of three hills (Muses, Pnyx and Nymphs), where a big channel covered by large blocks delimits northwards and westwards the opening of the square, directing the waters from the northern side of Pnyx hill to the road of Koile itself.

Figure 2. The Agora square from the west. (Archive of the Athens Ephorate of Antiquities)

At the north-eastern edge of the square the channel is connected in functional terms to a small road with five steps, just about as wide as the channel itself (ranging from 0.74 m to 1.05 m), which to the NW follows a small channel. This stepped road provided access from the Pnyx area to the square of the Agora, and was used to direct run-off from the eastern slope of the hill towards the main channel (Fig. 3). At the eastern end of that small set of steps and in the NE part of it, an oval basin (0.69 m long, 0.41 m wide and 0.46 m deep) with a narrow channel on its SE side carved into the bedrock was discovered under a destruction layer (Fig. 4–5).

Inside this oval basin, at a depth of 8 to 27 cm, in a homogenous layer of soil, were discovered 44 coins and tokens, four bronze rings, a gold crumpled foil, a copper bead, a lead ring, iron slag, large quantity of lead joins, lumps of lead and scrap iron rivets. At 27 cm deep the basin was sealed with a stone, and below it, to a depth of 46 cm, there were quite a few small stones and pieces of pottery (Fig. 6).

This group of coins revealed major differences in terms of dating, condition and the range of materials of manufacture; overall they can be considered to be of low value. There were four small Athenian silver fractions: an archaic obol (Davis 2014, 339), two Classical period obols and a silver trihemitetartemorion (Kroll 2011, 252–3) from the early fourth century BC (Cat. Nos 1 to 4, Figs. 7–10).

Among the rest there is one bronze jury token, which dates to the fourth century BC, together with 19 bronze coins and 20 lead tokens. Six coins have been definitely confirmed as Athenian, and were minted during the second half of the fourth century BC, such as the bronze coins with Triptolemos/piglet (Cat. No. 5, Fig. 11) and head of Athena/doubled-bodied owl (Cat. No. 6, Fig.12).

Figure 3. The westwards big channel of the Agora square and the stepped path from the NE. (Photo of O. Dakoura-Vogiatzoglou)

Figure 4–5. Basin carved in the rock. (Archive of the Athens Ephorate of Antiquities)

Figure 6. Pottery from the basin. (Photo of O. Dakoura-Vogiatzoglou)

Figure 7. Athenian AR Obol. Cat. No. 1. (Inv. No. 2691). (Archive of the Athens Ephorate of Antiquities)

Figure 8. Athenian AR Obol. Cat. No. 2. (Inv. No. 4805). (Archive of the Athens Ephorate of Antiquities)

Figure 9. Athenian AR Obol. Cat. No. 3. (Inv. No. 4806). (Archive of the Athens Ephorate of Antiquities)

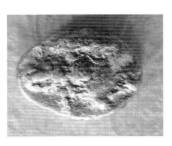

Figure 10. Athenian AR Trihemitetartemorion. Cat. No. 4. (Inv. No. 4807). (Archive of the Athens Ephorate of Antiquities)

Figure 11. Athenian Br. Cat. No. 5. (Inv. No. 2692–27). (Archive of the Athens Ephorate of Antiquities)

Figure 12. Athenian Br. Cat. No. 6. (Inv. No. 2692–29). (Archive of the Athens Ephorate of Antiquities)

Figure 13. Salamis. Cat. No. 17. (Inv. No. 2692–23).(Archive of the Athens Ephorate of Antiquities)

Figure 14. Megara. Cat. No. 19. (Inv.No. 2692–25). (Archive of the Athens Ephorate of Antiquities)

Figure 15. Antigonus Gonatas Br. Cat. No. 15. (Inv. No. 2692–21). (Archive of the Athens Ephorate of Antiquities)

Figure 16. Myrina of Lemnos Br. Cat. No. 16. (Inv. No. 2692-11). (Archive of the Athens Ephorate of Antiquities)

Two coins were minted on Salamis (Cat. Nos. 17–18, Fig.13), and date from the last decades of the fifth century until the late fourth century BC. Another two coins minted in Megara date from the second quarter of the third century BC (Cat. 19–20, Fig. 14).

A bronze coin of Antigonus Gonatas (Cat. No. 15, Fig. 15) is associated with the period Athens was occupied by the Macedonian king (Habicht 1995, 206). Another coin, minted at Myrina on Lemnos (an Athenian *cleruchy*) and dated between 167–86 BC (Cat. No. 16, Fig. 16), falls around 100 years after the previously mentioned coins.[1]

Almost all of the 20 lead tokens are in poor condition. They all appear to depict different subjects (where the image is discernible); one probably shows an amulet in the shape of an apotropaic eye (Fig. 17). However, most are exceptionally small (no more than 1 cm), which is the only uniform feature they seem to share. From the evidence of their metal (lead) and their size, they can be dated to the second century BC (See Lang and Crosby 1964, 84–5, pl. 20).[2] The purpose of these lead tokens has still not been elucidated, and any interpretation of them lies beyond the scope of this paper (See Dakoura-Vogiatzoglou, forthcoming).

As mentioned above, the small basin and the area around it were covered by a destruction layer containing numerous tile sherds under which quite a few shallow natural cavities were revealed. In one cavity, to the west of the small basin and adjacent to it, we found a silver obol, ten bronze coins and two lead tokens. Iron nails, iron slag and lead joints were also present. As a single destruction layer covered the area, the cavity mentioned was very close to the basin, and as the finds are uniform, we believe it necessary to examine them as a group in order to provide the most accurate and complete estimation of their chronology.

Figure 17. Lead tokens, in the middle the apotropaic eye.

---

[1] On the other seven coins the numismatic type (image) is not clearly distinguishable; some appear to have a head of Athena, but it is a daring leap to count those among the Athenian coins.
[2] See similar objects characterised as 'Seal impressions' in Davidson and Thompson 1943, 104–7 where the authors present 18 such seal impressions (13 lead and five clay) from the excavation on the Pnyx and characterise them as 'enigmatic objects' since no interpretation of their use is satisfactory. In the area of the hill of the Muses, possibly close to our excavation, clay seal impressions have been found in the past. None of our token types matches any of the examples provided.

Figure 18. Athenian AR Obol. Cat. No. 25. (Inv. No. 2680). (Archive of the Athens Ephorate of Antiquities)

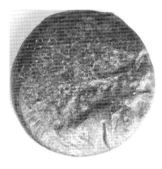

Figure 19. Athenian Br. Cat. No. 26. (Inv. No. 2684–6). (Archive of the Athens Ephorate of Antiquities)

Figure 20. Athenian Br. Cat. No. 27. (Inv. No. 2684–1). (Archive of the Athens Ephorate of Antiquities)

Figure 21. Corinthian Br. Cat. No. 30. (Inv. No. 2684–8). (Archive of the Athens Ephorate of Antiquities)

In addition to the silver obol from Athens (Cat. No. 25; Fig. 18), the bronze coins include an Athenian example dating from 340–320 BC (Triptolemos/piglet, Cat. No. 26, Fig. 19), another Athenian coin minted in the early 2nd century BC (Cat. No. 27, Fig. 20), a very worn, possibly Athenian coin, and a bronze coin from Salamis. Moreover, a bronze coin from Corinth (head of Poseidon/forepart of Pegasus minted in the final decades of the 3rd century BC (cat. No. 30, Fig. 21) was also included.

Figure 22. Lead token with a Pan seated on a rock. (Archive of the Athens Ephorate of Antiquities)

One of the lead tokens, which is small in size (like most in the pit), depicts a Pan seated on a rock on one side, and is better preserved than all the other tokens. (Fig. 22).

COMMENTS

A significant number of Athenian coins from the fourth century BC have been found, together with Athenian coins of the third century BC and non-Athenian coins (Megara, Corinth, Antigonus Gonatas). The best preserved is an Athenian coin from the first decade of the second century BC (Cat. No. 27), while the latest coin is a bronze from Myrina on Lemnos which was minted 167–86 BC (Cat. No. 16).

The presence of coins from Salamis (an Athenian cleruchy), Megara, Corinth, and from Antigonus Gonatas (who occupied Attica in 262 BC and maintained a Macedonian guard until 255 BC on the Hill of the Muses, a site very close to our excavations of the Koile road; see Habicht 1998, 200–2), reflects the picture presented by the excavations of the Athenian Agora (Kroll, 1993) and the Pnyx (Kourouniotes and Thompson, 1932, 211–213; Davidson and Thompson, 1943, 14–19 and 24–27), and by other archaeological sites that have been excavated in Athens.

The hypothesis that our group of coins is a hoard cannot be ruled out given the similar composition of a recently published hoard of 32 coins (two silver and 30 bronze) excavated at a residential commercial livestock settlement in the deme of Alai Aixonides in modern Voula, Attica (Giamalidi 2013, 27–30). However, the Alai Aixonides hoard does not contain issues from the second century BC and its burial has been dated to the period of the Chremonidian War.

The area where the coins were discovered lies a short distance to the north of the ancient road of Koile, very close of the eastern boundary of the assumed Agora of the deme of Koile where the remains of the historic settlement, carved in the rock, are quite dense. The inscriptions *SEG* 25 (1971), No. 148, and *SEG* 21, No. 527, refer to the double agora in the deme of Koile. Lauter (1982, 45) has speculated that the small carved areas with a carved bench along their length, located on the southern kerb of the Koile Road, directly opposite the spot where the coins were discovered, were used as shops. This theory was confirmed by excavations in 1997–2002. However, the fragmentary nature of the excavation does not allow us to recreate the landscape and to make decisive conclusions about the use of the area where the discovery was made. In any case, the heterogeneous objects from the carved basin do not permit us to easily decipher its use. Certainly, the way it was constructed suggests domestic or workshop use applicable most likely to a semi-outdoor area, judging by the large quantity of tiles covering the structure. Of course, it is difficult to explain how Archaic coins might come to be together with Classical and Hellenistic coins, as well as with a number of (Hellenistic) lead tokens, bronze items and shapeless masses, and lead strips. The idea that they were assembled through the action of water from the pipes is a convenient interpretation but stumbles on the fact that these objects were not deposited in layers. Moreover, although there is a concentration of lead items, it does not seem plausible that it was used as a workshop because this would not explain the presence of the other objects. An interpretation of this find as a coin hoard seems possible if the coins were collected in a purse made of some perishable material (which would have rotted away). The flow of water through the pipe and the deposition of other objects in the pit would have altered the original composition of the 'hoard', and helps explain the presence of second century BC coins. The lead tokens would in all likelihood have formed part of the group, just like the more precious and much earlier, silver coins.

Another, perhaps more attractive theory that heterogeneous objects were collected by some sort of scavenger in the area (which had lost its glamour) may better suit the evidence. In any event, the collection of objects in the carved basin indicates that it was no longer in use in the first half of the second century BC. That period coincides, in all likelihood, with the construction of the second phase of the Diateichisma, known as the White Poros Wall, which has been dated by Thompson and Scranton (1943, 358–60) to *c.*200 BC. On the basis of the most recent dating of the pottery by Rotroff, however, Conwell places this construction in the decade of conflict between Athens and the Achaean League after 166 BC (Conwell, 1996, 97; Theocharaki, 2007, 41–44).

The coins, coupled with the pottery finds from within the small basin and around it, which also date to the end of the third–first half of the second century BC, provide us with a *terminus ante quem* for the devastation of the Koile district. (Fig. 23). The area appears to have been gradually abandoned during the last quarter of the third century BC. But with the construction of the White Poros Wall, after 166 BC, the *extra muros* section of the deme of Koile appears to have been rapidly abandoned and the site of the living was taken by the

Figure 23. Pottery from the desctruction layer around the basin. (Photo of O. Dakoura- Vogiatzoglou)

homes of the dead (Dakoura-Vogiatzoglou, 2009, 226, 230–232; and 2012, 30–34). Nonetheless, it is likely that some daring individuals did continue commercial activities in the area of the Agora of Koile, trading with those people still using the road, and that these activities might be associated with the presumed Koile coin group.

ACKNOWLEDGEMENTS

Whole-hearted thanks to Mrs. Vasiliki Mylona, antiquities conservator at the Athens Ephorate for her extensive contribution to conserving and photographing the coins and for her constant support on all issues of supervision while the materials were being studied. Thanks are also due to Mrs. Eleni Stefanidou, photographer at the Athens Ephorate, for processing of the photographic material.

CATALOGUE OF COINS (E. APOSTOLOU)

A) from the small basin

Silver
Athens
1. Inv. No. 2691. Obol, 0.578 g
Wheel / Incuse square.
SNG München 6–7. Issued: 550–520 BC onwards.
2. Inv. No. 4805. Obol, 0.664 g
Head of Athena with an Attic helmet / AΘE, Owl.
SNG München 77–82. Issued: 454–404 BC.
3. Inv. No. 4806. Obol, 0.68 g
Same types.
SNG München 113–115. Issued 390–295 BC.
4. Inv. No. 4807. Trihemitetartemorion (= 3/8 obol), 0.25 g
Head of Athena with an Attic helmet / AΘE, Eleusinian ring.
SNG München 125–127. Issued: 390–295 BC.

Bronze
5. Inv. No. 2692–27. Very worn
Triptolemos in chariot / Piglet.
Kroll, 1993, cat. 38 or 48. Issued: 350–330 or 322/317–307 BC.
6. Inv. No. 2692–29. Very worn.
Head of Athena with an Attic helmet / Double-bodied owl.
Possibly resembling *SNG* München 132–137/8. Kroll, 1993, cat. 42–3.
Issued: 340–320 BC or 330–322/317 BC.

Fig, 24. Athenian Br. Cat. No 10. (Inv. No. 2692–28). (Archive of the Athens Ephorate of Antiquities)

Fig, 25. Athenian Br. Cat. No 12. (Inv. No. 2692–30). (Archive of the Athens Ephorate of Antiquities

Athens? 7–13
7–9. Inv. No. 2692–1, 3, 7. Completely worn.
Same obverse / Double-bodied owl (?).
SNG München 132–137/8; Kroll, 1993, cat. 42–3.
Issued: 340–320 BC or 330–322/317 BC.
10. Inv. No. 2692–28. Completely worn. (Fig. 24)
Head of Athena with a Corinthian helmet / Unidentified type.
Perhaps the same as Kroll, 1993, cat. 50, 52–54, 56, 58–59.
Issued: End of 4th – mid–3rd century BC.
11. Inv. No. 2692–18. Very poor condition.
Same obverse / Two owls (?).
Perhaps the same as Kroll, 1993, cat. 56 or 65.
Issued: Circa 270 or 229–224/3 BC.
12. Inv. No. 2692–30. Very poor condition. (Fig. 25)
Same obverse / Owl to r.
Perhaps the same as *SNG* München 152. Issued: 286–262 BC.
13. Inv. No. 2692–9. Very poor condition
Same obverse / worn.
Issued: 3rd century BC?

Token
14. Inv. No. 2692–22. (Fig. 26)
Head of Athena with an Attic helmet / capital Π.
SNG München 449. Issued: 4th century BC.

Fig, 26. Athenian Token Br. Cat. No 14. (Inv. No. 2692–22). (Archive of the Athens Ephorate of Antiquities)

Antigonus Gonatas
15. Inv. No. 2692–21. Worn.
Head of Hercules / Rider, monogram of Antigonus Gonatas under the horse. *SNG* Cop. 1142–1153. Issued: 277–232 BC.

Myrina, Lemnos
16. Inv. No. 2692–11. Very worn.
Head of Athena in Corinthian helmet / Upright quiver crossed by diagonal bow.
Svoronos 1923–6, pl.106, 27–8; Kroll, 1993, cat. 456. Issued: 167–86 BC.

Salamis
17–18. Inv. No. 2692–23, 24. Worn.
Head of the Salamis nymph / Ajax shield.
SNG München 465–470. Issued: End of 5th – 4th century BC.

Megara, Megaris
19. **20**. Inv. No. 2692–25, 26. Worn.
Tripod between two dolphins.
SNG München 486–487. Issued: 2nd quarter of the 3rd century BC.

Unidentified
21–24. Inv. No. 2692–5, 12, 17, 19.
Completely worn.

B) From cavity

Silver
Athens
25. Inv. No. 2680. Obol, 0.70 g
Head of Athena with an Attic helmet / ΑΘΕ Owl.
SNG München 77–82. Issued: 454–404 BC.

Bronzes
Athens
26. Inv. No. 2684–6. Very worn.
Triptolemos in chariot / Piglet.
SNG München 129–131; Kroll, 1993, cat. 38 or 48.
Issued: 340–320 BC, 350–330 or 322/317–307 BC.
27. Inv. No. 2684–1. Well preserved.
Head of Athena in Corinthian helmet / Zeus standing holding thunderbolt in r. hand; l. arm outstretched.
Kroll, 1993, nr.78. Issued: 196–190 BC.

Athens?
28. Inv. No. 2684–3. Very worn.
Same observe / Unidentified type.

Salamis
29. Inv. No. 2684–8. Extremely worn.
Head of the Salamis nymph / Ajax shield.
SNG München 465–470. Issued: End of 5th–4th century BC.

Corinth
30. Inv. No. 2684–8. Worn.
Head of Hercules / Forepart of Pegasus.
BMC 481. Issued: 223–196 BC.

Illegible
31. Inv. No. 2684–11. Extremely worn. (Fig. 27)
Griffin seated to r., in exergue, .[H]I . N? / Uncertain type.

Unidentified
32–33. Inv. No. 2684–2, 5. Exceptionally worn. (Macedonian?)
34. Inv. No. 2684–7.

Fig, 27. Illegible Br. Cat. No 31. (Inv. No. 2684–11). (Archive of the Athens Ephorate of Antiquities)

Table 1. Coin measurements

Fig.	Size
Fig. 7	7–8mm
Fig. 8	9–10mm
Fig. 9	7–8mm
Fig. 10	4–5mm
Fig. 11	14mm
Fig. 12	11mm
Fig. 13	15mm
Fig. 14	14mm
Fig. 15	16mm
Fig. 16	15mm
Fig. 18	16mm
Fig. 19	20–21mm
Fig. 20	20mm
Fig. 21	12mm
Fig. 22	10mm
Fig. 24	13mm
Fig. 25	14mm
Fig. 26	18mm
Fig. 27	11mm

REFERENCES

Consoli, V. 2011. 'La strada e la cd. agorà di Koile', in Greco, E. (ed.), *Topografia di Atene. Sviluppo urbano e monumenti dalle origini al III sec. D.C.*, vol. 2: Colline sud-occidentali – Valle dell'Ilisso (SATAA 1, Athens-Paestum), 348–351.

Conwell, D.H. 1996. 'The White Poros Wall: Character and Context', in Forsén, B. and Stanton, G. (eds.), *The Pnyx in the History of Athens* (Helsinki), 93–101.

Dakoura-Vogiatzoglou, O. 2008. 'Οι Δυτικοί Λόφοι στους Ρωμαϊκούς Χρόνους', in Vlizos, S. (ed.), *Athens During the Roman Period: Recent Discoveries, New Evidence* (Mouseio Benaki Suppl. 4, Athens), 247–267.

Dakoura-Vogiatzoglou, O. 2009. 'Η «δια Κοίλης» οδός', in Korres, M. (ed.), *Αττικής Οδοί, αρχαίοι δρόμοι της Αττικής*, (Αττική οδός, Athens), 220–235.

Dakoura-Vogiatzoglou, O. 2012. ' Ένα μοναδικό εύρημα: Τάφος αυλητρίδας στην Κοίλη' in *ΑΝΘΕΜΙΟΝ*, Ενημερωτικό Δελτίο της Ένωσης Φίλων Ακροπόλεως 23, 30–34.

Dakoura-Vogiatzoglou, O. 2013. 'Αναδιφώντας την ιστορία των Δυτικών Λόφων', in Oikonomou, S. and Dokka-Toli, M., *Αρχαιολογικές Συμβολές*, τόμ. Β: Αττική, Α' και Γ' Εφορείες Προϊστορικών και Κλασικών Αρχαιοτήτων (Athens), 193–212.

Dakoura-Vogiatzoglou O. Forthcoming. 'Tokens from the Koile Area', in *Tokens: The Athenian Legacy to Modern World*. Workshop at the British School of Athens, 16th–17th December 2019.

Davidson, G.R. and Thompson, D.B. 1943. Small Objects from the Pnyx: I, (*Hesperia Suppl.* 7, Princeton).

Davis, G. 2014. 'Where are all the little owls?' in Matthaiou, A.P. and Pitt, B.P. (eds.), *ATHINEON EPISKOPOS, Studies in honor of Harold B. Mattingly* (Athens), 339–347.

Ficuciello, L. 2008. *Le Strade di Atene* (SATAA vol. 4, Athens–Paestum), 99–102.

Giamalidi, M. 2013. 'The two numismatic 'hoards' and the coins from the S. & I. Sklavenitis S.A. plot in Voula', *NomKhron* 31, 17–44

Habicht, C. 1998. *Ελληνιστική Αθήνα* (Athens).

Kourouniotes, K., and Thompson, H.A, 1932. 'The Pnyx in Athens', *Hesperia* 1, 90–217.

Kroll, J.H. 1993. *The Coins* (The Athenian Agora 36; Princeton).

Kroll, J.H. 2011. 'The Reminting of Athenian Silver Coinage', *Hesperia* 80(2), 229–259.

Kroll, J. 2013. 'Salamis Again', in Grandjean, C. and Moustaka, A. (eds.), *Aux origines de la monnaie fiduciére* (Bordeaux), 109–116.

Lampert, S.D. 1997. 'The Attic Genos Salaminioi and the Island of Salamis', *Zeitschrift für Papyrologie und Epigraphik*, 85–106.

Lang, M. and Crosby, M. 1964. *Weights, Measures and Tokens* (The Athenian Agora 10, Princeton).

Lauter, H. 1982. 'Zum Strassenbild in Alt-Athen', *Antike Welt 13*: 4, 44–52.

Lazaridou, K. and Dakoura-Vogiatzoglou, O. 2004. *Hills of Philopappos – Pnyx – Nymphs, Brief history and tour* (Athens).

Rotroff S.I. and Camp J. McK. 1996. 'The date of the Third Period of the Pnyx', *Hesperia* 65, 263–294.

Svoronos, J.N. 1923–26. *Les monnaies d'Athènes* (Munich).

Theocharaki, A. 2007. *Ο αρχαίος αθηναϊκός οχυρωματικός περίβολος: ζητήματα μορφολογίας, τοπογραφίας και διαχείρισης*, (PhD thesis, ΕΚΠΑ, University of Athens). Available at https://www.didaktorika.gr/eadd/handle/10442/24494. 10/6/2017

Thompson, H.A. and Scranton, R.L. 1943. 'Stoas and City Walls on the Pnyx', *Hesperia* 12, 269–383.

Thompson, H.A. 1982. 'The Pnyx in Models', in Studies in Attic Epigraphy, History and Topography. Presented to Eugene Vanderpool (*Hesperia Suppl.* 19, Princeton), 133–147

21. THE ENIGMATIC TOOL FROM THE SANCTUARY OF POSEIDON AT SOUNION: NEW EVIDENCE

Zetta Theodoropoulou Polychroniadis and Alexandros Andreou

ABSTRACT

Monumental sculpture, architectural spolia, as well as diverse large and small - scale offerings were brought to light by the excavations of Valerios Stais (1897–1915) at the sanctuaries of Poseidon and Athena at Sounion. Several of these had been published by various scholars but the small finds have only been published in 2015 by Theodoropoulou. The excavation in 1907 of the bothros at the sanctuary of Poseidon revealed a group of small-scale objects, among which one stands out: a bronze cast tool, a punch, first published by Stais and later considered by other scholars. Their interpretations are reviewed in this collaborative research paper which sets the tool within the broader context of the metalliferous region of the Laureotike and the site of its deposition. The various possible uses of this tool are examined, while comparanda and epigraphic testimonia help to cast light on its most likely purpose. Its significance, the likely reason for its presence in the sanctuary and subsequent deposition inside the bothros before 480/479 BC are also discussed.

INTRODUCTION

This paper is the result of a wider research project into the sanctuaries of Poseidon and Athena at Sounion, and the finds of diverse material recovered by Valerios Stais during his excavations between 1897 and 1915,[1] conducted under the auspices of the Archaeological Society at Athens (Stais 1897, 16–18; 1898, 92–94; 1899, 12–13, 98–100; 1900a, 51–52; 1903, 13–14; 1906, 49, 85, 86; 1907, 102–104; 1908, 63; 1909, 117–118; 1912, 266; 1917, 168–213; 1920). Stais' aim was to recover whatever could be salvaged from the temple on the promontory, which until then was thought to be that of Athena. His assumption about the god to whom the temple had been dedicated was based on the testimony of Pausanias (1.1.1.).[2] In 1898 however, Stais' discovery inside the *temenos* of the military decree *IG* II[2] 1270 dated to the early third century BC, indicating that it was to be placed in the sanctuary of Poseidon, confirmed that the Classical temple had been dedicated to Poseidon and not Athena (Stais 1900b, 133–34). Stais went on to discover the sanctuary of Athena in 1900, situated on a low hill to the north-east of that of Poseidon (Stais 1900b, 122–131).

Stais' work in both sanctuaries was considered one of the major excavations of the time, but his brief reports in the Archaeological Society's journals lacked information on the find spots of most of the small-scale material. Stais' reports, nevertheless, had been the main source of reference for Sounion, until the recent publication of a monograph by this paper's first-named author which examines and interprets not only the unpublished small-scale material, but also the structures within both sanctuaries, casting light on their development and their significance to the socio-economic growth of south-east Attica (Theodoropoulou Polychroniadis, 2015).

The main subject of this paper is an enigmatic object, a tool, one of the many finds discovered in 1907 by Stais (1907, 103) inside the *bothros* at the sanctuary of Poseidon. Before discussing in detail the tool in question, its deposition in the *bothros* of the sanctuary of Poseidon should be considered within the broader context of the site.

---

[1] Paper presented at the International Conference on 'Mines, Metals and Money in Attica and the Ancient World' at the Epigraphic and Numismatic Museum at Athens, 20–22 April 2015. The authors wish to thank the members of the Organising Committee of the Conference for the invitation to present this paper, as well as the Scientific Committee for constructive suggestions and editing. They also wish to thank Dr. M. Lagogianni-Georgakarakos, Director of the NMA and Dr. G. Kavvadias, curator of the Vases, Minor Arts & Bronzes Collection for granting them permission to study and publish the bronze pendant NMA 13987 from the excavations at the Heraion of Argos, as well as Professor P. Arvanitakis for the drawings of the tool.

[2] Pausanias 1.1.1: "When you have rounded the promontory you see a harbour and a temple to Athena of Sunium on the peak of the promontory".

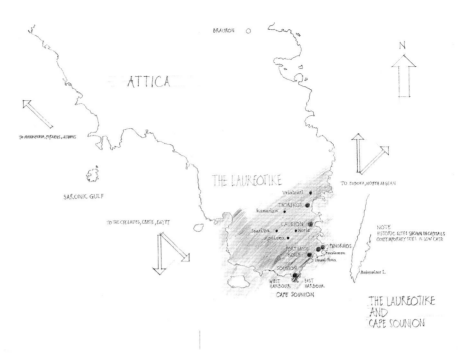

Figure 1. The Laureotike and Cape Sounion (Drawing P. Arvanitakis, 2012).

CONTEXT

The Laureotike, at the south-east tip of Attica, was one of the main centres of metallurgy in the Aegean (Salliora-Oikonomakou 2004, 73–82, 131–140; Goette 2000, 91–106; Kakavoyannis 2005, 91–108). Lead and silver are known to have been mined since the Early Helladic period (Fig. 1). Thorikos has revealed evidence of mining activity from the Late Neolithic onwards and was very likely the dominant settlement in the Laureotike, playing a leading role in the trade of raw materials in the eastern Mediterranean (Mussche 1998; Laffineur 2010, 26). In the eighth and seventh centuries BC, Phoenicians, gradually succeeded by Euboeans and Aeginetans, very likely using Cape Sounion as a landmark, were trading silver and other ores from the Laureotike to the East and West Mediterranean (Kroll 2008, 36; Thompson 2003, 95; 2011, 129–130).

At the southernmost tip of Attica, 13 km south of Thorikos, lies the rocky headland of Cape Sounion. The strategic and geographical position of this prominent landmark, commanding communication routes on both land and sea, as well as the rich ore-bearing area of the Laureotike nearby, were the main factors for its development through the centuries (Theodoropoulou Polychroniadis 2015, 8, 13). Archaeological and literary evidence suggests that 'the levelled summit' on the precipitous edge of Cape Sounion was a cult site at least from the end of the eighth century BC (Parker 1996, 18; 2005, 58; Osborne 1994, 35, 151; Theodoropoulou Polychroniadis 2015, 8, 104–108). By 700 BC, two cult centres had developed on the promontory: that of Athena and that of Poseidon, both most likely housing a hero-cult. Sounion grew into a major religious centre, evidenced by monumental sculptures, *kouroi* being placed in both sanctuaries around 600 BC. The dedicators, possibly wealthy Sounians, had a close connection with sea-trade and mining and sufficient funds to allocate to the commission of statuary, some of it colossal (Papathanasopoulos 1983, 20–25; Osborne 1985, 37; Flament 2011, 80–81). The sanctuary of Poseidon occupied part of the fortified area of the promontory and was surrounded by its own *peribolos* with its *propylaia* and two stoas. The erection of the Archaic temple around 490 BC represented a major investment. The funds required are likely to have come from the Athenian state, which between 508/7

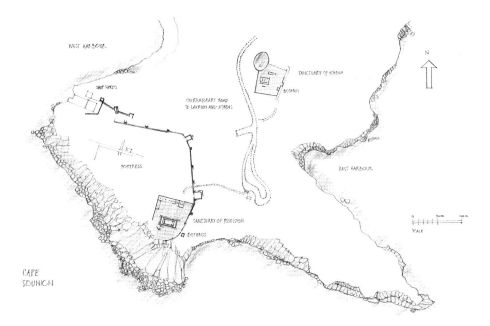

Figure 2. Cape Sounion, plan of the two sanctuaries and the two harbours. Poseidon bothros marked (Drawing P. Arvanitakis, 2012).

and 480/79 supported the establishment and expansion of sanctuaries in Attica, such as at Eleusis (Mylonas 1961, 78–91; Noack 1927; 48–70; Kokkou-Viridi 1999, 33–36; Paga 2015, 112), Rhamnous (Petrakos 1982, 136; 1999, vol. I, 192–194; Paga 2015, 112–114), and Mounychia in Piraeus (Palaiokrassa 1991, 42–50), arguably to consolidate its territorial and political boundaries (de Polignac 1995, 51–52; Parker 2005, 123).

BOTHROS FINDS

In 1907, at the south-east corner of the sanctuary of Poseidon, outside the old polygonal wall, Stais discovered a *bothros* which contained various offerings. They comprise ritual pottery, terracotta relief plaques, faience figurines, scarabs and seals, mainly dating from the late eighth to the early fifth centuries BC, that is before the erection of the Archaic temple whose construction, as mentioned above, started around 490 BC (Dörpfeld 1884, 329–333; Dinsmoor Jr, 1974, 12–16; Paga and Miles, 2016, 685, 687; Fig. 2). The largest securely documented assemblage inside the *bothros* is the metalwork comprising 24 copper-based artefacts which have been recently investigated with the use of portable XRF (Theodoropoulou Polychroniadis 2015, 6, 122–127; Theodoropoulou Polychroniadis, Orfanou 2019, 337–338). Due to the proximity of the Laurion mines, it is conceivable that at least some objects may had been locally manufactured. This assemblage comprises one human figurine, that of an eastern warrior god and two spiral rings, dated to the late eighth century BC, a figurine of a bull, dated to the mid-seventh century, as well as seven plain finger-rings, six functional arrowheads and a miniature one, one ex-voto spearhead, one ex-voto double axe, a cylindrical bead, a pair of tweezers and a nail cap, all dated to the seventh-sixth centuries BC.

One further item however, stands out from this assemblage from the *bothros* and is of considerable interest (Stais 1917, pl. 7; Theodoropoulou Polychroniadis 2015, 100–101, 123, 238). It is an intact, cast bronze object, the only tool recorded by Stais in *AE* 1917 as deriving from the *bothros* of the sanctuary of Poseidon. It resembles a double-ended hammer (Fig. 3). It is on display at the National Archaeological Museum in Athens (NMA 14926.1). It is well worth mentioning here that in the *bothros* and the artificial fill of the nearby sanctuary

Figure 3. Tool NMA 14926.1 (Photo: Elias Eliades, 2015).

of Athena, Stais recorded among other finds a further 23 metal objects. These comprise two silver and four lead rings, a miniature lead kouros, an ex-voto lead miniature mask, two iron swords, four pieces of jewellery made of bronze, three bronze animal figurines, two ex-voto bronze miniature shields and four ex-voto bronze miniature tripods (Theodoropoulou Polychroniadis 2015, 7, 89–93, 95–98, 100–103). More recent research at the National Archaeological Museum's stores by Theodoropoulou has revealed a further 279 unrecorded, unpublished metal objects which Stais discovered at Sounion. These are currently being studied by Theodoropoulou. Only 7 of these objects are copper-based, the others being mainly of iron (Theodoropoulou Polychroniadis, Orfanou 2019, 338–340, table 33.2). Stais hardly mentioned this assemblage except for weapons being found in the bastion on the east fortification wall of the citadel as well as in the artificial fill in the sanctuary of Athena (Stais 1917, 171, 208).

Of the 279 metal objects, several are identified as building construction elements, as well as fragmentary lumps of iron which may suggest the presence of a nearby foundry. Among the finds there are indeed weapons and two iron mattocks.[3] These tools obviously differ from the tool of this paper. From this report on the metal finds from the two sanctuaries at Sounion, the uniqueness of the bronze tool becomes self-evident, but what was its use?

THE USE OF THE HAMMER

The hammer is rectangular and bar-like in form, tapering to the ends with a rectangular perforation at its mid-point for the insertion of a wooden handle. Both ends are squared off

Figure 4. The two stamping ends of the tool (Photo: Elias Eliades, 2015).

[3] The material currently under study will be included in a forthcoming publication by Z. Theodoropoulou Polychroniadis.

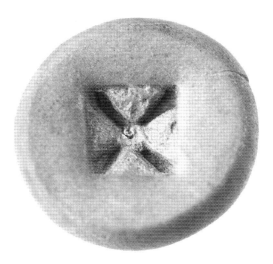

Figure 5. The imprint of the tool's end (Photo: Elias Eliades, 2015).

and worked to give four ridges, one running from each of the four corners of the square towards the centre. The ridges, which are very worn, particularly on one end of the hammer, do not, however, meet neatly at the centre (Fig. 4). The state of preservation of the ridges, 1.5–2 mm thick, proves that the tool had seen long service. On impact, the tool face forms a shallow sunken square, approximately 1x1cm, with a deeper X-like pattern inside it (Fig. 5). In his 1997 article, Kalligas, then curator of the Bronze Collection at the NMA, identified the tool as a punch die or 'χαρακτήρ', suggesting that both ends were used for minting purposes, and that the impressions created, "were identical with the emblematic-heraldic reverse of the earliest Athenian coins, the *Wappenmünzen*" (Kalligas 1997, 143).

If the hammer were indeed a punch-die, then this find would be of great importance, as few such items remain, as Hopper notes (Hopper 1968, 25, pl.2, nos 35a & b), and its deposition in the sanctuary of Poseidon would not have been unusual. Inscription *IG* II² 1408, the account of the treasurers of Athena on the Athenian Acropolis for the year 398/7 BC, emphasises the importance of tools related to the minting of coins. The punch-die and the anvil (ἀκμονίσκος) were safeguarded in the temple of Athena on the Acropolis in a box (Harris 1995, V34, 119). Inscription *IG* II² 1424a for the year 371/0 BC mentions that 4 iron anvils (ἄκμονες σιδηροί), 2 hammers (σφύραι) and 22 reverse and obverse dies (χαρακτῆρες) were kept in a box in the Opisthodomos of the Parthenon (Harris 1995, 58, no. 74).[4]

On impact, however, the impressions created by our hammer do not accord with those seen on the *Wappenmünzen*, as Sheedy later demonstrated, since it would have created the exact opposite of that found on the coins (Sheedy 2014, 24–25). Furthermore, the aperture in the centre of the tool (2x1 cm) would only allow for a slender wooden handle which would not have been robust enough for the task. The dimensions of this tool (length 13.2 cm and width 2.2 cm at its widest) as well as its light weight (267 g) may further support this objection, as argued by Sheedy (2014, 24–26; Fig. 6).

The tool therefore must have had some other use of sufficient importance to warrant it being dedicated and later placed in the *bothros*. Could it have been a punch to create decorative patterns on jewellery or other metal objects as Sheedy suggests?[5] In this case the

---

[4] Three further inscriptions from the Acropolis, *IG* II² 1438b, lines 23–24 (*SEG* XIX, 129), *IG* II² 1469, face B column I, lines 107–109 and *IG* II² 1471, face B column II, lines 56–57, dated to the fourth century BC, record in the accounts of the Treasurers of Athena and the other Gods (c.320 BC), the deposition in the Opisthodomos of the Parthenon of anvils, hammers and dies, one of the 21 reverse dies being broken ; Jones 1993, 116, no. 178, 118–120, nos. 185–186.
[5] Sheedy 2014, 26 notes the possibility "that the Sounion tool was employed in the manufacture of jewellery and toreutics should not be disregarded."

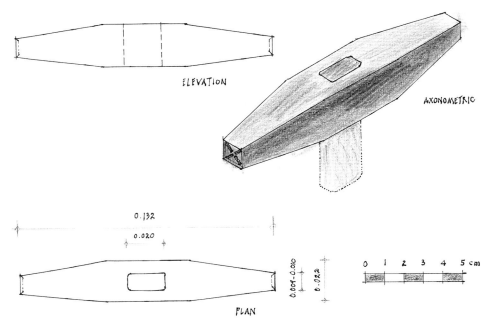

Figure 6. Drawing of the tool with dimensions (P. Arvanitakis, 2015).

impression would be struck on items such as rings, pendants or bronze vessels, which would require less force on the hammer blow. Alternatively, the tool may have been used to create impressed decorations on leather, or terracotta plaques and clay vessels. Such use was common practice, as is evidenced by a tool of the Middle to Late Geometric period recovered in 2001 during the excavations at Dipli Trapeza in Anchialos, ancient Sindos. It is made of bone with a stamp at its end. The excavators believe that the tool was used to decorate the rim of hand-made burnished bowls (Tiverios and Gimatzidis 2001, 305, 308, fig. 5). A fragment of a pithos from Crete, dated to the first half of the seventh century BC, bears cross-rosettes stamped on a raised band (Boardman 1961,114, pl. XLIII, no. 514). If this indeed were the use of the tool, then it may have ultimately been an offering to the god from a craftsman (Van Straten 1981, 95). However, the absence of dedicatory inscriptions would seem to preclude this interpretation. Our object moreover, cannot be regarded as a discard; it was deposited inside the *bothros*, among other intact valuable finds, as mentioned above. Its shape and size, as well as the significance of the location of its deposition together with other finds in that context, inside the sanctuary, suggest that its use was something other than anything hitherto proposed.

A NEW SUGGESTION

This is the enigma with which Theodoropoulou was faced while preparing her publication on the finds from the Sounion sanctuaries, and which ultimately led to this collaborative research with her colleague Alexandros Andreou, a curator at the Epigraphic and Numismatic Museum at Athens. There is another possible use. On due contemplation, the object is indeed a tool but not one necessarily to create decorative patterns. The tool may have been used as a stamp to mark proof of inspection, quality control or ownership. But of what? The following comparanda suggest an answer.

The Selinous hoard, discovered in 1985, included silver coins from South Italian and Sicilian cities, and from Corinth and Aegina – alongside four late Archaic silver ingots of great interest. Their discovery underlines the role played by ingots in the commercial circulation of silver and in the transactions before, as well as during, the early days of the circulation of coinage in the Greek world (Arnold-Buicchi Biucchi *et al.* 1988, 35). Silver round-cake ingot E from Selinous bears the stamp of an incuse square, measuring 1x1 cm; the motif is an X-like design and is almost identical to the Sounion one, both in design and dimensions, the important difference being that while the Selinous X motif is in relief, the Sounion one is sunken (Arnold-Buicchi Biucchi *et al.* 1988, 26, pl. 15 E). The origin of these ingots, which is of interest in our case, as well as the import of the stamped impressions, "Greek-style control or inspection stamps on them", according to Kroll, were elucidated after undergoing lead isotope analysis (Kroll 2008, 30; for similar disc shaped ingots, see Kroll 2011, 9–10, pl. 1; Liard 2009, 169). The lead isotope ratios for ingot E have been proven to correspond "very closely to ores from Laurion as they fall within the three-dimensional lead isotope field of analysed Laurion ores from both Thorikos and Agrileza", as Beer-Tobey *et al.* (1988, 387) noted. This finding proves that Athenian silver was exported to western Greece (see Birch *et al.* this volume). Ingots C and D, from the same hoard, also contained a significant portion of Laurion silver (Beer-Tobey *et al.* 1988, 387–388, table 1). Silver and litharge from the Laureotike were exported in large quantities from its main harbours. Such transactions are demonstrated by three finds of *Hacksilber* from Tel Miqne-Ekron in Cisjordan, dated to the seventh century BC. Results of lead-isotope analysis show that they all derive from the mines of Laurion (Thompson 2003, 92).

Another hoard discovered in Taranto in 1911 (*IGCH* 1874) contained coins from South Italian cities, from Sicily and Aegean Greece, unminted silver in the form of *Hacksilber*, but also chopped-up ingots (Babelon 1912, 1–40). It was the largest assemblage of silver bullion yet discovered from the ancient Greek world, and was possibly a banker's hoard, as Holloway noted (Holloway 2000, 6). The severed end of a stamped ingot was retrieved from this hoard and was published by Ernest Babelon after a sketch made by Gregory Vlasto. This and other parts of this hoard have long since been dispersed. According to Babelon, it was stamped with an incuse-square reverse coin punch from the mint of Selinus, evidence that in the late sixth century the Sicilian mint was both manufacturing ingots and minting coins at one and the same time (Babelon 1912, 32–33).

A bronze truncated pyramid-shaped pendant from the Argive Heraion, 3.8 cm high, with a 1.7 cm square base and a ring at its top (in diameter 6.8 mm) for suspension, was assumed by the excavator to serve the purpose of a seal (de Cou 1905, 264, pl. XCIII, no. 1557). On impact its engraved base produces an incuse square and within it four sunken ridges forming an X pattern, although the ridges do not meet at the centre. Their width varies between 1.7 and 2.7 mm. Its imprint is identical with that produced by both ends of the Sounion hammer (Fig. 7). The pendant from the Argive Heraion (NMA 13987) is therefore, the closest comparandum to our enigmatic tool, suggesting that it too, was used for stamping.

The above comparanda allow us to propose that the purpose of the small hammer was very likely for stamping silver, a task requiring a lighter, single stroke. However, the question raised *a propos* the Selinous stamped ingot may also apply to the Sounion tool: who had the authority to stamp silver?[6] It is known that there was some control of bullion arriving at the ports and markets of cities in the late Archaic period (Holloway 2000, 6). Metal bullion weighed out for use in transactions, a practice inherited from the Near East and dating from the second millennium BC, had preceded the introduction of coinage in the Aegean world (Kroll 1998, 229). In Attica as elsewhere, a pre-coinage period is recognised (for a full discussion with references, see Davis 2012, 127–158). Weighed silver was then the preferred precious metal used in trade transactions, as well as for lending at interest. The significance of silver, and its impact on one's wealth, is attested to in fragment 24 of Solon's poetry, where he remarks that: "the blessings of a man ranked an abundance of silver and gold first, before wealth in land and livestock". This statement led Rhodes to observe that it was quite

---

[6] For bullion stamping in Lydia and Ionia, see Kroll 1998, 230.

Figure 7. Pendant from the Argive Heraion. The object, its base and its imprint (National Archaeological Museum, Athens. Photo: Elias Eliades, 2015). © Ministry of Culture and Sports/ Archaeological Receipts Fund.

common for the Solonian-era Athenian elite to own large amounts of silver (Rhodes 1975, 7). It is worth noting that well after the circulation of coinage, uncoined silver was set aside, as attested in the fourth century BC inventory list of the Treasures of Athena, for conversion into coin in support of the Military Fund in an emergency (ἀσήμου ἀργυρίου τοὺς εἰς τὰ στρατιωτικὰ ἐξαιρεθέντος παρὰ ταμίου στρατιωτικῶν ... cf. Harris 1995, 125).

The late Archaic ingot E from the Selinous hoard proves that silver from Laurion was also exported, some of it in the form of ingots; it may have been traded further afield by Aeginetan traders (Kroll 2001, 83; Kroll 1998, 231; Liard 2009, 168). The fineness and weight were inspected and confirmed locally, by means of a stamp by officials. These last may have been either members of the local elite, Salaminioi settled in nearby Porthmos, or wealthy Aeginetan settlers, connected to the sanctuary of Poseidon (Davis 2014, 274–275; Theodoropoulou Polychroniadis 2015, 121–122). This local aristocracy gradually lost their primacy, first under the rule of the Peisistratids and soon after as a result of the Cleisthenic reforms, as the state took firmer control of sources of revenue (Flament 2011, 91). This is likely to be the moment when the hammer was withdrawn from use, possibly after being intentionally decommissioned. In preparation of the site for the erection of the Archaic temple, offerings including the hammer were carefully deposited in the *bothros* of the Poseidon sanctuary, the hammer as 'untouchably sacred' (ἐξάγιστον) as Parker eloquently translated it (Kosmetatou 2003, 73–79; Parker 1996, 125).

As noted above, the strategic position of the sanctuary was enhanced by two natural harbours, the western being the larger and more easily accessible. Literary sources from Homer onwards refer to the anchoring facilities of these harbours. Pilgrims, mariners, seafarers and merchants would all have disembarked here since it was the first port they would reach in Attica when sailing west, and the promontory was a highly visible landmark. Arguably they were taxed for the use of the harbours. A later inscription *IG* I³ 8 (Fig. 8), c.460–450 BC from Sounion, states in fragment b.12, lines 15–25, that landing taxes were imposed on every cargo ship that entered the harbour at Sounion, as a contribution towards the upkeep of the Poseidon sanctuary (Peek 1934, 35–39). By way of comparison, a fragmentary opisthographic lead tablet from Ephesus dating to the late seventh/early sixth centuries BC, discovered by Hogarth in 1904 in the foundations of the Archaic temple, records gold and silver bullion, money that was paid to the temple's treasury. Any silver collected as a harbour tax would have been "weighed out here" probably by the *nautikon*, as

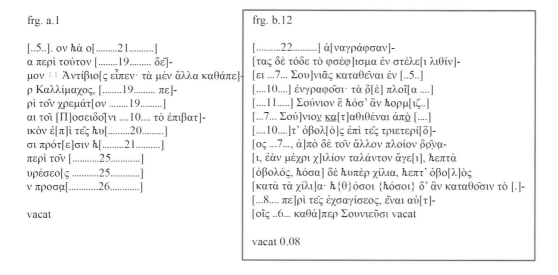

Figure 8. *IG* I³ 8

Inscription *IG* I³ 8

Kroll noted (Kroll 1998, 227–28; Kroll 2008, 20). It is reasonable to propose therefore that at Sounion too, harbour taxes were paid in silver. Before being stored in the sanctuary, such silver would very likely be weighed, tested, and stamped.[7] In whatever form it was received, silver may either had been heated in order to facilitate stamping, or the simpler method of heating one of the engraved faces of this tool, would be sufficient, on fairly light impact, to produce a sharp imprint.[8] Our tool therefore, may well have been used for this purpose rather than for stamping decorative patterns on metal sheets or jewellery. Its repeated stamping may justify the presence of the two identical engraved striking ends which would have prolonged the tool's life.

CONCLUSION

Based on archaeological and numismatic evidence and epigraphic testimonia, this study of the Sounion hammer allows the new proposition that the hammer was used as a means of stamping silver, most probably to confirm its fineness. When it was no longer needed, possibly when the state took control of revenues sometime in the latter part of the sixth century, it was deposited in the sanctuary as εξάγιστον. This study has also shed light on the importance of the promontory and its harbours, on aspects of the profile, status and the role of the local elite of the Sounians played in the trade of silver and other metals, as well as on the beneficial impact of mining activity on the political and economic development of the area in the Archaic period.

---

[7] Sanctuaries receiving precious metals and acting also as banks is well attested, see Holloway 2000, 10.
[8] This process has been elucidated and confirmed by Dimitrios Armaos, qualified metalsmith and gemologist, one of Greece's leading silversmiths (personal communication).

BIBLIOGRAPHY

Arnold-Biucchi, C. A., Beer–Tobey, L. and Waggoner, N.M. 1988. 'A Greek Archaic Silver Hoard from Selinus', *ANSMN* 33, 1–35.

Babelon, E. 1912. 'Trouvaille de Tarente' *RN* s. 4 16, 1–40.

Beer–Tobey, L., Gale, N., Kim, H. S. and Stos–Gale, Z. 1988. 'Lead isotope analysis of four late archaic silver ingots from the Selinus hoard', in Oddy, A. and Cowell, M. (eds.), *Metallurgy in Numismatics 4* (London), 385–390.

Boardman, J. 1961. *The Cretan Collection in Oxford: the Dictaean Cave and Iron Age Crete* (Oxford).

Cou, H. Fl., de 1905. 'The Bronzes of the Argive Heraeum', in W. Ch. Waldstein (ed.) *The Argive Heraeum* Vol II, (Boston, N. York), 191–340.

Davis, G. 2012. 'Dating the Drachmas in Solon's Laws', *Historia* 61(2), 127–158.

Davis, G. 2014. 'Mining money in the Archaic Athens', *Historia* 63(3), 257–277.

Dinsmoor, W. B. Jr. 1974. *Sounion* (Athens).

Dörpfeld, W. 1884. 'Der Tempel von Sounion', *AM* 9, 324–337.

Flament, Chr. 2011. 'Le Laurion et la cité d'Athènes à la fin de l'époque archaïque', *L'Antiquité Classique* 80, 73–94.

Goette, H.R. 2000. *Ο αξιόλογος δήμος Σούνιον* (Landeskundliche Studien in Südost Attika; Rahden).

Harris, D. 1995. *The Treasures of the Parthenon and Erechtheion* (Oxford; N. York).

Holloway, R.R. 2000. 'Remarks on the Taranto Hoard of 1911', *RBN* 146, 1–8.

Hopper, R. J. 1968. 'Observations on Wappenmünzen', in Kraay, C.M. and Jenkins, G.K. (eds.), *Essays in Greek Coinage Presented to Stanley Robinson* (Oxford), 16–38.

Jones, J.R.M. 1993. *Testimonia Numaria. Greek and Latin Texts concerning Greek Coinage.* Vol I: *Texts and Translations* (London).

Kakavoyannis, E., Ch. 2005. *Μέταλλα Εργάσιμα και Συγκεχωρημένα. Η οργάνωση της εκμετάλλευσης του ορυκτού πλούτου της Λαυρεωτικής από την Αθηναϊκή Δημοκρατία* (Athens).

Kokkou-Viridi, K. 1999. *Πρώιμες πυρές θυσιών στο Τελεστήριο της Ελευσίνος* (Athens).

Kalligas, P.G. 1997. 'Die from Sounion' in Sheedy, K.A. and Papageorgiadou–Banis, Ch. (eds.) *Numismatic Archaeology Archaeological Numismatics. Proceedings of an International Conference held to honour Dr. Mando Oeconomides in Athens 1995*, Oxbow Monographs 75 (Oxford), 141–147.

Kosmetatou, E. 2003. 'Taboo' objects in the Attic Inventory Lists', *Glotta*, 79 Bd. 1/4 H., 66–82.

Kroll, J.H. 1998. 'Silver in Solon's Laws' in Ashton, R. et al. (eds.), *Studies in Greek Numismatics in memory of Martin Jessop Price* (London), 225–232.

Kroll, J.H. 2001. 'Observations on Monetary Instruments in Pre-coinage Greece', in Balmuth, M.S. (ed.), *Hacksilber to Coinage: New Insights into the Monetary History of the Near East and Greece. A Collection of Eight Papers Presented at the 99th Annual Meeting of the Archaeological Institute of America*, Numismatic Studies no 24 (New York), 77–91.

Kroll, J.H. 2008. 'The Monetary Use of the Weighted Bullion in Archaic Greece' in Harris, W.V. (ed.), *The Monetary Systems of the Greeks and Romans* (Oxford), 12–37.

Kroll, J.H. 2011. 'A small find of silver bullion from Egypt', *AJN* 13, 2nd s., 1–20.

Laffineur, R. 2010. 'Thorikos Rich in Silver. The Prehistoric Periods', in Iossif, P.P. (ed.) *'All that Glitters...' The Belgian Contribution to Greek Numismatics, 29 September 2010–15 January 2011* (Athens), 26–40.

Liard, Fl. 2009. 'Les sources d'argent pour la frappe des monnaies grecques aux époques archaïques et classiques. Aperçu des dernières dècouvertes scientifiques et archéologiques', *RBN* 155, 159–176.

Mussche, H.M. 1998. *Thorikos: a minting town in ancient Attika* (Gent).

Mylonas, G.E. 1961. *Eleusis and the Eleusinian Mysteries* (Princeton).

Noack, F. 1927. *Eleusis:, Die Bau geschichtliche Entwicklung des Heiligtums* (Berlin).

Osborne, R. 1985. *Demos: The Discovery of Classical Attika* (Cambridge).

Osborne, R. 1994. 'Archaeology, the Salaminioi, and the Politics of Sacred Space in Archaic Attica,' in Alcock, S.E. and Osborne, R. (eds.), *Placing the Gods: Sanctuaries and Sacred Space in Ancient Greece* (Oxford), 143–160.

Paga, J. 2015. 'The Monumental Definition of Attica in the Early Democratic Period', in Miles, M. (ed.), *Autopsy in Athens: recent archaeological research on Athens and Attica* (Oxford),108–125.

Paga, J. and Miles, M. 2016. The Archaic Temple of Poseidon at Sounion, *Hesperia* 85, 657–710.

Palaiokrassa, L. 1991. *Το ιερό της Αρτέμιδος Μουνυχίας* (Athens).

Papathanasopoulos, G. 1983. *Σούνιον Ιρόν* (Athens).

Parker, R. 1996. *Athenian Religion: A History* (Oxford).

Parker, R. 2005. *Polytheism and Society at Athens: A History* (Oxford).

Peek, W. 1934. 'Griechische Inschriften', *AM* 59, 35–80.

Petrakos, V. 1982. "Ανασκαφαί Ραμνούντος", *ΠΑΕ*, 127–162.

Petrakos, V. 1999. *Ο δήμος του Ραμνούντος* vol. I (Athens).

Polignac, F. de 1995. *Cults, Territory and the Origins of the Greek City-State* (Chicago).

Rhodes., P.J. 1975. 'Solon and the Numismatics' *NC* 7th ser.15, 1–11.

Salliora-Oikonomakou, M. 2004. *Ο Αρχαίος Δήμος του Σουνίου* (Athens).

Sheedy, K. 2014. 'The Sounion 'Wappenmünzen die' Revisited', *Νομισματικά Χρονικά* 32, 21–32.

Stais, V. 1897. "Ανασκαφαί εν Σουνίω", *ΠΑΕ*, 16–18.

Stais, V. 1898. "Ανασκαφαί εν Σουνίω", *ΠΑΕ*, 92–94.
Stais, V. 1899. "Ανασκαφαί εν Σουνίω", *ΠΑΕ*, 12–13, 98–100.
Stais, V. 1900a. "Ανασκαφαί εν Σουνίω", *ΠΑΕ*, 51–52.
Stais, V. 1900b. "Ανασκαφαί εν Σουνίω", *ΑΕ*, 113–150.
Stais, V. 1903. "Ανασκαφαί εν Σουνίω", *ΠΑΕ* 13–14.
Stais, V. 1906. "Ανασκαφαί εν Σουνίω", *ΠΑΕ* 49, 85,86.
Stais, V. 1907. "Ανασκαφαί εν Σουνίω", *ΠΑΕ*, 102–104.
Stais, V. 1908. "Ανασκαφαί εν Σουνίω", *ΠΑΕ*, 63.
Stais, V. 1909. "Ανασκαφαί εν Σουνίω", *ΠΑΕ*, 117–118.
Stais, V. 1912. "Σουνίου ανασκαφαί", *ΑΕ*, 266.
Stais, V. 1917. "Σουνίου ανασκαφαί", *ΑΕ*, 168–213.
Stais, V. 1920. *Το Σούνιον και οι ναοί του Ποσειδώνος και Αθηνάς* (Athens).
Straten Van, V.T. 1981. 'Gifts for the Gods', in Versnel, H.S. (ed.), *Faith, Hope and Worship. Aspects of Religious Mentality in the Ancient World* (Leiden), 65–151.
Theodoropoulou Polychroniadis, Z. 2015. *Sounion Revisited: the Sanctuaries of Poseidon and Athena at Sounion in Attica* (Oxford).
Theodoropoulou-Polychroniadis, Z. forthcoming. ' Re-examining metal objects from the sanctuaries at Sounion',International Scientific Congress, Lemnos, 11–15 September 2019.
Theodoropoulou-Polychroniadis, Z., Orfanou, V. 2019. 'Copper-based offerings from the sanctuaries of Poseidon and Athena at Sounion, Attica: typological and analytical investigations', in Ph. Baas (ed.) *Resource, reconstruction, role, Proceedings of the XXth International Congress on Ancient Bronzes*, Tübingen, 17–21 April 2018, BAR series 2958, 331–343.
Thompson, C. M. 2003. 'Sealed Silver in the Iron Age Cisjordan and the "Invention" of Coinage', *OJA* 22, 67–107.
Thompson, C.M. 2011. 'Silver in the Age of Iron and the Orientalizing Economies of Archaic Greece: an overview', in Giardino, C. (ed.), *Archeometallurgia: dalla conoscenza alla fruizione*, Atti del convegno Carallino, Lecce, 22.25/5/2006 (Bari: Edipuglia), 121–13.
Tiverios, M. – Gimatzidis, St. 2001. "Ανασκαφικές έρευνες στη Διπλή Τράπεζα Αγχιάλου κατά το 2001", *ΑΕΜΘ* 15, 229–307.

22. METHODS OF CONSERVATION OF ANCIENT SILVER COINS USED AT THE NUMISMATIC MUSEUM, ATHENS

George Kakavas, Eleni Kontou and Nikoleta Katsikosta

ABSTRACT

This chapter presents a summary of treatment methods used by the conservators in the Numismatic Museum, Athens to treat and conserve ancient silver coins based on the three aims of conservation: revelation, investigation and preservation. It elucidates the challenges of conservation and shows the effects of the various methods. A case study is provided into how the curators are using X-ray fluorescence spectrometry to indicate the alloy composition and scanning electron microscopy to guide sophisticated laser cleaning. Some thoughts are offered on best practice in conservation.

INTRODUCTION

The conservation laboratory at the Numismatic Museum, Athens (NMA) was established in the 1980s, and specialises in the conservation of coins, lead seals, tokens and medals brought in from archaeological finds and by acquisition.[1] Since 2000 we have collaborated on five major analytical research programs with Greek and international institutions.[2] The expertise we have gained from these collaborations has given us a better understanding of the effects of cleaning and led to greater discernment in the choice of treatment method(s).

In this chapter, we present a range of methods we use for the treatment of ancient silver coins depending on the nature of the deterioration they have suffered over time. We look at the effect of conservation on the surface of coins, and provide examples of how we use scanning electron microscopy (SEM) and X-ray fluorescence spectrometry (XRF) in our work. Finally, we discuss 'best practice' and the dilemma of preserving authenticity while presenting some coins for identification, display and publication.

CONSERVATION OF ANCIENT SILVER COINS

CORROSION

Silver alloy coins are not chemically stable in the presence of oxygen or some other elements, particularly halides, common at earth surface environments (Table 1, cf. Selwyn 2004, 136; Bertholon and Relier 1990, 182).

Ancient coins develop surface corrosion, as well as post conservation treatment coins frequently develop atmospheric corrosion. Silver oxide is a thin white protective layer which develops in moist air. Silver cations can also react with sulfide ions in the environment (atmosphere or soil) to produce an insoluble black silver sulfide. The surface of silver coins is usually covered with a protective layer of variable thickness of silver sulfide tarnish (Stambolov 1985, 184). The tarnish changes in colour from white to yellow, brown, red and blue before turning black, the silver sulfide's final colour

---

[1] See Kakavas *et al.* on suspicious coins in this volume. Conservators Eleni Kontou and Niki Katsikosta have worked in the laboratory since the early 1990s.

[2] The research programs are: (1) 'A spring of silver, a treasury in the earth: coinage and wealth in Archaic Athens', a collaboration with the Australian Centre for Ancient Numismatic Studies, Macquarie University, Sydney, Australia, 2012–2015; (2) 'Cleaning coin collections by means of laser', a collaboration with the Physics Department, National Technical University, Athens, Greece and National Centre of Scientific Research, 'Democritos' (NRCPS), Athens, Greece, founded by the John S. Latsis Public Benefit Foundation, 2009–2010; (3) 'Investigation on Ptolemaic coinage by the use of X-ray Fluorescence analysis', a collaboration with the Departamento de Prehistoria y Arqueología, Universidad de Sevilla, Sevilla, Spain, between Spain, Italy and Greece, 2008–2009; (4) 'Characterizations and cleaning of metal artifacts by lasers', a collaboration with the Physics Department, National Technical University, Athens, Institute for Applied Physics 'Nello Carrara', Department of Electronica Quantistica, between Italy and Greece, 2005–2007; and (5) 'Characterizations and cleaning of metal surfaces by lasers', a collaboration with the Physics Department, National Technical University, Athens, between Greece and Poland, 2005–2007.

Table 1. Archaeological Silver corrosion products

Chemical classification	Chemical name	Mineral name	Chemical formula	Colour
oxide	silver oxide		Ag_2O	white/black*
bromides	silver bromide	bromargyrite	$AgBr$	yellow/brown
chlorides	silver chloride	chlorargyrite formerly known as cerargyrite	$AgCl$	white-gray
chlorides /bromides		embolite	$AgCl/AgBr$	white-gray
sulfides	silver sulfide			
		acanthite	α-Ag_2S	black
		argentite	β-Ag_2S	black

* For the colour and formation mechanism of silver oxide see also Stambolov 1985, 182–184.

(Ankersmit *et al.* 2008, 14). The intermediate state is termed iridescence. Spongy silver sulfide growth may also be observed (Stambolov 1985, 184).

In some excavation coins, a photosensitive grey-lavender, waxy, silver chloride forms on the surface ranging from infilling details of the design through to a thick crust. It sometimes carries inclusions from the soil. Some silver chloride crusts preserve the original surface between two phases - the outer silver chloride crust with soil inclusions and an inner layer comprising the partially mineralised silver matrix. A recent study on silver corrosion showed that the presence of silver chloride is associate with horn silver. Horn silver coins are stable and are of a greyish aspect. The main corrosion product is silver chloride that forms a brittle, finely granular layer (Marchand *et al.* 2014, 2). In fact, the UV radiation can reduce horn silver to silver; giving superficially a metallic sheen (Cronyn 1990, 234). In our experience, a silver coin typically retains its metal core, but is mineralised in areas such as the letters or details of the design. The original surface is displaced upwards keeping its silver appearance while underneath there are powdery or waxy silver corrosion products. This may then result in the loss of the surface details. However, environmental conditions may be responsible for the total mineralisation of the flan transforming it into silver chloride (Marchand *et al.* 2014, 5).

Rarely, there is a mixture of silver chloride and silver bromide that leads to the formation of either a protective patina and the preservation of the details of the surface or to a thick, sometimes swollen, crust and loss of details (Cronyn 1990, 231–2).

There are also cases where the surface of silver is covered by corrosion products of other metals, especially copper and iron. Copper corrosion products can derive from contact with a neighboring copper alloy object, but also as a constituent metal in the alloy, since copper corrodes preferentially and deposits corrosion products on the surface and between the silver grains. Furthermore, in the case of silver plated coins, where copper ions defuse through the silver plated layer, corrosion products such as copper carbonate hydroxide (malachite, $Cu_2CO_3(OH)_2$, green in colour) and copper (I) oxide (cuprite, Cu_2O, red-orange in colour) deposit on the surface (Cronyn 1990, 232).

Three distinct zones are normally exhibited in an excavated coin - an inner and relatively sound metal core; a compact layer of relatively pure corrosion products; and an outer mass of corrosion products of low density often growing through mineral particles including clays, organic remains or other material from the burial environment. The original surface may be found in between the two corrosion layers. (Seeley 1980, 7; Bertholon and Relier 1990, 187–90).

EXAMINATION

There are three aims of conservation: revelation, investigation and preservation. The terms 'preventive' and 'interventive' conservation have been adopted in conservation (Caple 2000, 33, 37–8).[3]

Preliminary examination of coins can provide valuable information regarding the alloy of the flan, the condition state or technological details, and even traces of organic material. Examination is usually performed by high magnification under a microscope (30x–90x), specific gravity estimation and X-ray radiography. Non-destructive analytical methods often used for coins include energy dispersive X-ray fluorescence spectrometry (EDXRF), scanning electron microscopy with energy dispersive spectrometry (SEM-EDX), neutron activation analysis (NAA), ion beam analysis as proton (or particle) induced X-ray emission (PIXE), electron probe microanalysis (EPMA), particle induced gamma-ray emission (PIGE), and laser-induced breakdown spectroscopy (LIBS). Furthermore, there are methods which require micro-sampling usually at the periphery of the flan where sampling will be less noticeable, mass spectrometry (MS) that is isotope analysis of lead or silver, or a cross section examination, such as metallography. Techniques that require a sample to be dissolved are inductively coupled plasma atomic emission spectroscopy (ICP AES), inductively coupled plasma mass spectrometry (ICP MS) and atomic absorption spectrometry (AAS). Techniques usually used for determination of the mineralogy of corrosion products are X-ray diffractometry (XRD) and Raman spectroscopy (Hein and Degrigny 2008, 125–40; Craddock 2009, 46–58).

TREATMENT

The reasons for conservation should govern treatment, especially the relative importance of identification, display or research. The method or combination of methods employed depends upon many factors, including alloy composition, type and extent of the corrosion. The required time for cleaning as well as the conservator's skill could be factors influencing the choice. Cleaning of silver coins aims to reveal the precious metal with respect to the original surface, but how far the cleaning should go and the final appearance are critical considerations. Each time tarnish is removed, the silver that reacted to form the tarnish is lost. Polishing also removes some of the underlying untarnished silver. After many cycles of tarnishing and polishing, so much silver may be removed that fine detail on the coin is lost (Seeley 1980, 5; cf. Selwyn 2017a).

Treatments reported in the literature mainly include pad cleaning, abrasive pastes (cf. Selwyn 2017), chemical cleaning with a variety of chemicals (Berthelon and Relier 1990, 203), mechanical cleaning (Cronyn 1990, 233), silver reduction with chemical reducing agent such as sodium dithionite (Stambolov 1985, 190–91), electrolytic reduction (Aldaz et al. 2013, 175–6; Degrigny 2010, 353), consolidative reduction (Charalambous and Oddy 1975, 219–221), hydrogen low-pressure plasma (Eckmann and Elmer 1994, 138–47) and laser cleaning (Drakaki et al. 2008; Drakaki et al. 2010). Although it is essential to know the effectiveness of the treatments used, it is also important to know about the methods used in the past, especially chemical agents and electrochemical cleaning (Stambolov 1985, 186–91; Plenderleith and Werner 1971, 239–43).

---

[3] Preventive conservation of coins includes environment monitoring and control, suitably tested materials for showcases, storage and even transport, collection assessments, disaster planning, legislative protection and advocacy. Interventive conservation includes preliminary examination and all invasive procedures and protection against future decay, followed by adequate recording of data, weighing and photographing before and after treatment, and reference to elements identified as organic residues, such as fibres.

METHODS USED AT THE NUMISMATIC MUSEUM, ATHENS

This section describes in detail each of the methods we use together with some examples of coins we have treated. In cases of hoards with many coins, it is essential to keep some untreated for future reference.

PADS WITH SOLVENTS

A soft microfiber cloth immersed in solvents, usually acetone or ethyl alcohol, can be used to remove effectively the silver sulfide tarnish of variable thickness from yellow to black in colour. It can also remove coatings or grease and dust. Cotton swabs immersed in solvents may be used, or alternatively a coin may be immersed in solvents and cleaned by a soft natural fibre brush. However, care must be taken as cotton swabs or dirty microfiber cloth may easily scratch the surface.

ABRASIVE POWDERS AND PASTES

Abrasive powders in a mixture with solvents can be used as pastes for the removal of the silver sulfide tarnish of variable thickness from yellow to black in colour (Selwyn 2017b). There are several alternative procedures. A soft and extremely fine abrasive powder of precipitated calcium carbonate is usually used, but sometimes it does not remove all the tarnish, especially on silver alloys. In these cases, we often use crystalline calcium carbonate in cotton swabs (Figs 1a and b) or by a soft natural fibre brush immersed in acetone and ethanol (Wharton *et al.* 1990). Choosing the proper crystalline calcium carbonate requires testing for its hardness, because even when buying from the same supplier, the product's composition can vary. The companies supplying these products classify them based on grain size or chemical purity. However, impurities with a higher hardness than the abrasive, even at very low contents, can scratch the surface of a silver coin. Cleaning is achieved with surface polishing in a circular motion. Spectacular results can be received in cases where the flan is very thin, and on medals. This procedure can be used in combination with another method; thus abrasive pastes can be used when most of the corrosion products have already taken off by mechanical or chemical means.

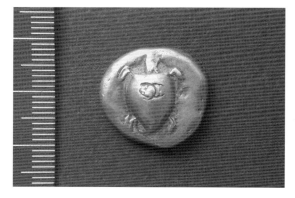

Figures 1a and b. Silver stater of Aegina from the Myrina – Karditsa hoard, 1970 (*CH* I, 25 = *CH* V, 11), c. 440 B.C., before and after cleaning with calcium carbonate impregnated cotton swabs

CHEMICAL CLEANING

Most of the methods that have been used over the years are based on the use of chemical agents. This is because silver is a noble metal and remains little affected by chemicals compared with other metals. Such cleaning requires considerable care during and after processing, but is preferable because it is relatively quick and cost-effective in the treatment of large numbers of coins in a similar state of corrosion. Its application may lead to side effects such as the stripping of the surface, the formation of cavities, the uncovering of silver grains and dendrites, and even the total loss of the design details when they are within corrosion crusts or layers. If not thoroughly rinsed, chemical cleaning may lead to further corrosion. In cases of intense corrosion, the silver ions of the corrosion products may be reduced forming a silver layer that covers the surface details. However, chemicals can also be used for silver dechlorination, which is known as stabilisation treatment (Cronyn 1990, 233; Argyropoulos 2008, 56). Chemical cleaning can be applied in conjunction with mechanical cleaning.

We commonly use the following methods (Berthelon and Relier 1990, 203; Cronyn 1990, 233):

- Complex agents such as ammonium thiosulphate, $((NH_4)_2S_2O_3)$ in a 5–15% solution with 1% neutral detergent to bind the impurities and entrain them to the solution, as no ionic Texapone N 70 or Lissapol (Lykiardopoulou-Petrou, M. 1996, 170). We prefer this for the removal of silver sulfide and chloride corrosion products (Figs 2a and b).
- Sequestering agents such as thiourea $((NH_2)_2CS)$ A 5–15% solution is used to dissolve corrosion crusts, without removal of the silver sulfide layer.
- In cases of copper corrosion products, chemicals such as formic acid (HCOOH), in a 5–10% solution (or up to 15%) can be used for the removal of copper carbonate hydroxide, green in colour and a 5–10% solution of EDTA $((HOOCCH_2)_2NCH_3CH_2N(CH_2COOH)_2)$ is suitable for removal of copper (I) oxide red-orange in colour.
- Coins from hoards that are stuck together by copper corrosion products and especially oxides which are quite insoluble, can be separated by a 5–10% solution of citric acid, $(C_6H_8O_7)$.

Figures 2a and b. Silver drachm of Athens, NM 2544, 550–520 B.C., before and after cleaning using a 10% solution of ammonium thiosulphate

MECHANICAL CLEANING

Hand tools can be used to remove all the crust or layers down to the original surface to reveal the details of the figure. The great advantage of mechanical treatment is that it is extremely selective and corrosion products may be precisely removed if layered; often a close approximation of the original surface is achieved. Abrasive or chemical cleaning may then follow. Mechanical cleaning needs considerable skill, because the metal surface can be scratched or damaged (Cronyn 1990, 233). Over the last ten years, the conservators in our laboratory have mainly used mechanical cleaning with flexible gold-plated pin picks under the microscope for the removal of silver crusts or layers to minimise the need for chemical cleaning and its side effects (Figs 3a and b).

Figures 3a and b. Silver tetradrachm of Alexander III (Makrupodi and Giannakoudi in press) before and after cleaning using a flexible gold-plated pin pick

LASER APPLICATION

Lasers represent a new approach to the treatment of ancient silver artefacts. Over the past decade, we have experimented with cleaning silver coins using lasers of several types, wavelengths, pulse duration and conditions. The most effective were those of Long Q-switched NdYAG (1064 nm, 100 ns pulse) for thick corrosion layers, and Q-switched Nd: YAG (266 nm, 6 ns pulse) for thin corrosion layers and copper corrosion products, both moistened with water. Cleaning of artificially corroded specimens has shown that a KrF excimer laser (248 nm, 10 ns pulse) can remove the superficial corrosion layer. Ultrashort laser pulses create minimal thermally and chemically induced alterations, higher spatial confinement and control (Siatou et al. 2006). Irradiation requires a XY micro-adjustable moving system of the coins on a stable base, which can give satisfactory results when the surface of the coin is covered with a thin and homogeneous layer of corrosion products, or with the use of an optic fibre beam distribution system that can have a useful effect on cleaning both homogeneous and heterogeneous layers of corrosion products (Drakaki *et al.* 2008; Drakaki et al. 2010).

CHEMICAL TREATMENT OF SILVER PLATED COINS

In cases of silver plated coins with copper cores, the silver layer can be treated chemically, while the copper core requires a combination of mechanical and chemical treatments (Figs 4a and b). Chemicals such as formic acid can be used for the removal of copper carbonate hydroxide which is green in colour. EDTA is generally suitable for the removal of copper (I) oxide, red-orange in colour, but in the case of plated coins it may not manage to remove copper (I) oxide from the silver surface before etching the original surface of the

Figures 4a and b. Silver plated drachm from the Piraeus Hoard, 1902 (*IGCH* 46), before and after chemical cleaning

copper core. Debased silver and silver-washed coins covered with copper corrosion products are also treated by chemical means, however cavities may appear from selective corrosion.

USE OF ANALYTICAL TECHNIQUES TO INFORM CONSERVATION PRACTICE – CASE STUDIES

Preliminary examination of coins under the microscope can provide valuable information regarding the alloy of the flan, the condition state or technological details, and even reveal traces of organic material. However, additional information can be obtained by other more sophisticated means of analysis. The Numismatic Museum possesses a shielded X-ray radiography system with a fluorescence screen, FAXITRON 43855 D, and in 2016 we acquired an X-ray fluorescence spectrometer, BRUKER M1 MISTRAL. We can access SEM-EDX through collaboration with Institutes such as School of Mining and Metallurgy Mining, National Technical University of Athens, which has a JEOL6380LV SEM.

SILVER REDUCTION

Firstly, we present the results of an investigation of Ptolemaic coinage using X-ray fluorescence spectrometry. This involved quantitative analysis with micro XRF of 82 silver Ptolemaic coins from the collection of Ioannes Demetriou into the origin of the ore (Kantarelou *et al.* 2011). Coins were selected considering their specific mints and not their state of preservation. Microscopic examination showed that their condition ranged from good to excellent. Their surfaces were covered by different kinds of silver corrosion products, mostly a thin, gray coloured layer of silver corrosion products, but some presented silver reduction - a coherent layer of metallic silver - while others had a thicker layer or were completely stripped off due to previously applied chemical cleaning. The coins being treated were also coated with varnish. During examination, the question arose whether or not to do more general cleaning in order to obtain more reliable results. We decided that since the coins came from a unique collection, they should not, just for the sake of analysis, have their patinas disturbed. A particular concern was the outcome of the cleaned area looking different from the remainder of the coin.

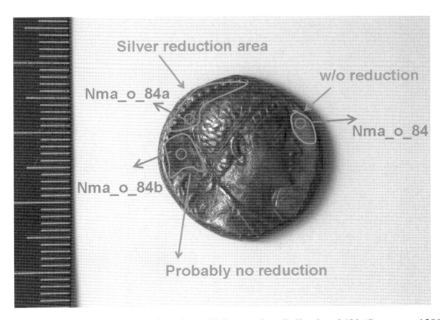

Figure 5. Coin #84, Silver tetradrachm of Ptolemy V, Demetriou Collection 242ᴬ (Svoronos 1289α). Points of analysis on obverse from silver reduction areas and from areas where reduction was not detected

Table 2. XRF analyses of three areas of Coin #84, silver tetradrachm of Ptolemy V, Demetriou Collection 242[A] (Svoronos 1289α).

Coin	Fe (wt%)	Cu (wt%)	Br (wt%)	Ag (wt%)	Au (wt %)	Pb (wt%)
Nma_o_84				98.293± 0.9	1.084± 0.004	0.448± 0.003
Nma_o_84a	0.235 ± 0.002	0.298 ± 0.002	0.041 ± 0.001	98.6 ± 0.9	0.073 ± 0.001	0.592 ± 0.006
Nma_o_84b	<0.066	0.205 ± 0.002		97.9 ± 0.9	1.06 ± 0.01	0.627 ± 0.006

To decide on the analytical approach, we selected certain coins and applied different treatments to small areas of each coin. We then compared the results of the analyses before and after treatment, which had involved cleaning with solvents and cotton swabs, or mechanical cleaning with a gold-plated pin pick and cotton swabs, or the application of calcium carbonate in cotton swabs immersed in acetone and ethanol over increased time spans. The results of the analysis for each coin show that the cleaning methods might give slightly different results depending on the areas of the coins which were analysed.

Nevertheless, we came across several cases where silver reduction was detected, such as coin #84, Ptolemy V, Demetriou Collection 242[A] (Svoronos 1289α), that had been treated in the past and had been coated with varnish. Fig. 5 shows the points that were analysed: NMA_o_84a, where reduction was observed, and NMA_o_84 and NMA_o_84b, where reduction was not detected.

The analyses given in Table 2 indicate that silver reduction may cause differences up to 1% in gold concentration, whereas the concentration of silver remains stable. Comparison of the results indicated that the selection of the best-preserved surface for performing the analysis is more essential than the choice of cleaning method to degrease it and remove any deposits. This indicates that the choice of reduction in interventive conservation should be applied wisely.

EVALUATION OF TREATMENT METHODS

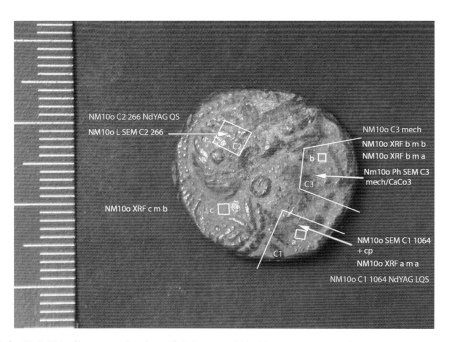

Figure 6. Coin #NM10, silver tetradrachm of Athens, c. 390–295 B.C., Π.Κ. serial number 35

As laser cleaning represented a new treatment method for us, we tested it on artificial specimens, then modern coins, and finally on coins in the museum collection chosen for research. Diagnostic examination techniques using optical microscopy, SEM and X-ray Fluorescence (XRF) spectrometry were applied for the analysis of the coins' alloys and corrosion products before and after laser treatment. Among the tests we performed was the application of the laser Long Q-switched NdYAG (1064 nm, 100 ns) held using an optical fibre beam distribution system. The obverse of coin #NM10, a silver tetradrachm of Athens, c. 390–295 BC, is covered by a thick layer of silver chloride that appears swollen especially on the details of the figure (Fig. 6). The initial SEM-EDX analysis on the corrosion products showed Ag (72.13 %), Cu (0.16 %), Sn (0.57 %) and Pb (0.36 %). On the area marked C1, laser LQS-Nd: YAG at 1064 nm at 2–4 J/cm^2 was applied with repeated irradiation moistened with water, while cleaning of the area marked C3 was carried out with a flexible gold-plated pin pick. The first attempt of cleaning using a LQS-Nd: YAG at 1064 nm, was made with a low energy density at 0.55 J/cm^2. During this procedure, a change in colour and texture of the corrosion products was observed (Fig. 6a), while this thick layer gradually acquired a metallic texture which was removed by mechanical means using a flexible gold-plated pin pick (Fig. 6b) which revealed the details of the surface (Fig. 6c). We evaluated the two methods under the optical and scanning electron microscopes, while determining the

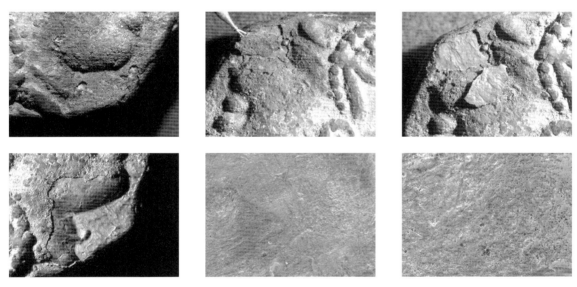

Figure 6a-f. Coin #NM10, Silver tetradrachm of Athens, c. 390–295 B.C., Π.Κ. serial number 35, C1: a) during laser application (8x); b) removal of irritated layer (8x); c) revealing the original surface (8x); d) after cleaning by 1064 nm LQS NdYAG, 4.00 J/cm^2 13–17 shots (8x) moistened with water; e) SEM image indicating the soft corrosion layer of the cleaning area (300x); f) SEM image indicating the soft corrosion layer of the cleaned area (1200x)

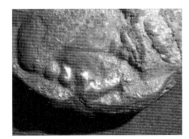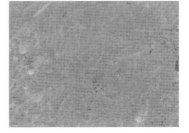

Figure 7. Coin #NM10, silver tetradrachm of Athens, c. 390–295 BC, Π.Κ. serial number 35, C3: a) after mechanical cleaning (5x); b) SEM image showing the surface after mechanical cleaning (300x); c) SEM image showing scratches caused by mechanical cleaning (1200x)

mineralogical and chemical composition of the various layers by SEM-EDX and XRF spectrometry. Microscopic examination at 30x–60x magnification showed that both methods had satisfactory results (Fig. 6d and Fig. 7a). Mechanical cleaning revealed the original surface displaced upwards with a glossy appearance, while the laser cleaning revealed the original surface displaced slightly downwards. SEM-EDX analysis showed that laser cleaning retained a thin layer of silver chloride containing Mg, Si, Ca, Fe, Cl and Br, meaning that it did not produce side effects on the original surface (Fig. 6e-f). SEM examination of mechanical cleaning detected light scratches, visible only at high magnification of 1200x, but not at 300x (Fig. 7b-c). Comparison of the two techniques regarding the detection of the original surface is of great importance. Laser cleaning revealed all the details of the original surface - slightly displaced downwards, while mechanical cleaning revealed the displaced original surface upwards. It is clear that in cases with swollen crusts, better results can be achieved by laser application.

EVALUATION OF THE SHAPE OF THERMAL EFFECT

The application of Long Q-switched, Q-switched, and Free Nd: YAG lasers may cause thermal effects on the original surface or between corrosion products and soil deposits which are usually not visible by the naked eye and cannot even be detected by examination under the stereomicroscope. To evaluate the laser application, it is necessary to detect these structures, their composition and extent. An ancient silver coin #NM18, silver drachm of Histiaea, Euboea, second half of 4th century B.C., Π.Κ. serial number 182, with surface composition Ag: 96.05 % and Cu: 2,23 % was used to determine the shape and extent of the thermal effect in terms of the energy density. While maintaining the spot size at 2 mm, four neighbouring areas on the reverse (Fig. 8, Fig. 9a-d) were irradiated by Free -Nd: YAG 1064 nm at 200 mJ, 400 mJ, 600 mJ and 800 mJ moistened with water. The stereomicroscope

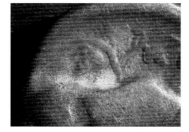

Figure 8. Coin #NM18, reverse, optical microscope image (10x), irradiated with Free -Nd: YAG 1064 nm with an energy density of 6,5 J/cm² - 25, 4 J/cm² moistened with water.

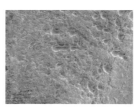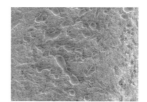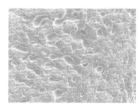

Figure 9. Coin #NM18, reverse, SEM images of area: a) irradiated with Free Nd:YAG 1064 nm, 200 mJ, spot size: 2 mm, 1 Hz, 1 shot (300x); b) irradiated with Free Nd:YAG 1064 nm, 400 mJ, spot size: 2 mm, 1 Hz, 1 shot (300x); c) irradiated with Free Nd:YAG 1064 nm, 600 mJ, spot size: 2 mm, 1 Hz, 1 shot (300x); d) irradiated with Free Nd:YAG 1064 nm, 800 mJ, spot size: 2 mm, 1 Hz, 1 shot (300x)

observation showed that the effect on the surface of the coin #NM18 varied from mild to intense, related to the energy density in magnification 30x–60x. Further SEM examination showed that the effect on area (a) (Fig. 9a), was mild within the spot with a few small droplets. However, on area (b) (Fig. 9b), droplets were observed in a parallel arrangement within the spot, whereas on area (c) (Fig. 9c), large droplets were observed in the spot. On area (d) (Fig. 9d) larger formations were observed overstepping the spot irradiated. This procedure was intentional, but in several cases stereomicroscope observation may not detect mild thermal effects. The SEM magnification required to detect the morphology of these structures starts from 150x or 300x up to 1200x, but sometimes even higher magnification up to 5000x is needed to clear the existence of formations caused by the thermal effects.

EVALUATION OF THE EXTENT OF THERMAL EFFECT

The next procedure was to study the temperature distribution in relation to the distance of irradiation point by Long Q-switched and Free Nd: YAG lasers of a modern silver alloy coin purchased by the National Technical University for the purposes of the program, in wet conditions (Fig. 10, Table 3). Measurements were made using an infrared thermometer (Marathon MM Series, Model MM2MH, Raytek), with a temperature range of 450–2250 °C and time response of 1 ms (which means that the temperatures may be higher than those recorded). Several measurements are close to, or exceed, the melting point of silver, and some exceed the melting point of copper. In addition, recorded temperatures are higher as far as 1 cm from the irradiation point. Greater temperatures were recorded using a Long Q-switched Nd: YAG laser, 130 mJ, with an attenuator, 1 Hz, 4 mm.

Figure 10. Modern silver alloy coin of the Ottoman Empire, Abdulhamid II, 1876–1909

Table 3. Irradiation of the modern silver alloy coin of Otoman Empire, Abdulhamid II, 1876–1909 by a Long Q-switched and Free Nd: YAG lasers: 1064 nm. Temperature measurements relative to the distance from the irradiation point.

Distance from shot	1064 nm, Free, 50 mJ, 1 Hz, 2 mm	1064 nm, Free, 50 mJ, 1 Hz, 4 mm	1064 nm, Free, 100 mJ, 1 Hz, 2 mm	1064 nm, Free, 100 mJ, 1 Hz, 4 mm	1064 nm, LQS, 130 mJ, with an attenuator 1 Hz, 2 mm	1064 nm, LQS, 130 mJ, with an attenuator 1 Hz, 4 mm
(a) on shot	650 °C	611 °C	760 °C	796 °C	830 °C	2100 °C
(b) 3.5 mm	678 °C	1311 °C	1300 °C	936 °C	1300 °C	990 °C
(c) 7.0 mm	1090 °C	627 °C	855 °C	662 °C	900 °C	600 °C
(d) 10.5 mm	680 °C	735 °C	902 °C	860 °C	578 °C	1060 °C
(e) 14.5 mm	750 °C	1225 °C	672 °C	951 °C	590 °C	999 °C
(f) 17.0 mm	960 °C	620 °C	815 °C	1131 °C	860 °C	970 °C

BEST PRACTICE

A well-known motto among conservation professionals is that "minimum intervention is the best intervention". This has led us to be careful in our choice of materials and techniques for the long-term care of coins in our collection, including decisions about whether or not to re-treat coins. Two questions derive from this: (1) which is the best practice or the best treatment method, and (2) is cleaning always necessary? With experience gained in many years in metal conservation, it is very difficult to answer the first question because all methods have advantages and disadvantages. Each silver coin has to be treated as an individual case. Thus, all the methods described above can be used individually or in combination. The second question is more easily answered. Cleaning is justified if there are soil deposits on the surface, active corrosion, or if the coin needs to be identified, displayed or published. Beyond the long-time tested methods, there is place for research using innovative technology to increase the choice of intervention methods.

REFERENCES

Aldaz, A., Espāna, T., Montiel, V. and Lopez-Segura, M. 2013. 'A simple tool for the electrolytic restoration of archaeological metallic objects with localized corrosion', *Studies in Conservation* 31/4, 175–176. *http://dx.doi.org/10.1179/sic.1986.31.4.175*).

Ankersmit, B., Griesser-Stermscheg M., Selwyn L., Sutherland S. 2008. 'Rust Never Sleeps: Recognizing Metals and Their Corrosion Products', Parks Canada Western and Northern Service Centre. *https://www.depotwijzer.be/sites/default/files/files/rust_never_sleeps.pdf*

Argyropoulos, V. 2008. 'Past and current conservation practices: The need of innovative and integrated approaches', in Argyropoulos, V. (ed.), *Metals and Museums in the Mediterranean: Protecting, Preserving and Interpreting* (Athens), 55–75.

Bertholon, R. and Relier, C. 1990. 'Les métaux archéologiques', in Berducou, M.C. (ed.), *La Conservation en Archéologie* (Paris, Masson), 163–221.

Caple, C. 2000. *Conservation Skills, Judgement, Method and Decision Making* (London-New York).

Charalambous, D. and Oddy, A.W. 1975. 'The consolidative reduction of silver', *Conservation in archaeology and the applied arts*. Preprints of the contributions to the Stockholm Congress, 2–6 June 1975, 219–227.

Craddock P. 2009. *Scientific Investigation of Copies, Fakes and Forgeries* (Oxford), 46–58.

Cronyn, J.M. 1990. *The Elements of Archaeological Conservation* (London).

Hein, A. and Degrigny, C. 2008. 'The application of non-destructive technologies for the damage assessment of metal objects', in Argyropoulos, V. (ed.), *Metals and Museums in the Mediterranean. Protecting, Preserving and Interpreting* (The Technological Educational Institute of Athens), 125–140.

Degrigny, C. 2010. 'Use of electrochemical techniques for the conservation of metal artefacts: a review', *Journal of Solid State Electrochemistry* 14, 353–61.

Drakaki, E., Evgenidou, D., Kantarelou, V., Karydas, A.G., Katsikosta, N., Kontou, E., Serafetinides, A.A., and Vlachou-Mogire, C. 2008. 'Laser cleaning experimental investigations on ancient coins', *Proceedings S.P.I.E.* 7027, *15th International School on Quantum Electronics, Laser Physics and Applications*, 7027071. Doi:10.1117/12.822443.

Drakaki, E., Klingenberg, B., Serafetinides, A.A., Kontou, E., Katsikosta, N., Tselekas, P, Evgenidou, D., Boukos, N. and Zanini, A. 2010. 'Evaluation of laser cleaning of ancient Greek, Roman and Byzantine coins', *Surface and Interface Analysis* 42, 671–4.

Eckmann, C. and Elmer, J.Th. 1994. 'Die Restaurierung und Konservierung archäologischer Bodenfunde aus Metall in einem Wasserstoff-Niederdruckplasma, in Heinrich, P. (ed.), *Metallrestaurierung, Beiträge zu Analyse, Konzeption und Technologie* (München) 138–147.

Kantarelou, V., Ager, F., Eugenidou, D., Chaves, F., Andreou, A., Kontou, E., Katsikosta, N., Respaldiza, M.A., Serafin, P., Sokaras, D., Zarkadas, Ch., Polikreti, K. and Karydas, A.G. 2011. 'X-ray Fluorescence analytical criteria to assess the fineness of ancient silver coins: Application on Ptolemaic coinage', *Spectrochimica Acta Part B* 66, 681–690.

Lykiardopoulou-Petrou, M. 1996. "Silver coins, production, deterioration, conservation", Character. (Athens), 165–176.

Makrypodi, S. and Giannakoudi, M. In press. "Θησαυρός πρώιμων ελληνιστικών χρόνων από το Άργος", *BCH Supplement* 57.

Marchand, G., Guilminot, E., Lemoine, S., Rossetti, L., Vieau, M., and Stephant, N. 2014. 'Degradation of archaeological horn silver artefacts in burials', *Heritage Science* 2:5. http://www.heritagesciencejournal.com/content/2/1/5, 2017.

Plenderleith, H. J. and Werner, A.E.A. 1971. *The conservation of antiquities and works of Art* (London).

Siatou, A., Charalambous, D., Argyropoulos, V. and Pouli, P. 2006. 'A comprehensive study for the laser cleaning of corrosion layers due to environmental pollution for metal objects of cultural value: Preliminary studies on artificially corroded coupons', *Laser Chemistry*, article ID 85324, doi:10.1155/2006/85324.

Seeley, N.J. 1980. 'Aims and Limitations in the Conservation of Coins, Numismatics and Conservation, Occasional paper No1', in Casey, P. and Cronyn, J. (eds.), *Numismatics and Conservation* (University of Durham, Department of Archaeology), 5–9.

Selwyn, L.S. 2004. *Metals and Corrosion. A Handbook for the Conservation Professional* (Ottawa).

Selwyn, L.S. 2017a. 'Silver - Care and Tarnish Removal', *CCI Notes* 9/7, Ottawa ON: Canadian Conservation Institute. *http://canada.pch.gc.ca/eng/1439925170396*.

Selwyn, L.S. 2017b. 'How to Make and Use a Precipitated Calcium Carbonate Silver Polish', *CCI Notes, No. 9/11*, Ottawa ON: Canadian Conservation Institute. *http://canada.pch.gc.ca/eng/1485381357043*.

Stambolov, T. 1985. *The Corrosion and Conservation of Metallic Antiquities and Works of Art* (Amsterdam).

Wharton G, Lansing Maish, S. and Ginell W. 1990. "A Comparative Study of Silver Cleaning Abrasives" *Journal of the American Institute for Conservation*, Vol. 29/1, 13–31.

ABBREVIATIONS

IGCH = M. Thompson, O. Mørkholm and C.M. Kraay (eds), Inventory of Greek Coin Hoards, New York, 1973.

23. THE ROLE OF THE NUMISMATIC MUSEUM OF ATHENS IN DETERMINING THE AUTHENTICITY OF COINS: THE CONTRIBUTION OF SCIENTIFIC ANALYSIS

George Kakavas and Eleni Kontou

ABSTRACT

The aim of this paper is to outline the procedures of the Museum in considering the authenticity of coins brought in for inspection or coins proposed as new acquisitions. We present four case studies. Here we wish to highlight the increasingly prominent role of scientific analysis.

INTRODUCTION[1]

The Numismatic Museum of Athens (henceforth, the 'Numismatic Museum') was founded in 1834 as the Royal Coin Collection, just a few months after the National Archaeological Museum had been established (Ministry of Culture–Numismatic Museum 1996, 15). The rapid expansion in the size of its collections right from the outset was due to the increase in excavations carried out under the supervision of the Greek State (which required that archaeological finds be protected and safeguarded), the growing number of donations made by collectors, confiscations made by the police and, more rarely, purchases from the market or from private individuals (Kakavas 2019). Today the Numismatic Museum is housed in the impressive Iliou Melathron building (Portelanos 2012, 449–464) designed by Ernst Schiller (Kardamitsi-Adami 2006, 99–109). It holds one of the most important numismatic collections in the world, with around 600,000 coins, large numbers of coin hoards, lead seals, medals and precious stones, jewellery, talents, obols, talismans and weights (Evgenidou 2010, 4). The Numismatic Museum plays a dynamic role in key aspects of protecting Greece's cultural heritage and its staff actively engages in scientific research.

The Museum's mission is to acquire, display and showcase, conserve, protect and safeguard coins and other related types of objects (such as lead seals, gems etc.). The Museum has many roles. It is legally required to be an educator (*Government Gazette of the Hellenic Republic*, No. 171, 28.8.2014). It provides the service of identifying coins from excavations in Greece. It also assists in the study of coins seized by the Hellenic Police. In order to properly perform its multifaceted role, the Numismatic Museum has developed successful partnerships between its staff and archaeologists and researchers in other institutions.

THE INVESTIGATION OF DOUBTFUL COINS

The Museum conducts research into the authenticity of all new acquisitions (Boz 2014, 219–225) as a matter of routine, since many of these objects do not have a known provenance or come from uncontrolled (unofficial) circumstances. The process followed when studying coins that appear to be of doubtful authenticity has a number of stages. Firstly, a macroscopic examination is performed; the coin is compared with similar examples published in corpora and, in particular, those within the Museum's own collections. The weight, flan and surface of the coin are carefully examined. This is followed by laboratory examination with a high magnification microscope to obtain more information concerning the processes by which the coin was manufactured. Here it is possible to identify the presence of surface striations caused by die stress (Craddock 2009, 183–184) during the striking process. If the coin was cast flow marks, 'seams' of excess metal between moulds, can form around the rim of the coin or cavities in the surface of the coin can result from trapped air bubbles. Moreover, with coins consisting of silver or copper and their typical alloys it is possible to identify the patina which has formed over time, either from burial in the soil or from being in a sealed burial environ-

---

[1] We wish to thank Dr Ute Wartenberg (ANS) for her contribution in preparing this text.

ment, or even, if the coin is counterfeit, as the result of the deliberate application of chemicals. Microscopic examination of gold and electrum coins may also permit the identification of surface depositions (rather than patina) created by the environment in which the coins were buried.

If necessary, further examination is carried out through an analysis of the composition of the coin's metal. Studies of the metal composition of the coin in question together with those of related coins may provide important indications when considering questions of authenticity. Counterfeiters and forgers in previous centuries, however, sometimes reused the metal of ancient coins to manufacture rare coins with types attractive to collectors (Kinns 1984, 5–6; Fleming 1975, p. 312, line 10, 108), a practice still common today. The results from elemental analyses of the metal will then need to be assessed in conjunction with information from typological and microscopic observations.

CASE STUDIES

By way of example we will look at four cases investigated by the Numismatic Museum in recent years.

1. The Mosses silver octadrachm.

The first case study concerns the identification of a silver octadrachm or tristater (29.29g) with the name of Mosses (Figs. 1–4), an individual (king?) probably to be associated with the Bisaltia region of modern-day Eastern Macedonia (Gaebler 1935, 145–6, No. 8–13).

Figures 1–2. Mosses octadrachm (32,5mm). Photos: Eleftherios A. Galanopoulos

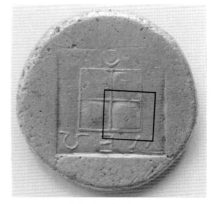

Figures 3–4. Photos of the same coin received from the Directorate of the Hellenic Police

Smaller denominations (drachms) of this ruler can be dated after 465 BC (Tzamalis 2012, 379–398, 542–544). In 2009 the Thessaloniki Security Issues Directorate of the Hellenic Police (the 'Police Directorate') received an anonymous tip that the coin was from an illegal dig at Vryonea in Serres (the Serres Court of Misdemeanours' Judicial Council determined later that the coin was illegally removed at the end of 2005). All the information came in an envelope with photos of the coin (Figs. 3–4), sent to the Police Directorate. The coin was to be sold in a public auction by the UK and Swiss firm Numismatica Ars Classica (henceforth, the NAC coin) (*Auction 52, 7 October 2009*, lot 110) (Figs. 1–2) (Tzamalis 2012, 381–382, photo 2.D). The Police Directorate notified the Ministry of Culture's Department for the Documentation and Protection of Cultural Goods. The coin was confiscated and subsequently held by the Zurich Police.

In order for the coin in Zurich to be repatriated to Greece it was necessary to determine if the coin from the auction and that in the photos sent to the Greek Police corresponded. Macroscopic examination confirmed that details such as the shape of the coin, die wear and other features were identical. In particular, one peculiar feature, two almost parallel lines in the area of the tail and hind legs of the horse, were present on both pieces, probably as a result of a crack in the die (Figs. 5, 6). On the reverse of the NAC coin (Fig. 2), in the centre of the indented square, is a central square divided into four sections and surrounded by an inscription. The section close to the Greek letters Σ and E has exactly the same degree of relief as that shown in the photograph in the Police Directorate's possession (Fig. 4). We noted that the surface of this section is higher than the surface of the central square's frame. Moreover, the traces of corrosion and indentations on the coin are exactly the same as those evident in the photograph. The same holds true for the evidence of mechanical stresses and all other features attesting to wear and tear.

Figure 5–8. Mosses octadrachm. Photos: NM, by optical microscope Fig. 5 (8x) and Fig. 7 (6x)

There is one difference. On the coin in the photograph we can see three dots in border which do not follow the line of the coin's dotted circle border; these are located directly slightly below the horse's leg (Figs. 7–8). The type of corrosion which might lead to the removal of a section of the dotted circle (the three dots) during cleaning occurs when the silver is converted into silver chloride in its mineral form, commonly known as horn silver or cerargyrite. In the longer term, UV superficially reduces this corrosion product to silver giving a metallic sheen (Cronyn 1990, 231–234). The fact that the three extra dots are not evident on the NAC coin (Fig. 2) may be due to their removal during cleaning prior to auction. Here we note that microscopic examination has revealed that a layer of original surface of the coin had been partially removed (which we believe included the dots). Furthermore, the same examination revealed that the auction coin had no signs of corrosion. The photograph of the coin from the Police Directorate reveal areas with residue products, primarily on the front (Figs. 3–4), indicating that cleaning and the creation of an artificial patina took place before the auction.

As a result of these studies the Mosses coin was repatriated to Greece in 2015 and has now been acquired by the Numismatic Museum (inventory No. ΒΠ 2216/2016). It was presented in detail by Dr George Kakavas during the International Numismatic Symposium "Mando Oeconomides", held at Athens, in April 20–21, 2016.

2. *An Athenian gold stater from a private collection.*

The second case discussed here is an Athenian gold stater minted by the tyrant Lachares in the early third century BC (296 BC), which was held in a private collection. The coin type and denomination are known from published corpora (eg. *BMC Attica-Megaris-Aegina, Athens* 129–131, Pl. V, 1–2) but the rarity of these coins has made them a target of modern counterfeiters. In studying the example brought to the museum for inspection we had concerns about details of the iconography (such as the absence of parts of the mouth and the oddly shaped eye of the goddess Athena) and the odd shape of the reverse. Since the two sides of the coin were struck off centre, part of Athena's helmet on the obverse and certain letters on the reverse were missing (Figs. 9–10). The coin was examined at high magnification under a stereomicroscope. No surface depositions were identified and no particular features relating to a casting process were found. The rim had been flattened, perhaps because the coin had been inserted into the frame of a piece of jewellery.

Given the rarity of the gold coinage of Lachares, we decided to compare the metal composition of this example with that of similar coins from the Museum's collections. Two were chosen: the forgery NM 2845 (Figs. 11–12) and an excavated coin from the Thorikos coin

Figures 9–10. Lachares stater, private collection (16.8mm). Photos: NM

Figures 11–12. Lachares stater (forgery), NM 2845 (16.3mm). Photos: NM

Figures 13–14. Lachares stater, NM Thorikos hoard/ 1968 (*IGCH* 134) 460/1969 (16.8mm). Photos: NM

hoard of 1968 (*IGCH* 134), NM 460/1969 (Figs. 13–14). The surface of the three coins was analysed using X–Ray Fluorescence (XRF). The choice of this specific analysis method, which has been widely used (Baer and Low 1982, 1) for generating reliable results when studying gold and silver coins (Fleming 1975, 110), meant that the analyses could be performed in Athens.

The XRF analyses were carried out by the Materials Identification and Analysis Lab of the Benaki Museum by the physicist Vasiliki Kantarelou. The portable milli-XRF device was designed and developed by the Materials Analysis Lab of the Institute of Nuclear and Particle Physics of the Democritus National Research and Physical Sciences Centre. The spectrometer consists of an X-ray tube with a rhodium anode (model XTF5011 from Oxford Instruments INC, USA, max. power 50 watt, voltage 50 kV and current 1 mA). The x-ray detector (XR–100 CR from Amptek, Inc, which contains a Si-PIN photodiode, 2-stage thermoelectric Peltier cooler and a preamplifier). The crystal was 6 mm^2 and 500 μm thick. The head of the XRF Spectrometer includes a fan to cool the tube and maintain a steady temperature and a system for focusing on the area being analysed. That system consists of two lasers placed so that where their beams intersect coincides with a point where the direction of the stimulated x-ray beam intersects the detector's axis. In that way the precise location of the head of the spectrometer in relation to the analysis point can be checked and, if needed, the measurements can be reproduced. To improve the quality of the spectral distribution of the stimulated radiation, the heard of the spectrometer has a filter selector. The filters consist of different materials placed in a suitable layout. Using filters significantly improves the analytical potential of the spectrometer, primarily in terms of the ability to identify concentrations of trace elements. They also offer very satisfactory minimum detectability thresholds for a relatively large range of atomic numbers. The diameter of the beam is around 2.5 mm. The beam of photons emitted from the source is focused using a collimator while a second collimator is placed on the detector's entry point. The coins were measured on both sides at a voltage of 40 kV and current of 40 μA for a period of 300s.

The results of the analysis of the three staters issued by Lachares are presented in Table 1. Microscopic observation revealed that iron found on the reverse of coin No. 2 (NM 2845) was from a surface deposition. The genuine stater from Thorikos has a lower gold content and more silver. The coin from the private collection (No. 1) has no trace of iron. The coin's gold, silver and copper content, and the absence of iron as an element of the composition of the coin, led to the conclusion that the amount of gold had been enriched (through flotation), a method in use at the time the coin was minted (Kotzamani *et al.* 2008, 47–48).

The gold stater, NM 2845 (No. 2) was first published as a forgery by Svoronos (1923–26, pl. 114.17), and this was confirmed by Kinns (1984, 27–28, cat. 29) who identified it as a product of the forger Caprara, alltough M. Oeconomides has accept it as genuine (Oeconomides 1996, 166, 241, n145). Kinns (1984, 28) lists no less than six examples, apparently all for the same set of dies. The coin from the private collection comes from a different set of dies.

Table 1. Compositional analysis using XRF of three staters of Lachares.

Coins	Analysis data	% Au	% Ag	% Cu	% Fe
(1) Gold stater of Lachares, private collection	PC_o	99.5 ± 2.0	0.33 ± 0.03	0.18 ± 0.02	0.00
	PC_r	99.3 ± 2.0	0.47 ± 0.04	0.24 ± 0.02	0.00
(2) Gold stater of Lachares, Numismatic Museum, NM 2845	NM2845_ o	99.7± 2.0	0.16 ± 0.02	0.14 ± 0.01	0.00
	NM2845_ r	97.5 ± 2.0	0.25 ± 0.02	0.18 ± 0.02	2.07 ± 0.10
	NM2845_r_ other spot	97.4 ± 2.0	0.17 ± 0.02	0.14 ± 0.01	2.29 ± 0.15
(3) Gold stater of Lachares, Numismatic Museum, Thorikos Hoard /1968, NM 460-1969	NM 460/1969_ o	95.5 ± 2.0	3.4 ± 0.3	0.81 ± 0.05	0.29 ± 0.02
	NM460/1969_o_ other spot	95.5 ± 2.0	3.2 ± 0.3	0.80 ± 0.05	0.50 ± 0.05
	NM 460/1969_ r	94.8 ± 2.0	3.9 ± 0.3,	0.75 ± 0.05	0.55 ± 0.10

At this point, the question of whether the Lachares stater from the private collection is authentic has been taken up by a scientific committee comprised of John Kroll, Ioannis Touratsoglou and Evangelia Apostolou following a decision from the Central Archaeological Council. What we have presented above, therefore, are the results of the initial investigations.

3. Silver stater of the Delphic Amphictyony.

Figures 15–16. Delphic Amphictyony stater, private collection. Photos: NM, by optical microscope on obverse (5x) and on reverse (8x)

The third case involves a coin from the Delphic Amphictyony held in a private collection. Preliminary research showed that the coin matched examples from the published corpora (*BMC Central Greece*, Delphi 22, Pl. IV, 13). The weight corresponded to other coins minted on the Aeginetan standard (11.93 g). Examination under a microscope at high magnification (up to 40x) showed that the coin's surface was full of uniform cavities, principally on the reverse, while the obverse had fewer cavities (Figs. 15–16). This was a cause for some concern. The presence of dents could be related to corrosion, or to the process of casting the flan, or even to formations arising from deliberate blows to the surface in order to create an aged look.

The Delphic Amphictyony silver staters, which have been well studied (Kinns 1983), most likely date to between the autumn of 336 BC and the spring of 334 BC. All dies for both sides are probably known. Two of the four coins from the Myonia hoard found in 1898 (Evgenidou 2010, 31) similar to the coin in question, inventory No. NM Myonia Hoard/1898 (*IGCH* 66) KZ´3, 12.27 g (Figs. 17–18) and NM Myonia Hoard/1898 KZ´4, 12.28 g (Figs. 19–20) were chosen for comparison. These three coins from the Delphic Amphictyony were examined using the XRF method. The analyses were again carried out at the Materials

Figures 17–18. Delphic Amphictyony stater, NM Myonia Hoard/1898 (*IGCH* 66) KZ´3 (26.2mm). Photos: NM

Figures 19–20. Delphic Amphictyony stater, NM Myonia Hoard/1898 (*IGCH* 66) KZ´4 (22.9mm). Photos: NM

Table 2. Compositional analysis using XRF of three staters of the Delphic Amphictyony

Coins	% Ag	Au ppm	Cu ppm	Pb ppm
(1) Stater of Delphic Amphictyony, private collection	99.6 %	19	29	44
(2) Stater of Delphic Amphictyony, NM Myonia hoard KZ 1	99.6 %	21	21	15
(3) Stater of Delphic Amphictyony, NM Myonia hoard KZ 4	99.6 %	53	38	27

Identification and Analysis Lab of the Benaki Museum by Vasiliki Kantarelou using the Milli-probe XRF spectrometer. The results of the alloy tests on all three Delphic Amphictyony coins are presented in Table 2 and show that all three coins have a similar composition, both in qualitative and quantitative terms.

4. Repatriation of five silver coins from New York in 2014 due to trafficking in antiquities (Inventory No. NM BΠ 2142).

Five coins returned to Greece in 2014 came from a group in the possession of a collector from Rhode Island, USA, Dr Arnold-Peter Weiss. Dr Weiss, who pleaded guilty to the charge of possessing stolen property, handed over twenty coins to the US authorities as part of a plea bargain. From this collection five coins issued by Greek mints were returned to Greece.

1. Locris, Locri Opuntii (*c.*356–338 BC). Stater, silver, 12.25 g (Figs. 21–22). Ex. Nomos AG, *Auction* 3, 10 May 2011, lot 81.
2. Thrace, Dikaia (*c.*515–480 BC). Stater, silver, 9.73 g (Figs. 25–26). Ex. Nomos AG, *Auction* 3, 10 May 2011, lot 40. May 1965, pl.1, 4 (this coin).
3. Euboia, Euboian League (*c.*375–357 BC). Didrachm, silver, 12.28 g (Figs. 29–30). Ex. Nomos AG, *Auction* 3, 10 May 2011, lot 85.
4. Boeotia, Thebes (*c.*405–395 BC). Stater, silver, 11.97 g (Figs. 33–34). Ex. Nomos AG, *Auction* 3, 10 May 2011, lot 83.
5. Boeotia, Thebes, (*c.*395–338 BC). Stater, silver, 12.00 g (Figs. 37–38).

A visual examination suggested to us that all five silver coins had seen very little circulation, for the types are in high relief and have sharp edges. Furthermore, the surfaces of all five coins appeared to be very similar. This could reflect the decision of the collector to select coins with the very best preservation. It was decided to seek further information about the metal of the coins through XRF analysis.

As the basis for a comparative study of metal composition, we began by obtaining data by the XRF analysis of matching coins from the same mints or similar issues that are held in the Numismatic Museum's collections. The following coins were used:

6. Locris, Locri Opuntii (*c.*369–338 BC). Stater, silver, Empedoklis Collection, 11.88 g (Figs. 23–24).

Figures 21–22. Locri Opuntii. Stater, silver, (12.25 g; 25.1mm). Photo: NM

Figures 23–24. Locri Opuntii. Stater, silver, Empedoklis Collection. (11.88 g; 24.8mm). Photo: NM

Figures 25–26. Thrace, Dikaia. Stater, silver (9.73 g; 18.1mm). Photos: NM

Figures 27–28. Thrace, Dikaia, Stater, silver, Empedoklis Collection (7.00 g; 19.6mm). Photos: NM

Figures 29–30. Euboia, Euboian League. Didrachm, silver (12.28 g; 22.8mm). Photos: NM

Figures 31–2. Euboia, Euboian League. Didrachm, silver, Empedoklis Collection (11.91 g; 22.1mm). Photos: NM

Figures 33–34. Boeotia, Thebes. Stater, silver (11.97 g; 24.1mm). Photos: NM

Figures 35–36. Boeotia, Thebes. Stater, silver, Empedoklis Collection (10.62 g; 19.0mm). Photos: NM

Figures 37–38. Boeotia, Thebes. Stater, silver (12.00 g; 20.2mm). Photos: NM

Figures 39–40. Boeotia, Thebes. Stater, silver. Kindynis Collection (11.85 g; 21.7mm). Photos: NM

7. Thrace, Dikaia (c.490–476/75 BC). Stater, silver, Empedoklis Collection, 7.00 g (Figs. 27–28).
8. Euboia, Euboian League (c.375–357 BC). Didrachm, silver, 11.91 g, Empedoklis Collection (Figs. 31–32).
9. Boeotia, Thebes (c.405–395 BC). Stater, silver, Empedoklis Collection, 10.62 g (Figs. 35–36).
10. Boeotia, Thebes. (c.395–338 BC). Stater, silver, Kindynis Collection, 11.85 g (Figs. 39–40).

The analyses were carried out at the Conservation Lab of the Numismatic Museum by E. Kontou under the guidance and supervision of analysts Mike Dobby and Dimitris Stamelos, using a M1 MISTRAL BRUKER NANO analyser. This analyser can measure elements with atomic numbers from 22 upwards (Titanium). The sample (measuring up to 100 x 100 x 100 mm) is placed in the measurement zone and is measured directly without any preparation. Using the microscope, the fine measurement point is identified (which may be over 0.3 mm). Technical characteristics: generator with a max. output of 50kV and 50W. X-ray source: tungsten. Analysis conditions: HV / 50 kV, Current / 800 μA, Time / 60 s, Colli1 / 700 mm, Colli2 / 700 mm. The results of the analyses carried out on the repatriated coins as well as the coins from the Museum's collections are set out in Table 3.

The results of these analyses show little difference between the metal of the five repatriated coins and the matching examples from the Museum's collection. We recognize that an extensive program of analysis for the coins of each mint will be needed to establish a set of expected compositional elements and the degree of variation. We also recognize that silver or gold obtained from sources not usually available (such as silver looted in war) can have different compositions, and this is to be expected. Nonetheless, these 'matched tests' can serve to alert us to differences that might warrant further examination of the coin (especially

Table 3. Compositional analysis using XRF of ten ancient Greek silver coins

Coins' data	Analysis data	Au c(%)	Ag c(%)	Pt c(%)	Cu c(%)	Fe c(%)	Pb c(%)	As c(%)
Stater of Locris. Locri Opuntii (c.356–338 BC)	NM_BP2142_1_o_a	0.6	94.4	0.0	4.4	0.0	0.3	0.0
	NM_BP2142_1_r_a	0.5	95.5	0.0	3.6	0.0	0.2	0.0
	NM_BP2142_1_r_b	0.4	94.8	0.0	4.3	0.0	0.2	0.0
Stater of Locris. Locri Opuntii (c.369–338 BC). Empedoklis Collection	NM_E_1_o	0.7	95.8	0.056	2.9	0.0	0.3	0.0
	NM_E_1_r	0.7	96.3	0.0	2.4	0.3	0.1	0.0
Stater of Dikaia. Thrace (c. 515-480 BC)	NM_BP2142_2_o_a	0.1	99.8	0.0	0.0	0.0	0.06	0.0
	NM_BP2142_2_o_b	0.1	99.8	0.0	0.0	0.0	0.06	0.0
	NM_BP2142_2_r_a	0.084	99.8	0.0	0.0	0.0	0.09	0.0
	NM_BP2142_2_r_b	0.089	99.4	0.0	0.0	0.4	0.06	0.0
Stater of Dikaia. Thrace (c.490–476/75 BC). Empedoklis Collection	NM_E_2_o	0.091	93.5	0.054	5.134	0.0	1.1	0.0
	NM_E_2_r	0.1	95.5	0.0	3.0	0.0	1.3	0.0
Didrachm. of Euboia. Euboian League (c.375–357 BC)	NM_BP2142_3_o_a	0.1	98.4	0.0	0.285	0.0	1.1	0.0
	NM_BP2142_3_o_b	0.1	98.5	0.0	0.250	0.0	1.09	0.0
	NM_BP2142_3_r_a	0.1	98.0	0.0	0.343	0.0	1.3	0.12
	NM_BP2142_3_r_b	0.097	98.0	0.0	0.398	0.0	1.4	0.0
Didrachm. of Euboia. Euboian League (c.375–357 BC). Empedoklis Collection	NM_E_3_o	0.0	98.1	0.0	0.000	0.0	1.8	0.0
	NM_E_3_r	0.04	98.8	0.0	0.000	0.0	1.1	0.0
Stater of Boeotia. Thebes. (c. 405-395 BC)	NM_BP2142_4_o_a	0.3	99.4	0.09	0.0	0.0	0.09	0.0
	NM_BP2142_4_o_b	0.3	99.4	0.08	0.0	0.0	0.09	0.0
	NM_BP2142_4_r_a	0.2	99.5	0.06	0.0	0.0	0.11	0.0
	NM_BP2142_4_r_b	0.3	99.4	0.06	0.0	0.0	0.13	0.0
Stater of Boeotia. Thebes. (c. 405-395 BC), Empedoklis Collection	NM_SEMP_D1_Tr37_o	0.06	98.9	0.0	0.7	0.0	0.3	0.0
	NM_SEMP_D1_Tr37_r	0.1	98.9	0.0	0.6	0.0	0.4	0.0
Stater of Boeotia. Thebes. (c.395–338 BC)	NM_BP2142_5_o_a	0.6	96.8	0.04	1.7	0.0	0.5	0.0
	NM_BP2142_5_o_b	0.6	96.6	0.0	1.9	0.0	0.7	0.0
	NM_BP2142_5_r_a	0.4	95.5	0.0	3.01	0.0	1.06	0.0
	NM_BP2142_5_r_b	0.4	95.8	0.05	2.5	0.0	1.04	0.0
Stater of Boeotia. Thebes. (c.395–338 BC). Kindynis Collection	NM_E_5_o	0.3	96.5	0.0	2.0	0.0	1.1	0.0
on	NM_E_5_r	0.3	96.3	0.0	2.2	0.0	1.0	0.0

if the composition suggests a modern alloy). The results can be archived for future studies of similar coins which might enter the Museum in the future.

CONCLUSIONS

In this brief study we have outlined some procedures for exploring the authenticity of coins brought to the Numismatic Museum of Athens. We wish to conclude by noting that while these procedures may allow us to detect forgeries, it nonetheless remains true that it is difficult to prove the authenticity of coins. The traditional methods by which coins are compared to the published records, especially die studies, will continue to be essential to attempts to uncover fakes. However, as technology improves, the contribution of scientific techniques of analysis will become more important. In future we expected that extensive data for the metal composition of entire coin series will become available. In the case studies presented above the Museum illustrates how it has actively fostered collaboration between its departments and external bodies in its efforts to respond to the increasingly more complex and technologically advanced counterfeiting common today. After the much-awaited acquisition of a new XRF spectrometer, the Museum has taken steps to establish a database for records of the metal composition of all coins in its collections. Although the study of suspect examples is not the key reason for the creation of a database of analyses, greater knowledge of metal composition may well prove to be critical in identifying forged coins.

REFERENCES

Baer, N.S., Low, M.J D. 1982. 'Advances in Scientific Instrumentation for Conservation: An Overview', in Brommelle, N.S. and Thomson, G. (eds), *Preprints of the Contributions to the Washington Congress, 3–9 September 1982, Science and Technology in the Service of Conservation* (London), 1–4.
Boz Z. 2014. 'Repatriation of Cultural Antiquities: Forming a Legal and an Archaeological procedure', *Proceedings of 3rd International Conference of Experts on the return of Cultural Property* (Athens), 219–225.
Craddock P. 2009. *Scientific Investigation of Copies, Fakes and Forgeries* (Oxford).
Cronyn, J.M. 1990. *The Elements of Archaeological Conservation* (London and New York).
Evgenidou D. 2010. (ed.), *The History of Coinage* (Athens).
Fleming, S.J. 1975. *Authenticity in Art: The Scientific Detection of Forgery* (London).
Gaebler, H. 1935. *Die antiken Münzen von Makedonia und Paionia, Die antiken Münzen Nord-Griechenlands Vol. III*. Macedonia and Paionia (Berlin).
Kakavas, G. Th. 2019. "Sponsors and donors in Public Museums: The case of Numismatic Museum" in Kakavas, G. (ed.) *Institution of Sponsorship from Ancient to Modern Times*, Proceeding of International Scientific Conference, Museum of Byzantine Culture, Thessaloniki, February 7-8 2014, 247–266.
Kardamitsi–Adami M. 2006. *Ernst Schiller 1837–1923, The Art of the Classic* (Athens).
Kinns, Ph. 1983. 'The Amphictioni Coinage Reconsidered', *NC* 143, 1–22.
Kinns, Ph. 1984. *The Caprara Forgeries* (London and Basle).
Kotzamani, D., Kantarelou, V., Sofou Ch., and Karydas, A.G. 2008. 'The golden kylix inv. no. 2108 of the Benaki Museum: Technical report', *Benaki Museum Journal* 8, 39–61.
Ministry of Culture–Numismatic Museum. 1996. *Coins and Numismatics* (Athens).
Oeconomides, M. 1996. *Greek art. Ancient Coins* (Athens).
Portelanos, A. 2012. 'Iliou Melathron. Heinrich Schliemann's house, a work by Ernst Schiller', in Korres, G., Karadimas, N. and Flouda, G. (eds.) *Archaeology and Heinrich Schliemann. 100 years from his death. Overview and Prospects. Myth - History–Science* (Athens), 449–464.
Svoronos, J.N. 1923–6. *Les monnaies d'Athènes*, edited by B. Pick (Munich).
Tzamalis, A.R. 2012. 'Les ethnés de la région "Thraco-Macédonienne". Étude d'Histoire et de numismatique (fin du VIe-Ve siècle)', (PhD dissertation, Paris IV–Sorbonne).

ABBREVIATIONS

IGCH = M. Thompson, O. Mørkholm and C.M. Kraay (eds), Inventory of Greek Coin Hoards, New York, 1973.